English Pageantry

An Historical Outline

The Old and the New

English Pageantry

An Historical Outline

BY

Robert Withington

VOLUME II

First published 1926, Harvard University Press.
Reprinted 1963, by arrangement with the Harvard University Press.
Published by Benjamin Blom, Inc., New York 52.
L. C. Catalog Card No.: 63-23191

Printed in U.S.A. by
NOBLE OFFSET PRINTERS, INC.
NEW YORK 3, N. Y.

CONTENTS

CHAPTER VI

CHAPTER VII

CHAPTER VIII

CHAPTER IX

CHAPTER X

ILLUSTRATIONS

ENGLISH PAGEANTRY

ENGLISH PAGEANTRY

CHAPTER VI

THE LORD MAYOR'S SHOW

§ 1. THE RISE AND PAGEANTIC DEVELOPMENT OF THE LORD MAYOR'S SHOW, 1209–1585

EARLY in the thirteenth century, King John granted a mayor to the citizens of London, who had hitherto been governed by bailiffs. The first man to hold this office was Sir Henry Fitz-Alwin, who was sworn in in 1209.[1] When the king granted the mayor, he stipulated that the officer should be presented for approval either to him or to his justices, who sat in his palace at Westminster; and from this stipulation originated the procession which has lasted to our own day.[2]

---

[1] *Annales Lond.*, i, p. 14. Stubbs, the editor, notes, (*loc. cit.*, n. 1) that Fitz-Alwin " had been mayor for many years, probably since 1191," yet he calls attention to Fabyan, who records that " Fitz-Eylwin " was sworn in as first mayor on Michaelmas day, 10 John (1209). Gregory's *Chronicle* (ed. from Egerton MS. 1995, for the Camden Society, by James Gairdner [London, 1876]) p. 60, notes that Fitz-Alwin, the first mayor, was installed in 1209. Cf. *ibid.*, p. 243 and note b. Cf. Tyrrell, p. 7; Grafton, p. 245; Stow, *Survey*, (1618) p. 915 f. The latter records Fitz-Alwin's mayoralty as beginning in 1189 (1 Rich. I) and continuing twenty-four years, to 15 John (1212). B. B. Orridge, F. G. S., in *Some Account of the Citizens of London and their Rulers* (London, 1867), prints a " Calendar of Mayors and Sheriffs " which begins in 1189 with Fitz-Alwin. Kingsford's Stow's *Survey*, ii, p. 384, dates Fitz-Alwin's term from 1191 or 1193. Cf. *ibid.*, p. 149.

Thomas Heywood (see *Works* (1874), iv, p. 270; v, pp. 264 and 360) says that Fitz-Alwin's twenty-four-year term began in 1210; J. G. Nichols, *Lond. Pag.*, is wrong in setting the date of the first mayor at 1215. Thomas Jordan, in the " epistle dedicatory " to Sir Joseph Sheldon in his 1675 pamphlet, says that Fitz-Alwin was mayor for " more than 24 years, *sans intermission;* " but neither here, nor in his 1676 pamphlet (on p. 6 of which he uses approximately the same language) does he assign a date for the commencement of the term. In the third " presentation " of Dekker's 1628 Show is John, who gave the city " a Lord Maior and two Sheriffes "; on p. 2 of his 1631 pamphlet he dates Fitz-Alwin's advancement to the mayoralty, Anno 1210. I need not add that none of these writers are authorities.

In 1889, the seven-hundredth anniversary of the mayoralty of London was celebrated. The " authorities concerning the Inauguration of the Mayoralty in the Year of Grace 1189, being the first year of King Richard I," are — as recorded in a pamphlet printed in March, 1889, — " *Liber de Antiquis Legibus; Liber Albus,* and Stow's *Survey of London.*"

[2] For accounts of the Lord Mayor's Show see — beside the contemporary chroniclers — Fairholt, *Lord Mayors' Pageants*, part i; Hone, *Anc. Mys.;* J. G. Nichols, *London Pageants;*

The Early Centuries

There were two ways of going from London to Westminster — one by the river and the other along the Strand. J. G. Nichols records that the newly-elected mayor and his companions "were accustomed to take their way on horseback, until Sir John Norman, the mayor in [1453], resolved to go by water. For this purpose, a stately barge was built at his private expense, and the companies imitated his example."[1] Perhaps it was the magnificence of the barge which was responsible for the oft-repeated tradition that Norman was the first mayor to make the journey by the Thames; whatever the reason for its persistence, Walderne, the mayor, seems to have made the journey by water, with the crafts, in 1422.

Fabyan records[2] that in 1251 the citizens were excused from presenting their mayor to the king, wherever he might be, but were allowed to present him to the "baronys" of the "exchekyr," who could receive his oath were the king away. This decision tended to give a "stability" to the procession, which was no small factor in its development; for the goal was fixed. When the king's Exchequer was not at London, or the Court was vacant, the mayor was presented to the Constable of the Tower, or to his lieutenant.[3]

So grew up the custom which later, as we shall see, became the famous "Lord Mayor's Show," and which — though its glories largely departed in the eighteenth century — is still a matter of interest to the citizens of London. In 16 Richard II (1392) one of the Bishop of Salisbury's yeomen stole from a baker; this aroused the people so that the bishop complained to the king, who deposed

Unwin, *Gilds and Companies of London:* Herbert, *History of the Livery Companies*, etc. The *Repertories* contain many items of interest; the pamphlets describing the shows between 1585 and 1708 are important, and there are many MS. accounts and minutes of committees in the Guildhall library. I may add that John Nichols gathered much material on the subject in the *Gent. Mag.* for 1824–25 (xciv, ii, pp. 113 f., 411 f., 514 f.; xcv, i, pp. 30 f., 131 f., 221 f., 321 f., 418 f., and the supplement, p. 593 f). These have been bound into a pamphlet (with some leaves of the *Biog. Dram.*) by Joseph Haslewood; it is in the Guildhall Library. Mr. Haslewood's MS. note in front of this volume, records that J. G. Nichols helped his grandfather in this task.

Gough, *Brit. Top.*, p. 339 f., gives an incomplete list of Lord Mayor's Shows of the seventeenth century, which is not without misprints and other inaccuracies. My own list in the Bibliography is not complete; but it is as full as possible.

[1] J. G. Nichols, p. 93. (He is only one of many writers to make this statement.)

[2] *New Chronicle* (1811) p. 337. Cf. Gregory's *Chronicle*, p. 67. Here the date of the mayor's presentation at the Exchequer is given as 37 Henry III (1252).

[3] Strype's Stow (1720) ii, p. 78. *Letter-Book* C, p. 174, has a record of the presentation of the mayor and sheriffs to the Constable of the Tower in 1303, when the Barons of the Exchequer were absent. This was "pursuant to the King's writ . . . 14 October 29 Edw. I. (A.D. 1301)." Again, in 1304, mayor and sheriffs were "admitted" by the Constable of the Tower. (*Ibid.*, p. 175 f.)

the mayor and both sheriffs. "And this was done a xiiij daies afore the feste of seynte John þe Baptiste. And than the kyng called to hym a knyght named sir Edwarde Dalyngrigge and made him warden and gouernour of the citee & chaumbre of London and ouer his people therynne, and so he kepte that Office but iiij wekes because he was so tendir & gentill vnto the citezeynes of London, wherfore the Kyng deposed him and made sir Bawdewyn Radyngton knight þat was counteroller of the Kynges housholde wardeyne & gouernour of his Chaumbre and of þe people therynne . . . vn to the tyme of the mayres electioun nexte. Than William Staundon was chosen mayre.[1] and þis Gilberte Mawefelde & Thomas Newenton Shirriefes. And than the Mayre and the ij Shirrieves & all the Aldremen with all the worthy craftes of London wenten on foote vn to the toure yate and þen come oute the Constable of the Toure, and gafe the mayre and þe Shirrieves her othe & charge as þey shulde haue take in þe Escheker of Westmynster in the kynges courte of his Justices & Baronns of þe Cheker, and þan wente they home ageyn."[2]

Considering the many opportunities which the guilds and civic officials had, of participating in "royal-entries" and Midsummer Shows, it is not hard to understand the possibility of their seeking to avoid the expense of adding pageants to the annual "riding" to Westminster, or to the Tower, when the mayor took the oath of office. But there was a certain state to these processions; even if they did not include pageants, they seem to have included minstrels; and the chief magistrate was accompanied by the beadle of his company, on horseback, his brother-aldermen, and other city functionaries, besides the crafts. The sheriffs were also accompanied by minstrels,[3] but there was no pageantry in connection with these "ridings" until the sixteenth century.

The processions on horseback continued until 1422. "On the death of Henry V," says Herbert,[4] "the sheriffs-elect, Eastfelde and Tattersalle, were

---

[1] Cf. above, vol. i, p. 131.

[2] Bodl. Ashm. MS. 793, fol. 128 *et seq.*

[3] Cf. the "Wardens' Account in the Reign of Henry IV., anno 1401," printed in the appendix of Heath's *Account of the Grocers' Company* (first ed., p. 310; third ed., p. 409). I copy some items:

"*Itm.* paie po^r. vij mynstrales po^r. chevaucher avec les viscom^t R. Chychley & S. Marlowe, xlvj*s.* viij*d.*"

"*Itm.* nous avons paie po^r. le chevache du John Walcote Mayr, po^r. vj mynstralles po^r. lo^r. saleire, xl*s.*

"*Itm.* po^r. lo^r. chaprōns and po lo^r. fessure, viij*s.*

"*Itm.* po. lo. dyner & po^r. vyn po. le chemyn, xxi*d.*

"*Itm.* po^r. un cheval po^r. le bedyl, iiij*d.*"

Perhaps the "vyn po. le chemyn" is for a conduit.

[4] Herbert, i, p. 98 (cited by Humpherus, i, p. 43). The date of this is 31 August 1422. "To take their charge" undoubtedly means their oath of office; it probably does not refer to any duties in connection with the royal funeral. But these funerals were — as Herbert

ordered not to ride on horse to take their charge at Westminster, as had been accustomed, but to go in *barges*, with their companies, which were the mercers' and the drapers,' which they did. The drapers are described, on this occasion, to have 'been *hooded in white, and needle pointed*,'[1] and the sheriffs' sergeants to have been 'gowned in the same.' The mercers wore 'their own clothing.'"

The sheriffs were not the only ones to make the journey by water. Herbert continues: "The brewers' records give the following interesting account of the king's funeral. '*William Walderne* was chosen mayor on St. Edmund's Day, when it was ordered that the aldermen and crafts should go to Westminster with him, to take his charge, *in barges, without minstrels*.'"[2] Apparently the royal obsequies followed closely the ceremonies of installing the mayor: "after the charge, to be present at the King's funeral." We read in the records of the Grocers' Company for 1 Henry VI, — Robert Otle[y] and Thomas Selove being wardens, — "Item, paie pur toutes lez torchez pur nostre art Encountre le morte de le Roy Henri V^e^, xxxix*s*. vj*d*. . . . Item paye a pers West pur dyuers Barges pur nostre art vers Westmenstre ouek le Meir et lez Scherevez pur ij anz et pur servoys pur lez bargeman, xvj*s*, viij*d*."[3] It became, apparently, a custom[4] for the mayor to go to Westminster by water very shortly after; but the "riding" was also kept up, as several entries show.

Humpherus records[5] "a serious conflict . . . on London bridge in the morning of the 30 October [1425] . . . the day of the Mayor's procession to Westminster. The servants of the Bishop of Winchester proceeding from his palace at Bankside, attempted to enter the bridge gate by force, but being repelled, they returned with a large body of archers and men at arms, and assaulted the bridge as a hostile city. All London was speedily in arms, headed by the protector, the Duke of Gloucester, but a further conflict was avoided by the prudence and mediation of the mayor and aldermen, who rode between the protector

(*loc. cit.*) points out — "a species of state solemnity, at which the attendance of the companies was generally required."

Stow, *Annals*, pp. 362 and 363, describes the journey from France with the body of the king, and records its arrival in London "about the tenth of November." Herbert, *loc. cit.*, notes that "the royal corpse was brought to London on Thursday, Nov. 5."

[1] Herbert does not give his authorities, which we may assume to be the records of the guilds he names.

[2] *Ibid.*, *loc. cit.* "Every householder," he goes on to say, "was charged to provide a black or russet gown and a black hood; and, after the charge, to be present at the king's funeral. Certain of the crafts were ordered to find 200 torches for the funeral. The brewers provided eight torches for the occasion, weighing 138 lb. of wax, price 51*s*. 9*d*. . . ."

[3] Kingdon, *Facsimile*, i, p. 149.

[4] *Ibid.*, i, p. 159, — the records of the Grocers from the day of John the Baptist, 3 Henry VI, to the same day the next year, — where among the items we find one "for bothyre (*boat hire*) to Westmynstre for terment (*the interment*) of þe kyng et diuerse tymes w^t^ þ^e^ meyre."

[5] *Hist. Watermen*, i, p. 44. We may assume that his authority is the records of the Company.

and the Bishop eight times, ere they could bring them to any agreement, as the feud between them had been of some standing, and had caused several affrays."

The Grocers' records, in the accounts extending from 5 June, 1427, to 6 July, 1428, show an item "For diuerse costis and mynstrelles atte Shirevis ridyng, summa iij*li.* xix*s.* iiij*d.*"[1] In 1432, the Grocers "Payd for hors here for owr bedull at *þ*e Rydyng of the Mayre and Sherevys," two shillings. The next year, they "paide for an hors at the Meiris and shrevis Ridyng for John Dalton," three shillings, sixpence.[2]

The Grocers' records for the period 25 July, 1434, to 26 July, 1436, show that there was — at any rate for the sheriffs — a water procession "at least nineteen years before their supposed introduction by Sir John Norman."[3] In 1435, the Grocers "paid be the handys of John Godyn For mynstralles and here hodys, and amendyng of Baneris And hire of barges wt Thomas Catworthe and Robert Clopton chosen Shirerevis, goyng be watir to Westmynster, iiij*li.*, vj*s.* iij*d.*" In the wardens' accounts of the Grocers' Company from 1437–1439, we find that they "payde For barge hyr to Westmester For the obyt of ye kyng and ye shrevys for ij yer, xix*s.*"[4]

These entries will be enough to show that the water-procession was common enough — with certain companies, at any rate — before Sir John Norman made the voyage to Westminster.

It is possible that the stir made by the voyage of Sir John Norman, in 1453, was due to the fact that he owned the barge, while hitherto, and for some time afterwards, it was usual for the companies to hire their barges. He seems to have been the first Draper to have gone by water to take his oath.

Fabyan and Stow note that on the morrow of Simon and Jude, "the accustomed daye when ye newe mayer vsyd yerelye to ryde with great pompe vnto Westmynster to take his charge,"[5] the Mayor, Sir John Norman, made his progress — "the first mayor that was rowed by water to Westminster to take his Oath: he caused a Barge to be made at his owne charge, and euery Company

---

[1] Kingdon, *Facsimile*, i, p. 166. As the "ridings" usually came in the autumn, this may be dated 1427.

[2] Kingdon, *op. cit.*, ii, pp. 227 and 230.

[3] Fairholt, pt. i, pp. 7, 8, and pt. ii, p. 243; cf. Herbert, i, p. 100 and note. Arundell, p. 297, points out that Fairholt has shown an earlier water-procession than Norman's, but he dates this procession 1436. Humpherus, i, p. 46, wrongly records this water-procession under the year 1434. Stow is copied by Orridge, p. 221, where he records that Catworth and Clopton were sheriffs in 1435.

My citation of these records is made from Kingdon, *Facsimile*, ii, p. 236. Besides the reprint in Fairholt, they may be found in Heath (3d ed.) p. 417. Fairholt is wrong in saying that they commence on 25 July, 1435; Kingdon (ii, p. 234) shows that they cover two years, (1434–36).

[4] Kingdon, *Facsimile*, ii, p. 253. This can hardly refer to the death of Henry V, unless the guild attended a requiem mass.

[5] Fabyan, *Chronicle* (1811) p. 628; cited by Fairholt, pt. ii, p. 243.

had severall Barges well-decked and trimmed, to passe along with him. For ioy whereof, the Watermen made a Song in his prayse." [1] It is, of course, possible that the largess which Sir John presumably distributed among the watermen accounts for their ballad. At any rate, tradition and the early historians are wrong in assigning to him the first civic journey on the Thames.

Humpherus notes [2] that in 1455 "the procession by water to Westminster . . . was accompanied by the barge of the Carpenters' company." Without stating his authority, he adds that "the company had had a barge for some years previously"; but Jupp, giving the same entries, says that the "first mention" of the Company's "attending at Westminster is in 1455." [3]

After Norman's journey, no Draper was inaugurated mayor until 1481; and in that year — for the first time — the books of the Company mention a mayor making his inaugural procession to Westminster by water.[4] "As Norman's barge was not then thirty years old," says Herbert, "it is not improbable that it might be used on this occasion. If so, we learn from the same and other entries that it was then customarily covered on civic triumphs with blue cloth (plunket), and on royal ones with red (murrey)." [5]

Under the year 1483, Humpherus records [6] that "from the commencement

---

[1] Stow, *Survey* (1618), p. 939. Herbert, i, p. 100, note, says that the Grocers hired a barge, not building one of their own until 1617. The entry for this year may be found in Kingdon, *op. cit.*, ii, p. 347 — paid "for j barge to Westmynster w[t] þe mayr to tak his charge, xv*s*, j*d*."

Various Lord Mayor's Show pamphlets by Heywood, Munday, Middleton, and others repeat Stow's error. Davey, i, p. 103, saying that Norman, "who was lame," invented the water-procession, is but one of the modern writers who have fallen into this error. Humpherus, i, p. 50 — citing Fabyan — dates the first appearance of Sir John Norman's barge, 1454.

Gough, *Brit. Topog.*, i, p. 675, notes that there is a drawing of Norman's Show on the river in the Pepysian Library. He is quoted by Fairholt, p. 8, n. 2; cf. *ibid.*, pt i, p. 114, n. 1, and pt. ii, pp. 244 and 284.

[2] *Op. cit.*, i, p. 51, citing the Carpenters' records.

[3] *Hist. Carpenters*, p. 31. Arundell, p. 297, cites the books of the Carpenters' Company to show that in 1460 (39 Henry VI) they paid four shillings for "hire of barge to Westminster with the shireves." This is also cited by Humpherus, i, p. 52, and Jupp, p. 31; the latter adds another item from the books of the Company, under date of 1471: "Itm. spent at tavern whan the mair cam fro Westm. ij*s*. iiij*d*."

[4] Herbert, i, p. 453. As Norman furnished his barge at his own expense, we should not expect to find it mentioned in the Company's books.

[5] Minstrels accompanied the mayor to Westminster this year, and "for a rewarde to the bargemen for going to Westminst[r] with the sheriffs to accompany the mayor aforesaid, ij*s*. iiij*d*," were given. (Entries from the Drapers' books, printed by Herbert, *loc. cit.*) "The sheriffs," Herbert adds, "were generally accompanied in their water-processions by minstrels or trumpets, with crimson or red hats, and headed by their marshal, in the Company's barge, decorated with banners, pennons, and streamers, fringed with silk and 'beaten with gold.'"

[6] *Op. cit.*, i, p. 59 f. — without giving his authority.

of the mayor's procession by water, the question whether the Merchant Tailors' or Skinners' Company should have precedence in the procession had been a matter of dispute; a great feud having existed between those companies, one barge always attempting to get before the other barge; this year the rival companies came to blows which resulted in bloodshed and loss of life. In consequence of this, the matter was referred to the mayor for arbitration, whereupon he decided that for the future the two guilds should alternately have precedence, and that each year on approaching Westminster, they should lash their two barges together and drink as a toast 'The Merchant Taylors and Skinners; Skinners and Merchant Taylors; root and branch, may they flourish forever.'

"For a long time this custom has continued, and latterly, when the procession by water became superseded by one on land, the two companies continued the friendly greeting, by inviting each other to a banquet every year."

The Sixteenth Century

In 1515, on 31 January, appeared "the order and direction taken . . . by the Mayor and Aldermen of and for all the Craftes and Mysteryes ensyuing, for they [*sic*] going as well as in all processions, as in all other going, standynge, and rydynge, for the businesses and causes of this citie. The seyd order and direction to be from hensforth fermely observed and kepte. Provided always that the Felyship whereof the Mayre for the yere according to the old custome shall have pre-eminence, in going afore all other Felyshippes in all places during the tyme of mayroltie." [1] The list of companies follows.

A fragment of what, to my mind, is rather a "royal-entry" than a Lord Mayor's Show, has been printed from a Trinity College (Cantab.) manuscript by Elizabeth D. Adams.[2] That this is a civic triumph, written for a London Salter in 1531 or 1542, I cannot accept: I have elsewhere suggested that, if it be not a provincial mayoralty show, it was probably part of the festivities with which a sovereign — perhaps Henry VII — was welcomed into some provincial city. The reference to salt — which is the salt of Wisdom — is purely figurative; various phrases suggest that civil strife has just ended; such a phrase as "your honor, worship, and royal majesty" would not be applied to a mayor, while "mayralte" might conceivably be used as a synonym for *reign* — particularly if the sovereign owed his position to the support of the people. The fact that the manuscript is in an early sixteenth-century hand does not rule out the possibility that the speech itself was delivered much earlier.

---

[1] W. M. Williams, *Annals Founders*, p. 213, quoting from the City's records.

[2] Elizabeth D. Adams, "A Fragment of a Lord Mayor's Pageant," in *Modern Language Notes* for May, 1917, p. 285. Cf. my note on this paper in *Mod. Lang. Notes* for December, 1919, p. 501. The "fragment" is reprinted from Trin. Coll. Cantab. MS. B. 15.39 (James's Catalogue, no. 181, pt. iii).

From the middle of the fifteenth century, there seems to have been an increase in the splendor of the water-progresses,[1] but no pageantry has as yet been introduced. As was the case with the "royal-entry," the soil is prepared for it by a growing ceremony and display in the procession itself. When the occasion was deemed worthy of such expense, the civic show received pageants both from the "royal-entry" and the Midsummer Show, to both of which the civic bodies contributed.[2]

In 1532, the Pewterers "pd. for the Barge hire whan the maire went to Westmenster to take his othe, xvj*s*."[3] Norman's barge seems to have been decayed in 1533, in which year the Drapers agreed to hire the great barge of the Archbishop of Canterbury "at such tyme as we shall have nede to occupy it, either with the mayer or sh^{r}'eves, or for any other busines."[4]

The passage in Hall, which describes the entry of Anne Boleyn, this same year, contains a phrase which has been misunderstood by some writers, and held to suggest that there were earlier mayoralty "shows" than I believe to have been the case. Henry wrote the mayor and citizens "to make preparacion aswell to fetch her grace from Grenewyche to the Tower by water as to see the citie ordered and garnished with pageantes in place accustomed [*i. e.*, at "royal-entries"; not at the inauguration of a mayor] . . . there was a common counsail called, and comaundement was geuen to the Haberdashers (of which crafte the Maior sir Stephen Pecocke then was) that they should prepare a Barge for the Batchelers with a wafter and a foyst[5] garnished with banners and streamers likewyse as they vse to dooe when the Maior is presented at Westminster on the morowe after Symon and Iude."[6] This last phrase refers, not to Lord Mayor's pageants, but to the barge; and we have seen that water-processions were common after 1422. We cannot assume from this passage that by 1533 there were pageants in the mayoralty shows.

"To a modern imagination," says Mr. Chambers,[7] "the type of civic pageantry is the annual procession and the installation of the Lord Mayor in No-

---

[1] Cf. above, vol. i, p. 160, for mention of the barges at the coronation of Elizabeth in 1487. There was also, on this occasion, a dragon spouting fire into the Thames.

[2] We have already noted (vol. i, p. 39) Sir Laurence Aylmer's pageant of 1516, which seems to have been part of the Midsummer Show of that year, though Fairholt calls it one of the earliest notices of a pageant exhibited on Lord Mayor's Day.

[3] Welch, i, p. 124.

[4] Herbert, i, p. 454. Mr. Edmund Wade, the archbishop's bargeman, was to furnish 28 oars and cushions, and to receive "for himself and . . . oars" at every voyage "when we shall have nede . . . wth ou^{r} compaignie in the lyvery, the sum of xxx^{s}."

[5] Fairholt, pt. i, p. 10, explains: "a barge, or pinnace, propelled by rowers." Cf. *The Knight of the Burning Pestle*, v, 2, 97: "next year I'll have him captain of the galley-foist, or I'll want my will."

[6] Hall, p. 798, cited by Fairholt and other writers. On this entry, see above, vol. i, pp. 180 ff.

[7] *Mediæval Stage*, ii, p. 165.

vember[1] . . . This was important enough from the middle of the sixteenth century . . . but its history cannot be taken much further back, and it is exceedingly probable that when the Midsummer Show came to an end in 1538, the pageants were transferred to the installation procession. The earliest clear notice is 1540, when a pageant of the Assumption, perhaps that which had already figured at the Midsummer Show of 1523, was used."[2]

Herbert quotes from the books of the Drapers, that the "election as Mayor of Sir William Roche in 1540 . . . is stated to have been 'with the gretyst and fayrest elec'ion amongst the co'es (commons)[3] that hathe byn sene.'" If there were a pageant on this occasion, we may assume it was that used in earlier Midsummer Shows.

The Ironmongers' books record, under date of 1540, "Payde ffor oure barge ffor ij. yers to Westmynster, xxxixs."[4]

Civic Pageantry at Norwich

We may note an example of civic pageantry at Norwich, just at the time when the Midsummer Show in London is becoming the Lord Mayor's Show. Were there more entries on this matter, it might more readily be presumed that these pageants were connected with the Midsummer Show (and perhaps they are); the civic pageants of Chester are mentioned in connection with this festival,

---

[1] The date was changed from the 29th of October with the change of the calendar in 1752. It is not clear that Walderne, mayor in 1422, took his oath on St. Edmund's Day (when he was elected); if he did, it is possible that the king's funeral upset the usual arrangements.

[2] Cf. Fairholt, pt. i, p. 14: "In 1540, the Pageant of the Assumption which had figured in the annual show at the setting of the Midsummer Watch in 1521–22, appears to have been borne before the Mayor from the Tower to Guildhall." Herbert, i, p. 457, is more cautious; this pageant "appears to have been that of the Assumption . . . whether it was precisely the same as at the Midsummer Watch, we are left to guess." The Assumption and St. Ursula were shown in 1522, (see above, vol. i, p. 40 and n. 3); Our Lady appeared in 1534 with St. Elizabeth (vol. i, p. 41).

[3] Professor Kittredge suggests *companies* which is a more likely expansion of co'es. But it must be admitted that Herbert had reason for his expansion into *commons*. Cf. *Liber Albus* i, p. 43, (Bk. i, pt. i) cap. xvi: "En droit del eleccion des Viscountz solent les Mair, Recordour, Audermans, et Communes assemblez le jour de Seint Matheu . . ." ". . . Et si contradursie sourde entre les communes . . ." [Cf. *ibid.*, iii, 1, fol. 12 a: "As concerning the election of Sheriffs — the Mayor, Recorder, Aldermen and Commons are to be assembled . . . And if any controversy arise between the commons as to the election . . ."] Cf. *Letter-Book* C, p. 174: in 1303 "John le Blund elected to the mayoralty . . . by . . . the whole Commonalty." Kemp, *Black Book of Warwick*, p. 4, makes the same expansion: "The Burgesses assembled in their coen (common) hall . . ."

It looks as if the "commons" were the regular name for the electoral body; so that the Drapers might well have spoken of the "greatest and fairest election among the commons." But the abbreviation seems a more natural one for *companies*.

[4] Nicholl, *Ironmongers*, p. 57.

as we have noted.[1] In 1556 and 1563, the Mayor of Norwich was clearly installed with pageantry. In 1540, "Thomas Nicholas, of his gode mynde, hath gyven to the Com̄naltie his Pagent called the Moremayd, the xxiiij^th^ day off Maye A° xxxij^nd^ R. R. Hen. viij., in the presens off Mast^r^ Sotherton & Thomas Conye."[2] The donor is probably Thomas Nicolles, who is mentioned in the list of Cordwainers admitted at the Feast of the Invention of the Holy Cross (3 May) 12 Henry VIII (1520).[3]

Whether or not it was a custom to exhibit pageants when the Norwich mayors took office is not clear; in 1545 there was "p^d^ for the chargis of a tryumphe made on trynyte sonday, for the peace concludyd between Inglond and Ffrance; & fyrst, for astyll[4] C . . . iiij*s*." There seems to have been no pageantry on this occasion, though the four waits received two shillings "for ther paynes," and "iij Menstrells at Crystechurche gate" were given "xij*d*."[5]

It is hard to say whether the pageantry in 1546 was in honor of the mayor, or not. There are some entries in the MS. *Chamberlain's Book* (for the years 1541 to 1550) under this year: "Item, to Robt. Nycholls, for his horses caryeng a pageant of Kyng Salamon about processyon, xij*d*.

"Item, to iij men that toke payn about the forsayd pageant, and to ij men that bare the moremayde, xx*d;* for sope, nayles, lyne, peynts, & other thyngs for the pageant, x*d*. . . .

"Itm, for mete & drynke for iiij persons with chargis of havyng the pageant out & inne, xiiij*d*."[6]

The Title "Lord Mayor" of London

About 1540 the title "Lord Mayor" was applied to the chief magistrate of London. There are no letters patent conferring the title upon him; "it was

---

[1] See above, vol. i, pp. 43 ff., esp. p. 47, n. 3.

[2] *Court-Book* v (1540–49) p. 4: cited by Ewing, p. 7. Hudson-Tingey, ii, p. 168, misprint the date 22 May, 1540; it is clearly 24 in the MS.

[3] *Old Free Book*, fol. 122 b. Cf. Hudson-Tingey, ii, p. 168, n. 2: "Nicholas was a cordwainer." *Ibid.*, ii, p. 230 (*Old Free Book*, fol. 162), enumerates the Norwich pageants: that of the "Tanners, Coryours, Cordwaners" is "Moises and Aron w^t^ the children off Israel and Pharo w^t^ his Knightes." [The same enumeration of pageants, made from the same source, may be found in *Norf. Arch.*, iii, p. 8.]

The "mermaid" is, perhaps, one of the inhabitants of the Red Sea.

Nicholas was neither Mayor nor Sheriff: see F. Blomefield (1806) iii, pp. 191 f., and 218 f., for lists of the mayors and sheriffs *temp.* Hen. VII and Hen. VIII; also Le Strange, *Norfolk Official Lists* (Norwich, 1890). In neither does the name of Nicholas, or Nichols, occur.

[4] Ewing notes "billet wood." (p. 11).

[5] *Chamberlain's Book* 1541–1550, fols. 214, 215. Printed in Ewing, p. 8 f.

[6] *Chamb. Bk.* (1541–50) fol. 249. Cf. Ewing, p. 13. The mermaid is presumably that given the city six yars before.

The election of mayor at Norwich (1 May) is described from a 1415 document in Hudson, i, p. 94 f. No pageantry is mentioned. A sword might be carried before the mayor save in the presence of the king (*ibid.*, i, pp. lxi and 32).

not definite but evolutionary in its origin, and . . .whereas the prefix had been more or less regularly adopted in the official minutes from about 1535, it did not come into general use in the outer world until some ten years later," says Mr. Beaven.[1] He refers to the expression "coram domino maiore," which was used in 1283,[2] and notes that before 30 May, 1545, Wriothesley never uses the title *Lord Mayor*, and after 8 June, 1545, he never uses anything else. Sir W. H. St. John Hope records [3] that in the minute-books of the Court of Aldermen and the Court of Common Council, the title was used as early as 1519, but not regularly until 1540.

1553 — The First Definite "Lord Mayor's Show"— Henry Machyn's Description

Henry Machyn, citizen and merchant-tailor of London, has left us an account of the first definite Lord Mayor's Show — that of 1553.[4] On 29 October, the new Lord Mayor [5] went "toward Westmynter [attended by the] craftes of London in ther best leveray . . . with trumpets blohyng and the whets [6] playng . . . a goodly fuyst [7] trymmed with banars and guns . . . waytyng of my lord mayre ['s] barge unto Westmynster [and] all the craftes bargers with stremars and banars [of every] craft, and so to the Cheker,[8] and so hom-wards; my lord mayre landyd at Banard Castyll[9] and [in St Paul's] chyrche-yerd dyd hevere [10] craft wher set in [array]: furst wher ij tallmen[11] bayreng ij gret stremars [of] the Marchand-tayllers armes, then cam on[12] [with a] drume and a flutt playng, and a-nodur with a great f [ife ?] all they in blue sylke, and then cam ij grett wodyn[13]

---

[1] *Aldermen of Lond.*, ii, p. xxxi. Cf. also *ibid.*, i, p. 407; ii, p. xxviii f. His careful researches on this subject allow him to speak with authority. I may refer, also, to Humpherus, i, p. 63; Sir W. H. St. John Hope's letter in the London *Times* for 10 December, 1901, p. 13, col. 6. (which is cited by Davey, i, p. 103.)

[2] *Letter-Book* A, fol. 30 b; Beaven, ii, p. xxviii f., and p. xxxi.

[3] In his letter to the *Times* already referred to.

[4] His *Diary* (1550–1563) has been edited by J. G. Nichols, from Cotton MS. Vit. F. v, for the Camden Society (no. xlii). It is referred to by Unwin, p. 275; Price, p. 92; Clode, ii, p. 113 f., &c. Cf. Fairholt, pt. ii, p. 244 f., and Nichols's note in the *Gentleman's Magazine* for October, 1833 (ciii, ii, p. 315 f.). This passage is on p. 47f.

[5] Sir Thomas White. (Nichols.)

[6] Waits (Nichols).

[7] Foist or pinnace (Nichols). Cf. above, p. 10, n. 5.

[8] Exchequer. (See Nichols's note e on p. 96 of the *Diary*.)

[9] This was reproduced in the 1913 Show; see below, p. 138.

[10] Every. (Nichols.)

[11] Cf. the "tall men" of the 1555 Show, who were "lyke wodys" — or "wild-men" — "alle in gren."

[12] One. (Nichols.)

[13] *Wood-men* or *savage men of the wood.* Next year written *vodys* (Nichols). These are obviously, "wild-men." Cf. above, vol. i, pp. 72 ff. — especially p. 77.

[armed] with ij grett clubes all in grene, and with skwybes borning [1] . . . with gret berds and syd here,[2] and ij targets a-pon ther bake . . . and then cam xvj trumpeters blohyng, and then cam [the Mayor's Company ?] in [blue] gownes, and capes and hosse [3] and blue sylke slevys, and evere man havyng a target and a gayffelyn to the nombur of lxx . . . and then cam a duyllyll,[4] and after cam the bachelars all in a leveray, and skarlett hods; and then cam the pageant of sant John Baptyst [5] gorgyusly [arrayed], with goodly speches; and then cam all the kynges trumpeters blowhyng, and evere trumpeter havyng skarlet capes, and the wetes [6] capes and godly banars, and then the craftes, and then the wettes playhyng, and then my lord mayre['s] offesers, and then my lord mayre and ij good henchmen, and then all the aldermen and the shreyffes, and so to dener; and after dener to Powlles . . . ."

This is a very interesting account of an early Lord Mayor's Show — the earliest definite one we have. It is interesting not only as showing the seed from which so many splendid triumphs developed, but also as giving us a glimpse of what the ancestry of the Show probably was. In the " royal-entry " the plat-

---

[1] Squibs burning.

I may note here that " squibs and crackers " in the streets were forbidden by a mayoralty precept of 25 October, 1684, [now preserved in the Taylor Collection of Broadsides in the Guildhall Library, (no. 99)]. The dates to which the prohibition applied were 29 October, 5 and 15 November. A mayoralty precept of 13 October, 1697 — preserved in the same collection, (no. 104) — provides that " no *Squibs*, *Serpents*, or any other Fire-Works, shall under colour of any Day of Solemnity, Festival, or other pretence whatsoever, be made, sold, flung or fired within this *City* or the *Liberties* thereof." In *Repertory* cxxiii, p. 574, (under date of 6 October, 1719) " it is ordered That the like number be Printed as was the last Year of a Paper to caution the Inhabitants within this City and Liberties against throwing Squibbs or other Fireworks be forthwith Printed and Delivered by the Beadles of the respective Wards to the several Inhabitants within the same." Notices in much the same words may be found in *Repertory* cxvi, p. 358 (21 Oct., 1712); *Repertory* cxvii, p. 396 (22 Oct., 1713); *Repertory* cxxxix, p. 345 (7 Oct., 1735), etc.; they were common enough during the eighteenth century; and Mayoralty Precepts of the early nineteenth century contain the same prohibitions. Cf. *e. g.*, no. 138 in the Taylor Collection (dated 24 October, 1816); nos. 139 and 140 (25 October, 1826 and 16 October, 1827); no. 143 (29 September, 1830) — which repeats the precepts of 1826 and 1827.

[2] Beards and side (*i. e.*, long) hair (Nichols). Perhaps what we call (side) whiskers.

[3] Caps and hose (Nichols).

[4] Devil (Nichols). It is almost impossible to say whether this figure is a survival of the miracle-play drawn into pageantry by the influence of the wild-man, or whether it helped to make the " wood-man " become wild. There is probably some connection between the two; and it is also possible that if this devil is not directly from the miracle-play, he has some connection with the Vice of the morality.

[5] The patron of the Merchant-Tailors. We may recall that St. John was given a trade symbolism by the Grocers in the " royal-entry " of 1392 (see above, vol. i, p. 131) and in the 1554 Show.

[6] Waits (Nichols); as is *wettes* just below.

forms were usually stationary; in the "midsummer show"— which began with the setting of the watch— there was marching, and the platforms and giants were carried about. St. John, as we have already noted, stood on a platform in 1392 (when a Grocer was mayor) to greet Richard II; Machyn's account shows that in 1553 he occupied a moving pageant at the inauguration of a Merchant-Tailor.[1] Giants are found in "royal-entries," it is true— but they originated in folk-custom; the devil here may have come— drawn by the influence of the "wild-man"— from the miracle plays.[2] Although "wildmen," waits, and henchmen were to be found in the "royal-entry," they were also in the Midsummer Show; and there is little doubt that the latter is the direct parent of the civic triumphs.[3]

1554 — Machyn describes the Show

In 1554, "a goodly pagant, a gryffen with a child lyung in harnes, and sant John Baptyst with a lyon, and ij vodys[4] and a dulle[5] with squybes bornyng," and music, accompanied the "nuw lord mayre of London, master Lyons groser."[6]

1555 — A Pageant and Four "Wodys"

The next year, "in Powlles cherche-yerde ther mett the bachelars and a goody pagyant[7] and a lxvi men in blue gownes, and with goodly targates and gaffelynes and a duwlle[8] and iiij talle men lyke wodys alle in gren, and trumpets playing a-for the mare."[9]

1556 — Sir Thomas Offley Installed in the Office of Mayor

The following year, on 28 October, the new mayor went to Westminster by boat, "and there was a godly pageant,"[10] but we are not told the subject. A few notices of the installation of Sir Thomas Offley may be found in Clode's volume. Directions were given "to see that the same men be fornyshed with children that shall then syng and playe upon instrumentes. And for apparellyng of them accordyngly, as by thadvice of my lord maiour electe shalbe thoughte

[1] In 1554, as we shall see directly, he appeared again, for a Grocer.

[2] At Chester— where the influence of the miracle-play on the Midsummer Show is marked— there were devils; which is one of the reasons why Henry Hardware put down the show in 1599 (see above, vol. i, p. 44).

[3] For further remarks on the "wild-man," see above, vol. i, p. 40, n. 5, and pp. 72 ff.

[4] Wild men (Nichols).

[5] Devil (Nichols).

[6] Machyn's *Diary*, pp. 72, 73. The lion is obviously appropriate.

[7] It looks as if this might have been stationary;— cf. the pageant which "stood" in Paul's churchyard in 1557.

[8] Devil (Nichols).

[9] Machyn, *op. cit.*, p. 96.

[10] *Ibid.*, pp. 117, 118; cf. Clode, ii, p. 262 f.

meate. And to devise other conceytes as woodwardes and other pastymes to be had with men castyng of Squybes of fyre afore the Bachelers." [1] In connection with the mayor's pageant, "'Mr. Leere, the schoolmaster of St. Anthony's received 10*s.* for the children which played at the Pageant.' This curious item is added, 'Paid for Rose water spent and occupied aboute the children and hym that rode upon the camyll, iiij*s.* ij*d.*'" [2]

1556 — A Provincial Mayor Installed with Pageantry

In 1556, the Mayor of Norwich was installed with pageantry. This is an interesting instance of what seems to have been an unusual occurrence; and as the account is to be found in a rare manuscript, it may be well to give some details of the occasion.[3]

There were three pageants, described in the *Mayors Book* as follows:

"This Paggeante was doone by the wagghts of the Cytte of Norwich. There was a Skaffoolld made at Sancte Peters of howndegate Churche-Styelle, rownnde like a pavillioun Richele adorned, full of targetts with a morien [4] on the toppe staunding naked, with a targett and a greate Darte in his haunde; wthin the wch stood an auncyente personage who represented Tyme, having the speche to the Mayor, as he cam forby, followinge the procession as ffolloweth." Here follow ten verses, composed by Mr. Boucke, schoolmaster.[5]

"There was in the persshe of S^c^ John's a greate pageant, stoundinge betweene Mr. Persses and Richard Bats, which was like a greate castell with a

---

[1] Clode, *Hist. Merchant-Taylors*, ii, p. 263.

[2] *Ibid.*, ii, p. 269, n. 2.

[3] The rare MS. is the *Mayors Book of Norwich*, which is kept in a safe in the Town Clerk's office. It is a pleasure for me to record my indebtedness to Arnold H. Miller, Esq., Town Clerk of Norwich, through whose kindness I was allowed to see this treasure. The paragraphs I cite are taken from pp. 139–143 of this MS.

A copy done by an eighteenth or nineteenth century scribe — not always accurate in minor details — may be found in the Brit. Mus. (Addl. MS. 27967 — see fol. 54). This MS. dates the event 1550, and is headed, "Pageants performed before Robt. Rugge, Mayor of Norwich, upon the day of his entering into the Office." Ewing, p. 14 f, prints the account "from the Corporation Books" — his version does not always agree with that in the MS. *Mayors Book.* He, too, says that these pageants were "exhibited on the Guildday of Robert Rugg, Mayor in 1550." The Norwich MS. clearly dates this 1556.

It is likely that this show was planned for the induction of Steward into his third term of office in 1556; the *Mayors Book* does not mention the name of Rugg in connection with these pageants. I feel certain that a scribe misread 1556 — or carelessly wrote 1550; and that afterwards the show was connected with Rugg who was mayor in that year.

Augustine Steward was mayor in 1534, 1546, and 1556 (see Le Strange, *Norfolk Official Lists*, pp. 107, 108).

[4] Ewing notes, *Moor.* This was, apparently, an image.

[5] It is possible that he spoke them as well. The MS. (p. 140) reads "yd Bucke." Perhaps yd = qd = quod (quoth).

greate gate thereunder like a Cytte gate, & ouer the gate a great castell with towers, made for Arms of the Cytte, & ye Lyon being cowched under the gate, & uppon every tower a Morian with his Darte & his targett;[1] & at the Castell gate stoode a personage richlie apperrelled like an orrator, who had thes words ffollowinge to the Mayor, which after he had spoken he gave the verses followinge, in paper foulde in a stycke of cannell,[2] with Rosemarye & gylleves gylte, & so passinge throwghe the Gate, all the greate ordenans with a grete nombre of chambers wer shott offe." Here follow eight verses.

"There was a pageante standinge in the pershe of St Andrews, against Willm. Barkhams, Richelie apparelled, wherein was an orratour & fower younge maydes Richelie apparelled, who represented the fower Cardenall vertews; and the orracon begonne with thes sentences followinge to the said Mayor & after they had all spoken, the orratour againe[3] to the said Mayor & presented him with A braunche with a Roll of ther declaracoun, clad in a braunch of Rosemarye." The Virtues were introduced by the orator in a four-stanza speech; each of the Virtues follows, with a twelve-line stanza, and the orator closes with six verses —

> "As wee do meane take in good parte
> This simple gyste geven with good harte."

Under this is written, "finis q^t^ Cordalle."[4]

It will be recalled that the four Virtues have appeared often in pageantry since they greeted Queen Margaret at Coventry in 1456; but Time makes his first appearance here. Three years later we find him welcoming Elizabeth at her coronation.

1557–60 — The London Shows

In 1557, a pageant stood in St. Paul's churchyard, and the mayor and aldermen, landing at Paul's wharf, passed it on their way to the Guildhall.[5] We know no details concerning it. Machyn makes no mention of a Lord Mayor's Show in 1558; in 1559 — the first year of Elizabeth's reign — on 31 September, the "nuw shreyffes of London toke ther barge to Westmynster to take ther howth, master Loge and master Marten, althermen, in the checker, and after home to dener with ther craftes."[6] On 28 October, 1560 — Chester being mayor — the Stationers were assigned a place following the Poulterers in processions on the Lord Mayor's Day.[7]

---

[1] Presumably images, as the other one.

[2] Cinnamon (Ewing).

[3] Supply *spoke.*

[4] Addl. MS. 27967 reads "Finis q^t^ & Cordalle," and the line is underscored in pencil, and queried. Cordalle may be the scribe — but I think it more likely that he is the author of the last set of speeches — perhaps the last two. The couplet cited above seems to show that mayors had not been often installed with pageants at Norwich.

[5] Machyn, *Diary*, pp. 155, 156.

[6] *Ibid.*, p. 213.

[7] *Repertory* xiv, fol. 552 b.

1561 — Sir W. Harper Installed

The Merchant-Taylors' records throw some interesting light on the 1561 Show.[1] Evan Davis, porter, agreed "that he shall and will provide to fynde with hym self xvj tall and stronge men [to] beare the pageant upon the morrowe after Symond and Jude next, and to see the same pageant broughte saffelye into this house that present day at nighte. And he to have for every of the said xvj men or portars xx*d*." Out of deference to the mayor the pageant showed five celebrated harpers; and is particularly important as showing the first instance of mythology in these shows.

"John Shutte shall make for this Company ageynst the feaste of Symond and Jude next, a pageant accordyng to suche a pattern (for drawing which, Gabitt received 5*s*.) as shalbe devised to answer the speches also here devised and delyvered to hym and also he to fynd ij men to be woodwardes to cast squybes or wilde-fyer the morrowe after the seid feaste of Symond and Jude next, and also to fynde the said wilde-fyer. And he to have of this house for the fynyshyng and makyng of the seid pageant and fynding the seid woodhousys xij*li*."[2]

That the figures of the various harpers on this pageant were alive, the following extracts from the Company's records show:

"Item paid for a crowne for Davyd, and trymyng of the regalles, and hyer of Mr. Shobman to attend upon the pageant xij*s*. vj*d*.

"Item to John Tayllour, master of the children of the late monastere of Westminster, for his children that sung and playd in the pageant, xxx*s*.

"Item paid to portars for settyng uppe the pageant in the hall upon the frame in the gallery, ij*s*. iiijd.

---

[1] See Clode, ii, p. 263 f.

[2] *Ibid.*, ii, p. 265. Cf. *ibid.*, ii, p. 267: "The pageant had reference to the Lord Mayor's name and the only description of it is this: 'On the toppe as a fane the Armes of the lord mayour electe on the one side thereof, and the armes of the merchant taillours on the other side thereof,

"'Under in the myddest David with his story aboute him.

"'On the right side Orpheus with his story before.

"'On the lefte Amphion with his story.

"'On the lefte side on the ende Arion, etc.

"'On the right side of thende Iopas, with his, etc.

"'Orpheus playeng upon his harpe, and trees, rivers, mountaynes as daunsinge and harkeninge.

"'Amphion so, with a Citie and the wall a buyldinge, and the stones as voluntary Ronninge to it.

"'Arion syttinge on a dolphin in the sea playeng on the harpe.

"'Iopas so, before a table of princes and every of theis (*sic*) to have his posie.

"'In all places of the pageant to have paynted the verses of 150th psalme.'"

" Item paid to Mr. More for the hyer of v harps and his child playing in the pegeant, xxjs." [1]

Apparently sixteen porters carried this pageant after the mayor,[2] and the pageant was kept by the company in its hall, after the show was over. The poetry was evidently written before the pageant was built by Shute; though perhaps not before the design for the structure had been made by Gabitt.

Machyn describes the day; " the nuw mare toke ys barge towhard Westmynster my nuw lorde mare master Harper, with the althermen in ther skarlett, and all the craftes of London in ther leverey, and ther barges with ther baners and streamers of evere occupasyon('s) armes; and ther was a goodly foist mad with stremars . . . and grett shutyng of gunes and trumpettes blohyng; and at xij of the cloke my lord mare and the althermen landyd at Powlles warffe, and so to Powlles chyrche-yarde, and ther met ym a pagantt gorgyously mad, with chylderyn, with dyvers instrumentes playng and syngyng; . . ." [3]

" A goodly pagantt with goodly musyke plahyng " greeted the lord mayor as he landed after his trip to Westminster in 1562; but we know none of the details.[4]

1563 — A Norwich Pageant

In 1563, the Norwich Grocers' pageant — originally used in their Whitsun play — was exhibited at a mayor's installation. " It was enquyryd by Mr Aldriche for ye Provysyon of ye Pageant to be preparyd ageynst ye daye of Mr Davy his takyng of his charge of ye Mayralltye." [5] This shows a miracle-play pageant — the Grocers' " tree," which represented Paradise — used with trade-symbolism on a civic occasion.

---

[1] Clode, ii, p. 269. The speeches are also in Clode, ii, p. 267 f. David, Orpheus, Amphion, Arion, and Iopas each spoke four lines in turn, explaining his " story " — which was probably painted behind each. Then David, Orpheus, and Amphion spoke again in praise of the harp. " Who wrote the speeches or composed the music is not disclosed " (Clode).

[2] It is, of course, possible that the porters were employed merely to carry the pageant from the Company's hall to St. Paul's churchyard and back.

[3] Machyn, p. 271; cited by Clode, ii, p. 244.

[4] See Machyn, p. 294. In a note, Heath (1869, p. 426) gives an order related to the dress of the bachelors, issued by the Court of Assistants in 1562. " . . . The Wardeyns of the Grocers, and the Wardeyns of the Bachillors to cesse both the livery of the bachillors, and all the Companie of the yeomanry for the furniture of the poor men's gownes, the pageant the first, and other great charges that must be done when my Lord Mayor elect shall go to Westminster, as to them shall be thought meet."

[5] " Mr. Aldriche " is probably the John Aldrich who was mayor of Norwich in 1570. For this cited passage see the Norwich Grocers' records of 13 May 1563 (copied by Kirkpatrick) in Fitch, *The Grocers' Play*, p. 22. [Cf. above, vol. i, p. 35, and n. 2.]

1566 — Sir Christopher Draper Inaugurated

When, in 1566, Sir Christopher Draper was inaugurated Lord Mayor of London, the pageant cost £18.[1] The Ironmongers' records give many interesting details. "October 1st. Richard Baker, paintoʳ staynoʳ, in the presence of this courte, was agreed wᵗ all for making of the pageant wᵗall, and all manner of things incident to the same, as well the carpenter and paynter's worke, except the children and their apparel; and for his paynes therein to have the some of sixtene pounds, and if it fortune him to be a loser at that price, it is agreed that he shall have xlˢ· more; and for confirmac̄on of this his promise the same Richard Baker hath hereunto put his hand."[2]

"At the same present tyme John Tailoʳ, Schoole mʳ of the children of Westmʳ, is also agreed wᵗ all for vj of his children to serve in the foresaid pageant, as well for the speeches as songs; and for his paynes in that behalfe to have the some of xlˢ·: and for performance hereof the same John Tailor hath put to his hande the same day and yeare abovesaid."[3]

Among the items in the accounts are:

"Item, paide to Richard Baker for the devise and makinge of the paggion, xviijˡⁱ·.

"Item, paide to Walter Browne for porters wʰ carryed the pagent, and hoggeshedes to reste the same uppon, sundry tymes, xlixˢ·.

"Item, paide to James Pele,[4] for seven paire of gloves for the children in the pagent, sixpence a paire, iijˢ· vjᵈ·.

---

[1] See Malcolm, *Lond. Rediv.*, ii, pp. 42, 43, (from the books of the Ironmongers' Company), cited by Fairholt, pt. i, p. 14; also Nicholl, *Ironmongers*, p. 83 f. Malcolm errs in giving the mayor's name as William; cf. Fairholt, *loc. cit.*, n. 2. Heywood, *Works*, (1874) iv, p. 287, and Herbert, ii, p. 591, give his correct name.

Jupp, p. 31, n., cites from the Carpenters' records, under 20 September, 1566: "Willyam Emerson servaunt wth Sr Thomas Gresham waterman promisethe to pve this copanye to Westmʳ to waite on the Lorde Mayoʳ for this yere for the some of xiij*s.* iiij*d.* and he to find eyshes."

[2] Nicholl, p. 85.

[3] *Ibid.*, p. 86.

[4] Hazlitt, *Livery Companies*, p. 310, n. 1, says: "probably the father of George Peele, the dramatist . . . He was possibly a glover, either by trade or freedom, as he supplied seven pairs at 6*d.* a pair for the children." Cf. Chambers, ii, p. 166 (referring to Malcolm and Hazlitt).

This is the same individual who is mentioned below, *sub anno* 1569. Nicholl (p. 88, n.) says: "He was contemporary with, and may have been a relative or elder brother of George Peele . . . Mr. Dyce, however, makes no mention of him in his biography of the dramatist . . ."

On his relationship to George, see Bullen's Peele, i, pp. xiii *et seq.* In 1565, George was a scholar at Christ's Hospital, of which his father was Clerk. James had, in 1553, published a black-letter treatise on book-keeping, and it was followed by another in 1569. That James Peele was the father of George was first announced by John H. Ingram, in the *Athenæum* for 2 July, 1881 (see Bullen's Peele, i, p. xiii, n.).

"Item, paide more to Mr. Pele, for his devise and paynes in the paggent xxx$^{s.}$.

"Item, paid to Mr Hill, Iremonger, for settinge up a frame of tymber to set the pagyent on, iij$^{s.}$ iiij$^{d.}$.

"Item, paide to Goodman Cave, joyner, for the setting upp the pagent in our hall, x$^{s.}$.

"Item, paid for a kylderkyn stande of ale, sent into Blackwell hall, for suche as tendyd on the pagent, iiij$^{s.}$." [1]

There were, on this occasion, twenty-eight "wifelers;" forty-eight men with wax torches, an ell in length, and an equal number armed with javelins. Two "woodmen" carried clubs and hurled squibs.[2]

1568 — A Pageant for Sir Thomas Rowe

In 1568, Sir Thomas Rowe, Merchant-Tailor, had a pageant of John the Baptist, the Company's patron saint; there were "other similar personages, amongst whom were four boys, who spoke complimentary speeches allusive to the name of the mayor. St. John's speech begins:

"*St. John* — 'I am that Voyce in Wilderness, w'ich ones the Jewes did calle.'

"*1st Boy* — 'Behold the *Roe*, the swift in chace.'" [3]

1569 — A Pageant Planned

In 1569, the Ironmongers "paid unto James Pele and Peter Baker, for the devise of a pageant, wch tok none effecte, xxvj$^{s.}$. viij$^{d.}$." [4] As the son often followed the father's footsteps, we may assume that Peter is the son of Richard Baker; Peele is the one who is mentioned in 1566.

On 25 October, 1573, the Court of Aldermen voted that the Lord Mayor-elect receive £50 toward the expenses of the pageants.[5] There is no detailed record of what these were; the Recorder, Fleetwood, in a letter to Lord Burghley, men-

---

[1] Nicholl, p. 87 f.

[2] Fairholt, pt. i, p. 56, note, quotes from Shirley's *Honoria and Mammon* (1652) saying, "He alludes to the wild men that cleared the way [for the Show] and their fireworks, in these words: 'I am not afear'd of your green Robin Hoods, that fright with fiery club your pitiful spectators, that take pains to be stifled . . .'"

For Herbert's notices of this 1566 Show, see *Hist. Liv. Comps.* ii, p. 592 and n.; i, p. 199. For a description of the Company's barge, or "foiste," see Malcolm, ii, p. 43 (Fairholt, pt. i, p. 17). Nicholl, p. 85, gives this extract from the Company's records: "It'm, agreed w^{t} Hugh Watts and Xp̃ofer Beck that they shall fynde us two woodmen, w^{t} clubbes, squibbes, and powder . . . and that to be done in all respectes as hath byn accustomed, and to be paid for the same xxxiij^{s} iiij^{d}."

[3] Herbert, i, p. 200; cited by Chambers, ii, p. 166. Cf. also Fairholt, pt. i. p. 20. J. G. Nichols, *Lond. Pag.*, p. 94, quotes John Day's *Order observed by the Lord Mayor*, etc., of 1568, which does not mention pageants.

[4] The records of the Company, printed in Nicholl, p. 98.

[5] *Repertory* xviii, fol. 285 b.

tions " a playe for our farewell," and feasts.[1] In 1574, on account of the plague, no feast was held at Guildhall, though the mayor went to Westminster by water.[2]

1575 — William Smith's Description of the Show

" A breffe description of the Royall Citie of London, capitall citie of this realme of England," was written by William Smythe, citizen and Haberdasher of London, in 1575. The manuscript [3] contains a detailed description of the Lord Mayor's Show of that period. The author tells of the chief magistrate's progress to Westminster by water " in most tryumplyke maner "; he describes the decorated barges, the arms of the various companies; the return — also by water — to Paul's wharf, after the mayor had taken his oath; and the procession through Cheapside. On this occasion " to make waye in the streetes there are certain men apparelled lyke devells and wylde men with skybbs and certayne beadells." [4] As a regular feature of the procession, Smith mentions " the pageant of (*sic*) tryumphe [5] rychly decked, whereuppon by certayne fygures and wrytinges, some matter touchinge justice, and the office of a maiestrate is represented." [6]

The costumes of the paraders are described, and the order in which they march; the procession included " certayne wyfflers in velvet cotes and chaynes with white staves." [7] And so " they passe alonge through the citie, to the Guyldhall, where they dyne that daye, to the number of 1000 persons, all at the charge of the Mayor and the ij Shereffes. This feast costeth 400*l.*, whereof the Mayor payeth 200*l.*, and eche of the Shereffes 100*l.*" [8]

In 1582,[9] there appears to have been no Lord Mayor's Show, on account of the plague; Sir Thomas Blanke, the mayor, was not presented to the queen until Sunday, 6 May, 1583, Elizabeth being then at Richmond. There were no pageants on this occasion.[10]

---

[1] His letter is published in *Prog. Q. Eliz.*, i, p. 355. In his *Diarium Heptomadæ* (October, 1573) he describes a change in the personnel of the City government.

[2] Holinshed, iv, p. 325.

[3] Printed by Haslewood, *Brit. Bibliog.*, i, pp. 539 f.; N. Drake, *Shaks. and his Times*, ii, p. 162 f. (Cf. also Fairholt, pt. i, p. 20 f. and note on p. 24; Chambers; J. G. Nichols and Hone, *Anc. Mys.*)

[4] Smith, quoted by Fairholt, pt. i, p. 21.

[5] Probably " pageant *or* triumph " — the two words were often used as synonyms.

[6] N. Drake, *loc. cit.*

[7] Drake, p. 163.

[8] Drake, *op. cit.*, p. 164. For an order of procedure on Lord Mayor's Day — of perhaps a slightly later date — see Strype's Stow's *Survey*, book v, p. 168.

[9] The " 1581 " pageant referred to by Herbert, i, p. 200, is clearly the 1585 pageant, written by Peele. (There is obviously a misprint in Herbert.)

[10] See *Prog. Q. Eliz.*, ii, p. 399.

Conclusion

In 1585, George Peele wrote the show for Sir Wolstone Dixie; his is the first printed pamphlet giving the speeches addressed to the mayor; and with it the civic triumphs enter a new stage of development. That words were spoken, before this show, we have seen; in 1553 there were "goodly speeches" which have not survived; those addressed to the Norwich mayor of 1556 have come down to us, and a fragment of those addressed to the London mayor of 1568. There were speeches in the 1561 Show, for Sir W. Harper, and there was music, if not speeches, in 1562. But Peele's pamphlet is the first known contemporary publication giving the verses addressed to the mayor; it is followed by a long line of descriptive booklets issued during the seventeenth century.

We may pause here, on the threshold of the period when the Lord Mayor's Show reached its highest development, to note that by 1585 these civic triumphs were well established as part of the ceremonies incidental to the inauguration of a new mayor. The ride to Westminster, which dates from the establishment of the mayoralty in 1209, was varied by a water-progress as early as 1422. By 1453, this had evidently superseded the "riding"; and a hundred years later the Lord Mayor's Show, as we know it, had begun. Taking pageantry from the Midsummer Show, and adapting the splendors of the "royal-entry" to the civic occasion, the installation of the chief magistrate of London grew in elaborateness, until it eclipsed the "royal-entry"; this development we shall now follow through the hundred and twenty-three years which lie between Peele's Show for 1585 and Settle's for 1708.

§ 2. THE SHOW AT ITS HEIGHT, 1585–1708: PEELE TO SETTLE

Peele's 1585 Show

The first "text" of a Lord Mayor's Show hitherto discovered, is that written by George Peele for Sir Wolstone Dixie, Skinner, mayor in 1585. The pamphlet [1] contains only the speeches spoken by the characters in the pageant; [2] it gives no description of the pageant or of the procession — a practice which grew up in later pamphlets. The "speech spoken by him that rid on a luzern [3] before the pageant, apparelled like a Moor" describes "this emblem thus in show signifi-

[1] A copy is in the Bodleian; reprints may be found in Dyce's (1829) ed. of Peele, ii, p. 147; Bullen's ed., i., p. 351; Price, p. 199; Nichols, *Prog. Q. Eliz.*, ii, p. 446; *Hist. Leicestershire*, iv, p. 496; *Harl. Misc.* (1813), x, p. 351; Strype's Stow's *Survey* (1720), ii, p. 136. Cf. also Greg, p. 22; Fairholt, *L. M. Pag.*, pt. i, p. 24; J. G. Nichols, *Lond. Pag.*, p. 100; Wadmore, p. 144; J. Nichols, in *Gent. Mag.*, August, 1824, p. 113; Hone, *Anc. Mys.*, p. 249.

[2] As Fairholt (*loc. cit.*), and others, have already pointed out.

[3] Lynx. This, with the Moor, is "a slender allusion to the company" of the Mayor, who was a Skinner. (Herbert, i, p. 200.)

cant": London, attended by her "well-advised magistrates," receives presents from the country; Thames,

> For London's good, conveys with gentle stream
> And safe and easy passage, what she can,
> And keeps her leaping fishes in her lap.

The soldier and sailor,

> . . . frankly both,
> For London's aid, are all in readiness,
> To venture and to fight by land and sea.

Science "is vowed to honour London with her skill," and the city herself is ready to yield all unto Elizabeth. The Moor ends by telling the Lord Mayor to guard the treasure he has received.

Speeches by London, Magnanimity, Loyalty, the Country, the Thames, the Soldier, the Sailor, Science and four nymphs — "the children in the pageant" — follow. London introduces herself and lauds Elizabeth; the others speak in turn, praising London and extolling the queen.[1]

We find here the symbolical figure of London which has persisted down to our own times. I have suggested the possibility of its connection with such figures as the 1486 Ebraucus, where the founder — an historical or pseudo-historical figure — comes close to symbolism.[2] The lynx and the Moor have a trade-symbolism which is, as we shall see, a very important element of the seventeenth-century mayoralty shows. Magnanimity, Loyalty, and Science are personified abstractions such as we have already seen in the "royal-entry;" the Thames is no new figure, and the Soldier and Sailor are practically abstract, in that they represent Force by land and sea. We should observe that here — as in former inaugural processions — there is but one pageant. This may have had an influence in changing the meaning of the word from *car* to *spectacle;* I do not believe that 'Sir Laurence Aylmer's pageant' of 1516[3] referred to a spectacle: the records probably meant the pageant-car itself; and in 1585 we find there is still only one car, though the show has become attached to the Lord Mayor's Day.

Peele's 1588 Show

That Peele was the author of the Show for 1588, is clear from the entry in the *Stationers' Register* under 28 October of that year:[4] "Entred for his [*i. e.*,

[1] It is to be presumed that the female characters were boys dressed up.

[2] See above, vol. i, p. 81 f.

[3] Herbert, i, p. 457, cited above, vol. i, p. 39. This was for a Midsummer Show, and is an example of the immediate source of the Lord Mayor's Show.

[4] Arber, *The Stationers' Register*, ii, p. 504. Fleay, *Biog. Chron. Eng. Drama, 1559–1642*, gives a list of Lord Mayor's Shows, ii, p. 402. He assigns — without giving his authority — the 1588 "device" to George Peele. Cf. also *op. cit.*, ii, p. 154.

Fairholt, pt. i, p. 26 (with whom should be compared J. Nichols, in *Gent. Mag.* for August, 1824, p. 113) notes that this "device of the pageant" was licensed to be printed by Richard

Richard Jones's] Copie vppon Condicion that it maye be lycenced, *ye device of the Pageant borne before the Righte honorable* MARTYN CALTHROP *lorde maiour of the Cytie of London the 29th daie of October 1588* GEORGE PEELE the Authour . . .vjd."

NELSON'S SHOW FOR 1590

The rare descriptive pamphlet of Thomas Nelson's Show for 1590 is in the British Museum; I have described it at length in a paper which appeared in *Modern Language Notes* for January, 1918. Here, it will be sufficient to repeat that there is little new in this show, although we see such characters as The Peace of England, Fame, Wisdom on one side supporting the State, Policy on the other side supporting the State, God's Truth, Commonwealth, Richard II, Jack Straw, another Commonwealth in the shape of Sir William Walworth — where we see a former mayor of London given an allegorical significance not unlike, perhaps, that which may have been given to the mythical-founder in the "royal-entry." History plays a part in the show, and at times — especially in Richard's cry to Walworth — the speeches suggest a formless play, partly historical, partly allegorical—a weaker *Kynge Johan.* We may presume that the mayor stopped before the pageant to hear the speakers; the conditions of presentation account for the lack of dramatic coherence.[1]

PEELE'S 1591 SHOW

The first Lord Mayor's Show to have a title is Peele's *Descensus Astrææ*, written for the inauguration of Sir William Webb, uncle of Archbishop Laud,[2] who entered into the mayoralty in 1591.[3] The presenter's speech eulogizes the mayor — not without a punning allusion to his name [4] — and flatters the queen.

Jones; he adds that no copy is now known to exist, "neither are the titles of any other than this one preserved between the years 1585 and 1591, though we may reasonably suppose that others were printed." In a note, he refers to Gifford's opinion that Munday contributed several during this period. I have not found a copy of the 1588 pamphlet.

[1] Nelson repeats the erroneous origin of the dagger in the City Arms, which is not Walworth's, but St. Paul's. He notes that Walworth won the Fishmongers their crest ("two armes bearing vp a crowne") and received a crest for himself. Jack Straw's speech ("Jacke Strawe the rebell I present, Wat Tyler was my aide . . . Yet for our bad ambitious mindes by Walworth we were tamde. He being Maior of London then . . . slew me first . . .") is exposition of history, connected with the guild, and not without a moral flavor.

[2] Bullen's Peele, i, p. 360. His wife was the daughter of Sir Christopher Draper (Lord Mayor, 1566); his sister Anne married Sir Wolstan Dixie (Lord Mayor, 1585).

[3] This pamphlet is in the Guildhall. It is reprinted in Dyce's (1829) ed. of Peele, ii, p. 155; in Bullen's ed., i, p. 361; the *Harl. Misc.*, x, p. 68, whence Gillespy reprints it, p. 66. Cf. Greg, p. 22; J. Nichols, in *Gent. Mag.*, August, 1824, p. 113; Fairholt, pt. i, p. 27; J. G. Nichols, p. 100. As usual, the pamphlet gives only the speeches — there was no prose description of the ceremonies of the day.

[4] "See, lovely lords . . . How Time hath turn'd his restless wheel about . . . and weaved a Web For your content."

As Astræa guards her flock from her seat on the top of the pageant, Superstition, a friar, and Ignorance, a priest, seek in vain to poison the fountain of truth,[1] beside which they sit. Astræa, " our Pandora fair, Our fair Eliza, our Zabeta fair," defends the fountain, her eye keeping Ignorance in awe. Euphrosyne, Aglaia, Thalia,[2] Charity, Hope, Faith, Honour, and the Champion, all praise Astræa, rather fulsomely; and the two Malcontents quail before her.

" In the hinder part of the Pageant did sit a child, representing Nature, holding in her hand a distaff, and spinning a web, which passed through the hand of Fortune, and was wheeled up by Time, who spake as followeth " — explaining that he winds " the Web that kind so well begins, While Fortune doth enrich what Nature spins." [3]

At the end of the descriptive pamphlet is a " speech on the water, delivered in the morning, at my Lord Mayor's going to Westminster." It was spoken " by one clad like a Sea-nymph; who presented a Pinesse on the water, brauely rigd and mand, to the Lord Mayor, at the time he took Barge . . ." This speech, says Fairholt,[4] " is rather high-flown in its diction, but it contains much poetic feeling, and a beautiful allusion to London, its greatness and stability, in the words; —

" ' The mortar of these walls, tempered in peace,
Yet holds the building sure.' "

Daw, citing from the oldest book of records in the possession of the Butchers' Company, notes " that there was no Barge money collected this yeare [1592] for that the Lord M. took his othe at the Tower Gate, and went not to Westminster, and so no Barge used." [5] There was, in this year, a plague in London; [6] and this seems to have made it necessary for the mayor to give up his show in 1593 as well. Sir Cuthbert Buckle, whose mayoralty began in this year,[7] was presented to the queen by the Recorder of London; but no place is mentioned in the speech, which was probably delivered at some suburban palace — perhaps Greenwich. Before the presentation took place, the mayor " hath beene presented before your Highnes Officer in that behalfe appointed, and hath sollemnly sworne his fidelitie to your most excellent Majestie and taken the accustomed oath for the due execution of his office . . ." [8]

[1] Also represented on the pageant.

[2] Cf. the 1533 pageant for Anne Boleyn, above, vol. i, p. 183.

[3] Pamphlet, p. 7. Cf. Bullen's Peele, i, p. 366.

[4] *L. M. Pag.*, pt. i, p. 29.

[5] *Early Hist. Butchers*, p. 23. " This appears," says Mr. Daw, in a note, " to have been the practice if the Court of Exchequer were not sitting." We have already noted instances of the mayor being presented to the Constable of the Tower in 1303 and 1304 (cf. above, p. 4, n. 3).

[6] Cf. *Prog. Q. Eliz.*, iii, pp. 130, 190, 214, 254 and n. 4.

[7] Cf. Strype's Stow's *Survey* (1720), ii, p. 138.

[8] Harl. MS. 852, fol. 2. This speech is reprinted by Nichols, *Prog. Q. Eliz.*, iii, 228 f.; he notes that Edward Drew, sergeant-at-law, was Recorder of London, 1592–1594.

The speech which begins "It is full three years past, my good lord, that by occasion of God's punishment the Cittizens of London have beene constreyned to forbeare their comeing to this Ho: place to accomplish their duety they owe to yor Lordship & this Honourable Court . . ."[1] follows the other address without a break. It was, however, delivered on the presentation of Sir John Spencer to the Lord Chief Baron[2] at Westminster in 1594. This sentence shows that for three years — since 1591 — no mayor had been presented at Westminster; which leads us to imagine that Sir Cuthbert Buckle had met the queen at one of her palaces on the outskirts of London.

1602 — The Merchant-Taylors' Show

From the "Court Minute" of 23 September, 1602, we get the following record of the Merchant-Taylors' Show of that year:[3] "Itt is concluded and agreed that against Symon and Jude's Day for the triumph before the Lord Maior, there shalbe preparacion made of a Pageon, a Ship, a Lyon, and a Cammell.[4] The Pageon being a thing ordinary, and th'other three doe properly belong unto our Companie, and are very fitt and answerable for this tyme, namely, the Ship in regard two Wor^{ll} Members of this Company are to bear great offyces in this Cittie for this nexte yeare ensuing, viz. Mr Robt Lee, Alderman, the hon^{ble} place of Lord Maior, and Mr John Swinnerton, Alderman, the place of one of the Sheriffes of this Cittie, and they both being merchants. And we, as well in regard of the Companies' Incorporacion and name of Merchantailors, as also in regard, the two said Wor^{ll} persons are merchants by profession, the shippe is proper and very apte for this occasion and tyme, and the Lyon being part of the Companie's Armes, and the Cammell the Companie's supporters. And our Master and Wardens are entreated to have a speciall care, that every thing maye be very sufficientlie performed, to the worship and creditt of the Company . . . not havinge had a Maior of our Company sithence Sir Thomas Rowe was Lord Mayor, being now thirty and three years since."

The emphasis in this show — the author of which has not yet been discovered — is on trade-symbolism. That the Merchant-Tailors were not niggardly in their celebration, is shown by the large amount of money they spent. There was evidently a water-show, for the ship is spoken of as distinct from the pageant, which was "a thing ordinary," — though it is, of course, possible that the ship

---

[1] Harl. MS. 852, fol. 2 — reprinted in *Prog. Q. Eliz.*, iii, p. 254 f.

[2] Sir William Peryam, [Nichols, *Prog. Q. Eliz.*, iii, p. 254, n. 2]. Both the *Cat. Harl. MSS.* i, p. 456, and Nichols, *op. cit.*, note that the presentation of Sir John Spencer begins here.

[3] Printed in Clode, i, p. 187.

[4] The ship cost £38; the pageant, £78, 17*s.*, 7*d.*; the lion and camel, £8, 16*s.*, 6*d.*; there were also "green-men," at £5, 3*s.*, 4*d.*; the barge, barge-cloth and "gallifoyst" cost £78, 3*s.*, 4*d.* The total expenses of the Merchant-Taylors' Company for this show, were £747, 2*s.*, 10*d.* The items are printed from the records of the Company, by Clode, i, p. 390.

was displayed on land; if this were the case, we have an early example of a show with more than one pageant. The "green-men," which appeared this year, as the accounts of the Company indicate, are, of course, nothing new.

On account of the plague, there was no show the next year. Sidney Young cites the records of the Barber-Surgeons' Company, for 22 October, 1603: "To the Wardens of the Companie of Barbor-Surgeons. *By the Maior.* Theise are to will and require you that you take speciall knowledge herby that for avoydinge of infeccion by assemblie of people this tyme of gods vizitacion It is thought meate therbe noe shewe made the morrowe after Simond and Judes daie next, it is intended that youre Companie be dischardged thereof for their Attendance for that tyme. This xxijth of October 1603. Sebright."[1]

1605 — Munday's "Triumphes of Reunited Britannia"

Munday wrote the show for the inauguration of Sir Leonard Holliday, Merchant-Taylor, in 1605. The pamphlet is entitled *The Triumphs of Reunited Britannia*,[2] — which, of course, refers to James's accession. In this show there is some of the mythical history of Britain, and Munday has inserted a good deal of symbolism. Opening with a dialogue between the master and the mate of the "Shippe called the Royal Exchange,"[3] in which the master expresses his joy at getting home, and the mate his pleasure in the fact that "our Master is Mayor," the show is continued by Neptune and Amphitrite on a lion and camel;[4] this pair first seated their son Albion in the land. Corinæus and Gogmagog — two huge giants, "for the more grace and beauty of the show" — were fettered by chains of gold to "Britain's Mount" — the principal pageant, which they appeared to draw. This mount, "triangular as the Island of Britayne it selfe is described to bee," contained children representing "under the shape of a fayre and beautifull Nymph, Britania hir selfe, accosted with Brute's divided kingdoms, in the like female representations, Leogria, Cambria, and Albania."

Britannia tells Brute, "her conqueror (who is seated somewhat lower, in the habite of an adventurous warlike Troyan)," that she had still continued her name of Albion but for his conquest of her virgin honor — and that she was glad he conquered her. Brute shows her her causes for joy — for he overcame "Goemagot" (or Gogmagog) and his "barbarous brood"; built Troya Nova, and beautified the land, which before was a vast wilderness.

The three virgin kingdoms seem to reproach him for his "over-much fond love" of his sons, in dividing one monarchy between them. He stays their re-

---

[1] Young, *Annals of Barber-Surgeons*, p. 111.

[2] Copies are in Brit. Mus., and Bodl. It is reprinted in Nichols, *Prog. James*, i, p. 564. Cf. also Greg, p. 21; Fairholt, pt. i, p. 29; J. G. Nichols, p. 100; J. Nichols, in *Gent. Mag.* for August, 1824, p. 114.

[3] Which may be the ship furnished by this company for the 1602 Show.

[4] Very likely those of 1602.

proof by showing the present united state of the land, divided by the first Brute; this glorious event is due to the second Brute — King James. For joy the three kingdoms deliver up their crowns and sceptres; and Troya Nova persuades fair Thamesis and the other rivers to sing pæans to the sovereign. Thames, the Queen of English Rivers, begins—and is followed by the Severn and the Humber.[1]

The history of the Merchant-Taylors' guild is recounted by Fame and her attendants;[2] and the show ends with speeches by Neptune and Amphitrite lauding Sir Leonard Holliday, and invoking divine blessings on "that second Brute, James our dread king."

This show is rather more connected than is apt to be the case in these civic triumphs; it is to be noted that much was made of history not purely that of the guild. This was due to the fact that James had to be complimented; and it is interesting to observe how many countries and rivers were personified, that honor might be done him. Ship, camel, and lion seem to have been brought over from 1602; they were, in fact, properties belonging to the company: but Gogmagog and Corinæus — who had, it will be remembered, appeared in the "royal-entry" of 1554[3] — seem to have been revived for the occasion.

The records of the company[4] throw an interesting side-light on this show. "This year, by reason of the great rain and fowle weather hap'ning and falling upon the morrow after Symon and Jude's day, being the day my Lord Mayor went to Westminster, the great costs the Company bestowed upon their pageant and other shows were in manner cast away and defaced. And therefore upon a general request made by the Batchelors the same shows were new repaired and carried abroad upon All Saints Day, at a cost of 64*l.*, 14*s.*, 1*d.*"

As an example of the way the word *pageant* is turning to mean *spectacle* — perhaps because the Lord Mayor's Shows had but one in these early days — we may refer to the epilogue of *Eastward Hoe* (1605): "See if the streets and the fronts of the houses be not stuck with people, and the windows filled with ladies, as on the solemn day of the pageant."[5]

The Show for 1609

The show to which Heywood, in the introduction of *Sinus Salutis* (his Show for 1635) refers, dating it 1607,[6] is really that of 1609. In the British Museum (*C. 33. e. 7* [*23*]) are to be found the last four leaves of the descriptive pamphlet, to which is prefixed a pencilled titlepage, as follows: "Camp-bell; or the Iron-

---

[1] The verse is iambic pentameter, in seven-line stanzas, riming ababbcc.

[2] Tapeinotės, Eros, Eleutheriotes, Sophrosyne, Agnites, Hypomene, Epimelia; Pheme rides before the chariot, which evidently contains the others.

[3] See above, vol. i, p. 191.

[4] Quoted by Clode, i, p. 188 n.

[5] Cited by Fairholt in his *Scrapbook* (in the Society of Antiquaries) vol. i.

[6] See the 1874 ed. of his works, iv, p. 288.

mongers Faire Field [a Pageant at the installation of Sir Thomas Campbell in the office of Lord Mayor of London, 29 Oct. 1609]." In pencil, on the margin of the first sheet, this is attributed to Munday.

In this show appear the Graces, various inhabitants of the sea, St. Andrew and St. George, " vnited now in enduring amitie." The former Saint rides a unicorn, the latter his dragon; both address the mayor.

Nicholl, citing the Ironmongers' records of 3 November, 1609, throws further light on this show. " At this court Mr. Anthonie Mundaye came into court, and the observations then made were theise, — that the children weare not instructed their speeches, which was a spetiall judgment of the consideration, then the musicke and singinge were wanting, the apparell most of it old and borrowed, with other defects, and the matter left to Mr. Leat's coming home, wch will be by the next courte." On 18 November, Munday was " a suitor for 5*li.* of increase over his bargaine, layinge his reason therefor in regard of his speeches made for the water; and had answere given that, in respect he performed not his speeches on land, nor the rest of his contracted service, the Companie were not to goe beyond their bargaine, and payd 45*li.*" [1]

1610 — Prince of Anhalt at the Civic Show

Christianus, Prince of Anhalt, witnessed the civic triumphs of 1610; " he surveyed the Cittie of London with great pleasure and admiration, and behelde the pleasant triumphs upon the water and within the Cittie, which at this time were extraordinary in honor of the Lord Mayor and Cittizens, and that daie this prince, with all his Germanyne trayne, were entertayned at the Lord Mayor's Feast, in the Guild hall, where hee manifested his former admiration . . . and sayd there was no state nor cittie in the world that did elect their magistrates with such magnificence, except the Cittie of Venice, unto which the Cittie of London commeth very neere." [2]

1611 — A Norwich Fatality

While not, strictly speaking, a civic pageant, that erected on the Norwich mayor's gate in 1611 deserves mention. " On the 18th of June (it being *gild-day*) a sumptuous *pageant* was prepared at the new Mayor's gate on Tombland, and certain *fire-works*, as had been usual, were fired off in the evening, some of which breaking, frighted the people (who were very numerous) to such a degree, that hurrying away in crowds for fear of hurt, there were no less than 33 persons

---

[1] Nicholl, *Ironmongers*, p. 143.

[2] Howes, Stow's *Annals* (1615 ed.), p. 908; cited by J. Nichols in *Gent. Mag.* for November, 1824, p. 411. Clode, ii, p. 311, is in error, in recording the election of Sir W. Craven to the mayoralty in 1610, when he says: " . . . by order of the king the Lord Mayor's Show, which had been for some years suspended, was revived." We have recorded the 1609 Show.

trodden down and pressed to death, as the *register* of the parish of St. *Simon* and *Jude* declares." [1]

1611 — Munday's "Chryso-Thriambos"

The reproof of the Ironmongers in 1609 did not dampen Munday's ardor, for in 1611 we find him in charge of the show for the Goldsmiths.[2] Prideaux, citing the records of the Company,[3] notes that John Lowen, one of the king's players, was "to perform the part of Lepstone in the show." He further records — from the same source — that Grinkin, the painter, was to provide for the show a tomb for Farrington, a former mayor; properties for Time; the chariot of the two kings drawn by two leopards; the "orpherie" drawn by two "victors," with places to contain Justice and her two daughters on the top, and for St. Dunstan. Evidently a trade-pageant, or "explanation of the Mystery," was to be included, together with two Moors, riding on unicorns (the supporters of the Company's arms); Grinkin was to have £75 for these, and Anthony Munday was to write the speeches. He received £80 for the following:

"Apparel for the kings in the chariot

"For Farington, the Mayor

"For Tyme

"For all other persons and children in the Mystery, and for all those that ride upon the beasts.

"For making-up the speeches, for expressing the meaning of the shows, both for Lepston, Farington, the kings, the boys and all the rest.

"For two books which are to be made and printed and to be delivered to Mr. Wardens for their disposal. Mr. Munday is also to bear the charge of the tyring and tryming of the children, and whatsoever else is requisite to be done by him for the managing of the whole business." [4]

By this time, clearly, there was more than one pageant in the show, although the trade-pageant continued to be the important one. This show seems to have included history and allegory, though some of the characters are not clear (the kings, for instance). St. Dunstan was the patron of the Company, and appears in later shows.

1612 — Dekker's "Troia Nova Triumphans"

Two items from the Merchant-Taylors' records [5] are of interest in connection with Dekker's Show for 1612. "Paid to Mr. Hemynge and Mr Thomas Dekker the poet, for the devise of the Land Shewes, being a Sea Chariott drawne by two

---

[1] F. Blomefield, iii, p. 364; cited by Ewing, p. 17.

[2] For mention of this, see Fairholt, pt. i, p. 32; J. G. Nichols, p. 100; J. Nichols, in the *Gent. Mag.* for Aug., 1824, p. 114; Greg, p. 20. I have not seen a copy of the descriptive pamphlet, which was entitled *Chryso-Thriambos, the Triumphes of Golde.*

[3] Prideaux, *Memorials of the Goldsmiths Company*, i, p. 116.

[4] Prideaux, i, p. 117.

[5] Printed by Clode, i, p. 335.

sea horses, one pageant called Neptune's Throne, with the seven liberall Sciences, one Castle called Envy's Castle, one other pageant called Virtue's Throne, and for the persons and apparel of those that went in them the sum of 197*l*. Also to Nicholas Sotherne and George Jackson the two master painters for the making, painting, gilding and garnishing of all the same several Thrones before mentioned and for new painting the Company's ship, the sum of 181*l*." The Mr. Hemynge referred to as Dekker's collaborator in this show is possibly the one who, eleven years later, shared the responsibility for the First Folio. The Company's ship, used on this occasion, may be that used by the Merchant-Tailors in 1605.

A description of this show may be found in Clode;[1] copies of the descriptive pamphlet are in the Bodleian and the British Museum; and Fairholt reprints it.[2] The first two "triumphs," or pageants, of this show represented Neptune in a sea-chariot with Tritons: and the four Winds "drive forward that Ship of which Neptune spake." Luna sits at the feet of the sea-god; and the Tritons ride on "foure severall fishes, viz: two dolphins and two mer-maids, which are not (after the old procreation) begotten of painted cloath, and broune paper, but are living beasts . . ." The Throne of Virtue contains in the most eminent place Arete, or Virtue herself. Beneath her sit the Seven Liberal Sciences — females, whose "habits are light roabes, and loose (for Knowledge should be *free*)." This throne is drawn by four horses which are ridden by Time, Mercury, Desire, and Industry. Desire seems to be a female; and Industry is "in the shape of an olde country-man." Both Neptune and Virtue addressed the mayor.

"A forlorn castle" — the third device — is built close to the Little Conduit in Cheapside; and as the Throne of Virtue approaches, there appear on the battlements Envy and her followers, Ignorance, Sloth, Oppression, Disdain and others. All are armed and ready to shoot at Virtue; Riot and Calumny, from their posts at the gate of the castle,[3] offer to stop Virtue's progress, but she dazzles and confounds them. They shrink back, and after she has passed, they shoot arrows into the air, which break out in fireworks.

On the mayor's return from the Guildhall to St. Paul's — the "shewes" marching back in the same order as before — Envy makes another stand. Virtue summons her people; pistols are fired, and Envy vanishes with her crew. It is impossible, when we read such descriptions as this, not to recall such fights and fortress-stormings as Elizabeth saw at Bristol; but this has a moral significance even more prominently brought out. It should be added that twelve horsemen, representing the twelve Companies, rode before the Throne of Virtue.

---

[1] *Op. cit.*, i, p. 335 f. This is the only Lord Mayor's Show to use New Troy in the title, although the historical element is much stronger in Munday's Show for 1605. (On this "history," see vol. i, p. 58, n. 2.)

[2] *L. M. Pag.*, pt. ii, pp. 7 ff. Cf. also Greg, p. 7; J. Nichols in *Gent. Mag.* for August, 1824, p. 114; and J. G. Nichols, p. 101.

[3] Note the moral allegory joined to "pageantized" chivalry.

1613 — MIDDLETON'S "TRIUMPHS OF TRUTH"

The next year, Middleton wrote *The Triumphs of Truth* in honor of Sir Thomas Middleton, Grocer.[1] At Soper-Lane end was a "Senate house" erected, upon which musicians sat playing. After a song, the Lord Mayor appeared from the Guildhall, and was greeted with a flourish. Then appeared from behind a silk curtain a "grave feminine shape . . . attired like a reverend Mother, a long white hair naturally flowing on either side of her . . ." She represented London, and addressed the mayor "after a comely grace, equally mixed with comfort and reverence." Then the waits of the city being there in service, his Lordship and the reverend Company were led forward to the waterside, where the river was decked in the richest glory to receive them.[2]

On the mayor's return from Westminster, the first "triumph" to attend his Lordship was Truth's Angel on horseback, and Zeal, the champion of Truth, "likewise the chastiser of Ignorance and Error" (symbolized by his scourge). Both the Angel and Zeal saluted the mayor; then they ranked themselves before his lordship and conducted him to Paul's Chain, where Error in a chariot, with his infernal ministers, awaited the mayor, to assault him. Their costumes showed the symbols of blind ignorance and darkness.

Envy, the champion of Error,[3] rode beside him, "eating of a human heart." With a long speech, Error greeted the mayor, enticing him to let his "will and

---

[1] Of the descriptive pamphlet of this show, two copies are in BM., one in the Gh., one in Bodl. It is reprinted in Dyce's ed. of Middleton, v, p. 213; Bullen's ed., vii, p. 229; *Prog. James*, ii, p. 679; Heath, (3[d] ed.) appendix, p. 443. Cf. also Bullen, i, p. xxxviii; Fairholt, pt. i, p. 32; J. Nichols, in *Gent. Mag.*, Aug., 1824, p. 114; J. G. Nichols, p. 101; Greg, p. 15; Hone, p. 246. In his introductory remarks, Middleton takes advantage of the opportunity to sneer at his brother-poet, Munday.

Under date of 8 July, 1613, "it is ordered that the Company of Grocers shall haue two convenient rooms one aboue another beneath in Leaden hall for the workmen to make their pageants and other devises in against the next Lord Maiors day." *Repertory* xxxi (i), fol. 129.

[2] See Herbert i, p. 200 (quoted by Dyce and Bullen) who says that Sir Thomas Middleton "was nearly the first who attempted an emblematical and scenic representation of his company in a water spectacle, consisting (in imitation of the pageant mentioned to have been exhibited by Sir John Wells to Henry VI) of 'five islands artfully garnished with all manner of Indian fruit trees, drugges, spiceries, and the like; the middle island having a faire castle especially beautified': the latter probably allusive to the newly established East India Company's forts, and whose adventures had contributed so much to enlarge the sphere of the grocers' trade." Just how much part the mayor himself took in planning the triumph is doubtful. This was Middleton's first show, and most of the credit of it should, surely, be given to the poet. The "imitation" of Lydgate's 1432 show is not close, and probably not conscious. (Cf. above, vol. i, pp. 141 ff.)

[3] Zeal and Envy recall the Elizabethan barriers — in moral-allegorical clothing. (Cf. above, vol. i, p. 111.)

appetite sway the sword" now that he has the power. Envy echoed Error; then Zeal, stirred up, forced their retirement, making way for Truth. When she comes in her chariot, Zeal presents her, and she claims the mayor — "Thou'rt mine!"

Then they all set forward — the chariot of Truth (who is attended by the Graces and Virtues) taking place next before his lordship; Zeal and the angel precede them, and the Chariot of Error follows the mayor, "as near as it can get"; and so to Paul's Churchyard, "where stand ready the five islands, those dumb glories that I spake of before upon the water." And on them were the Five Senses — Visus, Auditus, Tactus, Gustus, and Olfactus — with their proper emblems at their feet. There was also a King of Moors, his queen, and two attendants,[1] in a ship without sail or pilot, bearing the motto: *Veritate gubernor.* The king spoke, telling how he had been converted by the truth of the English merchants with whom he dealt; he is no longer an infidel. Then all in the ship bow "their bodies to the tempel of Saint Paul," while Error smiles 'twixt scorn and anger, exclaiming —

> What, have my sweet-faced devils forsook me too?
> Nay then my charms will have enough to do.

Time, the father of Truth,[2] charges the mayor always to listen to his daughter.

"Then the five islands pass along into Cheapside, the ship next after them; the Chariot of Truth," etc., to the Little Conduit, where there is "another more subtle object." This is "a mount triumphant, but the beauty and the glory thereof overspread with a thick sulphurous darkness . . ." — the mist, or fog, of Error, which ominously blemished London's Triumphant Mount. Four monsters — Error's disciples, Barbarism, Ignorance, Impudence, and Falsehood — sit at the corners. When Truth approaches, she drives the mists away with a "powerful command": the cloud rises, and turns into a brilliant canopy. The four monsters fall flat: London is discovered in the place of honor; above her sits Religion, with Liberality on her right, and Perfect Love on her left. In his right hand, the latter bears a spear, containing all the Twelve Companies' arms. On two heights sit Knowledge and Modesty, and at the back are Chastity, Fame, Simplicity, and Meekness. London, the scales of darkness fallen, gives her blessing to the mayor —

> The many ways that to blind Error slide
> Are in the entrance broad, hell-mouth is wide;
> But when man enters far, he finds it then
> Close, dark, and strait, for hell returns no men . . .

"At which words, the whole Triumph moves, in his richest glory, toward the Cross in Cheap, at which place Error, full of wrath and malice to see his mist chased away, falls into this fury." After his speech, the mist falls again;

[1] These have, doubtless, a trade-signification.

[2] Cf. the 1559 procession, above, vol. i, p. 202.

Truth again disperses it, and the Mount, glorious once more, passes to the Standard,[1] "about which place, by elaborate action from Error, [the mist] falls again, and goes so darkened till it comes to St. Laurence Lane-end" where Truth chases it away again, and is thanked by London.[2] Perfect Love banishes Excess from the feast of joy, and the Lord Mayor, with the Companies, passes to the Guildhall. On their return, the triumphs escort the mayor to St. Paul's — "Error by the way still busy and in action to draw darkness often upon that Mount of Triumph, which by Truth is as often dispersed . . ." Then, all returning home, this mount and the Chariot of Truth both were placed near Leadenhall, where London addressed the mayor. With Zeal's destruction of Error, the pageant ends — a flame shooting from his head consumes the Chariot of Error with its beasts.[3]

The gentle plot running through this show tempts us to call it a peripatetic morality-play; it would be interesting to know what proportion of the spectators saw the whole thing. Probably few did; hence the repetition of the "mist *motif*." It was, we may presume, a great temptation to a dramatist like Middleton to tell a connected story; but the conditions of presentation obviously made this impossible.[4]

---

[1] A Conduit in Cheap. Cf. *Michaelmas Term*, ii, 1,109 (Bullen).

[2] This repetition of the action is obviously so that all could get a chance to see the elaborate mechanism of the pageant, as well as to hear the simple lesson.

[3] They were obviously not alive. It may be added that the firework was made by Humphrey Nichols: the work of the Triumph was done by John Grinkin, "and those furnished with apparel and porters by Anthony Munday, gentleman." As in the case of the masque, the artificers were almost — if, indeed, not quite — as important as the poets. Their names are almost always to be found at the end of the printed descriptions, with the poet's acknowledgement of his debt. Sometimes — considering the conditions of presentation — the artificer is even more important than the author of the speeches.

Fairholt, pt. i, p. 37, remarks that the incident of Truth and Error "is an evident copy from that of Virtue and Envy in Dekker's pageant for the preceding year. The city poets did not scruple to repeat previous portions of pageantry occasionally . . ."

[4] Fairholt, pt. i, p. 56, n., quotes from Shirley, who makes fun of the Lord Mayor's Show. It may be remarked that, as far as is known, Shirley never composed one of these triumphs; and I have yet to see a scoffing reference to them in the work of any dramatist who did. We may add that they were taken much less seriously in the second half of the century; — a comparison of Evelyn's remarks with those of Pepys shows the different attitude, the former giving the older point of view.

A satire, perhaps based on the mayoralty shows, may be found in *The Seuen deadly Sinnes of London, Drawne in seuen seuerall Coaches, Through the seuen seuerall Gates of the Citie, Bringing the Plague with them* . . . (By Thomas Dekker; London, 1606.) "The names of the Actors in this old Enterlude of Iniquitie" are given just before the "induction": they are "Politike Bankeruptisme, Lying, Candle-light, Sloth, Apishnesse, Shauing, Crueltie — seuen may easily play this, but not without a Diuell." This is not a satire of the Lord Mayor's Show — and seems to be a combination of morality "spirit" with the "technique" of the pageant.

The Opening of the New River

No pageantry accompanied the ceremonies of the opening of the New River, this same year.[1] I mention this in passing, because the 1913 Show is supposed to have reproduced elements from this, as well as from the Show for 1613. We shall see, later, that very little of the latter was reproduced;[2] and none of Middleton's *Entertainment.* Echoes of the opening of the New River waterworks are to be found, however, in the figure of Hugh Middleton, who rode in 1913, as well as in the captive giant, who represented the river-god.

I do not intend to outline every Lord Mayor's Show of the seventeenth century. This labor has been rendered unnecessary by the work of Fairholt, which was well and faithfully done; I shall, therefore, limit myself to treating in detail only those shows which he has not mentioned, together with one or two important shows in decades widely separated, that the reader may see the lines along which these triumphs developed. As full a list as I have been able to make will be found in the Bibliography under the heading *Lord Mayor's Shows;* and bibliographical data have been collected under the name of each author.

1614 — Munday's "Himatia-Poleos"

The only noteworthy things in Munday's 1614 Show are first,[3] a long apology for having been led astray by Stow to call Fitz-Alwin a Goldsmith when he was a Draper; secondly, the figure of Richard I surrounded by many personified cities, each carrying the arms of the town he represents. The first pageant is a ship; and in the third pageant sits Himatia, or Clothing, surrounded by various trade and allegorical figures. Sir John Norman makes the speech on the water (in prose); and Sir Henry Fitz-Alwin also appears in the triumph. The Golden Fleece makes its appearance, and a shepherd addresses the mayor[4] in prose and verse.

---

[1] One of the copies of the 1613 Show in the B. M. has Middleton's description of these ceremonies bound with it [BM., *C. 33. e. 34*]. This is entitled: *The Manner of his Lordships Entertainment on Michaelmas day last . . . at that most Famous and Admired Worke of the Running Streame from Amwell Head into the Cestern neere Islington, being the sole Inuention, Cost and Industry of that Worthy Maister Hvgh Middleton of London, Goldsmith, for the generall good of the City.* London . . . 1613. This is reprinted by Dyce, v, p. 246, and Bullen, vii, p. 263; for mere mention of these festivities, see Clode, i, p. 339, and J. Nichols, in *Gent. Mag.*, for Aug., 1824, p. 115.

[2] See below, p. 138.

[3] On p. 5 of the BM. pamphlet. This has not, as far as I know, been reprinted; it is mentioned by Fairholt, pt. i, p. 37; cf. also Greg, p. 20; J. G. Nichols, p. 102.

[4] Sir Thomas Hayes, Draper.

1616 — Munday's "Lemon Tree"

A passing reference may be made to Munday's Show for 1616, which is outlined by Fairholt,[1] because the "lemon tree" which it contained, and which recalls the trade-pageant of the Grocers which we have seen so often, does not appear to have been a trade-pageant in this case. Rather was it planned to honor the Lord Mayor for this year who was Mr. John Leman, Fishmonger. It falls, therefore, in the category of such punningly appropriate structures as the three wells, in the "royal-entry" of 1432, when the Mayor was John Wells,[2] or the "Castle of Denhm" — out of compliment to Mr. Sheriff Denham — in the Midsummer Show of 1534.[3]

1617 — An Item from the City Records

Under date of 2 September, 1617, the Court of Aldermen thought meet "that the company of grocers may make their shewes for the Lord Maiors day in some convenient place one (*on*) the bankside of Gresham Colledg neere Broadstreete & that the Mr And wardens of the grocers shall presently conferr with the Mr & Wardens of the Company of Mercers concerning the same."[4] In this year, Dekker and Munday competed unsuccessfully with Middleton; the accounts of the Grocers contain these interesting items:

"Payde and given in benevolence to Anthony Monday, gent^n^, for his paynes in drawing a project for this busynesse which was offered to the Comytee, £5.

"Payde and given to Mr Deckar for the like, £4."[5]

---

[1] *L. M. Pag.*, pt. i, p. 40. Cf., for further details, Nicholl, pp. 177 and 180 f.

[2] See above, vol. i, p. 146, and n. 4.

[3] See above, vol. i, p. 41, and n. 2.

[4] *Repertory*, xxxiii, fol. 160. Copies of the descriptive pamphlet of this year's show — written by Middleton for George Bowles, Grocer — may be found in Gh., and BM. It was reprinted by Dyce, v, p. 607; Bullen, vii, p. 293 (in their editions of Middleton); Heath, (3^d^ ed.) appendix, p. 459. Cf. also Fairholt, pt. i, p. 43; Greg, p. 16; J. G. Nichols, p. 103; J. Nichols, in *Gent. Mag.*, Aug., 1824, p. 116.

[5] See Heath, (2^d^ ed.) p. 413, and my article in *Publ. Mod. Lang. Assoc.* for March, 1915, p. 111 f. For further items, see Fairholt, pt. i, p. 161 f. (appendix i) and Heath (3^d^ ed.) p. 425 f. An interesting item is found in Heath (3^d^ ed.) p. 428, under the head "*The Foiste and other Fire Works:*"

"Payde and given in benevolence to the fierman or greeneman over and about [above] his agreement, the some of 11 *s*."

It will be noted that "greenman" is here a synonym for "fireman" — he who casts squibs and other "fireworks" about.

Middleton received £282, but had to provide the pageants.

1618 — MUNDAY'S "SIDERO-THRIAMBOS"

Neither Fairholt nor Nichols know any pageant for 1618,[1] but the title of Munday's pamphlet is recorded by Greg,[2] and the original pamphlet may be found in the British Museum. It was written for Sir Sebastian Harvey, Ironmonger; and as it has not been reprinted, I shall outline it.[3] Munday first shows Lemnos, like a "goodly Myne," wherein sits Mulciber, god of mines and metals, with attendant Cyclops at work, "nimble and dexterious youthes" who sing as they labor.[4] At the four corners of the Isle, or Mine, sit four nymphs — Chrusos, Argurion, Calcos, and Sideros, figuring the four ages of the world. The two lizards of the Company's crest appear on the pageant, and "above them all is Jupiter, mounted vpon his Royall Eagle." Two estridges — supporters of the Company's arms — draw this "device." A cannon follows, with the "necessarie furnishment for charging and discharging, . . ." and "certaine gallant knights in Armour [5] . . . have the charge or guiding of this cannon." Jupiter, it may be remarked, was also in armor. A Leopard follows, and on him rides "an ancient Brittish Barde," guiding the Mount of Fame, wherein are Fame, Expectation, Hope, Justice, and Fortitude treading down Ambition, Treason, and Hostility, shackled in Ironmongers' manacles. Fear and Modesty, Vigilance and Providence,[6] Courage and Counsel also occupy places on the pageant. It may be noted that the bard's speeches — for he gives more than one, and speaks the last, "at night at my Lord's House" — are delicately flavored with lowland Scotch.

In 1623, Munday and Middleton worked together, the former planning the show upon the water, and the latter the show upon the land;[7] the next year John Webster wrote *Monuments of Honor* — the only Lord Mayor's Show, — so far as is known, — which he produced.[8] In 1625 comes the first break in the list of shows since 1609. That there was no show this year is made clear by Middleton's reference to Sir Allen Cotton, the outgoing mayor in 1626, whose

---

[1] See Fairholt, pt. i, p. 45, and J. Nichols, in *Gent. Mag.*, for August, 1824, p. 116.

[2] *A List*, etc., p. 20.

[3] The disbursements for this show, from the Ironmongers' accounts, may be found in Nicholl, p. 182.

[4] Every stanza of their song ends with *Acier Dure*, the motto of the company.

[5] Perhaps "armed-men" given a trade significance.

[6] Foresight.

[7] See my paper, "The Lord Mayor's Show for 1623," in *Publ. Mod. Lang. Assoc.* for March, 1915, p. 110 f.

[8] I have not seen a copy of the descriptive pamphlet, which is reprinted in Hazlitt's edition of Webster's *Works* (4 vols., London, 1857) iii, p. 225. Cf. also Greg, p. 25. (The show was written for John Gore, of the Merchant-Taylors' Company.) J. Nichols (*Gent. Mag.*, Aug., 1824, p. 117) had not seen a copy; Fairholt, pt. i, p. 51, notes its rarity.

arms were carried by one of the lions attached to the Chariot of Honor.[1] "At [his] happy inauguration," says the poet, "though triumph was not then in season — Death's pageants being only advanced upon the shoulders of men — his noble deservings were not thereby any way eclipsed."[2]

1628 — Dekker's "Britannia's Honor"

Breaking a silence that had lasted since 1612, Dekker's voice was again heard in 1628, when he wrote the show for the inauguration of Richard Deane, Skinner.[3] The first triumph "is called a Sea-Consort"; Amphitrite sits on a rock, built artificially in the water; mermaids attend her, sea-nymphs sit about the rock, "and in places convenient for them are bestowed our three famous Riuers, *Humber*, *Trent*, and *Seuerne*, aptly attired according to the quality of such Marine Persons, who play vpon Cornets." Amphitrite speaks, and there was a French speech planned, in case her Majesty honored the triumphs with her presence. London, a lady, is the speaker on the next pageant; her right hand rests on a tree,[4] twelve-branched, representing the Companies; various "scriptures" adorn the pageant. With London are Minerva, Bellona, Peace, Religion, Civil Government, Justice, Learning, Industry, and Honor.

The "Glory of Furres" is the third "presentation" — which has an obvious trade-significance. This was a chariot triumphant, drawn by two luzerns,[5] in which chariot were seated a fur-clad Russian prince and princess; an old lord, in furs; a judge, and a University doctor in furred robes, and other people with garments made — in whole or in part — with furs. Fame, who is also in this chariot, speaks.

"Brittannia's Watch-Tower" is the name of the fourth "presentation." Britannia is surrounded by Magnanimity, a Shipwright, Victory, Providence; and there are, in other prominent places, seated kings — Edward the Confessor, Richard I, John, Henry III — who had added to the civic freedom of the city.[6] Britannia addresses the mayor from this pageant.

The last triumph is the "Sun's Bower" — an arbor, where sits Sol, surrounded by the Seasons. Beneath is a wilderness stocked with fur-bearing

---

[1] See the preface to his *Triumphs of Health and Prosperity* (1626); in the Guildhall copy of the pamphlet, p. 7, before the speech of Government; in Bullen's edition of Middleton, vii, p. 408.

[2] The reference is to the plague and the death of James I.

[3] The descriptive pamphlet for this year, entitled *Brittannia's Honor*, may be found in the British Museum. It has not been reprinted, as far as I know; neither Fairholt nor Nichols knew of its existence.

[4] Called "New Troyes Tree of Honor."

[5] Supporters of the Company's arms. Cf. the "luzern" of the 1585 Show, (above, p. 23).

[6] Dekker notes that many kings have been free of the Skinner's Company, "whose names I forbeare to set downe, because they haue in former yeeres beene fully exprest."

beasts. A " scripture " in Latin [1] and English hangs from a bough of one of the trees. Sol addresses the mayor.

At night, Sol being veiled, London speaks the city's farewell to the new mayor. Dekker, at the end of his pamphlet, commends Mr. Gerard Christmas, and his son, Mr. John Christmas, for their " workes, that for many years, none haue beene able to Match them for curiosity." [2]

1629 — Dekker's " London's Tempe "

From the minutes of the Ironmongers' Company [3] we get the following information on Dekker's Show for 1629:

According to an order of Court, made the xj th of August last, theis present treated and agreed with Mr Crismas and Mr Decker and concerning the making of the pageants for the shew on the next Lord Maior's day; after, the said Xpmas and Decker presented them with a plott wherein was contayned six severall pageants, namely:

A Sea Lyon } for the water
2 Sea Horses }
An Estridge
Lemnions Forge
Tempe, or the Field of Hapines
7 Liberall Sciences

For the accomplishing whereof they demanded 200 *li*, which theis present conceaved to be an over value, and theruppon offered them 180 *li*, which they accepted for the making and finishing of the said pageants, to be furnished with children and speakers, and their apparell and necessaries thereunto belonging; land carriage by porters, water carriage by boats and watermen as is accustomed; the green-men with their fireworks; the musick for the pageant; and to give the company 500 bookes of the declaracion for the said shew: and the committee demanded that

Sea Lyon
The 2 Sea Horses, and
The Estridge

be brought into the Hall after the solemnity, there to be sett upp for the Company's use, whereunto Mr Crismas excepted, but was contented to deliver back the sea lyon and the estridge and desired to retain the sea horses to himself; all the rest he undertook to performe for the said some of 180*li* effectually and sufficiently to the Company's liking: In witness whereof they have hereunto subscribed.

Tho Dekker
Garrett Chrismas.[4]

---

[1] *Deus ecce Furentibus obstat.*

[2] Gerard Christmas, or Chrismas, was the engineer of many a Lord Mayor's Show. See his life in the *D. N. B.*

[3] Printed in Nicholl, p. 203 f.

[4] The signatures are reproduced in facsimile, in Nicholl, p. 204.

The Company's records further state that:

Mr Garratt Crismas desired to have theis things following, as is usually allowed by other Companies:

8 guides for the pageant; 8 blew coats and redd caps, with ribbin and staves.

For the lighting of the shew from Paules, 4 lbs of torches.

For the lighting of the shew to the water side 2 lbs of linkes.

For 24 staves and ribbins for 24 men that give their attendance that day.

For 2 scarfs for himself and his sonne, and the watermen are to have ribbings.

To which the Court assented, and Mr Garratt Xmas is appointed to take care for the provision of the children of the pageants, their breakefaste and dinner, as he in his discrecion shall think meete.[1]

The pamphlet, entitled *Londons Tempe, or the Feild* (sic) *of Happines*, which describes the show prepared for James Campbell, Ironmonger, may be found in the British Museum and the Bodleian. It has been reprinted by Fairholt [2] and from him by Nicholl; [3] there is no need of outlining it here.

On 18 January, 1629 (1630), the Court of Aldermen agreed that "whereas by order of this court made the xxii day of December last [4] Mr. Chamberlen was to satisfie vnto the severall companyes of this city especially vnto the inferior companyes their severall proporcions of mony with interest towards payment of the first 60 000*li* in that order mentioned it is now thought fitt and soe ordered by this court that such of the company as will make an abatement and defalcacion of the moneys they owe vnto the City toward the charge of Pagents &c. by vertue of a late Act of Common Councell shalbee satisfied and paid out of the Chamber of moneys their proporcions of money aforesaid." [5]

Additional items of information concerning the civic shows of the third decade of this century may be found in the *Repertories*. On 24 September, 1633, "it is ordered by this Court [of Aldermen] that Mr. Christmas and such others as are imployed for the making of the pageants and shewes against the Lord Maiors day shall have the present use of the rooms in the Greeneyard for the fynishing of the said workes." [6]

On 4 September, 1634, "it is thought fitt and soe ordered that the Greeneyard and roomes therein shalbe ymployed as formerly without hurt or preiudise to the same for the preparing and finishing of the Pagents and other devises

[1] See Nicholl, p. 206. [2] *L. M. Pag.*, pt. ii, p. 37 f.

[3] *Some Acct. of the Ironmongers*, p. 206 f. Cf. on this show Malcolm, ii, p. 43; Greg, p. 8; J. G. Nichols, p. 104; Fairholt, pt. i, p. 54; J. Nichols, writing in *Gent. Mag.* for November, 1824, p. 412, had not seen the pamphlet.

[4] Cf. *Repertory* xliv, fol. 81.

[5] *Repertory* xliv, fol. 90.

[6] *Repertory* xlvii, fol. 376 b. The show for this year, *Londini Emporia*, was written by Heywood: I have not seen either copy or reprint of the pamphlet, which is mentioned by Fairholt, pt. i, p. 57, and recorded by Greg, p. 10; J. G. Nichols, p. 105; and Herbert, ii, p. 659. The triumph was planned for Ralph Freeman, Clothworker.

against the next Lord Maior day "[1] John Taylor wrote the show this year for Robert Parkhurst of the Clothworkers' Company.[2]

On 8 October, 1635, "it is thought fitt and soe ordered by this Court for some reasons them moveing that from thenseforth noo pagents or other shewes for the Lord Maior day shall be made in the Greeneyard in Leadenhall, but that the Undertakers thereof shall provide some other place for the makeing thereof."[3]

1635 — Heywood vs. Taylor: a Matter of Money

Taylor, having done the 1634 Show, was underbid in 1635; we find in the Ironmongers' records for 2 October, 1635,[4] that "Robert Norman and John Taylor presented to the Court their project of five pageants for the Lord Maior's shew, for which they demanded 190*li*, and under that price they would not undertake it."

John Christmas and Thomas Heywood also presented their invention of five pageants for the said show, viz:

"One of the three celestiall goddesses, Juno, Pallas, and Venus.

"One of a Sagettary, because ye Sun entreth y^{t} day into the signe of Sagettary: both theise for the water and land.

"One antique pageant for pleasure.

"One of the castle of the god Mars.

"One of the harbour of happines.

"Which pageants they offered to make, furnish well and sufficiently to the Company's liking for 180*li.*, with children and speakers, and their apparell and necessaryes thereunto belonging, land carriage by porters, water carriage by boats and watermen as is accustomed, the green men with their fire-works, the musick for the pageants, with linkes and torches for the same, and to give the Company five hundred bookes of the declaracion of the said shew, which offer the courte accepted and agreed thereunto; and for performance thereof as abovesaid, the said Xp̃mas and Haywood have hereunto subscribed their names."[5]

---

[1] *Repertory* xlviii, fol. 419. In the margin stands "Greeneyard at Leadenhall to bee ymployed for makeing of Pagants."

[2] I have not seen — nor had Fairholt — a copy of the descriptive pamphlet for 1634; its title is recorded by Greg, p. 25; cf. also J. G. Nichols, p. 105; Fairholt, pt. i, p. 57; and J. Nichols, in *Gent. Mag.* for Nov., 1824, p. 413.

[3] *Repertory* xlix, fol. 321.

[4] Cited from Nicholl, p. 222 f.

[5] The agreement seems to have been signed by John and Mathias Christmas. In a note Nicholl records "for the project and invencion of Norman and Taylor, the Court appointed xx^{s} to be paid unto them." Various expenses connected with this triumph are printed by Nicholl, pp. 224–225.

The title of the show for this year was *Londini Sinus Salutis*. It is reprinted in Heywood's *Works* (1874) iv, p. 283 f.; cf. also Greg, p. 10; J. G. Nichols, p. 105 (referring to Malcolm, ii, p. 45); Fairholt, pt. i, p. 58; J. Nichols, in *Gent. Mag.* for Nov., 1824, p. 413.

The Civil War

I have been unable to find any mention of the shows for 1630 and 1636; but the longest break in the chain of seventeenth-century triumphs is that between 1640 and 1655. With Heywood's *Londini Status Pacatus* [1] the formal descriptions came, for a time, to an end; but there were flashes of brilliant ceremony, even during the period of the Civil War, on these civic holidays. For instance, in 1643, there seems to have been a certain amount of splendor when the mayor took his oath, even if there were no pageants. " Munday, the xxxth of October 1643 beeinge the Lord Maiour's daye, because the 29th was Sundaye . . . This daye the Wardens, Assistantes and Liverye of this Companye [the Goldsmiths] mett heere aboute 8 of the clock in the morneinge, and haveinge had some bread and drinck, they went to the Lord Maior's house to accompanye him to Westminster (but they should have mett him att Guildhall.) The Companye went from hence to his Lordship's house in such manner as the Wardens and Assistantes went on Simon and Jude's day [2] and from the Lord Maior's house the 4 almesmen (as on the other daye) leadeinge the waye, and the Clerke, and the Beadle and the youngest of the Companye formost, untill they came to the Guildhall gate, in Cateaton Street, where the Company of the Fishmongers, attendinge upon the old Lord Maior . . . . mett this Companye; and then the Fishmongers, the youngest of them goeinge formost, led the waye up St. Laurence Lane, and this Company followed them in the like manner unto the 3 Craynes wharfe, where this Companye's barge (which was borrowed of the Grocers') laye ready for them, in which they went to Westminster." [3] An account of the ceremonies of 1653 — also without pageants, but not wholly without splendor — may be found in the records of the same company.[4] At the Three Cranes Wharf were three barges ready, " but could not get to land by reason of the lowe tide and the winde against them." [5]

---

[1] Copies of which are in BM., B., and Gh. The pamphlet is reprinted in his *Works* (1874) v, p. 355; cf. also Greg, p. 11; J. G. Nichols, p. 106; Fairholt, pt. i, p. 60. Fairholt, p. 62, points out the aptness of the following passage in " the last city pageant known to exist before the unhappy civil wars had commenced ":

> " Let then our gratitude and pious cares,
> Strive to entaile them [*i.e.*, Peace, Prosperity, and Plenty] to us and our heires:
> Lest that too late (having stern War accited)
> We wish that Peace which (whilst we had) we slighted."

[2] The Saturday before, when the mayor took his oath before the companies at the Guildhall. See Prideaux, i, p. 216.

[3] The Goldsmiths' records, printed by Prideaux, i, p. 217.

[4] See Prideaux, ii, p. 48 f.

[5] *Ibid.*, p. 50.

1655 — Gayton's "Charity Triumphant"

Before the Cromwellian rule had passed, descriptive pamphlets of the Lord Mayor's Show reappear. That for 1655, by Edmund Gayton, begins the new series. It is a six-page pamphlet, with a three-page dedication, signed by the author; the other three pages contain a description of the show in narrative verse.[1] The preface is important:

"I cannot," says Gayton, "here set forth the reason of the late extinguishing these *Civick Lights*, and suppressing the Genius of our Metropolis, which for these Planetary Pageants and Pretorian Pomps was as famous and renouned in forraign Nations, as for their faith, wealth and valour. The Ingenie, Artifices, Mysteries, Shewes, Festivals, Ceremonies and Habits of a State being amongst the *Decora*, and unseparable Ornaments of it. Take away the *Fasces*, and the *Consuls* are no more feared, but scorn'd; Let fall the noble Sword of the City in any place, and you are sure the Mayor has there no Priviledge, no Livery, no distinguishing of Societies, and Fraternities, no Caps (in daies of old) no Prentices, no Truncks, no Citizens, no Robes, no Judges, no Maces, no Magestrate: And so for Anniversary Shews, and harmlesse and merry Recreations, without a moderate permission of them, [there is] very little content to the multitude. *Right Honourable*, I therefore, being the Son of a Citizen, Congratulate this Return of the City-Gallantry and manifestation of her severall Splendors in your Majority to your honoured self, it being most proper that the lost Beauty and Magnificence of the place, should be restored by One (if I mistake it not) a brother of the prime Company, and therefore most fit to lead, that so it being begun in the Virgin society, it may like Vestall fire never go out: And because the Scenicall Contrivement & Pageant Bravery is but an *Ephemeron*, or *Diurnall* birth and issue of one day, and so *Exit* till the next yeere.[2] Poetical fancy do's beg leave to supply that defect, and to inlarge the glory of your day (my Lord) to the period of your year; And because many a far off[3] will be glad to heare what they could not see, as some would willingly retaine and keep, what this day was seen by them.[4] This short Poem shall be to those that saw it, a Remembrancer, or representation, and to the remote Welwishers of the Cities honour, a written Pageant or *Pegma Metricum*, and so I address myself (my Lord) to your Virgin, whom I shal labour to make as famous, as your Honour has made her Dowagable . . ."

The Mercers' Virgin seems to have been the only pageant exhibited this year — what Fairholt calls "the old realization of the Company's arms — the crowned Virgin on horseback."[5] The mayor made the voyage to Westminster by water, and "thirty canons went off." Unfortunately the weather was bad:

---

[1] Copies may be found in BM. and Gh., and it is reprinted in Fairholt, pt. i, p. 170; cf. also Hone, p. 249; Fairholt, pt. i, p. 64; J. Nichols, in *Gent. Mag.* for Dec., 1824, p. 514; J. G. Nichols, p. 106. The latter notes that "this is not a description of the show" — meaning that it is not one of the regular descriptive pamphlets.

[2] Here is either an error in punctuation, or a verb omitted.

[3] Alluding, perhaps, to the Royal Family and nobles, then in exile.

[4] This period should be a comma; or a else a verb is again omitted.

[5] Fairholt, pt. i, p. 64. The verse in Gayton's description, "She how she rides! See how she comes!" would apply equally well to her if she rode in a car. There seem to have been no speeches.

The sight was rare, but envious clouds,
The glorious day in showrs beshrowds;
And Winds in Malice or in Love
To sport or court her [1] highly strove.

1656 — John Bulteel's "London's Triumph"

On 14 October, 1656, the Court of Aldermen ordered "that Mr Jarman [may] vse the place or Passage newly made out of Leadenhall into Limestreete for preparing the Pageant intended by the Company of Skinners against the Lord Maiors day.

"It is thought fit and ordered by this Court that Mr Jarman doe with all Convenient Speed proceed to make or fit a place or howse at thre Cranes for the Citie Barge there being not place to lay or preserve the same from Spoyle." [2]

Mr. Jarman, or German, was the artificer for several years; but the author of the 1656 Show is not so easily determined. Fairholt [3] records his initials, — J. B., — but did not see a copy of his pamphlet. There is one, now, in the British Museum,[4] and the catalogue of this library attributes it to John Bulteel.[5] The epistle dedicatory — signed I. B. — is addressed to the Lord Mayor, Sir Robert [6] Tichburn, and his Company, the Skinners. After a eulogy of the city, its government and antiquity, and an historical sketch of the office of mayor, the show is described.[7] "The loving members of the honourable Societie exercising Arms in *Cripplegate* Ground . . . march'd before him [the Mayor] to the three Crane Wharfe, where part of them under the Red Colours embarqued themselves in three severall Barges; and another part took water at Stone Staires being under green colours as enemies to the other: and . . . there began an encounter between each party, which continued all the way to Westminster." The Companies attended the mayor in their barges; "when the Barges wherein the

---

[1] The Virgin.

[2] *Repertory* lxiv, fol. 238.

[3] *L. M. Pag.*, pt. i, p. 64; cf. J. Nichols, in *Gent. Mag.* for Dec., 1824, p. 514.

[4] BM., *C. 33. e. 10* — in which Sig. B. 3 verso is slightly mutilated.

[5] There is nothing in the pamphlet itself to suggest that I. B. means John Bulteel, but inquiry revealed the fact that the BM. cataloguers made their assignment on the authority of *The Bibliographer's Manual of English Literature*, by Walter Thomas Lowndes. See the new ed., revised and enlarged by Henry G. Bohn, (London, 1864) i, p. 91, col. 2, where this "very rare" pamphlet is ascribed to Bulteel, though no authority is given. The pamphlet is also assigned to Bulteel in the *Handbook to the Popular, Poetical and Dramatic Literature of Great Britain* . . . by W. Carew Hazlitt (London, 1867) *s. v.* BULTEEL (p. 66); cf. also the *General Index to Hazlitt's Handbook and his Bibliographical Collections* (1867–1889) by G. J. Gray, (ed. W. C. Hazlitt [London, 1893], pp. 105 and 464); and the *D. N. B.*, *s. v.* BULTEEL.

[6] Fairholt misprints *Roger*, but in the first volume of his *Scrapbook* (in the SA. library) he corrects himself in a pencilled note. This mayor died a prisoner in the Tower; there are two portraits of him in Fairholt's *Scrapbook.*

[7] The pamphlet cited, p. 10 f.

Souldiers were, came right against *White-Hall*, they saluted the Lord Protector and his Councell, with severall peales of shott, which the Lord Protector answered with signal testimonies of grace and courtesie: and thence proceeding forward to Westminster-Staires, they gave another volley at the landing of the Lord Maior." While that official was taking his oath, the two parties of soldiers, after a short, sharp, encounter, arranged a truce; saluting the mayor and Cromwell, the barges returned; and the mayor, landing, "put an end to the Water solemnite; than which there hath not been a more gracefull fight upon the Thames ever since the city stood." [1]

Against the Old Change the first land pageant greeted mayor and Companies; "two leopards bestrid by two Moors, attird in the habit of their Country" stood on the pageant; and at the four corners sat four virgins with their hair dishevelled. "This seem'd to be the embleme of a city pensive and forlorn"; an old man, in black, threw off his mourning robes at the Mayor's approach, and bewailed the condition of his native place no longer, but burst into a speech of extravagant joy. After he had spoken, the pageant moved on before the mayor as far as the Mercers' chapel, "a Gyant being twelve foot in height going before the Pageant for the delight of the people. Over against *Soper-Lane* End, stood another Pageant also; upon this were placed several sorts of Beasts, as Lyons, Tygers, Bears . . . in a great Wildernesse; at the forepart whereof sate *Pan* with a Pipe in his hand . . ." [2] Here Orpheus played, and the wild beasts danced; "the Embleme of this Pageant seem'd proper to the Company out of which the Lord Maior was elected . . . A second signification of this Emblem may be this; that as *Orpheus* tam'd the wild Beasts by the alluring sound of his melody; so doth a just and upright Governour tame and govern the wild affections of men, by good and wholesome Lawes." [3] Orpheus addressed the mayor, after which the chief magistrate — preceded by the military — rode to his house in Silver Street.

"Now for a conclusion to the Triumphs of this Day, let me not deprive that worthy Architect Mr. *Jerman*, of a debt so justly due to his ingenuitie, as is the praise which he hath merited by the . . . rare inventions wherewith he did adorn this Day's Triumph." [4] The pamphlet ends with a congratulation to the mayor who "must needs be the most welcome Governour that hath for many years rul'd this city: who comes bringing in his hand the Olive Branch of *Peace*, restoring to the city those Ancient Customs of *Joy* and *Triumph*, which formerly gave it the Title of the most Fortunate, Plentiful and Flourishing Citie in the World."

---

[1] *Ibid.*, p. 11.

[2] *Ibid.*, p. 13.

[3] *Ibid.*, p. 14. (Does the expression *may be* mean that Bulteel had nothing to do with planning the show ?)

[4] *Ibid.*, p. 16.

1657 — Tatham's First Show; Jarman, Artificer

In 1657, John Tatham wrote his first show, entitled *London's Triumphs*, for Richard Chiverton, Skinner.[1] The records of the Court of Aldermen, under date of 13 October, 1657, read: " It is Ordered that Mr Jarman have Liberty to vse the roome in Leadenhall called the Pageant howse for preparing of some pageants intended for ye Lord Maiors day." [2] And under 28 October, " It is ordered by this Court that Mr Jarman and such as are Imployed by him shall and are hereby authorized to tye vp such signes in any of the streetes of this city as they shall see fitt for the cleerer passage of the pageants on the Lord Maiors day." [3]

There was, this year, " no Shew upon the Water, more then (*sic*) was the last year " — so that we may suppose the militia accompanied the mayor, and perhaps had a mock fight. At Cheapside Cross were the first land pageants — a rock and a wilderness. On the latter were beasts,[4] with a " Satyre " and a Pilgrim, or Traveller. On the other pageant was Fame, and " in the Chariot," [5] the four Continents — Europe, Asia, Africa, and America. The Pilgrim addressed the chief magistrate.

Near the mayor's house, in Dowgate, the second triumph awaited him — a sea-chariot, wherein sat Neptune with Luna at his feet, and two nymphs in attendance. Tritons surrounded his chariot. With a farewell speech by Neptune, the show was over.

Tatham wrote all the Lord Mayor's triumphs from 1657 to 1664 inclusive. As Fairholt outlines them all, we need not consider them here in detail. On 11 October, 1659, the Court of Aldermen " thought fitt and ordered . . . y[t] such convenient place of Gresham Colledge as Mr Jarman shall appoint, may be used for preparing the pageants, intended by the Company of Groc: against the Lord Maiors day." [6]

Evelyn and Pepys on the Shows

Both Evelyn and Pepys saw the 1660 Show; the former records: " Going to London, my Lord Maior's shew stopped me in Cheapside; one of ye pageants represented a greate wood, with ye royal oake and historie of his Majesty's

---

[1] A copy of this is in BM. Cf. Fairholt, pt. i, p. 65; J. G. Nichols, p. 107; J. Nichols, in *Gent. Mag.*, Dec., 1824, p. 514.

[2] *Repertory* lxv, fol. 199.

[3] *Ibid.*, fol. 211. The 1657 pamphlet ends: " The several Fabricks and Structures of the whole daies Tryumph, were performed by the Industry of Mr German, a man not onely excellent in his Art, but faithful in his undertakings."

[4] Alluding to the trade of the mayor, who was a Skinner.

[5] Apparently behind the rock, in the back part of the pageant.

[6] *Repertory* xlvi, fol. 320 b. A full list of Tatham's shows may be found in the Bibliography under his name.

miraculous escape at Boscobel."[1] Pepys writes: " . . . had a very good place to see the pageants which were many, and I believe good, for such kind of things, but in themselves but poor and absurd."[2]

Under date of 29 October, 1661, Evelyn wrote: " I saw the Lord Maior passe in his water triumph to Westminster, being the first solemnity of the nature after 20 years."[3] The water show this year was more elaborate than any since the days of Heywood. On his way to Westminster, the Mayor — Sir John Frederick — was accosted by a vessel, rigged and manned, near which was Galatea, a sea-nymph, drawn in a Sea Chariot by two Dolphins, which were ridden by Sirens who played on harps. Behind them were two Sea-Lions, ridden by Tritons, who played upon " retorted Pipes or Hornes antique." Other Tritons were around the Ship " wantoning in the water." On the mayor's approach, the Boatswain of the ship addressed him, and bade him hearken to the Captain's speech; then the mayor, with his attendant barges, continued to Westminster, while the " Ship, Furniture and annexed Sceans return, and are received at the place where the Ship first lanched, and from thence are conveyed through Pauls Church-yard into Cheapside where they make a stand near St. *Lawrence* Lane."

Evelyn mentions the show for 1662 under 29 October of that year,[4] when "was my Lo. Maior's show, with a number of sumptuous pageants, speeches and verses. I was standing in an house in Cheapside against the place prepar'd for their Maties. The Prince and heire of Denmark was there, but not our King."[5]

---

[1] *Diary*, ii, p. 118 (under 29 October, 1660). The pamphlet describing this show — entitled *The Royal Oake* — may be found in the BM. and Bodl; it is reprinted by Fairholt, pt. ii, p. 87. Cf. also *ibid.*, pt. i, p. 68, and J. G. Nichols, p. 108. What is apparently another version of this pamphlet (*The Several Speeches made to the Honorable Sir* Richard Brown, *Lord Mayor*, etc.) may be found in the Gh. and Camb. Univ. libraries.

[Cf. Withington, "A Civic 'Triumph' circa 1700," in *Journ. Eng. Germ. Philol.* for January, 1918, p. 125, n. 1, (where *Fairhold* should, of course, read *Fairholt*)].

[2] *Diary*, i, p. 270 (under 29 October, 1660).

[3] *Diary*, ii, p. 137. (Bray, the editor, refers to Nichols in *Gent. Mag.*, Dec., 1824, p. 516.) The original pamphlet for this show is in BM. and Gh.; it is reprinted in Heath (3d ed.) p. 475; cf. also Fairholt, pt. i, p. 68; J. G. Nichols, p. 108.

[4] *Ibid.*, ii, p. 153. Bray refers to Nichols in *Gent. Mag.*, Dec., 1824, p. 517. Copies of this pamphlet are in BM. and Bodl.; cf. also Fairholt, pt. i, p. 71; J. G. Nichols, p. 109.

[5] Cf. *Repertory* lxviii, fol. 205, under date of 7 October, 1662: " It is thought fitt and ordered by this Court [of Aldermen] that the Company of Clothworkers may make vse of such part of the Vnder Gallery of Gresham Colledge for preparing and fitting their Pageants against the Lord Maiors day, as shall bee most convenient for yt purpose." The 1662 Show — written for Sir John Robinson, Clothworker, — is printed without its author's name. The unusually apologetic preface ends: " My Lord, I have no better way of excusing my own *Insufficiency* then (*sic*) by attempting *little*, and making the *Brevity* of my discourse expiate the *Insipidnesse;* which I cannot perform more *Gratefully* to your or my self, then (*sic*) by telling you briefly, that I am your Lordships very much obliged Servant; But what my Name is, none shall know, but by your Lordships Revelation."

The Show for 1663

Pepys writes under date of 29 October, 1663: "The dinner, it seems, is made by the Mayor and two Sheriffs for the time being, the Lord Mayor paying one half and they the other. And the whole, Proby says, is reckoned to come to about 7 or £800 at most . . . I . . . took coach and through Cheapside, and there saw the pageants, which were very silly . . ." [1]

This show included an arbor, where Faunus — strange mixture of forester and woodman, in green and brown — sat surrounded by satyrs, who played on rude instruments, as they sang and danced for the people. These figures suggest, as I have noted,[2] the "drolls," and acrobats, which were common enough in the shows of this time, and which we found as early as the "royal-entries" of 1547[3] and 1554.[4] They may be a descendant of the "wild-man" tinged with mythology.

Pepys did not see the show in 1664, but his "boy and three mayds went out." Evelyn rather enjoyed himself this year:[5] "Oct. 29, 1664. Was ye most magnificent triumph by water and land of ye Lord Mayor. I din'd at Guildhall at ye upper table . . . The feast was said to cost £1000. I slipt away in ye crowd, and came home late." A notice of the civic show for this year may be found in the London *Intelligencer* for Monday, 31 October, 1664.[6] As it is rare, I quote it:

> London, Octob. 29. — This day the Right Honourable the *Lord Mayor* of the City of *London* (Sir *John Lawrence*) was sworn into the said Office, according to Custome, at the *Exchequer-Barre:* After which, having done the usuall duty of the Courts of *Common-Pleas* and *Chancery*, he return'd into the City, where the Solemnity of the day was perform'd with great Magnificence and in excellent Order. And for the greater Honour of the Spectacle, Their *Majesties Themselves* were pleased to vouchsafe it their presence, and were presented with a choice and sumptuous Banquet: but the glory of the Ceremony was much abated by the foulness of the weather.

On account of the plague there were no pageants in 1665. The mayor took his oath before the Lieutenant of the Tower, at the "further Gate of the Bulwark," and after the ceremony gave a dinner at his house.[7] There was a plague at Norwich this same year; for under date of 27 May, 1665, "it is ordered (in consequence of the Plague) that the Bellman doe make Proclamation every

---

[1] *Diary*, iii, p. 322. Tatham's show for this year, entitled *Londinum Triumphans*, was written for Sir Anthony Bateman, Skinner. A copy of the descriptive pamphlet is in Gh.; cf. also Fairholt, pt. i, p. 71; J. G. Nichols, p. 109; Wadmore, p. 145; J. Nichols, in *Gent. Mag.*, for Dec., 1824, p. 517.

[2] See above, vol. i, p. 77.

[3] See above, vol. i, p. 187.

[4] See above, vol. i, p. 194, and n. 1.

[5] *Diary*, ii, p. 172. This — the last of Tatham's shows — was written for Sir John Lawrence, Haberdasher. Copies of the pamphlet are in BM., Bodl., and Gh.; cf. also J. Nichols in *Gent. Mag.*, Dec., 1824, p. 517; Fairholt, pt. i, p. 71; J. G. Nichols, p. 109.

[6] No. 85, p. 704.

[7] See the London *Newes* for 2 November, 1665 (no. 89, p. 1082).

mercate day, betweene this and the Guilde, that ther shall be noe extraordinary solempnities, by henginge out cloaths, Pictures, Garlands or Streamers, this nexte Guilde, upon Tuesday three weekes. And this Order is made by the advice of ye Right Honble the Ld Lieu^{t} of ye City." [1]

1664-69 — Newspaper Accounts of the Solemnities

I have been able to find no descriptive pamphlets for the years which lie between 1664 and 1671; but on some of these years there were shows. The London *Gazette* for 28–31 October, 1667,[2] notes under date of 29 October: "This day Sir William Peck, Lord Mayor of the City for the ensuing year, attended by the Aldermen his Brethren, and the two Sheriffs, with several Companies of the Livery-men, came in their Barges to Westminster where, in the Court of the Exchequer, his Lordship took his Oath with the usual Solemnities." Had there been pageants on this occasion, it is probable that the newspaper would have mentioned them.

The same journal for 28–31 October, 1668,[3] notes that on 1 November, "Sir William Turner, Lord Mayor of the City of London for the year ensuing, went in his Barge to Westminster, attended by the Aldermen his Brethren, the Sheriffs, and the several Companies of the City in their Barges, and took the usual Oath administered on the like occasions." Again there is no mention of pageantry.[4]

1671 — Thomas Jordan's "London's Resurrection"

With 1671, a new writer of shows appears — Thomas Jordan, who wrote the civic triumphs from this year until 1685, when he was succeeded by Matthew Taubman. A full list of his pamphlets may be found in the Bibliography, under his name. He had been a writer of plays and masques from 1640 on; and Fairholt [5] notes that his poetry is chiefly remarkable for its allusion to contemporary events. An interesting thing about his productions is the "interludes," which were presented during the banquets in Guildhall.[6]

The title — *London's Resurrection* — suggests that no descriptive pamphlets had appeared for a few years.[7] The first pageant was "a Forests (*sic*) properly

---

[1] *Court Book* no. 23, fol. 247, cited by Ewing, p. 18.

[2] No. 204, p. 2, col. 2.

[3] The London *Gazette*, no. 309, p. 2, col. 2.

[4] I can find no mention of a Lord Mayor's Show — nor any reason why one should not be held — in the London *Gazettes* of October to November, 1670. There are, in the British Museum, no periodicals for 1666 and 1669.

[5] *L. M. Pag.*, pt. ii, p. 110.

[6] Strictly speaking, these are not parts of the shows themselves; but they are included in the descriptive pamphlets, and may be considered Jordan's answer to the demand for novelty or for further entertainment.

[7] This show of Jordan's — descriptive pamphlets of which are in HL., Gh., BM., and Bodl. — is reprinted by Fairholt, pt. ii, p. 113 f. For mention of it see also Fairholt, pt. i, p. 75; J. G. Nichols, p. 110, and Wadmore, p. 148.

Jacob Hall

accomodated with several *Animals*, *Sylvans*, *Satyrs*, and *Wood-Nymphes*, sitting and stirring in very good Order . . . And in the Front are two Negroes, richly adorned with Oriental Pearls and Jewels mounted upon two Panthers."[1] A wilderness, inhabited by birds and wild beasts, was to have been the first pageant,[2] but was — it seems — the second. On this was erected a " stately structure, formed in the figure of a pyramid, with four triumphal arches; " on the first of which sat Orpheus, in back of whom was a beautiful woman representing Amity; and on the highest part of the pyramid sat a " female negra " representing Africa.

Orpheus addressed the mayor, resigning to him his power of bringing concord to animals by harmony.

> . . . This City (which my *Pageant* doth express)
> May very well be call'd a *Wilderness*.
> A Wood where all the Wild and Brutish Creatures
> Lie lurking in the Dens of mens bad Natures;
> Which, if you can reduce, you will be fam'd
> For quelling more than ever *Orpheus* tam'd:
> No doubt but your endeavors will be shown
> And you'll perform it (if it can be done.)
>
> * * * *
>
> *Union* breeds *Peace* and Plenty in a Land
> But Cities self-divided, *Cannot stand*.

Then the mayor and his retinue went through Cheapside, and by the way the third [3] scene or pageant was presented. This was an imperial palace of Pleasure, in front of which sat four female figures, representing Justice, Temperance, Peace, and Plenty, with attendant nymphs. On the highest part was Fame, crowned and winged;[4] in her hand she carried a trumpet on which was hung the royal banner.

The mayor, having sufficiently viewed " this beautiful building " and the figures, continued his journey to the Guildhall; during the banquet, the waits sang " excellent musick."[5] Then " they make provision for a piece of drollery to be sung in parts and shapes " by Hoyden, a countryman of the West, Freeman, a citizen, and Billet, a soldier.

---

[1] Pamphlet, p. 3. The show, it may be noted, was written for Sir George Waterman, Skinner.

[2] See Fairholt's reprint, pt. ii, p. 118 and p. 138. Reference to the " postscript " on the latter page, shows us that Jacob Hall and his tumblers performed " near to the presence of the king, queen, duke, and other beams of the royal family, near Milk-street end." In the Guildhall pamphlet there is no mention of Hall.

[3] Called the second, in Fairholt, pt. ii, p. 120.

[4] All these figures were, apparently, alive, although none spoke.

[5] The first song, " consisting of three distinct Voices, with a chorus to each " was " purposely composed for my Lord Mayor's table."

Interludes at the Banquet

This is a musical dialogue with elements of farce — undoubtedly the audience laughed when Hoyden whipped Freeman. There is no plot, and the fun is primitive. Citizen and countryman, discovering that neither can get along without the other, agree to support the soldier; and the concluding chorus informs us that " a union well-grounded no malice can hurt."

After this " droll," the second course of the dinner was served; it was followed by another " representation to salute his Lordship, which consisteth of three parts, viz. — A Countryman, A Citizen, and Sedition, an old Instrument of Oliver's Faction." This appears to have been another musical show — the Countryman is the same Tom Hoyden of the last " droll; " he bemoans his fate, that ever he left the West Country. Enter Citizen, who has at first little sympathy for the gulled countryman, but who finally takes pity on him. As they are going out to eat, Oliver Faction — who loves to sow the seeds of strife — enters; he wonders why he, who — till lately — had been in great request, should now be left out of anything. After an argument with the citizen, he is whipped and ejected by Hoyden; Oliver finally promises not to hurt the city, and all unite in singing her glory.

The banquet and these interludes took all the afternoon. Dinner over, the procession of the morning marched by torchlight to the Skinners' Hall, where the pageant called the Wilderness made a stand, and Orpheus wished the Lord Mayor joy. Especial care was taken to lodge the silk-works and triumphs in some secure place, until they could be removed to Skinners' Hall " in regard they are of some weight, and the burthen of the day was heavy to the undertakers."

It may be remarked that the royal family witnessed this show; indeed, the king " graced the triumphs " of 1672, 1673, and — with many nobles — that of 1674 as well.[1] Almost a century later, " it was usual with the members of the royal family to witness the civic procession on Lord Mayor's day either from the leads of Whitehall, as it passed on the Thames, or from balconies in the city as it returned on land." [2]

Similarity of the Shows for 1672 and 1673

The marked similarity of Jordan's Shows for 1672 and 1673 [3] may not be due wholly to Jordan's inability to invent new material fitting to the Grocers' Company, for which both shows were written. His dedication to that Worshipful

[1] Cf. the title-pages of the pamphlets for these years, as recorded in the Bibliography.

[2] Fairholt, pt. i, p. 131. He quotes from the *Daily Gazetteer* of 30 October, 1741.

[3] On the former, see the descriptive pamphlet (in BM., Bodl., and Gh.); it is reprinted by Heath (3[d] ed., p. 488). Copies of the 1673 pamphlet are in Gh. and B.; it is reprinted by Heath (3[d] ed., p. 507). Cf. Fairholt, pt. i, pp. 74 f., 79 f.; J. G. Nichols, pp. 110 and 111.

Company, in the 1673 pamphlet, notes the fact that the Grocers have "undergone" the display of triumphs "these two years without intermission," and that it is their "fourth time of performance since the Happy Restoration of His Sacred Majesty . . . In such splendid actions," he continues, "although some Diminution of your Treasure, they are, and will be plentifully recompensed in the Addition of your Fame . . ." It is possible that Jordan had to use the same "silkworks and triumphs" he had used before. Both shows were opened by a negro boy, who, mounted on a camel, distributed fruits and spices to the crowd.[1] Effigies of the supporters of the Company's arms — the Gryphons — made up the second pageant in both shows; behind them, on a golden throne, sat Apollo in 1672, and the "god of Riches" with "the much ador'd Madam *Pecunia*, (a Lady of Great Splendor)" the next year. In both shows, the third pageant, near St. Laurence lane-end, was a "wilderness," or garden of fruits, in which were "drolls," — "tawny Moors," — who gathered fruits, and sang and danced the while: in 1672, "a proper Masculine Woman, with a tawny face," represented America, on a "steep Rock in a pyramidical Figure . . . eminently exalted above the tops of the Trees," — while in 1673, Pomona, attended by the Four Seasons, occupied the "eminent promontory." The 1672 pamphlet mentions giants, which do not seem to have appeared in 1673.[2]

1674 — Rules against Squibs; The "Spectator" on this Year's Dinner

In 1674, Jordan wrote the show for the Goldsmiths, upon the inauguration of Sir Robert Vyner.[3] It is needless here to outline the day's triumph; but we may remark that on 27 October, 1674, the Court of Aldermen, taking notice of the great disorders of apprentices and other boys continually committed by the throwing of squibs and other fireworks, which terrified and endangered all sorts of persons in their passage through the streets, ordered "that all the Marshalls men & Beadles of the four Hospitalls of this City doe attend the Right Hono[ble]

[1] On a silver throne, under a canopy of silver, sat an Indian Emperor in 1672: the next year Pallas occupied the "sublime seat of Soveraignty."

[2] On 15 October, 1672, the Court of Aldermen ordered "that the Guildhall & parts adjacent bee prepared for the Entertainment on the Lord Maiors day in such manner as hath been accustomed," (*Repertory* lxxvii, fol. 265 b) and on 23 September, 1673, "Upon a motion made unto this Court by the Lord Maior Elect whether it shall be thought fitting to invite his Majesty to dine at the Guildhall on the Lord Maiors Day next, and if it shall appeare to be the sense of this Court, that then his Ma[ties] inclinations may be understood in time, and the Citty the better inabled to make preparations for his Entertainment, It is by this Court recom̄ended to his Lordshipp in such matter as hee shall thinke fitting to understand his Maiestyes pleasure therein." *Repertory* lxxviii, fol. 285 b.

[3] Copies of this pamphlet may be found in SA., Bodl.; it was reprinted in 1835, and copies of this reprint are in Gh. and BM. Cf. also Fairholt, pt. i, p. 81 f.; pt. ii, p. vi; J. G. Nichols, p. 111.

the Lord Major this afternoon at five of the Clock to receive his Lo'pps. Comands touching some course to be taken for prevention of the said Mischiefs & Disorders." [1]

In the *Spectator* for Wednesday, 20 August, 1712, (no. 462) is printed an account of the Lord Mayor's dinner for this year, 1674. Charles II

more than once dined with his good citizens of London on their lord-mayor's-day, and did so the year that Sir Robert Viner was mayor. Sir Robert was a very loyal man, and, if you will allow the expression, very fond of his sovereign; but what with the joy he felt at heart for the honour done him by his prince, and through the warmth he was in with continual toasting healths to the royal family, his lordship grew a little fond of his majesty, and entered into a familiarity not altogether so graceful in so public a place. The king understood very well how to extricate himself on all kinds of difficulties, and, with a hint to the company to avoid ceremony, stole off, and made towards his coach, which stood ready for him in Guildhall-yard. But the mayor liked his company so well, and was grown so intimate, that he pursued him hastily, and catching him fast by the hand, cried out with a vehement oath and accent "Sir, you shall stay and take t'other bottle." The airy monarch looked kindly at him over his shoulder, and with a smile and graceful air (for I saw him at the time, and do now) repeated this line of the old song:

"He that's drunk is as great as a King,"

and immediately returned back and complied with his landlord.

Under date of 3 June, 1675, the Court of Aldermen, "being informed that the respective proporcons of the sumes of money payable by the Lord Maiors and Sherriffes towards the charge of the entertainm[ts] on the Lord Maiors Day for the years Last past are not yet fully made upp and discharged in the Accompts of the Chamber, doth order that all persons concerned doe forthwith pay into the Chamber their full proporcons of the said moneys with all convenient speed." [2]

1675 — Jordan Plans a Show for the Drapers

Of Jordan's Show for 1675, in honor of Sir Joseph Sheldon's inauguration, several descriptive pamphlets exist.[3] This was written for the Drapers' Com-

[1] *Repertory* lxxix, fol. 421. The king having accepted the Mayor's invitation to dine at Guildhall, a committee was appointed "for the providing & well-ordering of the Entertainment." (20 October, 1674.) *Repertory* cited, fol. 404 b.

[2] *Repertory* lxxx, fol. 205.

Under date of 26 October, 1676, the minutes of the Court of Aldermen record: "It is by this Court Referred to S[r] George Waterman Knt. and Alderman and other the Members of this Court concerned as Lord Majors or Sherriffes in the charge of the Entertainments at Guildhall or (MS. error for *on*) the Lord Majors day in the yeare 1671 And since to adjust and settle the Accompts thereof with Mr. Chamblen (*Chamberlain*) and forthwith to Pay all such sumes of money as they are severally in arrear and make up the full Complement of the sums charged upon them thereto and then make Report thereof to this Court." *Repertory* lxxxi, fol. 337.

[3] Copies may be found in Gh., Bodl. (2 copies) and BM. (3 copies — one lacking the title-page). For mention of this show see Fairholt, pt. i, p. 84 f.; J. G. Nichols, p. 111.

pany, and included a representation of the Golden Fleece. A " Scene of Drolls " was stationed near St. Laurence lane-end — a forest, or desert, properly accommodated with herbage, trees, bushes, birds and flowers. Sheep grazed therein, and Cotswold and Salisbury Plain shepherds played, danced, and tumbled in " excellent confusion."

From the Records of the Aldermen

On 17 October, 1676,

it was now agreed by this Court [of Aldermen] That on the Lord Majors day next the Right Hono^{ble} the Lord Major accompanied with my Masters the Aldermen do in their Return from Westminster Take Landing at Blackfryers Staires, and go from thence to Fleet Bridge by the End of the New Channell which is apprehended to be well accomodate for that purpose the usuall Landing place at Pauls Wharf and the Passage thence being now Obstructed by great Quantities of Stone laid there for the Convenience of St. Paul's Church.[1]

The Show for this year was written by Jordan; a copy of the descriptive pamphlet is in the Guildhall Library.[2]

On 23 October, 1677, the Aldermen ruled that

whereas complaint hath been made unto this Court that Boards and Scaffolds have heretofore been set up on the Lord Majors Day by the Inhabitants before their houses in the streetes and publicke passages of this City through which the Lord Major and Aldermen were to passe, whereby the Companies standing in those streetes have been greatly streitened for want of roome; It is now therefore ordered and strictly injoyned by this Court that noe Inhabitant in any street where the Lord Major and Aldermen are to passe, and especially in Cheapside, doe hereafter on the Lord Majors Day permitte any Boardes or Scaffolds to be set into the street without the ffront of their houses. And Mr. Oliver one of the Surveyors is desired to see that this Order be duely observed. And all Constables and other officers are required to be Assistant to him therein.[3]

Under date of 19 September, 1678, we find in the aldermanic records:

Whereas on the 16th day of October last upon the petition of the Master and Wardens of the Company of Stationers and a suggestion by them made that they had been disturbed in their standing on the Lord Major's Day before St. Paul's Schoole being the Place by them anciently used for that purpose, It was Ordered by this Court that the Members of the said Company should injoy their station before the said Schoole at that time as anciently, now upon a Petition presented unto this Court by the Master, Wardens and Assistants and Livery of the Company of Turners setting forth that their station on that day hath anciently been before St. Paul's Schoole under the Wall of the said School until they were disturbed therein

---

[1] *Repertory* lxxxi, fol. 319 b.

[2] For an outline of the show, see Fairholt, pt. i, p. 85 f.: cf. also J. G. Nichols, p. 112. We may note that, as in 1612, the Seven Liberal Arts (or Sciences) — which we have found in " royal-entries " (cf., *e.g.*, vol. i, p. 145, and n. 2) — appeared this year.

[3] *Repertory* lxxxii, fol. 289. Descriptive pamphlets of Jordan's show for this year are in Gh., Bodl., BM., (2 copies — one imperfect). Cf. Fairholt, pt. i, p. 87 f.; J. G. Nichols, p. 112.

the last yeare by the said Company of Stationers by vertue of the said Order, And upon hearing the proofes now offered to that matter by the said Company of Turners and what could be alleadged against the same by the said Company of Stationers who were here present It appearing unto this Court that the said Company of Turners had their Station anciently in the said place and that the said Suggestion made by the said Company of Stationers upon which the said Order was grounded that the same was their ancient standing was untrue It is therefore now thought fitt and Ordered by this Court That the said Company of Turners doe continue their Station on the Lord Major's Day in the place by them accustomed before St Pauls Schoole and as they did before the last year, And that the said Company of Stationers do likewise content themselves with their ancient standing And that the said Companies do not interfere or disturb each other in their said respective Stations.[1]

On the 10 October, 1678,

upon the motion of the right Hono^{ble} the Lord Major Elect [2] That the Company of Stationers (who are at present destitute of a sufficient roome for the station of their whole Company in the publick passage on the Lord Majors day) might be accomodated for that purpose in some convenient place near Ludgate, It is Ordered by this Court that Mr. Oliver do find out a convenient place for the said Company to stand in upon those Occasions and make report to this Court on Tuesday next to the end the same may be granted and established to the said Company by Authority of this Court.[3]

Five days later the court ruled

upon a motion now made unto this Court for and on the behalf of the Company of Barbersurgeons who by several Orders of this Court have been constituted and setled in the Ranke of the 17th Company of this City, It is Ordered by this Court that Mr. Oliver do hereafter on the Lord Major's Day accordingly dispose and ranke the said Company of Barbersurgeons as the seaventeenth in Order among the other Companies of this City.[4]

These extracts from the manuscript records of the London Aldermen are of particular interest for us, as showing the solicitude felt by the Companies in the annual civic show. Even those not directly concerned were anxious to take the subordinate part of onlookers; for the Companies which lined the streets contributed to the glory of the triumphs.

Jordan's Show for 1678 has been twice reprinted,[5] and there is no need of outlining it here. As in 1671, there was an interlude performed at the dinner, *in stilo recitativo*, the characters in which were Crab, a West-countryman, Swab, a seaman, and Self, a citizen. The scene was laid at the Royal Exchange: the quarrels of the characters are followed by union, for each is necessary to the others. While the characters are individualized to a certain extent, they point

[1] *Repertory* lxxxiii, fol. 295 *et seq.*

[2] Sir James Edwards, Grocer.

[3] The same *Repertory*, fol. 309 b.

[4] The same *Repertory*, fol. 311.

[5] Fairholt, pt. ii, p. 141; Heath (3^{d} ed.) p. 518. Copies of the original pamphlet may be found in Gh., (badly trimmed about the edges); HL.; Bodl. (2 copies); BM. (2 copies, one imperfect). Cf. also Fairholt, pt. i, p. 90; J. G. Nichols, p. 112.

to type figures: Crab — the Hoyden of 1671 — suggests Rus; Self — in 1671, Freeman — makes us think of a figure, Civis. The lesson — that city and country are mutually dependent — prevents us from losing sight of the underlying allegory. The " technique " of these shows is not unlike that of modern comic opera; song is combined with dialogue and dancing.[1]

1679 — A Newspaper Account of the Mayor's Installation

The vivid picture of a London crowd which Jordan gives in his pamphlet describing the 1679 Show, I have reprinted in "A Civic 'Triumph,' circa 1700."[2] It may be compared with Ward's description of London crowds two decades later.[3]

The Domestick Intelligence: or News both from City and Country Impartialy Related, for Friday, 31 October, 1679, (no. 34) gives an account of the show.

Wednesday last, the Twenty Ninth of this Instant *October*, being appointed for the Installment of the Right Honourable Sir *Robert Clayton* to be Lord *Maior* of *London*, to which he was unanimously Elected on *Michaelmas* day last past: His Lordship accordingly went in the morning to *Westminster* in great Triumph, attended upon with the Barges of the several Companies of the City, and being landed, his *Lordship* accompanied with the *Aldermen* and *Sheriffs* went into His *Majesties* Court of *Exchequer* in *Westminster-Hall*, where Mr. *Recorder* was pleased in a Learned and Elegant Speech, to discourse of the Excellent Qualifications

[1] Resembling Jordan's " interludes " is the " short representation performed before the Lord General Monk at Goldsmiths'-Hall, Tuesday, Aprill 11th. By three persons, An English-man, a Welsh-man, and a Scotch-man." (London, 1660.) This is in Guildhall (*A. 1.5*); dialogue precedes the songs, and here an " officer " represents the citizen of London.

Various speeches addressed to General Monk on his visits to the Companies of London may be found in the Bodleian. On Wednesday, 28 March, 1660, at Drapers-Hall, he heard one spoken " by one Representing the Genius of England " (Bodl., *Wood 398.4*); Walter Yeokney spoke, and perhaps wrote, the speech to Monk and the Council of State at Drapers-Hall on the same date (Bodl., *Wood 398.5*); W. Bard declaimed verses to the general at Skinners-Hall, 4 April, 1660 — beginning in the Cornish dialect, the speaker soon lapses into English (Bodl., *Wood 398.6*). Jordan wrote the speech which followed a song in four parts when Monk was entertained at the Goldsmiths-Hall, 10 April, 1660 — the speech was delivered by a " sea-captain," and is preserved in the same collection (*Wood 398.7*); Jordan also wrote that spoken before Monk, 12 April, 1660, at Vintners-Hall " wherein his illustrious virtues are shadowed forth under the emblem of a Vine." (*Wood 398.8*); the same author composed that spoken by Walter " Youkcny " (= Yeokney) on 13 April, 1660, at Fishermongers-Hall; "after a song of difference betwixt the Lawyer, the Soldier, the Citizen, and the Countrey-man . . . enter the Ghost of Massianello Fisher-man of Naples." (Bodl., *Wood 398.9*). In 1659, on 13 March, Monk was entertained at the Clothworkers-Hall, where a speech — preserved in the same collection (*Wood 398.3*) — was delivered.

It is clear that these pre-Restoration " interludes " of 1660, some of which were written by Jordan himself, are the forerunners of the later " interludes " at the inauguration banquets.

[2] *Journ. Eng. and Germ. Philol.* for January, 1918, p. 127.

[3] Cf. *The London Spy*, cited *ibid.*, pp. 128 f.

both of Sir *James Edwards* late Lord *Maior*, and also of the present Worthy Magistrate Sir *Robert Clayton*, who was now come to be sworn, and to enter upon that Honourable Charge; Mr. *Recorder* was also pleased to add that he was satisfied, and that it was without all Contradiction, that the present Magistrates and Citizens of this famous City, were as Loyal to His Majesty and the Government, as ever at any time heretofore, which they had fully demonstrated in these late times of Trouble and Danger, wherein they have appeared to be very Active and Careful for preserving the Peace and safety of the City against all Enemies whatsoever.

After which the Lord *Chief Baron* was pleased very excellently to discourse of this Great Office, and among many other worthy expressions, was pleased to Intimate, that the City ought yet to be carefull of the Designs of the *Romish* Party, whose *Jesuits* and *Priests* are never Idle in Contriving and Promoting the Destruction of His Majesties Person and Government. After his Lordship had taken the usual Oath, his Lordship went according to Custom to Visit the several Courts of Justice in *Westminster Hall;* and then his Lordship returned back in his Barge, and landed at *Black Fryers* Stairs, where the *Artillery Company*, belonging to the City, (who made a very Noble Appearance, in their Buff-Coats and Red Feathers,) Attended; and gave three Vollies of shot upon his Lordship's Landing, and then went to *Kingstreet* near *Guildhall*, where they waited till his Lordship came thither; his Lordship proceeded through St. *Paul's Churchyard*, and *Cheapside*, and was entertained with several Speeches from four Triumphant Pageants, which were provided at the Charge of the *Drapers* Company, (of which his Lordship was free) and represented some part of the *Drapers* Trade. His Lordship came then to *Guildhall*, where a Sumptuous Dinner was prepared, at which were the Lords of His Majesties Privy Councill, the Judges in their Scarlet Gowns, and several others of the Nobility and Gentry.

Such is a newspaper account of the annual occasion, of which Jordan, two years before,[1] said: " In all the Authors I have read, and all the most curious-observing Travellers I have conversed with, I have been answer'd, that in no City of *Europe* they have such *celebrious Triumphs* at the Inauguration and Instalment of their Magistrates, as the Lord Mayor of *London* . . ."

1680 — Jordan's " London's Glory "

A precept of the Mayor, dated 6 September, 1680, requires the Chamberlain, Common-serjeant, Common-Clerk, two Judges of the Sheriffs' Courts, four Common-Pleaders, the Comptroller of the Chamber, two Secondaries, the Remembrancer, Solicitor, two Bridge Masters, and four Attorneys in the Outer Court, to perform their duty in walking before the Lord Mayor and Aldermen, " Riding annually through the Streets of this City, on the usual days of Solemnity, such as are *Bartholomew Even*, to Proclaim *Bartholomew Fair;* on the 8th of *September*, to *Lady-Fair* in *Southwark;* on *Michaelmas-day*, and the day after; on *Simon* and *Judes-day*, and the day after; and three days in *Easter* to the *Spittle;* which are the Solemn days now used (there being some few other days

[1] Addressing his patrons, the Clothworkers, in 1677. (His descriptive pamphlet for this year's show is recorded in the Bibliography.)

wherein the like service was heretofore performed in Riding to *St. Pauls*, but the same is at present discontinued until that Church be rebuilt;) . . ." [1]

On 19 October of this year, " Itt is thought fitt & Ordered by this Court that the Masters & Wardens of the severall Companies of this City which have Barges & have usually attended the Solemnity on the Water at the Lord Majors-day bee Warned to appeare before this Court on this day sen̄ight." [2] *London's Glory* was the title of Jordan's show for this year, written to celebrate the inauguration of Sir Patience Ward, Merchant-Taylor.[3]

The 1681 Show also by Jordan

Sir John Moore, Grocer, was inaugurated in 1681; again the show was written by Jordan.[4] An account of it from *The Impartial Protestant Mercury* [5] is of interest.

> London, October 29. This day being the Anniversary Inauguration of the Lord Mayor of this Honourable City, the Right Honourable Sir *John Moor* repairing with the usual Splendor and Solemnity to *Westminster*, and being there Sworn, on his Return landed at Black-Fryars, and so proceeded in State to the *Guild-Hall*. Their Majesties, Attended with the Chief Persons of Quality of the Court, were pleased to honour the City with Their Presence, and appeared highly satisfied with Their Magnificent Entertainment: The Crowd of People in the Streets was extraordinary, and during His Majesties whole Passage thither, and going back, fill'd the Air with loud Shouts and Acclamations of Joy, and well Wishes for His Majesties long Life and Prosperity. So false, as well as wicked and malicious, are the Suggestions of those Ill Men, who would insinuate as if the Inhabitants of this Great and Honourable City were wanting in their Loyalty, or in that Obedience and Affection which is due to their Sovereign.

It will be recalled that England was politically excited at this period; we shall consider, in the next chapter, the " Pope-burnings " of the years following 1679 — suffice it here to note that, as Fairholt expresses it, " The Lord Mayor was at this period popular only with his own party, being in fact a mere political tool of the court. The infamous Charles . . . having among other acts of flagrant injustice suspended the charter of the city, he so managed that none but the servile creatures of his will should there have sway." [6] Further signs of this feeling are shown in the insane laudation of the king which makes the songs of

---

[1] See no. 94 in the Taylor Collection of broadsides in the Guildhall Library. Cf. *Repertory* lxxxv, fol. 219 b, *et seq.* for the order, made in the Court of Aldermen on 16 September, 1680, for printing the above precept.

[2] *Repertory* lxxxv, fol. 237.

[3] Copies of the pamphlet are in Gh., HL., BM., and Bodl.; cf. also Hone, p. 250 f.; Fairholt, pt. i, p. 92 f.

[4] Copies of the descriptive pamphlet are in Gh., BM., Bodl. It is reprinted by Heath, (3d ed.) p. 536 f.; cf. J. G. Nichols, p. 112 f.; Fairholt, pt. i, p. 95.

[5] No. 55 — from Friday, October 28, to Tuesday, November 1, 1681.

[6] Pt. i, p. 97 f.

the 1682 pamphlet noteworthy, and in the cessation of pageantry the same year, when some of the Companies refused to march in the procession.

1682 — No Pageants; but a Procession

In 1682, no pageants were exhibited, though there was a procession, described in a pamphlet entitled *The Lord Mayor's Show.*[1] The usual marching company, with banners, escorted the mayor from Guildhall to the Three-Cranes Wharf, where the water-procession began; Sir William Pritchard, the new chief magistrate, was saluted on his way to and from Westminster; on his return, he landed at Blackfriars, where the Artillery Company — of which he was president — gave him a volley, after which it led the way back to the Guildhall.

Various songs are printed in the pamphlet; one scorned the "tricks" and "plots" of the Whigs, and bade them farewell as they went out of office;[2] three "Loyal Songs" followed, from which the City Music were, apparently, to choose one for rendering.[3] Two catches, to be sung by the "loyal Spectators," end the collection. Hints of the trouble between the king and the city at this time, which is referred to by Fairholt, appear in the following account, taken from *The Domestick Intelligence:*[4]

London, Oct. 28. Yesterday the Worthy Sir *William Pritchard*, Lord Mayor Elect, accompanied with his present Lordship, many loyal Aldermen, and Mr. Recorder went to *White-hall* to wait upon His Majesty, by whom they were favourably received, His Majesty expressing His good liking, and high satisfaction in the Cities prudent Choice.

Most of the Companies are preparing to wait upon the Right Honourable the Lord Mayor to *Westminster* in their Formalities, in order to [attend] the Swearing the Lord Mayor Elect; and notwithstanding some are not a little solicitous to Eclipse the Triumph of the day (as we are informed,) by disswading their Brethren of the Livery from being present; yet such is the resolution of the Loyal and worthy Citizens, that nothing will be wanting that may conduce to the splendid Introduction of so worthy a Gentleman, as is to take upon him that great and Honourable Trust for the year insuing.[5]

---

[1] This pamphlet, which is mentioned by Fairholt, pt. i, p. 97, is in Bodl., (*Gough Lond. 122.24.*) The songs, which are printed after the account of the procession, were probably sung at the banquet following the inauguration of Sir William Pritchard, Merchant-Taylor. It is doubtful if these be the work of Jordan; though I have inserted this title with Jordan's shows in the Bibliography, he did not claim it. No "epistle dedicatory" precedes the account of the procession, which almost anyone might have written; if Jordan composed the songs, there is no sign of his authorship beside their commonplaceness.

[2] This was to be sung "to the Tune of *Sawny.*"

[3] One was a "New Song, which is set to an excellent Tune by Mr. *Pursell.*"

[4] No. 150 — "from Thursday, October the 26. to Munday the 30. 1682."

[5] The same issue of this periodical describes the administration of the oath to the mayor at Guildhall, (before the city authorities), and reports that in the afternoon of the same day the king was invited to dinner on the 30th, when the Mayor should go to Westminster. [Number 151 (from 30 October to 2 November, 1682) does not mention the ceremonies of the Lord Mayor's Day. It may be added that the election of the Lord Mayor, on 25 October, is described, *ibid.*, no. 149 (23–26 October, 1682.)]

1683 — Jordan's Pamphlet, "The Triumphs of London"

Jordan seems to have planned the festivities for Sir Henry Tulse, the king's appointee to the mayoralty in 1683; but there was no pageantry, and it is not clear that Jordan did anything but write a couple of songs for the mayor's banquet. *The Triumphs of London, performed on Monday, October xxix. 1683. for the entertainment of the Right Honourable, and truly Noble Pattern of Prudence and Loyalty*, Sir Henry Tulse, *Knight* . . . was printed at London in 1683;[1] from this pamphlet we learn that, the king having appointed Sir Henry Tulse to the mayoralty, Sir William Pritchard "issued forth his Precepts to summon the respective Liveries to attend His Majesty's new Lord Mayor . . . on *Monday*, the 29th of this instant *October*, 1683." There was a water-procession to and from Westminster, a military parade of the Artillery Company, and a march of the Companies, but nothing pageantic.[2]

1684 — Jordan's Last Civic Show

London's Royal Triumph for the City's Loyal Magistrate is the title of the last civic show which Jordan wrote.[3] It is outlined by Fairholt, in the *Gentleman's Magazine* for April, 1854.

There is nothing in the foreword of this pamphlet to suggest that there had been a break in the shows for two years: the "movements of the morning" are described in couplets; the Pleasure Boat saluted the mayor[4] with two broadsides; and everything took place as usual. The first pageant — described in verse — is the Chariot of Industry, where are twelve Virgins representing the twelve Companies; here Metropolis, "a majestic masculine woman" is the speaker.

---

[1] Copies are in Bodl. (*Gough Lond. 122.25*) and in Gh. (*A.1.5*). In pencil on the title-page of the latter copy is written, "by Thomas Jordan, city poet."

A picture at Windsor Castle, representing Charles II and his consort watching the Lord Mayor's procession by water in 1683, has been reproduced by the London Topographical Society, and a copy of the reproduction is in the Guildhall library. (The picture shows the City Barge, the barges of various Companies, and many spectators; it was reproduced in 1909, with permission of the king.)

[2] Two songs — entitled *A New Irish Song* and *The West-Countryman's Song, on a wedding* — are printed, with the music, in the pamphlet. The Honourable Artillery Company took part in many of the Lord Mayor's Shows; see the descriptive pamphlets, *passim*. For mention of the appearance of the Company in these triumphs, see Captain G. A. Raikes, *The History of the Honourable Artillery Company* [(2 vols.) London, 1878] i, p. 161, etc. In 1779, there was considerable friction between the Mayor and "the military glory of the nation," — cf. *ibid.*, ii, pp. 65 f., 424.

[3] Copies of the descriptive pamphlet are in Gh., Bodl., and BM. Cf. also J. G. Nichols, p. 115; Gillespy, p. 64; and Fairholt's letter to "Mr. Urban" (*Gent. Mag.* for April, 1854, pp. 380 f.) on this pageant, which he discovered (after the publication of *L. M. Pag.*), in the library of Sir Harry Verney, Bart.

[4] Sir James Smith, Draper.

The Mercers are represented by Mercatura; the Grocers by Aromatoria; the Drapers by Pannaria; the Fishmongers by Piscaria; the Goldsmiths by Aurifera; the Skinners by Pelicula; the Merchant-Taylors by Vestiaria; the Haberdashers by Minutaria; the Salters by Salina; the Ironmongers by Ferraria; the "Vintonners" by Vinitioria, and the Clothworkers by Lanaria — each character showing the arms and motto of the Company she represents. Two "Lyons or" draw the chariot: on one, rides a negro from India; on the other, a "West-Indian Cacick, or Lord." Metropolis explains the pageant.

The second — the "Fabrick of Fate" — had ten living figures on it, representing Good Fortune, Long Life, Strength, Riches, Beauty, Honour, Liberty, Pleasure, Fancy, and Agility. Here, a little musical dialogue took place — each contended with Fortune as to which quality was preëminent, and she answered each in *stilo recitativo.* The song of contention ended — somewhat abruptly, perhaps — in a general reconciliation; each character agreed that Fortune is the most necessary quality. She then addressed the mayor, who passed afterwards to the next stage, where sat princely shepherds and shepherdesses in a grove or grotto: they were Mucedorus, Pastora, Mirtillo, Jesemina, Sylvio, Dorinda, Tytero, and Corisca. After a song by Mirtillo, "in answer to his Friend, who had been labouring with Arguments to disuade him from Love, telling him that he mispent his Time in that unprofitable Passion," [1] Pastor Fido rose and saluted the mayor, after which Mucedorus and Pastora sang a "pastoral dialogue." [2]

As the mayor progressed, he came to the fourth pageant — "Downs of Delight" — where there were more shepherds and shepherdesses singing, dancing, piping, and tumbling: here were also spinners, carders, and other trade-figures. Then the mayor went to dinner, where a "Welcome Home" to the king and duke, upon their return from Newmarket, was sung, and instrumental music was performed; and so the day's festivities came to an end. There were no evening pageants.

1685 — Taubman's First Show

Matthew Taubman made his first appearance as a writer of civic triumphs in 1585; he composed the shows for the four following years,[3] all of which are recorded in the Bibliography. The four pageants provided for the inauguration of Sir Robert Jeffreys, Ironmonger, in 1685, cost £175, and the total expense for this show was £473, 4*d.*[4]

---

[1] It is not clear whether or not a *débat* actually took place. The friend may have argued in dumb-show, or the song may have been an answer to a possible argument.

[2] In this two-part song, the argument is very slight. There are six stanzas in all — the last being a "chorus," sung in unison.

[3] Fairholt, pt. i, p. 100 f., describes his work. He is, says Fairholt, p. 101, "much inferior to Jordan, being altogether a dull person enough."

[4] See Malcolm, ii, p. 48, and Fairholt, pt. i, p. 174. Copies of the descriptive pamphlet are in BM. and Bodl. Cf. Fairholt, pt. i, p. 101.

The first pageant contained eight females, representing Victory, Triumph, Honour, Peace, Plenty, Courage, Vigilance, and Conduct.[1] The next pageant, — a Sea-chariot of cerulean green, — contained Neptune, drawn by Tritons; Amphitrite, attended by Proteus, Glaucus, Thetis, and Galatea. The third was the Arch of Loyalty, surmounted by Fame who was attended by Loyalty, Truth Union, and Concord; a sea-lion, Tritons, and a negro suggested the "first commercial city in the world." Here Loyalty addressed the mayor.

In the fourth pageant music was combined with a trade appropriateness, in the labor of Vulcan and his attendants.[2] Among the characters on this pageant was "Polypheme. A Giant of large size, one great Eye in the middle of his Forehead . . . standing at the entrance of the Cave with a Crow of Iron in his hand to break the Rocks that hinder the access to the Mines, and a Sword in the other to prevent all others, but the Right Worshipful the Company of *Iron-Mongers* (whose peculiar Prerogatives it is) to enter."[3] Apollo and Cupids, Vulcan, Brontes, Steropes, and Pyracmon were also on this car; Vulcan addressed the mayor.[4]

Under date of 27 October, 1686, Evelyn writes, "There was a triumphant shew of the Lord Maior both by land and water, with much solemnity, when yet his power has ben so much diminish'd, by the losse of the Citty's former charter."[5] The show is outlined by Fairholt.[6] In 1687, Sir John Shorter, Goldsmith, was inaugurated as Mayor,[7] and the king and queen attended the banquet.[8]

---

[1] Triumph, Honour, Peace, and Plenty are the attendants of the other four. (*Pamphlet*, pp. 4 and 5.) Malcolm characterizes Victory's speech as "twenty-two vile doggerel lines."

[Malcolm, ii, p. 47, notes that "William and Mary honoured this spectacle by their presence," and that it was the "first civic celebration after their ascending the throne." This is an obvious error. James and his consort were present (*Pamphlet*, p. 12).]

[2] The mayor was Sir Robert Jeffreys, Ironmonger.

[3] *Pamphlet*, p. 10.

[4] Three songs — the last to the king, ("With a Health to our Royal *James*,") — were sung during the banquet.

[5] *Diary*, iii, p. 29.

[6] Pt. i, p. 102. Copies of the descriptive pamphlet are in Bodl., BM., and Gh.

The Mercers' Virgin — mentioned by Celia Fiennes (see below, p. 67) — appeared this year in glory. One is inclined to suppose that her chariot was new; for Taubman says, "the Magnificence of the Structure, the Elegancy of the Contrivance, and Costliness of the Work, has hardly ever yet been parallel'd." Allowing for the exaggeration common to these descriptive pamphlets, we may presume that the author would not have made such an emphatic statement if the chariot were old. The procession this year included "green-men."

[7] He died the following year. In Fairholt's scrapbook (vol. ii) is a MS. note from the Ellis Correspondence (vol. 2, p. 161) giving, under date of 6 September, 1688, the news of Sir John Shorter's death. "Few days before died Bunian, his Lordship's teacher, or chaplain, a man said to be gifted that way, though once a cobbler." And Fairholt noted below: "This was John Bunyan, author of the Pilgrim's Progress."

[8] See the pamphlet describing this year's show, copies of which are in Gh., Bodl., BM. On

1688 — No Pageantry, but a Magnificent Procession

Taubman's pamphlet for 1688 [1] has no "epistle dedicatory" addressed to a guild; a poetic address to the mayor "on the return of the Charter" takes its place. The Mercers, another foreword tells us, bore the charge of the entertainment; and a brief history of the Company is given. "Nevertheless though the Pageantry was omitted, there wanted nothing that could contribute to make it [2] Great both by Land and Water; nay, rather more Sumptuous in the Magnificence of their Cavalcade," which Taubman describes. "To supply the defect of the Pageants" the Artillery Company took part in the procession. Various banners and coats-of-arms represented St. George, King Richard II, Sir Thomas Gresham, and others; "at the time of Dinner, the Hall Echoing with *Huzza's*, and Healths to His Majesty, who returns the same to his Lordship; wishing him Success and Happiness . . ." [3] after which came a song in praise of James,[4] somewhat hyperbolical, perhaps, but hardly "abject trash."

In 1689, Sir Thomas Pilkington was raised from "Prison to the Pretorial Chair," and Taubman likened him to Daniel; "this," says the poet in his Epistle Dedicatory to the mayor, "is the Happy Day of Deliverance from *Pagan* and *Egyptian* Bondage, by Miracles and Wonders. When Idolatry, like a Deluge, had Over-spread the Land, and the Church, like the Ark, lay Tottering upon the Billows, then came the *Dove* with the *Olive Branch* of *Joy* . . ." [5] King William and Queen Mary dined at Guildhall this year.

---

the title-page of the latter copy is a pencilled "excessively rare," and the following MS. note regarding Shorter: "He had a new Quarter to his Arms giuen him by K. Iames 2d. for receiuing the Pope's Nunc [io] He was Grandfa[ther] to Catherine first wife of Sr R Walpole Earl of Orford." For mention of the 1687 Show, see Fairholt, pt. i, p. 103; J. G. Nichols, p. 116; Hone, p. 257. It included "green-men," and the Seven Liberal Arts.

[1] In Bodl. (2 copies). Cf. Hone, p. 260; Fairholt, pt. i, p. 105; J. G. Nichols, p. 116.

[2] That is, the show.

[3] *Pamphlet*, p. 11.

[4] The lack of pageants this year was, no doubt, due to what Taubman in his dedication, calls "the present Impending Storm, the Dread of a Foreign Invasion," which "has Obnubilated the usual Splendor of this Day's Solemnity." On account of the restoration of the charter, he calls this "Auspicious 88! *England's* great Year of Jubilee."

Conder, p. 235, gives some of the Masons' expenses for this show. The items include 17*s.* 6*d.* for whifflers, but no mention is made of pageants.

Fairholt, pt. i, p. 107, is unkind to Taubman who, he says, showed "a political versatility that would have done honour to the Vicar of Bray himself," for his flattery, (the "abundant and excessive expressions of loyalty,") to James gave way, in 1689, to "equally exuberant professions of loyalty and gratitude for the revolution." We should remember that these poets were hired, and had to write to please their employers — no one attacks a modern editorial writer for changing the opinions he voices, and which he does not pretend are his own. The similarity of the phrases addressed to different mayors and companies shows that much of the phraseology had become conventional.

[5] Copies of the descriptive pamphlet are in Bodl., BM., and Gh. A reprint of this show was made in 1761 (see Bibliography) and the pamphlet is also reprinted in *Somers Tracts*

1689 — Taubman Rejoices over the Revolution

Taubman hardly merits Fairholt's abuse; for the poet, writing for a patron who had opposed James, could not fail to praise the rule which had released him from prison. The writing of the city triumphs was a definite business proposition; it was understood that the poet was to praise the mayor and company who employed him. Taubman might have been less extravagant in his language; but no one can accuse him of being a turn-coat.

Elkanah Settle — "Last of the City Poets"

No trace of festivities in 1690 has as yet been found; Sir Thomas Pilkington still continued in office.[1] In 1691, Elkanah Settle wrote his first show, and continued — with some interruptions — to produce these triumphs until 1708.[2] A full list of these shows, as far as they are known, may be found in the Bibliography; they do not differ from those of his predecessors, but contain the same allegorical characters, the same trade symbolism, the same gods and goddesses, the same personified countries, cities, rivers. This is not surprising, for the pageants used in the civic shows were kept from year to year, each guild using its own property when it became necessary to inaugurate one of its members.[3] While the names of

(1751) 3d coll., iii, p. 33; (*ibid.*, (1812) xi, p. 584); cf. Fairholt, pt. i, p. 107; J. G. Nichols, p. 116 f.; Wadmore, p. 148.

Sir Thomas Pilkington was a Skinner.

Wadmore, p. 57, citing the Company's records, notes under 16 October, 1689: "At this Court it was determined that Pageants should be prepared against my Lord Mayors day and upon a 2nd question being put it was ordered that there should be four Pageants prepared on this occasion. Mr. Hayes appeared and proposed to make 3 pageants for two hundred Pounds; he was offered 180*l.* and as to the other 20*l.* to stand to the Judgm^t of the Renter Warden and he promised to bring a Perticular how he would performe the same."

[1] Fairholt, pt. i, p. 109; cf. *D. N. B.* li, p. 274. I can find, in the London *Gazette* for October and November, 1690, no mention of the Lord Mayor's Show for this year.

[2] For a detailed account of Settle's life and work, see F. C. Brown, *Elkanah Settle* (Chicago, 1910).

[3] "Salisbury Plain" and the "Arcadian Plain" appear often as such, and we know not how often under other names. We may note that the cut of the "Chariot of Justice" in the 1698 descriptive pamphlet is reproduced in that of 1708 — and neither description agrees exactly with the picture; the 1698 pamphlet describes it as "a triumphant chariot of gold." — The picture is reproduced by F. C. Brown, *op. cit.*, opp. p. 124, and forms the frontispiece of Fairholt's *Civic Garland*. As Gough (*Brit. Topog.*, p. 342) notes, there are illustrations of the 1692 and 1698 shows in the Pepysian Library at Cambridge University. Three of the pageants of 1692, with the Lord Mayor's Barge and a "wild-man," are in Pepys's *Collection of Prints and Drawings relating to London and Westminster* (put together in 1700) ii, pp. 277-279. Other pageants are illustrated, *ibid.*, pp. 282, 283.

It may be added that the "Chariot of Honour" of 1698, painted on glass by William Peckett in 1753, is preserved in a window in the old Committee Room of the York Guildhall. That Peckett should have chosen this subject to show his skill as an artist, indicates that the subject was a popular one.

the characters who occupied them could be changed — as the "drolls" appeared as shepherds for the Skinners, or as planters for the Grocers — there is not a large selection to choose from.

Unlike the "royal-entries," the Lord Mayor's Shows occur fairly regularly once every twelve months. This being the case, traditions grew up, which must have hampered the poets considerably. It is hard to find anything new, when one has to keep within a limited field.[1] This accounts, in large measure, for the similarity and consequent tediousness of this form of art; and we must also bear in mind that an uncritical audience was easily satisfied, and that the ephemeral nature of the production did not serve to inspire the poet to put forth his best endeavors. So we must not be too hard on Settle, whose shows probably served their purpose well enough.

Until 1695 there is no interruption in the list of Settle's shows,[2] and Brown says there were no shows from 1695 to 1698.[3] But it is possible that there were processions, without pageantry, during these years,[4] though the title of Settle's Show for 1698 — *Glory's Resurrection* — seems to indicate that there were none.

A Description of a Lord Mayor's Show *temp.* William and Mary

A vivid contemporary account — not from a glowing pamphlet by the author of the show himself — of a civic triumph at the end of the seventeenth century, may be found in Celia Fiennes's diary.[5]

> . . . ye old Lord Major Comes to meete ye new one and with him on his Left hand is Conducted on horse back in all their gouns of scarlet Cloth Lined with ffurr; all ye aldermen in Like Robes only differenc'd as their station, those of them wch have been Lord Majors weare

---

[1] Cf. the Harvard Class Day odes, where the poet is not only restricted to a certain subject, but confined to a certain meter.

[2] In 1692, William and Mary dined at Guildhall. Under date of 22 October, "it is agreed that the Lord Maior and this Court doe congratulate theire Majesties upon his Maties Returne and then humbly desire theire Maties to honour this City with theire presence at dinner at Guildhall on the Lord Maiors day next ensueing which was accordingly done And theire Majesties were graciously pleased to accept of the said Invitation," (*Repertory* xcvi, fol. 504.) Whereupon a Committee was appointed to prepare all things requisite for their entertainment.

[3] F. C. Brown, *op. cit.*, p. 124. On pp. 122 f., he lists Settle's shows with some comments. Conder, p. 238, notes that in 1695 the Standard-bearers and whifflers were ordered to attend the Masons on Lord Mayor's Day; the bill of fare for the Masons' dinner is given, *ibid.*

[4] I have not, however, found any mention of them. On 24 March, 1696, it was agreed by the Court of Aldermen that "the Processions and Entertainments on Easter Monday, Tuesday, and Wednesday be made and performed with the same solemnity as hath beene accustomed," (*Repertory* ci, p. 170,) but this throws no light on mayoralty processions.

[5] Published in 1888 under the title *Through England on a Side-Sadale in the Time of William and Mary.* I am indebted to Dr. Milton Percival for calling my attention to this book; the passage I quote begins on p. 242. With it, compare that by Ned Ward, in *The London Spy,* cited in my paper "A Civic 'Triumph' circa 1700" (*Journ. Eng. and Germ. Philol.* for January, 1918) and Jordan's picture of the crowd in 1679 (above, p. 57, n. 2).

a Gold Chaine Ever after, but those yt have not passed ye Chaire weare none. Ye Lord Major is allwayes one of ye aldermen and he has a great gold Chaine round his neck, the Sheriffs also weare a gold Chaine round their neck yt yeare. Thus on horseback they proceed two and two with all their officers. Ye Lord Major has his Sword bearer wch walkes before him with the Sword in an Embroyder'd Sheath he weares a Great velvet Cap of Crimson, the bottom and ye top of ffurr or such Like standing up Like a turbant or Great bowle in forme of a Great open Pye, this is Called ye Cap of Maintenance. This is ye Lord Majors Chiefe officer . . . He thus walkes before the Lord Major with ye water Bayliff beareing a Gold Mace &c. At Fleete ditch they Enter ye Barges wch are all very Curiously adorned and thus he is Conducted ye river being full of Barges belonging to ye severall Companyes of London, adorned with streamers and their armes and fine musick, and have sack to drinke and Little Cakes as bigg as a Crown piece. They Come to Westminster staires where they Land and are Conducted, the Lord Majors traines being borne up as well ye old as new Lord Major, they Enter Westminster Hall and are Conducted to ye severall Courts of justice where there is severall Ceremonyes perform'd. The new Lord Major is presented to ye King or those deputed to act under him and then is sworne, all which being over they are Conducted back to their Barges and soe to ye staires they took barge, where they are received by some of ye nobility deputed by the King who made some Little speech of Compliment and Give ye Lord Major and aldermen a treate of wine and sweet meates passant. They mount on horseback and returne only ye new Lord Major takes ye right hand and haveing by ye sheriffs invited ye King and Court to dinner, wch sometymes they accept but mostly refuse, because it puts the Citty to a vast Charge; they being then Conducted through ye Citty with Greate acclamations their own habits and trappings of their horses being very fine, and they haveing all the Severall Companyes of ye Citty wch walke in their order and gowns with pageants to most or many of their Companyes, wch are a sort of Stages Covered and Carryed by men and on ye top many men and boys acting ye respective trades or Employ^ts of Each Company, some in shipps for ye Merch^ts, and whatever Company the new Lord Major is off his pageant is ye finest and yt Company has ye precedency that yeare of all ye Companyes Except ye mercers Company, wch allwayes is the first and Esteemed ye Greatest, and when there is a Lord Major of yt Company their pageant is a maiden queen on a throne Crowned and with Royal Robes and scepter and most richly dressed, with Severall Ladyes dressed, her attendants, all on ye same pageant and wth a Cannopy over her head and drawn in an open chariot with 9 horses very finely accouter'd and pages that Ride them all, with plumes of feathers. After being drawn through ye Citty she is jnvited by ye Lord Major to a dinner provided on purpose for her, and soe many Rich Batchelors are appointed to Entertaine her that is a ranck among ye freemen. She has her traine bore up and is presented to Lady Majoris that salutes her as doth the aldermens Ladyes, all wch are Conducted in their Coaches to Guildhall.

The writer then tells of the banquet.

A Norwich Mayoralty Pageant of this Reign

The same lady describes a mayoralty pageant at Norwich,[1] where

there is a great many Cerimonyes in ye Choice and Swearing their Major: they Elect him the first day of May and yn prepare for his being sworne on Holly Thursday. They new washe and plaister their houses with in and without wch they strike out in squares like free stone. All ye streete in wch this mayor Elect's house, is very exact in beautifying themselves (*sic*)

[1] *Op. cit.*, p. 122.

and hanging up flaggs ye Coullrs of their Companyes, and dress up pageants and there are playes and all sorts of show that day — in Little what is done at ye Lord major of London show. Then they have a great feast with fine flaggs and scenes hung out, musick and danceing. I was in ye hall they keep their feast in and saw some of their preparations: for that day being about a fortnight to it.

After 1698, Settle's shows appeared regularly until 1702; between this year and 1708 there were no triumphs.[1]

A Contemporary Record of the Show for 1700

The rarity, as well as the interest, of this contemporary account of the Show for 1700 will justify my quoting it at length. I take it from the *London Post with Intelligence Foreign and Domestick*, from Monday, October 28 to Wednesday, October 30, 1700 (no. 219): [2]

Yesterday Sir Thomas Abney, the new Lord Mayor was sworn in Guild-hall, upon which the Sword and Mace-bearers kneeling, delivered the Sword and Mace to the Old Lord Mayor who presented the same to the New, after which Sir Richard Levit the Old, Treated all the Aldermen above, and Sir Thomas Abney the New Lord Mayor, Treated all those under the Chaire.

And this day, commonly called the Lord Mayors day, Sir Thomas Abney, the New Lord Mayor accompanied with some of the Aldermen, &c. made a splendid Cavalcade from Fishmongers-hall, up Grace-church-Street, down Cornhill and through the Poultry, being preceeded by 8 Men in Armour, Cap a pee on Horseback, the first of which carried, upon the top of a Pole, a Head, representing that of the Rebel Tyler, who was Stabb'd to the Heart in Smithfield (by Sir William Walworth, then Lord Mayor, and free of the Fishmongers Company) at the head of his Rebellions Crew: the second represented the said Sir William Walworth, and held a Naked Dagger in his Hand, the other 6 followed two by two. When his Lordship came over against Mercers Chappel, he was met by a Pageant representing a Ship, with the Cross-keys upon it, and some Men and Boys in it, drawing of a Net, in which came up a great many live Fish, which they flung among the Livery-men. This Ship carried 2 Masts, and was under full Sail, but dropt Anchor before his Lordship, when the Master made a Speech to him; after which, his Lordship proceeded further down Queen-street to the 3 Cranes, where being joyned by Sir Richard Levit, and the rest of the Aldermen, they Imbarqued on board their Barges; and went to Westminster-Hall, being accompanied by the Barges of the other Companies, one boat sailing to and again, round the New Lord Mayors Barge, and saluting his Lordship from time to time with 2 or 3 Guns; after having been sworn before the Lord Chief Baron, performed all the other usual Ceremonies at the Exchequer Bar, they returned by Water to Dorset Stairs; where, after having Landed, they were treated with a Noble Cold Banquet in the open Place, by the said Stairs, by the Lord Buckhurst Son to the Earl of Dorset; after which, the Lord Mayor, and Court of Aldermen, mounted on Horseback, began their Cavalcade through the City towards Guildhall, several of the Companies going before them with their Streamers displayed; as also the Artillery Company well Armed, and were followed by some other of the Companies. A splendid Entertainment was prepared in Guildhall for his Lordship. &c. and for those of his Company. The other Companies dined at their respective Halles. Besides the above-mentioned Pageant, there

[1] F. C. Brown, p. 36.

[2] Brit. Mus., newspaper room, *Burney 123*.

The City Barge, and Barges of Various Companies

were also 4 others, viz, one representing a Mairman and Maremaid,[1] very curiously done; one representing 2 Dolphins, with 2 Men on their Backs; one a Chariot cover'd with Scallop-Shells; and one a Tower or Temple, in the Pinacle of which sat a beautiful Woman richly apparall'd, who, I am told, also made a Speech to his Lordship.

The *English Post*, giving "an Authentick Account of the Transactions of the World, Foreign and Domestick," (no. 8 — from Monday, October 28 to Wednesday, October 30, 1700,) contains a paragraph narrating this event,[2] as does the *Post-Boy* of the same date, the final ten lines of which account Fairholt prints.

In 1708, Settle prepared a show, but the death of the Prince of Denmark prevented its production. Thus the spoken pageants came to an end.[3]

Concerning the Term "City Poet"

Settle is often called "the last of the City Poets," and this term *City Poet* is commonly applied, by Fairholt and other writers on this subject, to the authors of the civic shows we have been studying. Concerning this office, C. W. Wallace[4] notes that Ben Jonson was City-Poet; he says there was such a position, and refers to "documents in the City Record Office, Guildhall, London."[5] F. C. Brown remarks that "the city poet was usually chosen to prepare the pageants for the lord mayor's show, and whatever money he received was given by the company which employed him . . . It is stated by several biographers [of Settle] that the poet received a yearly pension from the City, and by one writer that this amount was £6, but no record has been found to justify such an opinion.

[1] See Nichols's edition of the 1616 Show, p. 16, and Shaw's Plate xi.

[2] This, and the *Post-Boy* (quoted by Fairholt, pt. i, p. 116) are in the same volume as the *London Post.*

[3] On 8 October, 1702, the Aldermen unanimously agreed that her Majesty and the Prince of Denmark be invited to dine at the Guildhall on the Lord Mayor's Day (*Repertory* cvi, p. 518); on 20 October, it was ordered that the streets be cleansed, and precautions taken against blocking the traffic with coaches or carts, so that the mayor's procession might not be obstructed or delayed, (*ibid.*, p. 525); on 22 October, the Committee of Entertainment was called to consider whether an invitation to the dinner could be made to the two Houses of Parliament, (*ibid.*, p. 543) and decided there wasn't room (*ibid.*, pp. 548 f.).

On 19 October, 1703, "This Court being now acquainted that Black Friers Staires is the fittest Place for the Right Hono^ble the Lord Major to land in his Returne from Westminster the next Lord Major's day, It is Ordered That his Lordship do land at the said Staires and from thence proceed in his Cavalcade." (*Repertory* cvii, pp. 574 f.) This does not, of course, prove that there were pageants this year.

On 17 October, 1704, "It is ordered that the Precept to the Companies to attend the Right Hono^ble the Lord Maior Elect and this Court in their Liveries on the Lord Maiors Day as also the Precept for keeping of a double Watch and Ward at the same time be sent out as usual." (*Repertory* cviii, p. 629.)

[4] *Evol. Eng. Drama*, pp. 18 f., referring to Overall, *Index to Remembrancia, 1579–1664* (1888) p. 305, etc.

[5] *Ibid., loc. cit.*, n. 2.

The records of the City of London contain nothing on the subject, and the chamberlain's accounts for the period have been destroyed by fire. There is little likelihood that the Corporation of London ever paid anything to the city poet, or bore any part of the expense of the lord mayors' shows. The amounts which the poets received for their work seem to have varied greatly.[1] Much depended, no doubt, on how well the company was pleased with the pageants, and on the financial ability and generosity of the new lord mayor . . ." [2] In 1617, Dekker, Munday, and Middleton apparently competed, the two former unsuccessfully, for the civic show; [3] in 1621 and 1623, Middleton and Munday collaborated.[4] The sums paid to the authors indicate that they had to furnish the materials for their shows; and the arrangement seems to have been made between them and the companies.

That the poets regarded the companies, rather than the city, as being their employers is shown by the Epistles Dedicatory prefixed to their descriptive pamphlets. I need call attention to but a few; in 1674, Jordan addressed the Goldsmiths, ("when by your own Indulgence more than my Desert, I was preferr'd to the Honour of this Imployment . . .") and in 1675, the Drapers, ("Gentlemen — your own Urbanity more than my Desert hath exalted my humble Genius to the Advancement of Designing and Describing this Days Triumph . . .") In his preface to the Drapers in 1676, Jordan calls the Company "my Worshipful *Patrons*, by whom I am employed and gratified." That the "city poet" was not required to give all his time to the city is shown by Jordan's preface to the Grocers in the 1672 pamphlet: ". . . if the nicety of some Mens Enquiry discover any thing that is irregular or superfluous, I hope you will justly impute it to the brevity of my time, my person being imployed in sundry places, as well as my Pen upon several Subjects."

---

[1] Brown gives an "Extract from Quires of Warden's Accounts of the Grocers Company, dated July 1692 to July 1693," which shows that Settle received £2, 3*s*. 6*d*.; and an account of the Vintners' Company for 1703 shows that he received £11, 1*s*.,6*d*. See Brown, *Settle*, pp. 122, n. 5, and 125, n. 4.

[2] Brown, *op. cit.*, p. 28. He notes, p. 29, that Settle was spoken of by a contemporary as "City Poet" in 1717 (Dennis, *Remarks upon Mr. Pope's Translation of Homer*, Preface); and that, as it was never recognized by the Corporation of the City of London, the office was allowed to lapse with its last occupant in 1724.

Cyril Davenport, in *The Connoisseur*, vi (1903) pp. 160–163, 210–12, says that John Taylor, "the water poet," was not officially appointed city poet, of whom the first was Tatham, who superintended the processions from 1657 to 1664. He records the succession of Jordan in 1671, Taubman in 1685, and Settle in 1691; but he gives no authorities for his statements. The names *Settle* and *City Poet* do not appear in the *Repertories* between 1691 and 1708.

[3] See above, p. 37.

[4] Withington, "The Lord Mayor's Show for 1623," in *Publ. Mod. Lang. Assoc.* for March, 1915, p. 112. Heming and Dekker collaborated in 1612 (see above, p. 31).

The Elements of the Lord Mayor's Shows of the xvii Century

Before we consider the development of this civic show in the eighteenth century, let us glance at the various elements which composed it in the period from Peele to Settle. Many of these will reappear in modern pageantry; this consideration, then, serves not only to review the past, but to connect it with the present.

It will not be necessary to emphasize the elaborateness which the physical pageant — the car — has reached; suffice it to remark that the ship and the "Paradise" of early days had developed into very complicated structures. In 1687, a ship of a hundred and forty-five feet in length, with twenty-two guns, rigging, anchors, and "a full complement of men," was shown among the pageants.[1] The trade-pageant was often very elaborate — a good example is the "plantation" in the Grocers' Show of 1678.[2] It must not be forgotten, however, that the author's imagination probably ran away with him at times, and lifted him above the facts.

Symbolism

Modern pageantry has a certain amount of symbolism; but it is nothing compared to that in these earlier shows. Naturally enough, in the guild productions, the emphasis is on trade-symbolism. Even in the days of the miracle-play, the bakers distributed their bread; the miracle-plays were given by guilds whose trade was appropriate to the show; many of the pageants in the early "royal-entries" bore the marks of the guilds which furnished them; as far back as 1298, the Fishmongers held a procession with what appear to have been moving pageants[3] indicative of trade. We should, then, be surprised if we did not find, in the shows of the seventeenth century, a symbolical representation of the guild whose brother is being inducted into the mayoralty.

Union of Mythology and Trade-Symbolism

A few examples will suffice to show the character of this trade-symbolism. In *London's Tempe*,[4] the fourth pageant is called the Lemnian Forge. In it, Vulcan and his servants work at an anvil; a fire is seen in the forge, and the bellows — with other fittings of a blacksmith's shop — are in evidence. As the smiths work, they sing in praise of iron, the anvil and the hammer, by the con-

---

[1] Cf. Fairholt, pt. i, p. 104; this ship was named *The Unity of London.*

[2] *The Triumphs of London*, reprinted by Fairholt. See *L. M. Pag.*, pt. ii, p. 164 f.

[3] The fishes. On this, see above, vol. i, p. 124.

[4] Dekker's Show for 1629, reprinted by Fairholt. The mayor of this year was a member of the Ironmongers' Company. Cf. above, p. 29f., where the same pun, made for Sir Thomas Campbell in 1609, is recorded.

cordant sounds of which Tubal Cain became the "first inventor" of music. Cupid and Jove[1] occupy the pageant also; and there is a dialogue between Jove and Vulcan, the former of whom upbraids the latter for making his men work on a holiday! He ends by saying that it is high time to get rid of Pride, Ambition, and Avarice — and that Iron is the only thing which can do this.

Here we find an interesting combination of mythology and trade; but this pageant does not contain all the symbolism of the show. The second "presentation" was a proud swelling sea, on whose waves is borne a sea lion, "in regard it is one of the supporters of the East Indian Company, of which his Lordship is free."[2] The fifth "presentation" — called "London's Tempe, or the Field of Happiness," with the usual pun on the mayor's name ("Le Beu Champe," — Champ bel — Campbell) — had on the top of all a lion's head, — the Lord Mayor's crest. In Heywood's *Londini Status Pacatus*[3] the fourth show is a chariot drawn by two camels; "and though the pelleted Lyons might have serv'd more properly to this place, as being supporters of the Armes belonging to the Right Worshipfull Company of the Drapers; yet these are as genuine to the purpose: to show his Lordships generall negotiation in all kinds of Merchandise whatsoever." We may recall the ship of 1602 — "proper and very apt for this occasion and time,"[4] — which appeared with the lion and camel, crest and supporters of the Merchant-Taylors arms. It is possible that this ship was later given another trade-signification, being made applicable to the Drapers under the name of the *Argo*.

The first pageant of *Porta Pietatis*[5] was presented by Proteus in a beautiful sea-chariot "decored with divers marine nymphs," etc. He sat on a tortoise, — which lives both on water and on land; symbolizing the fact that the mayor was a merchant, trading with Turkey, Italy, and France, as well as late governor of the East India Company. The first land show of this triumph was a shepherd with dog and hook; about him his flock, — some feeding, some resting, — occupied a platform adorned with flowers. The third show, symbolizing the merchants' trade, was a ship, full-rigged.

The "drolls," or singers, dancers, and tumblers, who occupied a stage in many of the seventeenth-century Lord Mayor's Shows, were commonly given a trade-complexion, being dressed as planters if the mayor were a Grocer, or as shepherds if he were a Draper, or as Cyclopes if he were an Ironmonger.

---

[1] Possibly these figures were attracted by Vulcan.

[2] Practically every show contained the animals which were crest and supporters of the arms of the Company who footed the bills. It is not necessary to emphasize this point.

[3] *Works* (1874) v, p. 368.

[4] Cf. above, p. 27.

[5] Heywood's Show for 1638; reprinted by Fairholt. The mayor was a member of the Drapers' Company.

Further examples of the union of mythology and trade-symbolism may be indicated. In Middleton's *Triumphs of Love and Antiquity*[1] we find "a wilderness most gracefully and artfully furnished with divers kinds of beasts, bearing fur . . . the presenter, the musical Orpheus . . . " who delivers a flattering speech.[2] Among the worthies who sat in the "Chariot of Honour," which opened Middleton's *Sun in Aries*,[3] were Jason, Hercules, Alexander, and Cæsar. Jason, "most proper by his manifestation," — the Golden Fleece, — addressed the mayor. In 1623, Munday introduced the *Argo* into Middleton's show for Sir Martin Lumley, Draper;[4] this subject has been popular with the Drapers since the entry of Charles V in 1522; the original reference to the *Toison d'Or* was quickly turned into trade-symbolism, and from the Midsummer Show it crept into the civic pageantry.[5]

In 1702, Bacchus appeared in the Vintners' Show;[6] in 1692, Neptune, Thetis, Mercury, and Pallas — as being the four requisite for the management of the Grocers' traffic "through all parts of the Universe" — appeared in the Temple of the latter.[7] These shows are full of mythology to which a trade-symbolism has been given, and it is useless to cite more examples.

The Companies Symbolically Represented

In Dekker's *Troia Nova Triumphans*[8] twelve men, representing the twelve "superior companies" — each carrying a shield with the arms of one of the guilds — rode as guardians of Virtue before her throne. The chariot of Industry, in Jordan's *London's Royal Triumph* of 1684 "contained twelve female characters, allegorical of the twelve companies, with appropriate names, habits, and shields."[9] In 1615, the principal pageant of the show represents London and her twelve daughters — the twelve Companies.[10] Symbolism permeates

---

[1] His Show for 1619, written for the inauguration of Sir William Cockayn, Skinner. Reprinted by Dyce, Bullen, and in Nichols, *Prog. James*.

[2] Orpheus appeared in similar surroundings in Jordan's Show for 1671, — cf. above, p. 51. The earliest instance of his appearance I have found in these triumphs is in 1561, when, with Amphion, Arion, Jopas, and David, he welcomed Sir W. Harper, the lord mayor. One might imagine that the presence of mythology in these shows was originally due to a pun on the mayor's name! On this 1561 Show, see above, p. 18 and n. 2.

[3] The Show for 1621, for Sir Edward Barkham, Draper. Reprinted by Dyce, Bullen; and Nichols in *Prog. James*.

[4] See my article, *The Lord Mayor's Show for 1623*, already cited. Jason, Medea, and the *Argo* appeared in 1615, (cf. article cited, p. 113, n. 2.)

[5] Cf. above, vol. i, pp. 40 and 176.

[6] Fairholt, pt. i, p. 121.

[7] The pamphlet is reprinted by Heath (3d ed.) pp. 551 f.

[8] The Show for 1612; see above, p. 32.

[9] Fairholt, pt. i, p. 100, citing Herbert. These are described in the pamphlet for this year; see above, p. 61.

[10] Munday's *Metropolis Coronata*, the Show for 1615, was reprinted by Nichols in *Prog. James*, iii, pp. 107 f.

these shows, and most — though not all — of it is naturally connected with trade. Even that, however, is softened by an appropriate mixture of classical mythology, or allegory.

PERSONIFICATION: — CITIES, CONTINENTS, RIVERS; TIME, THE SEASONS, AND MONTHS

In Jordan's *London in Luster* — the Show for 1679 — the twelve months surround Time; and Opportunity says: "The twelve months which these persons represent Contain the limits of your government; . . . the Shields (on which their honour much relies) Contain the Arms of the Twelve Companies. . . . Advance, true Virtue, punish every Crime, Y' have but a year to rule, *This is the Time.*" [1] Janus's speech in Heywood's *Londini Status Pacatus* [2] might have served as a model for it. The four seasons surround Janus, who speaks:

> "I, Janus, the year's father in my prime . . .
> Hither my servants, the four seasons, bring . . .
> These four succeeding seasons I resign
> Unto your charge; (which I before called mine)
> To the twelve months, most aptly may comply
> Your twelve chief companies . . ." [3]

In 1677, Jordan introduced "the Temple of Time," on which was Time himself, attended by the Four Quarters of the year, — Winter, Spring, Summer, and Autumn. Round about him sat six persons — a Minute, an Hour, a Day, a Week, a Month, and a Year.[4] It will be recalled that Time appeared in some of the "royal-entries" — notably in the first progress of Queen Elizabeth through London.[5]

The personification of cities — including such figures as the Genius of the City — was not unknown in Elizabethan pageantry; at Norwich, in 1578, "the Commonwealth of the Citie" and Norwich herself, appeared.[6] London appeared in Peele's Show for 1585;[7] in 1613, a "reverend Mother" represented the city in Middleton's *Triumphs of Truth.*[8] *Londons Ius Honorarium*, Heywood's Show for 1631,[9] included "the prime Lady seated in the first and most eminent place of the Chariot, [who] representeth *London*, behind whom, and on either side, diverse others of the chiefe Cities of the Kingdome take place: As

---

[1] See the descriptive pamphlet, p. 5; Fairholt, pt. i, p. 90 f.

[2] The Show for 1639; reprinted in his *Works* (1874) v, p. 355 f.

[3] *Op. cit.*, p. 365.

[4] *London's Triumphs* for 1677 has not been reprinted; but these characters are described by Fairholt, pt. i, p. 88.

We shall discuss Miss Rossetti's *Pageant of the Months* in a later chapter.

[5] See above, vol. i, pp. 201, and 202.

[6] See above, vol. i, p. 211. Elsewhere the relation of these figures to the "mythical founder" is suggested; see vol. i, p. 81 f.

[7] See above, p. 24.

[8] Reprinted by Dyce, Bullen, Heath, and Nichols in *Prog. James*, ii, pp. 679 f.

[9] *Works* (1874) iv, pp. 274 f.

Westminster, *Yorke*, *Bristoll*, *Oxford*, *Lincolne*, *Exeter*, &c. All these are to be distinguished by their several escutcheons; to them *London* being speaker, directeth the first part of her speech." Chester was personified in a "royal-entry" of 1610;[1] Britannia and Genius Urbis greeted James in 1604;[2] the "genious of the citie" welcomed Christian IV on his way through London.[3] London or the Genius of the City, sometimes under the name Augusta, appeared in the shows of 1628; 1639; 1662; 1689; 1694; 1700; 1616, and in *Civitatis Amor* (1616), when Charles was made Prince of Wales. In 1678, six Indian cities were "represented."[4]

Countries and Rivers appeared often in these civic shows; the four Quarters of the World were also common. In 1622, came "The Continent of India . . . replenished with all manner of spice-plants and trees bearing odour" on which a black person, representing India, called the Queen of Merchandise, was attended by Indians in antique habits. "Commerce, Adventure, and Traffic, three habited like merchants," follow the black queen's speech.[5] In 1605, Britannia, Leogria, Cambria, and Albania appeared; in 1691, Albion, Germania, Hispania, and Batavia. In 1671, Africa was represented by a "female negra;" Asia and Africa appeared in 1658; all four continents in 1694.[6]

A few examples of personified rivers may be given: the Thames, naturally, appears often, — we find him in 1585; in 1605, with the Severn and Humber; with the Tiber and Indus in 1694; and Neptune, with the Thames, Danube, Rhine, and Tiber occupied the second pageant of the 1701 show. The Boyne, Shannon, Rhine, and Danube, "signifying the present seats or scenes of war, of which the entire pageant is an emblem," appeared in 1691.[7]

Closely allied to such figures as India, London, and Africa, are the negroes, Indians, sea-captains, and sailors[8] who recall the mayor's trading interests, and the lands with which he deals.

---

[1] See above, vol. i, p. 230. The same year, Cornwall and Wales were personified at London, to welcome Prince Henry (vol. i, p. 231).

[2] See above, vol. i, p. 223.

[3] See above, vol. i, p. 228, n. 1. These last three instances of personification are not, it is true, taken from the civic shows; but they serve to indicate another thread which binds these triumphs to the "royal-entry," which they displaced.

[4] Fairholt, pt. ii, p. 162. There is no need of citing more instances.

[5] Middleton's Show for 1622 is reprinted by J. L. Pearson in *Shaks. Soc. Papers* (1845) i, p. 93; also by Bullen.

[6] It is not necessary to give more examples of these personifications. As we shall see, later, Britannia and France appeared in 1905; Egypt, Greece, Rome, and Britain in 1904; India in 1884, Australia in 1890, etc. Britain and the Colonies were personified in *Britannia's Muster* of 1910 (see below, p. 188).

[7] We shall find the Thames, Sabrina, Avona, and the Chelt, in the Gloucestershire Pageant of 1908. The New River was symbolized by a giant in the Lord Mayor's Show of 1913.

[8] Cf. on these last, the ship's master, mate, and boy of the 1605 Show; they are linked to symbolism by their ship, the *Royal Exchange*. Cf. the soldier and the sailor with such

A European, an Egyptian, and a Persian appeared in the 1659 Show;[1] in 1617 a Frenchman — in a French speech, followed by its translation — wished " le comble de toutes nobles et heureuses fortunes " to " Monseigneur le Maire " and " la très honorable société des Grociers." He was followed by a Spaniard, who gave his good wishes also in his native tongue; their joy was echoed by the silent joy of an Englishman, an Irishman, a Turk, a Jew, a Dane, a Pole, a Barbarian, and a Russian or " Muscovian."[2] Representing a country by a figure portraying an inhabitant of that country, is much the same thing as personification; but the personification is not, perhaps, so closely allied to symbolism or allegory.

Types Standing between Allegory and the Individual

Such figures as Hoyden and Freeman and Oliver in the Jordanian " interlude " may have suggested the allegorical figures of Rus and Urbs; but they are really men from the life of the times, and only as types tend to be symbolic. Like the Frenchman and Spaniard of 1617, and the foreigners in James's coronation triumph,[3] who tended to symbolize the nations they represented, rather than to stand out as individuals, Billet and Swab are types, as are the negroes and Indians, who are not far from Africa and India. Perhaps the six Cities of 1631 are on the line between symbolical representatives and representative types.[4] The technique of this older kind of pageantry prevents any character from being individualized — all must, of necessity, be colorless; hence, even those which tend to become individual are driven back into symbolism.

It is true that Hoyden and Freeman are not — strictly speaking — characters in the Lord Mayor's Show. The " interludes " were presented during the banquet, and the characters could have been individualized. That they are not, is partly due to the songs — and singing, as in the opera today, militates against " convincingness of characterization " — and partly to the fact that the " morality " flavor of the shows penetrated to these interludes, all of which teach the mutual dependence of town and country, and the need both have for the soldier. It is largely this didactic quality which keeps the characters in the interlude " typical."

---

figures as the Country, Thames, Loyalty, and Science in Peele's Show for 1585. They are at most types — and really abstractions. Hoyden and Freeman — in the Jordanian " interlude " — are types almost individualized.

[1] Reprinted in Heath (3d ed.) pp. 466 f.

[2] Middleton's Show for this year is reprinted by Dyce, Heath, and Bullen.

[3] See above, vol. i, p. 224.

[4] Always assuming, of course, that they are not *delegates* from the cities named. See above, p. 75.

Allegory

Openly symbolic, of course, are the allegorical characters which permeate these shows. Ever since Nature, Grace, and Fortune gave Henry VI " gostly giftes " at his coronation in 1432,[1] allegory has been an important part of this form of literary expression. We have seen that it was plentiful in the days before the Lord Mayor's Shows; and in them it is abundant. The strong morality-play flavor which these shows have, is entirely due to their allegorical seasoning. It is not worth while to cite many examples of this ingredient, for it is all-pervading.[2] Peele's earliest show gave us Magnanimity, Loyalty, and Science; in 1591 we find Nature, Hope, Faith, and Honour, while Superstition and Ignorance are represented by two of the Roman Church. In Dekker's Show for 1612, the second " land-triumph " was the Throne of Virtue, on the top of which sat Virtue herself, and beneath her the Seven Liberal Sciences.[3] In 1622,[4] in Soper Lane " two parts of the triumph stand ready planted; viz. the Throne of Virtue and the Globe of Honour, which Globe suddenly opening and flying into eight cants [5] or distinct parts, discovers in a twinkling eight bright personages, most gloriously decked, representing, (as it were,) the inward man . . . Clear Conscience, Divine Speculation, Peace of Heart, Integrity, Watchfulness, Equality, Providence,[6] Impartiality, each exprest by its own proper illustration."

In Tatham's Show for 1660, *The Royal Oak*,[7] the Lord Mayor is entertained at the end of Cheapside by a " sceane " which is a chariot drawn by a lion and a lamb; it is driven by Time, and contains Peace, Truth, and Plenty. The driver of the chariot addresses the mayor, showing that in time all come into their own, that treachery is discovered, and Treason cannot last.[8] From the

---

[1] See above, vol. i, p. 144.

[2] Occasionally the morality element is attached to mythology, as in Heywood's *Londons Ius Honorarium* (*Works* [1874] iv, p. 271 f.) where Ulysses, who personates a wise and discreet magistrate, delivers the speech upon the water. As the Mayor's barge goes between two rocks, representing Scylla and Charybdis, — on which are placed the Sirens, — Ulysses warns the mayor to keep the " even Channell and be neither swayde to the right hand nor left, and so evade Malicious envie . . . smooth visadgd flattery, and black mouthd detraction, sedition . . . all ambushing the god-like Magistrate."

[3] We have seen them in " royal-entries " as early as 1432 (see above, vol. i, p. 145) and in 1547 (see above, vol. i, p. 186,); and shall find them at Oxford in 1907, at Boston in 1908, (see below, pp. 223 and 283). They appeared in the 1612 Show (see above, p. 32); they surrounded Janus in the fourth pageant of the 1687 Show, and Minerva in the first pageant of that of 1676. [Neither of these has been reprinted; but mention of the Sciences is made by Fairholt, pt. i, pp. 85 and 104.]

[4] Middleton's *Triumphs of Honour and Virtue*, reprinted by Bullen, vii, p. 365.

[5] Pieces (Bullen).

[6] Meaning, of course, *foresight.*

[7] Reprinted by Fairholt, pt. ii, pp. 87 f.

[8] Fairholt, pt. ii, pp. 103 f.

next scene, the mayor is greeted by another Peace,[1] who — having with Truth been exiled — has now returned to flourish. Justice, Power, and Obedience were included in the show which Settle had planned for 1708.[2] These random selections from the earliest and latest of the Lord Mayor's Shows are enough so indicate how wide-spread the allegory is. With it we have the didactic character of the morality-play — a quality which is much weakened when speech disappears from the triumphs.

Allegory and History

Almost as pervasive as the allegory and mythology in these shows is the history — though this is usually confined to the past of the Company giving the show. Again, it will not be necessary to cite more than a few examples of this element, which is often linked to allegory, as in Middleton's Show for 1623, *The Triumphs of Integrity*. At the Little Conduit in Cheap stood a chariot "artfully framed and properly garnished . . . and on the conspicuous part thereof is placed the register of all heroic acts and worthy men bearing the title of Sacred Memory, who for the greater fame of this honourable fraternity [the Drapers] presents the never-dying names of memorable and remarkable worthies of this ancient society." Sir Henry Fitz-Alwin sat figured under the person of Government; Sir John Norman under the person of Honour; Sir Francis Drake under that of Victory; Sir Simon Eyre [3] under that of Charity; Sir Richard Champion and Sir John Milbourne under Munificence or Bounty; Sir Richard Hardell and Sir John Poultney under Justice and Piety.[4] The chariot was drawn by lions, the supporters of the Company's arms, mounted by two riders representing Power

[1] It was not uncommon to represent the same character twice in the same show.

[2] This has not been reprinted; cf. Fairholt, pt. i, p. 123.

[3] Simon Eyre was the name of the shoemaker-mayor of London in Dekker's *Shoemaker's Holiday*. The real Simon Eyre died 18 September, 1459; see Stow's *Survey* (ed. Kingsford, i, p. 154).

[4] Cf. Bullen's Middleton, vii, p. 342 for another list of the same worthies in very much the same language. *The Triumphs of Integrity* repeats *The Sun in Aries*. Fame sounds the praises of the Drapers in the latter show: Antiquity, "the register of Fame," contains "in her golden legend their names and titles."

In the 1626 Show (Bullen's Middleton, vii, pp. 403 f.) was a "Sanctuary of Prosperity" on the top arch of which hung the Golden Fleece (the mayor being a Draper) recalling Sir Francis Drake, "that most famous and renowned brother of this company . . . who never returned to his country without the golden fleece of honour and victory: the four fair Corinthian columns or pillars imply the four principal virtues, Wisdom, Justice, Fortitude, Temperance." (*Ibid.*, p. 406. These were usually personified.) A "speech in the Sanctuary upon the Fleece," lauds Sir Francis, "England's true Jason." Passing from this, the mayor and his company were taken to the Chariot of Honour, where Sir Henry Fitz Alwin illustrated Government, Sir John Norman, Munificence, Sir Simon Eyre, Piety, "*et sic de ceteris*," (p. 407). Again, lions, mounted by Power and Honour, drew the chariot. Fitz Alwin appeared in the 1615 Show.

and Honour.[1] Memory delivered the speech, calling to mind the advantage of a fame built on virtues over an age which " sits laughing upon heaps of gold."

In this same show appeared, in St. Paul's Churchyard, the Mount Royal, " on which are placed certain kings and great commanders, which ancient history produces, that were originally sprung from shepherds and humble beginnings: only the number of six presented; " which were Viriat, Arsaces, Marcus Julius Lucinus, Bohemia's Primislaus, the Emperor Pertinax, and Tamburlaine. A speech from the mount explained the part that Virtue played in raising the great from the humble.[2] Here the morality element attaches itself to history as (with Ulysses in 1631) it had to mythology.[3]

The historical element in these shows is doubtless an inheritance from the " royal-entry," stimulated by obvious opportunities for recalling the glorious past of the Companies.[4] In *The Sun in Aries*, Fame salutes the mayor from the " master triumph," the Tower of Virtue; and when he is done, " one in a cloudy, ruinous habit, leaning upon the turret, at a trumpet's sounding suddenly starts and wakes, and in amazement throws off his unseemly garments." His speech is an historical *résumé*, and a welcome to the mayor.[5] In the following year, Middleton provided a Chariot of Fame, " which awaits his Honour's approach near the Little Conduit in Cheap," where " Antiquity, a grave and reverend personage with a golden register-book in his hand," recalled the past.[6]

Sir John Hawkwood, an old Merchant-Taylor, appeared in 1680,[7] and again

---

[1] Bullen, vii, pp. 388 f.

[2] Such combinations as an allegorical Virtue treading an historical wrong-doer under foot — as seen at Edinburgh in 1503, for example — show the combination of allegory and history in the " royal-entry." The Liberal Sciences were sometimes — as in 1432 — represented by historical figures as well as allegorical, or symbolical, personifications.

In 1676, the second pageant was a Chariot "according to the *Scythian* mode of Building," upon whose eminent seat was mounted Tamburlaine; he was attended by Discipline, Conduct, Courage, and Victory, " properly arrayed." The chariot was drawn by two golden lions, the supporters of the Company's arms. Tamburlaine addressed the mayor.

In the same show, on the first pageant, at Minerva's feet was " a grave personage, representing Government, in the shape of the old Roman orator Cicero." (My citations are from the descriptive pamphlet; but mention of these matters is made by Fairholt, pt. i, pp. 85 and 86.)

Tamburlaine, as one of Marlowe's characters, appeared in the 1908 Show (see below, p. 135).

[3] See p. 77, n. 2.

[4] As examples of history in the " royal-entry," it will suffice to recall the six Henries at York in 1486; the Philips of 1554; Charlemagne in 1522; Edward and the nine Worthies at Coventry in 1456; Richard at Coventry in 1474, and Alphonso, Job, and Boethius in 1501.

[5] Bullen's Middleton, vii, pp. 344 f. In the Chariot of Honour, this same year, Alexander and Cæsar appeared with Jason and Hercules — a mixture of history and mythology.

[6] *The Triumphs of Honour and Virtue*, the Show for 1622. Bullen's Middleton, vii, p. 360.

[7] This pamphlet of Jordan's has not been reprinted; the figure of Sir John is recorded by Fairholt, pt. i, p. 93. The pamphlet reads: " On the lowest seat [of the first pageant, which

in 1693 — where he occupied a place on the fifth pageant.[1] Sir William Walworth was a popular figure in these shows. In 1616 he made an extraordinary resurrection, summoned from the tomb by the "Genius of the City."[2] The fifth pageant of this show was "a goodly Bower, shaped in forme of a flowrie Arbour, and adorned with all the Scutchions of Armes of so many worthy men, as have been Lord Maiors[3] of the Fishmongers Company and each mans name truely set downe on them. It is appointed first to stand in Paules Church-yard: And at such a place as is thoght most convenient. In this Bower is a faire Tombe, whereon in Armour lyeth the imaginary body of Sir *William Walworth*, sometime twise Lord Maior of *London*, and a famous Brother of the Fishmongers Company. The reason of this conceit, aimeth at that tempestuous and troublesome time of King *Richard* the Second, and the fourth yeare of his Raigne, whose life, Crowne, and Dignitie . . . were manfully defended and preserved by that worthy man *Walworth*." Five mounted knights in armour attended him;[4] "*London's Genius*, a comely Youth, attired in the shape of an Angell, with a golden Crowne on his head, golden Wings at his backe, bearing a golden Wand in his hand, sits mounted on Horsebacke by the Bower;[5] with an Officer at Armes, bearing the Rebels head on *Walworth's* Dagger." Upon the mayor's arrival, the Genius struck Walworth with his wand, and the latter arose from his tomb to address the new executive.[6] Sir William also appeared in 1700, when "a Cavalcade is Perform'd by several Persons Riding in Armour, *viz.* the first the Sergeant at Mace, Arm'd Ca-pa-pee (*sic*), bearing the Head of *Wat Tyler* on a Bloody Spear. The next the famous Sir *William Walworth*, Arm'd likewise Cap-a-pee, and the other Five being so many Aldermen, also all in Rich Armour; these all mounted on Manag'd Horses, most Richly Caparison'd, &c. march before the last Pageant, being the Fifth *Pageant*, the *Chariot of Honour*."[7]

---

is otherwise occupied by male allegorical figures] alone sitteth an ancient *English Hero*, habited in Antick Habiliaments of War, such as were worn by the Chief Commanders: under the Conduct of *Edward* the Third, when he conquered *France*, whose Name was Sir *John Hawkwood*, a *Merchant-Taylor*." Sir John addressed the mayor.

[1] See the descriptive pamphlet, which has not been reprinted. Fairholt had not been able to find a copy (pt. i, p. 112); one is now in the Brit. Mus.

[2] For a full account, with illustrations, see J. G. Nichols's ed. of *Chrysanaleia*, with Shaw's plates made from contemporary drawings. On p. 18 (plate v) this pageant is described.

[3] In the first pageant of Settle's Show for 1699, Triumph sat surrounded by the escutcheons of twenty Lord Mayors, members of the Haberdashers' Company.

[4] They represented the five knighted with him on the field, after Wat Tyler was slain. (See Nichols's ed., plates vii and viii.)

[5] *Ibid.*, plate x.

[6] The last grand pageant of this show, "drawne by two Mare-men and two Mare-mayds, as being supporters to the Companies coate of Armes [Plates xi and xii]" contained a victorious angel at the top, beneath whom sat Richard II, surrounded by impersonations of kingly virtues.

[7] Descriptive pamphlet, p. 5. Cf. Fairholt, pt. i, p. 116, citing the *Post Boy*. Cf. above, p. 68.

Fame occupied the highest seat of this "Chariot of Honour"; before her sat Richard II

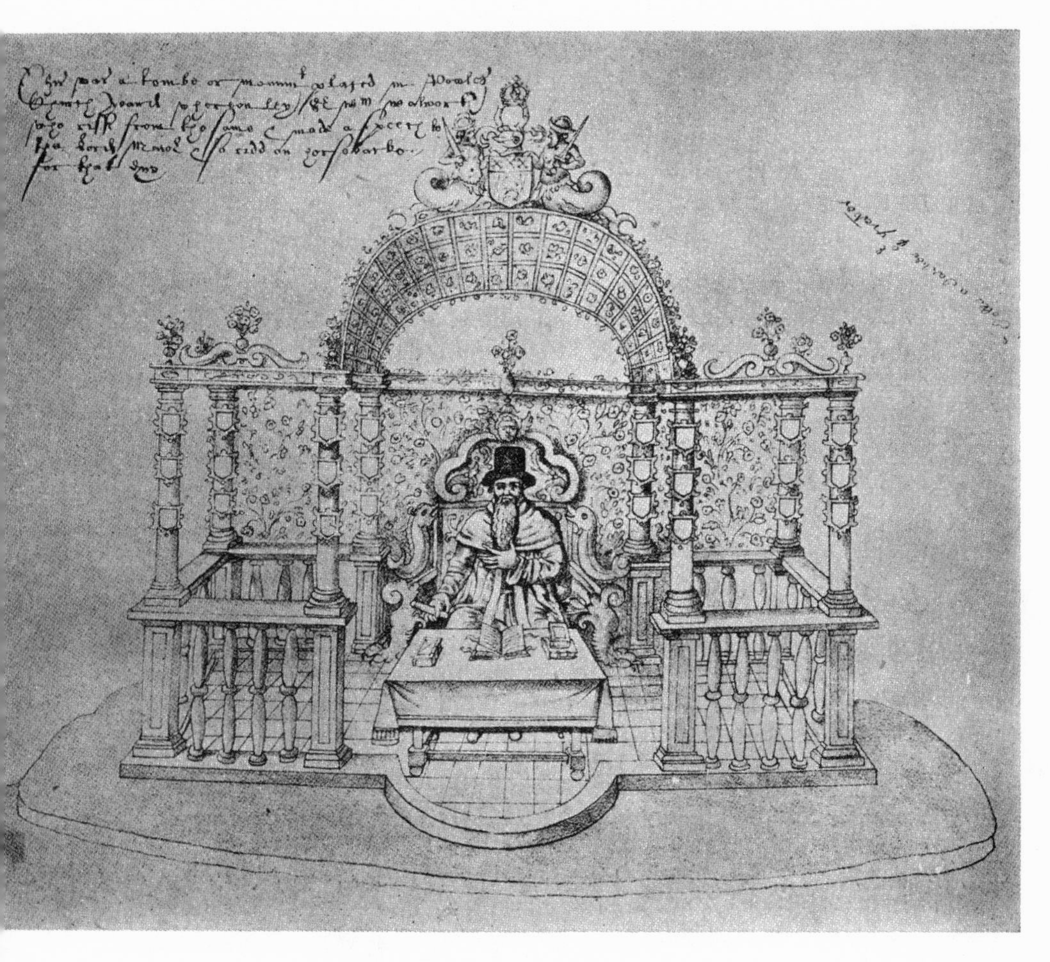

Sir William Walworth in the 1616 Show

In Dekker's Show for 1612, Fame welcomed the mayor, and gave a list of kings who had been members of the Merchant-Taylors' Company; in 1660, the mayor was entertained " by a pageant or scean " representing a royal tent, in front of which sat Henry VII holding the first charter of the Merchant-Taylors' guild. A " Soldier-senator " occupied a lower seat; his speech referred to the past great members of the Company, and gave thanks for the return of Charles.

There is — as we have noted [1] — considerable real and fictitious history retold in Munday's show for 1605; former mayors occupied the Castle of Fame or Honor in 1617, and in 1619 there was a Sanctuary of Fame, on which twenty-six bright-burning lamps represented the twenty-six Aldermen; Example, who sat on the structure, assured the mayor that he would find a place in the Temple where the members of his company who have preceded him in office were " enrolled. " [2]

The mayor was then taken towards the Parliament of Honour, near St. Laurence Lane-end, where Antiquity saluted him, and called attention to

> " . . . this mount of royalty, by kings grac'd
> Queens, prince, dukes, nobles, more by numbering gain'd
> Than can be in this narrow sphere contained;
> Seven kings, five queens, only one prince alone
> Eight dukes, two earls, Plantagenets twenty-one:
> All these of this fraternity made free," etc.[3]

" In former times," says Fairholt, "these pageants and their allusions connected themselves in no small degree with the history of the country, and its political movements; and shadowing forth as they do, the opinions of the metropolis, they are worthy of more attention than may be at first imagined, by persons who only know them through the expiring relics now yearly exhibited." [4]

---

trampling Insurrection under his feet. Conduct, Prudence, Temperance, and Vigilance sat around him, and in front Augusta bore the City sword, and the City Arms. Settle echoes the old error (*Pamphlet*, p. 6) in Augusta's speech:

> " *Walworth* made War and Conquest at a Blow
> With that Great Deed proud *Albion's* Annals fill'd,
> His bloody Steel adorns my Glorious Shield."

Fairholt points out (pt. i, p. 116, n. 2) that the sword of St. Paul — not the dagger of Walworth — is on the shield of London.

[1] Above, p. 29.

[2] Among them was Sir Henry Barton, who first had lights hung out in the city " for the safety of travellers and strangers." Sir Wolstone Dixie also appeared. It is not quite clear whether the mayors (named in Bullen's ed. of Middleton, vii, p. 322) were represented by living figures, or whether their names were written on the Sanctuary. Of course the emphasis on history is almost as strong if the latter were the case.

We shall see that former lord mayors and kings appeared in the 1884 Show; cf. also those of 1895, 1906, and 1913 (below, pp. 127, 132, and 138).

[3] Bullen's Middleton, vii, p. 324. The list is given more in detail, *ibid.*, pp. 325 f.

[4] *Op. cit.*, pt. i, p. ii.

Most of the history, which we have found so largely mixed with allegory that it is impossible entirely to extricate it, is brought into the seventeenth-century shows to glorify the Company which is meeting the expenses of the inauguration. Just how far the triumphs shadow forth the opinions of the metropolis is, I think, doubtful; it is even dubious how far they reflect the real opinions of their authors: but they are instructive as giving us a glimpse of the customs of the past, as showing us the kind of thing the people of the century swarmed to see.

Biblical Characters, and Saints, in the Shows

The "royal-entries" before 1500 included Biblical, as well as historical and allegorical characters; the early Lord Mayor's Shows were largely religious. John the Baptist appeared in 1553,[1] and again in 1554;[2] in 1561 David appeared with Orpheus and Amphion to honor Sir W. Harper.[3] In 1568 John the Baptist appeared again,[4] as the patron-saint of the Merchant-Taylors' Company.[5] Just as the morality-play substituted allegorical characters for the earlier individuals of the Biblical "mysteries," so in pageantry the development was from Biblical characters to abstractions. The reason for this is obvious; for unless a Biblical character were appropriate to the Company providing the show, he could not hold his place. Symbolism is at the bottom of these triumphs; and allegorical figures are more easily made symbolic than are Biblical characters.

It is not long before the only Biblical characters who appear are the patrons of the Companies; or — if we may class the saints with Biblical characters — the national patrons of Britain. In 1609, St. Andrew, riding a unicorn, and St. George, his dragon, appeared "vnited now in enduring amitie."[6] The seven Champions of Christendom appeared in the Show for 1681;[7] and the Mercers' Virgin was seen more than once,[8] — sometimes on horseback, more often in her chariot. The Eight Beatitudes appeared in 1623;[9] "near the entrance of Wood Street, the Imperial Canopy (being the Drapers' arms) is planted, and the rest about the Cross, — the Imperial Canopy covered the Eight beatitudes ('Beati pacifici,' being the king's word or motto, is set in fair great letters near the uppermost of the three crowns) as the King must not be forgotten in the tri-

---

[1] See above, p. 14.

[2] See above, p. 15.

[3] See above, pp. 18, and n. 2; 19, and n. 1.

[4] See above, p. 21.

[5] In 1553, a Merchant-Taylor was inaugurated; but in 1554 the mayor was a Grocer.

[6] See above, p. 30.

[7] This is reprinted by Heath (3d ed.) pp. 536 f. The saints are: George, for England; Andrew, for Scotland; Dennis, for France; Patrick, for Ireland; David, for Wales; James, for Spain, and Anthony, for Italy. The latter was the patron of the Grocers.

[8] The Virgin appeared with the Drapers' Company in 1638; with the Mercers' in 1655; in 1686; and in 1701. (See Fairholt, pt. ii, p. 75; pt. i, pp. 64, 102, and 117 f.)

[9] It will be recalled that they took part in Elizabeth's royal passage across London in 1559 (see above, vol. i, p. 201). These figures may be a development of the 1522 "scripture" (cf. vol. i, p. 177).

umph of his great substitute."[1] In the second pageant of Jordan's *London in Luster* — written for the Drapers in 1679 — sat David, attended by various shepherds and shepherdesses: Vigilius, Precaria, Canonicus, Evangelia, Orthodoxus, and Protestantia, among others.[2] His speech began:

> "I represent that shepherd whose abode
> Was Palestine, One who Divinely trod
> And said, My Shepherd is the Living God."

St. Martin, patron of the Vintners', received the mayor on his return from Westminster in 1702;[3] St. Dunstan, with a goldsmith's forge, and workmen about him, defied the devil — seizing him by the nose with his tongs — in the 1674 Show,[4] and St. Katharine, patroness of the Haberdashers, sat surrounded by her servants — some carding wool, some spinning, others knitting caps, while a shepherd kept his sheep in the background — on the "maine Pageant" of the 1620 Show.[5] In 1631, St. Katharine occupied a place in the Palace of Honour, whence she addressed the mayor;[6] and she appeared also in 1637 and 1699.[7]

Classical Characters

We have already noted the important part played in these shows by mythology; but occasionally we find classical characters which are rather historic than mythological. Pythagoras delivered the first speech and "Linvoy" in *London's Mirror;*[8] Aristotle, Plato, Socrates, and Diogenes, with "a Learned woman called *Diotema*" occupied the "Academy of Sciences" in 1681; Diogenes emerged from his tub to address the mayor,[9] — he is connected with the Grocers through his currant-butt.

There were forty lictors in Roman habits, with masked faces of silver, in Taubman's Show for 1686;[10] they escorted the "Imperial Triumphant Chariot

---

1 Bullen's Middleton, vii, p. 392.

2 See the *Pamphlet*, pp. 9–12, and Fairholt, pt. i, p. 91.

3 Fairholt, pt. i, p. 118. The saint is attended by twenty satyrs dancing before him; two persons in rich liveries walk by his horse; ten "halberteers" and ten Roman lictors escort him, and several cripples and beggars, supplicating for his charity, follow him. As Fairholt points out, Settle is blind to the absurdities of this group.

4 St. Dunstan is the patron of the Company. He appeared in 1611 (see above, p. 31); in 1687 (Fairholt, pt. i, p. 103); and was to have appeared in 1708 (*ibid.*, p. 123).

5 This is reprinted in *Prog. James*, iii, pp. 619 f.; cf. Fairholt, pt. i, p. 47.

6 Fairholt, pt. i, p. 56.

7 Cf. Heywood's *Works* (1874) iv, p. 308; Fairholt, pt. i, pp. 58 and 116.

8 Heywood's Show for 1637, reprinted in his *Works* (1874) iv, pp. 301 f.; cf. Fairholt, pt. i, p. 59.

9 See Fairholt, pt. i, pp. 96 and 97. He does not name the philosophers except Diogenes; but the names are recorded in the descriptive pamphlet.

10 See the descriptive pamphlet of this show, which was entitled *London's Yearly Jubilee;* also Fairholt, pt. i, p. 103.

of Roman form," in which sat the Mercers' patroness, the Virgin. This combination foreshadows the lictors, satyrs, and St. Martin of 1702.[1] In 1664, Magnanimity, surrounded by various animals under the protection of a lion, on which he was mounted, was "habited like a Roman general, in a buff doublet and scarlet breeches!"[2]

Music in the Shows

It is unnecessary to pick out the various instances of music in pageantry. Already in the days of the "royal-entry" the minstrel played an important part in the triumph; and — while not an integral part of these shows — music, both vocal and instrumental, was commonly found in these entertainments. Where it was particularly needed, of course, was with the "drolls," who alternated their dancing and tumbling with songs. In Dekker's *London's Tempe* we find the song of the smiths at the Lemnian Forge; Jordan's *Triumphs of London* for 1678 gives us a stout planter, "with a voice like a trumpet," who bellows forth a song from the Indian plantation.[3] Apollo and Orpheus were usually accompanied by minstrels; and occasionally a "musical dialogue" like that of 1684[4] would take place. The banquets at Guildhall are still accompanied by music — but they lie outside our field.

Dancing and Tumbling in the Shows

Another element, which is often found in these shows, though not an integral part of them, is the dancing and tumbling of the "drolls," who are usually given a setting suitable to the mayor's company. Mr. Dyamond "tumbled" in Tatham's Show for 1660, and Jacob Hall brought his troupe to at least one triumph;[5] but the writers of these entertainments did not, evidently, take kindly to the "drolls," for Heywood says that "the third Plat-forme is contrived onely for Pastime, to please the vulgar,"[6] and again, "the third Pageant

---

[1] See above, p. 83, and n. 3.

[2] See the descriptive pamphlet of the show, and Fairholt, pt. i, p. 72.

[3] See Fairholt, pt. ii, p. 168. [4] See above, p. 62.

[5] Cf., *e.g.*, Jordan's *London's Resurrection*, (Fairholt, pt. ii, p. 138.)

[6] *Londons Sinus Salutis; Works* (1874) iv, p. 292. As an example of the way the poets described these "drolls" when they wanted to make the best of it, let me cite Jordan's descriptive pamphlet for 1676: near St. Laurence Lane end was "a kind of Chase artfully contrived" with trees, grass, bushes, birds, flowers, shepherds, shepherdesses, and sheep on one part of the stage; and on the other side, persons at work: an old woman spinning yarn for woollen cloth; another carding wool; a third picking it; and in the middle, a crew of mad, frolicking shepherds, piping, dancing, and tumbling, "being intended for a description of Disorder, and an elaborate expression of Confusion; where since no Song can be heard, I have omitted it, because it would be rendered as ineffectual as the sound of a Lute in a Whirlwind."

In 1677, the fourth pageant was a "Jocular Scene" containing "a brisk Society of merry Labourers." Three masculine figures, representing Patience, Labour, and Diligence, occupied

or Show merely consisteth of Anticke gesticulations, dances, and other mimicke postures, devised onely for the vulgar, who are better delighted with that which pleaseth the eye, than contenteth the eare."[1] In the pageantry of our own day, under different circumstances of production, the dance has become — in America, at all events — very important; it is yoked to symbolism, and aims no longer solely to amuse.

These "drolls," who were sometimes shepherds, seem to have absorbed some of the characteristics of the older "wild-men." It may be observed that in 1686 the Mercers' Virgin was preceded by "twenty Savages or Green Men, with Squibs and Fireworks, to sweep the streets, and keep off the Crowd."[2] Of course, the "drolls" did not clear the streets: but they were not unlike the "hommes sauvages" of 1431.[3]

Conclusion

We have seen how the Lord Mayor's Show rose out of the "Midsummer Show;" how it borrowed much from the "royal-entry," and finally drove that form of pageantry almost out of existence. We have seen how it gradually grew in elaboration; how its course was interrupted by the Civil War; how, in the hands of minor poets, who had to use many of the same properties over and over again, it lacked novelty, and finally fell into decay in 1702. Settle tried to revive it in 1708, but the death of the Prince of Denmark prevented the performance of his show; and speech has never crept into this annual parade since. What its course has been for the last two hundred years, we shall discover in the next two sections of this chapter.

---

the most conspicuous position. At their feet were several workers, spinning, carding, &c., while others, "more jocose and at liberty sing a Song in Commendation of the *Cloth-workers-Trade*, and at the end of the Song, certain Rusticks, and Shepherd-like persons, Pipe, Dance, and exercise the activity of their limbs, in Gambolling, Tumbling and Capering . . . the whole *Pageant* being a piece of ingenious Confusion, or a Comical Scene of delightful disorder." (From the descriptive pamphlet for this year.)

We may refer to the "drolls" in Tatham's *Aqua Triumphalis* of 1662 (above, vol. i, p. 249) as well as to the tumblers in 1547 (i, p. 186); 1553 (i, p. 189); and 1554 (i, p. 193 f.). Perhaps the "hommes et femmes sauvages," who greeted Henry VI at Paris in 1431 (see vol. i, pp. 76 and 139) are related to the "drolls"; though they may not have sung, their acrobatic performance entitles them to consideration in this light.

[1] *Londons Mirror; Works*, iv, p. 312.

[2] *London's Yearly Jubilee;* cf. Fairholt, pt. i, p. 103. Cf. the "wodyn" of 1553 (above, p. 13 f.) and the wild-men of 1575 (above, p. 22.) There were lictors and "green men" and satyrs in the 1687 Show; cf. the descriptive pamphlet — Fairholt's account (pt. i, p. 103 f.) does not mention them.

[3] See above, vol. i, p. 139.

§ 3. THE DECLINE OF A TIME-HONORED CUSTOM, 1708–1858

With the Lord Mayor's Show of 1702, speech departed from the civic triumphs; for, though Settle planned a series of pageants for 1708, and wrote the speeches for them, the death of the Prince of Denmark prevented the exhibition. There seems to have been no interruption in the annual processions between 1702 and 1708; and we may presume that some of them were accompanied with pageantry, although speeches were done away with; the failure to employ the services of a poet would account for the lack of descriptive pamphlets. Since many Companies owned the "properties" of earlier pageantic "triumphs," it would not be surprising to discover that they brought them out on Lord Mayor's Day; and the description of that festival in Ned Ward's *London Spy* seems to lend color to the supposition that they did.

The passage in the rare volume to which I have just alluded, has been reprinted in the *Journal of English and Germanic Philology*, for January, 1918; it is vivid and entertaining, despite the satire. Exaggerated as it is, it is no worse than the laudatory accounts written by the poets who err on the other side, being too partial to the products of their brains; and Ward's fun is a good antidote to Settle's fulsomeness.[1] We may note that Ward does not mention speeches, as we might expect he would have done, had there been any.

Perhaps such attacks as this helped to bring the show into disrepute; at any rate, during the eighteenth and early nineteenth centuries it fell from the position it had held. It continued, however, to appeal to the people; and that the show is not dead today is largely due to the "mobility."

As a mere procession, the Lord Mayor's Show fails to interest us, and it seems to have been little else early in the eighteenth century. Fairholt records that Sir Gilbert Heathcote, in 1711, was the last mayor to ride on horseback at his mayoralty;[2] and says that since this year the mayor has ridden to Guildhall in a coach;[3] that before 1740, it was drawn by four horses, but that that year it had six.[4]

---

[1] With this passage should be compared the description by Celia Fiennes, (above, p. 66 f.) and Henley's "oration" of 1730, reprinted by Fairholt, pt. i, pp. 126 ff. The latter mentions pageants and the City Giants. I have quoted Ward's description of the latter (above, vol. i, p. 61) and his humorous picture of the City Waits (above, vol. i, p. 50, n. 2).

[2] Pt. i, p. 124; he cites Hone, p. 261, as does J. G. Nichols, p. 120. A writer in the *Athenæum* for 3 November, 1860, p. 585, notes, — like Hone, he fails to give his authorities, — that Sir Gilbert was the last mayor to ride; and further remarks that he was "that 'large-acred man,' whom Pope has immortalized, whom Addison has made known under the pseudonym of Freeport. . ."

[3] Hone, p. 261; Fairholt, pt. i, p. 124; Davey, i, p. 103. The *Repertories* and *Journals* are strangely silent on this matter of a state coach.

[4] Fairholt, pt. i, p. 130 f. He records, *ibid.*, that the coach may be found in the conclud-

1717 — A Pageantic Show at Adrianople

We may note in passing that in a letter, written on 17 May, 1717, Lady Mary Wortley Montagu gives an account of a pageant which she saw at Adrianople.[1] It included many features of the seventeenth-century Lord Mayors' Shows, among which " a man dressed in green boughs, representing a clean husbandman sowing seed," may be a development of some Turkish " green-man." " After him several reapers, with garlands of ears of corn, as Ceres is pictured, with scythes in their hands, seeming to mow. Then a little machine drawn by oxen, in which was a windmill, and boys employed in grinding corn, followed by another machine, drawn by buffaloes, carrying an oven, and two more boys, one employed in kneading the bread, and another in drawing it out of the oven.[2] These boys threw little cakes on both sides among the crowd, and were followed by the whole company of bakers, marching on foot, two by two, in their best clothes, with cakes, loaves, pastries, and pies of all sorts, on their heads, and after them two buffoons, or jack-puddings, with their faces and clothes smeared with meal, who diverted the mob with their antic gestures.[3] In the same manner followed all the companies of trade in the empire; the nobler sort, such as jewelers, mercers, etc., finely mounted, and many of the pageants that represent their trades, perfectly magnificent; among which, that of the furriers made one of the best figures, being a very large machine set round with the skins of ermines, foxes, etc., so well stuffed that the animals seemed to be alive, and followed by music and dancers. I believe they were, upon the whole, twenty thousand men, all ready to follow his highness if he commanded them. The rear was closed by the volunteers, who came to beg the honor of dying in his service. This part of the show seemed to me so barbarous that I removed from the window upon the first appearance of it. They were all naked to the middle. Some had their arms pierced through with arrows, left sticking in them. Others had them sticking in their heads, the blood trickling down their faces. Some slashed their arms with sharp knives, making the blood spring out upon those that stood there; and this is looked upon as an expression of their zeal for glory. I am told that some make use of it to advance their love; and when they are near the window where their mistress stands (all the women in town being vailed to see this spectacle), they stick another arrow for her sake, who gives some sign of approbation and encouragement to this gallantry. The whole show lasted for near eight hours, to my great sorrow, who was heartily tired, though I was in the

---

ing plate of Hogarth's *Industry and Idleness* series. A coach is mentioned by the author of *A Gigantick History* (see below, p. 90).

[1] *Letters of Lady Mary Wortley Montagu* (ed. Mrs. Hale, Boston, 1884, p. 87 f.). This letter is cited by Fairholt, *Civic Garland*, p. xix, n.

[2] These suggest the trade-pageants of the London guilds.

[3] Cf. the " drolls " of the London civic shows, and the earlier " devils " or " wild-men."

house of the widow of the captain-pasha (admiral), who refreshed me with coffee, sweetmeats, sherbet, etc., with all possible civility."

The trade-pageantry has much in common with the London civic shows; it is interesting as an example of a parallel development, if nothing more. Lady Mary's failure to suggest the obvious likeness, may be due to her unfamiliarity with the pageantry of her own capital; we often find things worthy of notice abroad which at home we ignore.

We have mentioned [1] the mayor's precepts against squibs in these early years of this century; they are important only as suggesting pageantry. In 1721, the Goldsmiths went to Westminster by water; [2] in 1722, the Masons were at some expense for the Lord Mayor's Day dinner; [3] on 24 October, 1727, "the Right Honourable the Lord Mayor Elect is desired to provide a New Crimson Velvet Gown at the Charge of this City to be wore on the Lord Mayors Day when their Majesties Honour this City with their presence with the Royal Family at Dinner and that the same be preserved for the use of this city on the like publick Occasions." [4]

1727 — Royalty in the City

On 30 October, Sir Edward Becher, Mayor-elect, with the late Lord Mayor, Aldermen, and Sheriffs went, in the City Barge, to Westminster and back. They progressed from Blackfriars to the Guildhall "with the usual solemnity." The royal family came to Cheapside about three in the afternoon, and saw the procession from a balcony near Bow Church.[5] They then went to Guildhall, where they were received by the Mayor and other city officials. The banquet on this occasion cost £4889, 4*s*.[6]

---

[1] See above, p. 14, n. 1.

[2] But there is no mention of pageants in the extract from their records in Prideaux, ii, p. 201.

[3] See Conder, p. 258.

[4] *Repertory* cxxxi, p. 459. Fairholt, pt. i, p. 133, records that the King, Queen, and princesses witnessed the procession this year from a balcony near Bow Church. He does not name his authority, which appears to be the pamphlet recorded in the Bibliography under the name of George II. This is my authority for the following paragraph; the account will be found there, pp. 45 f.

[5] Pamphlet cited in the last note, p. 48. This was "at *David Barclay's* an eminent Linen Draper (the only surviving son of the *Apologist*) at the *Black Bear* against *Bow Church.*" See *Verses on the Coronation of their Late Majesties . . . October* II, MDCCXXVII, &c., (London, 1761) p. 40, n. (This is bound with the volume cited above, in Fairholt's collection in the Library of the Society of Antiquaries.) On Barclay, see below, p. 96.

[6] An itemized account may be found in the pamphlet cited, pp. 54–6. After dinner, the royal guests returned to the Council Chamber, to be present at the ball; at eleven o'clock they returned in state to St. James's, the "Trained Bands" lining the streets, and the houses being illuminated.

We have referred to the remarks of Henley published in *The Lord Mayor's Shew, or the City in its Glory*,[1] and I shall not repeat the orator's words. Suffice it to say, that pageants, without speeches, seem to have been carried through the London streets about 1730; and that the giants appear to have graced the procession.

The *London Magazine* for October, 1732[2] notes that on 30 October, John Barber, Esq., the Lord Mayor-elect, was sworn "with the accustom'd Ceremony."[3] On Monday, 29 October, 1733, Sir William Billers, the Lord Mayor-elect, went from the Guildhall to Westminster "with the usual formalities";[4] but we can only surmise what they were.

No pageants are mentioned by Lord Mayor Perry, in his MS. *Diary;*[5] but he tells of going to, and returning from, Westminster by water in 1739; and, after landing at Blackfriars, "we proceeded to Guildhall in Procession of which I can give no account but that my own Company and the Artillery Company marched all the way before me."[6]

A Description of the Lord Mayor's Day, c. 1740

The Gigantick History has already been referred to, when we discussed the men in armor and the giants.[7] In the second volume of this microscopic work, Book iv is "an Account of My Lord Mayor's Show." I quote a few chapters.[8]

Chap. I. *Of my Lord entring upon his office.*

My Lord Mayor is the grand magistrate of this great city. He is yearly elected on Michaelmas day, and though the oldest Alderman, who has not served that office, is usually chosen, yet that is at the electors discretion.

On St. Simon and Jude's day, the 28th of October, let it happen to be Sunday or any other day; the Lord Mayor, Aldermen, Sheriffs, &c. meet at Guildhall about twelve a clock: and when the Lord Mayor elect comes, they all go to the Hustings court; where, after the common crier has commanded silence, the Town-clerk gives the new Lord his oath, and then the old Lord Mayor rises up, and gives the new his place: The Chamberlain first presents the

---

[1] Above, p. 86, n. 1. This pamphlet, from which Fairholt quotes, may be found in the Brit. Mus. (*605. d. 29.7*); it is recorded in the Bibliography under *Henley*.

[2] P. 369; on p. 368 the writer records the fact that 30 October is the anniversary of his majesty's birth.

[3] *A Rural Lay*, by a Gentleman in Norwich, is published, *ibid.*, for November, 1732 (p. 411); this is dedicated to the mayor. "The Pegasus in Grub-Street" also wrote a poem to him (*ibid.*, p. 412); but these verses do not seem to have been recited from a pageant.

[4] *London Magazine* for October, 1733, p. 529.

[5] Preserved at the Guildhall (MS. 15); a notice of the receipt of the *Diary* by the Court of Aldermen may be found in *Repertory* cxliii, p. 473.

[6] MS. cited, p. 11. Had there been pageants, he would, of course, have seen them.

[7] See above, vol. i, p. 47 f., and n. 5; p. 59; p. 61, and n. 4.

[8] My quotations are from vol. ii, pp. 97 f. (The first edition of this volume is dated 1740; though written for, and dedicated to, children, its description of a contemporary Lord Mayor's Show is probably accurate enough.)

sceptre to him, then the keys of the common seal, and lastly the seal of the office of mayoralty; and the sword bearer brings him the sword; all which the Mayor immediately returns. This ceremony being ended, they ride home in their coaches to dinner; the Aldermen who have been Mayors accompanying the old Lord Mayor, and those who have not served that office go with the new Lord. The next morning, the 29th of October, called *Lord Mayor's Day*, they meet together again, and proceed as follows.

Chap. II. *Of My Lord Mayor's procession to the water side.*

The Lord Mayor elect meets as many of his brethren the Aldermen as please to come, at Guildhall, about eleven a clock in the morning; all being invited: where having breakfasted, about 12 they set out in the following order.

Before the procession go officers to clear the way: Then the first in the cavalcade are the streamers of the company the new Lord is free of, born by sturdy watermen: next come the band of pensioners, as many in number, they say, as my Lord is years old, headed by their captain: and after them the gentlemen ushers, called *rich batchelors*, thirty in number, with white staves in their hands, and chains of gold about their necks, all in black clothes. Then comes the musick, *viz.* kettle drums, trumpets, hautboys, and other musical instruments; next the three banners; the King's in the middle, the City's on the right hand, and the Lord Mayor's on the left. Then comes the master of the city barge in his gown; and after him the champion, or master of defence, with his drawn sword in his hand; next to him march thirty or forty whifflers, dress'd up with ribbands, and white staves in their hands; who are followed by the two beadles of the old Lord's company; and then come the master, wardens, and livery men in their gowns. After them follow the new Lord's company in order, with all their attendants. And before the coach [1] come first the sheriff's officers, then the city musick, the city marshals on horseback, finely caparason'd; the city artificers, in furr'd gowns; and next before the coach, my Lord's officers.

And so they proceed to the end of King-street, Cheapside, where the old Lord Mayor's coach falls in next that of the new Lord. The swordbearer is at the right side in the new Lord's coach, with the sword in his right hand, and cap of maintenance upon his head; and on the left side of the coach, the common crier, bearing the mace.

After the old Lord's coach, come the Aldermen past the chair, in their coaches, according to seniority: next the Recorder, and after him the Aldermen who have not serv'd Mayor: Then come the Sheriffs, Chamberlain, Town-clerk, Comptroller, city Remembrancer, Common Hunt, city Solicitor, and city Counsel.

Being thus marshalled, they proceed with the greatest uniformity to the water side; and at the Three Cranes stairs they embark on board their state barge.

Chap. III. *Of the procession by water, &c.*

The barge being well provided with all things fitting for the voyage, the cockswain takes the helm, and the bargemen their oars, and so set forward towards Westminster; attended by a great number of the city companies in their barges, all with ensigns, streamers, *&c.* display'd; musick playing, and thousands of boats crowded with people, to see this gallant show; being all the way saluted with a discharge of the great cannon from the wharfs, and batteries on both sides the river, with a 'God send the ship a good voyage, and bless the Lord Mayor, and his honourable company.' And, if wind and tide are not too boisterous, in about one hour they reach Westminster stairs; where they are receiv'd by a large body of city grenadiers, who fire a volley to welcome their landing.

Then they walk to Westminster hall, where the new Lord Mayor is shewn the several courts; and having paid his respects to the Judges, *&c.* then sitting, he is sworn, according

---

[1] The mayor is supposed to have ridden in a coach after 1711; see above, p. 86 and n. 4.

to custom, before the Barons of the Exchequer. Then they go round the hall again, and invite the Lord Chancellor and Judges of the several courts to his Lordship's feast. This being ended, they return back to their barge; and are again saluted in their passage with a discharge from the great guns; and attended by several companies in their barges, with their streamers, banners, musick, *&c.* as in coming. And about three or four a clock my Lord lands, generally at Blackfriars stairs; where another large body of the honourable artillery company receive him and his attendants, and give them three vollies.

Chap.IV. *Of the Procession to Guildhall.*

From Blackfriars stairs they commonly proceed up the Ditch-side in their coaches to Ludgate hill; where the Nobility, Judges, *&c.* who are invited to dine with my Lord, join the procession: the artillery company, his Lordship's company, *&c.* marching before. And thus this solemn, magnificent, and grand procession is conducted with great regularity thro' the city to Guildhall, amidst thousands of men, women and children, who fill the balconies and windows, and line both sides of the streets, from the landing place, all up the Ditch-side, Ludgate hill and street, St. Paul's churchyard, Cheapside and King-street, to Guildhall.

When his Lordship comes near the hall, the commanding officers of the artillery company line both sides of the way, till my Lord, the Nobility, Judges and all the great personages who attend this grand show, enter the hall.[1]

If we may regard this description as accurate — and I do not see why we may not — it is clear that by the middle of the eighteenth century these shows had but one pageantic figure — the " armed man " — who may have a chivalric origin stimulated by his applicability to the Armourers', or even Ironmongers', Guild.[2] We may recall that, in 1700, Walworth was accompanied by several of his aldermen, in armor; that in 1681, the seven champions of Christendom were shown, and that Saints Andrew and George appeared in 1609. These are examples of the pageantic adaptation of an older figure, which survived well into the nineteenth century; by this time, he had become reduced to an " armed man," with no glamour of chivalry, history, or legend thrown about him.

The Show of 1740

No mention is made either of pageants or of Sir William Walworth in the account of the mayoralty procession which appeared in the London *Daily Post* of 30 October, 1740.[3] An account of this procession may also be found in the

---

[1] Chapter V of this book deals with the feast; Chapter VI — *Of the City Companies that grace my Lord's show* — makes no mention of pageants, but states that " some companies have stands built along the sides of the streets through which my Lord passes; where they seat themselves in order, and pay their respects to his Lordship, the Aldermen, *&c.* as they come by." (*Op. cit.*, ii, pp. 121 f.). [The seventh chapter, dealing with *The Man in Armour*, has already been quoted at length; see above, vol. i, p. 48.]

[2] There may be a hint of the older St. George and similar champion-figures in this character, as well as of the militia, who go back to the older " marching watch." Cf. the " giant-champion " of 1432 (above, vol. i, p. 143, and n. 6) and the discussion concerning the relationship of these figures (above, vol. i, p. 48, and n. 2).

[3] Herbert, ii, p. 51, cites under 1740 the same passage from the *Post-Boy* which Fairholt cites under 1700. This is, evidently, a misprint or oversight on Herbert's part. I can find no

Diary of Richard Hoare,[1] who says: "... what added magnificence to this day's shew was, that his lordship's coach was drawn by six horses, adorned with grand harnesses, ribbons, &c. a sight never seen before on this occasion... My late Lord Mayor chose to go privately in his coach by land to Westminster, where we met him in our barge, and after having paid our compliments to the several Courts in the hall, and passed through the formalities at the Exchequer Court, we got into our barge again by two o'clock; my late Lord Mayor returning back by himself in his coach as he came.

"But it so happened, that by the carelessness of our watermen, while we were in the hall, the tide had fell so low as to leave the barge aground, and it was ... past four o'clock before we arrived at Guildhall; our procession both by water and land being attended by the usual concourse of people."

The mayor's notice, making the arrangements for this show, may be found in the London *Evening-Post*, (from Saturday, 25 October, to Tuesday, 28 October, 1740, no. 2022). It reads:

Salter, Mayor.

Tuesday the 21st Day of October, 1740, and in the Fourteenth year of the Reign of King *George* the Second, of *Great Britain*, &c.

It is order'd, That the two Marshals of this City do take Care to give Notice to the several Constables of the Wards of Bread street, Castle-Baynard, Cheap, Cordwainer, Cripplegate Within, Farringdon Within, Farringdon Without, and Vintry, through which the Procession is to pass on the next Lord Mayor's-Day, that they take effectual Care to obey the Precept sent for a Double Watch and Ward of able Men well Weapon'd, to be kept on that Day; and that they dispose their said Watch at such Places, and in such Manner, that the publick Streets thro' which the said Solemnities are to pass be kept free and clear from all Obstructions or Hindrances to the said Procession; and that they do not permit any Cart, Dray or Coach to stand in the said publick Streets thro' which the said Procession is to pass; and if any Carman, Drayman or Coachman refuse to remove out of the said Streets, that they carry such Carman, Drayman, or Coachman to one of the Compters, and the Cart, Dray or Coach to the Greenyard, that they may be prosecuted for such their Offences; and they are to take especial Care that no Hackney-Coach, Cart or Dray be permitted to come into any of the said publick Streets thro' which the Procession is to pass, between Fetter-lane End in Fleet-street and Stocks-Market, after Twelve o'Clock at Noon on that Day; and the said Marshals are to take especial Care that the Passage down Queen-street to the Three Crane Stairs, be kept free and clear from all Coaches, Carts and other Hindrances, so that the Lord Mayor, Aldermen, and others in the Procession, may pass in their Coaches, without any Obstruction, to the Water-side; and that they cause the said Coaches to go in Order down one side of Queen-street to the said Stairs; and that as soon as his Lordship is set down there, his Coach to return up Queen-street again, and the other Coaches to do the like in Succession, so that all the Aldermen, and others, may be set down as near as possible to the said Stairs; and it is order'd, that a Copy hereof be publish'd in some of the Daily Papers.[2]

---

mention, among contemporary accounts, of the presence of Walworth or Wat Tyler in this show. Cf. Fairholt, pt. i, p. 130.

[1] Mentioned in the Bibliography; my extract is taken from p. 33.

[2] Cf. *Repertory* cxlv, p. 403, where this notice is written; the last words there read "some of the publick daily papers."

The order of procession on the occasion of the inauguration of Sir Robert Godschall, Ironmonger, in 1741, is given by Nicholl.[1] There were, however, no pageants on this occasion. A picture of the "Lord Mayor and the Livery Companies on their Way to Westminster in 1750," from "a picture belonging to the Corporation of London, hanging in the Guildhall Art Gallery," may be found in Stewart's *History of the Gold and Silver Wyre-Drawers*.[2]

1751 — The Alteration of Lord Mayor's Day to 9 November

In 1751, at the alteration of the style, the Lord Mayor's Day, which up to that time had fallen regularly on 29 October, was changed to 9 November, the present date unless the ninth happens to fall on Sunday.[3]

1757 — The Lord Mayor's Coach

The present Lord Mayor's Coach — almost entirely rebuilt several times, as it has been, at enormous expense—was built in 1757.[4] On 7 July, 1758, £860 were paid as "consideration money" for the coach —every Alderman paid £60, and the mayor £100, to the Coach Fund. In 1764, £227, 2*s*. 6*d*. were spent on the coach; and the next year, one Hutchinson agreed to mend the paint of the body, and paint the coat-of-arms, and new gild, "as at the first," the body and carriage, for £80, to make a new set of wheels for £20, and other repairs for £130 to £150. In 1768, £103, 4*s*. were paid to the Coachmaker for work done to the coach; and in 1773, £279, 10*s*. were paid to the Coachmaker — the itemized bills are in the Guildhall Records Office, where there are many others for various years. Among these papers is a letter from Berry & Barker, the coach-

[1] *Hist. Ironmongers*, p. 345.

[2] *The History of the Worshipful Company of Gold and Silver Wyre-Drawers* . . . Compiled by Horace Stewart (Illustrated). [London, 1891], p. 93.

[3] Cf. on this subject, Beaven, ii, p. xxviii; the *Handbook of Ceremonials, &c. for the Lord Mayor, Aldermen and other Corporation officers* (London, 1906) p. 24, n. 1, citing 24 Geo. II, c. 48, sec. 11; the change is recorded by Fairholt, pt. i, p. 133, — he dates it 1752; cf. Hone, p. 261.

Beaven, *loc. cit.*, gives various electoral and inaugural dates of mayors; since 1546 the election has been on Michaelmas Day (29 September).

[4] MS. Agreement for the building of the coach, kept in the custody of the London Town Clerk's office. Many of the following items come from bills preserved in the Guildhall Record Office, in the custody of the Town Clerk of the City of London. A brief description of the coach is in *The Illustrated News of the World*, 13 November, 1858, p. 317; cf. also Fairholt, pt. i, pp. 135 f.

Fairholt, (p. 136) says that the original cost of the coach was £1065, 3*s*. Cipriani, who painted the allegorical panels on it, was the artist who decorated the State Coach used by King George V and Queen Mary at their coronation in 1911; this coach, and the panels, are pictured in color in the supplement of the *Illustrated London News* for 1 July, 1911, following p. 33. Fairholt, pt. i, p. 135, n., says that the State Coach was built in 1762.

builders, which is worthy of reproduction; it is addressed "To Samuel Plumb, Esq[r]. No. 23. Foster Lane," and reads as follows:

Sr. To-morrow being the day on which our affair with regard to the State coach will in all Probability be determin'd; humbly beg leave to Entreat your Concurrence with those Gentlemen who sensible of the hardships we have laboured under are disposed of relieving us as much as in their power.

It is not only our Premier loss in the building of it, is a hardship but the misfortune we labour under of having (in the Opinion of a few) overcharged some articles which we have always been ready to answer to and have had Mr. Pinnock a Proper Judge, who has been ready for sometime past to answer any Taxation which any Gentleman or other might please to make.

Things have been in this Situation for three years past, and the account of course unliquidated, if the latter was all we suffer'd wou̅d chearfully sustain it, and scarce think it hard to wait 'till the Bank was able to Assist us.

But to loose (*sic*) the honour we have so long had of doing up and taking care of the Coach and unmerited lay (*sic*) under the Calumny of imposition is realy Excessive hard.

Nought has been spared, (we are sure) to deserve a Continuance, especially if it is considered it was our Resolution to finish it to the Satisfaction of the Gentlemen notwithstanding we knew the Consequences wou̅d be considerable to us more even than £200.

We built at no small Expence a Proper place of reception for it and provided every requisite to do it up annually, which we may boldly assert we have it in our power to do cheaper & better than any of the Profession (Partiality to any particular excepted). — We purchased at no small Expence a temporary State Coach new Gilt & decorated the same, submitting the Charge of the use of it to the Worshipful Aldermen: and having had the honour of giving Satisfaction to Every Gentleman 'till the Mayoralty of the late George Nelson Esq[r]. thought with Submission our fate the harder, as no other Complaint was made than the high charge of our bills, which on notice given were ready to submit to Arbitration and had the above mentioned Mr. Pinnock ready to attend any summons on that account.

This worthy Sir being realy the case most humbly beg you will take into Consideration & be assured that nothing in our power shall be ever wanting to be deserving of the continuance the worthy Aldermen have hitherto thought Proper to confer on

Sr., your very humble and most

Obliged Serv[ts].

BERRY & BARKER.

Leather Lane 21 September 1767.

1761 — A REVIVAL OF PAGEANTS

Unpageantic processions continued until 1761, when the Court of Common Council recommended pageants for the entertainment of their Majesties on Lord Mayor's Day.[1] A full account of the procession on 9 November, 1761, may

---

[1] Hone, p. 261; he continues (writing in 1823): "Although such revivals are inexpedient, yet, surely, means may be devised for improving the appearance of the present procession, without further expenditure from the city funds, or interfering with the public appropriation of the allowance for the support of the civic dignity."

The pamphlet describing Taubman's Show for 1689, entitled *London's Great Jubilee*, was reprinted in 1761, "for the perusal of the several Companies of London, agreeable to the

The Lord Mayor's Coach

be found in the contemporary *Gentleman's Magazine*[1] and *London Magazine* —from which last, because it is the rarer account, I shall quote:[2]

I must own that I look upon that part of the ceremony . . . which is presented to us on the water, as perhaps equal to what we read of in Holland or Venice. . . The skinners barge was distinguished from the rest by the outlandish dresses, in strange spotted skins and painted hides, of their rowers, &c. . .

Every house, indeed, from Temple-Bar to Guildhall, was crowded from top to bottom, and many had scaffolding besides. Carpets and rich hangings were hung out on the fronts all the way along. . . As the royal family passed by our window, I counted between twenty and thirty coaches belonging to them and their attendants, besides those of the foreign ambassadors, officers of state, and the principal nobility. . . . What was most remarkable, were the prodigious acclamations and tokens of affection shewn by the populace to Mr. Pitt, who came in his chariot, accompanied by Earl Temple. At every stop the mob clung about every part of the vehicle, hung upon the wheels, hugged his footmen, and even kissed his horses. . . .

I need not trouble you with an account of the city procession, (which was now left at liberty to shew itself) as it differed very little from that which you and I saw together, and has been seen for many years the same. The skinners, the ironmongers, and the fishmongers companies, were the only companies that had something like the pageants exhibited of old on this occasion: But, however clearly the symbols of the furred caps and spotted furr-dresses of the skinners company, or the dolphin and mermaid of the fishmongers, might be understood by the spectators, I must confess myself at a loss how to interpret the improvement made in the show of the armourers company. Besides the usual horseman in armour,[3] they presented us with a figure, standing erect in a kind of phaeton, drawn by four horses; this . . . represented an Indian warrior, because he had a bow in one hand, and a quiver of arrows flung across his back. But what has this to do with the armourers company? Or, are Indian princes ever carried in that manner? From the figure of the youth (whose complexion, made florid with rouge, was wholly European) one might rather suppose (as many did suppose) he was meant to personate Cupid, in allusion to the intrigue of the god of war, Mars, with his mother Venus, wife to the cuckold Vulcan, the founder of armourers: Or, (according to the ancient mythology) as some will have it, the pageant must have been designed to represent the chariot of Apollo, *i. e.*, the sun, the creator of all metalline substances, consequently iron. Whichever interpretation is approved of, there was certainly

---

Recommendation of . . . Sir Matthew Blakiston, Knt., Lord Mayor, and the Court of Common Council, held on Saturday the 3d of October, 1761;" this reprint — recorded in the Bibliography, s. v. *Taubman*, *sub anno* 1689 — is in the Soc. Antiq. and Brit. Mus. libraries. Cf. *The Guide to the Lord Mayor's Show* (London, 1761).

[1] *Gent. Mag.*, xxxi, p. 533 f., — for November, 1761, — cited by J. G. Nichols, p. 87. Cf. Fairholt, pt. i, p. 133 f.

[2] *Lond. Mag.*, xxx, pp. 597–601, — for November, 1761, — under the title: "Extract of a *Letter* from a Gentleman to his Friend in the Country, containing a full and circumstantial Detail of many Particulars, concerning *My Lord Mayor's Show*, and the *Entertainment* at *Guildhall*, &c."

[3] Cf. the 1761 *Guide to the Lord Mayor's Show*, which gives the Order of Procession of the Mayor on his Landing at Blackfriars through the City to Guildhall: it includes (p. 8), "Armourers and Braziers Company, preceded by a Man on Horseback in a complete Suit of Armour, with a Plume of Feathers on his Head and proper Attendants." This is no new figure; here, however, the trade-symbolism is more than usually marked.

no occasion for the burntcork strait stroke from beneath the youth's nostrils on the upper lip, and the serpentine line of beauty by the same pencilling on each corner of his lower one, to represent whiskers; as both Cupid and Apollo have always been described without any beard at all...

The account in the *Gentleman's Magazine* before referred to[1] gives other details:

The show on the water was very brilliant.... The state-coach was drawn by six beautiful iron-grey horses ... and all the companies made a very grand appearance....

The former [armourers and braziers] were marked by an archer riding erect in his car, having his bow in his left hand, and his quiver and arrows hanging behind his left shoulder, and a man in compleat armour. The skinners were distinguished by seven of their company being dressed in fur, having their skins painted in the form of *Indian* princes. The fishmongers pageants consisted of a statue of St. *Peter*[2] finely gilt, a dolphin, two mairmaids, and two sea-horses, which had a very pleasing effect. But the disagreeable circumstance of several livery companies waiting upwards of two hours in *Temple lane*, before the king, *&c.* could get by, made it almost dark before the lord mayor could pass the king in Cheapside.

The 1761 *Guide*[3] informs us that the king and queen were entertained by David Barclay, who had received George II in 1727. "It has been an antient Custom (which their Majesties upon this Occasion are most graciously pleased to keep up) to honour the City with their Presence the first Show after their coming to the Crown; and not only to see the Procession at a House in *Cheapside*, but afterwards to dine with the Lord Mayor at the Guildhall." And in a note, "The Kings and Queens who have honoured the City with their Presence upon this Occasion, have for many years been entertained at a Linendraper's in *Cheapside*, opposite *Bow Church*, now in the Occupation of Mr. *David Barclay*, a very wealthy and respectable Tradesman, and one of the People called *Quakers*, who with his Father-in-law (whom he succeeded in the House and Business) have entertained King *William*, Queen *Mary*, Queen *Anne*, King *George* I., King *George* II. and Queen *Caroline;* and will on this happy Day entertain their present Majesties King *George* III. and Queen *Charlotte;* an Honour that few private Persons can boast off (*sic*)."

The Later Eighteenth Century

After this occasion, the Lord Mayor's Show seems to have lost pageantry for a while; in 1762, (2 Geo. III.) "a committee was appointed to consider a recommendation of the Common Council to provide pageants for the ensuing Lord

---

[1] Above, p. 95, n. 1. This, I may add, is printed (without reference to the *Gent. Mag.*) in *The Citizen's Pocket Chronicle: containing a Digested View of the History, Antiquity, and Temporal Government of the City of London ... for the use of Citizens, Merchants, Lawyers, and Strangers*, (London, 1827), p. 335.

[2] Fairholt, pt. i, p. 134, notes "the patron Saint of the Company."

[3] Before referred to, (p. 95, n. 3). The extract is on p. 12 of the *Guide to the Lord Mayor's Show.* On Barclay, cf. above, p. 88, n. 5.

Mayor's day, when the Ironmongers resolved to adopt the course pursued by the other Companies; and no pageants were provided."[1] In November, 1768, a committee of the Merchant-Taylors' Company "taking into consideration the lord mayor's precept to attend the King of Denmark, on Friday next, directed that there should be no breakfast at the hall, *nor pipes nor tobacco*, in the barge, *as usual*, on Lord Mayor's Day."[2]

There is a description of Lord Mayor's Day in the *Gentleman's Magazine* for November, 1773; here we read that "the procession by water was as usual, but rather tedious, as the tide was contrary. The ceremonies at Westminster-Hall being gone through in the customary manner, the company returned by water to Black-Friars-bridge, where the Lord-Mayor landed at about three o'clock, and proceeded in solemn state to Guildhall. . . During the absence of the Lord Mayor, such of the city companies as have not barges paraded the streets in the accustomed manner; and the man in armour [was] exhibited to the delight of the little masters and misses, and the astonishment of many a gaping rustic . . ."[3]

1783 — A Pantomime on the Lord Mayor's Show

What appears to be a forerunner of the *tableau vivant* — which is related to our modern pageantry, particularly when the living pictures were historical — is found in connection with an "operetta" produced at the Theatre-Royal in Covent-Garden in January, 1783.[4] In the *General Evening Post*, we read:

On Saturday evening the Manager of Covent-Garden Theatre afforded a fresh instance of his attention to the publick, and his liberality in the mode of expressing his thanks for favours received. The Pantomime called *Lord Mayor's Day*, (having been rather hastily contrived,) when first performed, though allowed to be pleasant, was thought a more meagre entertainment than those previously brought out at Covent-Garden Theatre, in which Harlequin had been the hero. In order to remove the objection immediately, *half-price* was taken on the second night of representation; and now, effectually to do it away, the pantomime

[1] Nicholl, p. 347; he wrongly dates this 1761, when we have seen that there were pageants provided by three companies; "2 George III" was 1762. (The pageantry of 1689 was not reproduced in 1761.)

[2] Herbert, ii, p. 411, from entries in the Merchant-Taylor's books. (The italics are Herbert's.)

[3] *Gent. Mag.*, xliii, pp. 577 f.; this is referred to by J. G. Nichols, p. 121. There is nothing to tell us whether there was pageantry or not, beyond the pageantic figure of the "armed man." "As usual" and "in the accustomed manner" are non-committal.

[4] For accounts of this, see the [London] *General Evening Post*, 18–21 January, 1783; the *British Magazine and Review* (1783) pp. 60 f.; and a small pamphlet, preserved in the Guildhall Library, which gives the "Songs, Duets, &c. in the new pantomime called *Lord Mayor's Day; or, a Flight from Lapland*, as performed at the Theatre-Royal in Covent-Garden." This is an operetta, the characters in which are Sailor, Gobble, Polly, and Aërial Spirit. It is followed by "A Grand Historical Procession of the Several Companies with their respective Pageants, And the Chief Magistrates belonging to the City of London, from its Foundation."

has been enriched with the addition of a procession and pageant,[1] of a nature equally new, shewy, and apposite to the occasion. When processions are added to serious performances, we consider them as contemptible adjuncts to the drama, and always suspect, that the author means to dazzle our eyes with the glare of pageantry, because he is conscious he cannot satisfy our understandings with the plot, conduct and characters of his play; but when processions close a pantomime, our sensations are extremely different; pageantry appears then in right place, and is well employed in giving a striking termination to an entertainment, of which shew is one of the most essential properties. The procession of Saturday evening (as we have before observed) was perfectly in character for the occasion. . .

Then follows the playbill, which we shall quote from the Guildhall pamphlet:

1. A TROJAN bearing a scroll with '*Troynovant*.' The City so called by Brute (the lineal descendant of Eneas) who first built it.

2. BRUTE with Label, A. M. 2855 — The year of the city's foundation.

3. A BRITON with Label '*Lundain*' — The city so called from 'Llan Dian.' The Temple of Diana.

4. A BRITON bearing a Scroll with '*Caire Lud*.' — The city so called by King Lud, who in the year 3915 increased the city and built therein, to commemorate his own honor, the gate to this day called after him — Ludgate.

5. KING LUD, A. M. 3915.

6. } Two Sons { *Androgeus*.
7. } { *Theomanticus*.

These were sons to King Lud, and would have inherited his crown, but not being of age to govern at the death of their father, their uncle Cassibelan mounted the regal seat, in the 8th year of whose reign, Julius Cæsar landed in Britain, and after numbers of battles between the Romans and native Britons, Cassibelan paid tribute to Rome.

8. } Two ANTIENT BRITONS.
9. }

10. A ROMAN with a Scroll '*Augusta*.' — The city so called in Julius Cæsar's time.

11. } Two LICTORS with Fasces.
12. }

13. PREFECT. A. D. 44.

14. } Two ROMANS bearing The Eagle and S. P. Q. R.
15. }

16. A SAXON with a Scroll '*Londonceaster*.' — The city so called in the time of the Saxons.

17. PORTREVE, A.D. 654.— This title was given to the Chief Magistrate in the time of the Saxons.

18. A NORMAN with a Scroll '*Camera Regia*' — The city so call'd in the time of William the Conqueror.

19. GODFREY, the Portreve, bearing the first Charter, A.D. 1067. — In this year, being the second of the Conqueror's reign, he granted to Godfrey (a Portreve) in conjunction with William the Bishop of London the first Charter, viz. 'William the King friendly salutes William the Bishop, and Godfrey the Portreve, and all the Burgesses within London, both French and English. And I declare, that I grant you to be all law-worthy, as you were in the days of King Edward; and I grant that every child shall be his father's heir, after his father's days; and I will not suffer any person to do you wrong — God keep you.'

20. BAILIFF, A.D. 1067.— The Chief Magistrate, so called by the Normans.

---

[1] Note the use of this word.

21. HENRY FITZALWIN, A.D. 1189. FIRST LORD MAYOR of London.

Mercers, A.D. 1393 — Mayor, 2 Aldermen, 2 Common Councilmen, 2 Liverymen.

Skinners, A.D. 1325.

Grocers, A.D. 1344.

Vintners, A.D. 1340 — Bacchus, the son of Jupiter and Semele — God of Wine — he planted the first Vine in Egypt.

Drapers, A.D. 1438.

Weavers, A.D. 1104 — Penelope at her Web. The daughter of Icarius and wife of Ulysses, a princess of great chastity, who, during her husband's stay at the siege of Troy, when it was reported he was dead, was addressed by many suitors, and having promised to determine when she had finished a Web of Cloth, to delay the time, she undid in the night what she had finished in the day, and so amused them 'till her husband's return, when he slew them.

Fishmongers, A.D. 1537.

Dyers, A.D. 1472 — Iris in her Rainbow, the messenger of the Goddess Juno.

Goldsmiths, A.D. 1391.

Armourers, A.D. 1423.

Merchant Taylors, A.D. 1469.

Bakers, A.D. 1307 — Ceres, the goddess who first taught mankind to plough and sow, and reap and house their corn.

Haberdashers, A.D. 1502.

Butchers, A.D. 1604 —An ox dressed for sacrifice.

Salters, A.D. 1558.

Sadlers, A.D. 1281.

Cordwainers, A.D. 1438 — *Crispin and Crispianus* — the latter taking leave of the former, he going to the wars, and leaving his brother to follow the business of shoe-making. Supposed sons of King Logrid in Maximinius's time, who, seeking their lives, they were disguised by their mother, and travelling about at Feversham in Kent, were apprenticed to Robans, a shoemaker. They afterwards each of them married a princess.

Ironmongers, A.D. 1464.

Blacksmiths, A.D. 1577 — *The Cyclops at Work.* They were the sons of Neptune and Amphitrite, and assisted Vulcan in forging Jupiter's thunderbolts.

Woolmen, A.D. 1511 — *Bishop Blaise*, the inventor of Wool-combing.

Musicians — *Apollo* the God of Music, attended by his Priestesses, the antient Bards, and Doctors of Music.

[Then follow glees and dances, in honor of Music.]

Shipwrights, A.D. 1605 — *Noah's Ark.* The first vessel or ship built by the art of man.

Apothecaries, A.D. 1618 — *Esculapius*, the son of Apollo, the God of Health. Chiron taught him physic. He was killed by Jupiter for bringing Hippolitus to life. The Serpent and Dog symbolical of the arts of healing and physic.

John Norman, A.D. 1250 — *First Mayor* that was sworn at Westminster.

Henry Darcey, A.D. 1338 — *First Mayor* that had a mace borne before him.

Henry Picard, A.D. 1363 — Entertained at one time Four Kings, i. e. Edward III. of England, John of France, David of Scotland, King of Cyprus.

John Philpot, A.D. 1378 — Hired a thousand soldiers, who took John Mercer, a sea-rover, with all the ships he had before taken from Scarbro,' and fifteen Spanish ships laden with great riches.

William Walworth, A.D. 1381 — Banner with the City Arms. By the slaying of Wat Tyler in Smithfield, delivered the kingdom from a dangerous insurrection, and was knighted for it in the field.

Thomas Knowles, A.D. 1400 — New-built Guildhall, re-edified St. Anthony's church, and conveyed water to Ludgate for the use of the prisoners.

Richard Whittington, A.D. 1421 — Three times Mayor; founded the library of Grey-Friars, Whittington college, and almshouses, and whose executors built Newgate.

Robert Chichley, A.D. 1482 — Appointed, that on his birth-day a sufficient dinner should be given to 2400 poor Citizens, housekeepers, and also two-pence apiece.

Thomas Cook, A.D. 1462 — Knight of the Bath.

John Younge, A.D. 1466 — Knight Banneret.

John Shaw, Mayor, A.D. 1501 — First entertained the Aldermen and Citizens in Guild-hall.

William Fitzwilliams, A.D. 1506 — For his attachment to Cardinal Wolsey in his fall (who had been the means of his great fortunes) King Henry the Eighth knighted him, and made him a Privy Counsellor. He left the king by will his great ship with all her tackles, and his George set with diamonds, and collar of the Garter. At his death he was Knight of the Garter, Lord Privy Seal, and Chancellor of the Dutchy of Lancaster.

John Allen, A.D. 1554 — Gave a rich gold collar to be worn by the Mayor, and 500 marks for a stock of sea coal.

Thomas Gresham, A.D. 1566 — Built the Royal Exchange, and alms-houses for the poor.

The GRAND PAGEANT

A Triumphal Arch. On the left side, on a pedestal, is seen *Industry:* on the right *Commerce:* over which are two symbolical medallions. Through the Arch is seen *The Genius of the City*, crowned with a wreath of plane tree: in one hand a Goblet; in the other, a branch full of little twigs, to signify increase and indulgence. On his right hand,[1] The *Council of the City*, with a wreath of oak on his head and the fasces in his hand, as tokens of strength and civil magistracy. — On his left *The Warlike Force of the City*, with his helm on, and crowned with laurel, implying Strength and Conquest. — At his feet, *Thames*, the River God, leaning on his urn.

CHORUS

London, London, richest, noblest mart,
Seat of freedom, science, art;
Commerce spreads the swelling sail
Plenty's wafted in the gale.
Hail, London, great emporium of the world,
While Britain's thunder round the globe is hurl'd.

It makes little difference, here, that the history of this pantomime is not always accurate; what is important for us, is that here we have, in the form of *tableaux*, the elements of the earlier Lord Mayor's Show. Walworth, and other former Mayors; Apollo, and brother gods; Industry and the Genius of the City, have all appeared in these triumphs. We have a union of civic and national history; the pantomime does not glorify any one Company — it reflects an interest in London's glorious past.

After giving the above program, the critic in the *General Evening Post* continues:

The personages of this procession were all dressed in the characters of the time in which they lived, and before each of them a label, a scroll, or a pageant was carried, bearing their

[1] Note that the Genius is masculine.

THE GIANT GOG

THE GIANT MAGOG

name, or some allusion of the poets to their occupation. The figures in transparency were all painted as large as the life, and had a most grand and beautiful effect. The principal exhibited [were] *Penelope at her Web, Iris in her Rainbow, Ceres, Crispin and Crispianus, the Cyclops at Work in their Cave, Apollo, Esculapius; and a Triumphal Arch, with an emblematical painting in the centre, proper to the subject of the Procession.*

The idea of the paintings was furnished by Mr. Richards and Mr. Smirk, and all of them executed by the latter, in a style of great taste and excellence.

The audience expressed the strongest approbation at the whole of the Procession, and distinguished each of the transparencies with loud plaudits.

The glee introduced with so much applause, is the composition of the late Dr. Rogers (who lived in 1600); the other airs in the Pantomime and Procession, are by Handell, Lord Kelly Abel, Stamitz, and Shields, and have great merit.

The expense of preparing this splendid *spectacle* must have been very great, and the cost of continuing its representation cannot be inconsiderable, since more than 200 supernumarries (*sic*) are employed to walk in the Procession.

This occasion is not, of course, a Lord Mayor's Show; I have, however, included it here, chronologically, because it is based on the Lord Mayor's Show. For us, it is especially important as marking a stage between the civic triumph and the historical pageantry of the United States — which, in the form of *tableaux vivants*, antedates the Parkerian pageant of more recent times. Here, on a stage, without speech, we find procession and *tableau vivant* combined; the main emphasis is on civic history, but there are suggestions of symbolism and allegory.

We may remark that the symbolism and allegory are saved for the " grand pageant " at the end — mythology and history dividing the interest of the main part of the show.

The Ebb-Tide

The Barber-Surgeons " went out " on Lord Mayor's day for the last time in 1785.[1] I have found few references to the Lord Mayor's procession for the closing years of this century; but there are some interesting glimpses of the banquet to be gleaned from the MS. *Proceedings*[2] of the Committees for conducting the entertainments on this civic festival. Although not strictly connected with the subject, some of these items — hitherto unpublished — may be included here. In 1790, the committee "resolved that a card of Invitation [to the dinner] be sent to the Right Honble Edmund Burke, Esqr."[3] The waits — whose duties are not specified—received ten guineas; and the total cost of the celebration — most of which was for the dinner — was £1055, 19*s*. 9*d*.[4]

A MS. " Minute Book " preserved in the Guildhall Library gives many details concerning the procedure on the Lord Mayor's day during the last decade

[1] See Young, p. 421; and cf. below, p. 125.

[2] See the Bibliography, where these volumes are mentioned under this head.

[3] MS. *Proceedings* for this year, p. 21.

[4] *Ibid.*, p. 30. Mr. Jenkins seems to have provided only the music for the ball (*ibid.*, p. 13).

of the eighteenth century; there is no pageantry, in the strict sense, though the water processions were kept up regularly during these years.[1] On 4 October, 1791, " there being a sufficient number of Members present to form a Court of Assistants, tho' no such Court was called, the Master took the sense of the Members present, as an adjournment from the last Court of Assistants, whether the Company should go out in the usual procession the ensuing Lord Mayor's day, when on the question being put, the same was resolved in the negative." [2]

The expenses of the Lord Mayor's Day celebration in 1794, as recorded in the MS. *Proceeedings* of that year, amounted to £962, 16*s.* 7*d.*, of which the mayor paid £481, 8*s.* 3½*d.*, and each of the sheriffs £240, 14*s* 1¾*d.* Again no mention of pageantry is made; but the City Waits contracted " to provide a good Band of Music to attend the Lord Mayor and Company during the procession by Land and Water for the Sum of £8, 8*s.* And also to provide 18 Persons to play in the different Parts of the Hall during the Ball, and to continue playing untill the Company choose to leave off Dancing, for the Sum of £18, 18*s.*, making in the whole, £27, 6*s.*" [3] At the meeting of the committee in the Guildhall on 16 October, 1795, " Mr. Jenkins attended and contracted with the Committee to provide a good Band of Music to attend the Lord Mayor & Company during the Procession by Land and Water; and also to provide 10 Persons to Play in the different parts of the Hall during the Ball . . . for the Sum of £27, 6*s.* in the whole." [4] There is no mention of pageantry; the total cost of the celebration was £1011, 1*s.* 3*d.*[5]

In 1801, " Messrs. Ballet & Nash, City Waits, attended, & agreed to furnish 8 performers to play to & from Westminster for 8 Guineas, & 18 Performers to play for the Dancers in the several Rooms till dismist by Committee for 18 Guineas." [6] At the meeting of 27 October, 1801, " Mr. Mountague attended, and stated to the Committee that it was the wish of the Lord Mayor that a transparency should be exhibited in the Guildhall on Lord Mayor's day, that he the Lord Mayor had consulted the Sheriffs who said they should concur in anything that might be adopted by this Committee.

" Resolved. That this Committee approve the design marked no. 2 (representing Peace descending attended by Genii to bestow her inestimable blessings on the Four Quarters of the World) as fit for the transparency that the same be painted by Mr. Smirke,[7] & that he be paid for the same the Sum of 30 Guineas.

---

[1] Cf. this MS., pp. 18–28.

[2] From the Barber-Surgeons' records, cited by Young, p. 235.

[3] MS. referred to, fol. 6.

[4] *Proceedings* for this year, fol. 4.

[5] *Ibid.*, fol. 17.

[6] *Proceedings* of the Committee for this year, fol. 7. In 1801, as in the past, another band was hired for the dinner.

[7] Perhaps he who had planned the pantomime of 1783 (see above, p. 101); Peace and the Four Quarters of the World had appeared as living figures in more than one seventeenth-century Lord Mayor's Show.

"Resolved. That the word PEACE be exhibited in White Lamps over the Sheriffs Hustings." These entries show the development — or deterioration — from the pageant-car, with its living figures, to the painted transparency.

At the meeting of 6 November, 1801, it was "Resolved, that the Chairman & Secretary be desired to procure vocal performers on the best terms they can." It is recorded under date of 9 November, "The Lord Mayor, Aldermen & Sheriffs &c departed to Westm^r about 12 o'Clock when the Comm^ee proceeded to clear the Hall of Interlopers, & secure all the avenues, having previously badged the several attendants engaged for the service of the day. . . At three o'clock the Doors were opened & the company began to assemble, the Committee receiving them at the entrance, with their Wands decorated with Olive Branches, as a symbol of the restoration of Peace. The Lord Mayor, Aldermen and Sheriffs arrived about ½ past Four: & were followed by the Great Officers of State &c dinner was served at Six, to a Company as numerous as ever assembled at Guildhall: in fact the unusual splendor of the show; the fineness of the day, & the happy return of Peace, all contributed to invite those, whose situation in life entitled them to a seat; or whose interest could procure them a Ticket, to be present at the celebration of that day when the Chief Magistrate of the first City in the British Empire began the exercise of his magisterial functions. . .

"The company at the Sheriffs Hustings were much gratified by the melodious Voice of Mr. Incledon, who kindly & freely gave his assistance at a very short notice to forward the general harmony. . . The company continued enjoying the festive Dance, &c. with the utmost hilarity till ½ past 3 o'clock when, the last party separated; & the Committee having seen the hall cleared & perfectly secure from Fire retired to their respective habitations." [1]

The "order of procession" for the proclamation of peace, 28 April, 1802,[2] seems to include no pageants. The carriages of various city officials appeared, however, and the occasion may have resembled the annual civic show, which seems to have lost almost all — if not all — of its pageantic features. The transparency of 1801, and the olive-branched wands of the Committee, brought allegory and symbolism inside the Guildhall — a noteworthy fact.

Bell's Weekly Messenger for Sunday, 11 November, 1804,[3] recounts the mayoralty procession of that year. "The Goldsmiths' Company took precedence of the others in consequence of the Lord Mayor belonging to it. This Company put themselves to an additional expense on the occasion by introducing about twenty men . . . in full bottomed wigs and black cloaks, with cocked hats, and wearing round their necks gilt chains. The novelty of this exhibition, which was formerly a usual appendage to the Company, but long since discontinued, attracted general notice." Here we find a suggestion of history behind the dressing-up which must represent more than a costume-ball if it is to be real pageantry.

---

[1] MS. *cit.*, fol. 26 f.

[2] Preserved in the Guildhall (*Broadsides 11–13*).

[3] Cited by Prideaux, ii, p. 308.

1809 — The Usual Preparations; and the Rudeness of a Great Man.

At a meeting of the Lord Mayor's and Sheriffs' Committee held on 21 October, 1809,[1] " Mr. Warren of the West London Militia attended and was directed to supply a Band of 14 Musicians to attend the Lord Mayor in going to & returning from the water side which he agreed to do for the Sum of £8, 8*s*. . ." At the meeting of 31 October, " The Secretary was requested to write to Mr. Wm Taylor to request his Attendance on the ensuing Lord Mayor's Day as a Vocal Performer,"[2] and on 7 November it was " resolved that Mr. John Hayne have a personal ticket as a Gentleman qualified to assist in the vocal Performances."[3]

A parenthetical record may be made of the fact that in the committee's list of " Noblemen & Gentlemen who did not return any answer " to the invitation to the banquet, occurs the name of the " Rt Honble R. B. Sheridan."

1815 — Relics of Waterloo Exhibited

The year of Waterloo saw the revival of a figure not uncommon in the older pageantry, — the " armed man." The author of *Civic Honours*[4] tells us that " at the last Lord Mayor's Day, [1815] independently of two persons in complete armour, and a third partially armed, representing ancient Knights, with their attendants, 'squires, heralds, standard-bearers, &c. the procession was rendered very interesting by small parties of horse soldiers, arrayed as curiassiers, (*sic*), in the spoils so bravely won on the preceding 18th of June, at the ever-memorable battle of Waterloo! "[5] From this time on, the " armed man " becomes a common figure in these processions for many years; he is given no proper name, and can be regarded only as the skeleton of pageantic chivalry, or the shade of " pageantized " romance; but his direct ancestry seems to be in the Armorers' trade-figure.

In 1816, a precept of the Mayor[6] provides for the show, announcing the route of the procession, and forbidding squibs or other fireworks.[7] It further provides

[1] See the *Proceedings* of this year, p. 7.

[2] *Ibid.*, p. 21.

[3] *Ibid.*, p. 30. The names of four " vocal performers " — Messrs. Maynard, Ingle, Taylor and Terrail — are recorded on p. 32.

[4] This volume, published at London in 1816, is recorded in the Bibliography. The colored frontispiece of the book shows the men in armor, the Lord Mayor's Coach, and a bit of the crowd, in a drawing done after the style of Cruikshank.

[5] *Op. cit.*, p. 19. Mr. Marriott, whose name appears frequently in later *Proceedings* of Committees, received £80 for these " men in armour." (See the MS. " Expences at Guildhall on Lord Mayor's Day 1815," now preserved in that Library (MS. 148). No other sign of pageantry appears on the accounts; the total expenses amounted to £1448, 0*s*. 1*d*.

[6] Dated 24 October.

[7] This is preserved in the *Taylor Collection of Broadsides* (no. 138) in the Guildhall Library. (Cf. above, p. 14, n. 1.) It answers Herbert's query, (ii, p. 411, n. 2), as to whether

for the decoration of " the Fronts and Balconies of [the] Houses," with the best hangings or ornaments of the inhabitants; but makes no mention of pageants.

J. G. Nichols [1] records that when the mayor in 1816 returned from Westminster by land, the " High Steward of the City and Liberties of Westminster (Lord Viscount Sidmouth) thought proper to protest against such deviation from the usual practice, ' in order that the same course may not be drawn into precedent, and adopted on any future occasion.' "

" In 1817, the death of the Princess Charlotte of Wales having occurred three days before Lord Mayor's Day, the procession was omitted." [2]

1821 — Men in Armor and Mr. Marriott

The Secretary of the Committee for 1821 reported " that the Sub-committee had seen Mr. Marriott who informed them that it would not be consistent to have the Men in Armour without military, neither could he suggest any other procession but at an expence of at least from Three to Four hundred pounds." [3] Later

" Mr. Marriott . . . stated that he should be ready to provide Five Men in Armour with their Attendants on Lord Mayor's Day, the two in addition to the three which he had for several years furnished on previous occasions. One of the additional suits of armour was of a most splendid appearance, sent to this Country for the use of the Champion at the Coronation, but not used. The other new suit would be of a novel and striking description never introduced before. Mr. Marriott stated that in addition to his own men (about Twenty) he should require the attendance of Thirty six Mounted, Ten dismounted cavalry, Twelve Trumpeters, Two Kettle Drummers and six Chargers. Mr. Marriott said that the Charge for the Five Men would be One Hundred and ten Guineas. If only three, Eighty Guineas." And it was

" . . . Resolved. That the Lord Mayor Elect and the Sheriffs be requested to afford this Committee an opportunity of having a conference on the propriety of having the Men in Armour with the usual attendance of a Military before the final orders be given to Mr. Marriott." [4] At the next meeting of the Committee, the Lord Mayor-elect " stated that from a

---

the precept of 1768 " be not the last instance of the lord mayor's commanding the companies by precept."

A similar precept (no. 139 in the same collection) repeats practically the very words of the 1816 order; it is dated 25 October, 1826. That of 16 October, 1827 (no. 140) is phrased in much the same language — both forbid " squibs, serpents, or other fireworks." That of 29 September, 1830 (no. 142) to the Companies, does not mention fireworks; but that to the Aldermen of the different Wards, under the same date (no. 143 in the Taylor Collection) repeats the precepts of 1826 and 1827.

[1] *Lond. Pag.*, p. 121, (giving no authority). [2] *Ibid.*, *loc. cit.*

[3] *Proceedings* for this year, p. 17. On p. 13, we find that " Mr. Stokes was ordered to attend the procession to and from Westminster with his band (in all twelve persons) and to receive Eight Guineas. He was desired to take care that they all appeared in Uniform and were clean in their appearance."

[4] *Ibid.*, p. 21.

communication which he had with the proper authorities, he clearly understood that no Troops would be granted but the usual Guards. That in consequence of the opinion of the Sheriffs as well as that of this Committee that it would be improper to introduce those Troops and considering that it would not be consistent to have Men in Armour without the attendance of a Military he wished that they should not be engaged for the ensuing Lord Mayor's Day "[1] Whereupon, it was unanimously resolved, "That Mr. Marriott be informed that the Committee cannot enter into any Arrangement for the Attendance of the Men in Armour in the procession on the ensuing Lord Mayor's Day," — to which an amendment was made, adding the words, "At present."[2]

At a later meeting, "the Sheriffs attended and stated that they had seen the Lord Mayor Elect with whom they had again left the decision of having the Men in Armour with the usual Troops, who had informed them that he had had an interview with Lord Sidmouth on the subject of the attendance of the Military with the Men in Armour. His Lordship had referred to a letter sent last year in which it was stated that the Military could not be granted in any future year and that the said Resolution would be adhered to on the present occasion. That in consequence the Lord Mayor had acquainted the Sheriffs that he would agree to the Men in Armour being employed in such a way as the same could be arranged.

"Mr. Marriott having been sent for, attended and stated that last week he had received positive orders from the Lord Mayor Elect to get ready the Men in Armour in the usual way, his Lordship undertaking to obtain the attendance of the necessary Troops. In consequence of which he had been making preparations accordingly when on Saturday Evening last the Lord Mayor called in his way to Lord Sidmouth and promised to let Mr. Mariott (*sic*) know on his return the result of his application. . . Mr. Marriott was . . . asked whether he could provide the attendance of Four Men in Armour with suitable attendants at an expence of Eighty to One hundred pounds. He informed the Committee that it would be in his power and the said proposal received the approbation and sanction of both the Sheriffs . . ."[3]

At the next meeting of the Committee, the Lord Mayor-elect "stated that he never gave any positive directions to Mr. Mariott (*sic*), but only conditional orders on his own responsibility in case the usual number of Troops could be spared. The Lord Mayor Elect however not having been able to obtain the Troops he considered that he had given no orders on the subject. His Lordship added that subsequently he had withdrawn his objection to having the Men in Armour without Military the Sheriffs appearing to wish to have them. The Sheriffs however having referred the subject to the Committee, . . . his Lordship upon hearing the representation Mr. Marriott had made to the Committee as to positive orders having been given to him by the Lord Mayor Elect, His Lordship had refused to give any instructions in the affair and that he had nothing to do with it."[4] So there were no Men in Armor this year.

1822 — Men in Armor Reappear

In 1822, "the Lord Mayor Elect and Sheriffs signified their wish to have the usual Procession of Men in Armour, &c. and which was left to the Com-

---

[1] *Proceedings* for this year, pp. 25 f.

[2] *Ibid.*, p. 26.

[3] *Ibid.*, pp. 44, 45.

[4] *Ibid.*, p. 52. Four "Vocal Gentlemen" were engaged as singers (p. 38); they received thirteen guineas (p. 69); Mr. Marriott received "for trouble of attendance about Men in Armour," five guineas (*ibid.*); the dinner cost £906, 19*s*. 4*d*.; and the total expenses for the Lord Mayor's Day of 1821 were £1753, 16*s*. 3*d*. (pp. 69–70).

mittee to arrange." [1] It was resolved, "That Mr. Henry Marriott be requested to attend the next Meeting of the Committee with Estimates &c. respecting the Procession with Men in Armour and their Attendants." [2] At a later meeting, "Mr. Henry Marriott attended, and stated that he should be ready to provide the Men in Armour which he had for several Years furnished on similar occasions. And he had no doubt if Application was made to the proper Authority for sufficient Troops to form the Procession they would be readily granted. It was therefore moved and resolved unanimously That Mr Henry Marriott do attend the Procession in the usual way And that the Sum of Eighty Guineas be paid him to include the whole of his Expences And in the event of Troops not being obtained to assist in the Procession Mr. Marriott undertook to form a Procession which would be satisfactory to the Committee and suitable to himself at an Expence not exceeding the Sum before mentioned." [3]

On 24 October, 1822, "Mr. Remembrancer reported That he had seen Mr. Dawson the Under Secretary of State and Colonel Haverfield who informed him that the application for the Military to attend in the Procession was forwarded to the Rt. Hon. Robert Peel the Secretary of State for the Home Department who was absent in the country, and that an Answer might be expected before the next Meeting of the Committee." [4] Peel refused to order the attendance of either the Life or the Horse Guards, referring to a precedent.[5] "In 1820 the Lord Mayor Elect was informed by Sir Herbert Taylor by direction of H. R. H. The Commander in Chief that in future it would be necessary to discontinue the Attendance of the Military and last Year no Detachment was granted," reads his postscript.

"Mr. Marriott attended the Committee when he was informed that the Military would not be granted to assist in forming the Procession. He stated to the Committee that he had been preparing the necessary requisites for the Procession but as there were many necessary requisites . . . to be provided in equipping a certain number of Horsemen to form a Procession which should not be deficient in splendour and appearance from any former occasion the Expence would amount to £100 which the Committee agreed to give him.

"Mr. Marriott requested the use of the Magistrates Room and the adjoining Room in Guildhall Yard for the purpose of equipping his Men and depositing the Articles required for the Procession on the 9th Novr. which the Committee engaged to obtain for him for that purpose." [6]

---

[1] *Proceedings* for this year, p. 2.

[2] *Ibid.*, p. 4.

[3] *Ibid.*, pp. 13 f.

[4] *Ibid.*, p. 25.

[5] *Ibid.*, p. 33.

[6] *Ibid.*, pp. 33 f. Mr. Marriott was paid £100 for "Men in Armour as pr. Contract," and eight guineas for extra trumpeters and kettle drum (p. 75). Four men were engaged as "Vocal Performers" for the banquet (p. 28); they received — together — nine guineas (p. 76). The total cost of the entertainment this year was £1718, 2*s*. 8*d*. (*ibid.*).

At the end of the volume of minutes of the 1823 committee is preserved the "Order of Procession" for the 1822 Lord Mayor's Day parade. Besides the usual marching guilds, etc., it included an "Ancient Herald" and three "Ancient Knights," with their attendants — armorers, trumpeters, standard-bearers, and esquires, with yeomen of the guard. "The Suit of Brass Armour, worn by the First Knight," says the *Order of Procession*, "is the property of Mr. MARRIOTT. — The Suit of Steel Armour, worn by the second Knight is HENRY THE FIFTH'S, from the Tower. — The suit of Brass Armour, worn by the third Knight, is Mr. ELLISTON'S; all the Half Armour and Banners, are the property of Mr. MARRIOTT, and the former were taken from the French, at the Battle of Waterloo.

"The Arrangements of that part of the Procession connected with the Armour are under the direction of Mr. MARRIOTT."

Knights and attendants were inserted in this procession, like the modern "parenthetical" pageant. They were preceded by the Merchant-Taylors, in carriages, with their banners and attendants; they were followed by the Mayor, Sheriffs, and other civic officials. "At the Obelisk, Bridge Street, the Procession on its Return from Westminster in the State Barges of the several Companies of London, will be joined by the Carriages of the Royal Family . . . and other persons of Distinction invited to the *Banquet at Guildhall*." [1]

1823 — ARMED MEN THE ONLY PAGEANTIC FEATURE

The MS. minutes of the 1823 Committee record that on 13 October Mr. Marriott was called in; and "not being prepared with a Plan of the Procession for the Men in Armour, It was refer'd to a Sub Committee consisting of The Chairman, Secretary, Mr. Waithman, Mr. Whittaker and Mr. Richardson to arrange the same with him." [2] On 30 October, a letter from Mr. Elliston was read, "granting the use of his Armour to the Committee." At the same meeting, Messrs. Waithman and Whittaker reported that they had made the necessary arrangements for the procession of the Men in Armour, except the Trumpeters." [3]

A manuscript in the Guildhall Library, called *Ceremonies Observed by the Lord Mayor of London, 1824–25*, notes a water-procession on Lord Mayor's Day, 1824, to Westminster and return (fols. 7 and 8); no mention is made of land

[1] From the *Order of Procession*. Cf. on this year's show, Fairholt, pt. i, p. 137; in a note, he questions the authenticity of the ascription of armor in the Tower to Henry V.

[2] *Proceedings* for this year, p. 12.

[3] *Ibid.*, p. 32. "Humphries, for Men in Armour" sent in a bill of £33, 19*s*. (p. 56); it was resolved, "That in consequence of the Vocal Gentlemen who engaged to attend not being in the Hall in proper time, only Nine Guineas be given to them one of the Gentlemen not arriving 'till 9 o'Clock — the others not before 7 o'Clock" (p. 59). The total cost of the entertainment this year was £1237, 15*s*. 2*d*. (p. 58).

pageants, but Fairholt[1] says that the armor of 1822 appeared again. I have not seen any minutes of the Committee for this year. In 1825, at the meeting of the Committee on 7 October, it was resolved to provide four "Vocal Gentlemen," and to request Mr. Marriott's attendance, "on the subject of the Men in Armour."[2] A "transparency" at £2, 10*s*., was voted, to be provided by Mr. Pattrick;[3] and on 31 October, "the contractor for the Men in Armour attended to know what colour the Lord Mayor's Ribbons would be on the 9th November. Resolved, That he do attend tomorrow with a particular of the procession for the use of the Committee."[4] Mr. Callahan received "for Men in Armour and procession" £71, 8*s*.[5]

Armed men, or knights, and their attendants, appeared in other mayoralty shows of the period[6] — the only trace of pageantry we find. In 1827, as we have noted,[7] the two giants appeared; the *Order of Procession* for 1828[8] shows the usual guild-members, and four "ancient knights" preceded by two "ancient heralds." The humorous verses, published in 1830 under the name of "Thomas Dybdynne," and entitled, *A Ryghte Sorroweful Tragyke Lamentacyonne for ye losse of my Lorde Mayor his Daye! which was to have byn on ye ix of Novembyr MDCCCXXX, But dydd nevyr see ye Lychte, beyng Smothyred lyke unto a Fovle Abortyonne*, suggest that perhaps no show was given this year.

1833 — Mr. Marriott and the Committee; the Armed Men Again

The MS. *Minutes* of the Committee for 1833, under date of 1 November, record that

Mr. Marriott having been called in was requested to inform the Committee whether that part of the procession under his direction was equal to former years, replied that it was not; that in former years there were more Troops, Heralds, and Trumpeters, which gave to that part of the Pageant a more imposing appearance.

Mr. Figgins inquired what would be the additional expense of the necessary Heralds and Trumpeters, and how many more Troops would be required.

Mr. Marriott replied that in all about 25 Persons; that the expense would be about Twenty Pounds, and that the Pageant would be increased about one third. [It was thereupon resolved,] That Mr. Marriott do cause the said additions to be made and that his arrangements do equal in Splendour any former years.

That for the said additional improvements his contract be increased from Eighty Pounds to One Hundred Pounds.

---

[1] *L. M. Pag.*, pt. i, p. 137.

[2] *Proceedings* for this year, fol. 5.

[3] *Ibid.*, fol. 28.

[4] *Ibid.*, fol. 34.

[5] *Ibid.*, fol. 60; the total expenses were £1819, 11*s*. 4*d*. (fol. 61). Fairholt, pt. i, pp. 137 f., records that five knights appeared this year, in modern armor.

[6] Cf. Fairholt, pt. i, p. 138.

[7] See above, vol. i, p. 63.

[8] Preserved in Fairholt's *Scrapbook*, vol. ii, now in the library of the Soc. Antiq. Cf. the precepts for 1826, 1827, and 1830, mentioned above, p. 14, n. 1, and p. 104, n. 7.

A "Crown and Rays," which was the transparency the year before, was used again this year; the committee hired it for ten guineas and had it fixed in the East Window, and taken down, ("the same as last year,") — the price being for one night only.[1] On the 4th,

Mr. Depy Alderman referd to the additional engagement made by this Committee with Mr. Marriott in respect of adding to the procession a larger proportion of Troops and Heralds to precede the knights in armour, and Mr. Remembrancer having stated that any Troops required for the Procession had always been applied for by him, as from and for the accomodation of the Lord Mayor, and the copy of a letter from Sir Geo. Naylor, Garter King at Arms, addressed to Mr. Town Clerk dated[2] By desire of the Duke of Norfolk the Earl Marshall (requesting Mr. Town Clerk to lay the same before the proper Authorities) requesting therein that the use of Heralds wearing Tabords may be discontinued as tending to bring a very ancient service of His Majesty's Household into ridicule,[2] having been read from the minutes of the proceeding of the Committee conducting the entertainment for the 9th of Novr. as also a resolution of that Committee thereon

[Resolved] That for the reasons above given the Committee rescind the resolution of the 1st of Novr. in respect of increasing that portion of the pageant under Mr. Marriott's direction and that the contract do remain as originally agreed upon at the sum of £80. 0. 0.

The Remembrancer "was directed to make the necessary arrangements for the attendance of the marine Boys"; and on the 5th it was resolved that a dinner be provided for the forty boys who were to receive each a shilling in addition.[3]

The *Order of Procession* for this year is inserted in the MS. minutes, under 9 November; it included, beside the usual marching companies, three "Ancient Knights" with attendants. From the Guildhall, the procession went to the Tower, thence to Westminster by water; returning, the mayor landed at Blackfriars.

1837 — The First Year of Victoria's Reign

On the first Lord Mayor's Day after her accession, Queen Victoria dined at the Guildhall, according to custom.[4] Coming from Westminster in regal splendor, the young sovereign was met at Temple Bar by Mayor and Aldermen in all their civic glory; the senior scholar of Christ's Hospital delivered an address

---

[1] *Ibid.* The pages of this volume are not numbered; these arrangements were made on the first of November.

[2] Blank left in the MS.

[3] The cost of this item was £8, 16*s*. There were forty-one boys. Ten singers were agreed on at the meeting of 7 November; for his procession, Mr. Marriott received £85; the total cost of the entertainment was £2174.

[4] For particulars of this occasion, see a collection made by F. Hobler in 1838, now preserved in the Guildhall Library. It contains some rare folders and plates — many of them colored — tickets, *menus*, &c., together with the "Report to the Court of Common Council, from the Royal Entertainment Committee, presented 14 December 1837," and an *Order of Procession* (bound opposite p. 29). A rare panoramic view of the procession may be found in the Guildhall Library; a long account of the occasion appeared in the London *Times* for

at the door of the royal carriage,[1] but there was no technical pageantry on this occasion. The procession was a long and brilliant one; the banquet was elaborate, and in the evening, the city was illuminated.[2]

The Show for 1839

The MS. *Minutes* of the Lord Mayor and Sheriffs' Committee for 1839 contain the usual items. On 9 October, it was resolved that " the Men in Armour be engaged as usual for the procession on Lord Mayor's day, & that Mr. Marriott do attend the next Committee meeting with his terms for providing them." [3] On 14 October, " Mr. Marriott attended & offered to provide Men in Armour with their attendants, Banners, Troops & Trumpeters, the same as usual for the amount of One Hundred Guineas.

" Resolved; That Mr. Marriott's offer be accepted." [4] The Marine Society furnished forty boys, and five officers, with a banner, for the procession; [5] and an offer from the London & Westminster Iron Steam boat Company of the gratuitous use of one of its steam boats to tow the State Barge, if necessary, to its destination, was gratefully accepted.[6]

1841 — Pageantry Reappears: a Full-Rigged Ship

Besides the " ancient knights " and their attendants, there was, in the Show for 1841, the model of an East Indiaman, fully rigged and manned, on a car drawn by six horses.[7] It will be remembered that a ship appeared in many folk-processions, " royal-entries," and in the elaborate shows of the seventeenth century. This may be the immediate ancestor of the later ships which we shall find in subsequent Lord Mayor's Shows; it is an interesting example of the

---

10 November, 1837; the " Supplementary Number " (862) of *The Mirror of Literature, Amusement and Instruction* for Saturday, 11 November, 1837, gives an abridged version of the *Times'* account, and illustrates the banquet. Pictures of the City Giants are reproduced (*ibid.*, opp. p. 319) but they do not appear to have been carried in the procession.

[1] As Victoria passed St. Mary's, the charity children sang " God Save the Queen."

[2] The editor of the *Mirror* (supplementary number, p. 321) calls this a " solemn national pageant." It may be worth noting that a " handsome three-storied booth " was erected at the west end of Cheapside, for the boys of the City of London schools. After the scholars had quitted it, " the galleries " were occupied by about five hundred members of the Sacred Harmonic Society who sang " God Save the Queen " as the sovereign returned to Buckingham Palace.

[3] *Minutes*, p. 4.

[4] *Ibid.*, pp. 11, 12. A Star was provided this year for the Guildhall (p. 25); twelve vocalists and a piano were furnished for twenty guineas (p. 12).

[5] *Ibid.*, p. 27.

[6] *Ibid.*, p. 49. The total cost of this year's celebration was £2009, 17*s.* 1*d.* (p. 76).

[7] See Fairholt, pt. i, pp. 139 and 176. The *Order of Procession* for 1841 is reprinted, pt. i, pp. 175 ff.

resurrection of what we might call the "body" of pageantry, when the "knights" — representing nothing in particular — are mere masqueraders.

1842 — An Elaborate Show

In the *Illustrated London News* for 12 November, 1842, may be found an account of the Lord Mayor's Show for that year. The 9th of November was the anniversary of the birth of the Prince of Wales; and the double celebration was accompanied by the ringing of bells within and without the City. "The morning, too, was unusually fine, and altogether a Lord Mayor's Show has seldom . . . presented a gayer appearance than that of Wednesday. It is to be deeply regretted, however, that the festive procession did not pass over without a very serious accident to one of the 'men in armour,' who . . . fell from his horse near Blackfriars-bridge and broke his thigh."[1] The "men in armor" were again the only pageantic features; and the barges — instead of being rowed to Westminster by watermen — were towed by steamboats.

A short story by one Abraham Elder, entitled *Tommy Doddy: or the Grand Pageant*, appeared in *Bentley's Miscellany* for this year.[2] It describes, in the manner of historical fiction, a dinner given to the King and Queen, in 1633, at the Merchant-Taylors' Hall; the banquet was preceded by a "pageant," and the "hero" of the story is the son of the artisan who furnished the effigies. Neither as history nor as fiction is the production of great value; but it shows an interest in the civic pageants of the past felt in 1842, and is a rare instance of fiction based upon pageantry.

---

[1] Nov. 12, 1842, p. 424. The procession by water, from London Bridge, is pictured on this page; but the picture does not agree with the text, which (noting a departure from precedent in the embarcation at the Southwark end of London bridge) continues: "Here the 'silent highway' was witness to another departure from established rule, for some of the barges, in the place, as has been the custom 'any time these hundred years past,' of being propelled in the true and stately style of civic dignity, viz., by powerful sweeps in the hands of the renowned Thames watermen, were made fast to steamers, and 'tugged' up to Westminster . . . The state barge ran aground, and, as the tide was unusually low, a quarter of an hour elapsed before she could be got off . . . The appearance of the gilded barges on the water, when completely under weigh, was really very grand and imposing, particularly the state barge and the barge of the Goldsmiths' Company, which shone like immense masses of floating gold."

Pictures of the water-procession of 1843, the barge, and the show, with a humorous article, (illustrated by caricatures), on the "Characters" of the Lord Mayor's Day, may be found in the London *Pictorial News* for 11 November, 1843, pp.184 and 188. The official program of the show is printed, *ibid.*, p. 186; it included an "ancient Herald" and three "ancient Knights."

[2] See this publication, ix, pp. 281 f. I am indebted to Professor Kittredge for calling this to my attention.

WESTMINSTER ABBEY AND BRIDGE — THE DEBARKATION ON LORD MAYOR'S DAY

1845 — The Goldsmiths' Barge Used for the Last Time

Unmoved by the appreciation of the *Illustrated London News* in 1842, "on the 29th of October, 1845, it was resolved [by the Goldsmiths] 'That the Company do not join the procession on Lord Mayor's day by land or water,' and the barge was not used again." [1]

In 1847, Marriott and Smith received £105 for providing a "procession of knights, &c." [2] Four "ancient knights," an "ancient herald," with armourers, esquires, and standard-bearers appeared.[3] In 1848, it was resolved that the "Men in Armour be engaged as usual for the Procession on Lord Mayor's Day, and that Mr. Marriott of Fleet Street do attend the next committee meeting with his terms for providing them." [4] His terms (including a dinner for the mounted band) were £110, which were accepted.[5] The Order of Procession is bound with the minutes of the Committee [6] — four "ancient knights," fully attended, with an "ancient Herald, Habited in a Tabard," followed the marching companies and preceded the Lord Mayor: again the "parenthetical" character of this part of the show is to be noted.[7]

The minutes of the Committee for 1849 [8] give us details on the show for this year. It was resolved "that the procession take place as usual . . . and be as similar as possible to that of last year." [9] The Committee further resolved, "That the Fairlop Boat be engaged for the occasion; that the Men in Armour be engaged as usual for the Procession, and that Mr. Marriott [10] be written to attend the next Committee Meeting with his terms for providing them; that Mr. Remembrancer do apply to the Commander in Chief for the usual number of Troops and a Mounted Band for the Street Procession; that the Remembrancer do also make the usual application to the Board of Ordnance for Armour and

---

[1] *Prideaux*, ii, pp. 318 f. The "man in brass" and two "ancient knights" are pictured in the *Illustrated London News* of 9 November, 1844.

[2] See the MS. accounts for this year, in Guildhall MS. 149.

[3] Cf. *Illus. Lond. News*, 13 November, 1847, p. 308.

[4] MS. Minutes of the Committee for Conducting the Entertainment at Guildhall on Lord Mayor's Day, 1848, fol. 4.

[5] *Ibid.*, fol. 9. The route of the procession to and from Blackfriars Bridge is recorded (fol. 11); for the evening, Mr. Jolley offered to furnish twelve voices — three trebles (ladies) three altos, three tenors, and three basses — and to preside at the piano, for twenty guineas, — which offer was accepted (fol. 12). The expenses this year were £2471, 9*s.* (fol. 54).

[6] *Ibid.*, fol. 19. The bill for the 1848 "men in armor" was receipted by Henry Marriott. (*Ibid.*, fol. 58).

[7] Cf. the Shows for 1822, 1907, &c.

[8] Guildhall MS. 899.

[9] *MS. cit.*, pp. 6 f.

[10] Mr. Henry Marriott, for providing Men in Armour with Attendants, etc., received £115, 16*s.* (*ibid.*, p. 77).

Flags to be placed in Guildhall on Lord Mayor's Day; that the Remembrancer do apply to the Clerks of the Company's (*sic*) of which the Lord Mayor and Sheriffs are Members to ascertain whether they will attend in the Procession. Also to apply to the Marine Society for 40 Boys to join the Procession.

"That the Chairman be requested to provide a Dinner for the Boys . . . at Masons Hall Tavern at 2/6*d*. per head, and pay the usual gratuity of 1/ to each Boy...

"That Mr. Rathbone of 7 Portland Place, and Mr. J. Smithers of No. 4 Gregory Street, Pimlico, be applied to, requesting them to attend the next Committee to tender for providing the usual Band and Trumpeters in the Guildhall."[1]

The route of the procession was fixed as follows:[2] "From Guildhall through Gresham Street East to Basinghall Street, Fore Street, Moorgate Street, Princes Street, Cornhill, Gracechurch Street, and take water at London Bridge and to return from Blackfriars Bridge, Bridge Street, Ludgate Hill, St. Paul's Churchyard, Cheapside, King Street to Guildhall."

At a meeting of the Committee on 7 November, "the Barge Master attended and stated that in consequence of the Tide being low at the time intended for the Embarkation of the Procession it might be necessary to engage a Steam Boat to assist.

"Resolved — That the Secretary write to the Superintendent of the Iron Steam Boat Company to attend the next meeting of the Committee at 2 o'Clock.

"That Mr. Searle the Bargemaster be allowed the sum of £5 to be paid to the City Watermen as usual."[3]

1850 — A Change Made in the Show: Godwin's Letter

In 1850, George Godwin addressed a letter to the Lord Mayor-elect, giving suggestions for the improvement of the Show.[4] In view of its antiquity, he said, more taste and invention should take the place of dull routine; he suggests "emblems and works of art, accordant with its ancient character, and worthy of the present time. In lieu of the men in mock armour, who have had a long run, you might introduce, say three compositions typical of manufactures, agriculture, and the arts; and do honour, if it were by but a series of banners, to the great minds that have taught and raised the world, and to the past worthies

[1] Guildhall MS. 899, pp. 7–9.

[2] *Ibid.*, p. 28.

[3] *Ibid.*, pp. 43 f. At the end of the MS. may be found copies of the various bills. Twelve vocalists — as in 1848 — were provided at a cost of £21 (pp. 13 and 73); various military bands and trumpeters — both for the procession and banquet — were employed; the dinner — exclusive of wine — cost £1015; and the total cost of the entertainment amounted to £2366, 7*s.* 7*d.*, of which the mayor paid £1100, the two sheriffs £550 each, and the City Lands Committee £200.

A copy of these minutes, with an *Order of Procession* may be found in Guildhall MS. 35.

[4] The letter is preserved in the Guildhall. (See Bibliography, *s. v.* Godwin.)

who have specially served, adorned or otherwise improved the City. 'Peace has its victories as well as war.' . . "

This letter seems to have had an effect; the *Morning Post* and the *Times* for 2 November, 1850, announced: "The streets of the City will present a very curious and interesting scene on the approaching Lord Mayor's Day. Amongst the changes which are to be introduced upon that occasion in the great civic procession, will be the following appropriate substitutes for the trumpery exhibition of the men in armour at the head of the cavalcade. . ." The *Globe* of 7 November, 1850, foretells the changes in the procession, and observes: "It will be seen that the committee have most judiciously dispensed with the attendance of the farcical-looking 'ancient Knights, mounted and armed *cap-a-pie*, in suits of polished steel armour, and plumed,' and filled up the hiatus with something more pleasingly figurative of England's glory." [1]

Allegory and Symbolism Revived

"The New Lord Mayor's Show, 1850," is pictured in the *Illustrated London News* for 9 November, 1850; after musicians and trumpeters came Peace, mounted on a white horse; she was followed by Africa, Europe, America, and Asia, also mounted and appropriately dressed. Then came various animals — a horse, a camel, an elephant, and two deer — bearing fruits and produce of the different continents; then horses, bearing burdens representing Industry, the Arts, Manufactures, Commerce; and finally a car, drawn by six horses, representing a barge, manned by four sailors; Happiness sat therein on the world, Britannia at her feet. After this, soldiers and civic officials; then the Mayor in his coach.[2]

John Ashton [3] records this Show of 1850 from his own recollections of it. Its "novelty" commenced after the appearance of the late Lord Mayor. "First of all came Peace,[4] white-robed and white-winged, on a white charger . . . and in her train came Europe, Asia, Africa and America on horse-back." Then the animals above-mentioned, representing the four continents — a horse, carrying a trophy of all the arms of Europe; a camel for Asia, an elephant for Africa,

[1] The "pleasant change" in the Show for this year is recorded in the *Gent. Mag.* for December, 1850, p. 630.

[2] This *Illus. Lond. News* is preserved in Fairholt's *Scrapbook*, in the Soc. Antiq. library, vol. ii. A contemporary *Order of Procession* may also be found there, as well as in the Harvard Library. This shows no car, and mentions six "ancient knights" mounted and fully armed, each attended by two mounted squires bearing his battle-axe and mace. There seems to have been no water-procession this year, the route to Westminster being from Guildhall through Gresham-street, Princes-street, Lombard, Gracechurch, Leadenhall, Fenchurch, Gracechurch streets, Cannon-street East and West, St. Paul's Churchyard, Ludgate-hill, Fleet-street, and the Strand; the return was made through the Strand, Fleet-street, Ludgate-hill, St. Paul's Churchyard, Cheapside, and King-street to Guildhall.

[3] *Lord Mayor's Show*, p. 8.

[4] The show preceded the inauguration of the first International Exhibition in 1851.

and two deer for America; then came horses laden with attributes of Industry, Art, Commerce and Manufactures, as already related. "After this came the *pièce de résistance* of the show. A car, drawn by six cream-coloured horses, three abreast, containing four Sailors, and Britannia, most correctly habited, holding a branch of olive, whilst Happiness was seated on the summit of a huge Globe, flanked on either side by a Cornucopia."

A soliloquy by one who took the part of a "man in armor" in the mayoralty shows, lamenting his lot when these figures were abolished, appeared in *Punch* this year,[1] under the title, *The Lament of the Man in Brass.* With this show, we see the first sign of the new birth — a reappearance of the elements of the pageantic "triumph" at its height. The doom of the "armed man" has sounded.

But *Punch's* lament was a bit premature; in 1851, twenty-three "knights in armour" accompanied the Lord Mayor in procession.[2] Owing to the death of the Duke of Wellington, there was no show in 1852; and in 1853, the men in armor were replaced by personification and pageantic allegory.

1853 — More Personification

"... For reasons well-known to everybody, there has been an interregnum of twenty-four instead of twelve months since the last Lord Mayor's Show paraded the streets of London. ... Alderman Sidney, following in the footsteps of his aldermanic brother Musgrove, has lopped off the absurd portions of the spectacle, such as the knights in armour and other things equally ridiculous; and taking a hint from the more tasteful public processions in France and Belgium, has replaced them by picturesque personifications of 'Justice,' 'Industry,' 'Peace and Prosperity,' and so forth, and by living representations of the inhabitants of all foreign countries.." [3]

The Empire for 12 November, 1853, quoting from the *Times'* account of the show, notes that "the pageant was distinguished by several attractive features," and "was, in fact, one of the most successful that has taken place for some years past. The 'show,' thanks to the coöperation of Mr. W. Cooke, of Astley's Amphitheatre, was well arranged, and in some respects picturesque ..." In the *Weekly Times* [4] we read that "the committee for conducting the proceed-

[1] See vol. xix (1850) p. 206. Cf. *ibid.*, for a humorous account of Peace, the four Continents, Happiness, and Britannia, together with the rest of the show. Both these bits of humor are illustrated by Leech.

[2] See the *Illus. Lond. News*, 15 November, 1851, p. 606.

[3] Extract from an account of the Show of 1853, which appeared in the London *Weekly Times* for 13 November, 1853, p. 729, col. 1. Cf. the London *Times* for 10 November, 1853, p. 7, col. 3, for a full description of the show; and the *Illus. Lond. News* for 12 November, 1853, p. 405, for a page-picture of the procession. The car of Justice preceded horsemen representing "the Nations" — France, Russia, Germany, Italy, Turkey, etc., — each bearing a banner of identification. A cart, drawn by oxen, contained an Australian digger, followed by country-men and maids, representing Australia; and Peace and Prosperity occupied a car drawn by nine horses.

[4] Issue cited, p. 729.

THE LORD MAYOR'S SHOW — TWO ANCIENT KNIGHTS AND THE MAN IN BRASS

ings of the day consigned the allegorical representations in the procession to Mr. Frederick Fenton, the scenic artist of Sadler's Wells Theatre. . . . The novel part of the procession, in which Mr. Cooke's equestrian troupe was seen to very great advantage, excited general admiration. . . . The representatives of North and South America were amusingly tattooed and completely covered with dabs of various paints and occasioned much merriment. What, however, brought the laughter of the people to a climax, was the Australian digger . . ."

Perhaps this figure was humorous — of the class of the older "drolls"; but he was also symbolical — a personification, as it were, of Australia, as the tattooed characters were of North and South America. All of the British public were not amused by the show, nor did they all have complimentary things to say about it; I can here only refer to various letters in the *Times*.

Objections to the Show Voiced in the "Times"

"A Curate" protests against the lavish mayoralty banquet;[1] "Prisoner" voices his complaint of the show;[2] a protest against the "continuance of an absurd and ridiculous display" appeared from the committee of the coal trade;[3] "A City Broker" asks "how long is this foolery to be permitted?"[4] A letter, signed "Viator," complains of the obstructions caused by the procession;[5] another, from a sheriff, mentions the triumph with many uncomplimentary remarks;[6] and the *Weekly Times*[7] concludes that "the utilitarian spirit must prevail at last; and as this partiality for street pageantry is on the wane throughout the whole of England — in Ireland it is put down by the strong arm of the law — we think that the Lord Mayor's day may safely be left to itself and to the growing sense of the people of London . . . The whole thing will die a natural death, or be consigned to a desuetude, the natural result of indifference."

In 1856, the last water procession took place; the last entry in the *Repertories* concerning orders regulating barges on the Lord Mayor's Day appears this year.[8] On 13 October, 1856, together with the usual precept against squibs and other fireworks, we find it ordered "that the several barges to be rowed on the River Thames on Lord Mayor's day next be rowed from Southwark bridge and back to Blackfriars bridge, in procession, according to seniority, and that they

---

[1] Journal cited, 25 October, 1853, p. 8, col. 5.

[2] *Ibid.*, 7 November, 1853, p. 7, col. 6.

[3] *Ibid.*, 9 November, 1853, p. 7, col. 6.

[4] *Ibid.*, 10 November, 1853, p. 10, col. 2. The leader (on p. 6, col. 3 of this issue) is bitter against the Show; and the *Weekly Times* for 13 November, 1853, pp. 721 and 726, mentions the performance in no very enthusiastic terms, reprinting the *Times*' opinion.

[5] The *Times* for 11 November, 1853, p. 5, col. 4.

[6] *Ibid.*, 16 November, 1853, p. 10, col. 4.

[7] In the issue for 13 November, 1853, p. 721.

[8] *Repertory* cclxi, fol. 420.

do not approach too near this City's barge, thereby to endanger the lives of the passengers."[1]

Orders against squibs and other fireworks, for keeping the streets, over which the procession is to pass, clear from obstructions, and for the usual water-procession were made in 1857;[2] but the boats do not seem to have been used. The *Illustrated London News*[3] records that

> the pageant was not of a very imposing character, being shorn of much of its wonted pomp by the absence of the usual squadrons of dragoons. In point of fact, it was little more than a string of private carriages, interspersed with a military band or two, and slightly diversified by a few men in armour from Astley's. The ceremony deviated in an important particular from those of previous years, there being no water procession. The Corporation are no longer the only conservators of the Thames, and it was therefore resolved that the route should be entirely upon land.

Conclusion

By 1857, the Show had completely fallen from its high estate — its glory is, indeed, departed. The papers call it " little more than a string of private carriages "; a few " armed men " indicate but faintly the spirit of pageantry; the water-procession — which dated from 1422 — is no more. From the time when Ned Ward penned his gentle satire, to that of the more bitter attacks of the *Times* correspondents, a spirit of ridicule hung over the Show. Gradually getting less pageantic, it became little more than a procession, the chief figure in which — from our point of view — was the " armed man " or " knight," whose immediate ancestor seems to have been the trade-figure of the Armourers' Company already " usual " in 1761.[4] A connection with history was made, in 1815 and 1822, by equipping these figures with " half-armor " taken at Waterloo, and old suits of armor from the Tower; but they seem to have excited ridicule just the same, as in 1833 we find Garter King at Arms protesting against the use of heralds with them.[5]

In 1841, a ship appeared; this was a common accompaniment of earlier shows, but such pageantic features were rare in the century and a half which lies between 1700 and 1850. In the latter year, Mr. Godwin wrote a letter which bore fruit in the pageantry of 1850; but, with the exception of the show in 1853, this stimulation was deceitful, and a relapse to " armed men " followed. Bitter were the complaints of many correspondents in the *Times* of November, 1853; the

---

[1] *Minutes . . . of the Court of Aldermen* for 1856, (London, 1856) p. 72. A model of the last State Barge, built in 1807, is in the Guildhall Museum.

[2] *Minutes . . . of the Court of Aldermen* for 1857, pp. 54 f., under date of 13 October, 1857.

[3] For 14 November, 1857, p. 494.

[4] See above, p. 95 and n. 3. As these figures represented nothing in particular, they may hardly be said to be pageantic; rather they were masqueraders, from whom, to be sure, the raw material of the pageantic " soul " is drawn.

[5] See above, p. 110.

Show, however, survived the attacks levelled against it, and — as we shall see — editorial opinion has now changed regarding it.

One important fact in the history of pageantry during this period should be emphasized; in 1783, the show was carried into the theatre, and made the basis of a pantomime. The *tableaux vivants* of this production establish a connecting link between the figures carried through the streets on floats, and the historic "living pictures" of earlier American pageantry. Much history was recalled in the 1783 pantomime; and it was not the history of any one Company (as in the Lord Mayor's Show itself) but rather of London, in which all Companies and every citizen could take a just pride. Elements of mythology, allegory, and symbolism lent their aid; and the set of the final *tableau* recalled the street-pageant, or triumphal arch, of the Elizabethan "royal-entry."

In the years following 1857, the Lord Mayor's Show struggled from the depths into which it had fallen; the course of this regeneration we shall now trace.

§ 4. THE RENAISSANCE OF THE PAGEANTIC SHOW, 1858–1919

In spite of the ridicule and anger it had excited, the Lord Mayor's Show continued to exist even after the water-procession was abolished. Together with orders against fireworks, on 19 October, 1858: "it is ordered that the Commissioner of the City Police do take effectual care that the several public streets through which the procession is to pass on Lord Mayor's day next be kept free and clear from all obstructions and hindrances to the same."[1] Of what the Show consisted, we cannot be certain; but it did not, during the next decade, free itself from the ridicule with which it was, as we have seen, often greeted during the preceding century and a half; for, in 1867 it was again subjected to

[1] *Minutes . . . of the Court of Aldermen* for 1858, pp. 56 f. (The same notice appeared in 1857.)

In *The Illustrated News of the World* for 20 November, 1858, the arrival of the procession at Westminster is pictured (p. 328). The procession this year showed "nothing novel" (*ibid.*, for 13 November, p. 307) which indicates how quickly the public had got used to the absence of a water-procession.

Regarding the disposal of the State Barge, we read in the *Minutes . . . of the Court of Aldermen* for 1859 (London, 1859), p. 21, on 22 March: "Report, General Purposes Committee, upon the reference to consider the letter from Mr. Comptroller by direction of the City Lands Committee, to ascertain whether this Court desire that the housing of the Lord Mayor's State Barge should be still continued, and recommending that the Barge should be given over to the City Lands Committee to be sold. Read, approved and ordered." (Cf. *ibid.*, p. 16.) "The last of the Company's Barges" forms the frontispiece to Prideaux, *Memorials of the Goldsmiths' Company*, vol. ii; on the barge of the Skinners' Company, see Wadmore, pp. 137 f. — after spending £257, 14*s*. on it for repairs in 1855, the Company sold it, in 1858, for £75.

satire,[1] and its abolition was threatened. More than ten years later, however, the Lord Mayor and Sheriffs' Committee was meeting; and from their manuscript *Minutes* of 1879 we get some interesting information.[2] At the meeting of 15 October, " a letter was read from the Surveyor General's Department of the War Office, acknowledging the receipt of a letter from the Remembrancer requesting the issue on loan of armour to be used in the procession on the 10th November, and in reply calling attention to a letter from that Office in 1877 pointing out that the valuable specimens of armour which were then lent had been seriously damaged, and suggesting that imitation sets of armour of modern manufacture might be obtained for future use, and asking whether the Lord Mayor could not arrange to dispense with the valuable armour asked for." [3] As men in armour were hired from Messrs. Sanger and Son, and among the terms we find " Man in armour, lance horse and cloth for horse . . . £6; for armour for horse £4, 10*s* extra; for scale armour, £4 extra," we may assume that the suggestion of the War Office was acted upon.[4]

The keepers of Epping Forest announced their intention of marching; and Mr. Hart (the Chairman of the Coal and Corn and Finance Committee) wrote to ask if " the Committee could introduce anything in the procession illustrating the purchase of Burnham Beeches by the Corporation, and suggesting that a banner or banners should be carried by hired men." [5] The Metropolitan Board of Works was invited to send a detachment of firemen to walk in the procession,[6] and the Band and Boys of the training-ship *Exmouth* were authorized to take part in it.

The Commander-in-Chief was asked to allow " about 50 of the survivors of the detachment of soldiers engaged at Rorke's Drift to attend in the procession on the ensuing Lord Mayor's Day " but the request was refused, as, with some exceptions, the defenders of Rorke's Drift were still serving abroad.[7] This is an interesting effort; for it shows a tendency to substitute actual historical figures for the allegory which used to be so common in these shows. Is not a veteran more valuable, in rousing a spirit of pride, than a draped figure representing Glory ?

---

[1] See *The Prologue and Epilogue to the Lord Mayor's Show of 1867*, signed W. H. H., but published anonymously that year, at London. This is a humorous satire on the threatened abolition of the Show, and a lament for its past glories. The pamphlet is preserved in the Guildhall Library.

[2] Guildhall MS. 517.

[3] *MS. cit.*, pp. 21 f.

[4] Twenty men in armour with horses, lances, clothes for horses, etc., at £6 apiece were hired, (*ibid.*, p. 33). The route of the procession, to and from Westminster Hall, is given (p. 30).

[5] This suggestion was adopted, (*ibid.*, p. 34).

[6] *Ibid.*, p. 34.

[7] *Ibid.*, pp. 42 and 52. No vocal music was provided for the dinner, (pp. 20 and 44.)

1881 — Pageants and International Courtesy

In 1881, there were many triumphal arches, and the decorations were unusually splendid.[1]

An elaborate and imposing structure was erected at the corner of the Royal Exchange-avenue. A large pavilion had been constructed here, in front of which the procession halted, in order that the inhabitants of the ward might present an address through their representatives to the Lord Mayor.[2] The flag of the United States was displayed at various points, and it formed a feature in the procession, being escorted by a guard of honour . . . Upon arrival at Palace Yard, Westminster, the massed bands played the American National Anthem, 'The Star-Spangled Banner' . . . The procession was this year singularly free from eccentric features, which have the one merit of pleasing the lower elements in a London mob . . . The contingent of firemen, the boys from the Netley, and the American flag, called forth general enthusiasm.

1882 — The Last Time to Westminster Hall

In 1882, the mayor went to Westminster Hall to take his oath, for the last time, although his procession has entered the neighboring city often since then. Nothing particular marked this show, which was received " with all the cheering and goodhumour which is customary." The thoroughfares were gay with flags, and many of them were spanned by triumphal arches.[3]

1883 — The Mayor Takes his Oath at the New Law Courts — The Colonies in Pageants

The next year, we find the forerunner of a new era in the history of this civic pageant. In 1883, the mayor took his oath at the new Law Courts for the first time;[4] and the procession which accompanied him

contained no men in armour, or meaningless fancy costumes, but it included Grace Darling's boat, a life-boat with its crew, and a rocket apparatus, for saving lives from shipwreck; a trophy of the Fisheries, composed of nets, spars and oars, ropes, buoys, baskets and other fishing-gear, from the late Exhibition; and several trophies of India and the Colonies, which

---

[1] Cf. the *Illus. Lond. News* for 12 November, 1881, p. 470, from which I quote.

[2] Cf. the 1913 Baynard Castle — below, p. 138.

[3] Cf. *Illus. Lond. News* for 18 November, 1882, p. 530. Perhaps the glamour of the Show this year was dimmed by the return of soldiers from the war in Egypt (cf. the progress of the Horse Guards through London, *ibid.*, for 28 October, 1882, p. 440); at any rate the Show had no new features.

[4] *The Handbook of Ceremonials*, p. 24, n. 2, records that before 1881 the Lord Mayor was, in accordance with the charter of 37 Henry III, presented to the Barons of the Exchequer, and took the oath, or declaration, in that Court. Since 1881, he has been presented to Judges of the King's Bench division, and makes the declaration before them. (This volume cites Acts 44 & 45 Vic., cap. 68, sec. 17.)

On the mayor's going to the new Law Courts for the first time, see the *Illus. Lond. News* for 17 November, 1883, p. 478; various pictures of this year's Show may be found, *ibid.*, p. 473.

were original, if not quite appropriate in design. That of " India " consisted of natives standing among palm-trees, with a stuffed tiger above, followed by two elephants; that of " Canada," a backwoodsman, amidst pine-logs and piles of corn-sacks, with beavers and bears; that of " Australia," two red-shirted station-hands, with fleeces of sheep and bags of wool; a kangaroo and an emu, and a species of pelican, being perched a little higher. The vehicles upon which these colonial " exhibits " were set up, passed along the street; and they were succeeded by one which conveyed what was supposed to be meant as a representation of the supply of frozen fresh mutton from New Zealand. This was simply a row of twenty or thirty sheep carcasses, hanging up in much the same way as they do at a butcher's shop. The Committee of the Common Council, and others, appointed by the Lord Mayor and Sheriffs to arrange the procession, had given no sanction to any such exhibition; and it was certainly not provided by any person officially connected with the New Zealand Government Agency. The remaining parts of the procession were of the ordinary character, but there was a greater show of banners than usual, and more bands of music; the engines of the Fire Brigade, with their firemen, and the sailor boys of the Exmouth, made a very good figure.[1]

1884 — A Forecast of Modern Pageantry

The emphasis which modern historical pageantry places upon the educational value of the past, is foreshadowed by the publication of a pamphlet in connection with the Lord Mayor's Show of 1884.[2] The preface of this pamphlet reads as follows: " The publication of an Historical Pamphlet containing extracts from Standard Works on matters connected with the forthcoming Procession, demands a few words of explanation. It is only natural that many readers may have forgotten some of the ' memorable incidents ' they were taught in their school days, and the ' raison d'être ' of the publication of these extracts is to recall them to their recollection by depicting some of the scenes connected with the life and history of our renowned ancestors.

" The purpose of this year's ' Show ' is to bring before the minds of the public some of the glorious traditions of our ancient city — to show how, from time almost immemorial, the Corporation has been both loyal to the Crown and true to the People."

How this purpose was carried out is told in the *Illustrated London News* for 15 November, 1884.[3] " Most of the elaborate devices of the show were illustrations of national and civic history or tradition. There was a car drawn by twelve

---

[1] *Illus. Lond. News* for 17 November, 1883, p. 478. At the banquet in the evening M. Waddington, Mr. Gladstone, and Count de Lesseps were among the speakers.

[2] Extracts from Maitland's *History of London*, Thornbury's *Old and New London*, Stow's *Survey*, Allen's *History of London*, etc., compiled by Charles G. Nottage, inform the citizens of " a few memorable incidents in our civic history." (The Rt. Hon. George S. Nottage was mayor this year.)

[3] For illustrations of the Indian Empire Trophy, the Nile Expedition Boat, the Old Bow Church as before the Great Fire, and various Kings and Queens, with Barons, Knights, and Crusaders, see this issue of the *Illus. London News*, p. 469. The citation is from pp. 469 and 470.

ponies, with Dick Whittington beside the Highgate mile-post listening to Bow bells. . . Then followed a model of Bow Church as it was in old times with bell-ringers and a banner, and the figure of Sir Richard Whittington in all his civic dignity. William the Conqueror was represented, Richard Cœur de Lion, Richard II and Queen Elizabeth, all mounted and costumed after the habits in which they lived. . . Lord Mayor Walworth standing over the slain Wat Tyler provoked groans and hisses. A fairer spectacle was the car, drawn by four horses, carrying a raised daïs, upon which was a casket containing a fac-simile of the City's First Charter, A.D. 1067, guarded by citizens. . . A Nile boat, similar to those sent out to Lord Wolseley, was exhibited properly manned. . . There was a fine herd of camels, and, in recognition of our Indian Empire, Mr. Sanger provided also elephants ridden by representatives of Rajahs, and a car containing a picturesque group surmounted by a figure symbolical of India. . ."

This show — having a definite purpose — foreshadows the "educational pageant" of our own day. One cannot assume that much stress was laid on historical accuracy in this procession; but the emphasis on history is noteworthy. The past of one Company was glorified often enough in the seventeenth century; here the past of the City as a whole is brought before the people; and suggestions of the imperial greatness of Britain are made in the Nile boat, and the symbolical representation of India. The figures of the sovereigns furnish an element of chronicle-history.

1885 — An Historical Element in a Trade-Pageant

In 1885, the Gold and Silver Wyre-Drawers took part in the civic procession; as this was the first time that the Company had participated in the annual show, "a great effort was made to signalize the event in a fit and worthy manner, and thanks to the . . . generosity of Past-Master George Kenning, who, at his own expense, fitted up on Trolleys, a most picturesque and realistic representation of the Art of Gold and Silver Wyre-Drawing, as practiced at the time when the Company was Incorporated,[1] a display was made which was generally pronounced to be the chief feature of the Show."[2]

1889 — The Seven Hundredth Anniversary of the Mayoralty

In the *City Press* for 30 March, 1889, was printed a report of a meeting of the Court of Common Council, during which the matter of celebrating the seven hundredth anniversary of the mayoralty was discussed, and at which it was resolved "that the Court . . . do commemorate the event in a suitable manner . . ." The show for this year was largely historical, though there were no cars; and while the account of the procession in the *Illustrated London News* does not men-

---

[1] *I. e.*, 1623 — see Stewart, *Hist. Company of Gold and Silver Wyre-Drawers*, p. 32.

[2] *Ibid.*, p. 102.

tion the anniversary, one cannot help feeling that this was the form the celebration took.[1] The show included delegates from *le féderation des officiers et sous-officiers de sapeur-pompiers de France et d'Algérie*, as well as English firemen from twenty-nine provincial fire-brigades. The band and boys of the training-ship *Warspite* appeared in line; the Worshipful Company of Makers of Playing Cards marched with horsemen, "representing Knaves of the four suites (*sic*) of playing cards, in the costume shown upon the earliest existing playing cards — *temp.* about A.D. 1460," who bore the Company's banners. The Master of the Worshipful Company of Gold and Silver Wyre Drawers rode in a state carriage, escorted by two men in the costumes of the supporters of the arms of the Company. "The liveries and costumes are emblematical of the Gold and Silver Wyre Drawers' craft."

Groups illustrating the Sports and Pastimes of Old England followed other marching companies. A Hawking Party, in the dress of 1200; Shooting at the Butt, 1300; Quarterstaff, Tilting at the Ring, the Quintain, 1300; Maying, 1300; Preparing for the Tournament, showing the Queen of Beauty with her Maids of Honour, Heralds, Trumpeters, and armed Knights followed by their Squires; the Chase; the Lord of Misrule and his Court — mummers, musicians, jesters, etc. — were all shown. Many of these groups were costumed after illustrated MSS. in the British Museum; this suggests the desire for historical accuracy which is inseparable from a truly "educational" pageant.

Then came various English worthies who traced descent from Lord Mayors or Aldermen; they included:

1533 — *Queen Elizabeth* — Ancestor, Sir Geoffrey Bullen, Lord Mayor, A.D. 1457. Her canopy supported by Elizabethan gentlemen.

1561 — *Lord Bacon* — Ancestor, Sir Thomas Coke, Lord Mayor, A.D. 1462. Supported by yeomen of the period.

1594 — *John Hampden* — Ancestor, Ralph Warren, Lord Mayor, A.D. 1536. Supported by a party of Puritans.

1599 — *Oliver Cromwell* — Ancestor, Sir Thomas Marfin, Lord Mayor, A.D. 1518. Supported by soldiers of the Commonwealth.

1650 — *Duke of Marlborough* — Ancestor, Sir Thomas Leigh, Lord Mayor, A.D. 1558. Supported by soldiers of the period.

1676 — *Sir Robert Walpole* — Ancestor, Sir Edward Barkham, Alderman, A.D. 1580.[2] Supported by Lords (*temp.* Queen Anne).

---

[1] I can find, in the index of the *Times*, no other pageant which celebrates this anniversary. Cf. the *Illus. Lond. News* of 16 November, 1889, p. 613, for a picture of the Queen Elizabeth of this show; the "Procession of Lord Mayors of London" is illustrated *ibid.*, pp. 628 and 629. An account of Lord Mayor's Day, in much the same language as that used in the official program, may be found *ibid.*, p. 627.

[2] A Sir Edward Barkham was mayor in 1621. See the Bibliography, under Middleton, *sub anno* 1621: *The Sun in Aries*. This may have been the son of the alderman.

1708 — *Earl of Chatham* — Ancestor, Sir Thomas Leigh, Lord Mayor, A.D. 1558. Supported by Citizens (*temp.* George III).

1718 — *General Marquis of Granby* — Ancestor, Sir Baptist Hicks, Alderman, A.D. 1611. Supported by soldiers of the Whitehorse Hanoverian Regiment.

After this group came a " Procession of Lord Mayors," showing " one representative mayor of each of the seven centuries of the Mayoralty, supported by four Halberdiers of the period. This series is interesting as exemplifying the strange and peculiar changes in the colour and shape of the Mayoral robes." The Mayors who marched were: Sir Henry Fitzalwyn, (1190); Sir Gregory de Rockesby, (1285); Sir Richard Whittington, (1397); Sir Edmund Shaw, (1480); Sir John Gresham, (1547); Sir William Craven, (1611); and John Wilkes, (1775);[1] then followed the Aldermen, Sheriffs, the late Lord Mayor, and the new one, with much splendor.

1890 — The Show Includes Cars and Symbolism

Two steam fire-engines and a detachment of men from various fire-brigades followed the mounted band of the Royal Artillery in the Lord Mayor's Show of 1890.[2] After them came the band and cadets of the training-ship *Warspite*, followed by " a fully equipped life-boat . . . on its transportation carriage . . . drawn by eight horses." The Worshipful Companies of Pattenmakers, Clockmakers, Poulters, and Barber-Surgeons followed; then came cars " emblematic of the Markets of the Corporation of the City of London." Four city pages marched between each two. The first car, " Fruits and Flowers," contained figures of Pomona, the goddess of fruit, and Flora, the goddess of flowers, with their attendants; it was drawn by six horses, and accompanied by gardeners. The second, " Fish, Game and Poultry," showed " Neptune borne by sea-horses, Sportsmen, trophies of game, poultry, etc." It, too, was drawn by six horses; and fishermen and gamekeepers were in attendance. The third car was " typical of the Central Markets," and carried a shepherd and a shepherdess, surrounded by trophies; this car was also drawn by six horses, and was accompanied by farm-laborers.

Then came survivors of the Crimean War, in thirty carriages, each group indicated by a banner variously inscribed: *Crimean Heroes, 1854–1856; Alma, Sept. 20th, 1854; Balaklava, October 25th, 1854; Inkerman, Nov. 5th, 1854*, and *Sevastopol — Peace — April 29th, 1856*. Beside these veterans there rode the two trumpeters who sounded the charge at Balaklava. Here were no lay-figures dressed up to represent historical characters — but men who had greeted

---

[1] The dates are those of the program.

[2] My account is based on the *Official Program* of this year. The five cars in this show are illustrated in the supplement to the *City Press* for 12 November, 1890, p. 2. " The Pageant " is described in the same issue, p. 3.

History herself, and put their names in the book she is always writing, though they were privates, many of them, and obscure. Veterans were sought in 1879, as we have seen;[1] they appeared in several subsequent pageants[2]; not as a show, but that the public, gazing on men who had fought for their country, might be awakened to a keener sense of her glory, and a deeper love for her institutions. Such figures as these must have done a great deal to raise this annual civic triumph from the depths into which it had fallen; we laugh, perhaps, at the "ancient knight," — but we do not smile at the old soldier.

After more military bands came a car "representing the Arts." The central figure here was Music, who was surrounded by the nine Muses, and busts of great composers.[3] This float, likewise, was drawn by six horses, and was accompanied by four people in the garb of ancient Greek citizens. Ten halberdiers in demi-armor followed; then came a car entitled "The Colonies," in which sat the "figure of Australia, surrounded by figures emblematic of our colonies, supported on either side by heralds of England, Ireland, Scotland, and Wales. The car drawn by six dark-brown horses," was "accompanied by Colonists and Indian Mahouts." After officials of the city, the late Lord Mayor, another band, and the city trumpeters, came the Lord Mayor in his state chariot, bringing the procession to a close.

1891 — Cars, a Ship; History and Trade

Fire-engines; a life-boat; a car emblematical of the Guilds and City of London Institute; another car carrying the model of an Elizabethan ship — emblematical of Queenhithe (the ancient port of London); a car emblematical of the Principality of Wales, with Welsh girls in ancient and modern costumes, bards and Druids upon it; a car displaying the Welsh industries of Iron, Tin, Coal, and Slate; a car showing Edward I presenting the first prince of Wales to the Welsh chieftains at Carnavon in 1284, accompanied the Right Honorable David Evans, Lord Mayor, in 1891.[4]

1892 — Trade, History, and Allegory; Cars

The next year, after the marching Companies, came a car of the Fruiterers, with a trophy of fruit and flowers, drawn by six horses, and escorted by carters in costume. The second car, furnished by the Gold and Silver Wyre-Drawers, showed seven distinct branches of their trade, while specimens of their work

---

[1] Above, p. 120.

[2] Cf. *e. g.*, the Lord Mayor's Show of 1906; the Columbus Day parade at Boston in 1912. Who can doubt that future pageantry will make much of those who fought the Great War just ended?

[3] The next thing to personification.

[4] See the *Official Program* for this year.

formed the decorations. Both carters and workers were in the costume of *temp.* James I. The London and Provincial Fire-Brigades brought a "Manual Fire Engine, dated 1852," and one of the hand-squirts used at the Great Fire of London in 1666, together with a steam fire-engine of 1892. A car, entitled "Commerce and the Port of London," showed an "emblematical figure of Commerce, with Cornucopia and cereals, surrounded with groups representing the various countries. Sailors and Porters" were followed by two merchants on horseback. Then came a car "emblematical of the Goldsmiths' craft," drawn by six horses which were led by carters in the costume of 1561.[1]

1895 — Trade, History, Symbolism, and Cars

Again, in 1895, the Company of Fruiterers furnished a car — "Trophy of Fruit and Flowers."[2] — The Leathersellers brought "forty working Tanners, Lime Workers, Skinners, Leather Dyers, . . . carrying implements of their trade," and a "Car: containing a trophy of various Leathers and Workmen. A Leather Shaver at his beam, shaving a skin; a Leather Finisher graining and setting a skin; a Shoemaker at work, and a Harness Maker stitching a saddle. The Car covered with Skins, Heads of Animals, and Crocodiles, and canopied and festooned with Hides and Skins and surmounted by the Crest of the Company."

The band and cadets of the *Warspite*, together with detachments of firemen, appeared again; also the Epping Forest Keepers and their brethren. What is, however, of more interest to us, is a group of former Lord Mayors on horseback, each representing his epoch. There were six: Sir Richard Whittington, 1406; Sir John Gresham, 1547; Sir John More, 1612;[3] Sir Thomas Middleton, 1613; Brass Crosby, Esq., 1771; Samuel Birch, Esq., 1814. Five attendants and a banner-bearer, carrying his arms, escorted each magistrate; St. George of England followed them — he rode on horseback, attended by two esquires and twelve mounted knights in armor.[4]

Two cars, representing South Africa and India, followed. The first contained gold and diamond miners, African hunters and natives; it was escorted by six mounted Cape Volunteers in the uniform of 1853. The other — India Past and Present — showed Sir Thomas Smyth, founder of the East India Company, with two soldiers in the uniform of the East India Volunteers. A Rajah in his

---

[1] *Order of Procession* for this year.

[2] This, and the other cars of the procession, are illustrated in the *Official Program.*

[3] The dates are those of the program. Reference to the Bibliography, under Dekker, *sub anno* 1612: *Troia Nova Triumphans*, will show that the mayor that year was Sir John Swinerton. Jordan's Show for 1681 — *London's Joy* — was written for Sir John Moore.

[4] These figures die hard; but, when made symbolic, or attached to a pageantic figure — as St. George undoubtedly is — they become more closely related to pageantry, less mere masqueraders.

native costume; Indian merchants and the products of Indian workmanship appeared on the car, which was escorted by naval officers in the uniform of 1808.

Here we have trade and symbolism on pageant-cars, or floats; and between them an historical parenthesis, as it were, of equestrian mayors, with St. George.

1896 — The History of Uniforms

In 1896, the car " England and her Heroes " showed various army uniforms of different epochs; another car contained men in the uniforms of an admiral and sailors of the early nineteenth century; another showed " uniforms of various regiments in the early part of the present [*i. e.*, the nineteenth] century, with mounted gun." A stage-coach, " with ladies and gentlemen, guards and coachman, in costumes of 1796," preceded a motor-car — " old times " being thus contrasted with the present. The last " float " in this show carried a mounted Maxim gun, and men in the uniforms of 1896.[1] This is what might be called " expository history " — it is interesting to observe how far from a guild, or from London itself, this show has taken us. It can hardly have awakened civic pride; it appeals rather to a sense of national glory. These shows were preparing the way for the seed which Mr. Louis N. Parker was soon to plant;[2] it is probable that the emphasis on history — both civic and national, represented by former Lord Mayors or by the uniforms of a century ago — had much to do with the appreciation of Mr. Parker's work, which has little else in common with the kind of pageantry we have been considering.

1901 — Trade, Symbolism, and a Touch of History

There were three cars in the 1901 Show: the first illustrated the trade and commerce of London in the twelfth century; the second symbolized the Commonwealth of Australia, and was escorted by stock-riders; while the third represented the methods of weighing in use from the earliest times — brought to England by the guilds which united to form the Grocers' Company.[3] This

---

[1] See the *Order of Procession*, [which has been reprinted in *Mellin's History of the Lord Mayor's Show* — a pamphlet by Eric Broad (London, 1896)].

[2] It is due to Mr. Parker to say that he disclaims any influence from the Lord Mayor's Show. But however little they have affected him, there is small room for doubting that the people — at least in part — appreciated his work because of the training received at these processions. Both brought the past to the present; the Parkerian " folk-play," or pageant, did so in a more artistic fashion.

[3] This car is illustrated in a four-leaf pamphlet among the broadsides in the Guildhall Library, entitled " Why the Car of the Grocers' Company in the Lord Mayor's pageant of 1901 represented ancient modes of weighing." (See Bibliography, *s.v. Grocers' Company*.)

" The Grocers' Company, as custodians of the King's Beams and Weigh-house for more than three hundred years, have taken pains to represent the characteristics of the Company on their car which figures in the Lord Mayor's procession. The aim is to illustrate methods of weighing from the earliest times." A short history of the various methods follows.

was preceded by a group showing the early trade-connections of the Grocers' Company, illustrated by camels laden with spices and led by Arabs, with a mounted escort. In this show we find again the cadets and band of the *Warspite*, a life-boat, and a stage-coach of 1801 with motor-cars of a century later.[1]

1902 — Trade, Naval History, International Symbolism

In the 1902 procession, the Gardeners' Company was followed by a " Floral Car — representing the Garden Industry. The floor of the Car is laid out as a Flower Garden, with Rockery, etc. A canopy rising from the corners supports four cornucopiæ, filled with choice blooms; from the centre depends a basket of trailing creepers and flowers. The sides of the car are edged with smilax and draped with the colours of the Guild, on which are embroidered the arms of the Gardeners' Company. The Car is drawn by a team of Six Horses, and attended by the Gardeners in costume." Following the Haberdashers, came a car illustrating " The Dawn of Printing." A model of the first English printing-press was surrounded by a group representing Caxton showing proof to King Edward IV, the Queen, and Earl Rivers; a printer and his apprentice were included in this group. Around the car were the arms of Edward IV, and trade-marks of the leading printers of the period.

Following this, came cars illustrating the rise and progress of the British Navy; first, a model of the *Great Harry*,[2] escorted by men in the costume of sailors of the period; after the boys of the *Warspite* came a model of H. M. S. *Victory* (1805) also escorted by men in the costume of sailors of the period; finally, a model of H. M. S. *King Edward VII*, escorted by men dressed as sailors of the present. The next car, which followed the keepers of various forests, represented " The Anglo-Japanese Alliance "; it contained " an allegorical representation of Great Britain and Japan, with background of Japanese scenery; a boat in the foreground typifies the commerce between the two countries. Around the Car are emblazoned national armorial bearings and clusters of Roses and Chrysanthemums." This car, drawn by the usual six horses, which were led by carters in costume, was escorted by Japanese sailors.

Following the Spectacle-Makers, came a car " representing the Optical Industry of the 16th Century." It illustrated the use of nautical and astronomical instruments, " also scientific mechanics making and fitting spectacles. The Car is draped with the colours of the Spectacle Makers Company, with the Arms of the Guild emblazoned thereon."

It is worthy of note that, although the earlier pageantry had historical characters and plenty of trade-symbolism, we have not seen, before these modern

---

[1] My reference for this, and succeeding shows is, unless otherwise stated, the *Official Programs* or *Orders of Procession.*

[2] Destroyed by fire in 1553.

shows, a representation of the past in any trade. The illustrations of the Commerce of London of the twelfth century, of the Methods of Weighing from earliest times, and of the Optical Industry of the sixteenth century, seem to be new developments. The transition is, however, very natural; we have seen, in earlier centuries, the past of guilds portrayed by the former mayors who brought distinction to them; and we have been shown journeymen and masters at work at their trades, on many a pageant-car. Such figures as Caxton before Edward IV show the bridge between trade and history — elements which are united on the 1902 float. And with this union comes more than advertisement, more than entertainment; the past of a trade is used for instruction. This aim, or tendency, appeared in the Lord Mayor's Show of 1884; and in these floats of 1901 and 1902, we come a step nearer to the idea underlying the Parkerian "folk-play," where we deal, not merely with historical figures, but with the more social aspect of history.

1904 — History, Mythology, Allegory: One Underlying Scheme

The cars of the 1904 Show were four in number. A note in the *Order of Procession* for that year informs us that

"the general scheme of the ornamental cars is to represent, by reference to their chief characteristics, four of the most potent civilizing powers in the world's history, viz:
"Ancient Egypt — the Religion
"Ancient Greece — the Arts
"Ancient Rome — the Conquest
"Great Britain — the Bible, Navigation and Industry." [1]

On the first were "sphinxes guarding stairway leading to pillar supporting Statue of the God of the Nile placed under a canopy. On faces of pillar are wall paintings taken from the papyrus of Ani representing phases of the 'Adoration of the Nile,' which is further illustrated by group of Priests, etc." Followed a "Car representing Ancient Greece, Pillar, decorated with bas-reliefs, representing the Muses, at rear of Car, supporting Chariot drawn by two Grecian steeds, in which stands Apollo playing his Lyre. In front are grouped representatives of the Arts of Greece." The car representing ancient Rome contained the "'Columna Rostrata' supporting Statue of Victory. Group shewing Cæsar, accompanied by Roman Soldiers." And on the last: "Britannia seated high on Gothic throne supported by Griffins carrying City Arms, the British Lion crouched at her feet. In her right hand Britannia carries the trident while her left hand rests upon the open Bible, 'the secret of England's greatness,' and the names of some of the greatest pioneer exponents of the Bible in distant lands are mentioned, viz.: Livingstone (Africa); Morrison (China); Carey (India); Martyn (Persia). Allegorical figures representing Navigation and Industry. Representative Group of the British Colonies" completed the float.

It is to be remarked that here, for the first time, we have four floats related; one scheme of allegory underlies all. With all the symbolism and allegory which

[1] These cars are pictured in the *Order of Procession*.

we found in the seventeenth century, there was nothing which showed the singleness of purpose we find here; and this unity of design brings us another step nearer the Parkerian attitude.

1905 — International Symbolism, Allegory, and Suggestions of the Giants

The *Order of Procession* for 1905 contains illustrations of the three cars shown that year.[1] The first, recalling the Anglo-Japanese pageant of 1902,[2] represented *L'Entente Cordiale*. " This car shows two giant figures respectively representing Britannia and the French Republic [3] with hands clasped over a globe. At the corners are standing French and English Soldiers and Sailors. The Car is decorated by two giant Flambeaux of Peace, garlanded to the corners with gilt laurels and wreaths. The sides and base of the Car are draped with Union Jacks and Tricolours."

The next car was " designed to exemplify Peace and War. The rear, or Peace portion of the Car is a pedestal of granite with the word ' PAX ' marked in relief upon each side, and surmounted by a giant figure designed after the celebrated Statue of Liberty at the entrance to New York harbour. The base is decorated with a marble balustrade garlanded with flowers. The rear of the Car is draped with two large American ensigns.[4] In the forepart of the Car, at the foot of the Statue of Liberty, are two soldiers of Russia and Japan with rifles on the ground advancing on the summit of a ditch to give their hands in peace. At their feet are a dismantled cannon and broken wheels as if shattered by shell-fire. The base of the Car is decorated by Russian and Japanese flags."

" The central and upper part " of the third pageant, which represented the Colonies, " shows an Indian Trapper bartering furs with a Hudson Bay Trader. On one side of the Car is a typical Canadian Agriculturalist seated upon a real plough, with sheaves of corn and trophies of colonial produce near, and on the other side a New Zealand Agriculturalist with a live sheep, and samples of New Zealand produce. The four corners are occupied by typical Colonials and the Car is decorated with real fruit and the heads of animals."

---

[1] We may note that in 1905 came to life at Sherborne, England, the Parkerian " pageant " or " folk-play " which is discussed in chapter viii.

[2] See above, p. 129.

[3] If it be true that the personification of cities and countries came originally from the giant, through the giant-champion, Bruce, Ebraucus, to London and Africa, it is interesting to note here a return of the personified figure to the giant. This is, in all probability, pure coincidence; but it is none the less remarkable.

[4] In the illustration, printed in the *Program*, these appear to be the Japanese ensign and the Union Jack. The American flags and the Statue of Liberty refer, of course, to the Peace of Portsmouth.

Surely Dekker, Heywood, and Middleton would have smiled could they have foreseen how a peace signed in far-away New Hampshire, between the envoys of a Slavic and an Eastern Empire, would figure in the Lord Mayor's Show! The larger aspect of London, in her relations to the Empire, is emphasized in these later processions; as London, outgrowing its old boundaries, became less and less "the City" of old, it connected itself more and more with the Colonies, and with the Empire; and the history which is reflected — from the present as well as from the past — is rather that of the Empire and her Allies than of one London Company. The gigantic figures of Pax (or Liberty), Britannia, and the French Republic, recall the London, India, and Africa, of the older shows; but to these personifications has been added a suggestion of the civic giants. The latter represented what was believed to be history; the figures of 1905 were frankly symbolical and allegorical — yet the emotions of the crowd on seeing these huge images must have been akin to those with which the seventeenth-century mobs greeted their giants.

1906 — An Historical Parenthesis in the Show for this Year

A short historical introduction, with various illustrations — including "The Lord Mayor's Show from the famous picture by Hogarth [1] — opens the *Order of Procession* for 1906. Many of the features of this show are unchanged; there are the fire-engines, the life-boat, and the boys from the *Warspite*. A car, "carrying Cornish miners from the School of Mining, Truro," preceded the Ragged School Union and Shaftesbury Society, which was followed by a "car representing various Departments of the Society's Work." Then followed in carriages Crimean veterans representing the five regiments which took part in the charge of the Light Brigade.[2]

An "Historical Pageant representing notable Lord Mayors of London of the Past Seven Centuries, with their Retinues" brings us nothing new;[3] Henry Fitz-Alwin (1189–1212) represented the thirteenth century;[4] Sir John Philpot (1378) the fourteenth; Sir Richard Whittington (1397, 1406, 1419) the fifteenth; Sir Richard Gresham (1537) the sixteenth; Sir Thomas Myddleton (*sic*) (1613)

---

[1] This is the oft-reproduced final picture of the *Industry and Idleness* series.

[2] Cf. the Show of 1890, (above, p. 125).

[3] Cf. the Shows for 1884, 1889, and 1895. It will be recalled that in the seventeenth century, Lord Mayors appeared frequently in the procession; but they were famous predecessors of their guild-brother who was being inaugurated. In the more modern shows, the men owe their representation to no guild in particular; a civic broadness has taken the place of a natural exclusiveness.

The title — "historical pageant" — probably indicates an influence from the Parkerian pageants of Sherborne and Warwick, though there were "historical pageants" at Boston, (Massachusetts) in 1880, and Marietta (Ohio) in 1888.

[4] The dates are those of the program.

the seventeenth; John Wilkes (1775) the eighteenth, and Robert Waithman (1823) the nineteenth.[1] There were no cars with this part of the procession, which gives us history as a symbol of a glorious past — the "soul" of pageantry, which is an important element in the Parkerian work.

1907 — The Older and Parkerian Pageantry Meet

That the difference between the older and the Parkerian pageant is mainly one of technique, is shown by the ease with which the two were combined, when, in 1907, Mr. Louis N. Parker — who has been called the "father of modern pageantry" — planned an "historical pageant" for the Lord Mayor's Show. This insertion, or "interlude," in the procession was not a "folk-play" at all; and the conditions of presentation were not such that the show could be technically influenced by the "folk-play."[2] Mr. Parker's contribution to the procession is devoid of speech or action; "groups" take the place of his folk-play "episodes," and a symbolic car replaces the "final scene" — which is also symbolic — of his pageants. But this "interlude," if so it may be called,[3] shows the "folk-play" master's insistence on historical accuracy, his research, and the dramatist's desire for unity. *The Edwards of England*[4] is, after all, but an elaboration of such processions of former mayors as those of 1889 and 1906.

The Pageant begins with *Edward the Confessor* (crowned 1043) as closing the Saxon epoch. He is followed by *an Abbot* bearing the model of Westminster Abbey, which was built in his reign, and in which he was buried. Next comes *Godwine*, Earl of the West Saxons, the father of Eadgyth, the king's wife, and his two sons, *Tostig* the king's favourite, and *Harold*, who was himself chosen king in 1066. Edward the Confessor was a great benefactor to the Church, and by his gifts and endowments laid the foundation of the glory of St. Edmundsbury. The *Great Shrine of St. Edmund* is here shown. Behind it rides *William*, Duke of Normandy, whom Edward entertained at his court, and who returned in 1066 as William the Conqueror.

Group II

Edward I (1239–1307.) One of the greatest of our kings. He was a Crusader; he received the submission of the *Barons of the Cinque Ports;* was at war with *Simon of Montfort*, and created his son *Edward*, first Prince of Wales.

---

[1] Pictures of these mayors and their trains are published in the *Order of Procession;* and post-card illustrations of the groups may be found in the Guildhall and Harvard Libraries.

[2] I use this word in the Parkerian sense, meaning "a play given by the people." This form of art began — as I have already noted — in 1905; we shall treat it more in detail in chapter viii. With Mr. Parker's, pageantry adds to its list (which contains the names of Lydgate, Udall, Peele, Middleton, Webster, Dekker, and Heywood) another important name; he joins his fellow-dramatists, who, in the past, contributed much to the Lord Mayor's Show.

The reader must not confuse the Parkerian "folk-play," or pageant, with the earlier "folk-play," such as the mummers' play of Lutterworth, the sword-dance, or the Robin Hood plays.

[3] I have given it this name, because it is really a parenthetical insertion in the procession.

[4] It may be noted that the birthday of Edward VII fell on 9 November, (cf. above, p. 112.)

Group III

Edward II (1284–1327.) On his right rides *Piers Gaveston*, his favourite and foster-brother, with the ominous figure of the *Headsman* following close upon him; for Piers Gaveston was executed by the infuriated Barons on Blacklow Hill, near Warwick, in 1312. On the king's left rides his later favourite *Hugh Le Dispenser*, the younger. Behind them come the *Barons*, whose opposition to the king and his favourites made this one of the most turbulent and tragic reigns. Lastly *Henry Le Waleys*, first M. P. for London.

Group IV

Edward III (1312–1377) surnamed by Parliament 'The King of the Sea.' In his reign English Commerce had its beginning. He favoured *James van Artevelde*, a wealthy citizen of Ghent, and invited *Flemish Weavers* to settle in England, and *Genoese Merchants* to bring their wares. *Geoffrey Chaucer*, the poet of the 'Canterbury Tales,' flourished in this reign. During his reign the *First Cannon* is said to have been used. He instituted the *Order of the Garter* (which was then, and long afterwards, called the Order of St. George). His son, *Edward the Black Prince*, was so called after the Battle of Crécy, at which he was possibly accoutred in black armour. Edward III entertained *Knights from Spain, Cyprus and Armenia*, who had come to solicit aid against the Mahometans.

Group V

Edward IV (1442–1483.) He is closely followed by the *Earl of Warwick* (known as the 'King Maker') and by the *Duke of Clarence*, who, with Warwick, plotted his overthrow. Lastly the tragic figure of *Falconbridge* rides by, followed by the *Men of Kent* whom he raised in rebellion on behalf of Warwick.

Group VI

Edward V (1470–1483). The unhappy boy, who with his brother the *Duke of York* was murdered by the order of the *Duke of Gloucester*, afterwards Richard III.

Group VII

Edward VI (1537–1553.) The key-note of this reign was the revival of education. The boy-king himself was taught in all godly learning by his four tutors, *Richard Cox*, Bishop of Ely; *Sir John Cheke, M.A.*, *Sir Anthony Cooke*, and *Roger Ascham*, who was afterwards tutor to Princess Elizabeth and Latin Secretary to Queen Mary. He is followed by the *Earl of Hertford*, his uncle. A *Physician* representing the conversion of the Monastery of St. Bartholomew into St. Bartholomew's Hospital. He appointed as Court preachers *Nicholas Ridley*, Bishop of Rochester and London, *Hugh Latimer*, Bishop of Worcester, and *John Hooper*, Bishop of Gloucester and Worcester. Edward VI presented the *Palace of Bridewell* to the Corporation of London as a 'Workhouse.' A prominent figure in his short reign, and long afterwards, was *Sir Thomas Gresham*, who founded the first *Royal Exchange*. Edward VI converted the old Grey Friars' Monastery into *Christ's Hospital* (the Blue Coat School) in 1553, and founded many grammar schools, of which *Sherborne* (May 13th 1550) is reputed to have been the first.

Group VIII

The reign of His Most Gracious Majesty King Edward the Seventh is symbolized by a Car entitled '*The Harvest of the Peacemaker*.' It is a real Harvest Wagon, drawn by Eight Shire Horses, and bearing the fruits of *Peace*, who, owing greatly to the unceasing efforts of our Sovereign, is seen enthroned over the *Four Quarters of the Earth*."

This is the Parkerian interlude of 1907, which brought to the London crowds the raw-material of many chronicle-plays. Higher in artistic aim and historical accuracy than any previous Show, it gave to this institution the element which permeates our newer pageantry — the desire to turn entertainment to the uses of instruction.

1908 — "The Press, the Poets, and the Musicians from Chaucer to Milton"

The following year, the *Order of Procession* included an "historical literary pageant" by Mr. Parker, entitled *The Press, the Poets, and the Musicians from Chaucer to Milton*. Two Heralds led this section of the Show: then came Chaucer, followed by the Canterbury Pilgrims,[1] each of whom carried an identifying banner. William Caxton[2] came next, with a printing-press "(kindly lent by the Governors of the St. Bride Foundation), with Printers and a Printer's Devil at work." Sir Thomas Malory was followed by King Arthur and Sir Lancelot; Edmund Spenser by the Knight of the Red Cross, Sir Guyon, Sir Cambal, and Sir Talamond, Sir Artegall, and Sir Calidore, each of whom bore a pennant with his name, and the quality he represented, upon it.[3] Christopher Marlowe was followed by Tamburlaine,[4] Dr. Faustus, Mephistophilis, Barabas, Edward II, Henry of Navarre, Æneas, and Ascanius; Shakspere led many characters; Ben Jonson, Philip Massinger, and Robert Herrick followed; and then came John Milton, accompanied by L'Allegro, Il Penseroso, and Comus. All of these writers were — it will be noted — more or less intimately connected with London.

The Musicians' Company of London, (1472); Walter Halliday (First Master of the Company, 1472); Orlando Gibbons, Mus. Doc. (1583–1625); John Blow, Mus. Doc. (1648–1708); Henry Purcell, Mus. Doc. (1658–1695), and John Bull, Mus. Doc. (1563–1628) brought the pageant to a close. This show, like that of 1907, is an "interlude," or "insert," in the regular procession.

---

[1] A note in the *Program* states that "in arranging the procession of Literary and other celebrities, great care has been exercised in obtaining from all available sources the most reliable data as to the personal appearance, dress and habits of the various notabilities who are portrayed.... So far as concerns the dress of the different periods, the pageant may be looked upon as being probably the most authentic and correct series of historical groups that has ever been seen in London." Some of the characters in this part of the procession are pictured in the *Order of Procession* as well as in the *Program*.

This emphasis on accurate historical detail is one of the characteristics of the Parkerian pageant.

[2] Who appeared in 1902, it will be recalled.

[3] This might be thought to show a pageantic use of the older "men in armor;" I believe there is no connection whatever between the two.

[4] Tamburlaine, it may be remarked, appeared in the Shows of 1623 and 1676. (See above, p. 79, and n. 2.)

1910 — Famous Characters of Shakspere's London Plays

The procession of 1909 included Balaklavan survivors — who filled only two carriages — steam fire-engines, boy scouts, and the usual marching companies with their banners. There were no allegorical floats, or representations of historical figures.[1] But the Show of 1910 included an " insert " like those of 1907 and 1908.

Philip Carr was honorary master of the pageant this year; and his interlude consisted of " representative characters from scenes mentioned in Shakspere's plays as occurring in the streets of London." The events reproduced were: the return of Henry V and his army after the Battle of Agincourt, (1415); Sir John Falstaff and his companions leaving the Boar's Head Tavern at Eastcheap; Richard, Duke of Gloucester with King Edward V and the young Duke of York on their way to the Tower, (1483); King Henry VIII and Cardinal Wolsey going to the Papal enquiry concerning Queen Katherine at Blackfriars, (1528).[2] We find here a procession of some of the historical, and pseudo-historical, characters treated in Shakspere's plays. In 1907, we dealt with history, the raw-material of the chronicle play; in 1908, we saw literature viewed through the eyes of history; and here we get history seen through literary spectacles. These three processions indicate the influence on the Lord Mayor's Show of the modern historical " folk-play," or Parkerian pageant; and we have an interesting example of a later form affecting an earlier.

1911 — Army History and Naval Past Portrayed

Perhaps the Army Pageant of 1910 influenced the 1911 Show; at any rate, in this year the parenthetical " insert " — which we may call the " pageant " — illustrated, by means of groups, " five important epochs in the history of the British Navy and Army from the time of Queen Elizabeth." [3] The first group showed Sir Francis Drake, with officers and men who defeated the Armada; Sir Philip Sidney, with representatives of the land forces of his day. Group ii

---

[1] *Reminiscences of Bridge Ward and the Bridge of the World — London Bridge* (illustrated) prefaces the *Order of Procession* for 1909. The program for this year reproduces various old prints illustrating former pageants; and in this way history is emphasized.

[2] The *Official Program* of this show was reprinted in the Lord Mayor's Procession Number of *The County and City of London Observer*, for 9 November, 1910; but there are no illustrations of the Show in this paper. From a note we learn that the management of the *Festival of Empire* (cf. Bibliography) lent a number of properties and costumes used in the Lord Mayor's Show. It is hard to tell whether the characters here rode, or progressed on cars, reconstructing the scenes as *tableaux vivants*.

[3] How this kind of thing was done before the influence of the Parkerian work was felt, may be seen by referring to the Show for 1896. Both that, and this for 1911, may have felt an influence from the " Royal Military and Naval Tournament," which we shall touch on in the next chapter.

presented Admiral Blake, with officers and men "who drove Van Tromp from our seas"; and General Monk with "Ironsides" and pikemen of 1650; group iii portrayed Sir George Rooke and the captors of Gibraltar; the Duke of Marlborough, with mounted dragoons. In group iv, marched Admiral Boscawen, with sailors of 1747; and Lord Clive, with Dragoons and Grenadiers of 1757; and group v represented Admiral Lord Nelson, with officers and men of Trafalgar, and the Duke of Wellington, with soldiers of Waterloo.

Ever since 1585, when a Soldier and a Sailor accompanied the Genius of the City, the two branches of the service have been closely connected with London in the popular mind. A large part of the procession has for long been made up of soldiers; and with the tendency — visible at intervals from 1850 — to emphasize Britain rather than London, the ties between England and the Colonies, it is not surprising that the Army and Navy should be made the subject of a civic pageant. Now that the Great War is over, we may expect to find further glorification of His Majesty's Forces in more than one Lord Mayor's Show; indeed, before universal service was voted, troops were used as a means of stimulating recruiting.

1913 — A Change in the Attitude of the Press

It is interesting to compare the attitude of the press, in speaking of the Lord Mayor's Show of 1913, with that of 1853.

> "The glorious history of the City of London was again epitomized yesterday when the annual historical and military pageant of the Lord Mayor's Show proceeded from the Guildhall through the City... This quaint procession, with its curious conglomeration of potted history, can always be relied on to attract the whole of London and many from the provinces; and this year... the public imagination had been caught by rumours of a captive giant who was to be led through the streets, as in the Imperial triumphs of old Rome. . ." [1]

The leader in the *Times* for the 10 November, 1913, shows a marked contrast to that cited from the *Weekly Times* of 13 November, 1853.[2] After a brief *résumé* of the history of the Lord Mayor's Show, the editor continues:

> "No doubt many peaceable citizens, before as since, resented this noisy and even dangerous interruption of their trade. There is not lacking opposition to the custom even to-day. It is urged that the procession seriously obstructs the traffic, which is already as much as the City thoroughfares can cope with. This difficulty has to some extent been met this year by a commendable alteration of the route. Other critics, more revolutionary, complain of the expense and question the desirability of this civic parade. Objections on these grounds can, of course, be urged against any form of pageantry. None is in the strictest sense 'necessary,' and all is expensive. Such criticisms are nevertheless superficial. This is a time when the rule of 'common sense' is so strict that appeals to the emotions and imagination of the public are only too few. There is no method like the pictorial method for stimulating and fixing in the popular mind some notion of the past without which the present falls out of perspective.

---

[1] The London *Daily Chronicle* for 11 November, 1913.

[2] Cf. above, p. 117; and the editorial in the *Times* for 10 November, 1853, p. 6, col. 3.

This is the use, symbolical, suggestive, of all pageantry. The first City of the world is the last place where it could profitably be dispensed with. It is essential that its citizens should be reminded from year to year of some other aspect of their City's greatness than is provided merely in statistics of trade. The Tower holds as many secrets of the progress of London among the world's cities as does the Stock Exchange, and a picture drawn solely from one standpoint or the other would be incomplete. The unflagging interest of the public in the Lord Mayor's Show proves, at all events, that the vast majority are alive to its value and interest and true to civic traditions. There can be no gain in lessening the corporate spirit that still animates "the City" by impairing the authority and dignity attached to the yearly president of the community. The City Companies, by continuing to serve, in loyalty to tradition, the purposes for which they were founded, and by carrying on at the same time useful work of a more modern character, testify that even in matters relating to commerce it is possible to combine the old spirit and the new. According to EMERSON, "the use of history is to give value to the present hour and its duty." This use the Lord Mayor's Show can claim in some measure to perform. If some future Lord Mayor decided to revive the water pageant of olden days, this useful purpose would be equally well served and the complaint of interrupted business would be no longer heard."

Although announced, and reported, as a "reproduction" of the Lord Mayor's Show of 1613, that of 1913 was nothing of the sort.[1] Planned to observe the three-hundredth anniversary of the opening of the New River, the show included a giant — in which walked a man — who represented the River. He was led captive by a very small boy, dressed as a Crusader, who personified the Genius of London. At the corner of Queen Victoria Street and Upper Thames Street was a castle, representing the mayor's Ward — Castle Baynard — at which the Dean of St. Paul's read the new mayor a congratulatory address. There were the usual military bands, soldiers, boys of the Royal Merchant Seamen's Orphanage, Dr. Barnardo's Homes, and cadets from the *Warspite*. Among the Boy Scouts was young Dick Whittington as an apprentice. A real life-boat manned by the crew of Clacton-on-Sea took part in the procession; and a "trolley," or "float," accompanied the Boy Scouts, on which a group showed the duties of the Scouts in camp.

Sir William Walworth, attended by Knights, Sir Henry Fitz-Alwin, Robin Hood, with some of his men, five Moorish kings,[2] and Hugh Middleton, with mounted "wyfflers," and "waytes," rode in the procession, as did various City officers in the garb of the seventeenth century — the Common-Sergeant, Cham-

---

[1] For illustrations of the giant, the historical characters, the Boy Scouts' camp and the "reproduction" of Baynard Castle, see the *Illus. Lond. News* for 15 November, 1913, p. 783. "We are continually hearing," says that periodical, "that the most typical of London pageants, the Lord Mayor's Show, is a thing dead; yet every November it turns up again and draws great crowds to see it. This year's Procession proved no exception to the rule."

[2] Which, the *Official Program* tells us, "have reference to the Goldsmiths Company, of which Hugh Myddelton was a member." The supporters of the Goldsmiths' arms are not Moors but unicorns; apparently the 1613 Moors referred to Sir Thomas Middleton's wide commercial interests: (cf. above, p. 34).

berlain, Common-crier, Sword-bearer, and the two Sheriffs. Sir Thomas Middleton, with his immediate predecessor beside him, rode last of all. None of the dramatist Middleton's speeches was delivered; nor were any of Grinkin's pageants reproduced.[1]

1914 — The Show Incites to Patriotism

Just as no historical pageantry can bring the past so vividly before us as the figures of veterans who have participated in historical battles, so no amount of symbolism will arouse the fervor awakened by the sight of troops about to go to fight. The world was shuddering at the horrors of war when Sir Charles Johnstone took his oath in November, 1914. No pageantry accompanied him; but for the first time in the history of the Show there figured in the procession "the Empire troops from the Over-Sea Dominions come to help the Mother Country in a time of unparalleled stress."[2]

On the day after the Show, the *Times* published a leader which is worth quoting in full:[3]

> "November 9, 1914, will be for ever memorable in the long annals of the City of London. The shadow of the greatest war in history is over all hearts, and leaves our minds but little attuned to feasting. The flower of our manhood are at this hour wrestling in deadly conflict for all that we hold dear. All that the wisdom and the valour of our fathers have wrought for a thousand years is at stake; our fairest hopes, our noblest aspirations, hang upon the issue. The magnitude and the gravity of the struggle, and the consciousness that upon it depends the whole future of civilization in Europe, weigh upon the City of London and upon His Majesty's Ministers more heavily perhaps than upon any others. Yet it was decided, and in our judgment wisely decided, that neither sorrow for those who have fallen, nor cares or anxieties for the State should interrupt the accustomed ceremony with which the Lord Mayor takes possession of his office. The Lord Mayor drove in procession through the streets of London yesterday, as the King will pass in State to the Palace of Westminster to-morrow, because we hold it meet as an ancient nation that not even war should disturb our time-hallowed customs. We boast that our "culture" has its roots deep in the past, and these things are the outward symbols of the strong links that bind our race throughout the world to the inheritance which makes them what they are. The old Guildhall was built before the first Hohenzollern came to Brandenburg, and Lord Mayors have "kept their feast" there

---

[1] *The Evening Standard and St. James's Gazette* for 25 October, 1913, records that "this year there will be no symbolical cars and no private fire brigades. The proposal to include in the pageant representatives of the naval and military uniforms worn at Trafalgar and Waterloo, in which battles some of the Bowater family fought, has been dropped." The Lord Mayor for 1913 was Sir T. Vansittart Bowater, Bart.

[2] The London *Times* for 9 November, 1914, p. 10, col. 2. The *Order of Procession* is printed, *ibid*. In addition to the Canadian and New Zealand contingents, a detachment from the Newfoundland contingent of the Expeditionary Force also took part, with various London troops.

[3] The London *Times* for 10 November, 1914, p. 9, col. 1, under the caption *Lord Mayor's Day*.

since those days. Long before, King Edward III, and the Black Prince sat with their captive guests from Poitiers at a Lord Mayor's table. Many of our Kings and almost all our great sailors and soldiers have been entertained at the Guildhall by the Chief Magistrate of the capital. The memories of our struggles and of our triumphs gather thick about it. Queen Anne and George III., Chatham and Pitt and Nelson, are there on canvas or in marble. It is right to recall these memories at this time, not in any spirit of boastfulness or of overweening self-confidence, but in that temper of calm reliance upon the righteousness of our cause and of humble trust in the protection of Heaven, which the nation have exhibited since war was forced upon them.

"That temper was conspicuous in the ordering of the procession and in the attitude of the people of London yesterday. With a just sense of what is becoming, which the crowds thoroughly appreciated, the display was military only, and military in a stern and practical form. Troops, and troops in khaki, were the escort of the Lord Mayor and of the chief officers of the ancient City Companies. The Honourable Artillery Company, the London Territorials, the Royal Naval Reserve, and the contingents from the Dominions were all represented. The unusual quiet of the crowd until they appeared, and the enthusiasm with which they were cheered, again and again, as they marched past, struck all observers. These signs showed the earnestness with which we are facing the great ordeal of war, and the gratitude and admiration we feel for our champions. The Canadians, New Zealanders, and Newfoundlanders were greeted with special warmth. Londoners were eager to give them a welcome on this, their first, appearance in public, which should convey to our fellow-subjects beyond the seas something of the sentiments their love of the old country and the old flag kindles amongst us at home. The London Scottish, who have lately given their brother Territorials such a "glorious lead and example" at the front, were acclaimed with equal ardour. This year the joyous popular holiday has been a serious demonstration. The change is deeply significant to those who know our people.

"The speeches at the banquet teach the same lesson as the conduct of the crowds in the streets. They show that we are absolutely of one mind as to the justice of our quarrel and unanimously resolved to fight it out, at all costs and at all risks, until a righteous and an abiding peace has been won. For that end we have spared, and we shall spare, no efforts and no sacrifices. The services of our Allies, and of all who are fighting for the common cause, were amply acknowledged by more than one speaker."

The Show for 1915; a Promise of the Future

The "Recruiting" Lord Mayor's Show — with captured guns, is pictured in the *Illustrated London News* for 13 November, 1915.[1] Accompanying the scenes presented, is the following description:

The Lord Mayor's Show of this, the second year of the Great War, took exceptional and appropriate form, and was very successful despite the bad weather. It started at 11.30 from the Guildhall, earlier than usual because it was arranged that the Guildhall Banquet in the evening should begin at six o'clock instead of the customary seven. Included in the Procession were some German guns captured by our forces; a detachment of the Anti-aircraft Corps, with guns; a detachment of the R. F. C., with aëroplane; a detachment of the City of London National Guard; a Canadian Contingent; and Contingents representing Australia and New Zealand, South Africa and the West Indies. In addition were representatives of various regi-

[1] See that periodical, p. 617.

GUILDHALL BANQUET INVITATION — 1915

ments, the Royal Naval Division, the Royal Marine Artillery, and the Royal Marine Light Infantry. Other very prominent features were recruiting bands and, following the Lord Mayor and his escort of City of London Yeomanry, a Recruiting Column of considerable strength. Before the arrival of the Procession, recruiting meetings were held at various points of the route, and it was arranged that recruits should fall in in rear of the Guards detachment.

A promise of the future may be found not only in the "Royal Pageant on the Thames" of 4 August, 1919,[1] but also in Mr. Parker's Show for 1919. This took the form of "London's Welcome to Peace," and was built up around the League of Nations.[2] Children headed the procession, with a decorated car containing a large globe and the inscription, "You will build the new world." The "Herald of Peace" preceded a wain drawn by four horses, escorted by wagoners in long white smocks; in the wagon were the five continents of the world — Europe, Asia, Africa, America, and Australasia — who were followed by a long cavalcade of women representing the Allied States and neutral countries, each in her national costume or a symbolic one. London led the pageant, and Britannia closed it, with the Dominions — including Newfoundland, Canada, South Africa, Australia, India — and England, Scotland, Ireland, and Wales, in appropriate costumes. In the pageant, Mr. Parker expressed the union of the nations necessary to rebuild a world which the war had shattered.

This survey of the recent Lord Mayor's Shows indicates a gradual change in emphasis from the history of a particular Company to the history of the city as a whole, and of the Empire. No longer are past mayors revived because they belonged to a certain guild; though the Worshipful Companies still march carrying their banners and those of former illustrious members, the mayors who are represented are those who have helped to make the city great. Allegory and symbolism have reappeared — but they show Allied nations, and symbolize the Colonies across the world. The primary emphasis is still on entertainment rather than on education; for it is difficult to give lessons which will sink deeply into the popular mind, by means of a speech-less parade; but the sight of so many former worthies — admirals, mayors, generals, and sovereigns — must help to keep alive a pride in the past, which the historical "folk-play" could

---

[1] See the *Times* [weekly edition: for Friday, 8 August, 1919, p. 782] for mention of this greeting to the British Mercantile Marine. The Royal Barge, "the last survivor of many similar vessels which added to the gaiety of the river in the old days, was at once the most ancient as well as the most distinguishable of all in the procession." The writer in the *Times* finds symbolism in the display of house flags of the shipping lines, which recalled the vessels sunk in the War, and the brave fights put up by those which escaped. This pageant rightly belongs in the previous chapter, and one may leave further mention of it to the future historian of royal progresses.

[2] The *Program* of this show is in the Harvard Library. For mention of it, see the *Times Weekly Edition* of 14 November, 1919, p. 1065, and the illustrated section, p. i. (On p. iii are reproduced engravings of the Lord Mayor's coach in Cheapside [1768] and the Fishmongers' "pageant-chariot" of 1616.)

awaken only at rare intervals even if it could be satisfactorily given in a metropolis. What this "folk-play," or newer pageantry is, we shall consider in a later chapter; in this place, it is enough to indicate the fact that the Lord Mayor's Show — the chief aim of which, for centuries, has been to amuse the crowds — seems to be absorbing some of the new educational spirit; and with its higher aims, it has won back popular favor. The earlier programs are giving place to pamphlets, neatly bound and often illustrated,[1] which contain much interesting material beyond the mere order of procession. Even as far back as 1884, there was an educational purpose in the show; symbolism is still there, and personification — the latter more important, even, than it used to be; but the main element is history — of the past, to inspire pride in the present; of the present, to awaken effort for the future.[2]

Conclusion

We have, in this chapter, traced in fair detail the course of the Lord Mayor's Show from the time when London first had a mayor to the year 1919. We have seen how mayor and citizens rode to Westminster early in the thirteenth century; how, in 1422, the progress was first made by water — a practice that soon grew regular, and lasted until 1857. We have seen how, in the middle of the sixteenth century, the pageants which had been connected with the Midsummer Show were absorbed into the civic procession, and how this grew in importance until, in 1585, speech was added; how Peele, Munday, Dekker, Middleton, Heywood, and even Webster, wrote speeches for the Show, and planned the symbolism, history, and allegory which were to honor the mayor and delight the populace. We have seen the elaborate triumphs which took place, with few interruptions, from 1655 to 1702; and how Settle's final show — for 1708 — could not be given because of the death of Queen Anne's husband.

After Settle's day, the shows fell rapidly from favor; scoffers arose who — from the time of Ned Ward — satirized the civic procession with more or less venom. Yet royalty continued to grace the triumphs from time to time, and the strong popular demand for them kept the institution alive.

By the end of the eighteenth century, little of the old pageantry, save the water-procession, was left; early in the nineteenth, allegorical or symbolical "transparencies" were installed in the Guildhall; and the only pageantic features of the procession were the "knights in armor" who, originating, appar-

[1] Cf. the history of London Bridge published with the 1909 *Order of Procession;* and the history of Guildhall prefacing that of 1910.

[2] The soldiers in the 1914 Show stimulated recruiting enormously. Viewed in one way, these figures personified the history of the present more powerfully than anything else could have done; and they showed that — even in the dark days of the war — the appeal of the Lord Mayor's Show was far from dead.

"London's Welcome to Peace"

ently, from a trade-figure of the Armourers and Braziers,[1] soon became mere masqueraders, representing little in particular, and provided by successive Lord Mayor and Sheriffs' Committees, regardless of the Company to which the chief magistrate belonged.

In 1850, Godwin's letter to the Lord Mayor demanding an improvement in the Show, brought about the abolition of these figures — but in 1851, they returned in greater numbers than ever. Since the middle of the century the Show has become more and more pageantic; and when the armed men have appeared, they have been given a pageantic meaning. The Show survived the attacks levelled against it in the press of 1853; and, in 1884, we find it aiming not merely to give pleasure, but also instruction. For this reason there has been, in the succeeding years, a stronger and deeper emphasis on the treasured history of London, and on the City's present ties with the Colonies.

The Show has survived the War. It was used, before Parliament voted universal service, to stimulate recruiting; it proved an effective aid in stirring national pride and national determination. It is still a vital thing; and now that victory and peace have come to Great Britain and her Allies, we may expect that the annual procession, deeply rooted in the past as it is, will take on a new strength, nourished by the glorious chapters of England's history which have just been written — not only by the mother-country, but by the Colonies as well. The increasing vigor which the Show has displayed since 1884, the soberness of a nation emerging from a Titanic struggle, and the wealth of heroism which the war engendered, allow us to hope that in the future a more serious effort will be made to celebrate worthily the greatness of a capital whose glory does not decrease with age. Handicapped as she is by the " technique " of a street parade, Art has the material, and can find a method, of giving the London public yearly a dignified and adequate reminder of its rich Past and noble Present.

We shall see the emphasis on the educational value of a pageant more clearly marked in the " community dramas " which we shall discuss in a later chapter. These have adopted the name *pageant*, and are what most people think of when the word is used today. " None of the present so-called *pageants*," writes Mr. W. C. Langdon,[2] " have anything really to do with the mediæval pageant; they all alike have no right to the name. But the community-drama stole the word first; therefore its title should be respected . . . The modern pageant is a new thing . . . Mr. Parker simply took the name; he did not continue the thing. He made a new one."

---

[1] Possibly the trade-figure may have been adapted from an earlier chivalric or historical figure, or have been a development of the Marching Watch which was a usual accompaniment of the Midsummer Show. (Cf. above, vol. i, p. 47 f.)

[2] In a letter, dated 9 September, 1912.

We shall shortly turn to a consideration of the Parkerian "pageant" — its origin, development, and the different kinds of entertainments which claim the name today. Mr. Parker has frequently told me that he was not influenced by the Lord Mayor's Show at all; and while "none of the present so-called *pageants* have anything really to do with the mediæval pageant," there were undoubtedly features in common between the older and these newer forms.

The emphasis on history, which is so strong in the "folk-play" or "community-drama," returns to the Lord Mayor's Show as early as 1884; — it was common enough in the seventeenth-century shows, and was made the basis of a pantomime in 1783. The history of the more recent Lord Mayor's Shows deals, as I have repeatedly pointed out, with that of the community rather than with that of any particular guild; it is no incidental recalling of the past, but tends to be the framework on which everything else is built; London as a whole is glorified. There is, in this matter, a possible exchange of influence; the growing importance of history, from 1884 on, may have been — quite unconsciously — felt by Mr. Parker; or he may have been influenced by the same causes which produced it. And the historical element in the civic shows probably did much to prepare Mr. Parker's audiences to appreciate his work.[1]

Besides the civic processions of London, there were pageantic activities in the provinces, and these we shall examine in the next chapter. Some of these pageants are closely connected with folk-custom; others have a trade-origin, and we find some — long before the Parkerian "folk-play" — celebrating civic anniversaries. We must keep in mind the fact that these shows developed beside the London mayoralty processions, and may have had an influence on these, as well as on the Parkerian pageants. Many who saw the performance at Sherborne in 1905, had probably seen a certain number of the Lord Mayor's Shows since 1884, or recalled such occasions as the Ripon anniversary of 1886; if so, the history of these processions lived for them in a way it does not in books; and they could appreciate more fully a play based on history.

All this is, of course, mere surmise. There is no way of settling just what exchanges of influence may have taken place — but there were probably some, even if Mr. Parker's choice of the word *pageant*, when *folk-play* failed to arouse interest, was made without thought of the Lord Mayor's Show, or such proces-

[1] Similarities between earlier and later pageants do not necessarily prove an influence. The knitting women at Swansea in 1881 (see above, vol. i, p. 257) are probably not due to the spinners at Norwich in 1578 (see above, vol. i, p. 211); Robin Hood, "attended by 'Little John, Scathlocke, Much the Miller's sonne, Right-hitting Brand, Fryar Tuck and many more,'" appeared in Munday's 1615 Show [Fairholt, pt. i, p. 40]; he was also a common figure in the court masques of Henry VIII; he appeared in Parker's Sherborne Pageant of 1905, the Lancaster (Massachusetts) Pageant of 1912, and the Lord Mayor's Show of 1913. This does not mean that the Robin Hood plays, the Court disguisings, or the Lord Mayor's Shows influenced the modern pageants directly; or that Robin Hood did not come straight from the ballads to each.

sions as those at Preston, Coventry, Lichfield, and Ripon. In the old sense of the word, a pageant was — as we have seen — something "put together": giant, animal, stage, or wagon. To this background came hero, saint, patriarch, angel, knight — allegory, symbolism, history, and mythology, which have become, as the "soul" of pageantry, so necessary an element that often a procession may lose the cars or "floats" and — keeping the personified qualities or historical characters — still be regarded as pageantic.

In the next chapter, we shall examine some of the pageantry which lies outside the "royal-entry," and the Lord Mayor's Show. These celebrations are, in some cases, survivals of older ones: in others, they are due to the interest in the past, which is one of the characteristics of the nineteenth century — an interest which may be mirrored in the later London civic shows, as well, and which came — in pageantry — under the leadership of Mr. Louis N. Parker, to a full fruition in the Sherborne Pageant of 1905.

CHAPTER VII

SURVIVALS AND REVIVALS

WE have traced the development of "royal-entry" and Lord Mayor's Show, and have seen how the former declined when the latter was at its height; how the pageantry of London civic triumphs grew out of the Midsummer Show, which existed beside the earlier "royal-entries"; and how much the "formal" pageantry owes to the folk-celebrations, which often included one or more pageantic elements. Outside the pageants provided by civic authorities for sovereign and mayor, and the pageantic features borrowed by the courtiers for their masques and barriers, lie certain survivals and revivals of older pageantry which we shall examine before turning to the Parkerian work.

In this chapter we shall treat such pageants as those of Lichfield, Knutsford, and Grimsby, which have their root in folk-custom; such processions as those at Salisbury, Edinburgh, Preston, and Coventry, which seem to spring from trade; such political pageantry as the "Pope-burnings" of the time of Charles II, and of Colonial Boston, nearly a century later, as well as the "Orange Processions" of Belfast and other North of Ireland cities; "occasional" pageants, such as the Peace Celebration of 1814, the Ripon Millenary Celebration of 1886, the Liverpool Pageant of 1907 (which was not Parkerian) referring briefly to a couple of modern pageantic processions on the Continent.

We shall also consider the revival of the tournament in England, artificial as it is; and give a passing glance at the pageantic tournament at Compiègne of the days before the War. And, finally, we shall examine Christina Rossetti's *Pageant of the Months* — an example of a large class of productions wrongly called "pageants" — to show why it has no right to the name.

§ 1. FOLK-PAGEANTRY

We have already dealt with folk-pageantry,[1] and it will not be necessary to repeat what was said above; let me merely remind the reader that, in its simplest form, this folk-pageantry is practically a revel, or masquerade. This is what may be called the "raw-material" of pageantry — it is found whenever anyone dresses-up to represent someone he is not. The girl who goes to a fancy-dress ball as one of the Muses is — in herself — just as pageantic as if she were to occupy a car in the Lord Mayor's Show, and represent Clio, leading a detachment of famous chief magistrates. What makes her unpageantic at the ball is her surroundings. Such notices as those under the caption "Balls and

[1] See chapter i.

Pageants " in the London newspapers,[1] show that these masquerades are coming to have a central idea; one was planned, which should represent " famous men and women from B.C. 7000 to A.D. 2914 ";[2] but even these are rather outgrowths from pageantry, than pageants themselves. At best they have but the " soul " of pageantry — they lack the body, spirit, and technique of this form of art. From early days until the present, Court revels, artists' festivals and the like have been common enough; but they lie outside our field.

Artists' Revels with Pageantic Features

Sometimes, however, these revels add to the " soul " of pageantry the pageant-car. An example of this kind of thing may be found described in the *Illustrirte Zeitung* for 1852.[3] The artists' festival at Düsseldorf, on 12 June, 1852, included cars; the Venusberg, King Arthur, Percival, and other Knights of the Round Table, Eckhard, Tannhäuser, Venus, the devil, etc., appeared. A fight took place, but was stopped by Venus, who captured the knights and bound them prisoners with flowers. Costumes of the twelfth and fifteenth centuries mingled harmoniously together, " Märchenfiguren aus vielen Zeitaltern." As the *Zeitung* says, " Der Plan ist bunt und phantastisch "; and while the celebration has pageantic features, it more nearly resembles the carnival.[4]

These celebrations, though not unknown in England and America, are more common on the Continent. The Fleet Street Revel, and other artists' balls in England, commonly take place indoors, without pageantic accompaniments.

---

[1] Cf. *e. g.*, the London *Sunday Times* for 19 April, 1914.

[2] This was held at the Hotel Cecil on 4 May, 1914; among the characters to be presented were Lady Jane Grey, Garibaldi, the Hon. Mrs. Norton, Vittoria Colonna, Fanny Burney, &c. (Cf. the *Sunday Times*, *loc. cit.*)

[3] No. 477, (xix, pp. 119 f.).

[4] On 20 March, 1852, the first artists' festival in Hamburg took place. This is described in the *Illustrirte Zeitung*, xviii, pp. 360 f. (no. 466). A Meistersinger, a minstrel, Albrecht Dürer, and Till Eulenspiegel were among the characters. The " Winzerfest " at Vevey (7 and 8 August) celebrated every fifteen or twenty years, is described, *ibid.*, xvii, pp. 211 f. (no. 427). Here was a car of Bacchus, attended by boys dressed in leaves.

It is not uncommon for French students to have these pageantic carnival-processions. I saw that at Lyons on *Mi-carême*, 1910; there were cars filled with fancifully-dressed characters; and students with bags on the end of long sticks collected money from the crowd — with which, if I remember rightly, they were to defray the expenses of their ball. Cf. with such shows the entry of Bacchus into Lyons in 1627, which is described in a pamphlet entitled, *Entrée Magnifique de Bacchus avec Madame Dimanche Grasse, sa Femme, faicte en la ville de Lyon, le* 14 *feburier* 1627. Cf. above, vol. i, p. 77, n. 1.

In this procession, there were cars — and figures, personifying various inn-signs, spoke. The humorous character of the procession is suggested by " Le Mont de Parnasse Representé par Neuf Lavandières au Lieu des Neuf Muses," (*op. cit.*, p. 39) whose verses are in *patois*. The whole thing seems to have been a pageantic carnival, or revel, of which it is needless to give more examples.

These affairs suggest the older court "disguisings," in that they interest and appeal to a small group of the community; even when they borrow the pageant-car, they are hardly pageants.

Just as the "knights in armor" of the Lord Mayor's Shows ceased to be pageantic as soon as they ceased to represent King Arthur, Charlemagne, St. George, or even a trade-figure of the Armourers' Company, so the folk-mummers who represent no one in particular, fail to be pageantic. The small children in many American towns who on Hallowe'en dress up and go from house to house are simply mummers disguised; an historical suggestion makes the English child, with his "Guy," somewhat more pageantic. Only when a couple represents another who won the Dunmow Flitch a century and a half before, is there any pageantry in connection with that ancient folk-custom; and even then, the element is slight. One of the oldest folk-customs in England which has pageantic features is the Lichfield "Greenhill Bower"; let us examine this in some detail.

The Lichfield "Greenhill Bower"

The Origin of this remarkable and ancient Custom is uncertain. Some suppose it was first instituted, an. 657 by Oswius, . . . in memory of a Victory obtained by him (near this place) at the head of the Christians, over Penda . . .

Others conclude, that the Custom is founded upon an act, made in the 27th year of the Reign of King Henry the Second (1176) . . . by which it was enacted that the High Constables of every Town, &c. should oftentimes view the Arms and Armour of the Men in their Franchise or Liberty . . .[1]

In the time of William and Mary, Celia Fiennes described the show in her diary:[2] "They have [in Lichfield] a Custome at Whitsontide ye Monday and Tuesday Call'd ye green Bower feast, by which they hold their Charter. The Bailiff and Sheriff assist at ye Cerimony of dressing up Baby's with garlands of flowers and Carry it in procession through all ye streetes, and then assemble themselves at ye Market place and so go on in a solemn procession through the great streete to a hill beyond the town where is a Large Bower made with greens in wch they have their feast. Many lesser Bowers they make about for Conveniency of ye Whole Company and for selling fruite Sweetemeetes and Gingerbread wch is a Chief Entertainment."

---

[1] Jackson, *Hist. City and Cathedral of Lichfield* (1795) i, pp. 27 f., gives an account of the Bower. Cf. Harwood, *Hist. and Antiq. of Lichfield* (1806), pp. 352 f.; on p. 353, n., he reprints the statutes 27 Henry II (1176) and 13 Edward I (1285) "which enacted, that the high constables of every town should view, at stated periods, the arms and armour of the men within their district . . . The first Commission of Array, which we meet with, was issued in the reign of K. Henry V (Rymer, ix, pp. 254, 255) . . . The statutes of Array were repealed in the reign of James I when a military force superseded the necessity of such a measure; notwithstanding which, the Bailiffs have constantly held a manerial court on Green-hill, at the same time as the view of men and arms, according to ancient charter and prescription. It is now, however, an idle and useless ceremony, adapted for the amusement of children."

[2] *Through England on a Side Saddle*, p. 135.

Jackson's account of the ceremony, written about a century later, includes mention of " armed men " and morris dancers who escorted the city officers to the Bower, " where the stile and title of the Court is proclaimed by the Common Cryer . . . and all persons owing suit and service to this Court, anciently called, ' The Court of Array, or view of Men, and Arms ' of the Manour and Lordship of Lichfield, are required to appear, under pain of fine and amerciement. The Dozeners, or petty Constables, of the 21 Decennaries or Wards in the City, attend with emblems of their respective Trades, or other Devices . . . During the course of the Day, the High Constables, &c. perambulate the City, the Armed-Men Fire a Volley over each House; and the Evening concludes with a Procession, through the principal Streets, to the Market-place . . ." [1]

Harwood, whose account was published in 1806, attaches this to such folk-customs as the Midsummer Watch, which we have already dealt with.[2] " This Court," he says, " was anciently called ' The Court of Array or View of Men and Arms.' The public officers of the city attend, and various processions are made by the constables and dozeners of each ward; who, in these processions, anciently bore tutelary saints, but which [*sic*] are now converted into garlands of flowers, or emblems of their trade. They are attended by morrice (or moresque) dancers who appear in their shirts, with ribbands of various colours tied round their arms, and flung across their shoulders. They dance sarabands, chacons, &c. in imitation of the Moors . . ."

He considers that " the origin of this mixture of a religious and military custom, which is very ancient in the city," is probably due to the *campus martius*, " which was an annual assembly of the people upon May-day; when they confederated together to defend the kingdom against all foreigners and enemies, as mentioned in the laws of Edward the Confessor." [3]

About the year 1890 Mr. Councillor William A. Wood joined the Bower Committee, and from then on " official programs " have been issued.[4]

---

[1] Jackson, i, pp. 27 f.

[2] See above, vol. i, pp. 36 f. (I quote from his work, already cited, pp. 352 f.).

[3] The Bower of 1850 is described and pictured in the *Illus. Lond. News* for 25 May, 1850, p. 364. There are illustrations of the " knight," the morris dancers, and some of the civic officials, among whom is the Town Crier, who exercises his functions at Lichfield to this day. Photographs of this custom are in Stone.

[4] Thanks to Mr. Wood, a collection of these programs has been placed in the Harvard Library. The collection is not complete; with the exception of those for 1893 and 1895, all the programs date from the twentieth century; but it is hoped that *lacunæ* may later be filled. Every program since 1904 contains a brief notice of the antiquity of this celebration.

The following quotations are from various letters which Mr. Wood, then chairman of the " Bower Committee," wrote me in the autumn of 1913:

" There is no doubt," writes Mr. Wood, " that the celebration took its rise in the Courts of Array . . . In course of years the military portion of the proceedings was dropped, except for spectacular and picturesque purposes; and local and topical features were introduced . . .

We may sketch a few examples of this show between 1893 and 1914.[1] In the former year, as the custom is, the procession started from the Guildhall at one o'clock, and wound its way through the town to the " Bower House "; at the entrance to the Guildhall, the Mayor and Corporation reviewed it. The marchers were headed by boys on cobs or ponies, the winner of the first prize in the competition, leading; then followed Wombwell and Bailey's " World-Renowned Menagerie," with their brass band; historical and miscellaneous characters, (suggesting the carnival) followed — among them Shylock, Portia, Friar Tuck, Little John, Robin Hood; Buffalo Bill, Mexican Joe, a Toreador, a Chinaman, John Bull, a Yellow Dwarf, and Mephistopheles. Then came royal and political characters — the Prince of Wales, the Duke of Cambridge, Lord Salisbury, Mr. Gladstone, Mr. Chamberlain, and Lord Randolph Churchill.

" Tableaux Staged on Cars, Representing Nursery Tales " included Sleeping Beauty, (who was followed by Henry VIII, Wolsey, the Earl of Leicester and Sir Richard Varney); Cinderella, (followed by Cavaliers, Roundheads, Charles I and Cromwell); Red Riding Hood, (followed by George II, George III, and an officer of his time), and the Old Woman who lived in a Shoe. Then came " Morrice Dancers," a maypole, and the " Grand Mediæval Display of Ye Olde Court of Arraye, consisting of Knights and Men at Arms." In this division were trumpeters, heralds, a company of Halberdiers, bearing the City Halberds and Axes, " the Knight of Lichfield " and " the Knight of the Diocese," attended by squires; a Jester, a Knight in Black Armor, a Knight in Chain Armor, and a youthful knight of the time of Edward V, attended by his squires, and sup-

---

It is believed that the ' Bower ' is the last remaining regular representation of a Court of Array in England, and to Lichfield people and neighbouring districts, it still retains marvellous vitality, and is a perpetual source of pleasure and interest . . .

" . . . I don't think there has been any actual break in the celebration, since its inception; there have been years when little, perhaps, has been done, but I believe the ' Bower ' has been celebrated in some fashion continuously . . . From the earliest times, the City Trade Guilds took part in the Festival, and I well remember old flags, &c., indicative of the various Trades, being part of the paraphernalia; but from want of care in storage these have become lost.

" The Pageant Cars were introduced in the early 'nineties by Mr. C. J. Corrie, then City Surveyor; one of the first was a ' Stanley ' car, in the year after Stanley returned from ' Darkest Africa.' The Trade Exhibits on Cars were introduced afresh, about the same time, and these were arranged by individual firms . . .

" Like every other popular entertainment, it is getting increasingly difficult, owing to a variety of reasons, to keep the ' Bower ' going, and its arrangement entails much work and responsibility on the leaders, and, with the inevitable corollary, very little thanks. But from old association, and because of the benefit to the City in the way of business, a few enthusiasts besides myself manage to keep the Festival alive, and what is more, I think it was never more vigorously tackled than it is now."

[1] My authorities are the programs of the Shows; the procession which took place on Whitmonday, in 1914, I had the pleasure of witnessing.

ported by a company of youths on foot, clad in chain armor, and carrying spears and banners.[1]

Then came the Trades' procession, the Odd-Fellows' display, and those of other Friendly Societies; and, after a band, the Mayor, Corporation, Bower Committee, with other officials. " Humorous and comical characters " brought up the rear.[2]

Lichfield and Dr. Johnson

Although this includes historical characters, it suggests rather the carnival or revels than a pageant. The pageantic features, such as cars, historical or symbolical *tableaux*,[3] became more closely related to a central idea, and so more important, as the show developed. In 1909, the central idea of the " Bower " was the celebration of the two-hundredth anniversary of the birth of Samuel Johnson, " Lichfield's greatest citizen." Three of this year's *tableaux* were meant to illustrate his genius; " the first, devoted to ' Literature ' is a picturesque attempt to bring this about. The central figure (a female) is illustrative of classical scholarship; round her are grouped boy and girl scholars, four students bearing emblems marking phases in Johnson's learning, and at the rear a representation of a Doctor of Laws . . . A second Tableau represents ' Poetry.' There we see the muse of poetry attended by ' Fame ' carrying a torch, and grouped round these are ' Genius,' ' Song,' ' Art ' and ' Truth.'

" Another Tableau is illustrative of the ' Drama.' No more fitting figure could be found to occupy the seat of honour than Johnson's pupil and friend David Garrick, the greatest English actor of all time. Round him appear characters from some of Shakspere's most celebrated plays, including Shylock and Portia, Hamlet and Ophelia, Othello and Desdemona, and Orlando and Rosalind."

Beside these Johnsonian floats, there was a procession of notable sheriffs from 1553 to 1767 — one from each reign from Mary to George III. A *tableau* entitled " Boy Scouts," and another, " The National Service League," [4] followed.

---

[1] This section of the procession is strongly suggestive of the Lord Mayor's Shows of the early nineteenth century. The armed men here, however, are descended from the soldiers in whom the show found its origin.

[2] In the afternoon was a distribution of " Bower cakes "; an open-air band concert and an organ recital in the Cathedral.

[3] " Russia," " Japan," " Grace Darling," and the " Life Boat " are among the *tableaux* exhibited in 1904. They suggest the contemporary Lord Mayor's Show. " L'Entente Cordiale " was one of the *tableaux* in 1906; in 1907, " Peace " and " Imperial Unity " appeared, and in 1908 an attempt was made to illustrate in the procession, " various incidents, buildings, and individuals connected with the Siege of Lichfield in the Reign of Charles I, and with the stirring events of the Civil War." This may show the effect of the Parkerian pageantry on this old custom.

[4] Designed, a note in the program tells us, " to enforce on British men and boys the vital

A Coronation-Year Pageant

In 1911, the leading *motif* bore special reference to the Dominions of George V, this being Coronation year. England, Scotland, Ireland, and Wales, "the nucleus of His Majesty's possessions, from which springs his glorious Empire beyond the seas," were represented as follows: England, the Motherland, was depicted by "Britannia . . . forging on an anvil a chain of many links inscribed with the names of the Colonies innumerable which owe their birth and well-sustained being to the glorious deeds, both peaceful and warlike, of our ancestors. Four corner figures represented the chief divisions of the British Dominions — namely: Canada, Australia, India, and South Africa.

"Scotland, the land of the Firs, is well pictured by a female figure, 'Bonnie Scotland,' with her picturesque attendants in kilt, plaid and sporran.

"Erin, that charming and poetic ideal of the Green Island, represents Ireland, supported by pretty pictures of Irish girlhood . . .

"A unique incident is imported into the display by the choice of the Investiture of young Prince Edward as 'Prince of Wales,' as the picture designed to typify Wales.[1] Centuries have run their course since the last occasion on which a Prince of Wales was invested in state to the rank and dignity of his Office. The attempt now being made to illustrate this function may be useful in reminding us of the interesting event which is so soon to be enacted at Carnavon Castle."

The other features of the procession were much the same as usual: a military display of mounted men preceded the armed knights of the "Grand Court of Arraye"; and the trades' procession and fire-brigade display followed as usual.

"The chief products of Peace and Amity," were chosen for representation in 1912 — the Drama, Music, Painting, and Sculpture; but in 1913, the procession became more suggestive of the carnival, for the *tableaux* consisted of "The May Pole," "The May Queen," "Springtime," and "The Jack in the Green." In 1914, children showed "Little Red Riding-Hood," "Beauty and the Beast," "Sleeping Beauty," and "Cinderella." The knights wore "authentic Armour of great value and historic interest," which is kept in the City Museum save when worn in this procession. There appeared also some trade floats, boy morris dancers, and mounted characters in Elizabethan, Cavalier, and Foresters' costumes; after the "Bower" luncheon, athletic sports, and dancing on the green occupied the crowd till sunset; and in the evening there was a fair.

Such, then, is the Lichfield "Bower." On an old folk-custom, arising from a military review, was grafted a pageantic show which suggested carnival or revel. Recently — perhaps under the influence of the Parkerian pageantry —

---

principle that military training and habits should become an indispensable part of the education of every one of us."

[1] On this see below, p. 227.

this became more unified; allegory, symbolism, and history were not scattered broadcast through the procession, but were related to a central idea. This brought the show farther from the carnival, and made it a higher form of artistic expression — the Shylock and Portia at the feet of Garrick, in 1909, have some *raison d'être*, while the Shylock and Portia of 1893 — marching with Robin Hood and Buffalo Bill — have not. In studying this festival, we see clearly where the distinction between the pageant of the street and the carnival procession lies; not in the material, but in the purpose. At the end of the seventeenth century, the Lord Mayor's Show tended toward the carnival; this Fairholt observed, when he remarked: "The excessive absurdity of surrounding a Christian saint with a heterogeneous mass of attendants, composed of livery servants, Roman lictors, halberdiers, and, worse than all, twenty dancing satyrs with tambourines, seems never to have struck the mind of the last of the city laureates." [1] That this was not pure carnival is due to the relation of St. Martin and the satyrs to the Vintners' Company, to which belonged the mayor, Sir Samuel Dashwood.

The Knutsford "Royal" May-Day Festivities

From this festival of Lichfield, let us turn to the May-day celebration at Knutsford. As this does not date further back than 1864, it is rather a revival of older folk-custom than a survival, and need not detain us long. Organized by the Misses Clowes and Mr. G. W. Clarke, it later received the "hearty support of the late respected Vicar of the Parish"; in 1887, Edward VII and Queen Alexandra, then Prince and Princess of Wales, witnessed the celebration, and subsequently gave the Committee the right to use the prefix "Royal" in connection with it.[2] This festival is more closely connected with folk-revels than with pageantry, though it has pageantic features. In 1913, the procession included various *tableaux* on lorries, escorted by mounted boys and girls in costume; there was a Jack-in-the-Green,[3] and morris dancers danced through the streets with the procession. The characters suggested a peripatetic fancy-dress ball rather than a pageant; there were Flower Girls, Gypsies, an "Ancient Lady in a Sedan," King Canute,[4] Scotch Highlanders, the four Seasons, Italian nobles, Night, Spanish and Swiss girls, John Bull, Britannia, foresters, etc., in line. "Special Canadian Tableaux" included a "Trooper of the North West Mounted Police on Pony," "Miss Canada," "The Farmer," "The Lumberman," "The Miner," "The Fisherman" and "The Trapper"; on another lorry followed India, Australia, Africa, America, Yankees, Japanese girls, a Turk, a group of Courtiers, three Old English Officers, and Infant Hornpipe

[1] Remarks on the 1702 Show — Fairholt, pt. i, p. 119, n.

[2] Official program for 1913, p. 3. Cf. the Knutsford *Advertiser* for 1 May, 1914, p. 7.

[3] Cf. above, vol. i, p. 70.

[4] Knutsford is "King Canute's ford."

Dancers. Then came sailor girls with "Grace Darling and her Father";[1] and following them came cricketers, middies, admiral and sailors and a *tableau* "Alice in Wonderland." Maid Marian, Robin Hood, Will Scarlet, and foresters; heralds, with a Lord Chamberlain and Judge; pages, maids of honour, court officials and boy scouts escorted the "royal" May Queen and her attendants.

When the procession arrived at the Heath, various dances were performed, after which the public was allowed to enter the ring and dance.[2]

Although held on Whitmonday, the Milton procession of decorated cars and children seems to be a revival of May-day festivities. The twenty-seventh annual "fête" of the Milton Amalgamated Friendly Societies is illustrated, and briefly described, in the *Staffordshire Weekly Sentinel* for Saturday, 6 June, 1914. Various local firms provided "decorated turnouts"; a May Queen was crowned, and the whole affair seems to have resembled the more famous May-day celebration at Knutsford, which may be taken as the type of this kind of pageantry.

The fiftieth anniversary of this celebration was observed in 1914, and the May Queen of fifty years before rode in a carriage with her husband in the procession. A boy in armor represented "the Cheshire Champion"; "Miss Matty's tea-party" recalled *Cranford*;[3] the rest of the procession was much like that of the preceding year.[4] At the end of the formal dancing on the Heath — which, of course, included the Maypole dance — the townsfolk danced informally till dusk.

---

[1] In 1914, two children sat in a lorry on which was a boat. This *tableau*, it will be recalled, was not unknown in the Lord Mayor's Show and appeared at Lichfield in 1904.

[2] For details see the *Official Program* for 1913. Much the same procedure was observed on May Day, 1914, when I witnessed the procession; most of the participants were children, and the parade through the town was but the prelude to the more important part of the celebration — the dances on the Heath. (Cf. above, vol. i, p. 10.)

[3] Knutsford is the Cranford of Mrs. Gaskell's novel.

[4] The Knutsford *Advertiser* for 1 May, 1914, p. 7, gives a short history of the celebration, from which I give extracts. "... Pageantry in any form has an attraction for English folk, which is evidenced by the fact that for fifty years people have watched with interest the reproduction of the programme submitted at the festival for which Knutsford is so justly famous. This festival holds undisputed the position of being the most picturesque and fascinating of its kind, for its fame exceeding the limits of this country has reached the Colonies with the result that a tableau representing Canada was introduced two years ago ...

"The May-day Festival at the beginning was entirely a Church Schools organisation ..." It "was advertised only by blind 'Moses,' the old bell man, who went round the town in his uniform and tall hat, while he also requested people to sand the streets ...

"Records from the year 1870 reveal many interesting facts. The present run of the festival commenced in 1864, but for six years after that date no records were kept. It is extremely probable that the first of May was celebrated prior to 1864, but of that fact nothing authentic is known. At that time there was nothing to call forth the admiration it produces today, as its inception, like that of other institutions, was launched in quite an insignificant manner,

THE THRONE SCENE IN THE KNUTSFORD FESTIVAL

SURVIVALS OF MAY-DAY CUSTOMS; "A LABOUR 'KNIGHT'"

In some cities, children — many of whom have blackened faces — set up Maypoles in the streets, and, dressed in old bits of lace and paper crowns, dance about them. At other towns, processions of decorated wagons take place — usually without the allegorical occupants which give meaning to pageantry. In connection with such figures as the armed men of the London shows, the knights of the Lichfield "Bower," and the Knutsford champion, it is interesting to note that the "first May-day demonstration of Labourites in Warrington was held on Saturday [2 May, 1914] . . . A long procession with a couple of bands and numerous banners, paraded the town before the meetings, and particular attention was drawn by a 'knight in shining armour' mounted on a fine steed. He was a representative of the Sheet Metal Workers' Union . . ."[1]

THE SALISBURY GIANT IN MODERN TIMES

With the exception of the Jack-in-the-Green, who appears in the Knutsford May-day procession, St. Christopher of Salisbury is probably the only folk-figure in active service. I have already referred to his appearance in 1911;[2] since 1760 he has marched on these occasions:

1760. Accession and Proclamation of George III.
1763. Thanksgiving Day for Peace.
1784. Peace Festival at the Termination of the American War.
1798. Thanksgiving for the Recovery of George III.
1809. Jubilee of George III.
1832. "Reform" Festival.
1838. Coronation of Queen Victoria.
1842. Baptism of the Prince of Wales (Edward VII.).

---

the school children carrying out the proceedings in a degree that aroused merely local interest..."

An early procession is thus described in the columns of the *Advertiser:* "The procession started from the boys' school at the bottom of Adams Hill, preceded by the St. Cross Drum and Fife Band and the Crown Bearer and Sceptre Bearer. The Queen rode in a carriage... with an outrider arrayed in livery . . . At the tail-end of the procession was a milkmaid with a cow decorated with ribbons... The Queen's carriage was immediately followed by a Knight in ancient armour on horseback . . . In those days, the Crown-bearer and Sceptre-bearer did not wear any special dress, but appeared in the best mufti. The Crown was only of cardboard covered with gold leaf... Some of the costumes were lent by a travelling theatre proprietor named Snape, who supervised the painting of the faces with the exception of the sweep, who had to black himself . . ."

[1] Liverpool *Daily Post and Mercury* for 4 May, 1914, p. 8, col. 5.

[2] See above, vol. i, p. 56, n. 3; my authority for the information here given is Mr. Frank Stevens's paper, already mentioned, in the Salisbury *Festival Book*, p. 64, — from "official records."

1856. Peace Festival at the end of the Crimean War.
1863. Prince of Wales' Marriage.
1872. Visit of the Prince of Wales.
1887. Jubilee of Queen Victoria.
1892. Marriage of the Duke of York (George V.).
1897. Diamond Jubilee of Queen Victoria.
1902. Coronation of Edward VII.
1911. Coronation of George V.

When not in use, St. Christopher is kept in the Salisbury Museum. Mr. Stevens notes, in the article cited, that "Miss Child (*The Spinster in The Close*) gives an excellent portrait of the Giant and his attendants as they would have appeared in 1842 . . . The Giant appears to be smoking a pipe, placed between his lips doubtless by one of his 'merrie men.'"[1] This trace of the old Midsummer Show is worth recording among the survivals of folk-pageantry. Nor, on the Continent,[2] is all trace of the old folk-figures gone.

"Pack Monday" Fair in Dorset

Mr. H. V. W. Temperley, of Peterhouse, Cambridge, tells me that when he was a boy at Sherborne School, there was a great procession on the night of "Pack Monday fair," which included cars of the different crafts, and a bogus clergyman who carried a bogus Bible.[3] Interest in this procession is waning; it may have been extinguished by the new pageantry, which came into being at Sherborne in 1905.

Other Suggestions of Folk-Pageantry

We have already referred to the flogging of Judas Iscariot by foreign sailors at British ports[4] — a ceremony which keeps the religious flavor of its origin, and has apparently been widespread. In *Two Years Before the Mast*,[5] Mr. Dana refers to this custom, which, if not strictly "folk," is closely related to such

---

[1] St. Christopher is pictured, above, vol. i, opp. p. 62, and in the *Festival Book*, opp. pp. 59, and 64.

[2] See *L'Illustration* for July, 1846, pp. 279 f., for a pictured account of *Les Jeux de la Tarasque* at Tarascon. I have already referred to the giants in the war-swept area of northern France and Flanders; few of them are probably still in existence. (Cf. above, vol. i, p. 55, n. 2.)

[3] On "Pack-Monday fair," see Ditchfield, p. 245; this celebration dates from the time that the builders of the Abbey *packed* up their tools, having finished their work. The "clergyman" suggests the Boy Bishop, and recalls the anti-Popish feeling of Elizabethan days — but he may have been a later addition.

[4] Cf. above, vol. i, p. 16.

[5] (New York, 1841,) p. 159: "It was now the close of Lent, and on Good Friday she had all her yards a'-cock-bill, which is customary among Catholic vessels. Some also have an effigy of Judas, which the crew amuse themselves with keel-hauling and hanging by the neck from the yard-arms."

pageantry. Similarly, the ceremony of Crossing the Line[1] which includes the figure of Neptune, preserves a tradition, not without an element of pageantry. That it is still very much alive, the following description will testify:[2]

Four days later we crossed the Equator, and here the time-honoured ceremony of ' crossing the line ' took place. All who have not been over the line before, officers and men alike, have to be ducked and submitted to various other indignities before they can be considered ' freemen ' of the Sea King's domain.

On the previous night officers and men impersonating Neptune and his Court had paraded the ship with an impromptu band, and in the morning a huge canvas bath was rigged up on the fo'c'sle, with a rude throne for Neptune at one end. After lunch the fun began. The bears were already splashing about in the bath ready to duck the neophytes when Neptune and his staff had finished with them. One of our lieutenants was the first victim. The Sea King, gorgeously arrayed in red and yellow bunting, with a cardboard crown set on his hempen wig, asks each in turn if he has ever crossed the line before, but no sooner does the unfortunate open his mouth to reply, than a large brush dripping with whitewash is slapped in his face! He is then liberally whitewashed all over by Neptune's merry men and tipped over backwards into the bath.

Here the bears seize upon him and pass him along to the other end, each one ducking him as he goes, after which his ordeal is finished, and he can watch his messmates being served in the same way.

Our Gunnery Lieutenant at first hid, but he was soon routed out and carried, kicking and struggling, before the tribunal. He had reason to regret his attempt to shirk, for by this time the whitewash had run out, so he was treated to a plastering of black paint, sand, and water instead; and, further, given a spoonful of ' medicine ' made up of mustard, pepper, salt, oil, and sea-water all mixed together, after which he was duly tipped backwards into the bath!

The performance lasted until 4 o'clock, when we all went below, changed, and had tea.[3]

---

[1] Referred to, above, vol. i, p. 9 f.

[2] *From Dartmouth to the Dardanelles: A Midshipman's Log*, (London, 1916), pp. 98 f. We may note that Dana, who crossed the Line in 1834, escaped the " initiation ": cf. *Two Years Before the Mast*, (New York, 1841), p. 26: " Wednesday, October 1st. Crossed the equator in long. 24° 24′ W. I now, for the first time, felt at liberty, according to the old usage, to call myself a son of Neptune, and was very glad to be able to claim the title without the disagreeable initiation which so many have to go through. After once crossing the line you can never be subjected to the process, but are considered as a son of Neptune, with full powers to play tricks upon others. This ancient custom is now seldom allowed, unless there are passengers on board, in which case there is always a good deal of sport."

[3] The mother of the midshipman-author, who edited his log book, notes: " Maybe sober-minded people will think all this very silly — childish — almost improper, in view of the serious business on which they were engaged. But let it be remembered that, in the words of Kipling: ' The Navy is very old and very wise.' She cherishes her traditions, and knows well that the observance of an old ceremony in which officers and men take part without distinction of class tends to foster that immortal spirit of comradeship which is one of the most valuable assets of the service, and by no means the least important secret of our sea-power. For the rest, time enough to think of War when the call to ' action ' has been sounded off. They work best who know how to play."

Present-Day Mumming at Brooklyn

A sporadical manifestation of what may be a survival of more elaborate holiday pageantry is found at Brooklyn (New York) on Thanksgiving Day.[1] This, like the mumming found on Hallowe'en and in connection with the Guy Fawkes' celebrations, is confined to children, dressed up in costume, whose buffoonery and hilarity find expression in their progress from house to house — rarely singly, often in groups of ten or twelve. They invade front lawns, court-yards, or hallways, and give a " performance," which is little more than a succession of antics, popular songs, and " movie " representations, to which each one in the group contributes his bit. The program ended, each collects what he can from the spectators, in the way of pennies, or cake, fruit, and other sweets (the edibles are more in demand than the money, and are often put into the basket, which is part of the holiday garb); after which, the group moves on to fresh fields and pastures new.

Often the girls will give exhibitions of folk-dancing, learned in the public school or at the recreation center: frequently Russian peasant dances, the Highland fling, some Irish jig, or Swedish dance is skilfully interpreted on the city pavement by youngsters often arrayed in a manner at least suggesting the national costume of the country in question. A convincing effect is often obtained by merely tucking up a skirt or rolling stockings down below the knee and cocking the hat on one side; the illusion is there, if not the detail.

The boys usually prefer to dress up as " movie " heroes, and one often sees Charlie Chaplins and Bill Harts abroad; but pirates, Indians, cowboys, and colored comedians, are not neglected. Of historical periods, the Revolutionary is perhaps the favorite; the blue and buff Continental uniform is somehow achieved — topped by a cocked hat, it is at least recognizable. The bouffante skirt of the period, with lace kerchief and cap, is an attractive costume sometimes encountered. Present-day uniforms, Red Cross costumes, the dress of the boy-scouts, have been in evidence for the past year or two; but on the whole, the hybrid costumes are commoner, and the attempt to approximate historical costumes is rare.

In many parts of America, children dress up on Hallowe'en and visit the neighbors, sometimes playing tricks, such as carrying off gates, turning signs around, changing house-numbers, or exchanging various articles — as witches, in the past, were supposed to play roguish, if not malicious, tricks. Perhaps such mumming as that at Thanksgiving in Brooklyn, was transferred from Hallowe'en; though it does not include any of the tricks sometimes found elsewhere. Professor Paul R. Lieder, whose boyhood was spent in Brooklyn, haz-

---

[1] I am indebted to Miss Helen L. Lieder, of Brooklyn, for the following information. Her account indicates that what goes on today is rather mumming than pageantry.

ards the suggestion that if this mumming is not a legacy from the early Dutch settlers, it has come from New England. I may add that I have seen it on Hallowe'en in Bloomington, Indiana.

Revels at Grimston

Miss Edith Milner, of York, has told me of May-day revivals before 1867, in which she had taken part; similar to these was an outdoor *fête*, given by Lord Wantage in August, 1884, which inspired her to arrange at Grimston, Yorkshire, a pageantic festival early in September of that year. On this occasion the " Harvest wain " was covered with children; the Harvest Queen, Robin Hood, and other characters appeared; old English sports, and the Hobby Horse of folk-custom were revived. These revels are of importance because the Ripon pageant of 1886 owes its existence to them. And Ripon deserves detailed mention.

We see in these folk-festivals revived, the " raw material " of pageantry — or, to change the figure, the " unborn soul " of the pageant. There is no central plan to give the allegory or history a meaning; most of these celebrations tend rather to the carnival, which is pageantry without a central idea to give it unity. A tendency toward pageantry is seen in the celebration of the millenary anniversary of Ripon Cathedral in 1886; but it is worthy of note that the director of this festival is referred to as " master of the revels."

§ 2. " OCCASIONAL " PAGEANTRY

The Ripon Millenary Celebration of 1886

Because it is connected with the Grimston " revels," we may consider the Ripon Millenary celebration here, rather than defer it to its chronological place in this section. This show took place in August, 1886.[1] The town was hung with flags, and there were triumphal arches, flower-festooned; a procession of clergy, soldiers, magistrates, and civic authorities opened the festivities; Mr. Darcy Ferris, " master of the revels " marched with his committees. After service in the Cathedral, there was a luncheon for more than a thousand guests; in the evening, the " revels " began — Mr. Ferris, in Elizabethan dress, announced them from the market-cross.

Pageantic Revels

The proclamation having been read, the procession was formed in the market place. First came a group of torchbearers, then a drum-and-fife band, then a number of grotesque boy dogs, followed by a dancing band of satyrs and ogres. Behind these was a hobby-horse of the most approved and absurd appearance, and then, after more torchbearers and a huge symbolical banner, came the car of the Brewers' Guild. Around this were grouped a number

[1] Detailed accounts of this event may be found in the London *Times* of 26 August, 1886, p. 4, cols. 4 and 5; *ibid.*, for 27 August, p. 8, col. 1; for 28 August, p. 10, col. 1.

of stalwart fellows in appropriate red caps and aprons, while on the car were two huge casks, garlanded with evergreens. Following the brewers were the Oddfellows' lodges, marching four deep; then, after another banner, the Millers' car and the order of Foresters, then more banners, preceding in turn the Clothworkers' car and the Druids' Order. The Saddletree makers' car came next, and it is worthy of note that Ripon saddletrees have been as famous as Ripon spurs. At this point a somewhat more modern feature was introduced in the shape of the town fire engine, which broke the mediæval character of the procession. Following close on the fire engine, however, was the banner of St. Wilfred, followed by St. Wilfred himself on horseback, supported by two deacons and followed by six monks. Next came an old horn-blower and attendants in chariots, and a floral banner. The procession was closed by the master of the revels, his heralds, chamberlains and pages, the city banner, constables, bellman and beadle, and the mayor in a carriage with the chain and mace bearer. By the time the procession had formed, night had fallen, and the town was then lit up in all directions by most brilliant and decorative arrangements of colored lamps. The façade of the town-hall was brilliantly illuminated, and the triumphal arch at the head of Kirkgate was most picturesquely hung with Chinese lanterns. . . The lurid glow of the torches, the bright gleams of the coloured lamps, and the fitful shadows cast by the curling smoke on the faces and dresses of the actors in the pageant, served to make up such a picture of mediæval manners and customs, as set forth by the chroniclers, as to induce for a moment the belief that the veritable mummers had come to life again, and were disporting themselves at Ripon at the close of the nineteenth century.[1]

This evening's celebration is chiefly interesting for us in that it shows a large part of the community participating. Many of the characters appeared again in the Ripon Civic Pageant, which had a strong historical flavor. As this is much nearer our modern pageantry, it may be described in detail.[2]

The Ripon Civic Pageant — An Historical Procession Including "Wild Men," Allegory and Symbolism

The procession included

" wild men, marking the first period of known history, and looking wonderfully fierce, as, clad in skins, their limbs covered with hair, and their faces decked with woad, they strode along brandishing their clubs." Hobby-horse and jester followed; and the introductory part of the procession was brought to a close by a company of halberdiers and the master of the revels with his attendants.

The " first chapter was the Druidical period," and these priests came next, with foliage-crowned bards, carrying golden lyres. Arch-Druid, Vice-Arch Druid and Royal Arch-Druid with golden sickles and high golden head-dresses followed. Then came the Roman period — Hadrian and his empress in a Roman chariot, followed by Roman soldiers; then the Viking period — represented by a huge Viking boat, around which hung the shields of the crew, who sat or stood within, a shaggy lot of Norsemen. The Abbot of Melrose, with a model of the Monastery, led the Saxon period; he was followed by Prince Alefrid, behind whose attendants rode Queen Edelfleda, whose saddle was a tiger's skin. After her train — which included pages, nobles and Saxon ladies — came " a car bearing the ancient hornblower,

[1] The London *Times* for 26 August, 1886, p. 4.

[2] *The Times* for 28 August, 1886, p. 10.

attended by the executioner and gaoler, in type of the ancient rights of sanctuary and mortmain. It should be mentioned that the character of the hornblower was taken by an old man of ninety, who has blown the horn nightly in the market place of Ripon for the last seventy years. Following this car came that of St. Wilfrid," whereon was seated in a throne, supported by spears, King Egfried, attended by his brother Elwyn. Saxon soldiers accompanied the car of King Alfred, wherein sat Elswitha his Queen; then came Athelstan and Archbishop Odo; and the Normans were represented by Henry IV and his Queen, with Norman nobles, " who visited Ripon to escape the plague which raged at that time in London."

The prosperity of the town at this period was symbolized by a harvest group, and a car bearing a Queen of the Harvest with attendants in classic costumes.

Then came the first two burgesses of Ripon summoned for the Parliament of 1295. Robin Hood and his men followed, and behind them came Hugh Ripley, last wakeman of Ripon, with his lady. Then " cars of the city guilds, with operatives at work " preceded the heralds and banners of the knights of the tournament.[1] James I and his Queen accepting spurs from the Spurriers' Guild of Ripon, when he was on his way to his coronation at London, and " numerous other events in the history of the ancient city's existence were also represented in succession." Then followed the allegorical part of the procession.

This included the wife of the then Mayor of Ripon as the Genius of the City, with Charity and Loyalty in attendance. Maypole dancers, a Georgian farmer, with his wife on a pillion, shepherds and shepherdesses, sword dancers, and the civic procession of mayor and municipal dignitaries ended a mile-long procession. It marched to the ruins of Fountains Abbey, and filed before the crowd assembled there, later joining them to watch the play of *Robin Hood and the Curtal Friar*,[2] given on the traditional site of the famous event it recalled.[3]

In the afternoon there was tilting at the ring and quintain; and a tournament between armed knights on " armoured hobbies " took place, " much merriment being caused by the play made by the knights in their life-like horsemanship of their hobbies. With the ancient Yorkshire sword dance, the entertainment for the day came to an end." [4]

Although this procession included figures from the revel, it has many characteristics of later as well as earlier pageantry. The cars with their allegory and symbolism; the historical characters, from the " wild man," who represents the Early Briton, to the Georgian farmer; the care with which the site for the

---

[1] See below, and p. 185.

[2] Written by Augustin Dawtrey; Mark Landon, " who is justly celebrated for the part he has taken in previous revels and pageants, was a most admirable friar," and " the whole representation was eminently in keeping with the surroundings both of scenery and of the pageant grouped around the rustic stage." (*The Times, loc. cit.*)

[3] Cf. *The Times* for 27 August, 1886, p. 8, col. 1: " . . . The site selected for the representation of the play of *Robin Hood and the Curtal Friar* is immediately adjacent to the beautiful ruins of Fountains Abbey, and is supposed to be the identical spot on the banks of the Skell described in the ballad where the outlaw had his memorable encounter with the Curtal Friar, and where the two fought their long fight from ten in the morning till four in the afternoon." It was given before a crowd of 7,000 people who swarmed over the arena and the hillside without. (*The Times* for 28 August, p. 10.)

[4] *The Times* for 28 August, 1886, *loc. cit.*

Robin Hood play was chosen; the march before the crowd gathered in the open-air arena — even the preliminary service in the Cathedral — all these show it to be half-way between the older and newer pageantry, combining features of both. It is interesting to see a " folk-play " revived, with Robin Hood as one of the characters; for the older folk-play, or sword dance, is rarely connected with a pageantic procession.[1]

The Peace Celebration of 1814

Fireworks, " allegorical transparent Paintings," and allegorical statues formed part of the Peace Jubilee at London in 1814.[2] A fleet of boats on the Serpentine commemorated the Battle of the Nile;[3] a " revolving Temple of Concord " in Green Park was illuminated,[4] as were a Chinese bridge and pagoda. The fleet on the Serpentine took part in a mock fight[5] with ships flying American colors, which were, naturally, defeated; the British fleet subsequently attacked a French fleet, and again proved its superiority. Afterwards some of the ships were burnt, and fireworks concluded the show.

This exhibition recalls history, and reflects a national pride in the feats of British bravery. In this, it is connected with modern pageantry, even though the history recalled is recent. The allegorical paintings and the Temple of Concord echo the older pageantry of the seventeenth-century Lord Mayor's Show.

The celebration of peace was combined with welcomes to visiting royal personages, which seem to have been without pageantry.[6] Various illuminations were shown, however, and some of these transparencies were pageantic — for instance, those exhibited by H. Watson, at 35 Old Bond Street: in the center, one including Astræa, Britannia, Prudence, Victory, Marlborough, and Wellington; on the right, one representing *The Liberation of Spain*, and on the left, *The Magnanimous Emperor of all the Russians*.[7] Peace, Britannia, Ceres, and many

---

[1] Robin Hood, mounted on a hobby horse, is one of the figures in the Horn Dance at Abbot's Bromley — one of the few surviving folk-dances of the present day. Cf. Stone, *Festivals, Ceremonies, and Customs*, (1906), p. 18.

[2] This is described in the illustrated pamphlet recorded in the Bibliography under the heading *Peace Jubilee*.

[3] See the pamphlet referred to, plate 2.

[4] See *ibid.*, plate 4. The allegorical paintings described *ibid.*, pp. 49 f. were in this temple.

[5] Which is described, *ibid.*, pp. 54 f.

[6] I have mentioned the entry of Louis XVIII on 20 April, 1814, above, vol. i, p. 255; cf. for further description, *England's Triumph* (London, 1814; in Gh.), p. 34 ff. The visit of the Emperor of Russia and the King of Prussia, who arrived at Dover on 6 June, 1814, is described, *ibid.*, p. 89 f. This visit of the Allied Sovereigns to London, is " B " in scene vii of Part III of the London Pageant of 1911. (See *The Festival of Empire*, p. 132.)

[7] *England's Triumph*, p. 200. Cf. for other transparencies, *ibid.*, p. 197 f. These seem to have been exhibited on 9 June.

other characters, symbolical, allegorical, and mythological, whom we have met in pageantry, were represented on transparencies; but one deserves special mention:

> Among the various curious exhibitions in the streets during the late illuminations, there was one called the Agricultural Car, decorated with laurel, &c.; it displayed most of the implements used in husbandry. The reapers were within the car, with their scythes and sickles; their flags were supported on hay rakes, forks, &c. bearing this motto, 'We have cut down the Corn Bill.' We never remember to have seen so much joy and satisfaction expressed on all sides by honest John Bull; hats and handkerchiefs, huzzas and bravoes, gave the reapers a fine treat.[1]

1907 — Liverpool's Anniversary Pageant

Although given two years after Mr. Parker's Sherborne Pageant, the procession at Liverpool reminds us rather of the Ripon celebration, or of such shows as that of Lichfield, than of what we have come to regard as a "pageant" nowadays. But there is a suggestion of the Parkerian work in the underlying unity, which focussed the minds of the spectators on the city's history.

"Liverpool celebrated its seven hundredth birthday with a pageant which traced the development of the town from the year 1207 . . . The pageant was rather processional than dramatic, and its method differed somewhat from that of the accepted pageant ritual.[2] The history of the town was outlined in a great procession of symbolic cars which portrayed the commercial rise of the city, and its chief political events. The procession closed with the grand car of Liverpool which bore the goddess of the city, supported by Britannia, Erin, and characters symbolic of Science, Art, Music, Trades and Industries."[3]

Foreign Pageantic Processions of Recent Years

I shall not here attempt to trace any connection between such pageantic processions as that of Liverpool and those on the Continent; let me merely call attention to a couple of the latter, that we may not forget that such "occasional" pageants are not confined to England. In 1910, at Amsterdam, there was an "historical procession" in honor of the Princess Juliana, in which nine hundred people took part, and which included seven "chariots."[4] One of the features of the millennary celebration at Rouen, in June, 1911, was an historical procession,

---

[1] *England's Triumph*, p. 213. If these figures were not alive, the "treat" was not relished.

[2] What this is, we shall find out in the next chapter. Already, two years after Mr. Parker's first show, there was "an accepted pageant ritual"!

[3] *Illus. Lond. News* for 10 August, 1907, p. 191. Besides this car are illustrated here: "The Car with the Episode of the Surrender of Liverpool"; "Early Shipping — a Vessel of the Sixteenth Century"; "The Banner of Liverpool"; "The Car Commemorating the Slave Trade," and "Early Industries — the Everstan Windmill."

[4] Cf. the *Illus. Lond. News* for 4 June, 1910, p. 857. One feature of the "pageant" is pictured.

which included " les chars des arts et des industries normands "; the " drakar " of Rollo and his vikings was reproduced, among other things.[1]

" Un grand cortège historique . . . reconstituant l'histoire de la Normandie, et réunissant 1,200 personnages dont 400 cavaliers, a défilé dans les rues de Rouen au milieu d'une foule énorme. A une heure de l'après-midi, Rollon, figuré par un négociant rouennais, était arrivé par le Seine dans son drakar. Son costume et celui des guerriers vikings qui l'entouraient avaient été composé avec une grande exactitude documentaire," says the writer in *L'Illustration.* The procession awoke great popular enthusiasm.

The attempt to reproduce Rollo's costume with exactness, seems to point to an influence from the newer pageantry of England; and we may consider that this procession, as well as that at Liverpool in 1907, combines the spirit of the Parkerian work with the technique of the older pageants. We have seen at Ripon in 1886, and shall see at Boston in 1880,[2] stirrings of the newer spirit which finds in a civic anniversary a fit occasion for recalling the glories of the past.[3]

§ 3. TRADE-PAGEANTRY

Closely connected with folk-pageantry, are various trade processions with pageantic features. Examples of these may be found in Preston, Edinburgh, and Coventry. I have already mentioned the *guilda mercatoria* of Preston [4] which is said to date from the reign of Henry II; and we have discussed the 1802 and 1822 processions. In 1842, there were " floats " or pageants representing various trades when the " Preston Guild " was celebrated.[5]

The Preston " Guild " was not connected with the investiture of the mayor, which took place in October; [6] it has been held pretty regularly every twenty years from the middle of the sixteenth century,[7] usually in August or September,

---

[1] Cf. the *Don de Dieu* at Quebec in 1908, and the *Half-Moon* and the *Clermont* of the Hudson-Fulton Pageant of 1909, (below, pp. 241 and 242). For this Rouen procession, see *L'Illustration* for 17 June, 1911, p. 505: a photograph of the *drakar* landing on the banks of the Seine is reproduced.

[2] Cf. below, p. 239.

[3] Another French celebration of an historical event by means of pageantry more closely united to the older sort, is seen in the festival at Orléans for Joan of Arc. That on 6, 7, and 8 May, 1912, is pictured in *L'Illustration* for 11 May, 1912, p. 413. On the *fête* at Compiègne, see below, p. 187.

[4] See above, vol. i, p. 34.

[5] Cf. the picture in the *Illus. Lond. News* for 3 September, 1842, p. 276.

[6] *Hist. Preston,* p. 10. On p. 43 is given the list of years on which the Guild has been held: 1329, 1397, 1418, 1429, 1458, 1501, 1543, 1562, 1582, 1602, 1622, 1643, 1662, 1682, 1702, 1722, 1742, 1762, 1782, 1802, and 1822.

[7] *Ibid.*, pp. 9, 68, 96, 103. The Guild for 1762 (p. 104 f.), that for 1782 (109 f.) 1802 (110 f.) and the plan of that for 1822 (119 f.) are described. The names of the aldermen and grand

"commencing on the Monday after the decollation of St. John." [1] The Guild was held in 1882, and again in 1902, but without any great emphasis on pageantry.[2]

The "Shrewsbury Show," — which appears to have its origin in the Corpus Christi procession — has also been mentioned.[3] It lasted well into the nineteenth century.

Edinburgh Trade Procession in 1832

A trade procession, which seems to have been "occasional" and political as well, took place in Edinburgh, on 10 August, 1832.[4] Seventy-one guilds and other associations marched to celebrate "the triumph of the Great Cause of *Reform*" through the streets of the capital of Scotland. Most of the marchers carried only banners, but some showed examples of their workmanship as well; and the St. Crispin Society "are to turn out in all the splendour of the craft, with the king, his pages, and the various ministers of state, together with the British and Indian Princes, and their attendants, the Champion, &c."[5] With

---

seneschals on "guild years" from 1397 on, are given (*ibid.*, p. 97 f.). The institution may date from the time of Henry II, Duke of Normandy in 1172 (p. 68), but holds a charter from *temp.* Henry III (p. 9).

[1] *Ibid.*, pp. 9 and 71.

[2] Various triumphal arches of the "Guild Merchant" of 1882 are pictured in the *Illus. Lond. News*, of 9 September, 1882, p. 281. The municipal procession, and other celebrations are described, *ibid.*, p. 282. Among the scheduled entertainments, were "a grand tournament, or assault-at-arms, joined by soldiers of the cavalry and infantry," and a sham-fight, following a review of four thousand volunteers and other troops.

In the *Illus. Lond. News* of 1902, are pictured: the "Clerk proclaiming the Guild," on 23 August (30 August, p. 307); one arch, and the "State Progress of Earl Derby, the Guild Mayor, to church," on 31 August (6 September, p. 340); three cars in the procession of the combined trades — in which about ten thousand people took part, and every craft was represented: the exhibit of the Tin Platers and Wire Workers, that of the Textile Trades, and the living pictures (in frames) shown by the Picture-Framers. (13 September, 1902, p. 376.)

[3] See above, vol. i, pp. 32 f.

[4] There are two copies of the *Order of Procession* in the Brit. Mus. [*1882. d. 2 (17)* and *808. m. 16 (57)*]. An account of the procession, printed 11 August, 1832, is on a broadside also in the Brit. Mus. [*808. m. 16 (63)*].

[5] So the *Order of Procession*. The broadside says: "This body presented a most imposing spectacle in the magnificent pageant of King Crispin which was got up in a style of splendour hitherto unequalled." Does this imply that the procession was an annual, or, at any rate, a periodic affair?

Just as St. George became King George in many a later version of the mummers' play, so St. Crispin seems to have become King Crispin even without the aid of the Hanoverians. This may have been due to the Presbyterians' dislike for Romish saints; for St. Crispin figured at Shrewsbury in 1845. (Cf. above, vol. i, p. 33, n. 1.)

The "champion" is evidently a "knight in armor"; whether adapted from a trade-figure or an earlier chivalric representation, it is impossible to say. The chances are, that he can claim the former origin, if he does not show a survival of the civic muster.

the Printers, rode a "man on horseback working a Portable Press, and distributing the impressions to the surrounding spectators." Two cars followed — one, drawn by a horse, carried printers at work; the other, drawn by six devils,[1] showed a man working at a press. The Bookbinders exhibited a model of a standing-press "with a parcel of elegant bindings"; a Champion in armor, on horseback, supported by two Highland chiefs, accompanied the Wallace Youths' Society; the Highland Societies wore their full Highland costume; and five boys drew a car on which was a large Thistle, nearly ten feet high.

The Coventry Pageant — Lady Godiva

What may be a survival — or revival — of folk-pageantry, to which a memory of the distant past has been added, and into which a strong element of trade has been infused, is the procession which is often a feature of Coventry Fair.[2]

"The first record of a procession in which Lady Godiva was represented," writes the Town Clerk of Coventry, Mr. George Sutton,[3] "was in 1678, and the early processions appear to have been organized more or less under the auspices of the Corporation.[4] It has been held at intervals of a few years, more or less regularly ever since, though of later years the intervals have tended to become

---

[1] Probably these were printers' devils, and had not even a punning connection with the devils of the sixteenth-century Lord Mayor's Shows.

[2] On this, see Ditchfield, p. 245; Mary D. Harris, *The Story of Coventry* (in Dent's Mediæval Town Series) [London, 1911] pp. 19 f.; her *Life in an Old English Town* (in the Social England Series) [London, 1898] p. 10; Benjamin Poole, *History of Coventry* (1852); his *Coventry: its History and Antiquities* (1870); and the *Pamphlet* recorded in the Bibliography *s.v.* Coventry. Chambers, ii, p. 163, notes that Godiva was added to the Corpus Christi procession; he further suggests the possibility of the root of "the Godiva processions" being in the pre-Christian perambulations of the fields in spring (cf. above, vol. i, p. 25). Cf. also, on this procession, Fairholt, *Civic Garland*, p. xiv f.

[3] In a letter dated 19 January, 1914. "It was not . . . until the time of Charles II that the Godiva procession became a feature of Coventry fair. In 1678, we are told 'Lady Godiva rode before the mayor to proclaim the fair' and the custom thus inaugurated obtains to this day." Harris, *The Story of Coventry*, pp. 19 f. Miss Harris gives no authority for her statement; but in her *Life in an Old English Town*, p. 10, she uses the same words, citing Poole (1870) pp. 57–66. Poole, p. 58 cites (from Matthew of Westminster and Dugdale) the historical sources of the Godiva story; in neither is there mention of Peeping Tom, who seems to be a later fictitious addition. Poole reprints various treatments of the story in verse (pp. 60–64).

[4] "In this year (1677–8), in the Mayoralty of Mr. Michael Earle, there was a new show on the Summer, or Great, Fair, of followers — that is, boys sent out by the several companies, and each Company having new Streamers, and Lady Godiva rode before the Mayor to proclaim the Fair." Poole, p. 64, citing the Corporation Records. He notes that the fair had been established by a charter of Henry III early in the twelfth century (c. 1217 or 1218); it began on the feast-day of the Holy Trinity and continued for eight days; it was proclaimed with considerable parade by the civic authorities, even before Lady Godiva appeared.

greater. The last procession was in connection with the Coronation Festivities of 1911. I do not know when there is likely to be another, but it is usual to have a procession on the occasion of any general public celebration, such as the Coronation, or a Jubilee. . ."

As the show, during the nineteenth century, seems to have had more downs than ups, it may be interesting to examine its history, bearing the contemporary development of the London Lord Mayor's Show in mind the while. The procession of 1826 is described in a pamphlet which may be found in the British Museum.[1] The effigy of Peeping Tom is described: it is somewhat larger than life-size, and is of "considerable antiquity"; it is made of oak, and, in its original state, represented a man in armor. Some changes in painting, alterations in the fashion of its garments, and the loss of its hands have modified it considerably.[2] It is "to be seen at the corner of Hertford Street, in an opening at the upper part of the house."[3]

In 1826,[4] after the City Guards, came St. George, armed cap-à-pie; Lady Godiva followed the High Constable; then came the mayor and his attendants, and the aldermen and sheriffs. Various Companies and Societies followed; and the procession came to an end with the Wool-Combers, a shepherd and shep-

---

[1] *The History of Coventry Show Fair, with a Particular Account of Lady Godiva and Peeping Tom, and an Interesting Description of the Grand Procession;* (see the Bibliography, *s.v.* COVENTRY.) An engraving of the effigy of Peeping Tom is opposite p. 7.

[2] The writer of the pamphlet seems to think that the effigy dates from before 1678. One may hazard the guess that it was an earlier St. George, or some other chivalric man in armour, from an older show, to whom the individuality of Peeping Tom was attached.

On Peeping Tom, see *Life in an Old English Town*, p. 7, n. 3. "The name . . . occurs in the city accounts, June 11, 1773, when a new wig was obtained for the effigy." Miss Harris refers, on the origin of the character, to *D. N. B.*, *s.v.* GODIVA.

As recently as 1710 no less than forty armed men attended the mayor and aldermen at the Fair. (Pamphlet, p. 15, n. 1; Poole (1870) p. 66). "The City Guards, or men in armour who led the way, are intended to represent the armoured men provided by the ancient guilds and city companies, with each of which guilds or companies it was customary to send out their guards to accompany the mayor in making proclamation of the fair." (Poole, p. 66). "Their armour consisted of corselets, with and without skirts, back pieces and morions, and their offensive weapons either the characteristic English long-bow, or the variously formed bill . . . the whole assemblage being an interesting display of ancient armour, of which there are now but few remains." (Pamphlet, p. 15; cf. *ibid.*, n. 2: "This Armour has recently been very judiciously cleaned and restored.")

[3] Pamphlet, pp. 7 f.; see also Poole (1870) p. 59; *The Story of Coventry*, p. 342; Poole (1852) pp. 11 f. Baedeker's *Great Britain* (1910) p. 272, remarks that "'Peeping Tom' is pilloried in a bust at the corner of Hertford Street."

[4] Both the pamphlet and Poole (1870) pp. 65 f., print the order of the 1826 procession, which took place on 26 May. The latter remarks that this "is the last procession but one in which the mayor and corporation appeared in their gorgeous civic costume . . . their final participation in the pageant being in 1829."

herdess with dog and lamb; Jason, with the Golden Fleece; five wool-sorters, and Bishop Blaize.[1]

"The City Followers, whose original characters, probably, were those of pages or trainbearers . . . are habited in antique dresses, the singular costume of which produces a remarkable contrast to the shewy and tasteful style generally used in the decoration of this most interesting portion of the procession."[2] Concerning Lady Godiva, the pamphlet says: "The female representing the fair patroness of Coventry is usually habited in a white cambric dress, closely fitted to the body, and a profusion of long flowing locks . . . On some few recent occasions, indeed, changes of a most ridiculous nature have been made, by the addition of a sort of petticoat, thus destroying all the illusion of the personification, and sacrificing consistency at the shrine of mock-delicacy."[3]

After 1835, the civic element gave way to history. "Since the passing of the Municipal Act of 1835, the 'make-up' of the procession has borne comparatively

---

[1] These last four are evidently either trade pageants, or characters from trade pageants. The pamphlet (p. 22) records that the shepherd and shepherdess rode on horseback before 1824, in which year they "were first displayed underneath a large bower; . . . a living lamb supplied the place of the former artificial lamb" (held formerly in the lap of the shepherdess) "the dog attending upon the shepherd as usual; an alteration which gave such general satisaction that it was repeated in 1826, and is likely to become the regular practice in future."

From the description in the pamphlet (pp. 22 f.) Jason and the Bishop, we may presume, were alive. St. George appears because some authorities assert he was born in Coventry, or, at any rate, lived there. "In Percy's *Reliques of Antient English Poetry* it is recorded of him, that after his wonderful adventures abroad, he returned to England:—

"'Where being in short space arrived
Unto his native dwelling place,
Therein with his dear love he lived
And fortune did his nuptials grace.
They many years of life did see,
And led their lives at Coventre.'"

Much of Poole's material seems to come from the pamphlet, from which he differs but slightly in his account of this pageant. The latter, on p. 16, quotes from *The Birth of St. George* "printed by Bishop Percy," and adds the authority of the *History of the Seven Champions of Christendom* which records St. George's birthplace as Coventry. On p. 17, the above stanza is quoted from "another ballad printed in the same [Percy's] collection."

The characters mentioned in the text above, were, through inadvertence, attributed to Preston (above, vol. i, p. 35). The reader can make the necessary correction.

[2] *Pamphlet*, p. 18. Poole (1870) p. 66, says: "The little children denominated 'followers' . . . are supposed to have some affinity to the children introduced into the religious mystery plays in the character of angels. Great pains are still bestowed upon them by their parents and patrons in attiring them richly and tastefully, so as to make them appear as angelic as possible wherever the grand opportunity is presented." It should be remarked that children were commonly seen in the Lord Mayor's Show, and that the miracle-plays were nearly dead in 1678.

[3] *Pamphlet*, pp. 18–19. Already in 1827 the Victorian era had begun!

small resemblance to what it has previously been,[1] and it is always appointed to take place on the Fair Monday, instead of on Friday, the first day, as was the ancient practice." [2]

Dissatisfaction with the procession was voiced about the middle of the century. "Although a strenuous effort was made so lately as the year 1845,[3] by the whole clergy of the City, and the major part of the municipal authorities, backed up by a remonstrance from the Bishop of the Diocese, against the continuance of an usage alleged to be of so questionable a character, and so much at variance with the spirit of the age — all this resistance failed to defeat the popular resolution which had been taken to enforce the procession as usual. On this occasion, however, the style of the procession was so good as to afford no reasonable ground for objection to the observance of this ancient usage." [4]

---

[1] A pamphlet entitled *Peeping Tom and Lady Godiva; a Brief Account of the Origin and Mode of Conducting the Show Fair at Coventry.* (Coventry, 1839) in the Brit. Mus. (*12431. aa. 4*), gives the order of procession of the 1678 Fair, that of 1829, and says that the procession of 1836 differed but little from them.

[2] Poole (1870), p. 67. He continues: "The new corporation never took any part in it, and, consequently, it lost from that time all the brilliancy of the civic costume, the fine ancient regalia, and the stamp of authoritative sanction. The withdrawal of these, of course made the introduction of something else necessary, to fill up the void; and accordingly Godiva was now accompanied by the representatives of various personages whose names are historically connected with the city . . . so that, upon the whole, a very imposing and gorgeous procession is still provided whenever the undertaking is entered upon, which is much more seldom than in former years . . . first, on account of the expense, which amounts to a large sum, but which, since the withdrawal of the corporation from it [*i. e.* the show ?] devolves on very uncertain resources: and secondly, on the question of taste or propriety in reference to the representation of the chief personage, the Lady Godiva . . . and there can be no doubt that it [the opposition] has had the effect of causing more circumspection to be exercised than heretofore, in the selection of the person appointed to represent the great heroine, and also in bringing into use a decent costume in lieu of the former imitation of entire nudity. More than once, under the popular management of the pageant, females of professional reputation in the metropolis, have not hesitated to become the public representative of the far-famed countess. . .

"In the catalogue for the sale of the effects left by the late corporation, which were sold in the month of July, 1836, the following articles connected with the procession, are enumerated: namely — 'Lady Godiva's cap; Lady Godiva's pages' cap; Lady Godiva's side-saddle, cover and three girths; three city flags; four pair of fasces; two pairs of fasces, gilt head; fourteen fasces used in procession, in lots; two staves; six swords; six saddle-cloths, embroidered with silver; ten ancient vests, worn in procession; two followers' dresses; six ancient belts; two city followers' caps; four black horse-cloths, used in procession.' "

[3] Poole (1852), pp. 13 f.

[4] An engraving, (opposite p. 14 in Poole's 1852 volume,) published by David Lewin, of Coventry, resembles that in the 1827 pamphlet (published by Meridew and Son). Both show the procession passing the City Hotel, and both include Peeping Tom in the house on the opposite corner. W. F. Taunton's drawing, made in 1868 for Poole's 1870 volume (opposite p. 56), is a copy of one of the earlier illustrations.

The 1848 show is described in a contemporary publication;[1] it took place on 26 June. Lady Godiva was represented by Madame Warton of the Walhalla, London. Edward the Confessor (Mr. Warton); Henry VI and Queen Margaret, Sir John Falstaff, William and Adam Bottener, Sir Thomas White, and Sir William Dugdale appeared.[2] " An elegant sylvan car or bower, in which played a fountain," closed the procession: Strephon and Phyllis, with dog and flock, made up the pastoral scene.[3]

" After an interval of eleven years," the show was revived on 23 June, 1862.[4] The procession was led by two heralds; following them came a detachment of the First Life Guards; then the City Arms;[5] then, after the band of the menagerie, " St. George, the canonised pork butcher of Cappadocia, arrived *cap-à-pie* with feathers in his helmet . . . following the twelve men with tureens and porringers. St. George's attendant was dressed in the costume of a Templar."[6] Members of various city guilds came next, the " followers "of the companies being represented by richly-dressed children. After the yeomen, came a fire engine, with members of the volunteer fire brigade; the Ancient Order of Foresters; Robin Hood and Maid Marian, with Will Scarlet, Friar Tuck, and other merry men, preceded the Black Prince in black armor. After more bands and companies came Lady Godiva on a white charger; there were in the procession, also, Richard II, Henry IV, Henry VI and Margaret, Henry VIII, and Queen Elizabeth. After Sir John Falstaff and more soldiers, came " last of all, on a lurry (*sic*) and four, a youth and a maiden, — a handsome ' Florizell ' and a pretty ' Perdita,' — dressed as a shepherd and shepherdess, seated in a sylvan bower, and at their feet a sheepdog and a lamb."[7] The procession was over a

---

[1] See the *Era* for 2 July 1848, p. 6, col. 3.

[2] Poole (1870), p. 67, tells how these figures are appropriate. Falstaff was identified with Coventry by Shakspere; William and Adam Botoner (*sic*) were intimately connected with St. Michael's Church; Sir Thomas White was a great benefactor of the city; Dugdale was the eminent county historian of Warwickshire.

[3] *Era, loc. cit.* This pastoral scene evidently descends from the Wool-Combers.

The Godiva procession of 1851 is pictured and described in the *Illus. Lond. News* for 5 July, 1851, pp. 1 and 2. It included St. George and a May Queen.

[4] On this, see the London *Times* for 30 April, 1862, p. 12, col. 2; for 11 June, p. 6, col. 6; 25 June, p. 12, col. 2; the *Era* for 29 June, 1862, p. 15, col. 4; the *Morning Star* for 25 June, 1862, p. 6, col. 6. The latter (disagreeing with the *Times* for 25 June, p. 12, which, citing the *Express*, notes that on the 23d the procession was revived " after an interval of eleven years ") says " Eight years have passed since this famous Lady Godiva pageant was exhibited at Coventry." Cf also Fairholt's *Civic Garland*, pp. xiv f.; *Fun*, for 28 June, 1862, p. 144.

[5] A real elephant with a pasteboard castle on his back. Cf. above, vol. i, p. 68, n. 2 (on p. 69) and the drawing opposite p. 68.

[6] *Morning Star*, issue cited.

[7] *Morning Star*. Fairholt includes Jason and Bishop Blaize; the *Times* for 11 June, 1862, tells of plans to include Leofric, Earl of Mercia, the husband of Lady Godiva; a car emblematic of the Seasons, William and Adam Bottmer (*sic*) former mayors of Coventry,

THE LADY GODIVA PROCESSION

mile in length, and was made possible by subscriptions — about £200 had been raised by the end of April.[1] — The Committee spent nearly £300, and it is interesting to note that the costumes were all made in Coventry. Fourteen city guards, clad in suits of old armor in the possession of the Corporation, were a feature of the show.

The latest appearance of Lady Godiva was in 1911; "it has been decided to follow the precedent of the last Coronation festivities with regard to the costume to be worn by the representative of Lady Godiva in the procession on this occasion. Lady Godiva will be represented in silk fleshings, with a gauze cape carried under the left arm to the right shoulder, and having a long flowing wig covering the greater part of her figure."[2]

This procession seems to have its root in the Fair, though the latter may have attracted an earlier Corpus Christi procession; it soon took unto itself trade elements; and these have persisted, in spite of the emphasis on history which has grown since the civic authorities departed from the show in 1829. There is a tendency toward the carnival in the figures from fiction; but the pageant serves to keep the past of the city fresh in the minds of the inhabitants, and resurrects the worthies of civic history in much the same way as did the Lord Mayor's Show of the seventeenth century.

§ 4. POLITICAL PAGEANTRY

Every procession with an effigy to which a political signification has been given is, strictly speaking, a political pageant; from the multitude of such shows it will be sufficient to select, as representatives, the "Pope-burnings" of 1679–82, and the Orange processions of Belfast. We have already seen[3] that foreign sailors carried the image of Judas Iscariot through the streets of English ports, before they flogged it. A wickerwork representation which replaced the human victim of early sacrifices gave rise, folk-lorists say, to the folk-giant on one hand, and the saint's image on the other; and the change from religion to politics is made as soon as the effigy receives a political signification.

Brayley[4] notes that the Pope-procession "arose in Queen Elizabeth's reign,

---

and Sir William Dugdale, the antiquarian, besides those we have mentioned. *The Era* for 29 June, 1862, adds further notice of Sir Thomas White, a merchant *temp.* Henry VIII, and Mr. John Hales, a merchant *temp.* Edward VI. (Poole (1870), p. 67, notes that Hales founded the Free School.) All the royalties and celebrities were connected with Coventry history.

[1] *Times* for 30 April, 1862, p. 12, col. 2.

[2] The London *Times* for 10 March, 1911, p. 11, col. 3. On 14 February, p. 11, col. 5, the *Times* recorded (in an obscure paragraph) the decision to celebrate the coronation by means of a procession at Coventry.

[3] Above, vol. i, p. 16. Cf. above, p. 156, and n. 5.

[4] *Londiniana*, iv, p. 74.

and it was occasionally observed on the anniversary of her birth,[1] (viz. November the 17th,) till after the commencement of the last century, although not always with a similar degree of pomp and *uproariousness* . . . The most famous of these processions were those of 1679, 1680 and 1681." [2] Evelyn, in his *Diary* under date of 5 November, 1673,[3] says that the Pope was burned in effigy, after being paraded in triumph in the streets, to show the people's displeasure that the Duke of York altered his religion and married the Catholic Mary d'Esté, daughter of the Duke of Modena.

A contemporary account of the Pope-burning of 1679 is reprinted by Brayley;[4] the show consisted of a long procession with the Pope's image on a pageant.[5] A song, sung by "Cardinal Norfolk" and "Plebians" preceded the burning.

1680 — A Pope Burnt at London and at Edinburgh

The following year, there was an elaborate Pope-burning at London, of which Settle was in charge.[6] In the procession were nine pageants, with representatives

---

[1] Meaning her accession; she was born on 6 September — see Lord Herbert's *Henry VIII*, p. 510. *D. N. B.*, *s.v. Elizabeth*, dates her birth 7 September.

[2] I have found no mention of this kind of thing before 1673; but it is quite likely that the religious feeling of England in the hundred years before that date had received pageantic expression.

Various descriptive pamphlets dealing with these ceremonies (1679–82) are listed in the Bibliography, *s.v.* Pope-burning; the same sort of thing is found in Boston (Massachusetts) in the following century. See p. 176, below.

In Fairholt's copy of *London's Defiance to Rome* (preserved in SA) occurs this MS. note, *inter alia:* "In the Letters to & from the Earl of Derby (Lond. 1710) is an account of the Pope-burning in 1678, when Mr. Mountagu, a French agent, was in London. — 'It was the next Pope-burning day, he made me promise to show him the burning of the Pope. He came with a gentleman, that spoke English pretty well, to the Palsgrave head Tavern at five, where I stayed for him, and carried him within Temple Bar, to a Friend's house of mine; when he saw the Shew, and the great concourse of people which was very great at that time, to his great Amasement . . . At my return he seemed frighted, being afraid that some body that had been in the room had known him, for then he might have been in some danger, for had the Mob had the least intimation of him they had torn him to pieces . . . he wondered when I told him no manner of mischief was done, not so much as a head broke; but in 3 or 4 hours were all quiet as at other times.' " (I have not seen a copy of the book cited here; it is not in Gh., BM., SA., or Bodl.)

[3] Cited by Brayley, iv, p. 88.

[4] *Op. cit.*, iv, p. 73; cf. Scott's Dryden (ed. Saintsbury, 18 vols., Edinburgh, 1882–93) vi, pp. 237 f. A pamphlet entitled *Londons Defiance to Rome* [in SA and Bodl. (*Gough, Midds. 32*)] recounts this show. F. C. Brown, p. 61, notes Settle's part in preparing this pageantry.

[5] Fairholt, pt. i, p. 92, n. 2, mentions prints illustrating the Pope-burnings of 1679 and 1680, and notes that the former is reproduced by Brayley.

[6] On this, see *The Solemn Mock Procession*, (London, 1680) recorded in the Bibliography, *s.v.* Pope-burning; North's *Examen*, pp. 571 f. (cited by Brayley, iv, p. 80, and in Saintsbury's Scott's Dryden) describes the shows of 1680, 1681, and 1682 which North witnessed.

of various Catholic dignitaries on each. The parade was led by the captain of the Pope's guard; then came ten "Pioneers in Red Caps and Coats," who were followed by a "Bellman ringing, and saying in a loud doleful Voice, *Remember Justice* Godfrey." Then came a "dead Bloody Corps, representing Sir *Edm. Ber. Godf.*," supported by a Jesuit with a bloody dagger. There followed a banner showing Jesuits hanging on a gibbet with Mrs. Cellier,[1] "and all her other Presbyterian Plot-forgers."

Then came the first pageant, on which were figures of Mrs. Cellier, leaning on a meal-tub, and four Protestants in masquerade; after which rode an "Abhorrer" facing the tail of his horse. Four Franciscans occupied the second pageant; Augustine and Dominican friars, the third; Jesuits, the fourth. On the fifth were Bishops; on the sixth, Patriarchs, and the Pope's Master of Ceremonies selling Indulgences. The Pope himself occupied the seventh pageant, with the Devil at his elbow and the Emperor Frederick sprawling under his feet — two banners bore these inscriptions: *This is the King of Kings* and *Thou art our God the Pope.* On the eighth pageant rode the Empress Donna Olympia, with nuns; an inscription labelled them *Curtezans in Ordinary.* The ninth pageant bore a Bishop-Judge, surrounded by Monks, before whom a victim of the Inquisition was tied to a stake; round about were scattered racks and other instruments of torture.

From a pamphlet in the Fairholt Collection, we get these added details: A "vast *Bonfire* being prepared just over against the *Inner-Temple-Gate*, his Holiness after some Compliments and Reluctancies, was decently *Toppled* from all his Grandeur into the *Impartial Flames;* The crafty *Devil* leaving his *Infallibility-ship* in the lurch, and laughing as heartily at his deserv'd Ignominious end, as *subtile Jesuits* do at the ruine of *Bigotted* Lay-Catholicks . . . This Justice was attended with a *Prodigious Shout*, that might be heard far beyond *Somerset-House;* and 'twas believ'd the Eccho . . . reached *Scotland*, *France*, and even

---

Cf. also *London's Defiance*, p. 4; F. C. Brown, pp. 62 f., (citing Saintsbury's Scott's Dryden, vi, pp. 237 f.). North records that these processions were managed by the King's Head Club, or Green Ribbon Club.

Illustrations of the 1680 procession may be found in Fairholt's collection in the Society of Antiquaries; in the Brit. Mus. (*C.* 20. *f.* 6 [*26*]) is a copperplate engraving (advertised at the end of *The Solemn Mock Procession*) accompanied by a description. This is reproduced in F. C. Brown's *Elkanah Settle*, p. 62.

A ballad, entitled *London's Drollery* (in the Roxburghe collection, ii, no. 292) describes the nine pageants on this occasion.

[1] Brayley, *Lond.*, iii, p. 205, gives an account of "the Meal-tub Plot," discovered at the house of Mrs. Cellier, a midwife. "The people were rendered so indignant by the detection of the Meal-tub Plot, that they determined to express their feeling against the Papists in a marked way. Accordingly, on the seventeenth of November, the Anniversary of Queen Elizabeth's Accession, which at that time was a popular holy-day, the annual solemnity of *Burning the Pope* was performed with additional ceremonies of mock grandeur."

Rome itself . . . The same evening there were *large Bonfires* generally in the Streets and universal Acclamations, *Long live King* CHARLES, *and let Popery perish, and Papists with their Plots and Counter-plots ever* (as hitherto) *be confounded,* To which, every honest *Englishman* will readily say *Amen.*" [1]

The enmity against Catholics, which was particularly strong in 1680, seems to have spread to Edinburgh, where the University authorities tried without success to prevent the students from burning a Pope.[2] The undergraduates " took a Conceit in Imitation, as is supposed, of your Famous City of *London,* to Burn the *Pope* in *Effigie* . . ." The " cavalcade " of " his Holiness " (who was " attyred after his *Antichristian Manner,* with his *Miter, Keys,* &c. and settled in his *Throne* ") accompanied him: and the youths put " heresy " (*i. e.* gunpowder) in his belly, so that when the fire reached it, he blew all to bits.

The students who carried out this pageant were arrested and charged with disloyalty and rebellion. Their defence was published in a pamphlet dated February, 1681, and signed " N. M ";[3] the students did not mean rebellion, treason, or " an affront upon any person whatsoever other than the Pope." [4] Encouragement for the burning came from England: " the very same manner of expressing a detestation of Popery by Burning the Pope, has been practised in *London,* and in other places of *England,* without any *Imputation* of *Disloyalty* or *Sedition* that ever we heard of." [5]

LONDON BURNS OTHER POPES

In 1681, London repeated the show on 17 November. In this procession appeared " Sir Edmundbury Godfrey," besprinkled with blood, with a twisted napkin round his neck, and his head hanging on one side; there were effigies of

---

[1] *Londons Defiance,* p. 4. At the Lord Mayor's banquet, this year, the first song was called *The Protestant's Exhortation,* and the second was called *The Plotting Papist's Litany;* it began,

" Though our Plot be betray'd,
Let us pursue it,
We need not be dismay'd,
We will renew it; " etc.

No suggestion of unfriendliness to Papists occurred in the Show itself; see Jordan's descriptive pamphlet, which is outlined by Fairholt, pt. i, pp. 92 f.

[2] See " A letter from *Edenbrough* to a Friend in *London,* containing the Manner of Burning the *Pope* there in *Effigie* on *Christ*-Mass Day, &c." which is no. 4 in a collection entitled *Tracts Relating to the Popish Plot,* 1679–82. [B.M. *8133. h. 5 (1–10)*].

[3] *A Modest Apology for the Students of Edenburgh Burning a Pope, December 25, 1680, Humbly Rescuing the Actors from the Imputation of Disloyalty and Rebellion, with which they were charged in a Letter, &c.* . . (London, 1681); this may be found on p. 114 of a volume of tracts in the Brit. Mus. [*T. 2.* *(*28*)].

[4] *A Modest Apology,* p. 10.

[5] *Ibid.,* p. 8. On p. 12, the explosion of the Pope's effigy is recounted; and the rest of the letter is taken up with the account of the arrest of the students and of their defence.

friars, Jesuits, Cardinals, and the Pope, all of which — with the exception of Godfrey — were to be burned at Temple Bar, "according to the old laudable custom."[1] With the effigies were several painted "pieces" and fireworks. North[2] describes the Pope-burning of 1682, at which the statue of Elizabeth, "in the Nich of Temple-Bar" was "set out like an Heathen Idol."

As late as 1711, the 17 November was to have been celebrated by a Pope-burning; but the government seized the images, on which the Whigs had "laid out" £1000.[3] The processions lasted on this side of the Atlantic much longer. A ballad entitled *Plot upon Plot*[4] contains a notice of these political processions:

> "You for your Bonefires *Mawkins* drest
> On good Queen *Bess's* Day,
> Whereby much *Treason* was express'd,
> As all *true Churchmen* say,
> Against the *Devil* and the *Pope*,
> The *French* our new Allie,
> And *Perkin* too, that Youth of *Hope*,
> On whom *we* all rely."

With the beginning of the eighteenth century, these processions, having no civic ties (as had the Lord Mayor's Shows) passed from existence. Since then whatever political pageantry there has been, in England, has been incorporated with civic shows, or with such "occasional" pageants as we have examined here.

---

[1] On this, see *The Procession*, &c., recorded in the Bibliography, *s.v.* POPE-BURNING. (This is no. 8 in the *Tracts Relating to the Popish Plot*, and is also in the Bodl. (*Gough, Midds.* 32.)

[2] *Examen*, pp. 577 f.

[3] Swift, *Journal to Stella*, letter xxxv (17 November, 1711). See Scott's Swift (19 vols., Edinburgh, 1814), ii, pp. 409, 410. Cf. *Political Merriment* (1714), pp. 207 f. for a song ("to the Tune of *Bonny Dun-dee*") entitled: "*Queen* Elizabeth's *Day: or, the Downfall of the* Devil, Pope *and* Pretender." It is followed (p. 212) by an account of the "Mock Procession of Burning the Pope and the Chevalier *de St. George*, intended to be performed on the 17th Instant, being the Anniversary of Queen *Elizabeth* of Pious and Glorious Memory." On p. 214 is an explanation by one "Captain Tom" of the prevention of the "annual Protestation procession due to the memory of the glorious Queen Bess" scheduled for 17 November, 1711. It was intended to include in this a figure of the Cardinal Gualteri, various Friars, Jesuits, and Cardinals; and the Pope, "accompany'd by the Chevalier *St. George* on the Left, and his Counsellor the Devil on his Right." Also various link-men, watchmen, bagpipes, &c., &c. The effigies were to have been burned in front of Elizabeth's statue at Temple Bar. "After the proper Ditties were sung, the Pretender was to have been committed to the Flames, being first absolv'd by the Cardinal *Gualteri*. After that, the said Cardinal was to be absolv'd by the Pope, and burnt. And then the Devil was to jump into the Flames with his Holiness in his Arms. . ."

[4] Which is preserved in *Political Merriment* (1714) p. 82. (See Bibliography, *s.v.* BRINSDEN [BM. *238. g. 45*]). (I may note that the ballad contains an interesting allusion to Dean Swift.)

"Pope-Burnings" in New England

Much resembling these "Pope-burnings" of London, were the eighteenth-century processions at Boston, Massachusetts, in which effigies of the Pope and Devil were carried through the streets of the city, and then burned.[1] There is little doubt that these processions were connected with those of England: they seem to have lasted in some parts of New England until recent times, though the origins were forgotten, the customs changed, and the name corrupted almost beyond recognition.

In 1752, the General Court of Massachusetts enacted "that if any Persons to the Number of three or more, between Sun-setting and Sun-rising, being assembled together in any of the Streets or Lanes of any town within this Province, shall have any kind of Imagery or Pageantry for a Publick Shew, altho' none of the Company so assembled shall be arm'd or disguis'd, or exact, demand or ask any Money or Thing of Value, every Person being of such Company shall forfeit and pay the Sum of *forty Shillings* or suffer imprisonment not exceeding one Month, or if the offender shall be a Negro Servant, in Lieu of the Imprisonment he may be whip'd not exceeding ten Stripes, at the Discretion of the Justice before whom the Trial shall be.[2]

This act was passed because "many and great disorders have of late years been committed by tumultuous companies of men, children and negroes carrying about with them Pageants and other shews through the streets . . . of Boston . . . and besides the horrid profaneness, Impiety and other gross Immoralities usually found in such Companies a Person has lately been killed when orderly walking in the streets . . . and the aforesaid practices have been found by experience to encourage and cultivate a mobbish Temper and Spirit in many of the Inhabitants, and an Opposition to all Government and Order." [3]

Before 1752, both the North and South Ends of the town had their effigies; the marchers would meet and fight, the victors burning not only their own "pageants," but also those of the vanquished foe. In 1763, these processions

---

[1] *Publ. Col. Soc. Mass.*, xii, pp. 288 f. I am indebted to Professor Kittredge for this reference. Mr. Cunningham, in his paper on the *Diary* of the Rev. Samuel Checkley, there printed, further says that "Pope Night" was celebrated at Portsmouth, New Hampshire, as late as 1892; but that through a loss of the images, and changes in the customs, the origins had been forgotten, and the name corrupted to "Pork Night."

[2] *Massachusetts Laws*, 26 George II, chap. 6. (Boston, 1755–62, p. 104.) I am indebted to Professor Kittredge for this reference.

Because bonfires had been sometimes kindled in the streets and lanes of several towns, an act was passed making the building of bonfires in a street or lane, or within ten rods of any house or building, punishable by the same fine of forty shillings, or imprisonment. This act was to run for three years, and in 1758 was continued to 1 April, 1763, (*ibid.*, p. 348).

[3] *Temporary Acts and Laws of his Majesty's Province of the Massachusetts Bay (1736–1774)*, (Boston, 1763–74), p. 83; cf. *ibid.*, (1736–1762), (Boston, 1755–62).

were revived; but the accident of 1764, when a boy was killed, united the two processions, and the fights ended. In 1765, a Stamp-man joined the Devil and the Pope; and just before the Revolution, effigies of unpopular officers — such as Governor Hutchinson and General Gage — were added.[1]

I am indebted to Mr. Albert Matthews for the following information concerning early American pageantry. There was a procession of trades in Boston on 24 October, 1789, in honor of Washington's third and last visit to this town;[2] and the word *pageantry* was used in describing the Stamp Act riots which took place in Boston on 14 August, 1765. Early that morning were discovered hanging from a tree

> two Effigies, one of which by the Labels appeared to be designed to represent a Stamp-Officer [Andrew Oliver, Secretary of the Province], the other a Jack-Boot, with a Head and Horns peeping out of the Top, said by some of the Printers, to be the Devil or his Imp; but, as we are not acquainted with that Species of Gentleman, we cannot so well determine whether it was an exact Resemblance or not; . . . The Report of these Images soon spread through the Town, . . . About Dusk the Images were taken down, placed on a Bier, (not covered with a Sheet, except the Sheet of Paper which bore the Inscription,) supported in Procession by six Men, followed by a great Concourse of People, some of the highest Reputation, and in the greatest Order, ecchoing forth Liberty and Property! No Stamp! &c — Having passed through the Town-House, they proceeded with their Pageantry down Kingstreet, . . . to the top of Fort-Hill; where a fire was soon kindled, in which one of them was burnt; we can't learn whether they committed the other to the Flames, or if they did, whether it did not survive the Conflagration, being its said like the Salamander conversant with that Element.[3]

Another prohibition was made in 1797, when, on 10 March, *An Act for keeping Watches and Wards in towns, and for preventing disorders in streets and public places* was passed; the ninth section of the act reads: "Be it further enacted, That if any three or more persons . . . shall assemble together, having any imagery or pageantry as a public shew, . . . shall . . . demand or ask any money, . . . every person . . . shall, for each offence, forfeit and pay *eight dollars*, or be imprisoned not exceeding one month." [4]

---

[1] See Cunningham, in *Publ. Col. Soc. Mass.* for March, 1909 — the article cited above.

It is interesting to compare the Devil in these processions with those of the sixteenth-century Lord Mayor's Show (see above, p. 14f.). It is, however, probably not connected with that figure, being rather a copy of the political Devil who accompanied the Pope in the London processions we have just been considering.

[2] Mr. Matthews refers to the description of this in the *Massachusetts Centinel* of 28 October [1789] xii, 51/3.

[3] *Boston News Letter*, 22 August, 1765, p. 2/2. It is to be noted how discreetly the reporter conveys the information that the Stamp-Officer's effigy was that burnt. No treason is obvious here.

[4] *Laws of the Commonwealth of Massachusetts, passed at several Sessions of the General Court Holden in Boston*, iii, (n. d.), pp. 99–101. (The ninth section is on p. 101.) For this reference, I am indebted to Mr. Albert Matthews, who sent the information in a letter to Professor Kittredge.

Remarks on Effigies, Illuminations, and Pageantic Fireworks

The burning and flogging of effigies [1] suggest the popular superstition which plays such a large part in Rossetti's ballad of *Sister Helen:* this may be another development of the folk-custom which apparently lies behind the effigy and saint's image, if these come from the giant, which seems to have been a substitute for the human sacrifice. The bonfires become pageantic, when the figures burnt have a significance, and if the emotion expressed appeals to the witnessing crowd. The silent figures in a Lord Mayor's pageant appear to have foreshadowed the *tableau vivant*, which, in turn, led to such " illuminations " as that which celebrated Admiral Vernon's victory at Portobello, on 12 November, 1740 — the Admiral's birthday. Mr. J. G. Nichols [2] records a " pageant," with bonfires and illuminations, " representing Admiral Vernon and a Spaniard on his knee, offering him a sword; a view of Porto Bello, &c." [3] This seems to have been a painting, or perhaps, a *feu d'artifice*. The celebration of Vernon's birthday seems to have been widespread, [4] and to have consisted chiefly of bonfires and illuminations.

An example of what might easily have become pageantic *feux d'artifice*, I quote from a family letter, written from Newport, Rhode Island, in July, 1881:

---

[1] Cf., for further remarks on this subject, vol. i, p. 10, n. 5; p. 16; p. 51, n. 2; p. 56, n. 3; p. 229 (the 1606 burning of the Deadly Sins) and p. 241.

[2] *Lond. Pag.*, p. 120, n. 2.

[3] He adds: " It will from this be perceived that the modern successors of Pageants are the transparencies exhibited on nights of Illumination." What he means is, that the *feux d'artifice* (of which we have already made mention — see above, vol. i, p. 240 f.) developed from pageantry; the " successors " of the pageant are, of course, the " floats " of our own processions.

[4] See the London *Evening Post*, from Saturday, 1 November to Tuesday, 4 November, 1740 (no. 2023) which contains an account of the celebration, in the " Extract of a Letter from Bath, Saturday, Nov. 1." Effigies of Don Blass were burnt, " which afforded great Diversion to the Populace, among whom were generously bestow'd several Hogsheads of strong Beer . . ." At London and Lewisham, in Kent, the celebrations took the form of illuminations; bells were rung, bonfires were lighted, and fireworks set off. Warwick also celebrated the occasion (see *ibid.*, from 4 Nov. to 6 Nov. — no. 2026) in much the same manner; Essex and Peterborough celebrated later.

[On the possibility of *God Save the King* having been first sung by Henry Carey this year (1740) in a tavern on Cornhill, at a dinner given to celebrate Admiral Vernon's victory at Portobello, see W. H. Cummings, in the *Musical Times* for July, 1878 (vol. xix), p. 379. Mr. Cummings does not consider the evidence that Carey composed this song, reliable. We may refer to a letter, reprinted from the *St. James's Chronicle* by the *London Magazine* for November, 1761 (vol. xxx, pp. 597–601) in which the writer describes the banquet following the Lord Mayor's Show of that year, at which " the latter part of Mr. Handell's coronation anthem, *God Save the King, &c.*" was played while the mayor drank the king's health. On p. 608 of the same issue, the speech of the Christ's Hospital boy to the king is printed; at the end of the speech, " the boys in a grand chorus chanted, God save the King. Amen."]

"The latest novelty is 'day fireworks' . . . At the Casino, four mortars were placed in the ground, in an upright position. They threw bombs seven hundred feet into the air, where they exploded, showering paper balloons of various colors; gorgeous, air-filled men and women, butterflies and fish, some of which floated far away, while others came near enough for the boys to catch. At the same time, other bombs would explode into beautiful cloud-like figures, more resembling airy devil-fish against the clear blue of the sky, than anything else I can think of." Had these figures been given a significance, we might consider them related to such inanimate pageantry as the images which "did rise by a vice" in 1522,[1] or the painted Worthies of 1554.[2] And these are not unlike the images of the Deadly Sins, burned (as part of the entertainment) in 1606,[3] or the various *tableaux* suggested in the *Advis Necessaires pour la Conduite des Feux d'Artifice* of 1660.[4] From these to effigies which were burned as a spectacle for the entertainment of a crowd out of sympathy with the ideas held by the person represented, is but a step.

Guy Fawkes' Day after the War — Effigies Named

That dying customs have not been killed completely by the war, is shown by the following paragraph concerning Guy Fawkes' Day:[5]

During the war, Guy Fawkes Day was a suspended festival. Regulations bound up with national defence made a discharge of a squib or the soaring of a rocket a serious offense. Tradition this year was restored to its proper place, and young people, paying little heed to the chill, damp air, built their bonfires, exploded their crackers, and burned their effigies with old-time enthusiasm. Fireworks were dearer than in 1914, but purchases had been heavy, and the smell of gunpowder was pungent in many suburbs of London in the later hours of the day.

The choice of a subject for last week's effigy was curious. A year ago, the Kaiser would have been the children's selection for their Guy Fawkes Day figure, but the Kaiser seems to have been forgotten. Youngsters exhorted pedestrians in the streets "to remember the guy," but, where their processions escorted a scarecrow dummy, in three cases out of four the effigy in the chair was labelled "Pussyfoot."[6]

It was a matter for comment and for reflection on the high price of clothes that some of the effigies chaired through the streets were not life-like in size, and that in more than one instance "Pussyfoot" was a doll, camouflaged for the occasion, and probably guaranteed against a fiery destruction later in the day.

Effigies have long been burned on this anniversary, but they have a political significance rather than a folk origin. There is, however, a possible connection between such a mode of showing one's displeasure and the old belief expressed in Rossetti's *Sister Helen*, though the connection has doubtless long been forgotten.

---

[1] See above, vol. i, p. 177.
[2] See above, vol. i, p. 191.
[3] See above, vol. i, p. 229.
[4] See above, vol. i, p. 240 f.
[5] London *Times* — weekly edition, 14 November, 1919, p. 1065, col. 3.
[6] The nickname of an American agent of the Anti-Saloon League, at the time in England.

The Orange Processions of Ireland

As an example of modern political pageantry, we may glance at the Orange Processions of Ireland. The Orange Order was founded in 1795, after the Battle of the Diamond,[1] and the following year saw the first Twelfth of July Procession. "The Anti-Procession Act," continues Mr. MacArthur, "long ago imprisoned men for taking part in these July Processions, but of course this law has long since been repealed."

The anniversary of the Battle of the Boyne was celebrated by means of processions at various places during the nineteenth century; and these occasions served to keep alive the memory of past glories, as well as to strengthen Protestantism and political solidarity in the northern counties of Ireland.[2] In July, 1914 — less than a month before the beginning of the Great War, when it appeared as if England were facing a civil strife, which the European conflict averted — monster processions were held in various Orange districts. I shall here confine myself to that which, headed by the Unionist leader Sir Edward Carson, marched from Belfast to Drumbeg, where an enthusiastic meeting was held.[3]

The city of Belfast was decorated with flags and triumphal arches, with pictures of King William crossing the Boyne, Sir Edward Carson, and other his-

---

[1] My authority is a letter of Mr. William MacArthur, of Dublin, from whom I have received much information. He refers to *The Select Parliamentary Report on Irish Orangeism* (1835) which I have not been able to see. Mr. James Davidson, writing from the Grand Secretary's office of the Grand Lodge of Ireland, refers to the investigation at Castlewellan in 1849 — in connection with an Orange Procession, attacked at Dolly's Brae — which is treated by Richard Niven, in *Orangeism as it was and is*. He adds a reference to the report of the special committee of the Grand Orange Lodge, appointed to inquire into the matter, as well as to Sir W. Verner, *A Short History of the Battle of the Diamond* (London, 1863) neither of which have I had an opportunity to examine.

[2] Cf. Niven, *Orangeism*, p. 19: "Although it may be admitted on the part of any candid enquirer that the Orange Institution was justifiable and necessary, yet many, both those who are friendly to the Institution and those who are otherwise, think that the annual procession which takes place each 12th of July is in itself a cause for provoking angry collisions and keeping up an animosity that were better allayed. It may be so, still I think that the Orangemen are not to be blamed in the matter. They only perpetuate a memorable epoch in the history of our country which gave to all the inhabitants of the British Islands civil and religious liberty. Besides, before 1795 far more angry collisions occurred between the two parties. . ."

[3] Full details of various Orange processions of July, 1914, may be found in the Belfast *Weekly News* for Thursday, 16 July, 1914, which is my authority for the following remarks. Cf. also the London *Daily Sketch* of 14 July, 1914, for illustrations of the celebration which — the 12th being Sunday — this year took place on the 13th. "Today's procession was the first in which Unionists took as great a part as Orangemen," records this journal (p. 5). And again: "In other years 'the Twelfth' has been a festival. To-day it is a ceremony which combined a celebration of the past with a declaration of duty for the future." (*Ibid., loc. cit.*)

torical figures, living and dead. Such inscriptions as, " We prefer death rather than submit to Pope and Popery," " Ulstermen refuse to be sold by Asquith & Co. to the rebels of College Green," and " No Surrender and No Home Rule," were in prominent positions.

The only pageantic feature of the procession — and that was the most elementary of pageantry — were the banners which pictured historical scenes connected with the past of Protestantism.

The banners furnished a fine splash of colour, and in the brilliant, and broiling, sunshine which prevailed they were seen to excellent advantage. The designs symbolise the ideals and achievements of Protestantism. The picture of Queen Victoria presenting a copy of the Bible to one of her Indian subjects and telling him that it is the secret of England's greatness is one of the most popular subjects. Other designs relate to various phases in the life of Martin Luther, the burning of Latimer and Ridley, with the injunction of the former to his fellow-martyr — " Be of good comfort, Master Ridley, and play the man "; the landing of William at Torbay and Carrickfergus; the breaking of the boom by the Mountjoy; and the signing of the Ulster Covenant in the Belfast City Hall two years ago. The memory of many men — now, alas! no more — who served their day and generation faithfully is honoured in the Orange Institution, as the portraits on many of the banners show. Amongst those commemorated in this way are the late Marquis of Salisbury, Lord Beaconsfield, Colonel Saunderson, M.P.; Sir Daniel Dixon, Bart., M.P.; Sir Edward J. Harland, Bart., M.P.; Sir James Haslett, M.P.; Sir James Henderson, D.L.; Mr. R. J. M'Mordie, M.P.; Mr. William Johnston, M.P.; Rev. Dr. Kane, Rev. Dr. Cooke, Rev. S. M'Comb, and Mr. W. S. Baird, J.P. On the top of one flagpole a very neat model of the Mountjoy was placed. The Union Jack was prominent, and no patriotic emblem could have been more appropriate at this juncture. Nearly everybody one met with on Monday wore an Orange lily as a buttonhole, and the banner poles and drums which were carried in the procession were decorated with bunches of that much-esteemed flower.

During the three or four weeks preceding " The Twelfth " it is customary for many lodges to purchase new banners, and this year the number unfurled was, if anything, above the average. Amongst the new banners borne on Monday's procession were the following: . . life-size portrait of William III, in armour, with inscription " In glorious and immortal memory," in background scene representing the Battle of the Boyne, and medallions in four corners with portraits of Dr. Cooke, Dr. Kane, Mr. Wm. Johnston, and Colonel Saunderson; reverse side, life-size portrait of Oliver Cromwell in armour, with inscription " Trust in God and keep your powder dry," scene in background representing ships of the British fleet, with portraits as on obverse side. . . Portrait of the late Br. John Forsythe, and a representation of Castlereagh Presbyterian Church. . . Landing of William III. at Torbay, and " The secret of England's greatness."; . . . representation of the Battle of the Boyne in gold, five-pointed star. . . King William III. and the Relief of Derry; . . . William III. on horse, and the signing of the Ulster Covenant at the City Hall; . . . King William III. on horse, and representation of Britannia, with warship in the background; . . . Ruth and Naomi, representing Ulster's appeal to England, with motto, " Intreat me not to leave thee," reverse side shield set with diamonds, and representation of King William III; . . . William III. crossing the Boyne, surrounded with orange lilies, with mottoes " Civil and Religious Liberty," " Aughrim, Derry, Boyne; " above portraits of the late Prince Albert and Queen Victoria, a portrait of the late Mr. R. J. M'Mordie, M.P., Lord Mayor of Belfast, surmounted with crossed Union Jacks and rose, thistle, and shamrock; portraits above of Mr. Geo. S. Clark and Sir Edward Carson.

. . . Life-size portrait of late Field-Marshal Sir George White, V.C., with inscription, " Thank God, we have kept the old flag flying." . . .

The size of the procession may be judged from the fact that, although a fairly good pace was kept on the march, the brethren occupied over two hours in passing a given point.[1]

Here we have the " ghost " of pageantry; mere shadows of such historical events as were often reproduced by figures on moving cars. The " body " of pageantry is absent; the " spirit " is only suggested — yet the past is recalled and used as a spur to encourage the present. It is useless to multiply examples of this kind of procession; we mention the type merely because it is of interest to see what lies on the outskirts of this form of art — itself (until the Parkerian pageant) on the outskirts of the drama.

§ 5. PAGEANTIC TOURNAMENTS OF MODERN DAYS

This chapter would not be complete without some mention of the chivalric revivals of the nineteenth century; and, as tournament has played its part not only in the development of the masque, but also — though more indirectly — of the early pageant, it is only just to note the influence of the pageant on the later revivals of the tournament. One of the most famous, as well as the earliest, of these revivals was that at Eglinton, or Eglintown, Castle, Ayrshire, in 1839.[2] Rehearsals of the participants took place every Tuesday and Saturday at the Eyre Arms Tavern in St. John's Wood, for some time preceding the great day;[3] but it cannot be said that these pageanters were regarded with respect. " We

---

[1] Belfast *Weekly News* for 16 July, 1914, p. 5.

[2] See for mention of this in fiction, *Endymion*, by the author of *Lothair* (3 vols. — London, 1880), ii, chapters xxiii and xxiv (pp. 219–250). Montfort Castle is the name which Disraeli gives to Eglinton. Reference to the tournament is also made by George W. E. Russell, in *Collections and Recollections*, chapter xxxii, *Letter-Writing*. Cf. also various items in the London *Times*, as cited.

Regarding this affair, Mr. Russell says that Beaconsfield " conceding something to the requirements of art, ignores the fact that the splendid pageant was spoilt by rain. Two years' preparation and enormous expense were thrown away. A grand cavalcade, in which Prince Louis Napoleon rode as one of the knights, [while Louis took part in the sword play, he did not (unless under an assumed name) " ride as one of the knights," whose names are given in the *Times* for 31 August, 1839, p. 3, col. 4,] left Eglinton Castle on the 28th of August at two in the afternoon, with heralds, banners, pursuivants, the knight-marshal, the jester, the King of the Tournament, the Queen of Beauty, and a glowing assemblage of knights and ladies, seneschals, chamberlains, esquires, pages, and men-at-arms, and took their way in procession to the lists, which were overlooked by galleries in which nearly two thousand spectators were accomodated; but all the while the rain came down in bucketfuls, never ceased while the tourney proceeded, and brought the proceedings to a premature and ignominious close . . . The Queen of Beauty, elected to that high honour by unanimous acclamation, was Jane Sheridan, Lady Seymour . . ." (*Op. cit.*, pp. 316 f.)

[3] See the London *Times* for 9 July, 1839, p. 5, col. 4; *ibid.*, for 10 July, p. 5, col. 5., &c.

believe," says the reporter of the *Times*,[1] " next Saturday will . . . be the last day of the exhibition of the mimic knights and esquires . . . though if these doughty ' men at arms ' are not a little more *au fait* when the ' tournament ' is to take place, they will be miserably defective in their imitation of the knights of ' olden times.' " All of the combatants " appeared in full suits of armour, ' very grand,' and almost as fierce as the men in armour who ride in the ' Lord Mayor's Show ' . . . There were no serious accidents yesterday, and the whole business went off as such things usually do, somewhat dull and altogether silly. There were (*sic*) a group of attendants dressed like the buffoons at St. Bartholomew-fair, who were no doubt intended to represent the retainers of the jousting knights." The exercise consisted in running at a " dummy " knight — " a sort of iron scarecrow " — mounted on a wooden horse, and placed on small truck wheels on an inclined plane. " ' Dummy,' however, proved in the long run the best man of the lot, and sat with imperturbable patience whilst all the chivalry of the Eyre-arms attacked him in turn. There were many ladies present whose bright eyes encouraged the knights to the contest." [2]

A contributor to the *Times* [3] calls the attention of Lord Eglintown and " the noblemen and gentlemen who have engaged with him " to hold the tournament, that a tilt or tournament is an unlawful act, and if a participant be killed, " such killing is felony of manslaughter."

> " Now," wrote the correspondent, " I beg leave to remind the noble lords and gentlemen who seek to revive this antiquated and barbarous usage, that supposing death to ensue from their sport, and that they should be convicted of manslaughter, ' they would be liable to be transported for life, or for not less than seven years, or to be imprisoned with or without hard labour in the gaol or house of correction, not exceeding four years, or to be fined,' by stat. 9 George IV, c. 31, 89. . .
>
> " I am strongly inclined to think, that it is clear law that ' the Queen of Beauty,' and all the noble dames and demoiselles, who, as spectators, may be aiding and abetting at this illegal ' passage of arms,' will be guilty of a misdemeanour, and liable, in consequence, to the punishment of fine or imprisonment, one or both."

Another communication [4] recalls that " on the ceiling of the corridors in the Townhall at Nuremberg is a representation of a tournament, in which all the tilters are habited as Court fools. Allow me to suggest this to the heroes of St. John's Wood, as pointing out an appropriate costume for the approaching tournament at Eglintoun Castle."

As the time drew nearer, the encouragement became no greater. " The Duke and Duchess of Cambridge . . . have finally declined the Earl of Eglintown's invitation to be present at the tournament, the *éclat* of which has completely evaporated; indeed, *entre nous*, it is expected to be a very grand failure.

---

[1] 10 July, 1839, p. 5, col. 5. [2] *Ibid., loc. cit.*

[3] Whose letter in that paper, 11 July, 1839, p. 5, col. 2, is signed " no tilter."

[4] Signed " Robin Hood " — in the *Times* for 8 August, 1839, p. 5, col. 3.

Lord Hillsborough and one or two champions, from whose prowess much 'sport' was expected, will not be present; indeed, the authorities have given so many grave cautions respecting a breach of the peace, that the knights will not be allowed to 'bethwack' one another in good earnest, even if they had the inclination; so far as tilting goes, it will be what the ladies whispered the rehearsal was — viz. 'child's play.' As a tournament the whole affair will be a mere farce, but as a pageant[1] it will, doubtless, be very splendid, if it happens to be fine weather: but if it should rain, an enterprising speculator might realize something handsome by forwarding a good supply of umbrellas . . . for the use of the Knights and Squires."[2]

A "Glasgow paper," quoted by the *Times*,[3] says: "while it is requested that ladies and gentlemen will dress in costumes of the 14th and 15th centuries,[4] and that farmers and others will appear in Scotch bonnets and plaids, it is announced at the same time that no one will be refused admittance by the regular approaches. The lists is an enclosure 600 yards by 250 yards, with a barrier in the centre, where the combatants meet, 300 yards in length. There is a grand pavilion for the Queen of Beauty, and the distinguished Company connected with the amusements; while on each side seats are erected to hold 1,000, intended for the public, who will obtain admission to them by gratis tickets. The Queen of the Tournament, with her maids of honour and body guards, composed of ladies . . . equipped as archers, and the Irvine Toxophilite Society, are first in the procession; then follow Lord Eglintoun and the other knights, with their esquires and retainers. To give variety to the sports, 12 of the Irvine archers are to compete at butt-shooting within the lists . . . The arrangements are on the most costly and magnificent scale . . ."[5]

A long letter from Eglinton Castle, dated 27–28 August, appeared in the *Times* of the 31st;[6] it gave an account of the preparations for the event, and described the procession which left the Castle in mid-afternoon, and marched to the lists in the rain. A second letter, under date of 30–31 August,[7] relates

---

[1] *I. e.*, "spectacle."

[2] The London *Times* for 13 August, 1839, p. 5, col. 4.

[3] For 23 August, 1839, p. 5, col. 2.

[4] This suggests the "revel."

[5] The *Times* for 29 August, 1839 (p. 3, col. 4) cites the Glasgow *Chronicle* and *Constitutional*, which papers correct some of the details given above. The space inside the lists is 650 feet long and 250 feet wide; the barrier is 300 feet long and 4 feet 6 inches high. The "Queen of Love and Beauty . . . it is still said, is to be the Lady Seymour." The two smaller stands are to hold 600 each, and — on account of the immense number of applications — the Earl ordered another built to hold 1,000. Sixty or eighty thousand people could find places on the lawn, and, "if the weather prove fine," the *Constitutional* would not be surprised to see that number present. "Never, since the visit of George IV to Scotland in 1822, has anything taken place wherein the people of Scotland have displayed so great an interest as the present."

[6] See p. 3, col. 3.

[7] See the *Times* for 3 September, 1839, p. 5, col. 6.

how on the 29th, the weather forced a postponement of the tournament, and in-door swordplay — to which the public was not admitted — was indulged in. Prince Louis Napoleon " exhibited considerable skill in the use of his weapon " on this occasion. On the 30th, promise of fine weather drew great crowds to Eglinton; by one o'clock in the afternoon over 10,000 were assembled, and more continued to crowd in. About two o'clock the procession started from the Castle; " it was certainly a gorgeous and most splendid pageant." There was but one slight accident in the jousting; and after the tournament there was riding at the ring and the quintain; the *mêlée* closed the labors of the day, which were followed by a ball. At dinner, " Lord Eglintoun made a short speech . . . in which he expressed his hopes that tournaments would become fashionable amongst the nobility and gentry of the country; he had shown that they could be revived, and that tilting could be practised without danger. His lordship's address was received with great satisfaction by his numerous guests."[1] It is not apparent, however, that any of them adopted his suggestion, for these festivals did not become a common pastime of the English gentry.

At Ripon, in 1886, there was tilting at the ring and at the quintain, after the play of *Robin Hood and the Curtal Friar;* and following this, was a mock tournament between armed knights on " armoured hobbies " which caused " much merriment."[2] This may be — like the fight at Scarva — an adaptation of an old folk-custom.

The " Elizabethan Triumph " of 1912

Tournaments occasionally appear in the modern historical pageant — as we shall see — and it may be under the influence of these that the " Elizabethan Triumph " of 1912 took shape.[3]

" The organizers . . . made every effort to reproduce the full splendours of the mediæval tournament, as practiced in the early years of Queen Elizabeth. Ancient chronicles and other archives were carefully studied in order to preserve historical accuracy in every detail. The arrangements were based on the ordinances for the royal jousts drawn up for Edward IV by John Tiptoft, Earl of Worcester, and ordered by Elizabeth to be observed at tournaments held in her reign. The pageant began with the ' commynge into the Felde ' of various gorgeous processions — the Parade of the Knight Martiall, the Parade of the Queen of Beauty. the Parade of the Princess Errant, the Parade of the Knights, and the Ballet des Chevaux, Mr. F. R. Benson, as Herald of the Tournament and general ' producer,' aimed at representing a tournament as it was about 1580, when jousting had become a picturesque pastime . . ." The *Ballet des Chevaux* was followed by the actual jousts, announced by the Herald in the

---

[1] It was planned to continue the tournament on the Saturday (31 August), but the rain descended in torrents, and the wind blew a gale, so that the idea was given up.

[2] See above, p. 161. " Mock fights " are, apparently, not yet dead: cf. the " sham fight at Scarva," below, p. 186 f. and the American tournaments noted on p. 286.

[3] This is pictured in the *Illus. Lond. News* for 13 July, 1912, pp. 48 and 49. The Viscountess Curzon was chosen Queen of Beauty. (*Ibid.*, p. 58.)

time-honored form: "Oyez! oyez! oyez! Be it known, Lords, Knights, and Esquires, Ladyes and Gentlewomen: You are hereby acquainted that a superb achievement of arms and a grand and noble tournament will now be held . . . We proclaim that six knights of blood and of name have great desire to serve their ladyes, and say that they will juste at the tilt against all comers . . ."

This is a detached episode, or "interlude," of a modern pageant — such as that at Oxford;[1] or, more exactly, perhaps, a revival like that of Eglinton, done with the historical accuracy which modern pageant-masters, following the lead of Mr. Parker, have come to insist on. This accuracy was shown chiefly in matters of costume — for even the Elizabethan "barrier" had an element of danger which no one, of course, would care to duplicate.

The "Mock Fight" at Scarva

The "historic sham fight" at Scarva, of 13 July, 1914, may be the descendant of some folk-custom, to which a political significance has been given. I quote a contemporary account:[2]

Thousands of Loyalists from every corner of Ulster assembled at Scarva to participate in the celebrations connected with the historic sham fight. The 12th and 15th of July are recognised as the great Orange holidays of the year, but there is a seriousness about the celebrations of the "Twelfth" which is lacking on the day following. "Scarva Day" is a day set apart for enjoyment and recreation, and the little village on the borders of Counties Down and Armagh, with its memories and associations dear to the hearts of Orangemen, is the venue each year of a great gathering of holiday makers. Yesterday's celebrations were in accord with those of previous years, and were carried out with the utmost enthusiasm. From early morning special trains brought visitors from far and near, and towards noon a dense mass of people packed the village and the roadway leading from the station to Scarvagh demesne, in which the event of the day takes place. The procession of members of the Royal Black Preceptories was one of the largest on record, and a noticeable feature of it was the number of artistic banners displayed. Many fine bands were in evidence . . .

Each year the extensive and beautiful grounds surrounding Scarvagh House, the residence of Mr. Henry Thomson, D.L., are thrown open, and in them the sham fight is enacted . . He has . . . with his usual forethought and consideration, made arrangements that, no matter who may in the future occupy Scarvagh House, the privilege of holding the sham fight each year will be retained by the Orangemen . . .

In the afternoon the rival armies, clad in orange and green uniforms, and armed with muskets and blank ammunition, were marshalled in front of the house, and the "fight" commenced on the terrace, in the presence of a vast multitude. After a short encounter here for the benefit of the house party, an adjournment was made to a large field adjoining, where the battle proper was begun. For the next half-hour or so nothing could be heard but the roll of musketry, whilst from the outskirts of the dense crowd one could catch an odd glimpse of the waving plumes in the helmets of the leaders representing King William and King James, as they engaged each other in a sabre combat. The issue of the contest was in doubt for some time, first one side seeming to prevail, and then the other, but eventually William emerged victorious, his enemies captive, and the green flag hanging in ribbons from its standard.

---

[1] See below, p. 222 f.

[2] Belfast *Weekly News* for 16 July, 1914, p. 12, col. 8.

Le Tournoi de Compiègne

In England these tournaments are usually isolated; an example of a recurring tournament (like that, apparently, at Scarva) in France is seen in connection with the festival at Compiègne in honor of Jeanne d'Arc.[1] This has pageantic features; it includes knights and ladies in mediæval costume, a tournament, running at the quintain, and a procession. "La noblesse ici n'est pas simulée, car tous ces convives sont les descendants des vielles maisons dont ils portent les armoiries."[2]

It is obvious that such shows must tend to limit themselves — like the earlier tournament and the masque — to the court circle. Common folk have neither the skill nor the leisure to indulge in such sports, though the many thousand spectators of the Eglinton tournament indicate the interest of the people in these exhibitions. The history which is preserved in the festival at Compiègne tends to lift it toward true pageantry; the lack of any central figure or historical background tends to depress such tournaments as the 1912 "Elizabethan Triumph" to carefully planned "revels."

"The Royal Naval and Military Tournament"

Somewhat apart from these purely artistic tourneys stands the "Royal Naval and Military Tournament" which has taken place at London, practically without interruption, since its inception in 1879, when it was organized for the benefit of the military charities. Every year, for several weeks in May and June, the show is held — two "performances" are given daily — and various drills, military sports, and other contests, for which prizes are offered, are decided. The performers are, of course, limited to one class — the military — but the annual performances have a wide popular appeal. During recent years, the pageantic element has become more marked.

In 1887, the taking of a fortress was graphically presented; in 1888, a camp was surprised and attacked — and usually a picture of a soldier's duties in time of war, as well as of his tasks in time of peace, was part of these army exhibitions. In 1891, displays of fencing were given by *maîtres d'armes* of the French army; and Royal Engineers constructed a pontoon bridge "across a river of real water, in addition to the usual spar bridge." A Victorian team was this year sent from Australia to take part in the "tournament." In 1892, "representative instructors of the Italian army" fenced with foil and sabre; Indians and Victorians

---

[1] On this see the *Illus. Lond. News* for 29 May, 1909, p. 772, where photographs of the knights tilting at a barrier, Joan entering the town and riding through the streets, are published. Cf. also the Paris *Illustration* for 3 June, 1911, pp. 464 and 465, for pictures and a description of the show. "Nous sommes en plein quinzième siècle . . . Le programme va s'exécuter suivant toutes les formes en usage au moyen âge . . ."

[2] *L'Illustration, loc. cit.*

took part in 1893, and a detachment of Danish army gymnasts was expected, but they did not appear. The usual imitation of a battle was given — the scene of the fight being the Fort of Gilgit, taken some eighteen months before by a British colonel; the "hill-men" were British soldiers, dressed up to represent the enemy.

In 1897 — the Jubilee anniversary — were further Colonial representatives, "significant of the Imperial character of the year." The Dyaks and their savage dance formed a sharp contrast to the musical drill of the Third Dragoon Guards.

1897 — An Army "Pageant"

It is worthy of remark that the central feature of this year's spectacle was "The Pageant: Our Army, 1704–1882." This is outlined in the *Times:* "...Difficult as it is to devise a new pageant for every year, the organizers of 1897 may be congratulated on producing one ... never excelled. First the assembly looked upon types of the British Army as it appeared under Marlborough's command at Blenheim, special attention having been given to selecting the regiments which really were engaged ... From the glorious era of Blenheim we passed to that of Waterloo ... Next came representatives of the regiments which fought at Inkerman ... And last came the men who fought and won at Tel-el-Kebir ... On the whole, this was, and will be, recognized as a pageant of the first order; and the charge of the cavalry of four eras which ends it is stirring and effective." [1]

1910 — "Britannia's Muster"

This "pageant" furnishes an interesting parallel to the Army Pageant of 1910 — which is not, of course, a modern "folk-play." It is interesting to observe that in the latter year, the Tournament again became pageantic. "The Royal Naval and Military Tournament opened at Olympia on Monday last ... To quote the official description: '*Britannia's Muster* is no mere pageant.[2] It is the militant spirit of our Empire translated into flesh and blood ... India, Canada, Australia and South Africa grouped around Britannia, with the Navy and Army of all our lands formed into a square about them, speak of the allegiance of the Commonwealths and Dominions and Empires of our race to the Mother Country.' In the photograph may be seen the cars emblematical of India, Canada, Britannia, South Africa and Australia." [3] Where the 1897 pag-

---

[1] The London *Times* for 27 May, 1897, p. 6, col. 6. The early tournaments were, for the most part, held at the Agricultural-hall in Islington; of late years they have been held at Olympia. My information for the above paragraphs has been gathered from contemporary issues of the *Times;* the reader who is anxious to pursue the subject in more detail is referred to Palmer's *Index to the* Times, under *Military* and *Royal Military.*

[2] That is, *spectacle.*

[3] *Illus. Lond. News* for 25 June, 1910, p. 1007.

eant was historic, this was allegorical; and the cars added another pageantic element. After various drill " events " came the *pièce de résistance* — the *Muster*.

. . . Of the various displays that I have seen in the arena of the Naval and Military Tournament this is the most dignified and suggestive . . . Britannia, in the person of a young and pretty woman, mounted on a car, and supported by a lion, is drawn into the arena by a team the postillions of which are dressed in the costume of ' John Bull.' Halted in the centre of the open, Britannia's heralds summon with the trumpet the various units that hold inviolate her Empire. First come the representatives of the Home Military Forces. A car with an ostrich and a Kaffir heads the columns of Colonial Troops and Volunteers with whose names the South African War made us familiar. Then Australia answers call to the arms. Australia has a car with a gold-miner supported by a kangaroo at the head of its contingent. New Zealand follows Australia behind its own flag. The demand upon Canada produces a car in Arctic dressing. It is followed by a magnificent show of uniforms. The last demand that Britannia makes is upon the Indian Army. India is represented by a Maharajah reclining in State beneath a gorgeous canopy. He is followed by 18 detachments in the brilliant uniforms of the Indian Army.

This great muster is then marshalled in the arena round these triumphal cars. Then it is that the great thought that underlies Colonel Nugent's conception breaks upon the spectator. This huge arena is packed full . . . with the troops of our great Empire. Yet there are only five men from each unit. The immensity of our resources flashes upon one . . .[1]

In 1911, among the usual famous visitors to the Tournament, were King George V and Kaiser Wilhelm II of Germany. One of the features of this year's spectacle was " A Frontier Incident " — which showed tribesmen of North-West India stealing rifles, and the punitive expedition " whose main feature is the attack on and assault of a fort." This was not pageantry; it was rather a scene of expository drama.

1914 — A " Roman Pageant "

In 1914, however, there was a pageantic parenthesis inserted in the exercises of the Tournament. This was an " historical spectacle " which had a flavor of allegory; it consisted of

a prologue and three scenes. In the former a Roman tragedian discourses pleasantly through a megaphone with the Spirit of Luxury, and from their dialogue we learn, if we are close enough to hear, what is about to happen. Scene 1 transports us to Rome and before us passes the Imperial Triumph of Claudius, who has returned with his victorious troops after the conquest of Britain. The two consuls of the year, lictors, magistrates, senators, models of the captured city of Colchester and of Stonehenge, captured Britons much derided by the Imperial buffoon, the Emperor, the Empress, the Court, and lastly the troops of the victorious

[1] The London *Times* for 21 June, 1910, p. 10, col. 3. Cf. *ibid.*, col. 2: " The main object of the . . . Tournament is not to acquire funds for the enrichment of naval and military charities . . . The real object . . . is to encourage skill-at-arms in the Naval and Military Services . . . It is, therefore, a necessary and patriotic institution, apart from the fact that during the past decade it has handed over to the authorities many thousands of pounds for distribution amongst deserving naval and military charities."

army, all pass across the arena. In Scene 2 the Spirit of Luxury, whose appearance and evident appreciation of the good things of this world has caused him to be regarded with much favour by the audience, is awaked from sleep by the opposing megaphone and told that 300 years have passed, and that he is now on Hadrian's wall in the vicinity of Brampton.

The daily routine of Roman troops is shown, including some very striking drill carried out by a century of heavy infantry, in which modern guardsmen execute the most complicated movements to Latin words of command. The scene closes with an intimation that the legions are required in Germany, and a small party is alone left to guard the wall. Shrieks from terrified females now announce the approach of vast barbarian hordes, and the unhappy victim of good living has to fly for his life, while a great combat ensues in which the Roman soldiers fall gallantly at the post of duty unequal to the rush of the ancestors of our race. Space forbids a detailed description of the armament, which has been most accurately reproduced and which by itself is of sufficient interest to bring people to Olympia; but such pieces of ordnance as the carro-ballista, the ballista, and the onager — surely the first howitzer ever seen — may be mentioned as showing the research of the authors of the spectacle.[1]

This shows clearly an influence from the Parkerian pageant in its attempt at historical accuracy. The military character of these displays is, of course, always uppermost; and an example of the adaptation of the older pageantic material — cars and symbolism — to this spectacle is best seen in *Britannia's Muster* of 1910. A certain amount of historical instruction was furnished in 1897; these special celebrations are undoubtedly responsible for the pageantic additions to a show which lends itself readily to such interpolations. It can hardly be doubted that these exhibitions have played their part in developing the Services for the more serious work which they were soon called on to perform.[2]

---

[1] The London *Times* for 15 May, 1914, p. 14, col. 3. The arrangement of the scenes was made by Lieut.-Colonel Sir Mark Sykes, M.P.; special music was composed for the spectacle by Sir Charles Stanford.

See the London *Daily Telegraph* of 10 April, 1914, p. 11, col. 3, for the announcement of the "notable departure in regard to the chief spectacle" of the Tournament. This article notes Imogene and Cymbeline among "the captive royalties of the period," and says that "the last stand of the Romans will be shown with the death of Centurion Ausonius before the onslaught of the barbarian king . . . The rise of the Anglo-Saxons to power is indicated in the final setting, which shows the birth of a nation which was destined to build the greatest Empire since Rome . . ."

[2] An additional feature of interest was the appearance, at this 1914 "tournament," of a primitive "tank," which, two years later, perfected, created such havoc on the battlefields of France and Belgium. Had the spectators been able to see the future, the ungainly machine, looking not unlike a steam-roller, which laboriously clambered over all sorts of obstacles, would not have excited the thoughtless laughter it provoked.

There is no reason to suppose that the era of Peace will see a diminution of interest in these exercises, which are rendered none the less effective by the introduction of a pageantic element.

§ 6. CHRISTINA ROSSETTI'S "PAGEANT OF THE MONTHS"

As an example of the kind of thing called "pageant," without having any right to the name, let us consider Christina Rossetti's *Pageant of the Months.*[1] The foundation of this composition is the dance, and poetic song is the superstructure. The scene — a cottage with its grounds — remains unchanged throughout the act. Symbolism plays a considerable part in the poem — but that alone does not, of course, make a pageant; nor does the personification of the Months, whom we have met in more than one Lord Mayor's Show. The thing is, in reality, a masque: it is meant to take place on a stage, which is set to represent a room in a comfortable cottage; a fire burns on the hearth; the passage of a year is shown by the boys and girls, each of whom, as he comes in, displaces his predecessor. At the end, "while December sings his song, all the other months troop in from the garden, or advance out of the background. The Twelve join hands in a circle, and begin dancing round to a stately measure as the curtain falls." Under no definition of either modern or ancient pageantry can this composition find a place; the only suggestion of pageantic technique being the "march" of the characters, as each displaces his predecessor through the play.[2] The masque and the pageant have a common "soul"; but the stage-setting, the technique, and the spirit of this play remove it from pageantry in spite of its symbolical characters.

The four Seasons appeared at Knutsford in 1913; in Jordan's *London in Luster* (1679) the first pageant was called "The Triumph of Time" — and on the extreme top sat Time himself, surrounded by the Months and Opportunity; in Heywood's *Londini Status Pacatus* (1639) we find Janus and "foure Persons representing the foure Seasons; Spring, Summer, Autume, Winter; every one habited agreeable to his propriety and condition."[3] Again, in the third pageant of Jordan's Show for 1677, "stood Time, attended by the four Quarters of the year, and 'next to him and round about him sit six persons, representing a Minute, and Hour, a Day, a Week, a Month, a Year.'"[4] These figures, how-

---

[1] See *Poems* by Christina G. Rossetti (Boston, 1899), pt. ii, pp. 13–32. Cf. MacKenzie Bell, *Christina Rossetti: a Biographical and Critical Study* (London, 1898), pp. 224 f.: "'A Pageant and other poems' was published by Messrs. Macmillan in August, 1881 . . . The title-poem called 'The Months: A Pageant' runs to twenty-two pages, and is in the form of a masque, in which the 'personifications' of January, March, July, August, October and December are assumed by boys, and February, April, May, June, September and November by girls. The stage directions are ample and interesting, and, properly mounted, it should be a very picturesque little play for children . . . It is cheerful throughout, with not a single note reminding the reader of sorrow."

[2] The same desire to call a *masque* a *pageant* was shown in the welcome of Professor Duquesne by the Harvard architects in 1911. On this, see p. 287, below.

[3] *Works* (1874) v, p. 363.

[4] Fairholt, pt. i, pp. 88 f. Cf. above, p. 74.

ever, are not in themselves pageantic; in the civic shows they are the texts for sermons preached by Opportunity and Janus; at Knutsford, they are merely characters in a revel. In Miss Rossetti's masque, the Months act out, in their dances, their own symbolism, which is made clearer by their songs.

§ 7. CONCLUSION

We have, in this chapter, discussed various kinds of pageantry, most of which is still alive.[1] It must be kept in mind that the Lord Mayor's Show travelled beside these others; and while it is hard to give definite examples of cross-influences, it would be impossible to say that they did not exist. No connection is apparent between the " armed men " of the early nineteenth-century show and the tournament at Eglinton; or between *Britannia's Muster* and any show between 1907 and 1910; but it would be hard to prove that there was no memory of any symbolical float in the minds of those who planned the 1910 " Tournament."

The tradition of the older pageantry is kept up in such shows as we have seen at Salisbury, Coventry, Lichfield, and Knutsford. The 1907 Liverpool celebration seems rather to have drawn on this older form, though the Parkerian pageant, which arose in 1905, has affected many subsequent festivals. The spirit which animates the newer form is forecast in the Ripon anniversary procession of 1886; but the technique of this celebration is that of the old pageant.

The Corpus Christi pageantry, which may have been the source of that later attached to the Coventry Fair, probably goes back itself to such folk-customs as were revived in Knutsford, and have survived in the attenuated forms of Hallowe'en and Guy Fawkes' Day mumming. Even the political pageantry — insofar as it is confined to the burning of an effigy — may have a deep root in the credulity of folk that would burn a waxen image of an enemy to harm him; and the effigy itself may not be unrelated to the folk-figure which lies behind the civic giant. The need for national defence makes necessary the training of forces, and military exercises; these " musters " lie at the root of Midsummer Show, " Courts of Array," and — indirectly — of the " Tournaments " of our own day.

The difference between a pageant and a pageantic revel we have seen to consist in the central idea; in the former, history, symbolism, and allegory all point to one thing — the mayor who is being installed, or the guild which is providing the spectacle; the holiday which is being observed, or the event which is being recalled. A revel has no such unifying idea; and in proportion as the pageant admits distractions, by so much does it tend to drift to the revel. Shaksperian characters grouped around Shakspere are pageantic; but thrown wildly into a

[1] For the political pageantry of the seventeenth-century " Pope-burning," has a modern parallel in the July processions of the north of Ireland — though the pageantry is reduced to symbolical banners.

procession with other costumed figures unconnected with the dramatist, they become mere revellers.[1]

In 1905, at Sherborne School in Dorsetshire, under the guiding hand of Mr. Louis Parker, the modern pageant, or "folk-play," came into being. As this is a distinct form of art, we shall discuss it in the next chapter. We shall not find float, pageant-car, or giant; the procession through the streets gives way to one across a stage — usually (in England practically always) out-of-doors. Allegory is largely done away with, but we do not wholly lose sight of symbolism, in this new *genre;* and history is the breath of its life.

---

[1] It is, of course, unnecessary that each car of a pageant be closely connected with the others — though the closer the relation is, the higher is the art.

CHAPTER VIII[1]

THE PARKERIAN PAGEANT

Introduction

"ANY review of the uses of pageantry in past ages and of its development in recent time," writes Mr. William Orr,[2] "must recognize that, while certain elements are constant, the form of presentation and the manner of acting the scenes have varied greatly. The factors essential to true pageantry are the use of the costumes and practices of other days and the representation of important events in history as expressions of the manifold activities and aspirations of the human soul."

However true this may be of modern pageantry, I have ill done my task if the reader of the foregoing pages feels it to be true of the shows and triumphs we have been studying. Something of that spirit, to be sure, we have found in the Lord Mayor's Shows since 1884, and in a pageant like that of Ripon in 1886; at times, flashes of this emphasis on history — more or less recent — are seen in the later shows at Lichfield, Coventry, and Knutsford. But the older and newer pageantry are so different from each other, that to include the modern work in a consideration of the early, is almost like adding an appendix about fire-dogs to a treatise on the habits of the canine — to adopt the humorously exaggerated figure of Mr. W. C. Langdon.[3]

The Older and Newer Pageantry Compared

And yet the differences are not so great as at first appears; for, though the "body" and "technique" of the two have nothing in common, the "soul" and "spirit" of the two are much the same. It is true that there is, in the Parkerian work, little allegory, no mythology, and much less symbolism than in the older Lord Mayor's Show; but there is an increased emphasis on history, to make up for it. Though some of the Lord Mayor's Shows included historical

---

[1] For much material in this chapter I am indebted to Louis N. Parker, Esq., F. R. A. M., Officier de l'Instruction Publique; I take great pleasure in acknowledging my gratitude. The reader will find his papers in the *Journ. Soc. Arts* (22 Dec., 1905), liv, pp. 142 f., and in *New Boston* (Nov., 1910), pp. 296 f., mentioned in the Bibliography. Cf. also my *Manual of Pageantry*, Indiana University *Bulletin*, vol. xiii, no. 7. (15 June, 1915.)

[2] In the introduction to Bates and Orr, *Pageants and Pageantry* (Boston, and New York, 1912).

[3] In a letter, dated 28 January, 1913.

The Aborigines Sacrificing; in the Foreground, the Scir Burn

[Sherborne, 1905]

characters, and placed a certain emphasis on the glorious past of the chief magistrate's Company, this was done rather to glorify the present than to draw instruction from history. The presence of former renowned Lord Mayors, and the rehearsal of royal or noble names that appeared on the roster of the guilds, awoke feelings analogous to those with which a man reviews his distinguished ancestry.

It is for this reason that the pageantry of the past may be called "æsthetic," while that of the present is "educational." The first existed primarily to entertain; the second seeks rather to instruct. I would not imply that there is no entertainment in modern pageantry, any more than I would suggest there was no instruction in the earlier; there were often moral, as well as historical, lessons given in the seventeenth-century Lord Mayor's Shows — to those who could hear the speakers; but the chief emphasis is as I have said.[1]

The Aims of the Parkerian Pageant

Besides this aim — the education of a community in its own past — Parkerian pageantry is a protest against "modernity". "This modernising spirit, which destroys all loveliness and has no loveliness of its own to put in its place, is the negation of poetry, the negation of romance . . . This is just precisely the kind of spirit which a properly organized and properly conducted pageant is designed to kill," writes Mr. Parker.[2] Something of this spirit is seen in the more recent Lord Mayor's Shows, in the Ripon celebration, and we may catch reflections of it in the tournaments of 1839 and 1912. Insofar as the nineteenth-century civic shows aimed to preserve the romantic aspect of life, they prepared the way for the Parkerian work.

Pageant and Drama

Another difference between the early and the modern pageant is seen in their relations to the drama. At first a processional entertainment, quite undramatic, the pageant grew slowly into form; through the mists which usually surround the birth of a literary *genre*, we have seen folk-customs, with their attendant plays, dances, and games; the moving platforms and Biblical characters of the

---

[1] I must caution the reader not to confuse "modern pageant" with "pageant given in modern times." Owing to the poverty of our vocabulary, I must run the risk of being misunderstood; but I do not consider the Lord Mayor's Show of 1913 or the Lichfield *Bower* of 1914 "modern pageants." Rather are they survivals of the older pageants which have lasted to our days; and such revivals as we discussed in the last chapter are influenced by them. By "modern pageant," I mean the historical folk-play which came into being in 1905, and which forms the subject of this chapter. It is in order to avoid a confusion that I have named it after its founder; the reader will understand that "modern" and "Parkerian" pageantry are synonymous.

[2] *Journ. Soc. Arts*, liv, p. 143.

guild-plays; allegory, and the elaborate symbolism of tournament and "Court of Love"; the flattery and ingenious lavishness of the Lord Mayor's Shows — all, in one way or another, absorbed by the pageant. We have seen the interchange of influence between pageant, masque, and interlude — the masque, standing with luxurious feet where pageant and the drama meet.

But the new pageantry *is* drama. Mr. Parker, in the *Foreword* to the *Book of the York Pageant*, writes: "Dilettantes and quidnuncs prate about the National Drama. Here it is. Drama covering all English history from 800 B.C. to the Great Rebellion; written by Englishmen, set to music by Englishmen, costumed and acted by English men and women — acted by thirteen thousand of them — and listened to by over half-a-million spectators in twelve weeks. Drama lifting our souls to God, and our hearts to the King — is not that National Drama?" [1]

§ 1. THE BIRTH OF MODERN PAGEANTRY

It is generally recognized that Mr. Parker is "the inventor and founder of modern pageantry," [2] which came into being at Sherborne, in Dorsetshire, in 1905. As far back as the 'seventies or 'eighties the idea of giving a musical "folk-play" in the old courtyard of Sherborne School had appealed to Mr. Parker, who was then teaching there; but it was not until thirteen years after

[1] We must leave to a future study a consideration of the effect of pageant-writing on the technique of those dramatists who have planned pageants. The work of Dekker, Heywood, and Middleton must have been affected; Mr. Parker has told me that his own technique has been much influenced — but it must not be forgotten that he gave the pageant a dramatic quality it lacked.

Mr. Parker's own dramatic work before 1905 included plays which — like *Rosemary* and *The Cardinal* — dealt with the more or less distant past; and since 1905, he has composed such plays as *Drake*, and *Joseph and his Brethren*, which he calls "pageant-plays."

Mr. Nugent Monck's work — with the exception of his Norwich pageant, which was historical — is rather the production of plays on pageantic lines. He admits the debt of all pageant-masters to Mr. Parker, but told me that he was drawn into the work through his interest in reproducing miracle-plays and masques. A discussion of his work as a whole will have to be made elsewhere; his *Books of Words* are not easily accessible, and his departure for the front left me without a promised collection. Episodes in the life of King Arthur, which he wove into a "pageant-play," were produced under his direction in the grounds of "Abbey Lodge," Hanover-gate, Regent's Park, London, on the 8 and 9 July, 1914; this performance I attended — and while it was divided into episodes, given out-of-doors, and had other pageantic characteristics, the subject, and the limited audience, prevent its being considered true pageantry.

We shall discuss the "pageant-plays" of other recent writers in later section — see below, p. 229 f.; see also p. 208 for remarks on the pageant and the stage.

[2] Bates and Orr, *Pageants and Pageantry*, p. iv. Cf. Mr. Parker's *Foreword* to the *Book of the York Pageant:* "In 1905 I invented a new form of dramatic art with the Sherborne Pageant. After developing it at Warwick in 1906, at Bury St Edmunds in 1907, at Dover

he had left the school that the opportunity came for realizing his plan. The twelve-hundredth anniversary of school, bishopric, and town was to be celebrated in 1905; and Mr. Parker suggested that a "folk-play" be given to bring back the past glories of a see which antedated Salisbury.[1] The idea was received with approbation, and a year before the celebration was scheduled, preparations were begun. From a modest beginning, the scheme grew, so that — starting with a hundred performers — it ended with nine hundred.

It is important to note that this modern pageantry is not a development from the older; Mr. Parker is emphatic in saying he was not influenced by the Lord Mayor's Show, and that he does not approve of such street processions. While it is undeniably true that many of them are now inartistic — have, perhaps, survived their usefulness — still they have preserved the past, and have, very possibly, paved the way for an appreciation of the newer, and much higher, form of pageantry.[2] However that may be, Mr. Parker got his idea of a folk-play originally from such *Fest-* and *Erinnerungsspiele* as that of Tell at Altdorf, Luther at Worms, and the *Meistertrunk* at Bavarian Rothenburg.[3]

THE SHERBORNE PAGEANT OF 1905

The Sherborne entertainment was originally called a "folk-play,"[4] but the name was not understood, and the idea of a folk-play awoke no enthusiasm.

---

in 1908, and at Colchester in the present year, I close my pageanting career at York. That is as it should be . . .

"An enormous amount of pessimistic nonsense is talked about our undemonstrative nature, our depraved taste in art, our contempt for the drama, our ignorance in music, our commercial spirit, and so on. Let the acting that has been seen in these pageants, the costumes, the astonishing 'properties,' the arms and armour, the dances, the music, and all the self-sacrifice, self-effacement, surrender of leisure, on the part of thousands of voluntary workers, unnamed, unrewarded, often even unthanked, be the answer."

[1] Mr. W. B. Wildman was writing the history of the place, so that many historical details were accessible.

[2] Mr. Parker characterized the "pageant" at Coventry (in which — as he put it — a circus-rider takes the part of Lady Godiva, and is followed in her ride through the town by various motors, and tradesmen's floats) as a "distressing, ghastly affair." We should not whack our great-grandmothers over the head because they are toothless and wandering in their minds.

[3] Professor Baker, in a short article published in *New Boston*, (Nov., 1910), p. 295, calls this modern pageant "the revival of an old popular amusement that from the moment of its revival has been developing into something different from its origins." We have seen how the older pageantry, in the more recent Lord Mayor's Show, had been preparing the way for the newer form; we have Mr. Parker's word for the fact that there is really no connection at all between the forms, other than the mere accident of name. It is this unfortunate accident which has caused much confusion; there are, however, certain elements in common — even if the later is not derived directly from the earlier.

[4] With no reference to the earlier folk-plays or sword-dances.

So Mr. Parker sought for another name — a word that would appeal to every one; and revived the old term which meant nothing very definite to anybody, but which suggested delightful masquerading to the players. All their apathy vanished.

The Lord Mayor's Show had degenerated into fustian; it was given by hired performers, and had lost much of its old meaning.[1] The "pageant" at Sherborne — the first of a long line — was something new; it met with opposition and ridicule from outsiders; given in a small out-of-the-way town, under a pageant-master who himself hardly knew what he meant to do, the first modern pageant struggled into life.

As the preparations for the festival went on, great difficulty was found in interesting the press. The grandstand was erected, yet everything seemed to have been done for nothing, because no audience was in prospect. Ten days before the performance, the dress rehearsal took place; and by accident two newspaper men were present. Their notices brought fifty thousand people to the little Dorset village. All England took fire.[2]

§ 2. PRODUCING A PAGEANT[3]

Mr. Parker has insisted that all his pageants be done by voluntary labor. The "episodes" were written by local dramatists and poets wherever possible, and the music composed by local musicians.[4] All the costumes and all properties were produced by the inhabitants, voluntarily, without exception;[5] the poorer people were indemnified, but they were not paid a profit. The professional orchestras were the only people connected with Mr. Parker's pageants who were paid for their services.

---

[1] I quote Mr. Parker. The reader will soon see his dislike of "hired performers" — always part of the Lord Mayor's Shows. ("Degenerated into fustian" are hard words!)

[2] For pictures of the Sherborne pageant see the *Illus. Lond. News*, for 10 June, 1905, pp. 814, 815; and Stone, pp. 62 f.

[3] Many of the matters mentioned here are touched upon in my *Manual of Pageantry*. (1915).

[4] The choruses of all of Mr. Parker's pageants were written by James Rhoades, "a finished, though not a popular, poet." Especially noteworthy are the chorus in the Dover Pageant, preceding the entrance of Henry VIII, and that introducing the seventh episode of the York Pageant (see the *Book of Words* of the York Pageant, p. 113; another fine chorus is the *Triumph Song of York* [*ibid.*, pp. 126 f.]). Mr. Parker himself planned the pageants, chose the episodes, and edited the MSS. submitted — in one case, a five-act tragedy, offered by a local writer, was cut to a ten-minute episode.

It will be recalled that, in 1574, a Bristol schoolmaster became angry because local talent was slighted. (See above, vol. i, p. 207.)

[5] Mr. Parker demanded that each player furnish his own costume, as far as possible.

The Arena: with Remarks on the Site

Another important feature of these productions was that the arena, where the action took place, was kept like a first-class stage. The orchestra was concealed, and none of the " machinery " of the pageant was shown. The performances were directed by means of electric bells; some of the entrances — those at Warwick, for instance — took place a quarter of a mile from the grandstand. Everything ran like clockwork; and this was possible only because the arena — which varied between five and ten acres in extent — was strictly kept.

Mr. Parker has " rejected " from thirty to fifty towns, which applied to him for pageants, because they lacked suggestive backgrounds. He insisted always on finding the centre of historical interest in a town, and that was the site of the pageant.[1] While not presuming to criticize Mr. Parker's attitude — and no one will deny that the founder of pageantry as we know it has a right to speak authoritatively — many cannot help feeling that too strict a line may be drawn here. Conditions vary somewhat, it is true, between England and America; we have not got, for instance, charming old Abbey courtyards, around which our towns have grown up, and which have seen many, if not all, of the historical happenings our pageants celebrate. The impossibility of giving a pageant before, let us say Faneuil Hall, has driven American pageant-masters to country nooks on the outskirts of our cities; and this has had a slight effect, perhaps, on our pageants. No one will deny that if the site of a pageant be the scene of even one event reproduced, a great advantage is gained; that it is a necessity, is not universally admitted. Perhaps this is due to the fact that American pageants are not so strictly historical as are the English; to this point we shall return.

But even in England, pageant-masters do not all share Mr. Parker's views. " In selecting Cheltenham as the home of the Gloucestershire Historical Pag-

---

[1] In this connection, we may note the Pageant of Wales at Cardiff (pictured in the *Illus. Lond. News* for 31 July, 1909, supplement, pp. i and iv). Says that weekly: " The whole of the romantic history of Wales has been drawn upon for picturesque episodes and spectacles. . . The chief scenes are laid at Cardiff itself, at Agincourt and at Ludlow. We see the crowning of King Arthur, and the crowning on the battlefield of Bosworth of Henry Tudor; we see King Henry at the field of Agincourt, and, according to the programme, ' the Chief Constable of Glamorgan as Chief of the Ruffians! ' The good people of Wales have foregathered in the historic environment of Cardiff to celebrate ' the mighty heroes of a bygone time,' and they are particularly anxious to impress upon all beholders that this is a national, not a local, pageant; not a Pageant of Cardiff, but a Pageant of Wales . . ."

I may remind the reader that the play of *Robin Hood and the Curtal Friar*, at Ripon in 1886, was given on " the traditional site of the famous event it recalled "; (see above, p. 161).

On this matter of site, see also T. H. Dickinson, *The Pageant*, in *The Play-book* for September, 1914 (ii, 4), pp. 25 f., and Davol, *Am. Pag.*, pp. 145 f. (chapter ix).

eant," writes Hawtrey,[1] " some difficulty was felt, because the town is not one that possesses many historical associations. In each episode we have to assume that the scene represents a different locality. This demands a certain amount of imagination on the part of the audience . . . " — and imagination, it may be remarked, is a quality that audiences are usually very ready to give.

At York, the Dean urged the use of the space in front of the Cathedral for the pageant, and Lord Halifax warmly seconded him; but Mr. Parker wisely refused the site. Humor enters historical pageants, for it is in history; and one cannot present humorous scenes near a Cathedral, which was to be used as entrance and exit for appropriate characters. The offer, however, showed the spirit which lay behind the whole pageant — a spirit which was again shown in the final march, during which the cheers of the audience drowned the affectionate farewells of the actors to each other — farewells which showed the solidarity engendered by the pageant.

The English Church Pageant of 1909 — which was divided into two parts [2] — had a total number of nineteen " scenes "; the different episodes took place in various districts of England: for instance, the first scene was laid at " the Roman town of Calleva, now Silchester, in Hampshire "; the third, at " a Pictish village on the island of Hy, afterwards known as Iona "; the fourth showed " the open country a few miles from Canterbury "; the sixth, " the Frater or dining hall of the Old Minster at Winchester "; the ninth, " the island in the Thames by Runnymead." The fifth scene of the second part showed the coronation procession of Edward VI from Westminster Hall to the Abbey. Many of the scenes are laid in or near London; but it is not often that a pageant allows itself such latitude as we find here.[3]

The Pageant-Master

The personality of a pageant-master counts for a great deal; for the modern pageant is carried through by force of personal magnetism. Mr. Parker met indifference, discouragement, and opposition at the beginning; but each pageant ended in enthusiasm. Six thousand people took part in the York Pageant alone;

---

[1] In the *Foreword* to the *Book of Words* of the Gloucestershire Pageant.

[2] One beginning at three, and the other at eight o'clock; the first part consisted of ten "scenes," and the second of nine. (See the program of the Pageant for details.)

[3] It may be added that Mr. Parker disapproves of having the audience itself form the background for another part of the audience sitting across the stage — an ineffective practice not uncommon in America. Nor would he admit any artificial scenery in his pageants. Mr. Davol (*Am. Pag.*, p. 148) bids us " remember that little artificial scenery can be safely used in the open-air."

One American pageant of recent years not only used artificial scenery, but (when forced to change it) sent up a curtain of steam between spectators and stage, on which colored lights played, to make it opaque. (A clever way of solving *one* difficulty.)

and every one of them had to come in contact with the pageant-master. It will easily be seen that his position is no sinecure. It is true that Mr. Parker has created a new profession; but there is little danger that it will be overcrowded. Besides the genius of personality, the pageant-master must have a genius for organizing;[1] he must be able to do historical research, and turn the results of his scholarship into literary form; he must be able to make others work, and — while he leaves much to committees — he must never get out of touch with details; he must have the ability to assert his authority, and the tact to calm the quarrels of his subordinates without offending either of the offended; he must be versatile enough to do quickly whatever others have left undone; and he must have a constant supply of good-humor to meet the attacks of the pessimists, nor must he ever allow himself to get discouraged.

The Value of Accuracy

In all of Mr. Parker's pageants the details of history were carefully copied, so that the pageants became of great educational value. Precise words and music of old songs were dug out by antiquarian research; and not only were the audiences educated, but the performers as well. They had to search among old books to find out about flint weapons, Roman armor, and mediæval costumes; and all of this required much study. The work on a pageant began sometimes eighteen months before the production; the things collected and reproduced for the York Pageant — costumes, weapons, armor, horse-trappings, carriages, etc., — made a remarkable museum of real historical value; they were on exhibition weeks before the performance took place.

If pageantry is to have any influence as an educational force, it is clear that historical accuracy must be insisted on. Once let the public feel that they are being deceived, and you lessen their faith in the educational value of every pageant. The responsibility of pageant-masters in this respect is obvious.[2]

---

[1] A *Graphic Chart of a Pageant Organization Scheme*, supplementing *Bulletin 11* of the American Pageant Association, is reprinted in my *Manual of Pageantry* (1915), p. 4.

[2] Mr. Gilbert Hudson, who has served as pageant-master in several Yorkshire pageants, does not agree with this point of view. In a letter, under date of 30 November, 1918, he writes: "... Too much labour may be expended upon endeavouring to obtain 'accuracy' of costume, &c. To put on a scene in so-called 'accurate' costume is both impossible and wrong. For in all periods there are survivals and anticipations of fashion; and in old days garments were handed down (by will) from father and mother to son and daughter, as a common practice. The desire of gorgeous effect also leads to false impressions of a period; for no crowds of people at any time (except on definitely ceremonial occasions) were ever arrayed in all their best at once ..."

§ 3. CHARACTERISTICS OF THE NEW PAGEANTRY

The earlier triumphs were, as we have seen, given for the sake of entertainment. If the sovereigns or chief magistrates were not always amused by the shows provided for them, the populace crowded the streets in wonder and drank at the flowing conduits with gratitude, from the time of Perkin Revelour down. The new pageantry of our own day does not seek, primarily, to amuse. Perhaps it is an unconscious development of the Puritan conscience, which will not admit pure enjoyment, but seeks to find joy in edification. There are other characteristics of modern pageantry which are also characteristic of the times. It is, in the first place, essentially democratic.

The Democratic Aspect of the Modern Pageant

This democratic aspect of pageantry is, perhaps, more noticeable in England than in America. When Mr. Parker first undertook the Sherborne "folk-play," the headmaster of the School, Canon Westcott, agreed to take part in the performance. Mr. Parker thereupon insisted that everyone he asked should perform in the pageants he directed; he would take no refusal from anyone. All classes were called on, and all responded amazingly. Every kind of person, from peer to day-laborer, and even tramp, played together on a footing of absolute equality. High dignitaries of the Church of England joined ministers of other denominations;[1] and the pageants created a spirit of good-fellowship, sympathy, and brotherhood which did not fade from the community, long after the pageant was a thing of the past.[2] The German *Festspiele* are given by the tradesman-class;[3] but the English pageant brings all classes together, and gives each a chance to get the others' point of view, which arouses an understanding and sympathy between the classes.

The Pageant and the Community

Mr. Parker feels that the small place is the only fit place for a pageant.[4] There are so many interests in a big city, that everyone cannot give his attention and energy to it; and unless a town gives its whole life to a pageant, the

---

[1] Some non-conformist clergymen donned the robes of Romanist prelates with reluctance, to remove them with real regret.

[2] Mr. Parker possesses a beautiful illuminated address, expressing the gratitude and affection of those who participated in the Sherborne Pageant. Everyone who took part in the pageant signed it, including some old folks from the Almshouses, who — not being able to write — were obliged to "make their mark."

[3] There are, however, some exceptions, especially in the smaller towns, where everyone takes part.

[4] It is to be observed, however, that in December, 1905, he was looking forward to a great National Pageant of England, to be given at Windsor, or some other suitable site; the matter

pageant is nothing. It is obvious that it is much harder to develop community spirit in a metropolis than in a village; there are too many interests to weave together. And the solidarity which the pageant leaves behind it, is one of its chief gifts.

Many pageant-masters agree with Mr. Parker on this point. Not that a pageant can't be given in a large city; it has been often done (in America, perhaps, more frequently than in England) and been done successfully. But the fullest measure of success comes when everyone enters into the spirit of the occasion, and this is possible only in a smaller town. Pageants in cities are too apt to become the affair of one section or of one class; it is obviously impossible to make every inhabitant of a large center feel the personal interest in and responsibility for the pageant, which, in the town or village, helps the individual in many ways, and draws the whole community together.[1]

Mr. Gilbert Hudson, pageant-master of various Yorkshire pageants, writes that he regards the following as the chief social objects of a Pageant, or Folk-Play:[2]

1. The uniting of all classes and sorts of people in a task which all enjoy, and, by the healthy excitement arising from participation in dramatic scenes and in poetic utterance, the dissolving of artificial restraints and enmities among them, which the ordinary affairs of life seem inevitably to create.

2. The awakening or creation of a communal historical sense, which, however latent at times, shall yet persist as a general atmosphere of social life.

3. The instructing of people how to entertain themselves in each others' company, and as communities, in a rational artistic manner. The subservient benefits that spring herefrom need not enumeration.

Now it is much easier to achieve these objects in a small old-fashioned town (such as Thirsk or Pickering) than in a larger and more commercialized—may I say 'politicalized'?—

---

to be made up of various episodes from other more local pageants. (See *Journ. Soc. Arts*, liv, pp. 145 f.). Scotch and Welsh National Pageants there have been since that day; but the English is yet to come.

[1] What throws the *Masque of Learning* out of the strict field of pageantry, is that it does not deal with Edinburgh — or even Scottish — history, but with that of Education: a subject which of necessity must appeal to a limited set. The *Scottish National Pageant* of 1908 (see below, p. 214) has many non-Parkerian characteristics; but it is much nearer the ideal of Mr. Parker than is the *Masque of Learning*.

A Pageant of English Literature was given in the Town Hall of Oxford, during the week of 28 April, 1914, in aid of Home Missions. The ten episodes took the history of literature from Cædmon to Addison and Steele; various University people assisted; but the affair was far from having the community-appeal of the Oxford Pageant of 1907 — nor, indeed, was it so ambitious. (For a short notice of this, see the London *Times* of 27 April, 1914, p. 15, col. 6.)

We shall return to the "festival," or "restricted pageant," in the next chapter (see below, p. 281 f.). On the effect of pageantry upon the individual and the town, see the article already referred to in *Journ. Soc. Arts*, liv, p. 143. My material here is largely from conversations with Mr. Parker.

[2] In a letter of 25 November, 1918.

place like York or Scarborough. In the former cases, there is a better preservation of the old social traditions — a remnant even of the more philanthropic aspects of feudal conditions, — which enables the best-fitted, best-educated people to take the lead and set the example in matters of taste and organization, than in the latter, where modern industrial, political, and educative influences have upset the old social ideas, and have not yet produced any unifying idea in their place — and, I must fear, do not seem likely to, for the simple reason that they are founded not on any religion of human affections, but upon notions of mere worldly and economical advancement. . . . The commercialized town, besides, finds it difficult to undertake an artistic enterprise for its own, or a purely social sake, without any admixture of baser aims. At Scarborough the Pageant, in spite of all endeavors to the contrary, became continually involved with stupid designs of *advertising* the town, and of wishing to emulate other places in mere gorgeousness of exhibition.

But, putting all this aside, the social and moral results of a Pageant have always been to me a matter for satisfaction. People who take part in them seem to look back on them as among the great events of their lives, and to see their town ever after in a new light of historical and poetical illustration.

A semi-ironic, semi-appreciative, view of pageantry may be found in Sir A. T. Quiller-Couch's *Brother Copas*, the scene of which is laid in Merchester (Winchester) at the time of the pageant there. "Here, after all, thousands of people were met in a common pride of England and her history. Distort it as the performers might, and vain, inadequate, as might be the words they declaimed, an idea lay behind it all. These thousands of people were met for a purpose in itself ennobling because unselfish. As often happens on such occasions, the rite took possession of them, seizing on them, surprising them with a sudden glow about the heart, sudden tears in the eyes. This *was* history of a sort. Towards the close, when the elm shadows began to stretch across the green stage, even careless spectators began to catch this infection of nobility — this feeling that we are indeed greater than we know." [1]

International Good-Will Developed

Since these English pageants have always fallen in the holiday season, many Americans have attended them; American towns have been represented — as at Sherborne, Dover, and York — and a feeling of international good-will has been developed.[2] The articles in the American press have spread abroad the news of these amenities, and both countries have profited as the bonds between them have been strengthened.

---

[1] I am indebted to Mr. Francis W. Butler-Thwing for calling my attention to this book. The passage cited occurs in chapter xxiv. The Winchester Pageant was produced by Mr. F. R. Benson in June, 1908; pictures of it may be found in the *Illus. Lond. News* for 27 June of that year, pp. 956, 957. ("A Rehearsal" is illustrated, *ibid.*, for 23 May, p. 741.)

It is interesting to note that Sir A. T. Quiller-Couch had a hand in composing the Winchester Pageant — see below, p. 226, n. 1.

[2] Of course this aspect, though a common one, is not an essential of pageantry. It will be recalled that the more recent Lord Mayor's Shows symbolized allied and friendly Powers frequently.

In the Dover Pageant,[1] the episode of the coming of Henrietta Maria was written by a Frenchman, M. Louis Tiercelin, and played by a group of French teachers, who rehearsed at Douai. They went back from Dover full of enthusiasm, and wanted to give a pageant at St. Malo; but they ran up against political and social difficulties. Only in England, thinks Mr. Parker, can one get such a complete mingling of all classes as that seen in his pageants.[2]

The Pageant and the Individual

Not only does the modern pageant educate, and bring about a more solid community-spirit, and even develop international good-will, but it also brings to light latent — and sometimes undreamed-of — talents in the individual. All the costumes are made as cheaply as possible; and the inventiveness displayed is sometimes amazing. A young woman of Dover turned rejected "bowler" hats into splendid "steel" helmets, at a cost of twopence-halfpenny apiece; "chain armor" was made from thick twine, knitted and "metalized" at a very small cost. The average price of costumes, for the ordinary performer, was from one to two dollars; and the costumes were not only beautiful in themselves, but historically accurate. Many people were directed to arts and crafts owing to the incentive got in the pageants; to some a calling was given by their participation in these entertainments; new abilities were discovered, and the lives of a great number made the richer thereby.

Repetition of Performances

Although the idea of modern pageantry came from the German *Festspiele*, which are usually repeated once a year, if not oftener,[3] Mr. Parker thinks that the modern civic pageant cannot be repeated with advantage oftener than once every ten years; and he seems inclined to doubt whether any repetition is advisable. As most of these shows were planned to celebrate a particular anniversary, there has not been a tendency observable, as yet, to turn them into any such institution as the Passion Play at Oberammergau has become.

---

[1] See the *Book* of the Dover Pageant, pp. 54 f.

[2] He suggests that perhaps American pageantry suffers — less, indeed, in the smaller communities than in the cities — from the fact that the performers are apt to be of one social stratum. In England, the classes mix for the moment — and as they mix, a lasting sympathy may spring up; but as soon as the pageant is over, class lines are recognized, and the lower does not seek to presume on the upper, as it might, or, rather, as the upper might fear it likely to, in a republic like France or the United States.

Those pageants which are given by one class or group have been called "festivals" — in a new and specific sense of the word.

[3] The *Meistertrunk* at Rothenburg was, before the War, regularly given on Whitmonday, and sometimes once or twice a year in addition. The Oberammergau Passion Play is — like the early miracle plays of England — not pageantry.

The Cost of a Modern Pageant

Regarding the cost of a modern pageant, it may be noted that Mr. Parker's have varied from £5000 to £15,000. His guarantee funds covered all initial expenses — office-hire, advertisement in the press, circulars, etc. — and a possible deficit. As soon as the plan of the grandstand was ready, he opened his box-office. The stands usually seated about six thousand; the money began to come in even while the performers were working on the pageant, and a month before the first performance everything was sold.

The *Accounts* of the York Pageant are added in an appendix. They show total receipts of £14,439, 18*s.* 9*d.*, of which £11,612, 12*s.* came from the sale of grandstand tickets. The expenses amounted to £13,677, 9*s.* 2*d.*, of which the largest items were: grandstand, dressing-rooms, cloak-rooms, hire of exhibition, alteration at Museum Gardens, etc., £2,151, 6*s.* 8*d.*; costumes, £1,496, 1*s.* 3*d.*; advertising, printing, etc., £1,556, 6*s.* 7*d.*; the retaining-fee, royalty and expenses of the pageant-master, £1,744, 2*s.* 5*d.* The subscriptions were returned, and there was a balance of £762, 9*s.* 7*d.* in the treasurer's hands on 7 October, 1909.

Mr. Parker states [1] that the Sherborne Pageant made a profit of $5,000; that at Warwick, $15,000; one he wrote for the Duchess of Albany, $10,000 in only two performances; and that at Bury St. Edmunds, $7,000. The Dover Pageant — in many respects the finest spectacle of all — resulted in a loss, for various reasons. Mr. Parker strongly deprecates giving a pageant for any definite charitable object,[2] or to make money.

The Blight of Commercialism

Though the movement is so new in England, Mr. Parker points out that, even in 1914, it had already begun to decline. This, he says, is largely due to commercialism. The towns giving pageants usually made money, so other

---

[1] In *New Boston* (Nov., 1910), p. 298.

[2] The Church Pageant of 1909 was, according to Mr. Parker, a contradiction, for it was given by one class: the Army Pageant of 1910 was given under the auspices of the Army Charity. The profits of the Gloucestershire Pageant were to go to the Veterans' Relief Fund (see title-page of the *Book of Words*).

In the appendix to *Pageants and Pageantry*, Miss Bates estimates the cost of a school pageant (or "festival") with from a hundred and fifty to two hundred characters to be about $230 for two performances (*op. cit.*, p. 277). Mr. W. C. Langdon tells me that the cost varies with each place; at Warwick, Massachusetts, where everything was given, the cost was $10. Of course much depends on how carefully the pageant-master strives after historical accuracy, and how much material he has at hand.

We have mentioned the expenses of some of the earlier pageants in a former chapter. As a matter of comparison, it is interesting to recall that in 1617, Middleton received £282, out of which he apparently had to provide the show; that in 1685, the four pageants cost £175,

towns were anxious to have them. Mr. Parker emphatically declares that pageants should never be given for an object outside themselves; he always made it a condition of assuming charge of one, that the pageant should not be given for an " object," or charity. For either the entertainment is starved for the sake of profit, or there may be no profit — and then you are ridiculous. If, by any chance, there should be a profit at the end, and the people could all agree on a cause, the money could be turned over to it; sometimes the profits from his own pageants were used to make permanent memorials of the occasions.[1]

" War seldom enters, but where wealth allures "; and it is quite possible that thoughts centred on the box-office would kill any *esprit de ville* (if I may coin a phrase) which the pageant tends to develop; certain it is, that pageants exploited by ticket-agents and starved for the sake of a profit do not reach as high a plane as those managed with no thought of profit. The *Scottish National Pageant* of 1908 [2] was given " in aid of the Scottish Children's League of Pity," yet it has many features which show an influence from the Parkerian pageant.[3]

Whether we can rule an entertainment out of the field of pageantry purely because it is given avowedly for a charitable object, or even for the profit of the community (as the older pageants often were) is doubtful. The ideal pageant, perhaps, has no aim of this kind — does not even seek to pay expenses — but if the show is, in other ways, characteristic of pageantry, it has a right to consideration; even if the performers are paid, we can only deny that the production fulfils the high ideals of Mr. Parker. It may have what (for want of better terms) we have called the " body " and " soul " and " technique " of pageantry; if it lacks only the " spirit," it lacks what is not the least important element of modern pageantry.

---

the flag and streamers, £140, and the poet received £10 — the total cost of the show being £473, 4*d*. In the days when the only pageantic feature of the Lord Mayor's Show was the " men in armor," the cost averaged a hundred guineas. Evans, p. xxix, n. 2., says that the average cost of production of a masque at the time of James I was £1400 (or £6000 of our money); but Shirley's *Triumph of Peace*, performed at Whitehall 3 February, 1633-4, by the Inns of Court, cost much more. " The Charge of the whole *Masque* which was born by the Societies, and by the particular Members of it, was accounted to be above one hundred and twenty thousand Pounds." Whitelocke, p. 22. (Cf. above, vol. i, p. 118.)

[1] An account of the Army Pageant, which was opened at Fulham Palace on 20 June, 1910, by Lord Roberts, may be found in the *Times* for 21 June, p. 10, col. 1. The main object of this pageant seems to have been to raise funds for the Soldiers' and Sailors' Help Society: but " Lord Roberts hopes that the high ideals of the promoters of the Pageant will instil a sense of patriotism into the minds of the people, and cause them to do something, however small, for the good of their country." (*Ibid.*, col. 2.)

[2] See Bibliography, *s.v.* SCOTLAND.

[3] The legendary, mythical, elements are mixed with considerable Scottish history. From the program it is impossible to tell how much speaking there was; it is equally impossible to tell how much patriotic fervor was aroused by the view of former rulers and their courtiers. We do not know what proportion of the population — not of Scotland, but of Edinburgh —

§ 4. THE PAGEANT AND THE STAGE

I have already said that pageantry has revealed many latent talents among the participants; but of the thousands of people who passed through Mr. Parker's hands in connection with his pageants, only two sought to go on the stage. This seems surprising; but the reason is fairly obvious — for the pageant, although dramatic, is far removed from stage conventions. The individual actor is merged in the effect produced by the whole cast: there is no opportunity for conceit; all are working together for one aim.[1] Histrionic ability counts for little: many who said shyly that they "couldn't act," proved invaluable because they caught the spirit of an historical character, and presented him simply and naturally.

John Palmer on Pageantry

Mr. John Palmer[2] tells us that "much pious expectation has been aroused in the minds of many excellent people by local revivals of the masque or pageant. Arguing from these, and from one or two conspicuously successful efforts to raise crops of dramatic genius in villages of the countryside, it has been rashly prophesied that thither we must look for the true revival of the English theatre." And again:[3] "As to the masques and pageants which in the last few years have swept the country like an epidemic, no one who has borne a part in these enterprises is seriously able, on their behalf, to proclaim a national revival of dramatic art." Nor do they; Mr. Palmer seems to be unable to divorce the drama from the theatre; and he has quite missed the real significance of the interest in these historical pageants. "The greater number of these," he continues, "were country meetings of fashionable people playing the perennially delightful game known to children of all ages as 'dressing-up.' At best they were an elaborate fancy-dress ball." This, of course, is untrue of the Parkerian work; it is hardly true of even such celebrations as that of Ripon — though it is, quite likely, a just characterization of such festivals as that at Grimston which preceded it.

took part in the production of this "pageant"; it is obviously less of a "festival" than *The Masque of Learning*, in that it makes a more general appeal, and makes it through the history of the nation, rather than through that of an art. The fact that it has an ulterior aim — to make money for a charity — is not enough to rule it from pageantry.

[1] In England — and, to a certain extent in America, — the names of the actors do not appear on the program. This tends to subordinate the individual, as well as to emphasize the historical character he represents. The audience does not laugh to see the greengrocer in the garb of a Roman general, or make audible comments when Mary Ann appears as Queen Elizabeth. The identity of the neighbor is sunk in that of the personage he represents: many who are mute and inglorious become Miltons for an hour. Is it a wonder that life is never quite so humdrum for them after that?

[2] *The Future of the Theatre*, p. 167.

[3] *Ibid.*, pp. 172 f.

Had Mr. Palmer had the pleasure — as I did at York — of falling into conversation with a shopkeeper as he took the air in front of his shop, he would have seen — as I did — enthusiasm kindle as the talk came round to the pageant; he would have been taken inside, as I was, to see the spiked club which my interlocutor had, as an " ancient Briton," wielded five years before; he would have heard eulogies from the burly dealer in antiquities which would have made Mr. Parker's kind heart beat a little faster than usual... Here was no " fashionable " person talking about a " fancy-dress ball "! Of course, he liked the " dressing-up "; who doesn't ? But his chief joy was in the new spirit the pageant had brought to York; he never for a moment considered himself an actor, or expressed a desire to go on the stage, or even connected the pageant with the theatre in his mind.

To return to Palmer: " At worst they were conspicuous instances of precisely that deliberate cult of innocence and simplicity which is the last possible quarter whither we should look for a revival of the arts. They correspond with the activities of a large class of people who imagine they can recapture the sixteenth century by writing ' Merrie Englande ' upon invitations to a contest of brass bands — people . . . who imagine they are putting back the clocks of history by measuring time with a sundial." [1] They are rather the result of a popular interest in the history of England — or of such of it as centres about a given town. At their best, they are given by the townsfolk for the benefit of their fellow-citizens as well as of themselves; and civic pride and solidarity follow the lesson. At their worst, these pageants still teach a lesson in some kind of history (perhaps not always accurate, because some charity or business corporation is seeking to make money) and bring people together with a common aim. They are not a fad, but a legitimate form of entertainment and instruction — they are local chronicle-histories, given by the people and for the people; they are not training grounds for theatrical recruits, as Mr. Palmer hints; nor do they seek to " put back the clocks of history."

Pageant and Theatre

I should add that Mr. Parker has told me that managing a pageant is a great education, especially for stage-managerial work and play-writing. One gets an ability to turn almost anything into dialogue; he learns to save time, to cut out irrelevant matter, and to write crisp speeches. In a later section, we shall return to the subject of " pageant-plays "; here it will be sufficient to note that the accuracy of the historical pageant has not been unfelt on the stage.

Mr. Parker produced *Henry VIII*, from the pageantic point of view, for Sir Herbert Tree, and it had a long run; we shall refer later to his own *Drake*, and *Joseph* (which, as I have noted, he calls " pageant-plays "). Mr. Ambrose Lee,

[1] *Op. cit.*, p. 173.

the York Herald, directed "all the ceremonial of the monarch's crowning," and "the historical exactness in armour and heraldry of the knights and nobles present in Rheims Cathedral," when, in the autumn of 1913, Raymond Rôze produced at London his opera, *Joan of Arc*.[1] "The coronation of Charles VII, perhaps the most notable of the splendid 'living pictures' in the opera, compels enthusiastic applause by the gorgeousness of its many characters . . ." Everything was reproduced as accurately as possible, even to "those little hesitancies in the ceremonial on the stage upon which some of the critics have commented," which were perfectly in the picture since no rehearsal of the ceremony took place. "In the prologue of Mr. Raymond Rôze's opera there is an accurate representation of Joan's birthplace and home."[2]

This accuracy, sometimes seen in plays of a "pageantic" character, is undoubtedly due to the growth of interest in a careful reproduction of the past which owes its origin to the historical pageant.

§ 5. THE STRUCTURE OF THE PAGEANT

Unlike the peripatetic shows of earlier years, the cars of which were rarely related to each other, this modern procession of events across an out-door arena is bound together by a central idea. Each scene, which relates some past event in the history of the place, is called an "episode"[3] — it is not unlike an act in a play, the plot of which is the history of the town.[4] Of course the *dramatis personæ* change with the centuries; the place is the one thing which gives continuity to the performance; the "acts" are frankly episodic — hence their name.

There are eleven episodes in the Sherborne Pageant, all of which are, of course, closely connected with the history of the place. The first is "The Coming of Ealdhelm," 705; the second, "The Defeat of the Danes," 854; the third, "The Death of Ethelbald, and the Coming of Alfred," 860; the fourth, "The Benedictine Rule introduced at Sherborne," 998; the fifth, "William the Conqueror removes the See to Sarum," 1075; the sixth, "Roger of Caen lays the Foundation-Stone of the Castle," 1107; the seventh, "The Quarrel between the Town and the Monastery," 1437; the eighth, "The Foundation of the Almshouse," 1437. This is preceded by a Morris Dance, in which Robin Hood, Maid Marian, and their band take part; they play a small part in the action of the seventh episode. The ninth, "The Expulsion of the Monks," takes place in 1539; the tenth, "The School Receives its Charter," in 1550; and the eleventh, "Sir Walter Raleigh comes to Sherborne," in 1593.

---

[1] See the London *Standard* of 5 November, 1913, for "The York Herald's Explanation of the Pageants" — as the headline-writer calls the "living-pictures" of this opera.

[2] *Ibid.*

[3] In Mr. Lascelles's Quebec Pageant these scenes are called "pageants" — as if they were the successors of earlier cars or platforms; but most "pageanters" call them "episodes." Sometimes they are divided into scenes — cf. Mr. Parker's York Pageant.

[4] See below, p. 291.

THE DEATH OF KING ETHELBALD
[Sherborne, 1905]

Between every two episodes is a selection by the orchestra, followed by a few lines from the Narrative Chorus, who tell briefly what has happened since the last " act," or prepare for the scene to come.[1] At the end of the last episode, " the chorus rise from their seats and sing the Triumph Song," [2] and while they sing, a Maypole has been set up immediately behind them. The Dramatic Choir march on, and with them, a troop of children dressed as shepherds and shepherdesses; the choir sings " With a Laugh as we go round," from *The May Queen*, to which the children dance a Maypole Dance.[3]

Then comes the Final Picture.

> A stately Figure symbolical of Sherborne has been raised on a pedestal in the centre of the Quadrangle. In one hand she bears a model of Sherborne Abbey; the other reposes on a shield bearing the arms of the School. On her right stands her daughter, the American Sherborn, bearing in her hand the model of a caravel, and resting the other on the arms of the State of Massachusetts. Now the School marches through the crowd, singing the *Carmen Sæculare* (the Sherborne School song) . . . Then the combined Orchestras and Choirs play and sing the march in *Tannhäuser*, while all the characters of the previous episodes assemble round the pedestal. All the Performers together with the audience sing the first verse of the Hundredth Psalm . . . Now the Herald steps forward, and in a loud voice reads a *Message* of *Greeting* from Sherborn, Massachusetts, after which Performers and Audience sing the National Anthem.[4]

This is followed by the final processional march.

This pageant is an important one, for it was the model on which Mr. Parker built his others, and after which — to a greater or less extent — his fellow pageant-masters in England constructed theirs, though, as we shall see, there is considerable latitude in details. It combines drama, procession, and dance; each episode tells a complete, if simple, story; [5] though the procession does not wend its way through the streets of the town, it is none the less a procession; and the masque-features of music and dancing, which are scattered through the entertainment, give variety.

As the performance takes place on one spot, before the same audience, it allows the use of narrative dialogue; but the acting and speaking are of the simplest, the effects coming rather from the mass than the individual. The

---

[1] Mr. Parker has explained that the Narrative Chorus in his pageants has the function of the Greek chorus to a certain extent. It fills up the space between episodes — suggesting the passage of time — as well as introducing each one and commenting upon it.

[2] *Book* of the Pageant, p. 37; Mr. Parker wrote the music; Mr. Rhoades the poem.

[3] This serves to connect the modern pageant with such May-day festivals as that at Knutsford. The suggestion of folk-revels here and in the Morris Dance of Robin Hood recall other celebrations, not in themselves pageantic.

[4] *Book* of the Sherborne Pageant, pp. 38 f. In later pageants, the representatives of American cities were commonly delegates from America.

[5] In their relation to the whole, these " acts " remind us of the single plays that go to make up a miracle-play cycle; indeed, pageantry is in much the same stage of its existence as the drama in the days of the miracle-play.

" body " of the older pageantry has disappeared; but the " soul " remains, as does the wide, popular appeal which was the " spirit " of the earlier pageant. As for " technique," the modern work has drawn on dance, procession, and the drama itself, and so is a mixture of masque, the older pageant, and the play; and in this mixture the last element is the strongest.

A common, but not essential, accompaniment of the modern pageant, is the commemorative service often held in connection with it, not only in England, but also in America. Writing in 1910, Mr. Parker had called a pageant, " part of the great Festival of Thanksgiving to Almighty God for the past glory of a city and for its present prosperity. Such an interpretation removes the whole thing at once to a high plane and out of the atmosphere of the mere spectacular entertainment. The actual pageant should be — in the case of my pageants it always has been — opened and closed by great commemorative services on the previous and concluding Sundays in all the places of worship." [1]

§ 6. THE ELEMENTS OF THE PAGEANT

The Quality, the Type, and the Individual

There is a certain amount of symbolism in modern pageantry, and it would be hard to prove there was no connection between it and that of the older show.[2] The allegory which we found in the earlier pageant has, naturally enough, almost entirely disappeared from these historical " folk-plays "; in the former, every character remained symbolic because he could not, under the circumstances

[1] *New Boston*, for November, 1910, p. 296. In 1905, Mr. Parker had said (in the *Journal Soc. Arts*, liv, p. 144): " I confess I cannot conceive a pageant except as an incident in a great act of praise and thanksgiving . . ."

Quite the opposite view is held by Mr. Gilbert Hudson, the master of several Yorkshire pageants, who writes, in a letter of 2 December, 1918: " . . . In some of the Pageants, stress was laid by the person or persons in command on the theory that the Undertaking and Performance should be regarded as a Religious Civic affair; and in one case at least the proceedings were ushered in by a special cathedral service.

" This strikes me as profane nonsense, indicating (dare I suggest it ?) some solemn quackery on the part of the Instigator (perhaps of the Pageant Master in the first instance) and an *unwise* enthusiastic credulity in the people. I agree that a reverent and lofty ideal is to be held and worked for, but to mix up the methods of a Pageant Play with the ceremonies of a Church, seems an undesirable reversion to the grotesque pietism (which now affects us almost as sheer blasphemy) of the worser medieval Mystery plays.

" Therefore, as far as direct religious expression was concerned, I favored only the singing of a hymn by audience and performers at the end of the performance. And no hymn is fitter for all denominations to join in than ' O, God, our help in ages past.' "

[2] I do not mean that Mr. Parker took it directly from the Lord Mayor's pageants. It may well have been an unconscious borrowing, or even an indirect one; it is also possible, of course, that the same forces which were responsible for its earlier birth gave it an independent life — one entirely unconnected with the earlier symbolism.

of the presentation, be individualized. Fame, Honor, Envy, and Error must remain, in a street procession, qualities rather than persons. Even in Jordan's interludes, the characterization was so slight, that the countryman Hoyden and the citizen Freeman suggest rather Rus and Urbs than Tony Lumpkin and Simon Eyre.[1]

Was not this the case with the interludes of John Heywood? The Pedlar and the Pothecary are types, rather than individuals; and the abstractions of the morality-play were types. As soon as they became individuals, we ceased to have either morality-play or interlude (for the latter is, after all, only a morality-play with the moral aim left out); we ceased to deal with abstractions or types and got straight drama. No play can tell more of a *story* than a morality like *The Nice Wanton;* the difference between the play and the morality being that in the former the story is told by individuals; in the latter, by types. It is obvious that the more the characters are individualized, the higher is the form of art — the further it is from farce or melodrama.

Reasons for the Disappearance of Allegory

From modern pageantry allegory has practically disappeared; this is due to three reasons. First, the pageant is given on one spot, so that all the onlookers can see everything that happens. This gives a chance for characterization which the Lord Mayor's Show did not have. In the second place, the emphasis is on history; and to make history live, the historical characters must be alive. This was known to the writers of the seventeenth-century civic shows, who presented historical characters to their public, rather than allegorical abstractions, when they wished to recall the glorious past of the Mayor's Company. Even these historical characters, however, were usually little more than appropriately dressed and labelled lay-figures; the technique of the modern pageant enables us not merely to see the famous men of the past ride through the streets: we can see them doing something which their prototype had done; we can assist at the reproduction of an historical moment.

In the third place, the episodes of a modern pageant are dramatic, and a character in the drama is an individual. The more dramatic the Lord Mayor's Shows became, the more the characters drew away from allegory. Consider, for instance, the 1613 Show of Middleton's: there is a certain amount of drama in the strife between Truth and Error — between Envy and Zeal; and as they fight, these characters tend to get away from pure allegory.[2] They didn't, it is true, get far; but we must remember that conditions were such that they couldn't.

[1] Of course I use these names merely as representatives of countryman and citizen who are alive — as antitheses to Rus and Urbs.

[2] What they are *called* makes no difference. You can name a character Worldly Shame, or Pecunius Lucre, or Charles Marlow — it is all the same. What matters, is what he *does* — or rather, what he *is*. Error may be an individual; Audrey a type.

The modern English pageant is not a morality-play. Even in the days of the morality-play, the types tended to become individuals — the natural tendency on the stage. But Zeal and Envy, in 1613, were not on the stage. In the older pageantry, the types remained types because action was systematically shut out, and speech rigidly restricted to conventional flattery.

The little allegory and symbolism which survive in modern pageants are confined to the final picture, or to the narrative chorus — the parts of the pageant where action is in its lowest terms.[1] It is interesting here to note the strange assortment of characters which appeared in the *Scottish National Pageant* of 1908, to which I have before alluded. We find here such figures as the River Forth, Edinburgh — with Divinity, Law, Learning, Medicine, Valor, Commerce, Agriculture, Science, and various Arts — accompanied by a Monk, a Nun, Doctors of Divinity and Medicine, a Judge, Justice, Drama, and Music; and the Burghs of Scotland. There were also Celtic gods, Spirits of Light, Life and Joy, Demons, Goblins, Mortals, the Cuchulainn Cycle, the Ossianic Cycle, the Arthurian Legend, Romans, Vikings, and a group representing the Early Church. Then came historical groups from Malcolm III to "the Jacobite group of the '1745,'" including various English sovereigns between James I and George II. What these figures did, is not clear from the program; they may not have done more than march on — or across — the stage, though it is more likely that each group took part in some kind of dance. At all events, there was no historical play here: the cast suggests a cross between the masque and the older pageant.[2] The influence of the Parkerian pageantry seems slight.[3]

Symbolism in the Parkerian Pageant

In the so-called "futuristic pageants" of the United States, which we shall treat anon, there is much more allegory than in the English historical pageants; but in the latter a certain amount of symbolism persists. The figures personifying the towns in the Final Pictures lack individuality; these have come down from the *London* and *Britannia* of the older "triumphs." After the historical scenes, which give the audience a personal touch with the past through the individuals they have seen in each episode, comes the final symbolism. We have already mentioned the figure of Sherborne;[4] Hope and Colcestria have a short dialogue just before the "Final Tableau" of the Colchester Pageant;[5] at the

---

[1] In the narrative chorus of the York Pageant — to cite an example — semi-chorus I represents *Memory* and semi-chorus II, *Hope* (*Book of Words*, p. 3). We shall return to symbolism in a moment.

[2] *The Masque of the Seasons*, which was part of this pageant, will be treated later, (see below, p. 223 f.).

[3] Perhaps it was to shows of this kind that Mr. Palmer's remarks which I have cited, applied.

[4] See above, p. 211.

[5] *Book of Words*, pp. 65 f.

end of the Dover Pageant, " Enter Dover with the forty-four American and Colonial Dovers ";[1] at Warwick, " now enter the fourteen Colonial and American Warwicks, represented by young girls in appropriate costume. Lastly, enter a Stately Figure representing Warwick."[2] Here we have pure symbolism; and it is exactly like that which we find in the Lord Mayor's Show for the year 1631, when London was surrounded by Westminster, York, Bristol, Oxford and Exeter. With the exception of this personification — which, after all, is symbolism, insofar as it stands for cities — Mr. Parker does not favor inserting symbolical figures into historical pageants. We shall discuss, in the next chapter, the " futuristic pageant " so common in the United States; Mr. Parker, maintaining, as he does, that history is the most important element of pageantry, cannot advocate a substitution of allegory or symbolism.[3]

Rivers Personified and Individualized

Rivers, especially the Thames, were personified often enough in the seventeenth-century Lord Mayor's Shows;[4] we find them in the historical pageants of the twentieth century. Thames and Tide, who spoke the narrative links in the Chelsea Pageant, were characterized very slightly; and in the Introduction to the Chester Pageant — which " contains a good deal that was written by John Milton "[5] — the " persons " represented were Chester, the Gates, the Pinnacles, the Walls, Attendants on Chester, the Dee, with nymphs, Tritons, and fairies of the banks; here also there is little characterization.

---

[1] *Book* of the Dover Pageant, p. 69.

[2] *Book* of the Warwick Pageant, p. 60. Thirty American girls took part in this pageant. At Bath, the American girls, " special envoys from the United States," represented towns in Maine, New York, Illinois, New Hampshire, the Carolinas, South Dakota, Ohio, Kentucky, Missouri, Pennsylvania, and Michigan. " Two maidens representing the Canadian Baths . . . make their way towards the *Mother Bath* " (*Book* of the Bath Pageant, pp. 70 f.).

New York and Yorks situated in Tasmania, Alabama, Maine, Illinois, Nebraska, Pennsylvania, Queensland, Minnesota, North Dakota, Kentucky, Sierra Leone, Virginia, Ohio, and Ontario — besides Toronto, once called York — were represented at the York Pageant (see Solloway's volume, p. 73, n.).

[3] Both, or all three, elements were hospitably received by the older pageantry. Cf. above, vol. i, p. 220, for the account of Maria de' Medici's reception at Avignon in 1600. On this occasion we find the past of the city happily linked to its royal guests, by the introduction of those ancestors of both king and queen who played a part in the history of the town: and we noted a touch of " futurism." (It is rare that the future is suggested by anything except allegory or symbolism. Can one call the little Henri V " history " ?)

[4] It is enough to recall the Thames, Severn, and Humber in 1605; the Boyne, Shannon, Rhine, and Danube (" signifying the present seats or scenes of war, of which the entire pageant is an emblem ") in 1691; the Thames, Tiber, and Indus in 1694; Neptune with the Thames, Danube, Rhine, and Tiber in 1701; the Thames in 1585, and in the 1604 " royal-entry." Cf. also the Forth at Edinburgh in 1908. (See above, p. 214.)

[5] Mr. Hawtrey's *Foreword:* see the *Book* of the Chester Pageant, p. 11.

The Rivers and Streams of Gloucestershire

But the Gloucestershire Pageant demands more attention. Here the Chorus is made up of the Rivers and Streams of the county. They were rowed in boats upon the lake which stretched along the foot of the grandstand; and they came to and fro between the episodes, singing their songs and making the necessary explanations.[1] It matters not so much whether or not Mr. Hawtrey were directly influenced by the personification of rivers in the older show; for here the Rivers are characterized, and therefore tend away from the symbolism which pervaded it.

The four principal Rivers — the Thames, Sabrina, Avona, and the Chelt — are attended by various other Rivers and Streams of the shire, grouped in large boats. Father Thames speaks the opening words; and as he says, " We are the streams and rivers that do flow through Gloucestershire," the Chelt interrupts importantly —

" I am the Chelt.
Thames: Peace, unimportant brook!
Chelt: I unimportant! Isn't Cheltenham on the Chelt ?
Thames: This is Sabrina . . .
And this Avona . . .
I'm Father Thames . . . a true-born son of Gloucestershire.
This little fellow is the Chelt.
Chelt: All right!
I told them that. You don't think they forget.
Thames: All these around us are our tributaries;
Whose tuneful flow of rippling harmonies
Will soothe the ear with sweet old English songs.
Chelt: They are the small fry.
Sabrina: Silence, little Chelt."

Here is characterization obvious in the dialogue; we see the dignified figure of the Thames, and the pert Chelt, full of his own importance, hardly bigger than a tributary. This characterization is kept up between each episode; one or two more citations will suffice to show how far from symbolism we are taken.

Before the sixth episode, which is an " abbreviated scene " from *Comus*, Thames reads:

"Sabrina: an abbreviated scene from ' Comus,' by John Milton —
Chelt: Who was he ?
Sabrina: You ignorant, uneducated boy!

---

[1] Mr. Hawtrey, in his *Foreword*, says: " The task of explaining the subject of each episode in its turn is usually entrusted to a Narrative Chorus. I have ventured to make a slight change. The Chorus sing old English songs, or glees, not necessarily bearing on the following episode: while the explanation of what is to come is undertaken by representatives of Gloucestershire rivers who tell their tale in spoken dialogue."

Avona: Oh, Chelt! You've not read 'Comus'?
Chelt: No. Have you?
Avona: Have I? How dare you ask? Please, Father Thames,
Unfold the tale, in case there should be any
Beside this infant here, who know it not.
Thames: . . . Sabrina, beauteous stream, whom Milton loved,
She, she alone, has power to give release.
Chelt: I wonder Milton never thought of me.
Avona: Conceited little Chelt, I don't suppose
He ever heard of you.
Chelt: He must have been
An ignorant, uneducated man." [1]

And again, introducing Episode viii — the visit of George III to Cheltenham in 1788 —

" *Thames:* Now comes the reign of George the Third, a King
Whose memory we in Cheltenham hold dear.
Chelt, you shall tell the reason why.
Chelt: All right.
King George the Third together with his Queen and their three daughters
Came to this town when he was ill and drank the Cheltenham waters,
And to these waters George the Third declared himself a debtor,
Because he very soon became considerably better." [2]

Here is characterization which has killed symbolism: we do not see rivers, but four inhabitants of the county, acting as chorus. The Chelt, with his roguish conceit and impertinent interruptions, is akin to the morality " Vice "; and the Vice was one of the first characters in the morality-play to become human.

In the various figures of the cities, we have symbolism preserved; and some of the rivers remind us of predecessors in the Lord Mayor's Shows. All this symbolism is, however, confined to the Narrative Chorus or the Final Picture; and in the Gloucestershire Pageant the characterization which has taken history from the hands of lay-figures, has crept into the narrative chorus and banished symbolism.

The Historical Element in the Parkerian Pageant

We have already mentioned the part which early British history played in the " royal-entry " and Lord Mayor's Show of past centuries; in the Parkerian pageant it is, obviously, important.[3] If some of the history here made vivid is

---

[1] *Book* of the Gloucestershire Pageant, pp. 60 f.

[2] *Ibid.*, pp. 74 f.

[3] The Warwick Pageant is introduced by Druids; the Roman occupation of York forms the matter for the second episode of that pageant, in which Cartismandua and Caradoc appear; Caractacus appears in the Gloucestershire Pageant; Cymbeline and Caradoc (or Caractacus) appear in the first episode of the Warwick Pageant, and, with Gwyddyr, in the

not strictly accurate, we can hardly blame the pageant-masters; for, since the days of Geoffrey of Monmouth, we have almost adopted the mythical history of Britain as if it were fact.[1]

The Colchester Oyster makes its first appearance in the first episode of the pageant of that city, when the Britons discover the bivalve, and that it is good to eat.[2] The story of the Bear and the Ragged Staff is dramatically told in the second episode of the Warwick Pageant,[3] and Gwar says: " Now, look you, this . . . shall henceforth be our escutcheon, that all men seeing it shall dread Warwick's fist." How Dover got the motto *Invicta* is told in the second episode of the Dover Pageant.[4] Thus is history vivified.

The Pageant is a Modern Chronicle-Play

Modern pageants bear much the same relation to us that the chronicle-play bore to the Elizabethan audience.[5] The " historical exposition " is the soul of the Parkerian pageant; and, this being the case, the dialogue is important. Some there are, in America, who maintain that a pageant should be wordless, because in many cases it is impossible for the audience to hear; the Englishman feels that speech is so important that the audience should be restricted to those who can get within earshot.

In the Sherborne Pageant, Ealdhelm asks the chieftain, pointing to the spring, " My son, by what name is this water known ? " And the chieftain replies, " Sir, in our ancient tongue we call this water the Scir Burn — the clear stream. It is a holy place." [6] Thus the audience gets an etymological lesson with its history. It is obvious that the dialogue is important.

Older Chronicle-Plays Make Contributions to the New

Many of the older chronicle-plays are drawn upon by the modern pageant. In the York Pageant a condensed version of the Chandlers' play of the Angels

---

Colchester Pageant — which also includes, in a later scene, Boadicea, who is shown in the first episode of the Bury Pageant.

I may note that Taliesin appears before the Knights of the Round Table in Mr. Monck's pageant-play of *King Arthur*, before alluded to.

[1] The Trojans under Ebrauc appeared in the first episode of the York Pageant. (See Solloway's volume, p. 6, and the *Book of Words*, pp. 10 f.) Bladud appeared in the Bath Pageant of 1909 — as a character in a masque. (See the *Book* of the Bath Pageant, pp. 41 f.)

[2] *Book of Words*, pp. 9 f. The oysterbeds, (" fisheries ") play a considerable part in the pageant; " The Song of the Oyster " (*Book of Words*, p. 51) — written by the Mayor of Colchester — was introduced while Queen Elizabeth is at the Oyster Feast.

[3] *Book* of the Warwick Pageant, pp. 11 f. [4] *Book* of the Dover Pageant, pp. 15 f.

[5] Professor Baker, writing in *New Boston* (Nov. 1910) p. 296, remarks that modern pageantry " seems likely to be for us (in America) a combination of the Chronicle Play and the Morality." In England, the emphasis is on history; as we shall see, America permits much more allegory.

[6] *Book* of the Sherborne Pageant, p. 14.

The Coming of St. Ealdhelm
[Sherborne, 1905]

and the Shepherds was given in the closing scene of the fifth episode; the text was made from Miss Smith's *York Mystery Plays*,[1] and the scene was presented on a reproduction of a miracle-play pageant. This interesting union of the old and new pageants is noteworthy.[2]

One of the episodes of the Warwick Pageant, " based on scenes from Marlowe's *Edward the Second*," tells the story of Piers Gaveston in five pages;[3] episode v of the Dover Pageant is " compressed " from *Henry V*;[4] episode iv of the Gloucestershire Pageant is 3 *Henry VI*, v, 5;[5] and episode vi of the Bury Pageant is a " greatly condensed " version of 2 *Henry VI*, iii, 1.[6] No clearer evidence could be desired, of the fact that the English pageant-masters feel that they are doing the task of a chronicle-playwright.

The reason that these pageants cannot be called " chronicle-plays " — allowing for a change in the method of presentation — is that they deal with a place, whereas the chronicle-play presents the history of a person. The method of treatment is the same, but the matter treated is different. And it might be confusing to class them together, especially as there is such a divergence in the manner of presentation; though both have the " noble Patriotism " which Carlyle attributes to the one.

Comedy and History Combined

Just as Shakspere mingled comedy and history in *Henry IV*, so Parker, in the second episode of the Dover Pageant combines with history a dash of comedy:

" *Odo:* . . . Wherefore, Seneschal, summon the Cinque Ports.
Zack: What's cinque ?
Hob: How many fingers hast thou on the right hand?

---

[1] See the *Book of Words*, pp. 98 f., and T. P. Cooper's article on the Armorial bearings of the craft guilds and companies in the *Book* of the pageant (mentioned in the Bibliography, *s.v.* York).

It may be noted that the tenth scene of the first part of the English Church Pageant, showed a " Miracle Play and Pilgrimage Scene, c. 1350." The episode was divided into two parts, the first of which pictured " the market place of a country town, crowded with people. A band of pilgrims, on their way to the shrine of St. Thomas, are among them, and while they talk a cart enters, drawn by two oxen, bearing the curtained stage of a miracle play. The curtains are soon drawn and the Chester Miracle Play of the Shepherds is performed. At the end the cart is drawn off, and the pilgrims go out singing." (Program of the pageant, p. 11.)

[2] A rare post-card photograph of this scene has been given by Mr. Fred Arey of York to the Harvard Library. It is reproduced as the frontispiece of this volume.

[3] Episode vi. See the *Book* of the Warwick Pageant, pp. 27 f. " Piers de Gaveston in Scarborough Castle " is the seventh episode of the Scarborough Pageant (1912): some lines in this scene are taken from Marlowe's play. (See *Book of Words*, p. 25.)

[4] *Book* of the Dover Pageant, pp. 37 f. [5] *Book* of the Gloucestershire Pageant, pp. 45 f.

[6] *Book of Words* of the Bury St. Edmunds Pageant, p. 48. The *Foreword* notes that the scene is " drastically compressed."

Zack: Four. For one I cut off by mistake —

Hob: (*disgusted*) Oh — !

Flourish of Trumpets

Seneschal: All Mayors, Bailiffs and Barons of the Five Ports and their members, draw ye near and answer to your names as you shall be called, and give your attendance here at the Bredenstone upon the peril that shall fall of it.

As they are called, ENTER THE MAYORS, *etc., each with a* BANNER-BEARER *and banner and two* ATTENDANTS. *They form a great semicircle round the Bredenstone.* ENTER *the* CROWD *of* MEN, WOMEN *and* CHILDREN.

Seneschal: Dover — Sandwich — Romney — Hastings — Hythe — These be the Cinque Ports. Rye — Winchelsea — the two ancient towns. — Now certain of the Limbs or Members. Folkestone — Feversham — Margate — Fordwick — Deal — Walmer — Ramsgate — Lydd — Pevensey — Seaford — Tenterden.

Odo: Are all here?

Mayor of Hastings: All are here, my lord.

Odo: (*at the Bredenstone*) Hear now what rights and privileges our Sovereign Lord the King intends towards you, and what service he requires in return." [1]

And so the history lesson goes on. It makes an impression on us because we hear it, imaginatively, through the ears of those who are themselves taking part in it. The principle is the same as that used by the writers of the Elizabethan chronicle-play, whose audiences knew, for instance, that Richard III had lost the Battle of Bosworth Field when they heard him cry, " My kingdom for a horse!" They realized his defeat through his own realization of it. And this is what makes the history we learn by means of fiction impress us, and stay with us, long after the facts we have read in books have gone. Through our sympathy for, and interest in, the characters, we gain an interest in events.

In these pageants, history is made alive for us by the same method. They have an emotional appeal which is rarely equalled in the theatre. It would be a great play which could hold an audience for four hours, and leave such an impression that members of that audience became enthusiastic at the mention of the play five years later. Yet more than one pageant has accomplished this feat.

One can readily see that dialogue is important in these pageants. Although the action is built on broad lines, suitable for the open-air performances, the words of the historical episodes should be easily audible.

The Oxford Pageant of 1907 consisted of fifteen scenes and an Interlude or Masque; and of these sixteen parts, nine are dramatic scenes with words, and the rest spectacular only. " It is, perhaps, advisable to point out," says the prefatory note, " that a modern Pageant, like an historical play of Shakespeare, is often compelled, by reasons of space, time, and suitability for representation, to foreshorten history. The critic must not murmur if persons and events are found in a juxtaposition for which there is no absolute warrant in the chronicles,

[1] *Book* of the Dover Pageant, p. 16.

The Peasants' Revolt

or if fancy sometimes bodies forth possibilities which may never have been realities."[1]

This seems to be the only attitude to take regarding the use of history in the pageants. "Be accurate: but, if you can't be accurate, be as accurate as you can." Even Mr. Parker, whose insistence on the importance of historical accuracy in pageants is founded on the belief that laxity in this respect weakens them as educational vehicles, has allowed himself a certain margin. One does not, indeed, presume documentary evidence for Hob and Zack; but one wonders if Queen Elizabeth really attended the Oyster Feast at Colchester...

What is obviously unhistorical can do no harm; what is not obviously inaccurate should — in an historical pageant — be indicated, on the program or elsewhere.[2]

Where to Stop the Historical Survey

The ostensible aim of pageantry is to revive or maintain a memory of the past, giving the history of the town, and honoring its great men. One result of this is the education and development of the town's inhabitants (and the pill is not the less effective because it has a sugar coating!); but this is, after all, only a by-product.

In this historical survey, Mr. Parker stops at the time of the Civil War, or earlier.[3] He considered this necessary, as the Whig and Tory camps still exist in England, and feeling still runs high. It is unsafe, he believes, to come nearer than the middle of the seventeenth century; and he had to "skate rather carefully over Cromwell." At Colchester, where the siege was vital to the history of the town, he tried an experiment — from a dispassionate point of view he reproduced the shooting of the Royalists by the Roundheads in a scene strictly

---

[1] *The Book of Words*, p. 6. Cf. also the last paragraph of Mr. Langdon's foreword in the *Book of Words* of the St. Johnsbury Pageant, p. 5.

[2] It is, for example, unlikely that Dr. Johnson, Smollett, Boswell, and Goldsmith ever attended a *fête* at Ranelegh Gardens with George II — although such a thing would have been possible.

In Episode v of the Bath Pageant, the young Shakspere, who with Marlowe and others had been acting before the Queen, was presented to her. (Surely an unhistorical scene!) See *Book of Words*, esp. pp. 39 f.

[3] The Sherborne Pageant (1905) ends with Sir Walter Raleigh; the Warwick Pageant (1906) with the Fire of Warwick, (1694); the Dover Pageant (1908) with the arrival of Henrietta Maria, (1625); the Bury Pageant (1907) with "The New Age" (1533–1578); the Colchester Pageant (1909) with the siege of the town (1648); the York Pageant (1909) with the siege and surrender of York, to the Parliamentarians, "with all the honours of war," in 1644. The St. Albans Pageant (1907) ended with Elizabeth at Gorhambury, July, 1572; the Pickering Pageant (1910) with the defeat of the Armada (1588), and the Hertford Pageant (1914) with the visit of the Queen to the Castle in 1561. (None of the last three was Mr. Parker's.)

accurate, as well as amazingly dramatic and tragic.[1] The very words used at the trial and execution were repeated; and yet — though the people took the scene well — the episode did arouse feeling on both sides which, while not unpleasantly expressed, was obvious. Partly for this reason, and partly because the costumes of the Georgian period seemed dull and unromantic after those of earlier times, Mr. Parker deemed it best to emphasize the remoter past. Not all the other English pageant-masters, however, agree with him in this respect; but it is to be noted that when history was brought down to later times, contention is avoided, as Mr. Parker avoided it at Warwick.[2]

§ 7. MASQUE, INTERLUDE, AND JOUST IN THE MODERN PAGEANT

"The Masque of the Mediæval Curriculum" at Oxford in 1907

An interesting feature of many of the modern pageants is the "interlude." In the Oxford Pageant of 1907 we find *The Masque of the Mediæval Curriculum* — which is not a masque at all, but a modern attempt at a morality-play. This "masque" contains little dancing, though there is plenty of singing. The

---

[1] This final episode, the sixth, may be found in the *Book of Words*, pp. 54 f. "Every incident in the Pageant is based either on local tradition or on authentic history," says Mr. Parker in the *Foreword*, "and in many cases the characters repeat the actual words spoken by their prototypes. This is especially the case in Episode vi."

Concerning this scene (*Book of Words*, pp. 61 f.) Mr. Parker told me that the shooting was horrible in its realism. Regular soldiers — who often, by the way, acted in his pageants — took the parts of Cavalier and Puritan. The cavalry charges of this pageant were done by cavalrymen, and the effect was splendid.

[2] The Oxford Pageant (1907) included the visit of George III to Oxford in 1785; the Chelsea Pageant (1908) included a Royal *Fête* at Ranelegh Gardens in 1749, which was attended by George II, Dr. Johnson, Boswell, Smollett and Goldsmith, among others; the Gloucestershire Pageant (1908) showed the visit of George III to Cheltenham in 1788; the Winchester Pageant (1908) included the "Merry Monarch." The Bath Pageant (1909) showed the visit of Queen Charlotte to Bath in 1817; the Army Pageant (1910) included Badajos, 6 April, 1812; the West Dorset Pageant (1911) included the visit of Charles II to Bradpole in 1651, and the London Pageant (*The Festival of Empire*, 1911) showed "The Allied Sovereigns in London," 18 June, 1814. The English Church Pageant (1909) ended with the acquittal of the Seven Bishops in 1688, but contained groups representing eighteenth- and nineteenth-century Churchmen.

The Scarborough Pageant (1912) included several episodes after Queen Elizabeth's time: Episode x, "Surrender of the Castle to the Parliamentary Forces, 1645"; episode xi, "Discovery of Spa Waters, about 1620;" episode xii, "Release of George Fox from Imprisonment in the Castle," 1666; episode xiii, "Mr. Mayor is tossed in a blanket," 1688; and episode xiv, "A Miscellany, introducing: Gablers' Fair, Amusements, The Press-gang, Smugglers, Pirates, Fashionable Visitors, Local Celebrities and Eccentrics etc.; Time — the latter end of the eighteenth century (chiefly 1780–90)."

characters include a Prælector, a Vain Student and a Wise Student, the Court of Learning, with Divinity, Medicine, and Law and their trains, the Seven Arts [1] and the rout of Folly and Pleasure. These two, at the end, beckon luringly to the Vain Student; "he, hesitating for a little while, goeth to them. Turning him round with garlands they do drag him out singing, and then may one perceive Time following after them silently . . . When they have passed away, Time following, shall the Arts and Sciences, particularly Divinity, since he hath chosen her for his mistress, conduct the Wise Student forth in the opposite direction, preceded by the Prælector, who, when they are approaching the exit, shall let them pass him by, and then follows them out, and as they go they shall sing . . ." [2]

Another interlude, played before the Henry VIII and the Wolsey of this same pageant, showed a Knight (Youth) who slew the Dragon (Ignorance) and freed a maiden (Knowledge) whom the latter bore a prisoner on his back. A mimic castle, borne by four men within, appeared before the Spirit of the Age, attended by a number of dancing nymphs.[3] This entertainment — omitted in the performance because of lack of time — is a better imitation of a masque than was the other; for it has (besides song) dance, a moving castle, and a mock-fight — the roaring Dragon was killed with a goose-quill. The allegory tends, however, to give it a strong morality flavor.

"The Masque of the Seasons," in the Scottish National Pageant

Included in the Scottish National Pageant was a "Masque of the Seasons," the Argument of which reads as follows:

"'Time' leadeth in the masque; He enthroneth Queen Nature and placeth Pity and Valour on her right hand; Love and Beauty on her left.

"He surroundeth her with her Courtiers, and Attendants, Dawn, Day, and Night, the Stars, the Golden Hours, the Angels of Pity and the Babes they guard.

"He summoneth the Seasons in due order, Spring, Summer, Autumn, Winter, that they may present their gifts to Nature, and delight her heart with Song and Dance and Gaiety and set forth the Triumph of 'Good St. George over the Horrible Dragon of Cruelty.'" At the end comes, "The masque of Christmas and St. George and the Dragon," with Hestia, Father Christmas, Waits, Jesters, the Princess,[4] the Dragon, Mercy, Pity and St. George, the Horse, the Doctor, Turkish and True Knights. It is noteworthy that allegory is here combined with what is apparently a revival of the old folk-dance, although it is called "a play."

---

[1] Who appeared in 1432 (see above, vol. i, p. 145) and in 1547 (*ibid.*, p. 186); also in Dekker's Show for 1612, Jordan's for 1676, Taubman's for 1678. Cf. above, p. 77, n. 3.

[2] *Book of Words* of the Oxford Pageant, p. 62. This "Masque" was written by Professor Sir Walter Raleigh.

[3] *Ibid.*, pp. 74 f. J. B. Fagan was the author of this interlude.

[4] Presumably the figure of the maiden so often rescued by St. George in earlier days — as, for instance, in 1461 at Bristol (cf. above, vol. i, p. 152) and at Coventry in 1474 (*ibid.*, p. 154).

Given in six scenes, it shows the princess, fastened to a stake, attacked by the dragon and rescued by St. George, after which the " Ancient Mummers play St. George and the Dragon which is presented with quaint ceremony and circumstance by them. After which these and the whole Company with Nature and her Court form in procession and march out to brave music."[1]

It is interesting to observe that, whereas, in the Lord Mayor's Show — when there were interludes — the interludes tended away from the allegory which permeated the rest of the pageant, here the interludes tend toward allegory.

Folk-Revels of the Past Revived in Modern Pageants

But not all of the interludes in modern pageants are allegorical. That of the Winchester Pageant, called " St. Giles' Fair " is really a formless episode, giving a picture of a town fair in the time of Henry I.[2] The second part of the seventh episode of the Chester Pageant — which deals with the visit of James I to Chester in 1617 — shows " The Midsummer Revels " about 1620.[3] The revellers include the Waits, the Dragon, Elephant and Castle,[4] Maypole children, the Antelope, Ass and Unicorn, the Ship, the Merchants' Mount,[5] Morris Dancers, Jack o' the Green,[6] the City Giants, Guild Boys with banners, the Luce, the Camel, Hobby Horses, a Merry Andrew and Dairymaids, Elves and Fairies. In this episode, the revels consist almost entirely of dances: " enter the procession, which makes its way down to the front. Maypoles are set up on each side of the arena. The Revels open with a Maypole Dance . . . This is followed by a Morris Dance. Then comes a Dance of Dairy Maids. Then the Maypole Ribbons are unwound . . . Following this comes the Dance of the Elves and Fairies. The Revels then close with the Charge of the Hobby Horses."[7]

---

[1] From the program of the Scottish National Pageant.

[2] See *Book of the Words and Music* of the Winchester Pageant, pp. 35 f. The last episode of the Scarborough Pageant included the " Gablers' Fair." Cf. the *Book of Words*, p. 68.

[3] *Book* of the Chester Pageant, pp. 70 f. (A. E. Lovell, M.A., is the author of the entire episode.)

" May Day Revels " constitute scene v of part ii of the *Festival of Empire* — the London Pageant of 1911.

[4] See above, vol. i, pp. 66 f., and p. 170, and n. 5 of this volume.

[5] See above, vol. i, pp. 44–46, and notes.

[6] See above, vol. i, p. 70.

[7] *Book* of the Chester Pageant, p. 71. I may mention a few more examples of the masque-episodes in modern pageants: both gypsy and morris dances were included in the Potter Heigham Pageant of 1907; morris dancers appeared in the Colchester Pageant (see the *Book*, p. 30); and a Roman dance followed the Triumph of Claudius (*ibid.*, p. 13). Episode iv ended with a dance of the fishermen (*ibid.*, p. 41); a " stately dance " was performed in episode v, scene 1 (*ibid.*, p. 44); a " Rigadoon " was danced by children, after they had acted out the song of " Old King Cole " — who was brought on " in state " — for the entertain-

The Masque Imperial of the "Festival of Empire" Includes Allegory

The *Festival of Empire* ended with a "Masque Imperial," wherein the "allegory of the advantages of Empire" was shown. This, it is necessary to observe, gives a morality-play flavor to the whole pageant. The Genius of the World, the Voice of the World, Queen Need of Knowledge, with many Queen Needs of other things, Britannia, with the Spirits of her Meadows, Forests, Lakes, Mists, and Mountains (to name a few out of many) and the Queen of Wisdom were characters in this masque, which also included the Colonies.

Many of these masque-like episodes were mere revels; others contained allegory, with a morality-play flavor in some cases; and some prefaced a joust. In the second part of episode vi in the Winchester Pageant — showing the reception of the Emperor Charles V by Henry VIII — a morris dance entered, with Fool and Maid Marian, dragging a huge wooden horse.[1] After a dance, during which the morris men sang King Henry's song, "Pastime with good Companye," a grave man, crowned, stepped forward, in the dress of King Priam.

A Joust-like Masque at Winchester

. . . With his sceptre he strikes the horse. It snorts flame; opens, and a number of little Cupids with drums come pouring forth, beating an alarm. Other Cupids run with a band of silk, which they strain and set up as a tennis net . . . They toss balls to and fro across it, but scurry away as a trumpet sounds and from either entrance L and R six knights come riding, armed for the joust. Six are Greeks — Menelaus, Ulysses, Ajax, Pyrrhus, Sthenelus, Neoptolemus: six, Trojans — Paris, Deiphobus, Æneas, Pantheus, Hypanis, Polites. They pass the thrones to music, salute, and wheeling in two semi-circles ride back to their barriers. Then, at the sound of another trumpet, they gallop forward.

---

ment of Elizabeth (*ibid.*, p. 53). A "Stately Dance" and a morris dance welcomed Mary Tudor to Bury St. Edmunds (*Book* of that pageant, p. 57). Many dances occur in the York Pageant — a Roman dance (*Book of Words*, p. 27); a morris dance and a sword-dance (*ibid.*, p. 86); a dance by the children of York (*ibid.*, p. 100) and a "stately dance" by the Lords and Ladies of the Court before Anne, consort of James I, (*ibid.*, p. 112). Tymbesteres danced before King John of France and David Bruce of Scotland in the Hertford Pageant of 1914 (*Book*, p. 30); and there was a Pavane as well as a country-dance ("Bessy and the Clown on Plough Monday") before Queen Elizabeth in the last episode (*Book*, pp. 38–39). In the latter was a dragon and a hobby-horse.

"A Masque of Prince Bladud" forms a part of episode v of the Bath Pageant — depicting the visit of Queen Elizabeth to Bath in 1590. Hobby-horses, fairies, etc., take part. (*Book* of the Bath Pageant, pp. 41 f.) "The Faery Queen Masque" was performed before Elizabeth in episode vii of the Chelsea Pageant. (See the *Book* of that pageant, pp. 83 f., and the illustration opposite p. 77.)

[1] Pictured in the *Illus. Lond. News* for 27 June, 1908, p. 956, (picture 9).

A Joust. The Greeks prevail, and chase their opponents around the lists. At a sudden roll of drums, the king stands and lowers his warder, whereat all the knights form up and cross their lances.[1]

While many of these are not, strictly speaking, "interludes," they are akin to the formless episode, like the St. Giles's Fair of the Winchester Pageant. They give us pictures of the Court and folk life of the past, which need not be closely related to the life of one particular place. There were, it is true, revels at Chester in 1610 — but they were not confined to that year, nor were they confined to that place. Nor is there anything characteristic of the history of any town in a masque or joust.

The Modern "Interlude"

It is clear, then, that an "interlude" has — as far as modern pageantry is concerned — become something different from the dialogues that either John Heywood or Thomas Jordan wrote. Insofar as it breaks the slender plot[2] of a pageant, it has a right to the name. But the word is confusing when it can cover anything from a joust to what is practically a morality-play.

A Pageantic Masque at Edinburgh

In the reign of Henry VII, as we have seen, the pageant car was adopted by the masque; but it influenced only the setting — not the technique — of that form of art. In 1634, we found a masque with a pageant-attachment, as it were;[3] in 1912, we find a masque which seems to have been influenced by the modern pageant. *The Masque of Learning*, by Professor Patrick Geddes, was prepared to celebrate the twenty-fifth anniversary of the foundation of University Hall, Edinburgh, and was performed at the Synod Hall, in that city, on the 14, 15, 16, and 19, March 1912.[4] As Professor Geddes says in his Foreword, this *Masque*

---

[1] *Book of Words and Music* of the Winchester Pageant, p. 65. Sir A. T. Quiller-Couch is the author of this part of the episode.

Episode iv of the Bath Pageant — the visit of Henry VII to Bath in 1497 — ends with a joust. (See the *Book* of that pageant, pp. 28 f.)

[2] If we may use this word to suggest the story of a town.

[3] See above, vol. i, pp. 117 f.

[4] I am indebted to Mr. S. J. Hume for the *Book* of Professor Geddes's masque. A clipping from a Glasgow paper which I found in the copy he lent me, contains an account of the extension of the masque by the addition of new episodes. "Two masques have thus arisen — first, that of ancient learning, up to Celtic civilisation inclusive, and second that of mediæval and modern learning; and these will be given in successive weeks. . . Yet with this increase of spectacular interest, the main ideas of the whole, its historical interpretations, its educational suggestiveness, also, will, it is hoped, be all the clearer." This pageant, the same clipping asserts, led to the formation of the "Edinburgh Masquers."

The whole masque or pageant — both terms are very loosely used — is more of a "festival" than a real pageant; in spirit it recalls the Boston Normal School "Pageant," which

of Learning " consists of an historical pageant of characteristic scenes illustrative of the development of Higher Education, and of the origins and history of the University — each in its widest sense . . . The main presentment begins with the Oriental civilisations, and proceeds through Greek and Roman times, through Celtic and Mediæval periods to the Renaissance and the Encyclopædic age; and thence to the present day . . . Each sequence of scenes, with its typical and historic figures, is . . . in principle itself a pageant, expressing the essential genius of a race, or commemorating the main achievements of an epoch of civilisation . . . The final scene attempts to shadow forth the Opening Future of Education and Citizenship; and to suggest how Edinburgh and her many students may take an increasing part in this; City and University, Life and Learning, again, as of old, advancing hand in hand."

The Masque of Charterhouse

Akin to this pageantry which can appeal only to a small part of the community, and which, for this reason, has been more properly given another name, is the celebration of the tercentenary of the Charterhouse School in 1911, by the *Masque of Charterhouse*, performed on 8 July of that year. This set forth historical scenes from the past of the old school, and seems to have resembled, in several ways, the Pageant of Hollis Hall, presented at Harvard University in June, 1913.[1] Every incident of this masque " was concerned with the Charterhouse and her intimate life, and represented by men and boys to whom Charterhouse is a living reality."[2] This seems to have been rather a pageant than a masque; perhaps it was given the latter name because it appealed only to a small part of the community, rather than to the community as a whole.

A Word on the Investiture of the Prince of Wales

Mr. Parker thinks that the proclamation of the present Prince of Wales at Carnavon — in which careful attention was paid to past procedure — is an outcome of the love of the past developed by the educational pageant in England. It is, perhaps, more likely that both are the results of forces set in motion in the nineteenth century, though the historical pageant may have stimulated the Investiture of the Prince directly.[3]

is treated in the next chapter. The characteristically American " futuristic " element is also to be found in it, with the symbolism and allegory that are inseparable from a treatment of the age that is to come.

[1] On this, see below, p. 272. As far as I know there is no connection between these two pageants.

[2] A few ladies in " walking parts " appeared in the second scene; (the Hollis Pageant showed none). An account of the celebration in connection with this anniversary was published in the London *Times* for 10 July, 1911, p. 6, col. 1; a notice of it appeared in the same paper for 20 May, 1911, p. 6, col. 5.

[3] For pictures of this ceremony see the *Illus. Lond. News* for 22 July, 1911, especially

§ 8. PAGEANTIC TENDENCIES IN ENGLAND — THE "PAGEANT-PLAY"

Even before the war, pageantry seemed to be losing popularity in England; the years from 1911 to 1914 were not so prolific in historical pageants as had been those during the period 1905–1911; this is, it has been suggested, due in part to the commercializing of the pageant, but it is also due to a development in other lines of the forces which pageantry has put in motion. At first, England seized upon the historical pageant as a child seizes upon a new toy; then, the novelty having worn off, she threw it aside. But there are signs that it will become a cherished possession, none the less valued because kept less in evidence.

Already a revival — if one may revive what is not dead — seemed to be beginning in the summer of 1914, when, hardly a month before the war broke out, Hertford celebrated her thousandth anniversary. It is impossible to foretell the effect on pageantry which peace will have; but one can imagine the patriotism and national pride which will demand expression — and one sees the means of expression at hand.[1]

The pageantic spirit has been kept alive, in the years since 1911, in various ways. We have already noted the pageantry which has appeared in the Royal Naval and Military Tournament, and the tendency to "pageantize" the fancy-dress ball, by giving it a central idea. Such shows as the "Children's Welfare Festival," which was given at Olympia in April, 1914, and included the "Makers of England,"[2] keep alive — if it needs keeping alive — the "soul" of pageantry. The historical characters in this last festival gave a pageantic flavor to what would otherwise have been merely a children's masque.[3] These shows reflect

---

pp. 164, 165. This occasion was recognized in the Lichfield Bower of 1911 (which took place before the actual event).

We may note, in passing, "The renewal of a ceremony in abeyance for two and a half centuries: the King and Queen leaving St. George's Chapel for the return open-air procession after the special Garter Service at Windsor," which is pictured in the *Illus. Lond. News* for 6 July, 1912 (American edition), p. 7. "A special service for the Knights of the Garter was held in St. George's Chapel at Windsor on June 15, before their Majesties left for Harrow. The open-air procession was a novel feature of the ceremonies. It was revived last year, at the Investiture of the Prince of Wales at Carnavon, for the first time in the history of the Order since the days of Charles II . . ." (*Ibid., loc. cit.*)

[1] In both England and America pageantry was used, to a certain extent, and in various forms, not only as a means of raising money for war-charities, but as propaganda.

[2] Among whom were Boadicea, William I, Richard I, Elizabeth, Marlborough, Nelson, Wolfe, and Victoria.

[3] With the exception of the historical characters, the affair was a series of dances lightly related to each other in that they were all inspired by toys or fairy-tales; historical accuracy was not of primary importance, nor did the entertainment seek to awaken a patriotic pride in the past.

Another example of these children's entertainments is described in the London *Daily*

pageantry, applying it, as it were, to private or charitable ends, depriving it of its popular " spirit " and sometimes reducing it to its old form of *tableau vivant*, (though without the pageant-car and street-procession).

It is to be remarked that at the " Children's Welfare Festival " we see a pageantic interlude in a children's masque, reversing the commoner masque-interlude in the historical pageant.

The " Pageant-Play " and the " Play-Pageant "

There have long been spectacular plays, with large casts; but since the Parkerian pageant arose, the term " pageant-play " has come into being. This is still rather a vague term — it is used to cover many kinds of performances. The late Sir Herbert Tree's production of *Henry VIII* was an interesting performance which had a long run; Mr. Parker's more recent *Joseph and his Brethren*[1] was even more pageantic; his *Drake*—dealing with a national hero —was revived during the early days of the recent war, and awoke much patriotic enthusiasm. These plays show a tendency to bring the stage nearer the pageant, than the pageant toward the stage; in the first two, the method of production was pageantic — but *Drake* shows pageantic material as well. It is almost straight Elizabethan chronicle-history.[2]

" The Last Days of St. Benet's Abbey " at Potter Heigham

An interesting bridge between the historical pageant and the pageant-play is *The Last Days of St. Benet's Abbey*. which Mr. Parker wrote for the Norfolk town of Potter Heigham in 1907. This resembles an episode in a pageant, but it has a small love-story woven into it; the Narrator (a woman who takes the part of Chorus) gives prologue and epilogue, and interrupts at times to explain the progress of the story. The interest here is not confined to history; the germ of a plot is visible — and this makes it noteworthy, as a play given in the pageant manner.

Telegraph for 5 March, 1914: " A pageant entitled ' Children through the Centuries,' compiled by the Rev. C. V. R. Scott, will be given in connection with the Children's Union, Waifs and Strays Society, at the Royal Court Theatre on Thursday afternoon, June 25. There will be a series of scenes portraying historic and traditional incidents in connection with child-life including a symbolical scene arranged by Lady Beatrix Wilkinson, president of the Children's Union, and a patriotic scene, ' Children of the Empire,' arranged by Lady Muriel Herbert."

[1] Based on the Biblical story, this play had over forty speaking-parts, and hundreds of people in the cast.

[2] From the little I know of Mr. Nugent Monck's work, I should say that he applied the technique of the pageant to material not always pageantic. I have referred to his *Legends of King Arthur* — the only one of his " pageants " I have seen — (above, p. 196, n. 1). A good deal of his work lay in the revival of the masque — which lies outside our field.

The Plays of the Rev. Mr. Perkins of York

As an outgrowth of the historical pageant we may note the work of the Rev. Mr. F. L. Perkins, of York. He has written several " pageant-plays " or " play-pageants," either with the purpose of raising money for charitable objects, or — as with *Disinherited — ?* — to spread certain propaganda. The first, given at Thirsk in Yorkshire, on 25 and 26 June, 1907, owed its existence to the Sherborne Pageant as much as to anything;[1] all the parts were taken by the townsfolk,[2] and the matter of the " play " was the history of the town, scenes from which, to Elizabeth's time, were presented. Mr. Perkins prefers to call his productions " plays " rather than " pageants," because, as he says, the dialogue is important; but so is that of the Parkerian pageant — as we have seen — which is really a " chronicle-play of a town."

Up the Heights, a " play with a purpose," is really not a pageant at all; the only flavor of pageantry being an historical parenthesis showing Wolfe and the capture of Quebec. The play is a plea for missionary work in the Colony he conquered. *In Old Northumbria*, " an open-air play," was given at York in the summer of 1912; it showed four scenes of history which took place between 650 and 680 — one of which was re-enacted on the spot, outside the Minster, where the original happening took place.

On 17, 18, and 19, February, 1914, in the Festival Concert Rooms at York was presented *Disinherited — ?* : " a play-pageant in aid of the Church in Wales." I quote from the " Author's note ":

> " This play has been written in order to present to the eye (as well as to the ear and mind and heart) some of those facts with regard to the past and present work of the Church in Wales, upon which we base our urgent claim ' that the Church shall not be dismembered, and four of its Dioceses disestablished and disendowed.'
>
> " The limitations of a ' stage-play ' have compelled the Author . . . to abbreviate and condense matter of much historical importance. Lighter touches have been introduced here and there in order to counterbalance the dullness that might result from the scrupulous care that has been taken to suppress all references, however attractive, to persons or parties in the treatment of a subject which is at present, unhappily, part of a political programme."[3]

After " a reveille in aid of the Church in Wales " and a " prologue, to be spoken by the Angel of Wales," comes scene i — " A Point of Law " — which takes place in the library of Sir Richard Juxon, a Liberal Member of Parliament. To this defender of the Welsh Church Bill — whose wife has begged him in vain not to vote for the measure — the Angel of Wales appears in a dream, after he has fallen asleep with the reveille echoing in his ears. The Angel reveals to him the history of the Welsh Church, from 530 to 1914 in a series of episodes — which are not so called.

First, St. David blesses King Arthur " at early dawn "; the next scene shows " how the Church received lands — Guidnerth's gift, A.D. 590 "; the third, " Gerald, the Welshman,"

---

[1] My authority here is Mr. Perkins himself. (Mr. Gilbert Hudson " conducted, and partly wrote " this " pageant," he says, in a letter of 16 August, 1918.)

[2] Non-conformists as well as Church people.

[3] That is, the Welsh Church Disestablishment Bill, a policy of the Liberal Government.

c 1185 — which is based partly on Giraldus Cambrensis' *Itinerary through Wales*); the next, " A Measure of Disendowment. The Selling of the Monasteries, 1537," followed by " Another Measure of Disendowment, 1651–1653. The Puritan Failure." Finally we see " St. Teilo's Clergy House, Llanclwyd, 1914 " — a scene in a Welsh parish of the present. After this series of pageantic episodes, the scene returns to the M.P.'s library; Sir Richard, aroused by a message from the House, goes to vote against the Disestablishment of the Welsh Church. " And I shall vote that the Church, which has done so much and suffered so much, shall not be disturbed." Then, after an appeal by the Angel of Wales to the audience, the actors in the various episodes appear and all sing " O God, our help in ages past. . ."

This " play-pageant " was given by Church people in York, and it was planned to have others give it in various parts of England, in order to influence public opinion before the bill against which it was directed should be passed. Technically, it is not unlike Mr. Knoblauch's *My Lady's Dress;* though the material which lay between the first and last acts of the latter play was not pageantic.

The historical pageant has a well-defined technique, which is capable, it is true, of certain variations; and on the outskirts of this new art lie many possibilities — plots, masques, interludes — which may be combined into entertainments more or less pageantic. The spirit of the Parkerian work is also well-defined, but is capable of being diluted to almost any weakness; and in determining what is, or what is not, a pageant, both elements must be taken into account.

§ 9. CONCLUSION

This survey of the modern historical pageant in England makes clear two things: first, that Mr. Parker is not aware of any debt to the older pageantry; and secondly, that while Mr. Parker's productions may be considered the norm of the modern pageant, if you will, there may be a considerable variation from that norm. Of the older pageantry, only the " soul " exists in the newer — and that is somewhat modified; the " technique," and " spirit " have changed: the former is more that of the masque (or even of the theatre), and the latter is " popular," not only because given for the people, but by them, as well.

The older pageant was a procession in which symbolism, history, allegory, and mythology grew up, and had to be explained; the pageant itself was the platform or wagon on which these characters — appropriate to the occasion — stood. It always remained, even when, in the seventeenth century, speech was an important part of it, the least dramatic of all dramatic forms. Modern pageantry differs much from this, in that it is essentially dramatic. Like the masque, one episode follows another across the stage — a " procession of events " — while the audience remains seated in one place, and looks upon one arena. Each episode tells a story, but is more than purely expository; and the older allegory has largely given way to historical individuals.

Because each episode has a connected story to tell, the words are important; and the audience is often restricted — especially in England — to those who can hear what is said. Sometimes music and dancing are allowed to break the narrative chain [1] — but these two elements are more important in America — as we shall see — than in England.

Mr. Parker is, as we have noted, distinctly opposed to street-processions, and his pageants broaden the "popular" element, characteristic of the older shows. Not only was the first performance open to all free of charge,[2] so that the townspeople could see their pageant as easily as they saw their street parades; but a much larger proportion of the community took part in the Show. This awoke a local pride (almost of ownership) in the past of the town which the older pageant had failed to awaken.[3]

The earlier triumph was built around a person or an office, and aimed to amuse; in the modern pageant, the attention which, in former times was fastened on king or mayor, is focussed on the town — and the people are instructed, as well as entertained. There was symbolism and allegory in the earlier work; and a morality-element appeared in the "Be good and you'll be famous" of Antiquity, Time, or Fame to the Lord Mayor. This preaching — mixed with flattery as it was — did not affect the populace whose attention was held by the various "inventions" of the show; but the preaching and the allegory were there. In the modern work, lessons in history are presented with a dramatic effectiveness which is comparable to that of the Elizabethan chronicle-play,[4] and which impresses not only the local performer and auditor, but also the stranger from afar.

The modern pageant, then, shows the same progress over the earlier, that the chronicle-history showed over the morality.

English and American Pageantry

American pageantry differs from the English, in that it is less dramatic, more symbolic — as a rule — and seems to be freer to take some subject not strictly historical. In England, the emphasis of a pageant is on the past of the town that gives it; yet a strong community spirit is aroused, and the civic pride engendered is expected to bear some fruit in civic betterment. This result of pageantry

[1] It is hard to tell, from the account of the Quebec Pageant, just how large a part speech played in the presentation of the historic scenes; there was plenty of music and dancing in many of the episodes. (Of course the importance of speech does not determine whether or not a given entertainment is a pageant; it is merely a detail of technique.)

[2] His pageants usually "ran" for a week, and the first performance was, he tells me, open to all without charge. The whole town could thus see its pageant for nothing; the performance made a good "dress-rehearsal, and nothing was lost by the omission of street parades.

[3] Unless, perhaps, in the case of those shows whose annual recurrence made a civic holiday. Any established institution must awaken a sense of the past, even if it is subconscious.

[4] "Marlborough, you recollect, said, he knew no English History but what he had learned from Shakespeare." Carlyle, *The Hero as Poet.*

is, as we shall see, emphasized in America, so that what is almost a " by-product " of the English work, becomes the *raison d'être* of many American pageants. Hence the term " futuristic " pageant; hence, also, one reason for the increase of symbolism in the work done on this side of the ocean.[1]

England is not dead, and we are not wholly without a past; in the main, the difference between the pageants in England and America is due to the mental attitude of the two countries. As Mr. Parker says, England talks of the " good old times," and America of " the good times that are to come."

There are, of course, plenty of historical pageants given on this side of the water; but, whereas in England " the York Pageant " means a pageant giving the history of York, we cannot be sure whether " the New York Pageant " sets forth the history of that town or not.[2] In any case, we may be sure that the American pageant is likely not to confine itself to history, though this generalization — like every other — has its many exceptions. In America, we are more apt to build a pageant around an idea than a town.

Like many other things in this country, the pageant which came to us from oversea has become naturalized, and is changed to suit American conditions. But, like the modern English pageantry, its underlying spirit is educational. When we do not give dramatic expositions — or expository dramas — we fall back on symbolism; more often we combine the two, using, in the process, a considerable amount of allegory.

The new form of dramatic expression, which came into being with Mr. Parker's Sherborne Pageant of 1905, is, probably, the result of various forces which in the last century began to turn men's minds to the past. It owes no direct influence, however, to the pageants we have been studying — at least, it owns no debt. It has been a potent educational force, and has stimulated community-spirit; and now that the war is over, bids fair to spring into a new life voicing an enthusiastic patriotism.

The forms which this new mode of artistic expression is taking in America, we shall leave to the next chapter.

---

[1] In this connection, " futuristic " has no relationship with present-day movements in art and music. I mean simply " looking to the future."

[2] As a matter of fact, both in England and America, those pageants which officially bear the name of a place usually lay most of their emphasis on the his ory of that place. It will be recalled that there was much beside Scotch history in the Scottish National Pageant at Edinburgh.

YORK HISTORIC PAGEANT, 1909

EXECUTIVE COMMITTEE

ACCOUNT OF RECEIPTS AND PAYMENTS TO 7TH OCTOBER, 1909

RECEIPTS

	£	s.	d.	£	s.	d.
Subscriptions				1,598	10	6
Grand Stand Tickets —						
Pageant Week	10,273	5	6			
Rehearsal Week	1,297	3	0			
Preliminary Rehearsals	35	4	6			
Camera Permits	6	19	0			
				11,612	12	0
Book of Words —						
Sales	362	4	1			
Advertisements	22	10	0			
				384	14	1
Cloak-room and Lavatory Charges				9	15	9
Premiums for Souvenir, Post Card, Photographic, Cinematograph, and Bookstall Rights				145	0	0
Sales —						
Post Cards				3	5	0
Chairs				249	0	0
Costumes				301	0	1
Properties				107	14	7
Commission on Re-sale of Tickets				5	17	6
Bank Interest				22	9	3
				£14,439	18	9

PAYMENTS

	£	s.	d.	£	s.	d.
Grand Stand, Dressing-rooms, Cloak-rooms, Hire of Exhibition, Alterations at Museum Gardens, &c.				2,151	6	8
Yorkshire Philosophical Society —						
For use of Gardens — on a/c	200	0	0			
Dilapidations	100	0	0			
				300	0	0
Chairs (including Storage)				438	7	6
Wages of Joiners, Servitors, Commissionaires, Stewards, Cloak-room Attendants, and Cleaning Staff				424	8	10
Services of Military				334	13	0
Services of Police				38	7	0
Costumes				1,496	1	3
Properties				642	3	6
Hire of Wigs				250	0	0
Badges for Officials and Performers				52	19	6
Advertising, Printing, Stationery, Billposting, and "Press" Luncheon				1,556	6	7
Printing Book of Words				301	12	9
Master of the Pageant — Retaining Fee, Royalty, and Expenses				1,744	2	5
Music — Master of Music, Assistants, Instrumentalists, Vocalists, and Music Publisher, &c.				854	11	10
Master of the Dances				26	5	0
Ambulance Men and Gratuities				17	5	0
Rent of Pageant Houses and Rooms at Free Library, and Telephones, Rates, Lighting, Heating, Water, Cleaning and Furniture				471	6	4
Secretary				250	0	0
Salaries of Clerical Staff and Caretaker's Wages				265	2	0
Postages, Telegrams, Carriage, and Sundries				219	9	10
Small Accounts and Horse and Cab Hire				124	10	9
Expenses of Deputations to other Pageants				42	8	4
Agents' Commission on Sale of Tickets				41	0	5
Expenses of Lectures and Receptions				26	0	2
Auditors' Fee				10	10	0
Subscriptions Returned				1,598	10	6
				13,677	9	2
Balance in Honorary Treasurer's Hands				762	9	7
				£14,439	18	9

We certify that we have examined the Books and Accounts of the Executive Committee of the York Historic Pageant and prepared therefrom the foregoing statement which we certify to be correct.

(Signed) BARRON & BARRON, *Chartered Accountants*.

1, MINSTER GATES, YORK, 20th October, 1909.

NOTE BY THE AUDITORS.

The amount of £762 9s. 7d., in the hands of the Honorary Treasurer, does not represent the final balance, as a few costumes and properties have still to be disposed of, and a few accounts, including the expenses in connection with the final meetings, will have to be paid. In addition, certain Honoraria and Commission have to be paid in accordance

CHAPTER IX

PAGEANTRY IN THE UNITED STATES

ALMOST every American thinks he knows what a pageant is, and most of us have seen — if we have not taken part in — at least one. Here is no attempt to give directions for producing a pageant,[1] nor a list of all the pageants which have been produced in this country. Hardly a day goes by that one does not see in the daily papers accounts of a pageant just given or about to be given. The whole country is in a fair way to become pageant-mad; and in this madness pageantry has taken on many different shapes.

What I plan to do in this chapter is to divide pageantry into its three main classes, giving examples of each kind — not always from the best-known pageants. Perhaps when this survey has been made, we shall be able to define pageantry; at least the reader should be able to classify any pageant in which he has been particularly interested.

Strict rules for pageant-writing cannot be laid down. As a living language is constantly changing, and the rules thereof can never be absolutely fixed,[2] so pageantry cannot be strictly defined, for it is still in the making. It is a sign of the speed at which we live, that we demand definitions of this form of artistic expression when it is still in its infancy; but many tentative definitions have already been made.

It is possible that the reader may not be able to find, in the illustrative examples I shall give, any pageant which exactly conforms to the one he is trying to classify. But such a pageant must fall into one of two big classes: it was either peripatetic, or it was given in one place. These are the two great divisions; and we shall begin our survey of American pageantry with the pageantic procession.

§ 1. PROCESSIONAL PAGEANTRY

Historically, as we have seen, a pageant is a procession with floats or images carried about the streets, or a procession which marched from one stationary platform to another. On these platforms were various symbolic, or historical, allegorical, or mythological personages — so that even without speech, we find the " body " and " soul " of the older pageantry already joined. These pro-

---

[1] The interested reader may find hints on this subject in Bates and Orr's *Pageants and Pageantry*, Davol's *Handbook of American Pageantry*, Constance Mackay's *Plays of the Pioneers*, pp. 161 ff., my *Manual of Pageantry*, and Crawford and Beegle's volume.

[2] Greenough and Kittredge, *Words and Their Ways*, pp. 76, 77.

cessions have been, and still are, extremely common in America; although we have nothing which exhibits the continuity of the London Lord Mayor's Show.

The " Pope " processions in Boston [1] remind us of the earlier folk-processions with giants, although they are more " sophisticated "; [2] the Puritan's attitude toward the Pope, and that of the Revolutionary toward the royal governor are clearly marked.

At Boston, on 8 February, 1788, in celebration of the ratification of the Federal Constitution by the Massachusetts Convention, a big trade procession was held.[3] In the same year, " on Friday the *fourth day of July*, 1788, the citizens of Philadelphia in commemoration of the great event of AMERICAN INDEPENDENCE . . . presented the most brilliant and interesting spectacle that ever occurred in the annals of the new world, and which has scarcely been surpassed by the splendor of the ancient or modern triumphs of Asia or of Europe." [4] An historic event was reproduced — on the site of the actual happening — in New England, early in the nineteenth century.

EARLY HISTORICAL PAGEANTRY — THE FESTIVAL AT PLYMOUTH IN 1801

On 22 December, 1801, Forefathers' Day was celebrated at Plymouth, Massachusetts, by an " interesting piece of pageantry," which was preceded by a procession, headed by Captain Turner's independent company in complete uniform. The line of march led around the town; the procession escorted the clergyman to the meeting-house; and after divine service the company dined at Old Colony and Freedom Halls. During this celebration, " an Indian, dressed in the habiliments of a Sachem, met Capt. TURNER in the place where *Massasoit* was first discovered, and the emblems of peace and friendship, which were inter-

---

[1] Cf. above, p. 176 f.

[2] That is to say, no survival of the " human sacrifice " is seen here — nor is the effigy the descendant of any fertilization divinity. Massachusetts undoubtedly, as has been pointed out, inherited the custom from England.

[3] See the *Massachusetts Centinel of* 9 February, (viii, p. 169), of 13 February (viii, p. 174), cited by Albert Matthews, " The Term ' Pilgrim Fathers,' " in *Publ. Col. Soc. Mass.*, for December, 1914, p. 313, n. 5. (The *Massachusetts Spy* of 7 August, 1788, calls this the first of many processions to demonstrate joy.)

[4] Cited, from the *Columbian Magazine* (ii, pp. 391–400) for July, 1788, in *Publ. Col. Soc. Mass.*, for December, 1914, p. 313, n. 5.

The same note contains a passage from R. Davol, *Handbook of American Pageantry* (1914), pp. 27, 31: " A procession through the streets of floats on which historic occasions are rigidly impersonated by ' live people trying to look like dead ones ' is commonly called a pageant in America, for example at Philadelphia, or the Hudson-Fulton celebration . . . Research as to the beginning of modern American Pageants indicates that the spirit was manifest as early as 1627 at the Merry Mount revels . . ." The student of pageantry must be careful not to confuse the revel with the pageant — though the former, whether processional or not, contains the germ of the latter.

changed, brought into view, an interesting scene, that existed soon after the arrival of our ancestors. A sprightly ball at Old Colony Hall, in which the ladies, by their participation, heightened the social enjoyment, crowned the anniversary festival." [1]

PAGEANTIC PROCESSION AT ST. LOUIS IN 1847

The anniversary of the founding of St. Louis was celebrated 15 February, 1847, and included a pageantic procession.[2] Among the marchers "were four Indians, dressed in full costume, and mounted on horses, after the manner of the aboriginal tribes of this country. They very appropriately constituted the guard of honor, for the venerable President [3] had witnessed the day when the presence of friendly Indians had been, in fact, a guard and a protection to him.

"Succeeding the invited guests, came an admirable representation of the *Gen. Pike*, the first steam boat which arrived at St. Louis. . . .[4] Next followed a model, drawn on wheels, of that noble boat which boasts not only the name of the founder of St. Louis, but also that she was built in the city by St. Louis mechanics, and of St. Louis materials — the '*Laclede*.' In no way could the contrast between the *pioneer boat*, and those of the present day, have been more strikingly presented . . .

"Following, came the *Mayor* and city officers, two and two.

---

[1] From the *Columbian Centinel* for 30 December, 1801, pp. 2, 3, — cited by Mr. Matthews in the *Publ. Col. Soc. Mass.* for December, 1914, pp. 314 f. I am indebted to Professor Kittredge for calling the paper to my attention.

[2] A full account of this event may be found in a pamphlet entitled *Report of the Celebration of the Anniversary of the Founding of St. Louis on the fifteenth day of February*, A.D. 1847. Prepared for the *Missouri Republican*. Printed by Chambers and Knapp. 1847. [H. L., *US 25390.7.5*]. This is my authority for the following remarks.

[3] M. Pierre Chouteau, the President of the day, was "the only survivor of those who landed at this spot, with Laclede, on the 15th February, 1764." He rode in a carriage in the procession.

May we assume that these Indians were real ones — not men dressed up to represent the aborigines?

[4] Cf. the *Welcome* at Philadelphia (1882), the *Don de Dieu* at Quebec, (1908), and the *Half-Moon* and *Clermont* at New York, (1909). Cf. also the viking-ship at Rouen in 1911 (above, p. 164), and the *Argo* of the London Shows of 1615 and 1623 (above, p. 73 and n. 4) where trade-symbolism was linked with mythology. Cf. also the boats in more recent Lord Mayor's Shows, *e. g.*, that of 1891 (above, p. 126). These are, perhaps, developments of the "folk-ships" (cf. above, vol. i, p. 11 f.) to which an historical meaning has been given; if there be not an independent development, this connection is probably not consciously recognized. "This miniature representation was about 20 feet long; the hull, that of a barge, and the cabin, on the lower deck, run up inside of the running board. The wheels were exposed, being without a wheel house — she was propelled by a low pressure engine, with a single chimney, and a large *walking beam* . . . It was mounted on wheels, and drawn by eight white horses. The boat was manned by a crew of steam boat captains, who appeared in the dress usually worn by the officers and men, in their various stations . . ."

"To them succeeded the Fire Department, in the order of incorporation, and in all the splendor of their rich, but useful regalia . . . . Following this,[1] were a number of Indians, in full costume, who played well their characters. . ."[2]

After various other marching clubs and societies, "came a large company dressed in masques, in carriages and on horseback. This portion of the pageant excited no little amusement, from the grotesqueness of the dresses, and the variety of the characters. It would be impossible, in this place, to attempt a description of the various male and female, white and black, old and young, Yankee, French and other characters, presented and generally well sustained. Everywhere, they called forth the repeated cheers of the crowd." This suggestion of revels in the midst of the procession is not an uncommon feature of such parades, though it appears oftener in those celebrating a holiday — such as Mardi Gras or May Day — than an historical anniversary.[3] All this kind of thing needs to become pageantry is a central idea, and a weeding-out of those characters which do not fit it.

"M. Sutter, who was the first to establish an omnibus in the city, followed, with one of his omnibuses, drawn by four horses, filled with citizens.

"Henry Dolde's car, on which there was a profusion of bread, came next.

"Then came the *Public Schools* . . . In the line of Public Schools, was a banner which was prepared for the occasion, and presented to the schools, by the Board of School Directors. It was happily conceived and beautifully executed. On the one side, is Minerva, the Goddess of Wisdom, pointing with her left hand to the Temple of Science, placed on the top of a rugged mountain, with the Temple of Fame in the back ground — her right hand is resting on a shield. At her feet is a globe, and a telescope, levels, and various mathematical scientific instruments. Over this device, is the motto, '*Knowledge is Power.*' Surrounding this device are the words, '*St. Louis Public Schools.*'

"On the reverse, is a view of St. Louis from the Illinois shore — over which is placed the word *Excelsior*. . ."

Then came Masons, Odd Fellows, and other fraternal organizations — the Odd Fellows with a banner on which Charity was represented "dispensing blessings to the orphan." Such banners are worth noting only because they seem to show a development from the *tableau vivant* on the pageant-car; there have been, as we have remarked, painted scenes on pageants from very early times.

"Following these, came a large deputation of Brewers. 1st, a mammoth cask, sufficiently capacious to hold about eighteen barrels of beer, mounted on

[1] The banner of one of the companies. It may be remarked that the banner of the Washington Hose Company bore the likeness of the General and that of the Phoenix, the landing of Laclede; cf. the banners in the modern Ulster processions (above, p. 181).

[2] These were evidently white men, disguised.

[3] Attention may, however, be called to the centenarian procession at Bournemouth, pictured in the *Illus. Lond. News* for 16 July, 1910, pp. 90–91. It had various "satirical" features, and included many "chars," rivalling "Nice in gaiety."

The Boston Tea-Party

a car, drawn by four gray horses. On this car, was a representation of the King of Flanders and Brabant, fancifully said to be the inventor of beer, dressed in his royal robes, and bearing in his out-stretched hand an overflowing pitcher of the beverage . . . Then another cask of equal size, drawn by four gray horses. This cask was filled with beer, and around and on the car were the implements of brewing . . ." Others followed and " on each car were a number of brewers and . . . a good, round, portly representation of a hearty jolly beer-drinker . . .

" Immediately after these came the Coopers. They were preceded by a large new cask . . . drawn on a car by four horses. A master cooper, with his compass, sat astride of the cask, whilst several coopers walked by the side, holding ribbons attached to it . . ."

Other school children and University students followed with banners; " after the schools, came a printing press, in a car, and several boys engaged in working off, and distributing to the crowd, the following ode, composed for the occasion " by John P. Shannon.

Other trade societies followed, some of which bore banners showing various implements of their callings. The various exercises which took place after the procession had disbanded are described at length in the pamphlet from which I have cited.

The Boston Celebration of 1880

The two hundred and fiftieth anniversary of the settlement of Boston was celebrated with two " pageants," or processions with floats.[1] A " Civic, Military and Trades " procession was followed by an " Evening Procession " of two divisions — the first dealing with " History and Tradition," the second with " Allegory." Between each two cars marched torch-bearers, and the " floats " were lighted in various ways.

The Pennsylvania Bicentenary in 1882

" The foundation of the Colony of Pennsylvania . . . was commemorated on Oct. 22, and on three or four days following, with a Bicentenary Festival which drew great numbers of visitors to the city of Philadelphia . . . The festival proceedings . . . after a special Quaker religious service on Sunday, the 22nd, began next day with a rehearsal of this scene [Penn's landing at Chester, 22 October, 1682] in which Penn and his suite, represented in old-fashioned costume by the Chester Dramatic Company, landed at Penn-street wharf, Chester, the spot of the original landing; and the Governor of Pennsylvania received him, the United States squadron in the river saluting with its guns. After an address of welcome, with other services, 2000 school children sang patriotic songs, and Penn was escorted through Chester by a procession composed of civic and trade societies.

---

[1] See the *Celebration of the 250th Anniversary of the Settlement of Boston*, printed by order of the City Council; Boston, 1880; cf. esp. pp. 109–149, 153–162. The *tableaux*, or " floats," are illustrated.

In the procession was carried a model of Penn's original house at Upland, built in 1683, which still exists. Fireworks closed the Chester celebration at night, and the city of Philadelphia took up the course of festive performances and exhibitions in the ensuing days. There was a second landing from the old ship Welcome,[1] at the foot of Dock-street, where Penn actually came ashore, in that part of the river, at his first visit to America. His representative in this celebration was conducted to the landing place by Admiral Cooper, with the North Atlantic Squadron of the United States Navy, amid salvoes of artillery and the cheers of the populace. There was a grand parade, representing all the industries and trade societies of Philadelphia, to escort Penn through the streets. The subsequent nights were given up to illuminations and fireworks and the days to a succession of parades . . . Ships and locomotives were drawn through the streets, looms were shown in operation, and iron forges in active work. The mimic William Penn met with a gorgeous reception, not to forget the appearance of multitudes of Red Indians, for which sundry bands of city youths were attired in savage guise. It should be observed that in 1682, before the advent of the English Quakers, there were a few Dutch and Swedish settlers, the descendants of Protestant refugees from Europe, already dwelling on those Transatlantic shores.[2] The masquerading figures in the commemorative performance shown in our illustration [3] therefore include both Dutchmen and Swedes . . . the burly Dutch burgomaster, with other leading men of the community, proffers a friendly welcome to the founder of Pennsylvania in front of the Blue Anchor Tavern." [4]

Processional Features of the Quebec Celebration, July, 1908

Although Quebec is not in the United States, we may, perhaps, be permitted to call attention to the processional features of her tercentenary celebration. On Sunday, 19 July, 1908, there was a procession to the monument of Champlain; Quebec's usually quiet streets were alive with "men dressed in the military garb of Wolfe and Montcalm, courtiers of old France and primitive settlers of New France, her off-spring." [5] When the marchers arrived at the monument, a poem was read and various addresses delivered.[6] On the next day, Heralds-at-Arms, with watchmen in armor, marched through the city, "as in the days of Frontenac . . . proclaiming to the citizens the events of the day and the occurrences of the morrow." [7] British, French, and American warships met in the

---

[1] Cf. St. Louis, 1847; Quebec, 1908, New York, 1909.

[2] "The meek shall inherit the earth!"

[3] Cf. p. 520 of this number of the *Illus. Lond. News;* the source of the drawing is not indicated. It is, of course, not a photograph; but is it entirely fanciful?

[4] *Illus. Lond. News* for 18 November, 1882, p. 519.

[5] Carrel, *Quebec Tercentenary History*, p. 17. A triumphal arch, called "The Tower of Welcome," was erected in front of the archepiscopal palace. — This is illustrated, *ibid.*, p. 19.

[6] *Op. cit.*, pp. 19–24. [7] *Ibid.*, p. 25.

harbor, and the "acute struggles" of the past "were now marked but by pleasant friendship and common rejoicings." [1]

The other features of the tercentenary celebration will be noted later.[2] In connection with the *Don de Dieu* which appeared at Quebec, and the *Welcome*, at Philadelphia in 1882, the following paragraph is of interest: "The great pioneer's [Champlain's] first landing at St. John, New Brunswick, was reproduced on St. John's Day in 1904, at St. John. Our photograph . . . represents this ceremony, where an exact copy of Champlain's ship was used, as at Quebec this year." [3]

On 23 July, 1908, at Quebec, the Prince of Wales [George V] reviewed an "historical procession" [4] which included mounted heralds, men of the watch, Cartier and his soldiers, François I and his Queen, and many others. These seem to have been the characters of the "historical pageant," of which we shall make mention below; there were, apparently, no cars in this procession.[5]

Springfield Street-Pageant of 4 July, 1908

A Parade of Nations, "while of the float type, and civic rather than historical in character, was nevertheless the first parade possessing any notable civic value," was given under the direction of Mr. William Orr at Springfield (Massachusetts) on 4 July, 1908. It was listed by the American Pageant Association as particularly noteworthy "because of what it accomplished in arousing pageant spirit and introducing civic interest into other float parades, and in its own community." [6]

---

1 *Op. cit.*, p. 29.

2 See below, pp. 262 f.

3 *Illus. Lond. News* for 25 July, 1908, p. 125.

4 Described in Carrel, pp. 69 f.

5 On the morning of the 23d — "Champlain Day" — "once again the hardy explorer sailed up the St. Lawrence River, held a palaver with the Indians, and anchored before the rocks of Quebec." (Carrel, p. 53). He came in a model of the *Don de Dieu*, his original ship; the model was perforce made from a French merchant ship *temp.* Henri IV — there being no model or picture of the original *Don de Dieu* in existence (Carrel, p. 54). She sailed under her own sails; and Champlain and his crew were, of course, in the costume of 1608. Indians in their canoes escorted him ashore (cf. the illustrations in Carrel, pp. 56, 59, and 109).

On the 25th, the Prince attended the State Performance of the "pageants," or historical play; and the *Don de Dieu* was stationed on the river near Wolfe's cove, where she was plainly visible from the pageant grounds above. (Carrel, p. 86.)

6 American Pageant Association, *Bulletin 10*, 15 November, 1914. The pageant-parade of Philadelphia, 9 October, 1908, which was "historical in character," "clearly featuring the history of Philadelphia and the development of the community," is listed, *ibid.* It was prepared for Founders' Week by Dr. Ellis P. Oberholtzer.

The Hudson-Fulton Pageant at New York in 1909

A few more modern instances of processional pageants — or pageantic processions — will suffice to show how this form of celebration has developed. The Hudson-Fulton parade [1] was one feature of a celebration "whose purpose was the honoring of two world leaders of discovery and invention, who, in scattering the darkness of an unknown land and an unknown power have left something of profit for all men of all nations and of all times." This purpose links the celebration to the modern pageant which honors great men of the past rather than mayors of the present; but the chief emphasis is not on purely local history.

The military and naval parade — another feature of the festivities — was made up of the crews of "a thousand ships doing the marine honors to the resurrected *Half-Moon* and *Clermont*," [2] and expressed spontaneously "the brotherhood of men and the brotherhood of nations." [3] Historical and artistic exhibits, "admitted to be the largest and most significant of their kind ever offered to the student" were contributed by twenty-one public and semi-public institutions of the city.

> The two leading features of the shore program were the historical and military pageants. The first was probably the most ambitious assemblage of floats ever undertaken in this country, and as an example of decorative art and character portrayal, has never been surpassed.[4]

---

[1] On this, see Hugh C. Weir, "The Hudson-Fulton Pageant," in *The World Today*, for November, 1909, pp. 1204 f. A collection of postcards illustrating floats in this parade may be found in the Harvard Library. The *Half-Moon* is illustrated in Davol, p. 40, and part of the line of march, *ibid.*, p. 51. A car is pictured, *ibid.*, p. 215.

[2] Cf. above, p. 240, and n. 1.

[3] One may suspect that this bit of symbolism is read into the parade by Mr. Weir. But if it made this impression on the spectators, we see how the modern pageant has educated them to find for themselves the symbolism that lies dormant in everything.

The procession did give a flavor of the "international element" of which I have already spoken in connection with some of the English pageants. In the New York parade, foreign soldiers and sailors were greeted with American cheers; for the first time since 1783, British soldiers marched in the streets of New York; German military bands played American airs to the delight of the crowds, and much international good-feeling resulted, no one looking forward to August, 1914.

The parade of battleships — another feature of the celebration — has been loosely called a "pageant." Cf. also *The World Today* for September, 1909, p. 900, for an illustration of "England's great naval pageant on the Thames." Here, of course, the word means simply an "impressive, or spectacular, parade." The only pageantic features of the New York battleship parade, were the reproductions of the *Half-Moon* and the *Clermont*.

There were "military pageants" — or parades of soldiers — at Quebec in 1908.

[4] I am quoting Mr. Weir. The writer shows, it may be remarked, the Anglo-Saxon disposition to "understatement," which the rhetoricians call *litotes*. This is a characteristic of writers who describe pageants — both ancient and modern; for they are usually overcome with modesty in viewing the work of their own pen or the labors of their fellow townsmen. But the enthusiasm which pageantry arouses in the spectator is not one of its least valuable gifts.

Many of the floats were thirty feet long and forty feet high, the cost of the parade mounting to more than one hundred thousand dollars. The pageant was divided into four historical groups, the first dealing with the Dutch period, and the third with the seventeenth-century [1] life of the colonists. The fourth section was confined to the first fifty years of the past century.

The first float of the line, termed "The New York Title Car," endeavored to epitomize the three hundred years' growth of the city in picture form. The figure of the Goddess of Liberty was shown, with a monster record-book open in her lap. Before her were the models of an Indian canoe and a modern ocean greyhound. At the rear of her chair were an Indian wigwam and a twentieth-century sky-scraper.

In the Indian section there were floats showing the totems of the five nations: the deer, snake, tortoise, beaver, and otter; cars devoted to the methods and products of Indian field cultivation, others picturing the Indian seasons and dances, and one devoted to scenes from "Hiawatha."

One of the most interesting designs of the Dutch section showed the purchase of Manhattan Island from the Indians. Another showed the Huguenots receiving their title-deeds. A third pictured Bronck's treaty with the red men, while a fourth showed scenes on the old-fashioned bowling-green. Other floats were devoted to chapters in the life of Governor Stuyvesant. The last car in the section pictured the old Holland legend of St. Nicholas, with one hundred and fifty Dutch children marching behind, carrying toys.

In the colonial division, the subjects included "Old-time Punishments," "The Old Manor Hall in Yonkers," "The Trial of John and Peter Zenger," [2] "Pulling Down the Statue of George III," "Nathan Hale," "Washington Taking the Oath of Office," "Hamilton's Harangue," [3] "Washington's Coach," "Publishing the Constitution of the State of New York," and "The Legend of Ichabod Crane."

In the last division, devoted to latter-day history, one of the most pretentious floats was termed "The Fire of Knowledge," showing a pedestal holding a caldron of blazing coals, while around it were grouped the seals of the thirteen original states. The final car showed a huge figure of Father Knickerbocker receiving the great powers of the earth.

Reference to the Lieder Collection of postcards illustrating the floats in this pageant, shows another group which Mr. Weir's article does not mention. It is introduced by a "title-car" called "Carnival Pageant." "This car," reads the description on the reverse of the card, "is an ornamental car . . . It takes the fantastic shape of a dragon spouting flames, and surrounded by fire.[4] It

---

[1] Mr. Weir means, I think, the eighteenth century; or perhaps both were combined. The scenes from the seventeenth century were probably included under the Indian and Dutch periods.

[2] Mr. Weir means John Peter Zenger, who "edited a little paper called the *Weekly Journal*, in which he freely criticized the arbitrary acts of the royal government. In 1735 he was tried for libel, but acquitted in a verdict which is commonly said to have been the establishment of the principle of the free press." (Information printed on the back of the postcard (no. 26) illustrating this float; see the Lieder Collection in the Harvard Library.)

[3] On 18 July, 1795, at a mass-meeting to discuss the proposed Jay Treaty with Great Britain.

[4] We may compare — without claiming a direct connection between them — the dragons of 1487 and 1572 (see above, vol. i, pp. 161 and 205).

is simply fantastic in design, and is meant to prophesy the unconventional character of the floats which are to follow."[1] This section suggests such pageantic revels as those at St. Louis in 1847; it seems to be "carnivalistic" — if we may use the word — with an emphasis rather on amusement than on education.[2] The chief emphasis of the whole pageant, however, is on local history; and it has the aim of the modern "pageant-play" — to stir civic pride, and stimulate a desire for civic betterment.

Like the more recent Lord Mayor's Shows, this procession combines what we may call the "Parkerian spirit" with the technique of the older pageantry. It undoubtedly gave pleasure to the multitude which witnessed it; but it did more than that — it awakened an interest in the past, and an ambition for the future.[3]

---

[1] Among these floats are Germania, "an idealization of Germany . . . Germania, the central figure, holds the Imperial Crown in her hand. Beside her are the eagles, draped with the German colors. The nine figures represent the different states which make up United Germany"; William Tell; Lohengrin; The Death of Fafner; Ceres presiding over the float called "Harvesting"; Orpheus before Pluto; Father Rhine; Arion; Cinderella; the mythical Frost King; Humor; the Æolian Harp — which "is an idealization of the Æolian harp . . . one of the oldest musical instruments . . . The large figure holding the harp represents outdoor music." Other floats show gnomes, fairies, Europa; Egyptian literature and music; Tannhäuser, etc. The list includes foreign history, classical and Germanic mythology, fiction, and symbolism — in such figures as Germania, Europa, and Father Rhine — and it emphasizes the presence of foreign representation at the celebration.

[2] Granting, as some seem inclined to do, that the two are antithetical.

[3] Says Mr. Weir in his article already cited: "Behind the tinsel and the glitter of marching men and waving flags, the Hudson-Fulton celebration has struck a deeper and a graver note in American civilization than the entertainment of the moment. We have come to accept much as a matter of course the announcement that our great carnivals and great expositions are commemorative of an epoch of progress . . . Now that the Hudson-Fulton pageant is an event of the past, the vessels and soldiers have dispersed, the tinsel and bunting have been stored away, and the spectacle . . . has become a memory, are we to view it like a great conflagration that has dwindled to a heap of charred débris and dead ashes?

"Unless we have shown the nation and the citizen how better to use that power which the river of Hudson's discovery and the steamboat of Fulton's invention have given us, the recalling of that power and the exultation in its might have meant nothing. Unless a quickening of national pride shall come from the blare and the glitter of the marching regiments . . . unless we shall be spurred as a nation to guard better and use better the great national resources typified by such a river as the Hudson, and the great mechanical inventions typified by such a craft as the steamboat, the fortnight of New York's pomp will be but a mockery.

"Has the Hudson-Fulton celebration left such a lesson and such an impetus in its wake? I think it has."

Time alone can answer this question positively; the influence — direct and indirect — of such a show can never be measured.

The Boston Columbus Day Parade of 1912

Although but recently established, Columbus Day may become, in many places, the occasion for an annually recurring pageant. One such parade at Boston approached the spirit of the Lord Mayor's Show more closely than American parades usually do; but he would be rash who should attempt to define the debt that it owes to the London civic "triumph."

The procession which, on 12 October, 1912, marched through the streets of the Massachusetts capital, took three hours to pass a given point. With the exception of the "town crier," who led the way, and shouted at intervals, there was no speaking. Preceding the rest of the procession by some fifteen minutes, this "prelude" to the parade passed over the route; the crier, dressed in Colonial costume, was followed by twentieth-century newsboys "illustrating the modern method of imparting information to the public."[1]

Every so often the town-crier stopped, rang his bell, and shouted:

"Hear ye! Hear ye! Good People! The Grand Parade and Pageant in honor of the great discoverer Christopher Columbus approacheth. Give earnest attention thereto in decent and peaceable manner, and thereafter peaceably depart unto your homes.

"The Twentieth Century newsboys follow!

"God save the Commonwealth of Massachusetts!"

And as he walked on, the street became filled, with the energetic "newsies" who cried "Papers! Extra!" with as much enthusiasm as if they were really trying to sell their journals.

After this bit of symbolism, the parade proper began. The first division was led by a group of real Indians[2] on horseback: then came various detachments of United States troops, State militia and veterans of the Civil War — those who were too old to march riding in motor-barges.[3] Behind them came the first float, entitled "One Country — one Flag." This was followed by the Sons of Veterans, the Spanish War Veterans, the Prince Heinrich Veteran Society, and the British Naval and Military Veterans. With the German and British flags came the first hint of one of the dominant notes of the parade — its cosmopolitanism; the other note sounded was patriotism; and the "melting-pot *motif*" was emphasized by the fact that beside every foreign ensign — and there were many — was borne the American flag.[4]

---

[1] For further details than I give here, the reader is referred to the Boston press for 12 October, 1912. It is preferable, in looking up matters of this kind, to take the accounts which appear after the event, rather than those which recount the proposed program, not all of which materializes.

[2] Cf. the Indians at St. Louis in 1847, at New York in 1909, etc.

[3] Cf. the veterans in the Lord Mayor's Shows of 1890, 1906, and 1909.

[4] Incidentally, this blending of the two dominant notes of the parade fulfilled the require-

The second division was almost entirely made up of the Knights of Columbus, many of whom were Irishmen. An interesting group was that wearing the uniforms of soldiers of important periods in the nation's history — 1776, 1812, 1861, 1898 and 1912.[1] The banners of the various councils of the Knights of Columbus lent variety and color to the procession; and one could not help feeling the patriotic fervor — here as marked as anywhere else in the parade — with which the recent anarchistic outrages in Lawrence were rebuked.

The Boston Equal Suffrage Association furnished a float showing " Isabella's Part in the Discovery of America." Here an historical interest was linked to present-day politics by the plea of equal rights for women which accompanied it.[2] Six horses drew the pageant-car representing " The Landing of Columbus," which had been provided by a large dry-goods firm of the city; and the same number of horses drew that of the Dorchester Historical Society, representing " The First School in America." Other floats in this division were: " General Washington Reviews the first Stars and Stripes ";[3] " Washington Unfurls the first Stars and Stripes at Dorchester Heights,"[4] and " The Evacuation of Boston."[5]

Great enthusiasm was awakened in the crowd by the passage of a man on stilts. Towering above everything as he strode down the street, he reminded one of the London giants. The banner of the Order of the Sons of St. George, which depicted that saint slaying the dragon, added another reminiscence of the pageantry we have already studied, but it is probable that there is no direct connection between these things and the older English shows.

Children dressed in red, white, and blue, waving American flags, passed by in three motor-barges. These representatives of the Mission Church evoked a patriotic response from the crowd, in whose minds an anarchistic outbreak at Lawrence was still fresh. Indeed, much of the enthusiasm at the parade was undoubtedly due to this memory; but it was none the less stirring or impressive on this account.

---

ments of the law. No foreign flag can be carried by a procession without an American flag beside it.

[1] Cf. the Cape Volunteers of 1853 in the Lord Mayor's Show of 1895; and the historical naval exhibition in that of 1902. Past uniforms of the British Army and Navy were shown in the Lord Mayor's Show of 1911, together with various great generals and admirals.

[2] Many of the crowd appreciated the unconscious humor of the band which preceded this float, in playing a popular song entitled " You Great, Big, Beautiful, Doll " as they marched before the City Hall.

[3] Provided by the Betsy Ross Club, Civic Service House.

[4] Furnished by a large mercantile firm of the city; it was an " autofloat," (motor-pageant) and carried the thirteen original States, represented by girls in Colonial costume.

[5] This was also an " autofloat," and was furnished by the Citizens' Association of South Boston.

The third division closed with a float showing a "Children's Playground," contributed by the Park Department of the city. "Ancient and Modern Counting House" — the float of the Library Bureau — was little more than a trade-pageant.

Italians made up the fourth division of the parade; many secular and religious societies took part — some of them in the costume of Garibaldi's soldiers. A humorous illustration of contemporary European history was furnished by a Turkish prisoner who was led firmly by two uniformed Italians; his sheepish smile suggested that he did not find captivity irksome. Among the floats in this division was one provided by the New England Telephone Company in honor of the two discoverers, Columbus and Bell; the telephone poles, instruments and switchboard emphasized the fact that history was linked to trade. Another float, furnished by the Italian societies of the North End, represented "Marconi and the Wireless Telegraph" linking together the nations of the earth, which were represented by their coats-of-arms around the car.

The fifth division was truly cosmopolitan. The "feature," or chariot which opened it, was called "The World's Contribution to Boston." A few Indians were followed by Italians, Germans, and the Swedish Singing Society; then came the Armenians, with a float entitled "Armenian Rug-Making." Russians and Syrians followed; then came members of the "newest republic," with their new flag. "Old China and New" was succeeded by three gorgeous floats: the first was a Chinese Garden; the second contained a Chinese band; and the third was filled with Chinese women and children in the elaborate costumes of their land. The Scotch, in picturesque Highland dress, followed the Lithuanians, and preceded their floats which contained Scotch dancers, and a representative from many clans, in plaid and bonnet. The Charitable Irish Society furnished a jaunting-car, in which was Uncle Sam with his own children and those whom he had adopted. The Canadian representatives, the Finnish societies, a barge containing the Germania Singing Society; "Greek Janissaries" and Polish Societies brought up the rear.

The work against the "white plague" was shown by a float which the Consumptives' Home exhibited; "Père Marquette and the Indians," was the subject of the Young Men's Catholic Association float; the modern fire apparatus — including a motor fire-engine — preceded the old "hand-tub" dragged by members of the Firemen's Veteran Association of Charlestown;[1] floats representing the ringing of an alarm, and "A Fire Breeder"[2] had their educational value; a gigantic cigar-box on a motor truck advertised a local tobacco house; and

[1] Cf. the fire-engines in the Lord Mayor's Shows of 1889, 1890, 1891, etc., — also the fire brigades at St. Louis in 1847. Cf. especially, p. 127, above.

[2] This showed a mass of inflammable waste material piled high; and beneath it a placard — "Does your cellar look like this?"

from another trade-pageant, provided by a well-known firm of bakers, loaves of bread were tossed to the crowd.[1] Various " public work " wagons, representing the departments of the city, brought the parade to a close.

I have not enumerated every float in this parade, but I have given enough to show the complexity of the pageant. Its primary aim was, like that of the older triumphs, to entertain; it was planned with the help of the director of public celebrations,[2] and was witnessed by a holiday crowd. Although Columbus had no direct connection with Boston, the occasion was made not only an opportunity to recall his courage and our debt to him, but also — as in the Hudson-Fulton pageant — an opportunity to represent some scenes from the history of the city. There were lessons taught by the parade — and not the least forcible appeal was that which awakened patriotism. Few could fail to be impressed by the sight of so many races marching under one flag. Lessons that we learn unconsciously are apt to linger the longest; so the impression made on a crowd which does not realize it was being edified will probably bear more fruit than that caused by a loud trumpeting of some educational aim. Here was history, which did not merely evoke past glories; trade-symbolism there was, too; and bands and soldiers and thousands of marching civilians. In such a parade as this we see the " melting-pot " itself, in which a new nation is being formed from the people that come to us from over-sea. Such a pageant furnishes a " snap-shot " of the process, as it were: and having seen it, we turn away not merely entertained, not educated solely — but inspired. Though the material here is largely old, the spirit is that of the newer pageantry; and the procession itself symbolizes America — *e pluribus unum.*

THE NORRISTOWN PAGEANT OF 1912

More closely related to such processions as those of St. Louis in 1847, and of Philadelphia in 1882, is the Historical Pageant of Norristown (Pennsylvania) held to celebrate the centennial of the borough.[3] The celebration began on Sunday, 5 May, 1912, with special services in all the churches; on the Monday was a " public school pageant, with the thousands of children in costumes varied and historic . . . Civic Day was observed on Tuesday, Industrial on Wednesday, and Firemen's on Thursday. This last was the largest parade of the week's celebration, which closed with Military Day. Friday, the most beautiful day of all so far as the weather was concerned, was Historical Day . . . The Historical

---

[1] Cf. various seventeenth-century Lord Mayor's Shows — *e. g.*, those of 1616, 1672, 1692, — and the printers at St. Louis in 1847.

[2] I was unaware that such an officer existed in Boston, until I read of him in this connection; see the afternoon edition of the Boston *Traveler-Herald* for 12 October, 1912, p. 2, col. 8.

[3] This is fully described in an illustrated volume by the Rev. Theodore Heysham, Ph.D., (Norristown, 1913) which is my authority for the following remarks.

Pageant was the feature of the afternoon. It was then that Norristown saw herself for the first time in pageantry . . ." [1]

This historical procession was divided into five parts, consisting of thirty-two " scenes "; *Early Inhabitants and Settlers* showed Indians,[2] Dutch, Swedish, Welsh, and English Quakers,[3] German, Scotch and Irish settlers. *Colonial Norristown* opened with a float reproducing an old Log Cabin; [4] a float called " Indian Trail " was followed by " Trappers and Traders," and a living-picture represented the Norris and Trent Purchase, 1704.[5] Then came a float or pageant-car, showing " The Public Sale of Norriton Plantation, 1771." Other historical scenes were represented on floats furnished for the most part by local business houses; [6] many of these pageants are illustrated in Dr. Heysham's book.

The third part dealt with the *Revolution*, and showed Continental and British soldiers, the French Allies, " The Spirit of '76," and a float with Betsy Ross.[7] Among the historical figures were Washington, General Clinton, and General Peter Muhlenberg. The fourth part showed *Norristown after 1812;* and included such floats as " Governor Snyder signing the charter," which made Norristown a borough on 31 March, 1812; [8] a float appealing for women suffrage, models of the Old Academy and various churches; the " old Pat Lyon " fire-engine — built in 1812 — the first fire-engine owned by the town; " Old Ironsides," the first engine built by the founder of the Baldwin Locomotive

---

[1] Heysham, p. 11. He continues: " Pageantry is unintentionally presumptuous, consciously spectacular, always dramatic. It deals with history as though it were something that could be handed out in chunks. It asks society to line up in a sort of historical ' bread line ' that it may satisfy its hunger for reality as the historical fragments are passed along the line.

" Pageantry, however, is not to be criticized because of its presumption nor yet because of its spectacular and dramatic characteristics. It must of necessity repeat the methods of the kindergarten and the stage. The purpose of the pageant, as of the kindergarten and the stage, is the same — to please and to instruct. In the pageant the living must impersonate the dead and the dead must appear to live again."

We shall return to a definition of pageantry later (see below, p. 291); one may be permitted to question how dramatic a street-procession, even if pageantic, is — in the ordinary sense of the word *dramatic*.

[2] " Impersonated and equipped by the Beaver, the Tecumseh, and the Minne Kaunee Tribes of Red Men."

[3] " A model of the old Plymouth meeting house, contributed by members of the Friends' Meeting of Norristown, appeared in the pageant. This model is now preserved at Plymouth Meeting House." A model of Old Norriton Church was also carried in the pageant.

[4] Illustrated in Heysham, opp. p. 23, as is the Trapper's Hut. Cf. " Raising the first Meeting House " — a float in a night pageant at Cadillac, (Michigan) — illustrated, Davol, p. 54.

[5] Illustrated, in Heysham, opp. p. 25.

[6] Churches, schools, business men and their employees took part in the different living pictures; men of the National Guard marched as Revolutionary soldiers.

[7] These are illustrated, *op. cit.*, opp. p. 37.

[8] Illustrated, *ibid.*, opp. p. 41.

Works, which was also the first to run from Philadelphia into Norristown (15 August, 1835).[1] The Sons of Veterans appeared in a scene entitled "Mexican War."

Rebellion and Later was the title of the fifth part, which began with "Responding to the call of 'Father Abraham,' 1861–64,"and "Departure of the Troops." A float representing "Abolition" followed;[2] then came veterans of the Civil War, and a scene representing the Spanish-American War of 1898. The final float [3] corresponded to the symbolical end of many a community drama; it was called "The Holy City" and "represented the three great ideals of human society and modern civilization — religious peace, industrial peace, and national peace. The three virtues, faith, hope, and charity, or love, are symbolized by the three ladies clad in Grecian costumes on the throne. The children point the way to the representatives of Religion — a Jewish High Priest, a Roman Catholic Cardinal, and a Protestant clergyman. Their prayer is 'that all may be one.' Just beyond are symbolized Capital and Labor; Peace and War, with the goddess of peace presenting the symbol of peace, the olive wreath. It is the prophecy of the future as it was the song of the angels . . ."[4]

This pageant is noteworthy as an example of those which combine the technique of the older triumph with the spirit of the new — which centre around the history of the community. It is to be observed that there is no suggestion of the carnival; that the only touch of allegory or symbolism is in the final car. All elements of the town coöperated, making this a pageant given by the community; it dealt entirely with local history, and was, therefore, a pageant of the community; it took place on the streets, and was distinctly a pageant for the community; but the technique is that of the Lord Mayor's Show. What drama may be found in the representation of the past, was here in living-pictures; but the procession was an expository setting-forth of history rather than a dramatic performance in the true sense of the word.

Sports and the raw-material of pageantry were combined at Little Compton, Rhode Island, in 1914, as described in a pamphlet preserved in the Harvard Library.[5] The important element of community-effort makes this worth noting, although the central idea which gives artistic unity to a pageantic show, was not emphasized. Each section of the township furnished a group — "any sort of group that should bring to the parade grounds a brilliant bit of color."[6] The parade included floats, some of which were appropriate — e. g. the first group, representing "The Sea," which included Neptune, the Spirit of the Sea, with eight little girls to personate the waves: a whale-boat on wheels, "manned by stout urchins in oilers, hauling in seines . . .

---

[1] The engine is pictured, *ibid.*, opp. p. 49.
[2] Illustrated, *ibid.*, opp. p. 53.
[3] Illustrated, *ibid.*, opp. p. 55.
[4] *Op. cit.*, p. 55.
[5] Georgiana B. Withington, *A Children's Parade* (1915).
[6] *A Children's Parade*, p. 4.

Toilers of the Sea

" In sharp contrast to these ' Toilers of the Sea,' were the ' Playfellows of the Sea,' on the next float . . . This group ended with a Marconi apparatus . . . and [was] called the peaceful ' Conqueror of the Sea.'

" With war-whoop and prancing came the next group. Chief Assowan and Queen Sachem Awashonks, with their Braves, their Squaws, and their wig-wam bearers . . ." [1] These had an historical connection with the town: but the Early Settlers (one of whom wore the wedding suit of his great-grandfather) were unnamed; types, rather than individuals. The Mother Goose characters, the Rainbow, with a Pot of Gold, Captain Kidd, a Circus Group, and other like figures, suggested the carnival: Uncle Sam, Columbia, a reproduction of " The Spirit of '76 " and " the tiny ' Angel of Peace,' who took the prize in the baby-carriage group," furnished the patriotic and allegorical figures necessary for all good pageants. Another parade was held the next year, and the occasion was apparently to become an annual celebration when interrupted first by epidemics, and then by the war. Possibly with the advent of peace, the parade will revive — perhaps with a unity of plan which will bring it indubitably into the field of pageantry.

After all, it was the aim, rather than the technique, of this parade, which was important. " It was pretty, later, to see these classic figures dancing on the green, outlined against the setting sun, but fairer was it by far to see the sweet courtesy of the descendants of the Pilgrims, towards the children of the recent immigrants, who were mingled in this pretty group.

" The wonderful afternoon lights, and long shadows on the beautiful upland meadow, the shaded village street, the gay groups and happy faces, the prancing horses and mild oxen, the sweet music and merry laughter, what a memory-picture it is!

" More lasting, even, than this attractive picture will be the remembrance of the spirit of helpfulness and neighborly kindness, which pervaded the town during the weeks of preparation . . ." [2] Summer cottagers and the all-year-round inhabitants, prominent citizens and recently-arrived immigrants, all took part; and the occasion did much to bring the community, as a whole, together.

A War-Time Fourth in New York

That the war did not dampen pageantic enthusiasm in New York City, is shown by the following item from the Paris edition of the London *Daily Mail*, of 10 July, 1918, published under the heading: July 4 Pageant Winners. *First Prize Won by Poles:*

New York, Monday. The gold medal for the most artistic floats [tableaux] and the best arranged pageant in New York's Fourth of July parade has been awarded to the Poles. The silver medal goes to Syria, and the bronze medal to Portugal. The committee selected for

---

[1] *A Children's Parade*, p. 6 f.

[2] *Ibid.*, p. 9.

special praise the Navy float entitled "Help your country." This represented a shipload of survivors pulling away from a submarined liner.

Diplomas of merit were awarded to Chinese, French, British, Italian, and Swiss representations, and honorable-mention diplomas to Czecho-Slovaks, Greeks, Americans of Hungarian origin, Japanese, Norwegians, Russians, Spanish, and Ukrainians.

This shows not only the value of pageantry for propaganda, but also that the "melting-pot *motif*" of such parades as the Columbus Day pageant at Boston in 1912 is bearing fruit. There must have been some central idea underlying the New York pageant of 1918; varied as the contributions seem to have been, the show was not, evidently, a revel — like the "grotesque" section of the St. Louis procession of 1847, or the "carnival pageant" in connection with the Hudson-Fulton celebration of 1909.

A Word on "Pageantic Revels" in America

Turning to examples of pageantic processions which suggest rather revels than true pageantry, let us mention very briefly a few. The circus-parade, usually a glittering show which includes moving wagons, lies outside our field because it does not soften a commercial appeal with even a semblance of allegory or symbolism. "The Quaker City's Curious Carnival — New Year's Eve Parade in Philadelphia; one of the oddest and most brilliant pageants in the United States,"[1] and the Mardi Gras celebrations at New Orleans and elsewhere, illustrate the processions with cars and disguising that seek only to entertain. Body and soul of pageantry are both here — but there is apt to be little coherence in the show, the unifying spirit of which is not — as in the London Lord Mayor's Shows, and such as we have been examining in this chapter — a civic occasion; rather an annually recurring holiday to which little deeper meaning is given. A May-day procession with floats, which bids fair to become an annual show, was started at Indianapolis in 1914; in Canada, various towns celebrate the 24 May (the Queen's Birthday) or 1 July ("Dominion Day") with "callithumpian" processions,[2] which are parades of "horribles" with a trade-element added.[3] In many Canadian towns, the Orangemen celebrate the 12 July with a procession which includes the pageantic figure of William III — usually mounted on a white horse. Historical accuracy of costumes, however, plays no part in these shows, which seem to be rather popular celebrations of an historic date than more de-

[1] Illustrated in *Leslie's Weekly* for 18 January, 1912, p. 69.

[2] The word is derived from a humorous combination of κάλλος and *thump* (cf. the *Webster* and *Century* Dictionaries). Mr. J. M. Kerrigan, of Dublin, tells me that there is a club in that city called the "Noble Order of the Callithumpians," which does not, however, give processions.

[3] At Woodstock, Ontario, they occur on 24 May, and have been in existence about fifty years; in several small Nova Scotian towns they occur on 1 July. I am indebted to various Canadian graduate-students at Harvard for this information.

veloped pageants, such as the pageantic processions with which Springfield (Massachusetts) and other towns have, of late years, been celebrating Independence Day.

THE "VEILED PROPHET" AT ST. LOUIS

As an example of the pageantic revelry which is so common in this country, as well as abroad, let us consider the processions which precede the St. Louis "Veiled Prophet" balls.[1] Since the autumn of 1878, "the Veiled Prophet and his faithful followers have appeared on the streets of St. Louis in a pageant of magnificence and splendor, 'casting sunshine and flowers' to the multitude." In 1878, the "Festival of Ceres" was given, showing seventeen floats;[2] twenty-two floats illustrated "The Progress of Civilization" in 1879;[3] the same number "The Four Seasons" in 1880. In 1886, "Scenes from American History" were exhibited,[4] and in 1887, twenty-two floats showing "The History of the Bible." "Children's Lore," in 1888, contained various floats which we have seen at Knutsford, Lichfield and elsewhere.[5] In 1892, twenty-two floats gave the "History of Louisiana Territory"[6] and in 1897, "Old Time Songs" were

---

[1] For more details than I shall give here, see Frank Gaiennie's article in the *Encyclopædia of the History of St. Louis* by William Hyde and Howard L. Conrad (New York, Louisville, and St. Louis, 1899), pp. 2370 f. I am indebted to Mr. Charles A. Cox of St. Louis for a typewritten copy of the article, the original of which I have not seen. "The organization has gone on in the same manner since 1897," wrote Mr Cox in 1913.

[2] Enumerated by Mr. Gaiennie as follows: 1, Glacial Period of Winter; 2, Chariot of the Sun; 3, Primitive Animals; 4, Fiends of Darkness; 5, The Centaur; 6, Flora; 7, Proserpine and Pluto; 8, Golden Globe; 9, Demeter; 10, Triptolemus; 11, Plowing; 12, Fruits; 13, Bacchus; 14, Industry; 15, Wealth; 16, "The Veiled Prophet," and 17, Silenus.

[3] Various trades and industries were symbolized.

[4] The twenty-one floats showed more coherence than is usual in a pageantic revel; but the history was not confined to St. Louis. Symbolism was there, in "America," "Missouri," and "King Cotton"; among the other floats were: the Discovery of the Northmen; the Landing of Columbus; Columbus received by Ferdinand and Isabella; Ponce de Leon and the Fountain of Youth; Meeting of Cortez and Montezuma; King Nezahualcoyotl at Tezcoco; de Soto discovering the Mississippi; Pocahontas and John Smith; Hendrik Hudson; Burning of the Dutch Village; Landing of the Pilgrims; Washington Crossing the Delaware; The Heroes of '76; Daniel Boone; Hunting the Buffalo; Statue of General Jackson; Westward Ho! and the invariable "Veiled Prophet."

[5] Little Red Riding Hood; Bluebeard; Aladdin in the Cave; Humpty-Dumpty's Misfortune; various floats showing scenes from *Alice in Wonderland;* Uncle Remus's Tar Baby Story; Santa Claus on the Roof Tops; Mother Goose; Old King Cole, and Cinderella were among the floats that year. Cf. the pictures of the "Mother Goose" pageant at Greensboro (North Carolina) in Davol, p. 57.

[6] Some of the floats were: America; Europe; Asia; Africa; Mexico; South America; Oceania; Missouri; Veiled Prophet; Father of Waters; Death of de Soto; Arrival of Pontiac; Reception of Père Marquette and Joliet; LaSalle taking possession of Louisiana Territory; Founding of the city of St. Louis; Visit of Lafayette to St. Louis; Native Missourian inaugurated President of the United States.

illustrated with the same number of cars. There is no need to go into detail here of the shows which run in unbroken sequence from 1878 to 1897,[1] nor need we discuss here the masked ball which follows them.

In spite of the allegory, symbolism, and even history which can be found in these processions, they lie on the outskirts of pageantry, because they have no connection with the town, and are given by a social organization. Insofar as the subject of the triumphs approaches local history, they tend towards pageantry in its higher forms; the fact that the shows are not given by the community as a whole puts a barrier between this and a pageant like that of Norristown. The tendency toward the carnival is shown by the fact that a Queen is chosen at the masked ball which follows the parades.[2]

A "Carnival" at Revere in September, 1912

To illustrate the formless "raw material" of pageantry, I may allude to a "carnival" which took place at Revere (Massachusetts) early in September, 1912.[3] This apparently had a trade-origin. "Ten artistic floats will be features of the grand carnival parade, or pageant, to take place each night during the Mardi Gras celebration at Revere Beach from Tuesday to Saturday of next week. The royal float will convey the King and Queen of the carnival. A different royal couple will be picked for each night. Other floats will represent Fame, Beauty and the Beast, the Flying Dutchman, the Man in the Moon, Robinson Crusoe, the Martians, Slumberland, the Sun Princess, and Revere Beach."[4]

Pageantry "with a Purpose"

Another development of pageantic material in processions deserves a word. Just as the pageant-play has been turned to political uses—as in *Disinherited—?*[5] — so the pageantic procession occasionally takes unto itself a political complexion. Allegory, or symbolism, was used by the Socialists of Boston during the campaign of 1912, when a figure, richly dressed in silk hat and furs, repre-

---

[1] And, as far as I know, to the present day.

[2] Since 1890, *tableaux* have been a feature of several balls.

[3] I cite a paragraph from the Boston *Herald* of 30 August, 1912; the heading reads: "Ten Floats to Appear in Revere Carnival — Different King and Queen for each Night of *Fête*." On carnivals, see the *Theatre Magazine* for February, 1911, p. 43.

[4] It is worth calling attention to the phenomenon which permits the use of *Mardi Gras* in the paragraph quoted above. The phrase is hardly appropriate for a parade that is to be repeated five nights of the first week in September; but it shows the influence which is behind such an entertainment.

[5] See above, p. 230 f. (The "Pope-burnings," both in England and America, may be considered political pageantry of a kind, as are the Orange processions.) This is not far removed from propaganda.

senting Capital, was drawn through the streets by the Elephant, Donkey, and Bull-Moose — emblems of the Republican, Democratic, and Progressive parties. The implied political doctrine was emphasized by the transparencies of the torch-light parade which followed. In the woman-suffrage procession at New York on 9 November, 1912,[1] there were chariots and floats representing the States where women vote; " Our Plank " — a float intended to convey the idea that the vote is for the benefit of all sorts and conditions of women — contained woman-physician, college-girl, trained-nurse, tenement-house mother and " rich butterfly," each in appropriate costume. Another float showed " China, the land where women vote "; it contained twenty-five women in Chinese costume, with lanterns. Men helmeted, dressed in silver armor and carrying shields emblazoned with the name of the State each represented, walked by the horses' heads; and many thousand people, some of them in costume, accompanied the procession.[2]

A " pageant-procession," followed by an " allegory," made up the suffragette " show " in Washington on 3 March, 1913.[3] The following year, " the greatest suffrage demonstration that Washington has ever seen filled Pennsylvania avenue and other streets leading from Lafayette Park to the Capitol, where an army of women and girls besieged Congress . . . Every State of the Union was represented in the parade. The petition brigade numbered 531, and marching with them were a hundred girls with garlands, a chorus of a thousand, ten bands, divisions of suffrage cavalry, and girl heralds, besides the rank and file of the women's suffrage organisations and a delegation from Pennsylvania of the Men's League for the Suffrage, swelling the total to about five thousand . . .

" Then came colour-bearers and behind them a Pageant of Spring with its white-robed girls typifying spring, youth and hope. The cavalry section, with brilliant banners of purple, white and gold, was headed by Miss Elsie Hill, of Connecticut. In contrast with the Amazonian pomp of mounted suffragists were the more sober and business-like ranks of the women workers, in bodies according to their callings — writers, actresses, doctors, stenographers, farmers, waitresses, milliners, and, as if to defy the taunts of ' the Antis,' home makers marching under their banner." [4]

---

[1] See the New York *Tribune* of that date, p. 6.

[2] Cf. the Suffragettes' London march, pictured in the *Illus. Lond. News* for 25 June, 1910, p. 1011. Picture 2 emphasized " the fact that many suffragettes have been in prison as a result of their political beliefs "; it showed " Miss Howey in prison dress on the only car in the procession."

[3] On the " allegory," see below, p. 284 f.

[4] The London *Observer*, for 10 May, 1914, p. 11. Cf. the " Pageant of Spring " with the masques mentioned above, p. 191, and below, p. 284.

"Pageantry for Returning Heroes"

Under this title, the *Literary Digest* for 12 April, 1919, records — with illus trations — the welcome planned by New York City for her troops returning from overseas service. Here the pageantry recalls the Elizabethan triumphal arch — the structures erected at London in 1559[1] and at Norwich in 1578,[2] for instance. The troops themselves were not pageantic: like those of war-time Lord Mayor's Shows, they were history itself, not a representation of historical characters, nor symbolical figures representing History. An observer, quoted from the New York *Times* by the *Literary Digest*, remarks: "The three phases of the decorations were evident last night. At the Public Library with the Court of the Heroic Dead, a mourning note was struck, while victory was the *motif* at the Victory Arch, and joy and thankfulness at the Arch of Jewels, at Sixtieth Street. Thousands and thousands of crystal prisms gave out the colors of the rainbow last night at the jeweled portal, which consists of an arch of two shafts, each eighty feet high, the portal itself being a hundred and thirty feet wide. About thirty-two thousand pieces of prisms in ruby, jonquil, olivin, and ultramarine blue surround a sunburst of nine thousand pieces to bring out the coats-of-arms of the Allies . . ." An interesting discussion of the effectiveness of the architectural features of these "pageants" is summarized in the same issue of the *Literary Digest*. A selection from a letter which appeared in the New York *Tribune*, I quote:

> Street pageantry and decoration, being for an occasion, are not architecture, which is for continual and daily use and enjoyment. Therefore, such decoration should not be made even remotely to resemble architectural art, for if it does so, it immediately and inevitably enters into competition with the surrounding architecture, with which it cannot hope to compete, but which it may nevertheless outrival by reason of its gaiety, its brilliance, and by a beauty of an entirely different sort.
>
> Instead of being treated to an exhibition of pageantry and decoration as an art in itself, we were confronted with imitation architecture of an ancient, uninspired, cumbersome sort; false in fact, false in taste, and actually obstructive to the aim and end of it all, which was to enhance and adorn the spectacle of marching troops.
>
> It was false in fact because it was lath and plaster made to imitate enduring stone. It was false in taste because it echoed the taste of imperial Rome by way of imperial France. It was obstructive because it actually obstructed the movement of the troops and the vision of the spectators.
>
> The trump-cards in the decorator's pack, color and movement, were played scarcely at all. . .

It is encouraging for the future of pageantry in the United States, to know that public interest can be aroused enough to discuss matters of beauty — in connection with triumphal arches erected for street parades. The Dewey reception of 1899 — also a "military pageant" — is compared (by a writer in the

[1] Cf. above, vol. i, p. 200.

[2] Cf. above, vol. i, p. 211.

New York *Evening Sun*, who is quoted in the *Literary Digest*) with the return of the New York troops; he finds a loss of the picturesque in the olive-drab uniforms of the present day. The Dewey Arch, on the site of which the Victory Arch was erected, is pictured in the same number of the *Literary Digest*.

This survey — incomplete as it is — is sufficient to show us the range of processional pageantry. In its least developed form, it is the carnival procession pure and simple. Sometimes it takes on a suggestion of history, either national or local, but — being given by a small group — is not of the community. Sometimes it is used for propaganda; sometimes it combines history with an ill-assorted carnivalistic *mélange;* sometimes it approaches the Parkerian work, as at Norristown, where the community furnished scenes (which were practically speechless " episodes ") dealing — with one exception — with the history of the community; and the exception included symbolism, frequently found at the end of the " community drama." It is obvious that the greater the unity of the underlying plan in these proceessions, the larger the share of the community in preparing and producing them, the more care that is given to get historical accuracy, the greater the civic pride and the desire for civic betterment awakened by them — the higher they rise in the scale of pageantry. It may not be fair to judge the Lord Mayor's Show by these standards; but they may be applied with justice both to the processional pageant and the " community drama " in the United States.

§ 2. THE COMMUNITY DRAMA

We have seen that Mr. Parker wanted to call his pageants " folk-plays," but that this name did not awaken enthusiasm. As the German *Erinnerungsspiele* serve to keep alive some episode in the history of a town, so the old " folk-plays " of England recall some pre-Christian festival — the Robin Hood plays are supposed to go back to a fight between Winter and Summer; or some event in the past of the community — the Hox Tuesday play of Coventry, for example, is thought to commemorate a victory over the Danes.

When, early in the eighteenth century, speech died out of the Lord Mayor's Show, the characters in these triumphs were, presumably, wheeled through the streets silent on their pageant-cars.[1] In 1783, as we have seen, figures from the Lord Mayor's Show appeared on the stage of a London theatre; the transfer was not difficult. Probably — although more evidence is needed to prove the matter conclusively — the silent group which portrayed an historical event on some pageant-car in a street procession, lies behind the group which did the same thing in a hall.

---

[1] Only one in each group had delivered speeches in the days when the services of a poet were required; even in the days of the " royal-entry," the groups on the pageants had never been far removed from the *tableau vivant*.

In 1882, William Penn was the chief figure in a pageantic procession at Philadelphia; in 1888, scenes from the early history of the colony were presented in Centennial Hall, at Marietta, Ohio.[1]

The Marietta Pageant of 1888

Ten " tableaux " made up this pageant,[2] most of them, apparently, nothing more than " living pictures " of scenes from the early history of the new colony. It is hard to tell just how much speaking there was; but there seems to have been some.[3] Musical selections separated the *tableaux*. The first scene showed the landing of the French at the mouth of the Muskingum on 16 August, 1749; the last was a minuet at Blennerhassett's, in which Aaron Burr and various other historical characters took part. There was no symbolical or allegorical character in this pageant.

The Plymouth "Historic Festival" of 1896

At the end of the nineteenth century, these " historic festivals " or " pageants " were common enough. The rarity of the program of that given on the last week of July, 1896, and again in 1897, at Plymouth, Massachusetts, warrants its reprinting. " The performances were given in a large hall which was used as an armory, and would easily accommodate fifteen hundred people," writes Mr.

---

[1] It must be borne in mind that Mr. Parker recognizes no debt to the " living pictures " of the street procession; and that, while American pageantry of the twentieth century recognizes its debt to the Parkerian work, there was no direct influence from America on the modern pageant in England. The origin of, and influences upon, the German *Erinnerungsspiele* cannot be taken up here; these provide a fruitful field for further research.

[2] A full account of this pageant (the " manager " of which was Mrs. Edward E. Phillips) is given in the *Report of the Commissioners of the National Centennial Celebration of the early Settlement of the Territory Northwest of the River Ohio*, which is recorded in the Bibliography, *s. v.* Marietta. The celebration was held there 15–19 July, 1888; the " pageant " (the word is used in the *Report*) was produced on 17 July, in Centennial Hall.

Cf. also for mention of this pageant, Bates and Orr, *Pageants and Pageantry*, pp. 12, 13, and Davol, *Am. Pag.*, pp. 31 f.; on p. 33 a scene is illustrated. Mr. Davol notes that the pageant was repeated at Cincinnati the October following.

[3] *E. g.*, in tableau iv: " General St. Clair . . . enters the ' bowery ' near by and his commission as Governor is read." (*Report*, p. 29); in tableau viii, scene 2: " A woman with children, . . . Mrs. Moulton, (was) missing. — ' Is she killed ? ' ' No,' said Lydia, ' mother has stopped to put things a little to rights.' " (*Report*, p. 31.) " In this tableau," the program continues, " the original Campus Martius bell, which rang the alarm in 1791, will be used."

Historical accuracy was sought for, and the community drawn upon for actors and heirlooms. An historical loan-collection (with which may be compared those at York and New York in 1909) was a part of the celebration, and indicates the " educational " spirit which is so prominent in the modern work.

Lord.[1] "There were no speeches. . . . The affair was planned principally by Miss Margaret MacLaren Eager of New York, who at that time had charge of many historical pageants, as they were called. She arranged the *tableaux*, selected the persons, determined the costumes, and had the entire responsibility for the preparation of the scenes, and acted as stage manager.

"The general management of the affair was in the hands of a large committee of which I was chairman. The nominal purpose of the pageant was to secure funds to provide a new bell for the First Church, the old one having been injured in the fire which destroyed the church, and sufficient funds were raised to recast the old bell and place it in position. The pageant, as the program shows, involved no writing as the actors had no speaking parts . . ."

The character of this entertainment is shown by the program; the thing was called an "historic festival," and entitled *Old Plymouth Days and Ways*.

WEDNESDAY AND FRIDAY EVENINGS

Scene 1. Scrooby, Farewell of Gov. Bradford.
2. Festivities of Holland Peasants. Tableau, the Embarkation of the Pilgrims from Delft Haven.
Scene 3. Indian life. An Indian Hunt Dance. Tableau, the Landing of the Pilgrims on Plymouth Rock.
Scene 4. A service in the Old Fort.
Scene 5. A Pilgrim Wedding.
Scene 6. A Ball of 1760. The Flag Dance.

THURSDAY AND MONDAY EVENINGS AT 8

Tableau, the Embarkation from Delft-Haven.
Scene 1. Indian Life. An Indian Hunt Dance. Tableau, the Landing of the Pilgrims. Tableau, the Treaty with Massasoit. Tableau, home of John and Priscilla.
Scene 2. David Alden's family. (Descendants of John and Priscilla.)
Scene 3. A Tea Party of 1770. The Flag Dance.
The Civil War — Scene 1, Departure of troops. Scene 2, A camp scene. Scene 3, Return of troops.

SATURDAY MATINEE AT 2:30

Scene 1. Scrooby. The farewell of Wm. Bradford.
2. Festival of Holland Peasants. The Embarkation from Holland.
Scene 3. Indian Life. An Indian Hunt Dance. Tableau, the Landing of the Pilgrims.
Scene 4. A Pilgrim wedding. A drum dance.
5. A Ball of 1760. The Flag dance.

---

[1] I am indebted to Mr. Arthur Lord, of Plymouth and Boston, for the opportunity of transcribing the program of this festival. My quotations are from a letter of his dated 25 February, 1915.

SATURDAY EVENING AT 8

Scene 1. Scrooby. The farewell of Gov. Bradford.
Tableau. The Embarkation. An Indian Scene. Indian Hunt Dance. Tableau, The Landing. A Pilgrim wedding. Tableau, Home of John and Priscilla. David Alden's family. A Tea party of 1770. A Flag dance. Return of the troops.

THURSDAY, FRIDAY AND MONDAY AT 2:45

Scene 1. A dancing school of the olden time.
2. The flags of all nations.
3. A quilting party of 1812. A drum dance.
4. A sailor dance.

Here were living pictures, dances, and perhaps scenes acted in dumb-show. Symbolism may have played a part in such a scene as "the Flags of all Nations"; and there may have been a stirring of local pride due to the historical scenes portrayed — most of which, it will be remarked, emphasized the customs of the people, although Governor Bradford, Massasoit, John and Priscilla Alden, and other historical characters, appeared. But the purpose of the "festival" was not to awaken civic pride; it was to get a bell for the church...

THE BOSTON "HISTORICAL FESTIVAL" OF 1897

Miss Eager directed the "Historical Festival" which was given in Music Hall, Boston, 22–30 April, 1897, under the auspices of the Boston Teachers' Mutual Benefit Association.[1] This consisted of various scenes or living pictures[2] given by different groups as follows: "Boston, England. St. Botolph's Church where John Cotton preached. English villages and their Merry-makings. John Cotton. Thomas Dudley and others enter and discuss the matter of transferring the Charter and Company of New England to New England . . .[3] Cambridge, England. Meeting of the twelve men chosen to weigh and consider the matter of transferring the Charter and Company to New England . . ."[4] Then came "The wharves at Southampton, England. Tableau. 'Departure of the Puritans.'"[5] Students of the English High and Latin Schools gave the next scene, which was entitled "Indian Home Life," and showed "'Blaxton' wel-

[1] The souvenir program of this — with the names of those who took part, and the characters each represented — is in the Harvard Library (*Thr. 1211.70*). This pamphlet is my authority for the following remarks.

[2] It is impossible to tell from the program how great a part was played by speech.

[3] This was "under the auspices of Boston Art Students." The characters included Puritans and Villagers, a May Queen, Gregory and Jester, together with the historical figures.

[4] This scene was "under the auspices of members of the Tavern Club"; the cast of characters included some well-known names. (Cf. program, p. 23.)

[5] This was "under the auspices of the Gov. Thomas Dudley Family Association"; Mr. Sanford H. Dudley took the part of Governor Thomas.

coming Winthrop and his followers to Shawmut." An early Town Meeting (1633) was next presented "under the auspices of Boston Masters," and then the Colonial Dames showed "Puritan Home Life. The welcome given to Margaret Winthrop and John Eliot," and "Copley's Studio," which "tableau represents a lady of the period sitting for the artist in his studio in Boston. A few of her friends accompany her." A social gathering in provincial days, with old-time dances, made up the next episode; after which members of Battery A gave "The Boston Massacre," and "The Removal of the Troops."[1] The "Interior of the Green Dragon Tavern — Meeting of the Sons of Liberty" was produced under the auspices of the Old South Historical Society, who also gave "The Old South — the 'Tea Meeting,'" and "On Board the Dartmouth — the Boston Tea Party." The Mary Draper Chapter, D.A.R., gave "On the Road to Roxbury. Mary Draper's Home. The Eve of the Battle," and a company of the English High School regiment showed Paul Revere and the minutemen at Lexington. "Washington's Entrance into Boston" was presented by members of the Ancient and Honorable Artillery Company;[2] and the reception at Governor Hancock's mansion, on 10 August, 1790 (on the arrival of the *Columbia*, the first American ship to sail round the world) was under the charge of "ladies of the William H. Prescott Club." The Daughters of the Revolution gave "the Lafayette Reception, 1824," and the State Department of the Woman's Relief Corps and the G.A.R. showed the departure and return of troops in the time of the Civil War. With the Flag Dance and three "Children's Scenes,"[3] the festival came to an end.

As at Plymouth, there was some dancing in this pageant, but the emphasis was more on history — and the whole show seems to have been given at every performance. The "flag dance" may have been the same as that of Plymouth, and the quilting party may have been another "stock scene"; but the important thing to note here is that, although given for an object, many different groups — historical, educational, and social — took part in the festival, thus tending to link the community together.

1901 — Historical Scenes at Yale

In his account of the Yale Bicentennial,[4] Professor Henry S. Canby recalls that in October, 1901, "five thousand Yale men, costumed to represent the historic ages of the University, marched . . . from the campus aglow with orange

---

[1] This latter scene was laid in the Governor's Council Chamber, and included Lieutenant-Governor Hutchinson, Samuel Adams, citizens, officers, and the council.

[2] An off-shoot of the London Honourable Artillery Company, which figured in more than one Lord Mayor's Show.

[3] Which showed "Master Tileston and his School of ye Olden Time," "A Quilting Party," and "Ye Miniature Navy."

[4] *The Book of the Yale Pageant*, pp. 105 ff. The second scene of the fourth episode was planned to represent the academic procession of the Bicentennial.

lanterns, and set about with great bowls blazing with burning rosin, through the streets of New Haven . . . On Tuesday evening, the graduates filled an amphitheatre built about a stage upon which the undergraduates presented scenes from the history of Yale. This was the first open air presentation of historical scenes under modern conditions, and may earn for Yale the name of 'Mother of Pageants.' Classes were grouped together, and in the waits between the scenes each introduced its favorite old-time songs . . . At the end of the evening, the audience of nine thousand stood bareheaded singing the Doxology, as at the end of Chapel service, while bombs burst overhead and stars of fire rained through the elm tops — thus, so said an observer afterward, 'praising God and raising hell,' in good Yale fashion."

Perhaps because this was overshadowed by "the more formal aspects of the Bicentennial," or perhaps because it was exclusively for a Yale audience, this "pageant" seems not to have exercised much direct influence on others. There were historical scenes (though not out-of-doors) at Marietta in 1888, and at Boston in 1897.[1] And history had been reproduced out-of-doors at Plymouth, in 1801.[2]

Quebec Pageant of July, 1908

With the birth of the Parkerian pageant in England, new influences began to be felt. No longer were living pictures and pantomimic scenes illustrating historical events — the kind of pageant which developed in America at the end of the nineteenth century — sufficient. The Sherborne Pageant of 1905 had been three years a memory when one of the first of the more elaborate shows was produced on this continent — that which took place at Quebec in 1908.[3]

Mr. Frank Lascelles, the master of the pageant which celebrated the tercentenary anniversary of the founding of Quebec in July, 1908, had been the master of the Oxford Pageant of 1907; the connection between this and the Parkerian work in England is, therefore, not hard to trace. At five o'clock on the afternoon of 21 July, the first regular performance of this part of the celebration began;[4] the technique is in general like the English pageants, but we may go

---

[1] See above, pp. 258 and 260 f. [2] See above, p. 236 f.

[3] Although this chapter deals chiefly with pageantry in the United States, we may, perhaps, be allowed to cross the frontier without offending our northern neighbors. I have already mentioned various pageantic processions which accompanied this tercentenary celebration, (see above, p. 240 f.).

[4] For further details than I give here, see the *Historical Souvenir and Book of the Pageants of the 300th Anniversary of the Founding of Quebec, the Ancient Capital of Canada*, 20–31 July, 1908 (illustrated). (Montreal [1908]); Carrel, *The Quebec Tercentenary Commemorative History* (illustrated). (Quebec, 1908); *Les Fêtes du Troisième Centenaire de Québec*, 1608–1908. (illustrated). (Quebec, 1911), where *Les Spectacles Historiques* are fully described on pp. 369 ff.

Besides the illustrations in these volumes, I may note that the *Don de Dieu* is reproduced

into some detail, in view of the historical importance of this one. It will be observed that some freedom is allowed in the matter of site; [1] that speech is not so important as in some of the English pageants; [2] but that the spirit of the Parkerian work is kept.

The first episode dealt with Jacques Cartier, and the founding of Quebec, 1534–6. Much of this — though not all — appears to have been in pantomime and song. The second scene — Cartier at the court of François I — seems also to have been largely pantomime; what words may have been spoken were not, probably, very important. The second "pageant" — or episode — took place at the Louvre; Henri IV gave Champlain a commission to set out for la Nouvelle France. Again trumpets, music, song, and dance seem to play more important a part than dialogue. The second scene of this "pageant": "1620 — Samuel de Champlain brings to Quebec his young wife, and is received by the Garrison of the Fort, and the friendly Indians who perform the Calumet dance in their honour." The third episode,[3] — "1639: Mère Marie de l'Incarnation reaches Quebec with the Ursulines and Jesuits and is received by the Governor," — was followed by one which showed how in 1660 Adam Dollard, Sieur des Ormeaux, and his companions in arms at Long Sault kept the fort against the Iroquois. The fifth episode was the reception by Mgr. de Laval of the Marquis de Tracy, the Lieutenant-General of Louis XIV; the sixth, "Daumont de Saint-Lusson takes possession of the country of the West, in the name of the King of France." Phips appeared in the seventh episode; and the "Battles of the Plains of Abraham" [4] followed; the last "pageant" or episode was the "march past" of characters and a final chorus.

As the two armies of Montcalm and Wolfe stood facing each other, "from a thick bush in the centre of the field were seen to emerge a cluster of white doves — emblems of peace. They were released, but uncertain of their freedom, hesitated, then soared overhead, as if cementing the unity of the two armies below." [5]

---

in the *Illus. Lond. News* for 25 July, 1908, p. 125, and by Davol, in *Handbook Am. Pag.*, p. 40. The pavane danced in this pageant is illustrated, *ibid.*, p. 197.

[1] *E. g.*, the "second pageant" (or episode) takes place at the Louvre; and though "c'est à Montréal que Jacques Cartier lut l'évangile selon saint Jean aux sauvages groupés autour de lui," (*Les Fêtes*, p. 371) it was thought good, to show the Christian spirit of the discoverer, to introduce the scene as if it had happened at Quebec.

[2] *E. g.* "Il est arrivé qu' à la scène l'on dut couper certains dialogues, abréger certains discours; nous les citerons aussi intégralement que possible." (*Les Fêtes*, p. 376.) Cf. Carrel, pp. 131 f., for a description of the pageant in scenario form. On pp. 154 f. some of the dialogue (between the English and Frontenac) is reprinted. Dialogue in English, Latin, French, and even in the Indian tongue, seems to have been delivered; we may suppose that the meaning of the scenes was largely brought out by action.

[3] Illustrated in *Les Fêtes*, opp. p. 400.

[4] Wolfe against Montcalm (1759) and Lévis against Murray (1760).

[5] Carrel, p. 86.

With the laying of wreaths on the monument — " to the honor of Wolfe " by one of Montcalm's men, and " to the honor of Montcalm " by one of Wolfe's — the pageant came to an end.[1]

The pageant given at Lancaster (Massachusetts) on 4 July, 1912, was a development of the " tableau pageant." It consisted of four scenes from the history of the town, presented on the village green. It was not entirely without speech, although that played a very minor part.[2]

The Peterborough Pageant of 1910

Turning from the purely historical pageant, like that of Quebec, we find that —although it was the affair of the whole town — the Peterborough (New Hampshire) Pageant was " a tribute to Edward MacDowell." [3] It " tried for the first time to express a town's history in music written by a former citizen, and aimed to bind the different episodes in a closer unity than is common," says Professor Baker, the master of the pageant.[4] The emphasis is, perhaps, more on the impersonal element of history — what may be called its social side — than is common with historical pageants. The attention which music and dancing received seems to place this much nearer the masque than the historical " folk-play " usually gets; but the " popular " quality of the pageant saves it. There is, perhaps, a good deal of masque-technique; but the fact that the townspeople took a personal pride in the pageant separates it from such shows as the Bohemian Club " Jinks." [5]

The pageant opens with an invocation, in which Muses and Dreams appear. An Indian idyl follows; and then we have an episode dealing with " the conditions in North Ireland compelling the emigration of the settlers." In this we see the impersonality of the history; Boy, Old Woman, Young Woman, Old Man, Pedlar, Peasants, Puritan, Children, Soldiers — the list shows us that we are dealing largely with the supernumeraries of history. In these episodes, Sir William Tenney, Lady Tenney, and Horton are the only individuals named.

" The Departure " and " The Landing " are followed by " The Burial of the

---

[1] Carrel, p. 88. A "pageant ball" or "historical ball" seems to have been little more than a fancy-dress ball, though most of the costumes were " historic." " Everything else was of today, but the spirit was that of history — the history of the times and peoples that made the Dominion — the history which one is pleased to think of — the history whose thoughts are studied and the garb of whose period is worn. In a thankful manner the spirit of the age was imbued and its garb donned.

" The spirit of pageantry and history filled Quebec and even in their enjoyments Quebecers learned, for the ball was a lesson and a pleasant one." (Carrel, p. 122.)

[2] The program of this pageant may be found in the Harvard Library.

[3] *Book* of the Peterborough Pageant, p. 5.

[4] In *New Boston* for November, 1910, p. 295.

[5] On this, see below, p. 286.

A Scene from the Peterborough Pageant of 1910

Chieftain." [1] "A Colonial Wedding" — again with unnamed characters [2] — shows "a custom of these early settlers at weddings . . . The scene illustrates also the essential part spinning played in the daily life of the time. It is a fact that the women carried their wheels with them even to festivities." [3]

A dance illustrating an old legend concerning a whimsical negro who was the village cow-herd, forms episode viii; this is followed by "The Call to Arms, April 18–19, 1775." "Working the Hand-Looms, 1810," recalls the building of the first cotton mill, a hundred years before the pageant; "The Deserted Farm" [4] again deals with nameless characters. Then comes a "Dance — in Autumn."

The final episode is the welcome of Peterborough to its returning soldiers in 1865: then a dance — "Peterborough welcomes People of other Nations and the Muses to her Woods and Hills" — after which Peterborough reviews the historical groups — Settlers, Indians, Colonials, Revolutionary figures, the Milling group, the people of the Civil War period, and the Foreign Races — and receives the English, Canadian, and New York Peterboroughs.[5]

This pageant combines history, mythology, and symbolism; it employs dance and music, as well as dialogue; it portrays the past of the town, and uses in the portrayal the musical utterance of a great man. We can see that in certain details it differs from the Parkerian norm; but it does not lose its right to the name of pageant for all that.

"From Cave Life to City Life" — at Boston in 1910

A pageant which combines history and allegory — which has, one might say, a symbolic structure built on a foundation of history — is the Boston "Civic Pageant" of 1910, entitled *From Cave Life to City Life.* We may examine this somewhat at length, because it differs from the Parkerian pageant widely.[6]

---

[1] It looks from the program, or *Book* of the pageant, as if each scene were made up of pantomime and singing — the music based — of course — on MacDowell's compositions, which were arranged by Mr. Chalmers D. Clifton. Mr. Baker tells me there was more speaking than would appear from the *Book;* the dialogue has not been published.

[2] Save for "Old Black Baker."

[3] Cf. the illustration (from another pageant) in Davol, p. 125. Pictures of "Dreams" (on p. 19) and of a solo-dancer in this pageant (on p. 168) may be found in Davol.

[4] Cf. episode ix of the Thetford Pageant, (the *Book* of that pageant, pp. 50 f.).

[5] This ending — with its symbolism and "march past" — is more Parkerian than is usual in America. The song which the chorus sings during the final march expresses the hope characteristic of the "futuristic" pageant.

[6] The program of this pageant was published in the "pageant number" of *New Boston* (November, 1910), i, no. 7, pp. 273 f. Miss Lotta A. Clark was "Director of the Pageant." Besides the illustrations in this pamphlet, the Knights of Economy, and other pictures, may be found in Davol.

Although this "Pageant of the Perfect City" — to give it its subtitle — was not arranged to celebrate any civic anniversary, it was given by a thousand citizens of "greater Boston" as part of the "civic advance campaign" to awaken municipal pride, to quicken a public spirit of coöperation, and to stir the community life to better things. The pageant was given in the Boston Arena on the evenings of 10, 11, and 12 November.

A Prologue, in which Father Time invites Labor, Progress, Success, and Prosperity, Peace, and Happiness to assist man in his work, was followed by episode i — the Cave Dweller at the first hearthstone.[1] An "interlude" — which was a dance symbolic of the welcome which Vineland extended to the Norsemen — separated the first and second episodes; then followed "Life in the Indian Village." Another solo-dance — the Dance of the Waves — introduced the third episode, which showed, in three scenes, "The Colonists and their Settlement for Freedom in the new Land"; scene i, the struggle for existence — including a fight with the Indians; scene ii, "Strength and Progress. An early Thanksgiving"; and scene iii, "The Resistance to Tyranny," with "The Governor's Reception,"[2] at which a minuet was danced.

After a five-minute interval, episode iv — "Present Success and Future Improvement" — was introduced by a solo-dance entitled "The Passing of the Indian." In the fourth episode, there were four scenes dealing with the past, present, and future, together with "the assimilation of the nations." The characters here were symbolical personifications. The pageant came to an end with a solo-dance, and the singing of a patriotic hymn.

"The present Boston Pageant works by contrasts," says Professor Baker,[3] "aiming to suggest future possibilities by placing in juxtaposition that in the past which was inept and uncomfortable, and the commonplaces of life today undreamed of by our forefathers." The illustrated evolution is meant to stimulate a demand for realities which might seem ideal, he continues, by showing that the commonplace of today was undreamed of even a hundred years ago.

Much which the program of the pageant contains was, it should be remarked, omitted in the actual production; and much of the symbolism of the final assembly was not clearly brought out.

---

[1] While the majority of the episodes did not contain speeches, they were not living-pictures in the sense of being presented by people who remained motionless. The spectators sat on three sides of the Arena, and the acting took part on the floor in the middle; when scenery was needed it was placed at the far end, under the musicians.

[2] Until the second scene of this episode, when Jonathan Edwards, the minister, reads the Thanksgiving proclamation, no historical figure appears. As at Peterborough, many of the characters have no names, being designated simply as "the Captain," "the Minister," "Colonists," etc. With the "Town Crier" and "Minister" (named Jonathan Edwards on p. 284 of the program; without a name on p. 290) in the second scene of episode iii, appeared "The New England Conscience"; "the Dance of the Devil and the New England Conscience" of the Taunton Pageant of 1911 is illustrated in Davol, p. 168.

[3] In the number of *New Boston* already cited, p. 295.

The fact that the spectators sat on three sides of the hall, tended to destroy much of the effect — for more than two-thirds of the people had no background against which to see the pageant, save that furnished by their fellow-citizens across the " stage." The first two episodes, given in pantomime, were effective; but the solo-dances, which were highly symbolic, meant little to many of the on-lookers, who soon wearied of the gliding figure of the dancer, graceful as it was. The first scene of the third episode — with its fight between settlers and Indians — was effective;[1] but the second scene (where inaudible speech was introduced) contained too much material,[2] and divided the attention of the spectators in much the same way as does a four-ring circus. The fourth episode — a review by Boston and the suburban cities, of present success and future improvement — was nothing but a kermess. The Town Crier was jostled out of the way by newsboys; pillions, Sedan chairs, and coaches were distanced by an electric motor-car which whirled about the hall until the spectators grew dizzy, and bore before us the name of the manufacturer with a commercial zeal worthy of the Lord Mayor's Show at its worst.

The " present city " included in its historic past the Indians and Colonists who had appeared in earlier episodes; the " future city " showed " Dust Clouds bringing Disease Germs," " Flames " (extinguished by the " Knights of Economy ") and other symbolical figures represented by children, appropriately dressed, who danced as in a ballet. The final scene, " The Assimilation of the Nations," was frankly a ballet, in which each group — dressed in the national costumes of Scandinavia, Scotland, Ireland, Holland, Russia, Hungary, Italy, and Greece — joined, dancing, as best they could, the peasant dances of each country. A final solo-dance — " Aspiration " — brought the pageant to an end; the friends of the pageanters swarmed from their seats to the floor of the arena, the band struck up a waltz, and the rest of the spectators, on their way to the doors, looked down on a fancy-dress ball.

This pageant combined history and symbolism; but the historical characters were — as has been noted — types rather than real men. Some actual characters were, of course, presented; but few of the men who live in the history of Boston appeared. Peter Faneuil, John Hancock, Samuel Adams, James Otis, Cotton Mather, and many others were conspicuous by their absence; " Colonist Captain," " Ezra," " Minister," " Jotham," " Sally," " the Rev. Arthur Brown," " Lord Marrington," and other equally well-known characters took their place. " The New England Conscience " appeared in the first two scenes of the third episode, and the combination of history and symbolism was not a happy one.

---

[1] This recalls such musters as that held at Bristol in 1574, and the fight between cavaliers and Puritans at Colchester in 1909.

[2] " The party now breaks up into four separate groups: 1. The Dame School. 2. A spinning school. 3. A quilting party. 4. The singing school . . ." (*New Boston*, p. 285.)

From Ab to the Governor's Reception we had history of a sort; but it was "typical" rather than actual. Then the pageant became a huge ballet; the vast floor was covered with moving figures in gay costumes, reviewed by Boston and her suburbs. The "Spirit of America," a gauze-clad figure with waving arms, was, perhaps, the quintessence of symbolism; but just what idea she was intended to illustrate, a large proportion of the spectators could not easily have told, had they lost their programs. There is a danger in being too subtle before an assembly not carefully chosen — many of whom were more interested in John and Mary than in the Disease Germs or Dust Clouds they were supposed to represent; and this danger was not avoided in *From Cave Life to City Life.*

The failure — if failure there were — to arouse a civic pride and a desire for civic betterment, is easily accounted for. Many groups from Boston and its suburbs were herded together in this affair; but when a community has a population of a million and a half, it is impossible to arouse in each individual a keen interest in, and a sense of responsibility for, the pageant; and this feeling is necessary for the complete success of a modern civic pageant. Mr. Parker maintains that pageantry should be limited to the smaller communities; when it is transported to the metropolis it becomes a kind of "festival" or "group-pageant," even if the subject-matter is of general civic interest.

Another reason for the weakening of the civic appeal — if, indeed, it were weakened — is that the great moments of Boston's history and the great men of Boston's past were not reproduced. Instead, were typical scenes, which might — in most cases — have happened anywhere in New England; and personified abstractions,[1] which surely belong to no one place. Undoubtedly more civic spirit was aroused by this Boston pageant among the performers than among the spectators — and it would be hard to prove that none was awakened in those who witnessed this pageant. Here is a matter which only time can settle; and no one in America should condemn even an abortive attempt to foster this needful, and all too rare, desire to improve our civic conditions.

Assuming that civic betterment did not result from this pageant, and that it gave birth to no tightening of community ties, can we deny it a right to the name? What is the *sine qua non* of pageantry? Is there one? These questions we must try to answer later; here it is enough to point out that although the distinction made between "pageant" and "festival" is arbitrary, this is an example of the kind of thing that is between the two. The group that gave it was not "exclusive" — many associations, historical, religious, and educational, united;[2] but it is hard to get a group that is "inclusive" in any large city. Technically, this drew much from the masque; and the amount of allegory,

---

[1] With the "futuristic" pageant we shall deal later. Here I wish merely to point out that there is not the inspiration in a dancing figure called "Dust Cloud" that there is, for instance, in the representation of General Washington.

[2] The Indians were a professional *troupe* of real Indian actors.

characteristic of many American pageants, tends — as we shall see — to relate them to the morality-play.

THE PAGEANTS OF LAWRENCE AND TAUNTON, 1911

" The Lawrence *Pageant of Progress* was modelled on the *Pageant of Education*," writes Mrs. Dallin, the author of the pageant.[1] " It was a great deal bigger in conception. Its central figure was Lawrence, represented as an Industrial City. Her attendants were the Civic Virtues; and the history of the city and its activities was symbolically represented. Thus there was a dance of river maidens and foam sprites; and other elements connected with Lawrence were introduced.

" Then followed by means of various groups — symbolic and picturesque — the story of the progress of the world, industrially, educationally, etc., giving especial prominence to industrial progress, because the city of Lawrence is an industrial city . . ."

This seems to have been a pageant dealing with history rather through symbolism than in terms of historical characters. More historical — and yet with a good deal of symbolism and allegory — is the Taunton (Massachusetts) Pageant of July, 1911.[2] This was entitled *A Pageant of American History — a Living Lesson in Patriotism;* it opened with Father Time and dancing fairies; the first episode presented " American Indians at home," and " the Landing of Columbus." Episode ii showed Cavaliers and Puritans in Taunton, England; then came an interlude — the " Dance of the Waves " — which recalls the Boston Civic Pageant of 1910;[3] after which a second scene showed the beginnings of Taunton in New England. The first scene of episode iii took us to the Court of George III; but the second brought us back to Taunton Green on the eve of the Revolution. An interlude (" the Devil and the New England Conscience " — the latter of whom was, it will be recalled, a character in the Boston Civic Pageant) introduced the last episode — scene i, the return of the soldiers at the end of the

---

[1] In a letter dated 3 August, 1912. I have not seen the program of this pageant, which was given in 1911. The *Pageant of Education*, to which she refers, was that given in 1908 at the Boston Normal School; this we shall consider later — see below, p. 281 f.

Am. Pag. Assoc., *Bulletin 22*, 15 July, 1915, records the pageants produced in America during 1911. That of Lawrence is characterized as " a pageant dealing more particularly with educational and industrial progress, with most of the participants chosen from the higher school grades. In form it differed from the ordinary pageant in that it opened with a processional [*sic*] disclosing all the pageant groups, and in that the episodes were not of a local historical character."

[2] The program of this pageant is in the Harvard Library, bound as an appendix to chapter ix in the second volume of my MS. thesis. Various illustrations of the pageant are in Davol, pp. 10, 62, 76, 101, 131, 168, and 185. Cf. also, for a short characterization, Am. Pag. Assoc., *Bulletin 22*, 15 July, 1915.

[3] Cf. above, p. 266. It will be noted that the unity of place is not kept.

Civil War, with the "Prophecy of the New America"; scene 2, folk-dances by local nationalities — French-Canadians, Irish, Scotch, Italians, Portuguese, and "Polanders." The final dance — the "Spirit of America" — recalls the Boston Civic Pageant again.

We may note the "futuristic" quality of this pageant, as well as the latitude in history which the author allowed himself. Neither Columbus nor George III had much to do with Taunton directly.[1] If the pageant failed to awaken as much community-spirit as it would have done if all the scenes had been taken from purely local history, yet surely such a pageant, given on the national holiday, must have aroused a sense of patriotism which undoubtedly bore fruit.[2]

The Pageants of Thetford (1911) and St. Johnsbury (1912)

As other examples of pageants which are both historical and symbolical, we may mention those which Mr. W. C. Langdon produced at Thetford and St. Johnsbury in Vermont.[3] In both, the histories of the towns make up the main part; and both contain, in addition, symbolical characters.

The pageant of Thetford, which was given in August, 1911, opened with "a dramatic dance symbolic of the three nature-elements of Thetford — the mountains, the river, and the intervale." Mingled with these three Spirits, Indian braves and squaws danced until the White Man arrived. Historical episodes — some of which contained dialogue, and others of which were pantomimic — followed; and the pageant was brought to an end by the Spirit of Thetford, the Spirit of Pageantry, America, Vermont, and the neighboring States.

"The Power of the Wilderness" — a figure which recalls the early "wild-man," and the Sylvanus of Elizabethan entertainments — opened the St. Johnsbury Pageant.[4] The Spirits of Mountains, Forests, Rivers, and Valleys joined him, and the group was put to flight by the Spirit of Civilization. Dialogue and pantomime — rather more of the former than at Thetford, I think — were used in the historical scenes which followed; and, at the end, America, Vermont, and the surrounding States appeared again. But instead of a personification of St. Johnsbury, we have the figures of St. John de Crèvecœur and the Knight of St. Johnsbury, with his train of the Knights of St. John.[5]

---

[1] Undoubtedly, the fact that the pageant was given on 4 July, was responsible for the inclusion of much American history which had little local significance.

[2] There is nothing in the program to tell us what part speech played in the pageant, which contained a considerable amount of dancing.

[3] The *Books* of both are in the Harvard Library.

[4] This took place in August, 1912. I may note that a picture illustrating the Thetford Pageant is in Davol, p. 210, and that illustrations of the St. Johnsbury Pageant may be found, *ibid.*, pp. 150, 186.

[5] Which represented the various towns of Caledonia County and of the Passumpsic River and upper river valley. Two squires on foot represented the two villages of St. Johnsbury Centre and East St. Johnsbury.

Both of these pageants may be termed "futuristic," in that they view the past with an eye on the present, and the present in a hopeful mood. Mr. Langdon tells me that he has tried to show the people not only what they have, but how to use it; and at Thetford the pageant committee is still in existence — the centre of much effort for local improvement.

The Pageant of Keene, 1913

Living-pictures, pantomime, and speech were all used in the historical pageant which was given in the City Hall of Keene (New Hampshire) in February, 1913,[1] under the auspices of Ashuelot Chapter, D.A.R. A hundred and fifty performers took part, including a number of school children.[2]

After the overture and a "processional" by the school children, "the Indians in the Forest" — "which . . . gave an excellent and necessary picture of the wilderness to which the first settlers came" — was followed by a dance, "The Spirit of the forest, heralding the pioneer."[3] Various historical scenes, called "acts," followed; they were separated from each other by musical selections more or less appropriate. "Act 8" — which preceded that showing the departure of the first regiment for the Civil War, and followed the *tableau* entitled "The Minute Man" — was an "allegorical picture" representing Keene and her industries. "Keene, seated in a graceful chariot, was splendidly personified . . . and the dances of the Elements . . . were of rare beauty and excellence and all of them typical to a marked degree. The costumes of the dancers were a splendid feature . . . The dancers, each typical of the impersonation sought, were the embodiment of grace, beauty and skill . . .[4]

"A recessional or march around the hall by all the characters of the evening . . . came next, after which all who had taken part reassembled on the stage and were grouped for a final tableau of unusual scope and detail because of the

---

[1] I am indebted to Professor Rudolph Altrocchi of the University of Chicago for a copy of the Keene *Evening Sentinel* of Friday, 21 February, 1913, where a full account of the pageant is printed.

[2] "The historian, Rev. J. L. Seward, D.D., who selected and wrote out a historic story from which pictures of notable events in the history of the town, from its beginning, could be pictured, did his part well. The director, Mrs. Robert P. Hayward, . . . the stage manager, Mr. Fred E. Howe, and several who assisted him, were particularly efficient . . ." Keene *Evening Sentinel*, *loc. cit.*

[3] "The allegorical and historic scenes which follow," says the program printed in the *Evening Sentinel*, "were announced and explained, in several instances with brief quotations from early records, by the prolocutor, Mrs. W. H. Prentiss."

[4] The figures were: Keene, Water Power, Monadnock, Fire, Agriculture, Fur, and Pine. To quote the program: "In this scene Keene and her attendants formed the central group, while the industries of Keene, personified by six graceful dancers typifying the elements of her productions, in turn enter, dance around the stage and present to Keene the elements which they represent."

large number [of] the impersonators of the scenes of the evening entering into it. The Goddess of Liberty . . . was the central figure, standing on a high pedestal in the rear . . . As the curtain went up, the orchestra and children struck up 'The Star-Spangled Banner,' the audience rising, and joining in the chorus." [1]

Allegory, history, symbolism, dancing, and *tableau* all contributed their share to this pageant.

"An Dhord Fhiann" in New York, 1913

As an example of an historical pageant which interests a part of the community only — not merely because it was given in a metropolis, but also because it does not deal with the history of the place — let us note the Irish Historic Pageant, entitled *An Dhord Fhiann*, which was produced under the auspices of the American Committee of the Gaelic League of Ireland in New York on 7 and 8 May, 1913.[2] The matter treated is Irish history from the Feis at Tara (mid-third century) to the Convention of Dromceatt (at the end of the sixth century); there is little symbolism, and though the history may be considered legendary, the pageant is historical. It is interesting to note that the history deals in no way with New York; its limited appeal makes this production as much a "festival" as is *The Masque of Learning* or the Boston Normal School pageant; at best, this is on the line between pageant and festival despite its historical material.

The Hollis Hall Pageant of 1913

Another pageant, historical in material, but with an appeal to a comparatively small body of the community — even of the Harvard community — is the Hollis Hall Pageant which was given, under the direction of Professor George P. Baker, on 14 June, 1913,[3] to celebrate the hundred and fiftieth anniversary of the Harvard dormitory. The subject-matter dealt with the history of the hall, rather than of the college; a small proportion of the undergraduates took part in the pageant — though the opportunity to do so was shared by all; but the number of participants was not confined to those rooming in Hollis itself. The University community did not feel a personal interest in, or responsibility for, the success of the pageant, which was produced primarily for Hollis men — past and present; but many of the college public witnessed the performance.[4]

This stands on the line between "festival" and a pageant dealing with the history of a community. Technically it was the latter; as regards the spirit of its production it belongs rather to the "festival." Harvard history crept into the pageant; but the chief emphasis was on Hollis history.

---

[1] *Evening Sentinel*, as cited.

[2] The program is in HCL. This pageant was by Anna T. Craig.

[3] The program of this pageant is in the Harvard Library.

[4] Cf. with this, the Charterhouse tercentenary, of 8 July, 1911 (mentioned above, p. 227). The celebration included a "masque" — which was, like this one, rather a pageant or festival.

One unusual feature deserves to be mentioned: it was given by men primarily for men (though women were allowed to witness it). No female character appeared — allegory, symbolism, and history were all expressed by masculine characters, who told the story of the college dormitory, and what the life there has meant to generations of college men, to a college audience.

The St. Louis Pageant of 1914

In the Pageant and Masque which were given at St. Louis in May, 1914, we find allegory and history separated.[1] The pageant began " with an imaginary realistic scene in the life of the Mound-Builders " and carried continuously " the actual local history down to the Doniphan expedition;[2] while the masque was a wholly independent poetical and symbolical drama designed to show the inner significance of the existence of the city and its humanity, in their broadest cosmic relations, and to indicate its destiny and the quality of its influence in the future. The pageant began in the daylight and concluded in the evening dusk with some assistance from the very remarkable and effective electric lighting system employed, while the masque, beginning after dark, was wholly dependent upon artificial light, through which effects of the most beautiful and striking character were obtained."[3]

As there was no " exclusiveness " in cast or audience, and as dancing seems to have played almost no part in this " masque " of Mr. MacKaye's, one may feel that, strictly speaking, it has no right to the name, the use of which tends to confuse. Rather than a masque, it is a poetical " morality-play " or " allegorical drama "; and this production is particularly noteworthy in that it shows a tendency to keep apart the two elements of the American pageant, which often is — as we shall point out[4] — a combination of chronicle-history and morality-play.

---

[1] On this, see *The Book of Words of the Pageant and Masque of Saint Louis. The Words of the Pageant by Thomas Wood Stevens; the words of the Masque by Percy MacKaye.* (St. Louis, 1914); also Arthur Farwell, *The Pageant and Masque of St. Louis; a People's Drama on a National Scale* (illustrated), in the American *Review of Reviews* for August, 1914, pp. 187–193; scenes from the masque are illustrated in Davol, pp. 15 and 39.

[2] There were three " movements " or episodes; — a Prophet separated the first and second, and a Watchman, the second and third — like members of a " chorus." The " Pierre Chouteau," who figured in the second episode of the pageant — which included the landing of Laclede — was the Pierre Chouteau, who — the last survivor of Laclede's party — rode in the pageantic procession at St. Louis in 1847. (See above, p. 237, n. 3.)

[3] Farwell, article cited, p. 190. It may be mentioned that a knight chosen by *St. Louis* overcomes *Gold* in a tournament (see *Book of the Words,* pp. 93 f.). We find here much the same union of allegory and tournament as in 1581, when the Foster-Children of Desire assaulted the Queen's heart; but then, allegory was approached through the tournament, while in this " masque," the tournament is approached through allegory.

[4] See below, p. 291.

THE YALE PAGEANT OF 1916

The Yale Pageant of 1916 is noteworthy as being perhaps the most important American pageant in which an institution was joined by the larger community surrounding it, to produce that which, but for such collaboration, must have been — technically, at all events — a "festival." The occasion was the two hundredth anniversary of the removal of the College to New Haven from Saybrook, where Yale had been founded in 1701; the history reproduced was chiefly Yalensian, though the city figured in "The Founding of New Haven," the "Kansas Volunteers," and in various other episodes, such as the Governor's Foot Guard of 1775, and the Town and Gown Riots of the early nineteenth century, where citizens and collegians fought with and against each other.[1]

---

[1] See the *Book of the Yale Pageant*, edited by George H. Nettleton. This contains the episodes of the pageant (each of which was by a different author) and numerous essays on Yale achievement. Mr. F. H. Markoe, a Yale graduate, was the master of the pageant.

An outline of the pageant shows the relation of history and symbolism — the latter being chiefly confined to the "interludes."

Prelude. The scene is laid in Wales, and shows the wedding of Margaret ap Ienkyn (grandmother of John Yale, the founder of the family) in 1485.

First, or Colonial, Episode.
- Scene i. The Founding of New Haven.
- Scene ii. The Founding of the College.
- Scene iii. The Removal of the Books from Saybrook.
- Scene iv. The First Commencement at New Haven.

First Interlude.

The Passing of the Arts and Sciences from the Old World to the New.

Second, or Revolutionary, Episode.
- Scene i. The Demanding of the Keys to the Powder House, and the March to Cambridge, 1775.
- Scene ii. The British Invasion of New Haven in 1779.
- Scene iii. The Martyrdom of Nathan Hale.
- Scene iv. President Washington's Visit to New Haven in 1789.

Second Interlude.
- An allegory of War and Peace.

Third, or Early Nineteenth Century, Episode.
- Scene i. Town and Gown Riot.
- Scene ii. The Burial of Euclid.
- Scene iii. The Kansas Volunteers.
- Scene iv. The Death of Theodore Winthrop.

Third Interlude.
- The Wooden Spoon Prom.

Fourth, or Modern, Episode.
- Scene i. Panels of Modern Yale.
- Scene ii. The Yale Bicentennial.
- Scene iii. The Yale Battery.

Finale. Yale, the Mother of Colleges and Men.

SCENES FROM THE PAGEANT OF BLOOMINGTON AND INDIANA UNIVERSITY — 1916

[An example of the pageant in which, as in the Yale Pageant, the past of an educational institution is combined with that of the community in which it is situated, and of which it is a part. The two men kneeling at the altar (in the lower picture) are the Governor of the State and the President of the University; it is not uncommon to find city and state officials taking part in pageants.]

Yale, like many another institution of learning, is in spirit a community: and it is often difficult to separate such a community from the larger one about it. The pageant was produced in the Yale Bowl, but all the scenes were not laid in New Haven: the Prelude, for instance, took place in Wales; "The Founding of the College," at Branford; "The Removal of the Books," at Saybrook, the early seat of the College; the execution of Nathan Hale (Yale, 1773) at New York.

The fourteen "panels," with which the fourth episode opens, are *tableaux vivants;* [1] and the mock-funeral of Euclid is an academic parallel to the earlier Pope-burnings. Such pageantry as this student-ceremony included, between the late eighteen-twenties and 1860, was reproduced in the second scene of the third episode of this pageant — recalling the mediæval pageant-car which reappeared in the York Pageant of 1909.

The first two interludes are allegorical: the third reproduces a "prom of bygone days, when ladies built a yard around themselves, and gentlemen wore tight trousers of incredible length." [2] It is worthy of note that the performers of the Civil War scene — "The Death of Theodore Winthrop" — were veterans. "These are no dressed-up mummers, but the very men themselves: Grand Army men, some two hundred of them; their old blue uniforms hanging loose over shrunken shoulders — and their rusty old Springfields at the carry . . . And then something happens. For ten minutes those two hundred or so old gentlemen of our fathers' time have been going through what for them was not play-acting but the very truth itself. For ten minutes they have stood there remembering; and their memory reaches out and strikes the watching multitude like an invisible wave. As the long column plods toward the stands, the grim gray heads held high and the thin fife piping a cracked hymn tune, thirty thousand people are on their feet and uncovered, not knowing why or how; and the applause rises and swells and crackles into one deep roar! Someone whispers: 'God! look at their faces!' And we look, and read things written there. These men did not keep us out of war. They faced it, and brought us through on the right side. They were too proud to fight with words alone. They fought with more than words; and the fire of things we cannot understand shines on their steady faces. In all the Pageant there has been nothing like this; for the rest was allegory and reminiscence; but this is resurrection." [3]

The final *tableau*, for which Mr. Lawrason Riggs wrote verse far above the commonplace, included a "symbolic float of the University (occupied by Repre-

---

[1] They were evidently not produced for lack of time; see Brian Hooker's account of the pageant, p. 14.

[2] Brian Hooker's description of the Pageant, in the (illustrated) supplement to the *Yale Alumni Weekly* of 27 October, 1916, gives a full account of every episode. This one is pictured on the cover.

[3] Hooker, *loc. cit.*, pp. 11 f.

sentatives of the three Official Departments . . .) "[1] on which "Mother Yale" was the chief figure. This combination of the older and newer pageantry is not often seen. "Then into the Bowl pours in procession of multitudinous movement and color the whole Pageant at once: all places and times together, spirit and substance, hero and jester, history and tradition and dream . . ."[2]

An International Pageant

Closely allied to the "community pageant" in spirit — although the community in question includes the English-speaking nations — is the celebration of the three-hundredth anniversary of the voyage of the *Mayflower*, scheduled for the summer of 1920. We have noted international features in the Lord Mayor's Show, and international participation in at least one Parkerian pageant;[3] but hitherto there has been no "international pageant." The one planned for 1920 will begin in England, and the *Mayflower* will repeat her trip across the Atlantic. The celebration will be continued at Provincetown and Plymouth; and — if the plans are carried out — the observance of the anniversary will include "all English-speaking peoples," the Colonies joining the United States and the mother-country in honoring the Pilgrims.

An account of the proposed plans from the New York *Times* will give some idea of the scale on which the occasion will be celebrated:

A nation-wide celebration commemorating the landing of the Pilgrims three hundred years ago will mark the present year. But, indicating its deeper importance, is the fact that the United States alone will not celebrate this important event in her early history. All English-speaking peoples will participate, in official, institutional and community exercises, and Great Britain, Canada, and Australia will take part in commemorating what the Pilgrims stood for.

Beginning with the 1st of May in England, according to the plans of the Sulgrave Institution, the activities will commence later at the old port of Leyden, Holland, and then in the United States. Again the Mayflower will sail from England, following the route of the Pilgrims of old, touching at Leyden and next at Provincetown, Mass., which, in August, will be the scene of celebrations. Later Plymouth, Mass., will hold the centre of the stage.

It is expected that the events marking this tercentenary will be distributed throughout all parts of the United States, and will touch all sections and classes of people, from highest officialdom down to little private groups of people, social clubs, embracing in that downward sweep institutions, schools, organizations, and societies.

Boy Scouts and Girl Scouts will naturally make a rush for the Indian drama, Indian games and dances with native songs. Schools and colleges will devote themselves to impressive pageants. . . .

Celebrations in England are being arranged by the Sulgrave Institution, which takes its name from the ancient seat of the Washington family, Sulgrave Manor, North Hants, England. At this manor a special celebration will mark the Tercentenary. The English committee includes the Archbishop of Canterbury, Viscount Bryce, Viscount Grey, David Lloyd George, Cardinal Bourne and the Lord Mayor of London.

---

[1] Illustrated in the *Yale Alumni Weekly*, before referred to, p. 20.

[2] Hooker, *loc. cit.*, p. 14.

[3] Cf. above, p. 205.

John A. Stewart is chairman of the New York Board of Governors,which includes, among others, Brand Whitlock, James M. Beck and Charles W. Eliot. The Advisory Committee includes J. P. Morgan, Samuel Gompers, the Rev. Dr. William T. Manning, Cardinal Gibbons, Gen. John J. Pershing, Major Gen. Leonard Wood, Franklin K. Lane, and William Howard Taft.

The plan is a vast one, and in order to achieve good results patriotic and dramatic societies, organizations and institutions everywhere will have to start ahead of time, and put forth serious effort. Community Service officials have already done some work in this connection, and through the department of pageantry and dramatics, they plan to offer still further assistance to communities undertaking celebrations . . . .[1]

Having examined various kinds of "community-drama," and seen how it is capable of variation from the norm of the Parkerian work, let us, before we conclude this section, take note of some pageants which are not successful.

"From Kingdom to Colony" at Marblehead in 1912

From Kingdom to Colony was presented at Marblehead (Massachusetts) 6 and 7 August, 1912; it was given "for the benefit of the Marblehead Historical Society."[2] This, though breaking one of Mr. Parker's cardinal rules — that a pageant should never be given to make money — is not enough to take it from the field of pageantry.

The Prologue opens with the arrival of John and Anne Devereux[3] from Berwick Castle, England. Scene i (1649) is laid in the camp of the Naumkeag Indians, near Forest River. Characteristic Indian dances introduce the "drama," which begins with scene ii, at the house of John Devereux. Part ii consists of a "Ribbon Ballet"; and so the Prologue ends.

Part iii begins with "Act 1: time 1774." The first scene shows "The Beginning of the Revolutionary War. Home of Joseph Devereux. Miss Helen True will sing 'Flow Gently, Sweet Afton,' and 'The Last Rose of Summer.'"[4] After the cast of characters comes the announcement that "Mrs. R. M. Cook as 'The Spirit of the Night,' will sing 'The Fairy Lake.' (By courtesy of White, Smith Co., Publishers.)."

Part iv is "The Old Time Darky Jubilee"; Part v: "Act II. Scene 1. Dorothy's visit to Nurse Lecrow's cottage. Scene 2. Meeting of Dorothy and Cornet Southorn in the woods." Part vi consists of the Dance of the Seven Star Sisters,[5] and with Part vii we return to the play: "Act III. Scene 1. Home of Mistress Horton. Wedding of Mary Broughton and

---

[1] New York *Times*, Sunday, 7 March, 1920, (editorial section, p. 4). Professor George P. Baker, of Harvard University, has been commissioned to write the book on which the Pilgrim Tercentenary Pageant will be based. (*Harvard Alumni Bulletin* for 26 February, 1920, p. 499.) This pageant will be given at Plymouth in 1921. (This is not the celebration planned for the summer of 1920, which commemorates rather the voyage of the *Mayflower*, and the coming of the Pilgrims, than the settlement of Plymouth.)

[2] My authority for the following remarks is the program of the "pageant" which is in the Harvard Library: "The Historical Pageant and Drama 'From Kingdom to Colony.' Book by Mary Devereux; dramatized by Mrs. Marie J. Morgan; produced by George Lowell Tracy."

[3] Qy.: ancestors of the authoress of the book?

[4] Cf. below, p. 280.

[5] Allegory or symbolism suggesting vaudeville...

Jack Devereux. Dancing of Minuet . . . Scene 2. Abduction of Dorothy by Southorn. Marriage of Dorothy to Southorn by strategy. Scene 3. Arrest of Southorn as English Spy at Grey Horse Inn (just inside the American Lines). Scene 4. Arrival of Dorothy and Mary at Grey Horse Inn. Dorothy pleads with Gen. Washington for Southorn's life. Scene 5. Dorothy and Southorn's departure for England.

Part viii. Flower Festival and Maypole Dance.[1] The Marriage of Cornet Southorn and Dorothy. General Washington and his Staff. The Floats. "Yankee Doodle," "Signing the Declaration of Independence," "The Thirteen Original States."

"The chorus will sing 'Ode on Science,' 'Revolutionary Tea,' 'The Ship of State,' . . . and 'Hail Columbia.'"

This "pageant" has, apparently, several different elements.[2] Dancing plays a considerable part in it,[3] as does music. A thread of connected story seems to run through the performance, in spite of numerous interruptions (without which it would be considered a melodramatic "costume-play"[4]) telling the story of a group of figures. At all events, the place is not the hero;[5] it is not clear from the program just what part Marblehead plays in all this; it seems rather to be a pageant of the Devereux family! There is a certain amount of — can one say fantasy? — in the persons of "The Spirit of Night" and the "Seven Star Sisters"; they seem to have no connection with what has gone before or what comes after. There is symbolism, or personification, in the Thirteen States; and history in the Declaration of Independence. These are surely pageantic, and it is, perhaps, with these in mind that the authors added *pageant* to the *drama* of their title.[6]

As we have already seen in the case of Taunton, the history in a pageant need not be a part of the actual town history, so long as the town is affected by it.[7] This is clear enough in those scenes which deal with the departure of the colonists before the town was founded — examples of which are seen in the Pageants of

---

[1] Here, as during the Minuet, the chorus sang.

[2] It is always difficult to judge a performance of this kind from the program.

[3] Cf. *e. g.* Parts ii, iv, vi, and viii.

[4] Which appears to be the dramatization of an historical novel. Surely pageant and drama are growing close together!

[5] Cf. below, p. 291.

[6] I should, perhaps, add that the program does not state how much of the "drama" was pantomime — if any was. The program is disfigured with advertisements — a necessary accompaniment of the commercial spirit which "benefits" usually have.

As Norristown gave history in a procession, so here we find elements of the carnival on the stage. The program does not state whether this performance took place indoors or out; but that makes no difference as far as we are concerned. Plenty of pageants have been given under roofs — cf., *e.g.*, that of Marietta in 1888 and that of Keene in 1913.

[7] The tie between the history portrayed and the place of its portrayal is almost too slight in the case of the Irish Pageant at New York to give the performance the right to the name of pageant. Yet the material thereof is history; and as the scenes given extended over three centuries, one cannot well call the production a "chronicle-play."

Peterborough, and Lancaster (Massachusetts). This seems to be an American development; in England pageant-masters confine themselves more closely to scenes which took place in the town itself.[1]

If the historian may become critic, he must maintain that this "pageant," *From Kingdom to Colony*, is not a pageant in the strict sense of the word, because it does not deal with Marblehead history first and foremost; because the historical characters introduced are subordinated to fiction; because the "interludes" are interruptions which tend to destroy the unity of the work.[2] Criticisms have been made regarding anachronisms and other inaccuracies in the costuming and production of this affair; we have noted the importance of accuracy in historical pageants, in order to keep the confidence of the audience, and the educational value of these productions.

"How Not to Do It"

"An approach to the ideal pageant was given in a humble way at Warwick, Massachusetts, (1912). To celebrate the 150th anniversary the town appropriated ten dollars; the townspeople did the rest and returned two dollars to the treasury."[3] The "ideal" conditions of which Mr. Davol speaks seem to be confined to the financial, and perhaps the æsthetic, side — the educational left much to be desired.

"Funeral Honors for General Washington before the Continental Troops" furnished a scene in the Pageant of Oxford (Massachusetts);[4] and one wonders when any town in the State received the body of the late President. Such inaccuracies as these are common enough in American pageants, which are nevertheless hailed as a great educational force. While some undoubtedly are educational, it must be confessed that many more have that aim; too often, however, well-meaning but busy school-teachers or church-workers plan shows like that described in the opening chapters of Booth Tarkington's *Penrod*, which do more harm than good.

In this connection, we may note a letter by Mr. J. C. L. Clark, dated at Lancaster (Massachusetts) on 7 September, and printed in the Boston *Herald* for 12 September, 1912:

From press notices I learn that the coming historical pageant at Warwick, Massachusetts, is to include a scene entitled "The naming of Mount Grace." This episode is to represent

---

[1] Though some, as has been shown, allow themselves more latitude in this matter.

[2] Were the Devereux characters historically important in early Marblehead, the above criticism of the "pageant" would still hold, because they are not shown in connection with the development of the town. The pageant-writer ought not to produce an episode dealing with the private affairs of any historical personage he may wish to represent. This should be fairly obvious.

[3] Davol, pp. 37 f. A scene from the pageant is given, *ibid.*, p. 89.

[4] Illustrated in Davol. p, 120.

"the burial of Grace Rowlandson, who, with her mother, has been captured by the Indians. The child dies on the march and is carried for two days in her mother's arms," etc. In view of the publicity of the matter, will you allow me to point out that this derivation of the name "Mount Grace," and, indeed, the whole incident so far as Warwick is concerned, is so utterly baseless that it is hard to see how such a belief originated? It is true that when Mrs. Rowlandson was taken captive at Lancaster, February 10, 1676, she carried in her arms her little daughter, a child of six, who had been wounded in the fighting. The child's name was not Grace, but Sarah. It is also true that eight days later, February 18, the child died. But this occurred while the Indians and their prisoners were camped at Menameset, or Wenimesset, as Mrs. Rowlandson calls it. This "Wenimesset" was a stronghold of the savages in what is now the town of New Braintree. Far from being permitted to carry away the body of her child, the distracted mother in her wonderfully vivid and pathetic "Narrative" — the sole authority for the details of her captivity — tells of its burial near the spot where it died: "I went to take up my dead child in my arms to carry it with me, but they bid me let it alone; there was no resisting, but go I must and leave it. When I had been at my master's wigwam, I took the first opportunity I could get, to go look after my dead child; when I came I askt them what they had done with it? Then they told me it was upon the hill; then they went and shewed me where it was, where I saw the ground was newly digged, and there they told me they had buried it." It was more than a fortnight later, between March 3 and 5, that the party passed through the southwestern part of the present town of Warwick. In short, "Grace" Rowlandson never existed; she is simply an eponymous heroine, and as mythical as Romulus . . .

A correspondent of mine who has made a study of the whole subject of pageants and folk-festivals declared that a whole book might be written on how not to give pageants. Some instances of how not to do it occurred in a recent much-lauded spectacle, given under the dignified auspices of an historical society, in which a Puritan divine of (I believe) the year 1649 appeared in a stove-pipe hat, a negro house-servant of the Revolutionary period wore modern trousers and the duck jacket affected by barbers and bar-tenders of the present day, and a fair maiden sang "The Last Rose of Summer" in 1774, five years before Tom Moore, the author of that song, was born!

But bad as are anachronisms like these, the case is far worse when the imaginings of an "adventurer in historic disquisition," as H. S. Nourse scoffingly termed the inventor of the Mount Hope story, are actually made the basis of a dramatic representation before the eyes of the people. And this because a thing so presented takes on an added reality forever, and because the great value of popular pageantry is educational — the imparting of a knowledge of, and an enthusiasm for, the noble past of one's home region. If the promoters of the Warwick Pageant regard their responsibilities, this episode of "The Naming of Mt. Hope" will be dropped in toto from their program. One foresees in the near future a time when serious lovers of history may well sigh, O Pageantry, what crimes are committed in thy name!

One wonders sometimes if modern pageants in America are fostered in a spirit of true respect for history. Too often, it may be feared, the carnival spirit enters into them — a spirit, by the way, perfectly legitimate if it does not hide itself behind history, or behind an incompetent pageant-master who has not had Wolf's "scientific teaching,"[1] and is easily led from the path of accuracy. If

[1] "'I call all teaching *scientific*,' says Wolf, the critic of Homer, 'which is systematically laid out and followed up to its original sources . . .'" [cited by Arnold, in *Literature and Science* (*Discourses in America*, ii.)].

this tendency toward the presentation of pseudo-history continues, the "community drama" in America will cease to be an educational force; and no community can be tied together or inspired to progress and civic betterment by the production of a carnival.

Many pageant-masters hold that folk-lore material and local legends may be admitted as integral parts of a pageant. The figures of Gogmagog and Corineus, of Ebrauc and Bremmius and Gurgunt, show that this was the case in the past; but those who emphasize the importance of the educational appeal in pageantry maintain that what is real should be clearly separated from the legendary.

§ 3. THE "FESTIVAL"

Beside the community-drama, various forms of which we have mentioned, lies a vast body of so-called pageantry which does not occupy the community as a whole, and yet which is given under conditions more or less pageantic. To this has been given the name of "festival." The line between the two is sometimes hard to draw; although dealing with historical material, both the Irish Pageant of New York and the Hollis Hall Pageant at Harvard had, as we have seen, an element of restricted interest characteristic of the "festival." The celebration of the three-hundredth anniversary of the Charterhouse School, in 1911, furnishes — as we have pointed out — an English parallel to the pageant of Hollis Hall.[1]

Normal School Pageant at Boston, 1908

There is a kind of pageant which deals with the history of an art or science rather than of a community; one of the best — as well as the earliest — examples of this is the *Pageant of Education*, with which the State Normal School dedicated its new building at Boston in June, 1908. This was, in no sense, a civic or community affair, but rather the production of a limited circle; an English — or more strictly, a Scottish — parallel may be found in Professor Geddes's *Masque of Learning* which we have already discussed.[2]

---

[1] The Oxford Pageant of 1907 had a wider appeal; that at Oxford in 1914, was a "festival." (See above, pp. 203, n. 1, and 227.)

[2] See above, p. 226 f. For three illustrations, and mention, of this Boston festival, see Bates and Orr, *Pageants and Pageantry*, pp. 17, etc. A picture may also be found in Davol, p. 79.

Mrs. Dallin, the author of this festival, writes me that Mr. Percival Chubb was responsible for interesting the Twentieth Century Club of Boston in pageants, and through it, indirectly, the committee at the Normal School who were charged with providing some entertainment to present at the dedication of the new building.

"To complete this record, it might be stated that the Pageant of Education was actually undertaken before American pageantry began to be influenced by the English historical pag-

Mrs. Colonna Murray Dallin was entrusted with the task of planning " some sort of procession or *tableaux* suitable to present on such an occasion. My first thought," she writes,[1] " was to try to represent the fresco of ' Education ' by Puvis de Chavannes at the Sorbonne, and let the figures in it form a procession; but on examining the picture, that seemed, of course, impracticable without too great modifications of costume, etc. Then the idea came to me, as the air was full of echoes of English pageants, that the history of education might be presented in pageant form."

Technically, this festival had a processional element, for the characters in each episode marched across the improvised stage in the courtyard of the new building; the procession was broken by " interludes " — dances, rites, and choruses — the purpose of which was " not only to add rhythm, charm, and variety to the spectacle, but to mark by forcible contrasts the changes in ideals from era to era. They aim to suggest that education is development not only of the intellect but of the emotional nature and of the body." [2]

Historical characters, from Moses to Pestalozzi, represented the different epochs; such symbolical characters as Alma Mater and the Foreign and American Universities, joined allegorical figures — Knowledge, Inspiration, Truth, Science, History, Learning, Peace, Prosperity, and Happiness. The Vernacular, followed by Shakspere, Dante, Racine, Goethe, and Cervantes; the Classics,

---

eant — from which type this particular pageant radically differed." Am. Pag. Assoc., *Bulletin 22*, 15 July, 1915. Miss Lotta A. Clark was " Chairman of the Festival Committee," and Mrs. Dallin, " Designer of the Pageant," on this occasion. (*ibid*).

[1] In a letter, dated 3 August, 1912. She continued: " This idea was gradually worked out, and the process was very delightful. Naturally, in trying to give the broadest idea of educational development, the song, the dance, and the religious rite wove themselves into the scheme.

" Then, too, after once dividing the pageant into episodes, the interludes were needed to give contrasts and reliefs; and the songs, rites, and dances were found to express certain phases of life and thought more effectively than any other element that could be used in pageantry.

" I had never seen a pageant anywhere, so that the structure of the Normal School pageant was original, in a way." Mrs. Dallin attempted " to represent the development of an idea from its earliest expression through its manifold changes throughout the ages. This I tried," she continues, " to present in both the *Pageant of Education* at Boston, and the *Pageant of Progress*, presented at Lawrence."

Regarding symbolism, Mrs. Dallin says: " I was forced into this in the work on the *Pageant of Education*, because I was obliged to use women for members of various groups. For instance, instead of representing Scholasticism and Theology in the Middle Ages by representative schoolmen and theologians, I used symbolic figures . . ." It is interesting to note that symbolism and allegory grew spontaneously in Mrs. Dallin's pageants, though they are common enough in the earlier shows. It should be remarked, however, that a considerable number of men took part in the festival, and that historical figures appeared as well as the symbolical.

[2] Cited from the program of the " festival."

accompanied by Erasmus and Melancthon; the Seven Liberal Arts,[1] adapted from the frescoes of Simon Memmi in the Spanish Chapel of Santa Maria; Scholasticism, Theology, Romance, Poetry, and Music appeared. There were also types, such as the Dame-school teacher; Knight, Lady, and Page, representing Chivalry; and troubadours, representing Minstrelsy. One symbolical group consisted of wood-nymphs, whose dance — based on regular kindergarten games — was meant to suggest the transition from autumn to spring — a school year.

Other Pageants of Limited Appeal

This suggests, both in spirit and technique, the masque, rather than the pageant. Dancing occupied a large part of the attention of the audience; and the festival was given by a limited group. A similar entertainment — Mr. Thomas Wood Stevens's *Pageant of the Italian Renaissance*, which took place at Chicago, 26 and 27 January, 1909 — may be noted as another example of a group which soon became numerous. This " festival " has been characterized as " an unusual pageant, performed by the art students in Statuary Hall of the Art Museum; and although localized to the backgrounds of Italian architecture there provided, it nevertheless clearly displayed community development. It is one of the finest pieces of pageant writing yet accomplished in America or England, and is perhaps the first of a type that might be termed ' Epic Pageants ' — although so far as it dealt with periods of civilization or culture, it became related to the *Pageant of Education*, of which — because of this added epic quality — it was a more literary development." [2]

The *Cayuga Indian Feast*, given on the north shore of Beebe Lake " at sunset in the time of Strawberries, May 27, 1914," seems to have been a festival; indeed, in the descriptive pamphlet [3] it shares the name with that of *pageant*. Various manners and customs of the Indians were illustrated; the action was in pantomime; and while the scenes were based on historical events (the spring of 1737 is the time chosen) the show is at best one episode in a larger pageant which was not given. What the relation of the performers to the community may have been, it is impossible to tell from the pamphlet.

The bulletins of the American Pageant Association contain mention of many of these " Pageants of Ideas," and it is not necessary here to dwell on them. Suffice it to say that, as they are usually given by a group in a community, rather than by the community as a whole, they fall into the class of " festivals."

Technically the " festival " is nearer the masque than the drama; it makes its appeal through the symbolical dance, rather than through the historical episode. This is, indeed, not unexpected; for as soon as we get drama, the symbol-

[1] Already found more than once in early " royal-entries " and the Lord Mayor's Show.

[2] American Pageant Association, *Bulletin 12*, 15 December, 1914.

[3] Which is preserved in the Harvard Library.

ism tends to fade, as it did from the morality-play, the more dramatic they became. As long as pageant-masters put an emphasis on allegory and symbolism, they are bound to see that the shows do not become so dramatic that these qualities are imperilled.

Such performances as the symbolical *Pageant of the Year* given by the students of the Brookline (Massachusetts) High School are reminiscent of Christina Rossetti's *Pageant of the Months* which we have already considered.

A somewhat similar production is described in the Boston *Herald*,[1] under the heading: "150 Women to Take Part in Cambridge Pageant — Y. W. C. A. to Give 'Festival of the Seasons' on Thursday Night — Spectacle will Resemble 'Caliban.'"

> A novelty, entitled "The Festival of the Seasons," is to be given by the Cambridge Young Women's Christian Association at the association grounds Thursday evening, which will resemble in some respects the famous "Caliban."
>
> Over 150 women will take part in the performance, most of them members of the association . . . The production starts with old Mother Earth sending out two babies, to typify life. Spring is the first episode, which starts with homage to Isis . . . Miss Ethel Vincent and Miss Ada Rahn represent the old year being banished. Then comes the awakening of Spring. The powers of the earth and sky are called upon to arouse the sleeping flowers. Thus the pageant starts, with singing, dancing, verse, and tableaux, one season making way for another. Youths and lassies, the May Queen, the villagers, the foresters, Maypole dancers, lords and ladies, Little Boy Blue, Mother Goose, and April Fool are represented in this first season.
>
> Summer brings the pantomime of the Sun Goddess, the Japanese dancers, the philosophers, the Sleeping Beauty, the Flowers and Bees, the Haymakers, and patriotic features. Autumn brings forth Grain and Fruit Bearers, Autumn Leaves, the Flight of the Birds, the Dance of the Winds, and the Whirlwind Pantomime. Winter has its Snow Flakes, its Skaters, Christmas with Santa Claus, Red Cross Demonstration, and Carol Singers . . .
>
> This affair will close the entertainment activities of the association for the season.

This, like the other shows we have just mentioned, is rather a masque than a true pageant; it includes many characters which we have seen at Lichfield and Knutsford, but these alone cannot bring it into pageantry. There is, apparently, enough unity to keep it from being a mere carnival; but it is given by a limited group in the community, and must have appealed to a limited audience.

The Women-Suffrage Masque at Washington, 3 March, 1913

What should have been called a "masque," given by a group in the community as propaganda for women-suffrage, took place on the steps of the Treasury Building at Washington on 3 March, 1913. The plan of this entertainment was announced as follows:[2]

---

[1] Boston *Herald* for Monday, 2 June, 1919, p. 6.

[2] I quote from the Boston *Transcript* of 6 February, 1913: an eye-witness of the event tells me that it is a very good account of what happened.

For illustrations of this masque, see Davol, pp. 29, and 61.

. . . The Show on the Treasury steps is technically an "allegory," while the rest of the demonstration is technically called the "pageant-procession." The story told in the procession itself will show the actualities of much that woman has struggled against and is still struggling to achieve, as well as what she has attained, while the ceremonies at the Treasury Building will symbolize the ideals toward which both men and women have been struggling . . .

The southern steps of the Treasury Building are a flight mounting some twenty or thirty feet and broken by a landing, easily fifty feet square, on which the evolutions of the characters in the *tableaux* will take place. Surmounting the steps are the lofty columns of the Treasury Building. The audience will be seated on stands erected on the little park about the Sherman statue just across the street from the steps. Between the audience and the steps the pageant will pass.

When the pageant starts, a mile or two away down Pennsylvania avenue, a trumpet will be sounded, and this note will be taken up at intervals along the line of march until it reaches the two trumpeters dressed in purple and gold who are stationed on the plaza of the Treasury Building. These trumpeters announce in a fanfare that the ceremonies are about to begin, and immediately, while the band plays *The Star-Spangled Banner*, the commanding figure of Columbia emerges from behind the shadows of the great columns. On each side of the great platforms which flank the steps an American flag is unfurled. Columbia slowly descends and takes a stand on the plaza below. The allegory then proceeds as described by Miss MacKaye, as follows:

Again the trumpets are sounded, and Columbia, turning toward the massive columns from which she has just emerged summons to her presence the first of her followers, Justice. Obeying this command Justice and her attendants appear in robes of purple and violet lightened by the faintest touch of blue. To the majestic strains of the *Pilgrims' Chorus* they formally descend and make their obeisance to Columbia.

Columbia then turns again and summons Charity. The serene and benignant strains of Händel's *Largo* announce her coming. Gently and nobly she descends the steps, preceded by two little children who strew her path with roses. Following her closely comes a group of youths and maidens in tender grays and blues, and, enfolding some of these in her simple mantle of deeper blue, Charity takes her place.

With the crashing of cymbals and brass in the *Triumph March* from *Aïda*, a flying figure in glowing crimson appears — Liberty — unfettered and free. She poises for an instant at the top of the steps and then, with swift running feet she sweeps on to the plaza below, beckoning her attendants to follow her. Thereupon a company of gay and brave young girls troop out from between the columns and with floating scarfs of crimson, rose, and gold, weave a glorious dance of joy and freedom.

This last tumultuous and breathless entrance is followed by a moment's silence, to be broken by the clear note of the horn — the only sound to intrude upon the stillness. Presently, to soft and tender strains of music, a serene and beautiful figure in white and silver appears bearing in her hands her emblem, the Dove of Peace. Halting at the head of the steps, she releases the bird and watches its flight as it mounts to the heavens. Then she descends — always to the strains of softest music — surrounded by another group of girls with golden cornucopia, laden with glowing fruits — Plenty follows Peace. And now it is Columbia who makes obeisance, and, with reverent gesture, welcomes this beneficent and longed-for follower to her place.

One more figure is still to come — Hope, bearing the promise of the future. Peering shyly from behind the columns, her gauzy veil falling between her and the world, a tender girl looks forth. With increasing courage she ventures out, only to disappear again and reappear, like a bright spirit. At last she boldly leaves her hiding place and springs lightly down the steps, followed by a group of laughing girls, in softest greens and rainbow colors. Together they chase and elude each other, and swing and sway until their dance is broken in upon by a joyous troop of children — Hope's dear reliance. Following her radiant figure the young girls weave the mazes of their dance, while the happy children toss their golden and iridescent balls, till they, too, join the others in the final *tableau* to greet the great procession, which with band and banner, sweeps by triumphant.

"A Pageant of Progress"

A Pageant of Progress, which celebrated the seventy-fifth anniversary of Mount Holyoke College, represented the liberal arts and sciences. Each department of the college produced a section of the show.[1] With some historical characters, there were many from fiction, and much personification — Radium, Helium, the Telegraph, Flora — and the emphasis was not primarily on history. Like the Hollis Hall Pageant, this was given by one sex;[2] but the material was not taken directly from the history of the college, and the technique was more closely related to that of the masque. Thus this falls under the head of "festival."

On the borderland we find many shows which resemble the pageantic festival somewhat, and yet, for one reason or another, are outside the pale. The revels at Merry Mount show the germ of pageantry which may be found in almost every folk-celebration; the tournament at Philadelphia during the Revolution,[3] together with the tournaments of the Southern States before the war,[4] reflect the same germ among a higher class. The Bohemian Club "Jinks," which began in 1878, are invented and performed by a limited circle for audiences restricted by privilege;[5] as Mr. Garnett says: "Although the drama and the opera were the progenitors of the Bohemian grove-play, in its ultimate form it bears a greater resemblance to the masque than to either . . . It may be safely said that no constructor of a midsummer high jinks, no writer of a grove-play, ever used a masque for his model. We find, therefore, in California, in the first years of the twentieth century, an independent occurrence of the masque type brought about by an entirely different set of conditions from those that produced the original examples of this *genre* nearly four hundred years earlier."[6]

---

[1] This occasion is described in an illustrated article by Elizabeth C. Porter in the *Outlook* for 23 November, 1912, pp. 653 f.

[2] A much larger proportion, however, of the undergraduate body took part in it, than was the case at Harvard.

[3] Illustrated on the cover of Davol's volume: for mention of this, see Davol, p. 31.

[4] For mention of these see T. H. Dickinson, *The Pageant* in the Wisconsin *Play-book* for September, 1914, p. 13. According to Professor Dickinson, that which took place near Baltimore in 1840 was directly due to the tournament at Eglinton, which we have already discussed (see above, p. 182 f.); one of the last of these tournaments was given at Front Royal (Virginia) in 1866.

[5] On the Bohemian Club "Jinks" see Porter Garnett's volume, *The Bohemian Jinks*, published by the Club at San Francisco, 1908; also the Am. Pag. Assoc. *Bulletin 8*, 15 October, 1914.

[6] Garnett, pp. 33, 34.

The Duquesne "Pageant" of 1911

When the Harvard architects welcomed, in April, 1911, Professor Duquesne who had come from the École des Beaux Arts to the chair of architectural design at the Massachusetts institution, they called their entertainment a "pageant." Given in the big living-room of the Harvard Union, before an audience of invited guests, the affair lacked the "popular" element which we have seen to be necessary to pageantry in its truer sense. While there was an attempt made to show the development of architecture by means of symbolic figures — such as the Spirits of Gothic, Renaissance, and Byzantine Architecture — the dance was at the heart of the entertainment, which was more exactly a masque with an interlude, and was more closely related to the revels of artists and students, which take place on both sides of the Atlantic, than to pageantry. There was no educational aim to this entertainment; the symbolism was appropriate, but neither the distinguished guest of honor nor the audience, made up largely of architects and professors, derived much information from the masque. This, in itself, is, perhaps, not enough to throw the entertainment out of the realm of pageantry; but the fact that it was given before an invited audience, by a limited number of students from one department of an institution of learning, and consisted largely of dancing, brings it into the field of the masque.

A performance wherein history and dance were almost inextricably mixed, and which combined a "Kirmess" with scenes at the Court of Spain, among American Indians, in Colonial Days, and before the Civil War, was given for the benefit of the Home for Incurables at Cincinnati in the Emery Auditorium, 16, 17, and 18 April, 1914.[1] This has little right to be called a pageant; it stands half way between the masque and the carnival, and is interesting only as an example of what often lays claim to the title of *pageant*.

An example of the "pageant of limited appeal" is that "depicting the celebration of Our Lady's Feast in Ireland, Italy, France, and America," which was presented at Æolian Hall, New York City, by a hundred members of the Young Women's Catholic Patriotic Club, on 16 May, 1919, in honor of the organization's first anniversary.[2] Not only is this a "pageant" based on religious material, but it apparently substituted distance in place for the distance in time characteristic of the episodes of the historical pageant. Both the subject-matter and the fact that it was presented by an association, membership in which is limited, put this production in the field of the so-called "festival."

---

[1] The souvenir program of this occasion may be found in the Harvard Library [*Thr. 1211.80*].

[2] An item announcing the event appeared in the New York *Times* for 16 May, 1919. The tickets were on public sale, but the entertainment did not affect the community life of the metropolis.

Masque and Pageant in America

As *masque* and *pageant* differ chiefly in spirit and technique, we find, in America, a confusion arising between the two as the difference in technique diminishes. The modern American pageant allows considerable dancing, and singing plays a large part in the entertainment; there are some who would exclude speech, and get all their effects from song and pantomimic action. The modern "pageant" (not of the processional type) is given in one place — either indoors or out; the masque admits allegory and symbolism, and there is no reason why it should exclude historical characters — provided, of course, that they are not out of place in a dance. The modern pageant is founded on history, and a certain amount of this element is necessary. Mr. Parker represents one school which insists on the spoken word, a maximum amount of history, with little symbolism and little dancing. In America, there is a tendency to replace speech by the "broader effects" of music and dancing; but music and dancing alone — even if symbolic, and "popular" — show the technique of the masque on which the spirit of pageantry has been imposed.

Although, broadly speaking, the "soul" of both is the same, yet the technique of the masque absorbs allegory and symbolism more readily, while the modern pageant — being dramatic — deals almost entirely with historical characters. It is clear why this must be so; for when we show an historical scene, we must use historical characters. Were we to replace the Puritan and Indian by Civilization and the Wilderness, the scene would cease to be historic and would be symbolic. History is, perhaps, the flesh that covers the bones of symbolism; but the pageant in its strict form deals with that flesh, and only suggests the bones that lie beneath.

The "Victory Pageant" which was given by the Rhode Island Normal School on 29 May, 1919, shows an interesting combination of pageantic material with the spirit and technique of the masque. It is really rather a patriotic festival than a pageant: for, like the Boston Normal School "pageant" of 1908, it appealed to a limited group in the community; it expressed itself rather by the dance than by the historical "episodes" characteristic of the Parkerian pageantry. The material had no particular connection with the school producing it — and was not appropriate to any special locality or field of activity — such as "education," which formed the background of the Boston Normal School festival. This is not, of course, saying that it could not have been a very effective spectacle. The "Synopsis of Scenes" gives a good idea of the matter treated, and one can see that it could be easily adapted to any other place or group.[1]

---

[1] The program of this "pageant" — from which I quote — is in the Harvard Library. The show was adapted from *The March of Democracy*, a masque for Victory Day celebrations, by Charles B. McLinn, in the *Historical Outlook* for January, 1919, pp. 29 f. The pageant "is not original, but is adapted, with new headings, from a play written for a western institution

After the March, and the Prologue, comes Part I, " Our Allies before the World-War," in which England, Russia, Italy, Belgium, Serbia, and France are represented by Folk-Dances.[1] — Part II, " Autocracy Dominant," shows a Herald preceding Autocracy, who drives before him frightened refugees: in his train follow War, Fire, Famine, Rapine, Terror, Death, and Greed. An " Interpretation of the Grief of the World " was given in a dance.

Part III — *America's Crusade for Democracy.* Soldiers and Sailors escort the States of the Union. *America enters with her train:* Humanity, Red Cross workers, Liberty, Food Supply, War Gardens, Mines, Miners, Liberty Loan, Liberty Bonds, War Savings Stamps. *America recalls her Past:* Roger Williams, The Spirit of '76, War of 1812, Civil War, Spanish-American War, Immigration. *America summons her Resources:* Food Supply and War Gardens, Mines and Miners, Liberty Loan, Liberty Bonds, and War Savings Stamps. *America Proclaims her Ideals:* Democracy, Truth, Light, Law, Justice, Equality, Fraternity, Freedom of Thought, Opportunity, Suffrage, International Faith, Peace.

Part IV — *Democracy Triumphant.* Victory. Chorus: "The Star-Spangled Banner." March.

The history here — with the exception of the Rhode Island figure of Roger Williams — is universally American: propaganda is not lacking (Suffrage) and would have been stronger had there been at the time, a campaign for Liberty Bonds or food conservation. The marches introduce and close a show in which dancing apparently plays a large part. The whole school was generally represented in the cast.

The more successful pageants in America keep the two elements separate; no scene can be wholly satisfactory when the two are mixed. And a pageant at its best should include the whole community; when fewer participate, the celebration, even if it deals with history, tends to become a " festival."

The " Pageant-Play "

The " pageant-play " — like the political pageantry of the Pope-burnings — is not likely to be local in its appeal; we have seen that the Pope was burned at London, at Edinburgh, and at Boston. In such a category would fall productions like Mr. Percy MacKaye's *Caliban,* which was less concerned with local history than with drawing a community together; it was produced in the Stadium of the City College of New York in 1916, and the next year, shortly after the United States had associated herself with the Allies in the Great War, was repeated in the Harvard Stadium, for the benefit of the American Red Cross and the Harvard R. O. T. C.[2] This, Mr. MacKaye called a " community masque,"

and published in an educational magazine . . ." From a letter written by Miss M. L. Brown of the Rhode Island Normal School.

[1] This scene is based on *The Drama of the Powers,* a " dialogue " by Douglas Horton, in the *Historical Outlook* for March, 1919, pp. 132 ff.

[2] See *Community Drama,* pp. 51 ff., and p. 62. Mr. MacKaye applies the term " community masque " to his spectacle, and most of the writers of the press-notices included in the appendix to the volume cited, use the same term, which is more appropriate for a show based on Shaksperian material, and in which the community effort was of chief importance.

objecting to the use of *pageantry*, as a misleading term;[1] the motive and method behind it — "the Christian motive of efficient 'neighborliness,' and the art method of dramatic organization "[2] — are intended to distill the organized, constructive imagination which peace lacks. War, holds Mr. MacKaye, organizing for competition, creates a national mind: the Community Drama, organizing for coöperation, harmonizing community with community, nation with nation, may create an international mind. There are many who believe, with Mr. Parker, that local history is the best, if not the only, material capable of uniting solidly a community, which shares the past in common heritage; that too much symbolism fails, and that it is not enough to join in giving a show, but that the show must be worth giving, and have the particular appeal which only one's *own* show can have. This Mr. MacKaye recognizes when he says: "The difference is between *mine* and *ours* . . . '*My* pageant' is inconceivable. '*Our* show' is the typical vernacular of every civic festival."[3]

Such a feeling must weaken, if it does not entirely disappear, before pageants written for any community which lacks the energy or the originality to bring forth its own. "Books of historical pageant-plays "[4] — the characters of which are of necessity types (sometimes combined with allegory or symbolism) — remind us of machine-made goods, which drive out the better hand-made products, with a gain in efficiency and convenience hardly equivalent to the loss in quality and art. Closely allied to this kind of thing is the "pageant-ceremony" devised by Mr. MacKaye at the request of the Citizenship Day Committee of New York to welcome newly naturalized citizens in the City College Stadium, and "designed to be at the service of whatever American community, committee, school, or civic society may desire to use it."[5] Here the historical characters are limited to national figures "chosen not from one era but out of the total tradition of our liberties"; symbolical figures, such as Liberty and America, and types, such as new citizens and folk-dancers, join them. The "ritual" may be applied to any American community; and may be repeated as often as occasion arises.

While pageantry is a powerful weapon of propaganda, and may be a strong tool in the hand of the sociologist who seeks to develop community-spirit by its aid, there is a danger that, in seeking to "educate," pageant-masters in America may forget the value of local history, which, in some pageants, is almost crowded out to make way for nameless types or purely allegorical figures, characteristic of the older masque.

---

[1] *Community Drama*, *p.* 39. [2] *Ibid.*, Preface, p. xii. [3] *Community Drama*, p. 20 f.

[4] Such as *Plays of the Pioneers*, by Constance d'Arcy Mackay. In this volume, *The Pioneers* "forms the lyric interlude in the Pageant of Pioneers now in rehearsal in some of the smaller farming communities of the Dakotas and other Western states. This pageant is not a pageant of a given place, but of a movement — the Pioneer Movement — with episodes adaptable and applicable to any locality that has witnessed the coming of the pioneers, their vicissitudes, and final triumphs." (*Op. cit.*, p. 12.)

[5] *The New Citizenship*, p. 8.

The Coronation of Charles VII of France

§ 4. DEFINITIONS OF "PAGEANT," AND CLASSIFICATION OF PAGEANTIC SHOWS

We are, perhaps, ready now to define a *pageant*. Several definitions have been made, and some of these we shall cite. To begin with Mr. Parker's: "Let me say here what a pageant is *not*. It is not a circus. It is not a procession. It is not in any sense a display of professionalism ... It is the representation of the history of a town, in dramatic form, from the earliest period to some later point, forming a fitting climax. This is set forth in verse and prose of the most direct sort, and is embellished with choruses, songs, dances, marches, and every legitimate spectacular adjunct. It is acted in some beautiful and historical spot, which is left without any artificial embellishment whatever. It is acted by the citizens of the town themselves, their wives, their children and their friends ... It is acted in a spirit of simplicity and reverence, and the audience must bring the same spirit in watching its progress. It is not a stage play. It is a lofty and dignified panorama of the town's history. And it is ... an act of local patriotism. And out of local patriotism grows that wider patriotism which binds the sons of England together ... But it is more still. I confess I cannot conceive a pageant except as an incident in a great act of praise and thanksgiving ..."[1] And again —

"It is a great drama representing the history of a city ... It is a powerful, historical object lesson."[2]

These passages show what the Parkerian standard is; and, indeed, most of the English pageants not directed by Mr. Parker strove toward these ideals. As I have already stated, the pageant in England is a chronicle-play; it awakens civic pride by portraying history. But these definitions do not apply to all the American pageants we have been studying; here, the art has undergone certain changes, as we have seen. "Pageantry," says Professor Baker, "seems likely to be for us [in America] a combination of the Chronicle-Play and the Morality, a free dramatic form which teaches, though not abstractly, by stimulating local pride for that in the past which makes the best incentive to future civic endeavor and accomplishment. Already in the communities where it has been tried, it has quickened patriotism, strengthened civic pride, and stimulated or revealed latent artistic powers."[3]

Mr. W. C. Langdon, subsequently president of the American Pageant Association, wrote in 1912: "I feel very strongly that the word *pageant* is used for so many different kinds of festal activities that it has but little definitive value left it. My definition of a real pageant is a drama in which the place is the hero and the development of the community is the plot. It is community drama, as

---

[1] *Journ. Soc. Arts*, liv, p. 144.

[2] *New Boston*, for November, 1910, p. 296.

[3] *New Boston*, November, 1910, p. 296.

distinguished from individual drama." [1] Mr. Davol [2] notes that American pageants lean more towards symbolism and prophecy than do the English, and continues: "Two types of standard pageantry now in vogue are: First, what we may call the academic pageant,[3] given in schools and colleges as a means of visualizing history and of Americanizing the foreign-born element of the population by a dramatic appeal.

"Secondly, in a larger way, comes the community, or anniversary, pageant. . . . the community pageant, as a whole, never failed to inspire finer fellowship or make for life more abundant."

Good as these definitions are for the historical pageant of modern times, which came into being with that at Sherborne in 1905, none of them seems quite inclusive enough. "Logically, for the benefit of the public, it is essential that some discussion should clear the atmosphere and decide just what we do mean by a *Pageant*," writes Miss Mary P. Beegle.[4] "This distinction in the use of the term is not a mere matter of terminology, but it rather becomes a question of the entire purpose of pageantry. Just what are we trying to do with the pageant in the community? This question requires a definite answer, because the commercial pageant, for instance, even when a beautiful artistic production, still remains a commercial venture in distinction from the type of community drama which it is the object of the [Association] to foster.

"Yet, so far as the public can see, the commercial pageant apparently fulfills the superficial aspects of the true pageant, and it is only through education and publicity that the many individuals composing the public may be made to realize the significance of pageantry as a new and possible art for the people, of which the final aim is Social Service . . . .

"It is not right to assume that the highest social value of the pageant may only be gained from a spirit of loyal coöperation. If the pageant is lacking either in artistic or dramatic qualities it is a failure, for the reason that such a pageant does not establish a true standard . . . No slovenly or inartistic performance may be excused on the ground of the splendid spirit aroused through the work, or by the fact that the people have had a chance to express themselves. Pageantry must set a high standard of production. It may be simple; but it must be well done, or it cheats not only the audience but the performers . . . .

"The question, it would seem, is one of purpose; if the purpose is to bring into the lives of the people a new form of recreation that awakens a sense of

---

[1] I quote from a letter. Cf. Am. Pag. Assoc. *Bulletin 11*, 1 December, 1914.

[2] *Handbook of Am. Pag.*, p. 28.

[3] Practically what we have called the "festival" for want of a better name.

[4] Am. Pag. Assoc., *Bulletin 7*, 15 September, 1914. Cf. Am. Pag. Assoc., *Bulletin 53*, 1 December, 1917, for "a set of tentative definitions of the principal types of modern community celebrations." These include *pageant, community drama, masque, festival,* and *processional.*

beauty and pride in the community, it is necessary that we have a clear idea of what we mean that new art to be called."

THE AIM OF PAGEANTRY

Mr. Parker has very clearly stated the purpose of the English pageant; does that of the American differ? It may, I think, be agreed that the aim of pageantry is to interest and educate the people; to arouse a civic pride and a community spirit, patriotism, humility, and a love of the beautiful; and to show the community what it can itself accomplish toward this end. Unless the desire to give a pageant comes from the community itself — perhaps aroused by the work of a neighboring town — no really successful pageant can result.

"FUTURISM" IN PAGEANTRY

It is not my purpose here to discuss the methods by which pageantry can best accomplish these aims. Professor Dickinson has touched upon the matter: "Too easily assuming a lack of glories in the past, some directors are centering their attention in the present, and throwing into high relief the wonders of present 'achievement.' To me the glorification of the present comes with a bad grace. And with even poorer grace comes the custom of some of presenting the past as a crude and shameful background for presenting 'enlightenment and progress.' Aside from the poor taste of this attitude, it is quite lacking in truthful perspective.[1] Without reverence there can be no art. And in self-vaunting there can be neither art nor social welfare. The good pageant is one that strives to make us worthy of our yesterdays by enriching their promise.

"There is a theory that the future can be effective material for pageantry. For this theory William Chauncy Langdon makes himself responsible when he speaks of the drama of the community being 'carried down to the present and on into the future to reflect in advance the gleam of those ideal conditions which the new country-life movement is so successfully bringing into realization.' A theory so idealistic as this needs respectful consideration. But it is clear that if there is any value in the theories we have been working out for the pageant, episodes of the type suggested by Mr. Langdon would fall to the ground through their extra-dramatic character. It is greatly to be doubted whether the future could be so realistically treated as to be interesting. Put to such a use, the pageant becomes the vaguest kind of symbolism, dealing with no clutches or soul-stirring contests, or reminiscent ceremonies, but done up in the white mist of a future that the more sceptically-minded of us would fear as we fear the heaven of our youth."[2]

---

[1] Professor Dickinson here refers to American pageantry.

[2] *The Play-book* for September, 1914, p. 28.

Pageants Classified

Three kinds of pageants are indicated in *Pageants and Pageantry* — the parade, the out-door performance, and the indoor entertainment, "made up of scenes so related as to possess unity."[1] I have classified pageants differently. It makes little difference whether a pageant be given outdoors or in; the chief question is, is it "popular," or of limited appeal? Assuming that the theme shows unity,[2] does it have the popular element which lies in "the freedom of the people of the community *to take part* in it?"[3] If not, it is a "festival,"[4] no matter how easily the public may get tickets. This is a fundamental distinction between the dramatic pageant and the "festival." The production of a limited group naturally draws a selected audience; and it makes no great difference whether this audience sits in the open air or in a hall. The "popular" element is the "spirit" of pageantry; the masque has always appealed to a limited circle. In early times, the "technique" of the pageant was the procession — now it is the procession of events dramatically presented; while the "technique" of the masque has always been the dance. The "festival" shows the spirit of the masque combined with the technique of the pageant, as the older "folk-play," or mumming, suggests the spirit of the pageant joined to the technique of the masque. The production of a community appeals to the community, and has the true "popular" quality necessary for a pageant.

Then, of course, there is the second type of pageant — that which is not given against a stationary background. At one time this included speech: speech may in time come back to it. If it is given merely to entertain, using no history and little symbolism — even if it shows frank commercialism — it is still a pageant. It may not be a high form of pageantry,[5] but nothing can take from it the name that belongs to it by right of inheritance. This kind is, even today, capable of great things; at its worst, it is carnivalistic hodge-podge.

---

[1] Bates and Orr, p. 5.

[2] The theme may be the growth of national spirit, the struggle of a people for liberty, the progress of a science or of education (to cite *Pageants and Pageantry*, p. 5). "Naturally such an instrument [as the pageant] does not pass unnoticed by those who have a program to promulgate. Already people are using it to establish a number of cases from the right of women to the vote to the necessity of 'swatting the fly.'" Dickinson, *op. cit.*, p. 27.

The larger the theme, the less likely it is to appeal to a limited group. Every pageant is, of course, given by a group; but the members of such a group should be chosen from as large a field as possible. The more representative it is of the community, the nearer it comes to fulfilling the ideal conditions of a pageant.

[3] As Mr. Langdon phrases it, in a letter dated 28 January, 1913.

[4] This is what Professor Dickinson (*op. cit.*, p. 28) calls "the Pageant of Idea"; it deals with that which may be greater than the community, but which interests only a part of the community, not being a common interest of all.

[5] A melodrama may be rough and uncouth, but it still belongs to the drama.

These, then are the two classes of modern pageants — the processional and the dramatic.[1] The division may be graphically represented as follows:

A.	B. Related episodes given in one place	
Street processions with floats containing figures of allegorical, symbolical, and historical significance.	1 Of the town; by the town; a main element being history	2 Of a science or art; by a restricted group

In this table, A represents the oldest branch of the family — one that has, perhaps, seen better days, but which does not deserve to be snobbishly frowned upon. B1 represents the " historical pageant " or " community drama," while B2, representing the " festival," is an offshoot from it, and really is not entitled to be called pageant at all. It is sometimes hard to tell whether a given production should be placed in B1 or 2; *An Dhord Fhiann* and the Hollis Hall Pageant dealt with historical episodes of interest to a small part of the community; the *Pageant of Progress* dealt with science and art, yet interested all of an isolated collegiate community; *From Cave Life to City Life* treated history in terms largely symbolic, and failed to appeal to an entire metropolitan population. All so-called " pageants " given in large cities tend to become " festivals " — especially when any other subject than the history of the community is dealt with.

Although sometimes called " pageants," such productions as the Bohemian Club " Jinks," and the Harvard masque in honor of Professor Duquesne, are outside of the field altogether. They show a further development of the tendencies indicated by the " festival."

In the definitions of Mr. Parker, Professor Baker, and Mr. Langdon which I have cited, history plays an important part. That it is an essential for those pageants which fall into group B1 will be readily admitted — and accuracy is, as I have said, of prime importance where historical episodes are concerned. Unless the allegory and symbolism common in the American pageants are rigidly kept to the interludes, the pageants will go over the line to the " festival "; for, as has been pointed out, allegory and symbolism are naturally expressed in the dance, and militate against history unless they are kept subordinate to it.

Because a carnival procession contains no unity of any sort, historical or symbolic, it has only the " raw-material " of pageantry. The emotions aroused

[1] Professor Dickinson, in the *Play-book* (from which I have already cited), p. 14, divides pageantry into two main classes: the " so-called Continental or Processional type in which the event and the ceremony are presented in a moving procession of floats and symbolic figures in costume," and " the English or dramatic type, in which the action takes place on one spot, or on a series of related spots, in the form of a plot loosely constructed of a series of authentic episodes in dramatic form, usually comprising speech, action, and suggestive setting."

by such a show are transitory. The same inborn desire for spectacular display underlies the " educational " pageant; but here we have come to look for something more. If our pageantry is more than mere entertainment, it is because we like to feel that we are not simply amusing ourselves; this is an age which cannot fully enjoy Niagara because it thinks of the unharnessed power going to waste.

With the development of history — an element which has been growing in importance in recent Lord Mayor's Shows — pageantry has become a new force. In America, we have linked history to morality-play abstractions — a dangerous thing to do if we wish to keep the educational value of the pageant. But, as Professor Kittredge has said, this is an age of symbolism and abstraction; we no longer talk of " learning a trade " —we create an abstract Vocational Education; we speak of Efficiency as if he were an intimate friend. A few years ago we personified Gold and Silver in a political campaign. Pageantry readily adapts itself to this state of mind; and that is one reason why, in America, it is a mixture of chronicle-history and the morality-play. The other is, as I have already stated, because we wish to portray the future, and can do so only by means of abstractions. But the tendency must be kept under control, or the new form of artistic expression, which seems so vigorous now, is doomed.

CHAPTER X

CONCLUSION

HERE, then, we end our survey of English pageantry. We have traced its course through details monotonous in their repetition, from the mists of folk-custom to the chaotic conditions of the contemporary pageantry in the United States. We have seen how, in pre-Christian times, the folk marched with images of animals, and figures of men — survivals of the human-sacrifice practiced by primitive peoples. This is the basis of the pageantry which was so common in the middle ages, and is not yet dead. The Church made use of the figures, turning them into saints' images; and the guilds used the animals as trade-symbols. In 1298, both saint and fishes accompanied a London guild when it celebrated the victory of Falkirk.

The common misapprehension concerning the importance of the miracle-plays in the history of the pageant we have helped to dispel. It is true that these performances would be pageants, were they not something more; but they must be considered dramatic productions — given, if you will, under pageantic conditions. Pure pageantry arose in the folk-celebrations and the "royal-entry": often enough, in the provincial towns especially, the pageant-car of the guild miracle-play was pressed into service to furnish a suitable platform from which some appropriate Biblical character could address the visiting sovereign. Only then did the miracle-play element become pageantic.

The folk-giant, who lasts to this day in the figures of Gog and Magog and the Salisbury St. Christopher, seems to have occasionally taken the form of a champion. At least once the giants appeared in a "royal-entry" with the appropriate names of Hercules and Samson. Perhaps the Bruce, who greeted a Scottish queen early in the sixteenth century, was a folk-giant under an historical disguise; history was first attached to the London giants in 1554, when Gogmagog and Corineus welcomed Philip of Spain to his wife's capital.

From the "Court of Love" literature — perhaps by way of the pageantic tournament — came the castle, which we find in an English "royal-entry" in 1377; in 1432, Lydgate introduced allegory into the pageant, and early in the sixteenth century, mythological characters made their appearance.

The habit of masking, common alike to court and folk, showed itself in the tournament which earlier than 1300 had begun to grow less serious. Allegory soon developed, and the seed from which grew the Elizabethan tilt and barrier was planted. It was not long before the informal masquerades of the court were elaborated into more formal entertainments built around the dance, which, in the reign of Henry VII, had borrowed the car from the pageantic procession.

This developed into the elaborate background against which the later Tudor and Stuart masques took place, and which, in its turn, became the chief source of our modern scenery.

Perhaps the pageant gave allegory to the morality-play, though this point needs further investigation. It is possible that, having received allegory from literature at the hands of John Lydgate — at a time when the morality-play was in its infancy — the pageant showed how the qualities could be personified, and gave a hint to the morality-play writers.[1] It seems quite clear that *The Castle of Perseverance* and *Mary Magdalene* owe something to the " materialized love allegory " of the tournament, but I do not press the matter of the morality-play's debt to the pageant.

Mythological characters are first found in Scotland just after 1500; I suggest that they came from France. In 1522, Jason and Medea welcomed Charles V to London; and in 1533, Udall and Leland employ Mercury, Paris, and the three goddesses in the reception to Anne Boleyn. Pageantry, like every other form of artistic expression in the early sixteenth century, reflects the Renaissance spirit.

Between the end of the thirteenth century and the reign of Elizabeth, pageantry was chiefly developed in the " royal-entry." Perhaps this development was aided by influence from the " groote Ommeganck " of Antwerp, and similar shows on the Continent; but one may suggest that there was an influence also in the opposite direction. It is not the purpose of this work to trace connections between the pageantry of England and that of Belgium, France, and Italy; that such existed is plain, but details of this exchange must be left to future studies.

After the middle of the sixteenth century, when the " Midsummer Show " - a survival of old folk-custom — began to die out, the pageants were transferred to the Lord Mayor's Day " riding," which had been going on annually since 1209. In 1422, the mayor first made the journey to Westminster by water; and this method of transportation gradually became — with some interruptions — the rule until 1856. The pageants of the " Midsummer Show " were combined with the " water-triumph " and thus the Lord Mayor's Show grew up.

George Peele wrote the words for the first Lord Mayor's Show of which the speeches have come down to us. Among the poets who followed him were Munday, Dekker, Heywood, Middleton, Webster, Jordan, Tatham, Taubman, and Settle, with whose Show for 1708 — which was not presented, owing to the death of the Prince of Denmark, Queen Anne's husband — speech departed from the triumphs of the Lord Mayor.

By the end of the eighteenth century, and during the first half of the nineteenth, the civic show at London consisted of little pageantry beyond the " armed men "; but of late years there has been an attempt to revive the older glories;

[1] It is, of course, also possible that the morality-play and the allegorical pageant are independent developments of the same tendency.

and allegory, symbolism, and history have reappeared on pageant-cars, or floats. In the first years of the war, the Show was used to stimulate recruiting, and the regiments which marched therein — themselves historical — replaced figures dressed up to represent historical characters.

In 1783, figures from the Lord Mayor's Show appeared on the stage of a London theatre; and thus the *tableaux vivants* were, for the first time, transferred from the street-pageants to a hall. The material dealt with was chiefly history; and it is not difficult to see the connection between the pageantic procession and such living-pictures of history which appeared in the United States at Marietta in 1888.

These make a convenient link between the old and newer pageantry. Of the old — the technique of which is the procession — there are survivals not only in the Lord Mayor's Show, and the celebrations at Knutsford, Lichfield, Coventry, and other towns in England, but revivals in America — at Boston, Springfield (Massachusetts), Philadelphia (in 1908) and Norristown (in 1912), to name a few of many examples. The carnival processions of many places show the " raw material " of pageantry, without the unity which is essential for the higher forms of art.

The new " pageant," however, is something quite different. With the exception of the final march at the end, it has kept none of the processional features we have come to associate with the pageant. It is a chronicle-play, differing from the Elizabethan chronicle-play only in the fact that the hero is a town, not an individual. Just as John Lydgate may be called the " father of pageantry," because he brought the form into the field of art, so Mr. Louis N. Parker is the " father of the modern pageant," which came into being at Sherborne in 1905.

This new form of pageantry traces its ancestry not from the old, but from the German *Erinnerungsspiele*. We have noted how the more recent Lord Mayor's Shows, by emphasizing not the history of some guild but the history of the city, prepared the public for this " historical community-drama " which is now called " pageantry." These plays — for they are really plays — tell the history of a community in episodes; they are produced by the members of a community, and have a great educational value, care being taken to make the reproductions historically accurate.

This modern " folk-play " is to our time what the chronicle-play was to the people of Shakspere's England. It vitalizes history. From the mother-country, it spread to the American continent; and in the United States, it absorbed the historical *tableaux vivants*, giving them pantomimic action, in many cases speech, and often an open-air setting.[1]

[1] As has been shown, there is more emphasis on symbolism and allegory in the American work than in the English. This is due to several causes, and has resulted in giving us the " futuristic pageant," or pageant which looks to the future, rather than to the past.

A further development has taken place on this side of the ocean; for the "pageant" given by a school, or small group in a community, instead of by the people as a whole, has lost its "popular" aspect. These entertainments — the subject of which is usually of less general interest to the majority of the people than would be the history of their town, and which frequently trace the development of some art or science which interests the group producing them — have been called "festivals." They have the spirit which underlies the masque — which is given by and for a restricted circle — and at times their technique approaches that of the masque.

Professor A. Chaurand, of the Lycée Ampère, Lyons, in a letter of 28 May, 1918, wrote: "... À Lyon, nous avons une nouvelle création de la Croix Rouge américaine: un asile pour les enfants des réfugiés, établi dans la maison très somptueuse, mais assez laide, de l'ancien consul Allemand. J'ai vu une demoiselle américaine, fille d'un professeur de Princeton, qui fait partie de cette mission. Elle m'a dit que l'on procéderait d'abord par une cérémonie: the rite of cleansing the uns' home with lustral water. Mais tout cela est vide de sens; et je pense que vous devez passer de bien mauvais moments, et qu'il est hors de saison d' essayer de rire. Je crois bien, cependant, que vous avez dû remarquer que le Français aime beaucoup rire, même dans les ombres de la vallée de la mort ..."

It is interesting to observe that this Frenchman does not take the symbolism of the ceremony which the Red Cross had planned, as seriously as the Americans do. That such a rite seems trivial, given the sufferings of the French, cannot be denied: "lustral water" could not cleanse France from the Huns! Perhaps there is an excuse for those who were for so long in actual contact with the realities of War, if they felt the absurdity of such a ceremony at that time. One does not dance in a house of mourning: but one could not condemn dancing itself, if a few misguided individuals were to attempt it.

In America, then, we have three types of pageantry — or, rather, two, one of which is subdivided. We share with England and the Continent, the procession with moving platforms on which historical and symbolical figures are carried through the streets; we share with England the historical "community-drama," modified on Parkerian lines from the German *Erinnerungsspiele;* and the more restricted "festival" (less commonly found in England) which approaches sometimes the masque, and at others the "pageant-play."

Broadly speaking, there is pageantry whenever people dress up to represent something they are not, in real life. Thus, we find pageantry in a Lord Mayor's Show of 1913, which includes Sir Thomas Middleton : we do not find pageantry in a civic procession of 1915, which includes heroes back from the Flanders front. In the first, we have someone representing an historical character; in the second, we have history itself.

But the above definition, taken alone, would admit a carnival procession, or a fancy-dress ball, into the realm of pageantry. I have already called these the

" raw-material " of the pageant, and have stated that what kept them out of our field was the lack of unity exhibited by such a spectacle. Some of the Lord Mayor's Shows — when that procession was at its lowest artistic level — suggested a carnival; the final *tableau* of a Parkerian pageant would suggest a fancy-dress ball, had there not been preceding scenes, which found a unity in the town, the history of which had just been set forth. The primary aim of the Parkerian work was to depict this history; but the discovery was made that in so doing, a community solidarity was developed, which, like many by-products, became almost as important as the main product.

In America, sociologists, and propagandists of all sorts, have seized upon the by-product as a fulcrum from which to apply their " uplift." Placing a strong emphasis on the necessity of imagination in dealing with present-day problems of American life, and intent on distributing as much imagination as possible among the population of our country, many pageant-masters and pageant-writers show a tendency to exchange history for symbolism, allegory, and nameless type-figures. The danger of this development is, that fact may become so diluted with imagination, that it will fail to awaken a community spirit. When we show an historical scene, we must use historical characters; when we replace the Puritan and the Indian by Civilization and the Wilderness, the scene, ceasing to be historic, becomes symbolic. Symbolism and allegory tend to express themselves by the dance, and no community can be spurred to civic endeavor by frisking figures of Faith, Hope, and Charity! Unless the symbolism is kept subordinate, the interest in the pageant will wane, and the production will become a " festival " — given only by a small group in the community.

Important as the spectacular element in pageantry is, it is by no means the most important. Mr. Percy MacKaye lays great stress on " the handsomeness of war " in his suggestion that community drama could prove a substitute for war.[1] " Statesmen and military leaders," he writes, " utilize the full potency of the imaginative arts born of the theatre, and employ for their ends the ecstasy and pomp of music and pageantry with a perfection of ' stage management ' that would stagger a Reinhardt. Symbolism they call to their aid, to provide for patriotism her radiant flags and uniforms. The art of the music-maker peals in brass to the multitude. Poetry and dance stride forth, like strange colossi, in the public squares, exhorting the populace with rhythms of marching regiments, that leap forth like glorious stanzas on the breath of the rhapsodist. A choral shout — as old as the chanting of Homer — invokes and unifies the nation." The armies of peace, as he calls the social workers, " have, with few exceptions no adequate symbols of their service — no banners, uniforms, fighting hymns, rhythmic marches, pageantry of spiritual meanings made sensuous . . . . Drab — that is their disease."[2]. As a " moral equivalent " of war, Mr. MacKaye suggests the community drama: " The present time is peculiarly auspicious for

[1] *A Substitute for War*, pp. 26 ff.

[2] *A Substitute for War*, p. 35.

this widened civic scope of the theatre's art. On the one hand, that art itself — rekindled from within by the constructive discoveries of its creative artists in production, architecture, music, and the dance — stands at the threshold of a splendid renascence. On the other hand — stirred from within by the portentous menace of world war — civic ardor has never been more deeply roused than now to discover effectual means for combating the enemies of society — poverty, disease, unemployment, political corruption, and all the hosts of embattled ignorance. To this war against all social and economic causes of war dramatic art offers a popular symbolism of magnificent scope and variety; it offers a new method of social science."[1] Mr. MacKaye's aim is that of Mr. Parker — perhaps carried to a further development — but his method differs: for Mr. Parker, basing his pageants on history, sought to give an artistic performance which would leave the town better for having taken part in it; Mr. MacKaye, emphasizing symbolism, seeks to give an artistic performance which will not only leave the community more closely knit, but will also organize militant social service as an effectual substitute for war. The future alone can show whether history or symbolism will prove the more potent force.

The greatest change between the older and newer forms of pageantry — greater even than that of technique — is this change in purpose. The pageantry of the past existed chiefly to entertain the crowds; it was as innocent of an ulterior motive as were the early folk-plays, which unconsciously kept alive pre-Christian customs. There was, however, in these old shows, a certain allegorical and historical element which indicates that the pageantic "dressing-up" was not wholly purposeless. Often it was appropriate in the case of the "royal-entries"; often it recalled the past, in the case of the Lord Mayor's Shows. But its chief aim was not instruction.

That of the present mingles with its entertainment a desire to educate, to spur on to better things. It seeks to inspire a greater community spirit, to awaken a local patriotism. Being a form of art very close to the people, it reflects the spirit of the age closely, and for this reason, if for no other, is it worth studying. The instincts to which pageantry appeals are deep-rooted; and it is instructive to watch the development of these instincts in a people. There is, it must be admitted, a tendency, in the United States, at any rate, to take from pageantry the spontaneous and unconscious charm of folk-custom, and render it too sophisticated and unnatural under the chaperonage of pageant associations and similar conventionalizing groups; but perhaps this, also, is in the spirit of the age.

Dangerous as it is (from the point of view of pageantry) to produce those shows which can be fitted or adapted to any place — as the *Canterbury Pilgrims* were made applicable to Gloucester, Massachusetts — Mr. MacKaye's article

---

[1] *A Substitute for War*, pp. 42 ff.

on *The New Fourth of July*, in the *Century Magazine* for July, 1910 (pp. 394 ff.), has some interesting suggestions for fitting pageantry to an Independence Day celebration in any community. Taking the Pittsburgh celebration as a basis, the writer advocates an application to other cities of the processional pageant, a children's parade, an historical military parade, folk- and pantomime pageants, etc., all of which are described and outlined. It is worthy of note that Mr. MacKaye emphasizes the desirability of attaching to such a celebration whatever of local history or custom would tend to give it individuality: and urges each community to " make much of the tradition of your own locality." In these days of standardization for the sake of efficiency, it is, perhaps, to be expected that pageants will tend to be machine-made.

Pageantry is nothing new, though the modern pageant is not a revival of the earlier. Both are only different expressions of the same desires. The modern pageant is a higher form of art, having unity; but it lacks the spontaneity of folk-custom. The community, not the guild, is the center around which it is built; its history and symbolism deal with the town, not with the craft. The fact that people look to it for education and inspiration, puts a responsibility on the modern pageant-master which the writers of the earlier shows did not bear. Yet these processions of older times played an important part in the life of England from the days of Chaucer to those of Dryden.

Pageantry, both of the past and of the present, has been connected with the celebration of some event. At first, this event was a folk-festival, or a Church holy-day; the welcome of a sovereign, or the installation of a mayor; now it is a national holiday or some civic anniversary. In addition, pageantry is more and more being used to give publicity to some idea — as a form of propaganda. Our review of the subject has been chiefly a review of the centuries in holiday mood; and, as Bacon has said, " such shews . . . are not to be neglected."

At all times — from the earliest " Midsummer Show " down — pageantry has been, to use Mr. Percy MacKaye's phrase, " poetry for the masses."

BIBLIOGRAPHY

BIBLIOGRAPHY[1]

ABBREVIATIONS

B	Bodleian, Oxford.
BM	British Museum Library, London.
C	Library of Cambridge University.
Gh	Guildhall Library, London.
HL	Library of Harvard University.
RS	Rolls Series.
SA	Library of the Society of Antiquaries, London.

Adams, Elizbeth D. "A Fragment of a Lord Mayor's Pageant," in *Modern Language Notes* for May, 1917.

[Agincourt]. *See* Nicolas.

American Pageant Association. *Bulletins*, 1913, *et seq.*

Amerie [Amory], Robert, *see* Davies.

An Dhord Fhiann, *see* Irish Historic Pageant.

Annales Londonienses, *see* Stubbs.

Annales Paulini, *see* Stubbs.

[Anne]. *See* Campion.

Antiquarian Repertory, *see* Grose.

Aqua Triumphalis, *see* Tatham (sub anno 1662).

Arber, Edward. *An English Garner.* (8 vols.), Westminster, 1877–96.

Archæologia. Published by the Society of Antiquaries. London, 1770 — in progress.

Arlington Pageant. 6, 7, 13 June, 1913. By Mrs. Colonna (Murray) Dallin. [Program in HL].

Army Pageant, Book of. Edited and arranged by F. R. Benson and A. T. Craig. London, 1910. [The pageant was held at Fulham Palace, 20 June–2 July, 1910.]

Arundell, Thomas. *Historical Reminiscences of the City of London and its Livery Companies.* London, 1869.

Ashdown, *see* Hertford.

Ashton, John. *Lord Mayor's Show in the Olden Times.* Compiled from various authentic drawings and ancient MSS. The drawings are by F. C. Price. London [1883].

Astle, *see* Grose.

Athenæum, The. London, 3 November, 1860 [no. 1723, pp. 581–585], "A Full and Particular Account of the Lord Mayor's Procession by Land and Water." (Street Boy.) [A sprightly essay, full of entertaining gossip.]

Aungier, G. J. *Chroniques de Londres, depuis l'an 44 Hen. III jusqu'à l'an 17 Edw. III.* Edited from Cotton MS. Cleop. A. vi. for the Camden Society (xxviii), London, 1844.

Avesbury, Robert de. *Chronica.* Edited by E. M. Thompson. (RS 93) London, 1889.

Axon, W. E. A. *Chester Gleanings.* Manchester, 1884.

Baker, David E., *see* Jones.

Baker, George P. "Pageantry," in *New Boston* for November, 1910. [HL]

Baker, George P., *see* Hollis Hall, *and* Peterborough.

Bannatyne Club, *see* Edinburgh.

[1] This does not pretend to be a complete bibliography of the subject; and I have made no attempt to list the modern English and American pageants. This list is rather to elucidate the references in the footnotes.

Barber-Surgeons, *see* Young.

Barriffe, William. *Mars, his Triumph:* or the Description of an Exercise performed the xviii of October, 1638, in Merchant-Taylors Hall by certain Gentlemen of the Artillery Garden, London. London, 1661. [Gh, *A. 1. 5.*]

Bates, E. W., and Orr, W. *Pageants and Pageantry.* Boston and New York, 1912.

Bateson, Mary, *see* Leicester.

Bath, (celebration of Charles II's Coronation.) *See* William Smith.

Bath Historical Pageant. Frank Lascelles, Master. 19–24 July, 1909. *Book of Words.* Bath, 1909.

Beatty, Arthur. "The Saint George, or Mummers' Plays: a study in the Protology of the Drama," in *Trans. Wisconsin Acad. Sci. Arts and Letters* (October, 1906), vol. xv, part ii, pp. 273 f.

Beaven, Alfred B. *The Aldermen of the City of London.* (2 vols.), London, 1908–13.

Beegle, Mary P., *see* Crawford.

Benson, F. R., *see* Army, *and* Winchester.

Besant, Sir Walter. *Mediæval London.* (2 vols.), London, 1906.

Bickley, F. B., *see* Bristol.

Bieling, Hugo. *Zu den Sagen von Gog und Magog.* Berlin, 1882.

Blomefield, Francis. *An Essay towards a typographical History of the County of Norfolk,* &c. (6 vols.), London, 1805–07. Continued by Parkin (vols. 7–11), London, 1807–10.

Blomefield, Reginald T. "Inigo Jones," in *The Portfolio* for May, 1889 (pp. 88 f.), and June, 1889 (pp. 113 f.).

Bond, E. A., *see Chronica de Melsa.*

[Boston, Massachusetts]. *Celebration of the 250th Anniversary of the Settlement of Boston.* Boston, 1880. [HL, *US. 13176. 25. 5.*] *See especially* pp. 109–149, 153–162. Various "floats," or tableaux, are illustrated.

[Boston, Massachusetts]. *Historical Festival.* Music Hall, April 22–30, 1897 (under the auspices of the Boston Teachers' Mutual Benefit Association). Margaret M. Eager, director. Boston, 1897. [HL, *Thr. 1211. 70.*]

[Boston, Massachusetts]. *See New Boston* (for the "Civic Pageant" of 1910, entitled, "From Cave Life to City Life").

Bourbon, Étienne de. [Stephanus de Borbone.] *Anecdotes,* &c. (Edited by Albert Lecoy de la Marche.) Paris, 1877.

Brand, John. *Observations on Popular Antiquities.* Newcastle-upon-Tyne, 1777.

Brand, John. *Ibid.,* edited, with large corrections and additions, by W. C. Hazlitt. (3 vols.), London, 1870.

[Brand, John]. *Dictionary of Faiths and Folk Lore.* [Built on Brand and Ellis, *Pop. Antiq.*] (2 vols.), W. Carew Hazlitt. London, 1905.

Brayley, Edward W. *Londiniana.* (4 vols.), London, 1829.

Brewer, E. C. *Dictionary of Phrase and Fable.* London, 1895.

Brewer, J. S., and J. Gairdner. *Letters and Papers, Domestic and Foreign, of the Reign of Henry VIII.* (21 vols.), London, 1862–1910.

Bridport, *see* West Dorset.

[Brinsden]. *Political Merriment: or Truths told to some Tune.* Faithfully Translated from the Original French of R. H. S. H. H. S. F. A. G. G. A. M. M. P. and Messieurs Brinsden and Collier, the State Occulist, and Crooked Attorney. . . . By a Lover of his Country. London, 1714. [BM, *238. g. 45.*]

Bristol, The Little Red Book of. Edited by Francis B. Bickley. (2 vols.), Bristol and London, 1900.

Brittannia's Honor, see Dekker (sub anno 1628).

Broadley, *see* West Dorset.

Brotanek, R. *Die Englischen Maskenspiele.* Vienna and Leipzig, 1902.

Brown, Carleton F. "Lydgate's Verses on Queen Margaret's Entry into London," in *The Modern Language Review* for April, 1912.

Brown, F. C. *Elkanah Settle, his Life and Works.* (Illustrated.) Chicago, 1910.

Brown, P. Hume. *History of Scotland.* Cambridge (England), 1899.

Bruce, John, *see* Hayward.

Buck, Sir George. *The History of the Life and Reigne of Richard the Third.* London, 1646.

Bullen, *see* Middleton, *and* Peele.

B[ulteel] J[ohn]. (*Show for 1656.*) *London's Triumph;* or the solemn and magnificent reception of . . . Robert Tichburn, Lord Major, after his return from taking his oath at Westminster . . . October 29, 1656. London, 1656. [Sig. B. 3 verso slightly mutilated in the BM copy (*C. 33. e. 10*)].

Burckhardt, Jacob. *Die Cultur der Renaissance in Italien.* (Fifth edition, "unveränderter Abdruck der vierten Auflage, besorgt von Ludwig Geiger," 2 vols.), Leipzig, 1896.

Ibid., see Middlemore.

Bury St. Edmund's Pageant. Louis N. Parker, Master. 8–13 July, 1907. *Book of Words.* Bury [1907]

Also: *Pageant Souvenir, 1907.* (Illustrated.) [This volume contains, among others, articles on "Bury St. Edmund's" (L. Willoughby); "Organizing the Pageant" (F. T. Carter); "Costumes" (Arthur Hood); and "Art-Work and Craftmanship" (A. R. Christopherson). Mr. Parker wrote the Introduction.]

Butchers, *see* Daw.

Calendar of Close Rolls preserved in the Public Record Office. (29 vols.), London, 1892 (in progress).

Calendar of Letter Books, see Sharpe.

Cambridge History of English Literature. (14 vols.), Cambridge (England) and New York, 1907–17.

Campion, Thomas. *A Relation of the late Royal Entertainment given by . . . the Lord Knowles . . . to our most Gracious Queene, Queene Anne, in her Progresse toward the Bathe, vpon the seuen and eight and twentie dayes of April, 1613.* London, 1613.

Carpenter, John, *see* MacCracken.

Carrel, Frank, *see* Quebec.

Cavendish, George. *Life of Wolsey.* (Third edition; Morley's Universal Library.) London, 1890.

[Cavendish, W., Duke of Newcastle]. *The Country Captaine, and the Varietie.* Two Comedies, Written by a person of honor. Lately presented by His Majesties Servants, at the Black-Fryers. London, 1649. *The Covntry Captaine,* A Comoedye . . . The Hague, 1649.

Cayuga Indian Festival. Beebe Lake, 27 May, 1914. *The Story of the Pageant.* [Ithaca, 1914.] [HL]

Ceremonies observed by the Lord Mayor of London, 1824–25. [Gh, *MS. 510.*]

Chambers, E. K. *The Mediæval Stage.* (2 vols.), Oxford, 1903.

Chambers, Robert. *The Book of Days.* (2 vols.), London and Edinburgh, 1863–64.

[Charles I]. *Ovatio Carolina.* The Triumph of King Charles, or the Triumphant Manner and Order of Receiving his Maiesty into his City of London on Thursday the 25th Day of November, Anno Dom. 1641, upon his safe and happy Return from Scotland . . . London, 1641. [Gh. Reprinted in *Harl. Misc.*, v, p. 86.] *See also* John Taylor.

[Charles II]. *See* Tatham; Ogilby; *England's Joy*, in Arber, i, pp. 25 f.; and, *A True Relation of the Reception of His Majestie and Conducting him through the City of London . . . on Tuesday the 29th of this instant May, being the Day of his Majesties Birth.* London, 1660. [B]. Also, *The Cities Loyalty Display'd*, London, 1661. [B]. Cf. vol. i, p. 243, n., above.

[Charles V]. *See* Dupuys.

Chelsea Historical Pageant. J. H. Irvine, Master. 25 June–1 July, 1908. Old Ranelagh Gardens, Royal Hospital. *Book of Words*, &c. Chelsea, 1908.

Cheltenham, *see* Gloucestershire.

Chester Historical Pageant. G. P. Hawtrey, Master. 18–23 July, 1910. *Book of Words.* Chester, 1910.

Chester, *see* Morris, *and* Ormerod.

Chester's Triumph, *see* Davies.

Chestre, Thomas. *Chestre Launfal.* Edited by Joseph Ritson. Edinburgh, 1891.

[Christian IV]. *See* H. Robarts; also, *The King of Denmarkes welcome: Containing his arriual, abode and entertainement, both in the Citie and other places.* London, 1606. [BM, *C. 33. e. 7 (5)*].

Chronica Monasterii de Melsa. Edited by E. A. Bond. (RS 43) London, 1866–68.

[Cincinnati]. *Grand Kirmess and Historical Pageant*, under the supervision of Lila Agnew Stewart . . . April 16, 17, 18 [1914]. [HL, *Thr. 1211. 80*]

Citizen's Pocket Chronicle . . . for the use of Citizens, Merchants, Lawyers, and Strangers. [Introduction signed " J. S. F."], London, 1827.

Civic Honours; or a Succinct Historical Display of the Origin, Establishment, Prerogative and Mode of Election of the Chief Magistrate of the City of London; together with some particulars of his inauguration and Show (both by Land and Water) . . . London, 1816. [Gh, *A. 1. 5.*]

Civitatis Amor, *see* Middleton (sub anno 1616).

Clark, Lotta A., *see New Boston.*

Clode, C. M. *Early History of the Merchant Taylors' Company.* (2 vols.), London, 1888.

Cocheris, H. *Entrées de Marie d'Angleterre, femme de Louis XII, à Abbeville et à Paris.* Paris, 1859.

Colchester Pageant. Louis N. Parker, Master. 21–26 June, 1909. *Souvenir and Book of Words.* Norwich and London [1909].

Cole, C. A., *see Elmhami Liber.*

Collier, J. P. *The History of English Dramatic Poetry to the Time of Shakespeare, and Annals of the Stage to the Restoration.* London, 1879.

Commelinus, *see* Monmouth.

Conder, Edward, Jr. *Records of the Hole Crafte and Fellowship of Masons.* (Illustrated.) London, 1894.

Cooke, John. " Green's Tu Quoque," in Dodsley, *Old Plays*, vii, pp. 1 f. London, 1825.

Coopers, *see* Firth.

[Coronations]. For information regarding coronations between the times of James I and William and Mary, *see* the collections of broadsides and pamphlets in the Bodleian Library. [*Wood, 398* and *Ashmole G. 10 (3–19)*.]

Country Captain, *see* W. Cavendish.

Courthope, W. J. *History of English Poetry.* (6 vols.), New York and London, 1895–1910.

Coventry Leet Book. Edited for EETS by Mary D. Harris. (3 vols.), London, 1907–09.

[Coventry]. *See* Harris, Poole, Sharp; *and,*

The History of Coventry Show Fair, with a particular account of Lady Godiva and Peeping

Tom, and an interesting Description of the Grand Procession. (Illustrated.) Coventry, n. d. [? 1827.]

Craig, Algernon Tudor, *see* Army Pageant.

Craig, Anna Throop, *see* Irish Historical Pageant.

Craig, Hardin. *Two Coventry Corpus Christi Plays.* Edited for EETS by H. Craig. London, 1902.

Crawford, J. R., and Mary P. Beegle. *Community Drama and Pageantry.* New Haven (Connecticut), 1916.

[Croke, Sir George]. *The Reports* of Sir George Croke, Knight, Late one of the Justices of the Court of Kings-Bench . . . of such Select Cases as were adjudged . . . the time that he was Judge . . . Collected and written in French by Himself; revised and published in English by Sir Harebotle Grimston, Baronet . . . London, 1657.

Cummings, W. H. " God Save the King," in the London *Musical Times* (xix), 1878.

Cunningham, F., *see* Jonson.

Cunningham, Henry W. " Diary of the Rev. Samuel Checkley, 1735," in the *Publ. of Colonial Society of Massachusetts* for March, 1909.

Cunningham, Peter. " Extracts from the Accounts of the Revels at Court," &c. [*Publ. Shaks. Soc.*] London, 1842.

Current Newspapers. The contemporary accounts of pageants in the London *Post-Boy, Daily Post, Evening-Post, Standard, Times, Graphic, Illustrated London News, City Press, Era, Morning Star, Pictorial News,* &c.; the Paris *Illustration,* the New York *Evening Post, Times,* the Boston and other American papers, give much interesting information on the subject. I have indicated, at various points in the text, my indebtedness to these sources.

Dallin, Mrs. Colonna (Murray), *see* Arlington.

Dana, R. H., Jr. *Two Years before the Mast.* New York, 1841.

Davey, Richard. *The Pageant of London.* (2 vols.), London, 1906.

[This book, illustrated by John Fulleylove, is a history of London, giving much information about the city at second hand.]

Davidson, Charles. *English Mystery Plays.* New Haven, 1892.

Davies, R. *Extracts from the Municipal Records of the City of York.* London, 1843.

Davies, Richard. *Chester's Triumph in honor of her Prince.* As it was performed upon S. George's Day, 1610. Reprinted by the Chetham Society. Manchester, 1844. [Cf. *Prog. James,* ii, p. 291.]

Davol, Ralph. *Handbook of American Pageantry.* (Illustrated.) Taunton, Massachusetts [1914].

Daw, Joseph. *A Sketch of the Early History of the Worshipful Company of Butchers of London.* [London], 1869.

Deering, Charles. *An Historical Account of Nottingham.* Nottingham, 1751.

Dekker, Thomas.

The Magnificent Entertainment, given to King James, Queene Anne his wife, and Henry Frederick the Prince, vpon the day of his Majesties Tryumphant Passage (from the Tower) through his Honourable Citie (and Chamber) of London, being the 15. of March 1603. As well by the English as by the Strangers: With the speeches and Songes deliuered in the seuerall Pageants . . . Tho. Dekker. London, 1604. [Gh, B, BM]

[A second edition (entitled *The Whole Magnifycent Entertainment,* etc., " printed at London by E. Allde for Tho. Man the yonger, 1604 ") is in B (*Gough Lond. 122. 3* and *Douce D. 206*); this is reprinted in Somers, *Tracts* (1751) third collection, i, p. 116; *ibid.,* (1810), iii, p. 1; *Prog. James,* i, p. 337 f. Another edition was printed at Edinburgh in 1604; this is in BM (*C. 33. d. 26*). On the fly leaf of the BM copy is a pencilled note:

"This Edinburgh edition is of the greatest rarity," and opposite the title page are the two words in pencil, "Very rare"].

(*Show for 1612*). *Troia Noua Triumphans.* London Triumphing, or the Solemne . . . Receiuing of . . . Sir John Swinerton . . . into the City of London . . . the 29. of October, 1612. All the Showes, Pageants, Chariots of Triumph, with other Deuices (both on the Water and Land) here fully expressed. By Thomas Dekker. London, 1612. [BM, B. Reprinted in Fairholt, *Lord Mayor's Pageants*, pt. ii, p. 7; cf. J. G. Nichols, *Lond. Pag.*, p. 101; Greg, p. 7; *Gent. Mag.*, for August, 1824, p. 114.]

(*Show for 1628*). *Brittannia's Honor:* Brightly Shining in seuerall Magnificent Shewes or Pageants, to celebrate the Solemnity of . . . Richard Deane, At his Inauguration into the Majoralty . . . on Wednesday, October the 29th. 1628. At the particular Cost and Charges of the . . . Skinners . . . Inuented by Tho. Dekker. [London, 1628.] [BM]

(*Show for 1629*). *Londons Tempe, or the Feild* [sic] *of Happiness.* In which Feild are planted seuerall Trees of Magnificence, State and Bewty, to celebrate the Solemnity of . . . James Campebell, At his Inauguration into the Honorable Office of Prætorship, or Maioralty of London, on Thursday the 29 of October, 1629. All the particular Inuentions, for the Pageants, Showes of Triumph, both by Water and land being here fully set downe, At the sole Cost and liberall Charges of the . . . Ironmongers. Written by Thomas Dekker. [London, 1629.] [BM, B. Reprinted in Fairholt, pt. ii, pp. 37 f.; Nicholl, p. 206; cf. Malcolm, ii, p. 43; Greg, p. 8; J. G. Nichols, p. 104.]

The BM copy is not perfect; after 14 pp. of print come four of MS, preceded by a pencilled note: " Written by the late Mr. Rhodes & to be implicitly trusted." On the fly leaf: " Given to me by the Duke of Devonshire after I had procured him a perfect copy of this Pageant. J. Payne Collier. 13 Nov. 1847."

Delpit, J. *Collection générale des documents français qui se trouvent en Angleterre.* Paris, 1847.

Descensus Astrææ, see Peele (sub anno 1591).

Dickinson, Thomas H. " The Pageant: a Study of its History, Principles, Structure and Social Uses," in *The Play-Book* for September, 1914. Madison (Wisconsin), 1914.

Dictionary of Faiths and Folk-Lore, see Brand.

Ditchfield, P. H. *Old English Customs Extant at the Present Time.* London, 1896.

Dodsley, *see* Cooke.

Douët-d'Arcq, *see* Monstrelet.

Dover Pageant. Louis N. Parker, Master. 27 July–1 August, 1908. *Book of Words.* Dover, 1908.

Drake, Francis. *Eboracum; or, the History and Antiquities of the City of York,* &c. London, 1736.

Drake, Nathan. *Shakespeare and his Times.* (2 vols.), London, 1817.

[Dublin]. *See* Gilbert, *and* Molloy.

Dugdale, Gilbert. *The Time Triumphant,* Declaring in briefe, the ariual of our Soueraigne liedge Lord, King Iames into England, His Coronation at Westminster: Together with his late royal progresse, from the Towre of London through the Cittie, to his Highnes mannor of White Hall. Shewing also, the Varieties and Rarieties of al the sundry Trophies or Pageants, erected aswel, by the worthy Cittizens of the honorable Cittie of London: as also by certaine of other Nations . . . By Gilbert Dugdale. London, 1604. [B. Reprinted in *Prog. James*, i, pp. 408 f.; Arber, *Eng. Garner*, v, pp. 648 f.]

Dunbar, William. *Poems.* [Ed. Laing.] (2 vols.), Edinburgh, 1834.

Dupuys, Rémy. *La Triomphante et Solennelle Entrée de Charles-Quint en sa ville de Bruges, le 18 Avril 1515.* (Illustrated.) Bruges, 1850. [Reprinted from a contemporary volume by the Société d'émulation de Bruges.] [SA]

Dybdynne, Thomas. *A Ryghte Sorroweful Tragyke Lamentacyonne for ye Losse of My Lorde Mayor, hys Daye* . . . London, [1830]. [Gh]

Dyce, *see* Middleton, Peele, *and* Webster.

Eager, *see* Boston.

[Edinburgh]. *Extracts from the Records of the Burgh of Edinburgh, 1403–1589.* (With index, 5 vols.), Edinburgh, 1869–92.

Documents relative to the Reception at Edinburgh of the Kings and Queens of Scotland, A.D. MDLXI–A.D. MDCL. Published by the Bannatyne Club. [The documents are chiefly taken from the Registers of the Privy Council of Scotland, and the records of the City of Edinburgh.] Edinburgh, 1822.

Elder, John. *The Copie of a Letter sent in to Scotlande, of the ariuall and landynge, and most Noble Marryage of the most Illustre Prynce Philippe, Prynce of Spaine, to the most excellente Princes Marye Quene of England* . . . (Black Letter.) London, 1555. [Gh, *A. 1. 5*]

[Elizabeth]. *See* Hayward, J. Nichols, Furnivall, *and* Garter. *Also,*

The Honorable Entertainment gieuen to the Queenes Maiestie in Progresse, at Eluetham in Hampshire by . . . the Earle of Hertford. 1591. London, 1591. [BM, *C. 33. e. 7. (9)*]

The Passage of our most drad soueraigne lady Quene Elyzabeth through the Citie of London to Westminster the daye before her coronacion. (Black Letter.) London, 1558. [Gh]

The Royall Passage of her Maiesty from the Tower of London, to her Palice of Whitehall with all the Speaches and Deuices, both of the Pageants and otherwise, together with her Maiesties Seuerall Answers and most pleasing Speaches to them all. London [1558–59.] [BM, *C. 33. e. 7 (11)*]; another edition [BM, *C. 33. e. 7 (15)*] is dated 1558. A 1604 edition may be found in B [*Wood, 537*]; for reprints, or other mention of these pamphlets, see Arber, iv, pp. 217f.; pp. 224f.; *Prog. Q. Eliz.*, i, pp. 38f.; Greg, p. ix; Chambers, ii, p. 172.

Ellis, Sir Henry, editor. *Ceremonial of the Marriage of Mary, Queen of Scots . . . with the Dauphin of France.* (Roxburghe Club publ.) London, 1818.

Elmham, Thomas de. *Vita et Gesta Henrici Quinti.* Edited by Thomas Hearne. Oxford, 1727.

Elmhami Liber Metricus de Henrico Quinto. Edited by C. A. Cole. (RS 11) London, 1858.

Emerson, O. F. "Legends of Cain," in *Publ. Mod. Lang. Assoc.* for December, 1906.

Encyclopædia Britannica. (Eleventh edition.) *Arts.* "Drama," "Masque," *and* "Pageant."

England's Comfort and London's Joy, see Taylor, J.

England's Triumph: being an account of the Rejoicings, &c., which have lately taken place in London and elsewhere. Including the Restoration of Louis XVIII, the Proclamation of Peace, and the Visit of the Emperor of Russia, and the King of Prussia, &c., &c. London, 1814. [This is in Gh (*A. 8. 4*); an account of the visit of the royal guests to the Guildhall, in June, 1814, was printed for the Corporation, and may be found in the Guildhall Library (*A. 4. 5*). No pageantry, in the technical sense, accompanied this visit.]

English Church Pageant. Hugh Moss, Master. (This pageant was held at Fulham Palace, 10–16 June, 1909.) *Handbook*, edited by C. R. Peers. (Illustrated.) [London, 1909].

Official Handbook. (Illustrated.) London [1909].

Épervier d'Or, see Rosny.

Evans, H. A. *English Masques.* London, 1897.

Evelyn, John. *Diary.* Edited by William Bray. (4 vols.), London, 1879.

Ewing, W. C. *Notices and Illustrations of the Costume, Processions, Pageantry, &c., formerly displayed by the Corporation of Norwich.* (Illustrated.) Norwich, 1850. [This volume is usually cited under the name of its publisher, Charles Muskett. A MS. note in the Norwich Museum copy of this work shows that it was prepared by W. C. Ewing, who was a well-known antiquary of Norwich in the nineteenth century.]

Fabert, Abr. *Voyage du Roy à Metz, l'occasion d'iceluy.* (Illustrated.) Metz, 1610. [SA]

Fabyan, Robert. *New Chronicle of England and France,* &c. Edited by Henry Ellis. London, 1811.

[Fairholt, F. W.]. A catalogue of a collection of works on Pageantry, bequeathed to the Society of Antiquaries of London, by the late F. W. Fairholt. London, Somerset House, 1869.

Fairholt, F. W. *Gog and Magog.* (Illustrated.) London, 1859.

Fairholt, F. W. *Lord Mayors' Pageants.* (Percy Society publ.) London, 1843–44. [In the second part of *Lord Mayors' Pageants* (referred to in the text as Fairholt) are reprinted Dekker's Shows for 1612 and 1629; Heywood's Show for 1638; Tatham's for 1660; and Jordan's for 1671 and 1678.]

Fairholt, F. W. *The Civic Garland.* (Percy Society publ.) London, 1845.

Farmer, J. S. *See Marriage between Wit and Wisdom.*

Farwell, Arthur. "The Pageant and Masque of St. Louis," in *The Review of Reviews* for August, 1914. Illustrated.

Festival of Empire, see London.

[Fiennes, Celia]. *Through England on a Side Saddle in the Time of William and Mary.* Being the Diary of Celia Fiennes. London, 1888.

[Firth, James F.]. *Historical Memoranda, Charters, Documents and Extracts from the Records of the Corporation and the Books of the* [*Coopers'*] *Company, 1396–1848.* London, 1848.

Fitch, R., *see Grocers' Play of Norwich.*

Fleay, F. G. *Chronicle History of the London Stage, 1559–1642.* New York, 1909.

Folk-Lore, see Ordish.

Folk-Lore Journal, see Rowell, *and* Sawyer.

Fordun, Johannis de. *Scotichronicon.* Edinburgh, 1759.

Founders, *see* W. M. Williams.

Foxe, John. *Acts and Monuments.* Edited by S. R. Catley. London, 1838.

Frazer, Sir J. G. *The Golden Bough.* (5 vols.), London, 1911.

Froissart, John. *Chronicles.* Translated by J. Bourchier; reprinted from Pynson's editions of 1523 and 1525. (Ed. Johnes), London, 1812.

From Cave Life to City Life, see New Boston.

From Kingdom to Colony, see Marblehead.

From Dartmouth to the Dardanelles. A Midshipman's Log. London, 1916.

Furnivall, F. J. *Ballads from Manuscripts.* Edited for the Ballad Society. London, 1868–72.

Furnivall, F. J., and R. E. G. Kirk. *The Account of W(illiam) Combes and Richard Ryche for putting up Lists and Scaffolds for Jousts in West Smithfield, 30 January, 1442.* [Chaucer Society publ. 2nd Series, 36.] London, 1903. *See also* Manning.

Gaiennie, Frank, *see* St. Louis.

Gairdner, James, *see* Brewer, Paston, *and* Stow.

Garnett, Porter. *The Bohemian Jinks.* San Francisco, 1908.

Gar[ter], Ber[nard]. *The Ioyfvll receyuing of the Queenes most Excellent Maiestie* into her Highnesse Citie of Norwich, The things done in the time of hir abode there: and the dolor of the Citie at hir departure. Wherein are set downe diuers Orations in Latine . . . and certaine also deliuered to hir Maiestie in writing: euery of the[m] turned into English. London, n. d. [There is no name on the title-page; the dedication, however, is signed by "Ber. Gar. citizen of London." Reprinted in *Prog. Q. Eliz.*, ii, pp. 136f.; cf. Greg, p. 8.]

Gatfield, George. *Guide to Printed Books and Manuscripts, relating to English and Foreign Heraldry and Genealogy: being a classified catalogue of works of those branches of literature.* London, 1892. [BM, *B. B. T. d. 15;* pp. 268–284 give titles on ceremonials, processions and tournaments.]

Gayton, Edmund. (*Show for 1655.*) *Charity Triumphant, or the Virgin-Shew:* Exhibited on the 29th of October, 1655. Being the Lord Mayor's Day. London, 1655. [Gh, BM. The three-page dedication is signed by Emd. Gayton; the other three pages consist of narrative verse, describing the show. Reprinted in Fairholt, pt. i, p. 170; cf. also, *ibid.*, p. 64; J. Nichols, in *Gent. Mag.* for December, 1824, p. 514; Hone, p. 249; J. G. Nichols, p. 106.]

Geddes, Patrick. *The Masque of Learning.* Edinburgh and Chelsea, 1912.

Gentleman's Magazine. London, 1731–1907.

Geoffrey, *see* Monmouth.

[George II]. *A Particular Account of the Solemnities used at the Coronation of his Sacred Majesty King George II (Our late most Gracious Sovereign) and of his Royal Consort Queen Carolina. On Wednesday the 11th of October, 1727. Also . . . an account of their Majesties Entertainment at Guildhall on the Lord Mayor's Day following.* London, 1760. [SA]

See Guide, *below*.

[George IV]. *Historical Account of his Majesty's Visit to Scotland.* Fourth edition. Edinburgh 1822. [SA]

This volume includes illustrations of the King's landing at Leith (15 August); the Royal Procession passing Picardy Place (on the same day); view of the Grand Procession to the Castle (22 August); and the banquet given to the King (with plan of the same) on 24 August. The visit was made in 1822.

Gesta Henrici Quinti. Edited for the English Historical Society by Benjamin Williams. London, 1850.

Gifford, William, *see* Jonson.

Gigantick History of the Two famous Giants and other Curiosities in Guildhall. (2 vols.), London, 1741. [These two small volumes, which are kept in the Guildhall Library safe, are very rare. What is apparently the first edition of volume 2, is dated 1740; the third edition, "corrected," of volume 1, and the second edition of volume 2, were published in 1741.]

Gilbert, Sir John T., editor. *Calendar of Ancient Records of Dublin, in the possession of the Municipal Corporation of that City.* (7 vols.), Dublin, 1889–98.

Giles, Rev. J. A. *See* Paris, Matthew of, *and* Monmouth, Geoffrey of.

[Gillespy, Thomas]. *Some Account of the Worshipful Company of Salters.* London, 1827.

Gloucester, Robert of. *Chronicle.* Edited by W. A. Wright. (RS 86) London, 1887.

Gloucestershire Historical Pageant. G. P. Hawtrey, Master. Cheltenham, 6–11 July, 1908. *Book of Words.* Cheltenham, 1908.

Godefroy, Théodore. *Le Cérémonial de France.* Paris, 1619. [SA]

Godwin, George. *Suggestions for the Improvement of the Lord Mayor's Show.* A letter addressed to the Lord Mayor-elect, Mr. Alderman Musgrove. London, 1 October, 1850. [Gh, *A. 1. 5.*]

Goldsmiths, *see* Prideaux.

Goldwell, Henry. "A briefe declaratio[n] of the Shews," &c., 1581. [Reprinted in *Prog. Q. Eliz.*, ii, p. 310. Cf. Greg, p. 9.]

Goodwin, Alfred T. *Court Revels.* [Reprint of Harl. MS. 69 — an account of the 1501 "disguising." Shaks. Soc. Papers, i, pp. 47 f.] [London], 1844.

Gough, Richard. *Anecdotes of British Topography.* London, 1768.

"Greenhill Bower," *see* Lichfield.

Grafton, Richard. *Chronicle or History of England. To which is added his table of the Bailiffs, Sheriffs and Mayors of the City of London, from the year 1189 to 1558 inclusive.* London, 1809.

Greg, W. W. *A List of Masque, Pageants, &c.* London, 1902.

Grego, Joseph. "The Artistic Aspect of Lord Mayor's Shows," in *Gems of Art*, pp. 8f. (Illustrated.) New York [Cassell Publ. Co.] n. d.

Grocers, *see* Heath, *and* Kingdon.

[Grocers' Company]. *Why the Car of the Grocers' Company in the Lord Mayor's Pageant of 1901 represented ancient modes of weighing.* (With an illustration of the car.) London, 1902. [Gh, *Broadsides 7. 66.*]

Grocers' Play of Norwich. From a MS. in the possession of Robert Fitch, Esq. Norwich, 1856. [Cf. also, *Norfolk Archæology*, v, p. 29.]

Grose, F., and Astle, T. *Antiquarian Repertory.* Compiled by F. Grose and T. Astle. (4 vols.), London, 1807–09.

Grosley, Pierre Jean. *Londres.* (3 vols.), Lausanne, 1770.

Ibid., translated by Thomas Nugent, *q. v.*

Gross, C. *The Gild Merchant.* (2 vols.), Oxford, 1890.

Groot, J. J. M. de. *Religion of the Chinese.* New York, 1910.

Guide to the Lord Mayor's Show: or, the Gentleman and Lady's Companion to that Magnificent Procession . . . To which is added A particular account of their most Sacred Majesties [George II and Queen Caroline] Entertainment at Guildhall on October 29, 1727 . . . London, 1761. [SA]

H., W. H. *Prologue and Epilogue to the Lord Mayor's Show of 1867.* London, 1867. (A humorous satire on the reported abolition of the Show, and a lament for its past glories.) [Gh, *A. 1. 5.*]

Hall, Edward. *Chronicles*, &c. [Henry VI to Henry VIII.] London, 1809.

Halliwell-Phillipps, J. O., editor. *John Lydgate's Minor Poems.* Percy Soc. Publ. London, 1840.

Hamilton, *see* Wriothesley.

Hammond, E. P. "Lydgate's Mumming at Hertford," in *Anglia*, for June, 1899, pp. 364 f.

Handbook of Ceremonials, &c. A revised edition of the Book of Ceremonials of the City of London, as reprinted in proof in 1882. Issued under the direction and with the approval of the Privileges Committee of the Court of Aldermen, For the Guidance of the Lord Mayor, the Aldermen, the Sheriffs and the Corporation officers, &c. Guildhall, 1906. [Gh, *A. 8. 3.*]

Harleian Miscellany, vol x [London, 1813] contains Peele's Show for 1591 (pp. 68 f.); Peele's Show for 1585 (pp. 351 f.); Petowe's *England's Cæsar* [1603] (pp. 342 f.). [*See* Oldys.]

Harris, Mary D., *see Coventry Leet Book.*

Also: *Life in an Old English Town.* "A history of Coventry from the earliest times compiled from official records." Social England Series. London, 1898.

Harris, Mary D. *The Story of Coventry.* [In Dent's *Mediæval Town Series.*] London, 1911.

Harrison, Stephen. *Illustrations of the Pageants in the 1604 Coronation Procession of James I.* Together with two odes, by Thomas Dekker and John Webster, and the Speeches of Gratulation. [London, 1604.] [Gh.] The copy of this rare pamphlet preserved in the Guildhall lacks the title-page and one plate: on the cover is written in pencil what is probably a copy of the title-page:

"The Arches of Triumph Erected in honor of the High and Mighty Prince James the first of that name King of England and the sixt of Scotland at his Maiesties Entrance and Passage through his Honorable Citty & Chamber of London upon the 15th day of March, 1603." [Cf. Dekker (sub anno 1604)].

Harrod, Henry. "A few Particulars concerning early Norwich Pageants," in *Norfolk Archæology*, iii, pp. 3 f. Norwich, 1852.

Harwood, Thomas. *The History and Antiquities of the Church and City of Lichfield.* Gloucester, 1806.

Haslewood, Joseph, and Sir E. Brydges, Bart. *British Bibliographer.* (4 vols.), London, 1810.

Hasted, Edward. *History and Topographical Survey of Kent.* Canterbury, 1800.

Hatton, Edward. *New View of London.* (2 vols.), London, 1708.

Hayward, Sir John. *Annals of the first four years of the reign of Queen Elizabeth.* Edited from Harl. MS. 6021 (3) by John Bruce for the Camden Society. London, 1840.

Hazlitt, W. C. *Livery Companies of the City of London,* &c. London, 1892. *Also, see* Brand, *and* Warton.

Hearne. *See* Elmham, *and* Sprott.

Heath, John Benjamin. *Some Account of the Worshipful Company of Grocers.* [First edition, 1829; second edition, 1854; third edition, 1869.] London.

[Henley, John]. *The Lord Mayor's Show: or, the City in its Glory.* Now first published from an Original Manuscript of the late ingenious and facetious Orator John Henley, M.A. "Surely every Man walketh in a vain Shew." Psalm xxxix: 6. London, n. d. [BM, *605. d. 29* (7).]

[Henri IV]. *See* Fabert.

[Henry V]. *See* Cole, Elmham, Kingsford, *and* B. Williams.

[Henry VI]. *See* MacCracken.

[Henry VIII]. *See* Brewer, *and* Baron Edward Herbert.

Herbert, Edward, first Baron Herbert of Cherbury. *Life and Reign of Henry VIII.* Reprinted from Kennet's folio edition of 1719. London, 1870.

Herbert, William. *History of the Livery Companies.* (2 vols.), London, 1834–36. [Referred to in the text as Herbert.]

Hertford Pageant in connection with the Millenary Celebration, 914–1914. 29 June–4 July, 1914. *Book of the Words and Lyrics,* by Charles H. Ashdown, Master. Hertford, 1914.

Heysham, *see* Norristown.

Heywood, Thomas. *Dramatic Works.* (6 vols.), London, 1874.

(*Show for 1631*). *Londons Ius Honorarium.* Exprest in sundry Triumphs, pagiants and shews: At the Initiation or Entrance of . . . George Whitmore, into the Mayoralty of the . . . City of London. All the charge and expence of the laborious proiects, and obiects both by Water and Land, being the sole vndertaking of the . . . society of Habburdashers. London, 1631. [B; Heywood's name does not appear on the title-page, but he signs the Epistles Dedicatory to Mayor and Sheriffs. The show is reprinted in his *Works,* iv, pp. 263 f.; cf. Greg, p. 10; J. G. Nichols, p. 104; Fairholt, pt. i, p. 54; J. Nichols in *Gent. Mag.,* for November, 1824, p. 412.]

(*Show for 1632*). *Londini Artium et Scientiarum Scaturigo.* [I have not seen a copy of this pamphlet. Cf. Greg, p. 10; J. G. Nichols, p. 105; J. Nichols, in *Gent. Mag.,* for November, 1824, p. 412; Fairholt, pt. i, p. 57; Hone, p. 267.]

(*Show for 1633*). *Londini Emporia, or London's Mercatura.* [I have not seen a copy of this pamphlet, either. These shows are not reprinted in the 1874 edition of Heywood's *Works;* but cf. Greg, J. Nichols, J. G. Nichols, and Fairholt, as cited above — and Herbert, ii, p. 659.]

(*Show for 1635*). *Londini Sinus Salutis.* [Reprinted in *Works,* iv, pp. 283 f.; cf. Greg, p. 10; J. G. Nichols, p. 105 — referring to Malcolm, ii, p. 45 — Fairholt, pt. i, p. 58; *Gent. Mag.,* for November, 1824, p. 413.]

(*Show for 1637*). *Londini Speculum: or, Londons Mirror,* Exprest in sundry Triumphs, Pageants and Showes, at the Initiation of . . . Richard Fenn into the Mairolty of . . . London. All the Charge and Expence of these laborious projects both by Water and

Land, being the sole undertaking of the . . . Habberdashers. Written by Tho. Heywood. London, 1637. [Gh, B. Reprinted in *Works*, iv, pp. 301 f.; cf. Greg, p. 10; J. G. Nichols, p. 106; Fairholt, pt. i, p. 59; *Gent. Mag.*, for November, 1824, p. 413.]

(*Show for 1638*). *Porta Pietatis, or The Port or Harbour of Piety*, Exprest in Sundry Triumphes, Pageants, and Shewes, at the Initiation of . . . Sir Maurice Abbot, Knight, into the Mayoralty of . . . London. All the Charge and expence of the laborious Projects both by water and Land being the sole undertaking of the . . . Drapers. Written by Thomas Heywood . . . London, 1638. [SA, Gh, B, BM. Reprinted in Fairholt, pt. ii, p. 57; in *Works*, v, pp. 259 f. Cf. Greg, p. 11; J. G. Nichols, p. 106; Fairholt, pt. i, p. 60, and *Gent. Mag.*, for November, 1824, p. 413.]

(*Show for 1639*). *Londini Status Pacatus: or, Londons Peaceable Estate.* Exprest in sundry Triumphs, Pageants, and Shewes, at the Innitiation of . . . Henry Garvvay, into the Majoralty of . . . London. All the the Charge and Expence, of the laborious Projects both by Water and Land being the sole undertakings of the . . . Drapers. Written by Thomas Heyvvood. London, 1639. [BM, B, Gh. Reprinted, *Works*, v, pp. 355 f.; cf. Greg, p. 11; J. G. Nichols, p. 106; Fairholt, pt. i, p. 60; *Gent. Mag.*, for November, 1824, p. 413.]

Historical Account of his Majesty's Visit to Scotland, see George IV.

[Hoare, Richard]. *A Journal of the Shrievalty of Richard Hoare, Esq., in the years 1740–41.* Printed from a MS. in his own handwriting. Bath, 1815.

Holinshed, Raphael. *Chronicles.* (6 vols.), London, 1808.

Hollis Hall Pageant. George P. Baker, Author and Master. 14 June, 1913, at Hollis Hall, in the Harvard College Yard. Cambridge (Massachusetts), 1913. [HL].

Hone, William. *Ancient Mysteries Described.* London, 1823.

Hooker, Brian. "The Pageant," in the (illustrated) supplement to *The Yale Alumni Weekly* for 27 October, 1916. (New Haven, Connecticut.)

Horton, D. "The Drama of the Powers," in *The Historical Outlook* (Philadelphia) for March, 1919.

Hotton, John C., *see* Larwood.

Howes, E., *see* Stow, *Annals.*

Hudson, Gilbert, *see* Pickering *and* Scarborough.

Hudson, Rev. William, and J. C. Tingey, editors. *Records of the City of Norwich.* (2 vols.), Norwich and London, 1906–10.

Hudson-Fulton Celebration. New York, 1909. [Post-card illustrations of floats in HL. For a description of this pageant, *see* Wier's article, listed below.]

Humpherus, Henry. *History of the Origin and Progress of the Company of Watermen and Lightermen.* (3 vols.), London, n. d.

Irish Historic Pageant. *An Dhord Fhiann.* Anna T. Craig. Produced at New York, 7 and 8 May, 1913. [New York, 1913.]

Ironmongers, *see* Nicholl.

Irvine, J. H., *see* Chelsea.

Ives, John. *Select Papers*, &c. London, 1773. [Reprints of MSS. in the possession of the editor.]

Jackson, John, Jr. *The History of the City and Cathedral of Lichfield.* (2 vols.), Lichfield [1795.]

[James I]. *See* Dugdale, Dekker, Jonson, Harrison, Millington, *and* J. Nichols.

[James II]. *An Account of the Ceremonial at the Coronation of their Most Excellent Majesties King James II and Queen Mary At Westminster the 23 of April, 1685* . . . London, 1685 [A broadside in B (*Gough Midd. 32*); no pageantry was connected with this ceremony.]

Jarman, Herbert, *see* St. Albans.

Jeffrey, *see* Preston.

Jones, Stephen. *Biographia Dramatica.* [Originally compiled by David E. Baker.] London, 1812.

Jonson, Ben. *Works.* Edited by William Gifford and F. Cunningham. (3 vols.), London, n. d.

Jon[son], B[en]. *His part of King James his Royall and Magnificent Entertainement through his Honorable Cittie of London, Thursday the 15. of March, 1603; so much as was presented in the first and last of their Triumphall Arch's* . . . London, 1604. [Gh, B.]

Jordan, Thomas.

(*Show for 1671*). *London's Resurrection to Joy and Triumph,* Expressed in Sundry Shews, Shapes, Scenes, Speeches and Songs in Parts, Celebrious to the much-meriting Magistrate Sir George Waterman Knight, Lord Mayor of . . . London. At the Peculiar and Proper Expences of the . . . Skinners. The King, Queen and Duke of York and most of the Nobility being present. Written by Tho. Jordan. London, MDCLXXI. [Gh, HL, BM, B (4 copies); reprinted in Fairholt, pt. ii, p. 113. Cf. Fairholt, pt. i, p. 74; J. G. Nichols, p. 110; Wadmore, p. 148.]

(*Show for 1672*). *London Triumphant: or the City in Jollity and Splendour:* Expressed in various Pageants, Shapes, Scenes, Speeches and Songs. Invented and performed for Congratulation and Delight of . . . Sir Robert Hanson, Knight, Lord Mayor of . . . London. At the Cost and Charges of the . . . Grocers. His Majesty Gracing the Triumphs with His Royal Presence. Written by Tho. Jordan. London, 1672. [Gh, BM (2 copies); B (2 copies); reprinted in the appendix of Heath (3d edition), pp. 488f. Cf. Fairholt, pt. i, pp. 74 f.; J. G. Nichols, p. 110.]

(*Show for 1673*). *London in its Splendor:* consisting of Triumphant Pageants, whereon are Represented many Persons Richly Arrayed, Properly Habited, and significant to the Design. With several Speeches, and a Song, Suitable to the Solemnity. All prepared for the Honour of the Prudent Magistrate, Sir William Hooker, Kt., Lord Mayor of . . . London: at the Peculiar Expences of the . . . Grocers. As also, a Description of His Majesties Royal Entertainment at Guildhall, by the City, in a plentiful Feast, and a glorious Banquet. Written by Tho. Jordan. London, 1673. [Gh, B (2 copies, one imperfect); reprinted by Heath (3d edition, appendix, pp. 507f.) Cf. Fairholt, pt. i, pp. 79 f.; J. G. Nichols, p. 111.]

(*Show for 1674*). *The Goldsmiths Jubile: or London's Triumphs:* Containing a Description of the several Pageants: on which are Represented Emblematical Figures, Artful Pieces of Architecture, and Rural Dancing: with the Speeches spoken on each Pageant. Performed Octob. 29, 1674 for the Entertainment of . . . Sir Robert Vyner, Kt. and Bart., Lord Mayor of . . . London: At the proper Costs and Charges of the . . . Goldsmiths. The Kings Most Sacred Majesty and his Royal Consort . . . honouring the City with Their Presence. Composed by Tho. Jordan. London, 1674. [SA, B. In the BM are two, and in the Gh, one, of the 1835 reprints. Cf. Fairholt, pt. i, pp. 81f.; pt. ii, p. vi; J. G. Nichols, p. 111.]

(*Show for 1675*). *The Triumphs of London,* Performed on Friday, Octob. 29, 1675, for the Entertainment of . . . Sir Joseph Sheldon, Kt., Lord Mayor of . . . London. Containing a true description of the several Pageants, with the Speeches spoken on each Pageant. Together with the Several Songs sung at this Solemnity. All set forth at the proper Costs and Charges of the . . . Drapers. Designed and Composed by Tho. Jordan, Gent. London, 1675. [Gh, B (2 copies), BM (3 copies — one lacking the title-page). Cf. Fairholt, pt. i, pp. 84 f.; J. G. Nichols, p. 111.]

(*Show for 1676*). *London's Triumphs:* Express'd in sundry Representations, Pageants and Shows, performed on Monday, Octob. 30. 1676, at the Inauguration and Instalment of . . . Sir Thomas Davies, Kt., Lord Mayor of . . . London. Containing a true Description of the Several Scenes and Habits of the Representers, with the Speeches spoken on each Pageant. All the Charge and Expences of the Industrious Designs being the sole Undertakings of the . . . Drapers, being the Second Year without Intermission. Devised and Composed by Tho. Jordan. London, 1676. [Gh. Cf. Fairholt, pt. i, pp. 85 f.; J. G. Nichols, p. 112.]

(*Show for 1677*). *London's Triumphs:* Illustrated with many Magnificent Structures & Pageants. On which are orderly advanced Several Stately Representations of Poetical Deities, sitting and standing in great Splendor on several Scenes in Proper Shapes, with Pertinent Speeches, Jocular Songs (sung by the City Musick) and Pastoral Dancing. Performed October 29, 1677, for the Celebration, Solemnity and Inauguration of . . . Sir Francis Chaplin, Knight, Lord Mayor of . . . London. All the Charges and Expences of the Industrious Designs, being the sole Undertaking of the . . . Clothworkers. Designed and Composed by Tho. Jordan, Gent. London, 1677. [Gh, BM (2 copies, one imperfect), B. Cf. Fairholt, pt. i, pp. 87 f.; J. G. Nichols, p. 112.]

(*Show for 1678*). *The Triumphs of London.* Performed on Tuesday October xxix 1678 for the Entertainment of . . . Sir James Edwards, Knight, Lord Mayor of . . . London. Containing a true Description of the several Pageants, with the Speeches spoken on each pageant. Together with the Songs sung in this Solemnity. All set forth at the Costs and Charges of the . . . Grocers. London, 1678. [Gh (copy badly trimmed around the edges), HL, BM (2 copies, one imperfect). B (2 copies). Reprinted in Fairholt, pt. ii, p. 141; Heath (3d edition), appendix, pp. 518 f. Cf. also Fairholt, pt. i, p. 90; J. G. Nichols, p. 112.]

(*Show for 1679*). *London in Luster; projecting Many bright Beams of Triumph:* disposed into Several Representations of Scenes and Pageants. Performed with great Splendor on Wednesday, October xxix, 1679. At the Initiation and Instalment of . . . Sir Robert Clayton, Knight, Lord Mayor of . . . London. Dignified with divers delightful Varieties of Presentors, with Speeches, Songs, and Actions, properly and punctually described. All set forth at the proper Cost and Charges of the . . . Drapers. Devised and Composed by Tho. Jordan, Gent. London, 1679. [Gh, HL, BM (2 copies), B (2 copies). Cf. Fairholt, pt. i, p. 90; J. G. Nichols, p. 112.]

(*Show for 1680*). *London's Glory, or the Lord Mayor's Show:* Containing an Illustrious Description of the several Triumphant Pageants, on which are represented Emblematical Figures, Artful pieces of Architecture, and Rural Dancing, with the Speeches spoken in each Pageant; Also Three New Songs, the first in praise of the Merchant-Taylors, the second the Protestants Exhortation, and the third the plotting Papists Litany, with their proper Tunes either to be Sung or Play'd. Performed on Friday October xxix. 1680. For the Entertainment of . . . Sir Patience Warde, Knight, Lord Mayor . . . At the proper Costs and Charges of the . . . Merchant-Taylors. Invented and Composed by Tho. Jordan, Gent. London, 1680. [Gh, HL, BM, B (3 copies); cf. Fairholt, pt. i, pp. 92 f.; Hone, pp. 250 f.]

(*Show for 1681*). *London's Joy, or the Lord Mayor's Show:* Triumphantly Exhibited in Various Representations, Scenes, and splendid Ornaments, with divers pertinent Figures and Movements: Performed on Saturday, October xxix. 1681. At the Inauguration of . . . Sir John Moore, Knight, Lord Mayor . . . With the several Speeches and Songs which were spoken on the Pageants in Cheapside, and sung in Guild-Hall during Dinner. All the Charges and Expences of the Industrious designs being the sole undertaking of the . . . Grocers. Devised and Composed by Tho. Jordan, Gent. London, 1681. [Gh, BM (2 copies, one imperfect), B (2 copies). Reprinted in Heath (3d edition, pp. 536 f.); cf. Fairholt, pt. i, p. 95; J. G. Nichols, pp. 112 f.]

[? Jordan, Thomas]. *The Lord Mayor's Show:* being a Description of the Solemnity at the Inauguration of . . . Sir William Pritchard, Kt., Lord Mayor of the City of London; President of the Honourable Artillery-Company, and a member of the Worshipful Company of Merchant-Taylors. Perform'd on Monday, September xxx. 1682. With several new Loyal Songs and Catches. London, 1682. (6 pp.) [B (*Gough London 122.24*). Cf. Fairholt, pt. i, p. 97; there seems to have been no pageantry on this occasion.]

It is doubtful whether Jordan is the author of this pamphlet, or the songs therein; at any rate, he does not claim the authorship on the title-page, nor is there any " epistle dedicatory " which he might have signed.

(*Show for 1683, see Triumphs of London.*) [Jordan seems to have planned the festivities for Sir Henry Tulse, the King's appointee to the Mayoralty in 1683; but there was no pageantry, and it is not clear that Jordan wrote more than a couple of songs for the Mayor's banquet.]

(*Show for 1684*). *London's Royal Triumph for the City's Loyal Magistrate:* In an Exact Description of several Scenes and Pageants, Adorned with many Magnificent Representations. Performed on Wednesday October xxix. 1684. At the Instalment and Inauguration of . . . Sir James Smith, Knight, Lord Mayor . . . Illustrated with divers Delightful Objects of Gallantry and Jollity, Speeches and Songs, Single and in Parts. Set forth at the proper Costs and Charges of the . . . Drapers. Devised and Composed by Tho. Jordan, Gent. London, 1684. [Gh, BM, B. Cf. J. G. Nichols, p. 115; Gillespy, p. 64; Fairholt in *Gent. Mag.* for April, 1854, p. 380.]

Journal d'un Bourgeois de Paris, see Tuetey.

Journal. The MS. minutes of the Court of Common Council of the Corporation of London. In the Guildhall Archives.

Jupp, Edward Basil. *An Historical Account of the Worshipful Company of Carpenters.* (2d edition, with a supplement by W. W. Pocock.) London, 1887.

Jusserand, J. J. " A Note on Pageants and ' Scaffolds Hye,' " in the *Furnivall Miscellany,* (pp. 183 f., with two illustrations.) Oxford, 1901.

Kelly, William. *Notices, &c., of Leicester.* London, 1865.

Kelly, William. *Ancient Records of Leicester.* Read before the Literary and Philosophical Society, Leicester, on 24 February, 1851, and printed in a selection of papers . . . in June, 1855. [*See* pp. 31–103.] Leicester and London, 1855.

Kelly, William. *Royal Progresses and Visits to Leicester, from the reputed foundation of the City by King Leir,* B.C. *844, to the present time.* Leicester, 1884.

Kemp, Thomas. *The Black Book of Warwick.* Warwick [1898.]

[King, Daniel, publisher]. *The Vale Royall of England,* &c. Performed by William Smith and William Webb, gentlemen . . . London, 1656. [*See* Ormerod.]

Kingdon, John Abernethy. *Facsimile of the First Volume of MS. Archives of the Worshipful Company of Grocers of the City of London, A.D. 1345–1463. . . .* (2 vols.) [London,] 1886.

Kingsford, C. L. *Chronicles of London.* Oxford, 1905.

Kingsford, C. L. *English Historical Literature.* Oxford, 1913.

Kingsford, C. L. *Henry V.* London, 1901.

Kingsford, C. L., *see* Stow, *Survey.*

Kirk, R. E. G., *see* Furnivall.

Kittredge, George L. " Who was Sir Thomas Malory ? " in *Harvard Studies and Notes in Philology and Literature* [v, pp. 85 f.] Boston, 1896.

Knighton, Henry. *Chronicles.* Edited by J. R. Lumby. (RS 92) (2 vols.), London, 1895.

Kraus, Carl. "Das gotische Weihnachtsspiel," in Paul-Braune's *Beiträge* [xx, pp. 224 f.] Halle, 1895.

Lancaster, Massachusetts, Pageant. Joseph L. Smith, Master. 4 July, 1912. [Program in HL].

Langdon, William C. *See* St. Johnsbury, *and* Thetford.

Langford, C. F., *see* West Dorset.

Larwood, Jacob, and John C. Hotton. *The History of Signboards.* London, 1867.

Lascelles, Frank. *See* Bath, London, Oxford, *and* Quebec.

Lawrence, W. J. "The Mounting of the Stuart Masques," in the *English Illustrated Magazine,* November, 1903 [illustrated]. Revised and reprinted, under the title: "The Mounting of the Carolan Masques," in *The Elizabethan Playhouse and Other Studies.* Philadelphia and Stratford-upon-Avon, 1912.

Leather, Ella M. *The Folk-Lore of Herefordshire.* Hereford and London, 1912.

[Leicester]. *Records of the Borough of Leicester. Being a series of Extracts from the Archives of the Corporation of Leicester, 1103–1327.* Edited by Mary Bateson. Revised by W. H. Stevenson and J. E. Stocks. (3 vols.), London, 1899–1901. *See also* Kelly, *and* J. Nichols.

Leland, John. *Collectanea.* (6 vols.), London, 1770.

Leland, John, *see* Udall.

Letter Books, see Sharpe.

Liber Albus. Edited by H. T. Riley. (RS 12) London, 1859–62.

[Lichfield]. *See* Harwood, *and* Jackson.

Lichfield Greenhill Bower. Official Programs for the years 1893, 1895, 1904–09, 1911–14 in HL. [Gift of Mr. Councillor William A. Wood of Lichfield.]

[Lille]. *See* Rosny.

[Little Compton, Rhode Island]. *See* Georgiana B. Withington.

Littlehales, H., editor. *The Mediæval Records of a London City Church* (St. Mary at Hill), A.D. 1420–1559. [EETS. 125.128.] London, 1905.

Liverpool's 700th Anniversary Celebrations. *Words and Music. August, 1907. Great Historical Pageant and Tableaux in Wavertree Park and Grounds* . . . Liverpool, 1907.

[Lloyd, Lod.]. *Hilaria: or the Trivmphant Feast for the fift of August.* London, 1607. [Dedicated to the King by Lod. Lloyd.]

Loftie, W. J., *see* Torkington.

Logan, W. H., *see* Tatham.

Lomas, Sophie C., *see* London, Pageant of.

London Magazine. (10 vols.), London, 1820–24. New Series. (10 vols.), London, 1825–28.

[London, Pageant of]. *The Festival of Empire.* Frank Lascelles, Master. May, 1911, at the Crystal Palace. *Souvenir, containing 29 Coloured pictures; with Historical Presentment of the Scenes.* Edited by Sophie C. Lomas. London, 1911.

[Lord Mayor's Coach]. Chromolithograph of the coach, with description. Made in 1872. [Gh, *Broadsides 5.20.*]

Lord Mayor's Minute Book of Ceremonials, 1791–1800. [Gh, *MS. 1121.*]

[Lord Mayor's Show]. *See* Fairholt; J. G. Nichols; *and also* Ashton.

"The Lord Mayor's Show," in *Bentley's Miscellany* (1854), pp. 577–80. [A light essay on the subject, reflecting an opinion held by some today.] London, 1854. [Gh, *L. P. 53.16*]

Lord Mayor's Shows, *see* Official Programs.

Lord Mayor's Shows :

A CHRONOLOGICAL LIST OF THE AUTHORS OF THE SHOWS, 1585–1708

(The descriptive pamphlets are recorded under the names of the writers in the bibliography)

1585..........Peele.
1588..........Peele.
1590..........Nelson.
1591..........Peele.
1605..........Munday.
1609..........Munday.
1611..........Munday.
1612..........Dekker.
1613..........Middleton.
1614..........Munday.
1615..........Munday.
1616..........Munday.
1617..........Middleton.
1618..........Munday.
1619..........Middleton.
1620..........Squire.
1621..........Middleton.
1622..........Middleton.
1623........Munday and Middleton.
1624..........Webster.
1626..........Middleton.
1628..........Dekker.
1629..........Dekker.
1631..........Heywood.
1632..........Heywood.
1633..........Heywood.
1634..........Taylor.
1635..........Heywood.
1637..........Heywood.
1638..........Heywood.
1639..........Heywood.

1655..........Gayton.
1656..........Bulteel.
1657..........Tatham.
1658..........Tatham.
1659..........Tatham.
1660..........Tatham.
1661..........Tatham.
1662..........Tatham.
1663..........Tatham.
1664..........Tatham.

1671..........Jordan.
1672..........Jordan.
1673..........Jordan.
1674..........Jordan.
1675..........Jordan.
1676..........Jordan.
1677..........Jordan.
1678..........Jordan.
1679..........Jordan.
1680..........Jordan.
1681..........Jordan.
1682..........Jordan.
1683..........Jordan.
1684..........Jordan.
1685..........Taubman.
1686..........Taubman.
1687..........Taubman.
1688..........Taubman
1689..........Taubman.

1691..........Settle.
1692..........Settle.
1693..........Settle.
1694..........Settle.
1695..........Settle.
1698..........Settle.
1699..........Settle.
1700..........Settle.
1701..........Settle.
1702..........Settle.

1708..........Settle.

Luard, H. R., editor. *See* Paris *and* Westminster.

Lydgate, John. *See* C. F. Brown, Halliwell-Phillipps, Hammond, *and* MacCracken.

[Lyons]. *Entrée Magnifique de Bacchus avec Madame Dimanche Grasse, sa Femme, faicte en la ville de Lyon, le 14 feburier 1627. . . .* Lyons, 1838.

Lysons, Daniel and Samuel. *Magna Britannia.* [vol. Cheshire.] London, 1810.

MacCracken, H. N. *The Minor Poems of Lydgate.* [EETS. ES. 107.] London, 1911.

MacCracken, H. N. "King Henry's Triumphal Entry into London. Lydgate's Poem and Carpenter's Letter," in Herrig's *Archiv.* [cxxvi, pp. 75f.] Braunschweig, 1911.

Machyn, H. *Diary.* Edited by J. G. Nichols, for the Camden Society. [xlii.] London, 1848.

Mackay, Constance d'Arcy. *Plays of the Pioneers. A book of Historical Pageant-Plays.* New York and London, 1915.

MacKaye, Percy. *The Civic Theatre.* New York and London, 1912. [Especially ch. vi, pp. 161–177; app. iii, pp. 280f.; app. iv, pp. 288f.; and app. v, pp. 306f.]

MacKaye, Percy. *Community Drama; Its Motive and Method of Neighborliness.* Boston and New York, 1917.

MacKaye, Percy. *The New Citizenship: a Civic Ritual.* New York, 1915.

MacKaye, Percy. *A Substitute for War.* New York, 1915.

MacKaye, Percy. "The New Fourth of July," in the *Century Magazine* for July, 1910.

McLinn, C. B. "The March of Democracy — a Masque for Victory Day Celebrations," in *The Historical Outlook* for January, 1919. (The Rhode Island Normal School "Victory Pageant" was based on this masque and on the "drama" listed under D. Horton's name.)

Madden, Sir F., editor, *see* Paris, Matthew of.

Magnin, C. *Histoire des marionnettes en Europe.* (2d ed.), Paris, 1862.

Magnus, Olaus. *A Compendious History of the Goths, Swedes & Vandals, and other Northern Nations.* Written by Olaus Magnus, Archbishop of Upsall . . . London, 1658.

Maidment, J., *see* Tatham, *Works.*

Maidstone, Richard de. "De Concordia inter Regem Ric II et Civitatem London." In *Political Poems and Songs*, edited by Thomas Wright. (RS 14) (2 vols.) London, 1859–61.

Maitland, William. *The History of Edinburgh from its Foundation to the Present Time.* Edinburgh, 1753.

Maitland, William. *The History and Survey of London from its Foundation to the Present Time.* (2 vols.) [3d edition]. London, 1760.

Malcolm, James P. *Londinium Redivivum.* (4 vols.), London, 1803–07.

Manning, Robert, of Brunne. *Ye Story of Inglande.* Edited by F. J. Furnivall. (2 vols.), (RS 87) London, 1887.

Manly, J. M. *Specimens of pre-Shaksperian Drama.* (2 vols.), Boston and London, 1897.

[Marblehead Pageant]. *From Kingdom to Colony.* 6 and 7 August, 1912. Produced by G. L. Tracy; book by Mary L. Devereux; dramatized by Mrs. M. J. Morgan. [Program in HL.]

[Margaret]. *See* C. F. Brown, *and* Withington.

[Marietta, Ohio, Pageant]. *Report of the Commissioners of the National Centennial Celebration of the Early Settlement of the territory Northwest of the River Ohio.* [The pageant was held at Marietta, Ohio, in July, 1888.] Columbus, 1888.

Markoe, Francis H., *see* Yale Pageant.

Marriage between Wit and Wisdom. Tudor Facsimile Texts. Edited by John S. Farmer. London and Edinburgh, 1909. Cf. also vol. ii of J. O. Halliwell-Phillipps, *A Supplement to Dodsley's Old Plays.* (4 vols.), Shaks. Soc. Publ. London, 1853.

Mars his Triumph, see Barriffe.

[Mary]. *See* Cocheris.

[Mary, Queen of Scots]. *See* Ellis.

Masons, *see* Conder.

Massachusetts, Temporary Acts and Laws of (1736–62). Boston, 1755–62.

Matthew Paris, *see* Paris, Matthew of.

Matthew of Westminster, *see* Westminster, Matthew of.

Matthews, Albert. "The Term Pilgrim Fathers," in *Publ. Colonial Society of Massachusetts,* for December, 1914.

Melsa, *see Chronica.*

Menestrier, Claude François. *Traitê des Tournois, Ioustes, Carrousels, et Autres Spectacles Publiques.* Lyons, 1669. [SA]

Merchant-Taylors, *see* Clode.

Middlemore, S. G. C., translator. J. Burckhardt, *The Civilisation of the Period of the Renaissance in Italy.* (2 vols.), London, 1878.

Middleton, Thomas. *Works.* Edited by A. H. Bullen. (8 vols.), London, 1886.

Middleton, Thomas. *Works.* Edited by the Rev. Alexander Dyce. (5 vols.), London, 1840.

(Middleton)

(*Show for 1613*). *The Triumphs of Truth:* A Solemnity vnparaleld for Cost, Art, and Magnificence, at the Confirmation and Establishment of . . . Sir Thomas Middleton, Knight; in the Honorable Office of his Maiesties Lieuetenant, the Lord Maior of . . . London . . . October 29. 1613. All the Showes, Pageants, Chariots; Morning, Noone, and Night-Triumphes. Directed, Written, and redeem'd into Forme, from the Ignorance of some former times, and their Common Writer, By Thomas Middleton. London, 1613. [Gh, BM (2 copies), B. Reprinted in Dyce, v, pp. 213f.; Bullen, vii, pp. 229f.; Heath (3d edition) appendix, pp. 443f.; *Prog. James,* ii, pp. 679f. Cf. Bullen, i, p. xxxviii; Greg, p. 15; Fairholt, pt. i, p. 32; J. G. Nichols, p. 101; *Gent. Mag.,* for August, 1824, p. 114.]

Civitatis Amor. The Cities Loue. An entertainement by water, at Chelsey and Whitehall. At the ioyfull receiuing of that Illustrious Hope of Great Britaine, the High and Mighty Charles To bee created Prince of Wales, Duke of Cornewall, Earle of Chester, &c. London, 1616. [Gh, BM. Reprinted in Bullen, vii, p. 269; Dyce, v, p. 249; *Prog. James,* iii, p. 208. Cf. Greg, p. 16.]

(*Show for 1617*). *The Tryumphs of Honor and Industry.* A Solemnity performed throughout the City, at Confirmation and Establishment ot . . . George Bovvles, In the Office of his Maiesties Lieuetenant, the Lord Mayor of the famous Citty of London. Taking beginning at his Lordships going, and proceeding after his Returne. . . . October 29, 1617. London, 1617. [Written for the Grocers' Company. In Gh and BM (imperfect copy); reprinted in Bullen, vii, p. 293; Dyce, v. p, 607; Heath (3d edition) appendix, p. 459. Cf. Fairholt, pt. i, p. 43; Greg, p. 16; J. G. Nichols, p. 103; *Gent. Mag.,* for August, 1824, p. 116.]

(*Show for 1619*). *The Trivmphs of Loue and Antiquity.* An Honourable Solemnitie performed . . . at the confirmation of . . . Sir William Cockayn, Knight, in the office of . . . Lord Maior of the Famous Citie of London . . . By Tho. Middleton, Gent. London, 1619. [BM, B. Reprinted in Bullen, vii, p. 311; Dyce, v, p. 271; *Prog. James,* iii, p. 570. Cf. Greg, p. 17; Fairholt, pt. i, p. 45; J. G. Nichols, p. 103; *Gent. Mag.,* for August, 1824, p. 116.]

(*Show for 1621*). *The Svnne in Aries.* A Noble Solemnity performed through the Citie at the sole cost and charges of the . . . Drapers, at the confirmation and establishment of their most Worthy Brother . . . Edward Barkham in the high office of . . . Lord Maior . . . the 29. of October. 1621. By Tho. Middleton, Gent. London, 1621. [BM. Reprinted in Bullen, vii, p. 335; Dyce, v, p. 291; *Prog. James,* iv, p. 724. Cf. Greg, p. 17; Fairholt, pt. i, p. 48; J. G. Nichols, p. 103; *Gent. Mag.* for August, 1824, p. 116.]

[Cf. Bullen, i, p. lviii: "Among the Conway papers in the Record Office is a MS: 'Inventions by Thomas Middleton being a musical allegory, performed for the service of Edward Barkham, Lord Mayor of London, when he entertained his brother aldermen at a feast in the Easter holidays, Apr. 22, 1622.' I have reprinted it for the first time; it has little merit." This is, of course, not the Lord Mayor's Show for this year; and is a masque rather than a pageant. It may be found in Bullen, vii, pp. 369 f.]

(*Show for 1622*). *The Triumphs of Honor and Vertue.* [BM (lacking title-page). Reprinted by Bullen, vii, p. 353, and by James L. Pearson in *Shaks. Soc. Papers*, ii (1845), p. 93. Cf. Greg, p. 18. It is not mentioned by Dyce, Fairholt or J. G. Nichols. The show was written for the inauguration of Peter Proby of the Grocers' Company.]

(*Show for 1623*). *The Triumphs of Integrity.* [Reprinted from Dyce, v, p. 303, by Bullen, vii, p. 381. This show was written for the inauguration of Sir Martin Lumley, of the Drapers' Company. I have not seen a copy of the original pamphlet. Cf. Greg, p. 18; Fairholt, pt. i, p. 49, and below, Munday (sub anno 1623.) On the relationship between Munday and Middleton in this show, see Withington, "The Lord Mayor's Show for 1623," in *Publ. Mod. Lang. Assoc.*, for March, 1915.]

(*Show for 1626*). *The Trivmphs of Health and Prosperity.* A Noble Solemnity performed through the City at the sole Cost and Charges of the Honourable Fraternity of Drapery, at the Inauguration of . . . Cuthbert Hacket, Lord Major . . . By Tho. Middleton, Gent. London, 1626. [Gh. Reprinted in Dyce, v, p. 319; Bullen, vii, p. 399. In the Gh copy is noted: "Perhaps the rarest of all the City Pageants; no copy but Garrick's was known to Loundes." Cf. Greg, p. 18; Fairholt, pt. i, p. 52; J. G. Nichols, p. 104; *Gent. Mag.*, for November, 1824, p. 412.]

M[illington], T[homas]. *The True Narration of the Entertainment of his Royall Maiestie*, from the time of his departure from Edenbrough; till his receiuing at London: with all or the most speciall Occurrences. Together with the names of those Gentlemen whom his Maiestie honoured with Knighthood. At London, printed by Thomas Creede for Thomas Millington, 1603. [The preface " to the Reader " is signed T. M. The pamphlet, which is preserved in B., is reprinted in Arber, viii, p. 485, and in *Prog. James*, i, p. 53. Nichols seems to have used another edition, for there are slight textual differences between his version and the pamphlet in the Bodleian.]

Minute Book, see Lord Mayor.

Minutes of Committees for conducting the Entertainment at Guildhall on Lord Mayor's Days, see Proceedings.

Molloy, J. F. *Romance of the Irish Stage.* (2 vols.), London, 1897.

Monck, Nugent. *The Pageant-Play of King Arthur.* [London, 1914.]

[Monk, General]. For broadsides containing speeches addressed to General Monk at various dinners given him by the London Companies in March and April, 1660, see the collection in the Bodleian. [*Wood, 398 (4–9)*.]

Monmouth, Geoffrey of. *Historiæ Regum Britanniæ in Rerum Britannicarum.* Edited by Hieronymus Commelinus. Heidelberg, 1637.

Monmouth, Geoffrey of. *Hist. Reg. Brit.* Edited by J. A. Giles for the Caxton Society. London, 1844.

Monstrelet, Euguerrand de. *Chronique.* Edited for the Société de l'Histoire de France by L. Douët-d'Arcq. (6 vols.), Paris, 1857–62. *Ibid.*, " continued by others . . . to the year MDXVI," translated by T. Johnes, and printed " At the hafod press."

Morris, Rupert H. *Chester in the Plantagenet and Tudor Reigns.* Chester, [?1894.]

Moss, Hugh, *see* English Church.

Mount Holyoke, *see* Porter.

Munday, Anthony.

(*Show for 1605*). *The Trivmphes of re-united Britania.* Performed at the cost and charges of the . . . Merchants-Taylors, in honor of Sir Leonard Holliday, Kni. to solemnize his entrance as Lorde Mayor of the Citty of London, on Tuesday the 29. of October. 1605. Deuised and written by A. Mundy, Cittizen and Draper of London. London, [1605]. [BM, B. Reprinted in *Prog. James*, i, p. 564. Cf. Greg, p. 21; Fairholt, pt. i, p. 29; J. G. Nichols, p. 100; *Gent. Mag.*, for August, 1824, p. 114.]

(*Show for 1609*). In BM [*C. 33. e. 7 (23)*] are to be found the last four leaves of the description of the 1609 Show, to which is prefixed the following pencilled title-page: " Camp-bell; or the Ironmongers Faire Field (a Pageant at the installation of Sir Thomas Campbell in the office of Lord Mayor of London, 29 October 1609)." In pencil, on the margin of the first sheet, this is attributed to Munday.

London's Love, to the Royal Prince Henrie, meeting him on the River of Thames, at his returne from Richmonde, with a Worthie Fleete of her Cittizens, on Thursday the last of May, 1610. With a breife [*sic*] reporte of the Water Fight, and Fireworkes. London, Printed by Edw. Allde for Nathaniell Fosbrooke, and are to be solde at the West-end of Paules, neere to the Bishop of Londons gate, 1610. [Gh, BM. This is by Munday; *see* Dr. C. W. Wallace, in the London *Times*, 28 March, 1913, p. 6 col. 1.]

(*Show for 1611*). *Chryso-thriambos, the triumphes of Golde.* [Cf. Greg, p. 20; Fairholt, pt. i, p. 32; J. G. Nichols, p. 100; *Gent. Mag.*, for August, 1824, p. 114. I have not seen a copy of this pamphlet.]

(*Show for 1614*). *Himatia-Poleos.* The Trivmphs of olde Draperie, or the rich Cloathing of England. Performed . . . at the charges of the . . . Drapers at the enstalment of Sir Thomas Hayes . . . in the high office of Lord Maior of London . . . the 29. day of October. 1614. Deuised and written by A. M. Citizen and Draper of London. London, 1614. [BM. Cf. Greg, p. 20; Fairholt, pt. i, pp. 37f.; J. G. Nichols, p. 102; *Gent. Mag.*, for August, 1824, p. 115.]

(*Show for 1615*). *Metropolis Coronata, the Trivmphes of Ancient Drapery:* or, Rich Cloathing of England, in a second Yeeres performance. In Honour of the aduancement of Sir Iohn Iolles, Knight, to the high office of Lord Maior . . . on Monday, being the 30. day of October, 1615 . . . Deuised and written by A. M. Citizen and Draper of London. London, 1615. [Gh, B, BM. Reprinted in *Prog. James*, iii, p. 107; cf. Greg, p. 20; Fairholt, pt. i, pp. 38f.; J. G. Nichols, p. 102; *Gent. Mag.*, for August, 1824, p. 115.]

(*Show for 1616*). *Chrysanaleia: The Golden Fishing: Or, Honour of Fishmongers.* Applauding the aduancement of Mr. Iohn Leman, Alderman, to the dignitie of Lord Maior of London . . . on Tuesday, being the 29. day of October, 1616 . . . Deuised and written by A. M. Citizen and Draper of London. London, 1616. [Gh, B, BM. Reprinted, *Prog. James*, iii, p. 195; cf. Greg, p. 20; Fairholt, pt. i, p. 40; J. G. Nichols, and *Gent. Mag.*, *loc cit.*]

The Fishmongers' Pageant, on Lord Mayor's Day, 1616. Chrysanaleia, the Golden Fishing, devised by Anthony Munday, Citizen and Draper. Represented in twelve plates by Henry Shaw, F. S. A., from Contemporary Drawings in the possession of the . . . Fishmongers. Accompanied with various illustrative documents, and an historical introduction by John Gough Nichols, F. S. A., Citizen and Stationer. Printed for the Worshipful Company of Fishmongers. [London], 1844. [Gh, BM, HL.]

(*Show for 1618*). *Sidero-Thriambos. Or Steele and Iron Triumphing.* Applauding the aduancement of Sir Sebastian Haruey . . . to the dignitie of Lord Maior . . . on Thursday . . . the 29. day of October, 1618. Performed . . . at the charges of his kinde Brethren, the . . . Ironmongers. Deuised and written by A. M. Citizen and

Draper of London. London, 1618. [BM. Cf. Greg, p. 20; not mentioned by Fairholt or J. G. Nichols.]

(*Show for 1623*). *See* Middleton (sub anno 1623). *The Trivmphs of the Golden Fleece.* Performed at the cost and charges of the Auncient and Honourable Societie of the Drapers. For the enstaulment of their Worthy Brother, Mr. Martin Lvmley in the Maioralty of London. On Wednesday . . . the nine and twentieth day of October, 1623. Written by A. Mundy, Citizen and Draper of London. London, 1623. [BM. (*C. 33. E. 7(6)*)]

[Münchausen, Baron]. *The Surprising Travels and Adventures of Baron Munchausen . . . A new and complete edition. . . .* London, 1823.

A Sequel to the Travels and Adventures of Baron Munchausen. [Printed as vol. ii of the above.] London, 1823.

Murimuth, Adam. *Continuatio Chronicarum.* Edited by Edward M. Thompson. (RS 93) London, 1889.

Muskett, Charles, *see* Ewing.

Neilson, William A. "Origins and Sources of the Court of Love," in *Harvard Studies and Notes in Philology and Literature* (vi), Boston, 1899.

Nelson, Thomas. (*Show for 1590*). *The Device of the Pageant:* Set forth by the Worshipfull Companie of the Fishmongers, for the right honorable Iohn Allot: established Lord Maior of London, and maior of the Staple for this present yeere of our Lord 1590. By T. Nelson. London, 1590. Black-letter. [BM (*C. 38. d. 25.*) *See also* Withington, "The Lord Mayor's Show for 1590," in *Mod. Lang. Notes* for January, 1918.]

Nettleton, G. H., *see* Yale.

New Boston. From Cave Life to City Life. Pageant Program Number, November, 1910. Lotta A. Clark, Mistress of the Pageant. [HL]

Newcastle, Duke of, *see* W. Cavendish.

Nicholl, John. *Some Account of the Worshipful Company of Ironmongers.* Compiled from their own Records, and other authentic sources of information. London, 1866.

Nichols, John. *History and Antiquities of the County of Leicester.* (4 vols. bound in 8), London, 1795–1811.

Nichols, John. *Progresses, &c., of Queen Elizabeth.* (3 vols.), London, 1823. [Abbreviated: *Prog. Q. Eliz.*]

Nichols, John. *Progresses, &c., of King James the First.* (4 vols.), London, 1828. [Abbreviated: *Prog. James.*]

Nichols, John. Various articles on the Lord Mayor's Shows of the seventeenth century, in the *Gent. Mag.*, from August, 1824 to May, 1825.

Nichols, John Gough. *London Pageants.* London, 1831. [Referred to in the text as J. G. Nichols.]

See also Machyn, *and* Munday (sub anno 1616).

Nicolas, Sir Nicholas Harris. *History of the Battle of Agincourt.* (Second edition), London, 1832.

Norfolk Archæology. Norwich, 1847 *et seq.*

Norman, Philip, *see* W. Rendle.

[Norristown, Pennsylvania]. *History of the Centennial Celebration*, &c. (1812–1912.) By the Rev. Theodore Heysham, Ph.D. (Illustrated.) [Norristown] 1913.

North, Roger. *Examen . . .* London, 1740.

[Norwich]. *See* Ewing, Fitch, B. Garter, W. Hudson, *and Norf. Arch.*

[Nottingham]. *See* Deering.

Nugent, Thomas, translator. *A Tour to London, or new Observations on England and its Inhabitants.* (2 vols.), London, 1772. [*See* Grosley.]

Oberholtzer, E. P. "The Philadelphia Historical Pageant of 1912," in the *Alumni Register of the University of Pennsylvania* for January, 1913.

Oberholtzer, E. P. "Historical Pageants in England and America," in the *Century Magazine* for July, 1910.

O'Curry, Eugene. *On the Manners and Customs of the Ancient Irish.* Edited by W. K. Sullivan. (3 vols.), London and New York, 1873.

Official Programs of nineteenth- and twentieth-century Lord Mayor's Shows. [The collection, given by Bernard Kettle, Esq., J. Dixon Taylor, Esq., and D. J. Hile, Esq., of the Guildhall, to HL, includes the programs of the shows for 1850, 1884, 1889–92, 1895–96, 1901, 1902, 1904–11, 1913 *et seq.* Many of the programs are illustrated. (HL, *Thr. 1211.61.*)]

Ogilby, John. *The Relation of His Majestie's Entertainment, Passing through the city of London to his Coronation: with a description of the Triumphal Arches, and Solemnity.* By John Ogilby. London, 1661. [Gh, B (2 copies.)]

Ogilby, John. *The Entertainment of . . . Charles II in his passage through the City of London to his Coronation . . . To these is added A Brief Narrative of his Majestie's Solemn Coronation . . .* By John Ogilby. (Illustrated.) London, 1662. [Gh]

Ogilby, John. *The King's Coronation:* Being an Exact Account of the Cavalcade, with a Description of the Triumphal Arches, and Speeches prepared by the City of London for his late Majesty Charles the Second . . . Also the Narrative of his Majesties Coronation . . . Published by William Morgan, his Majesties Cosmographer. London, 1685. [Gh, B (2 copies.)]

Ibid., reprinted by the heir of Andrew Anderson. Edinburgh, 1685. [Gh]

Oldys, William, and Thomas Park. *The Harleian Miscellany.* (10 vols.), London, 1808, etc.

Ordish, T. F. "English Folk Drama," in *Folk-Lore* (ii, 3, p. 314; iv, 2, p. 149), September, 1891 and June, 1893.

Ormerod, George. *History of the County Palatine and City of Chester.* (With a republication of Sir Peter Leycester's *Cheshire Antiquities* and Daniel King's *Vale Royal.*) Second edition, revised and enlarged by Thomas Helsby. (3 vols.), London, 1882.

Orr, William, *see* Bates.

Orridge, B. B. *Some Account of the Citizens of London and their Rulers.* London, 1867.

Ovatio Carolina, see Charles I.

Overall, W. H., editor. *Accounts of the Churchwardens of the Parish of St. Michael, Cornhill . . . from 1456 to 1608.* [London, 1871.]

Overall, W. H., and H. C. Overall. *Analytical Index to the series of records known as the Remembrancia, Preserved among the Archives of the City of London. A.D. 1579–1664.* London, 1878.

Oxford Pageant. Frank Lascelles, Master. July, 1907. *The Book of Words.* (Illustrated.) [Oxford, 1907.]

Pageants, *see* Lord Mayor's Shows.

Palmer, John. *The Future of the Theatre.* London, 1913.

Parker, Louis N. "Historical Pageants," in *Journ. Soc. Arts* for 22 December, 1905 (liv, p. 142.) London.

Parker, Louis N. "What is a Pageant ?" in *New Boston* for November, 1910. Boston.

Parker, Louis N. *See* Sherborne, Dover, Warwick, Bury St. Edmunds, Colchester, *and* York. Also: *Last Days of St. Benet's Abbey.* A Village Pageant-play. Given on 7 and 8 August, 1907, at Potter Heigham (Norfolk).

Paris, Matthew of. *Chronica Majora.* Edited by H. R. Luard. (RS 57) (7 vols.), London, 1880.

Ibid., translated by the Rev. J. A. Giles. London, 1852.

Paris, Matthew of. *Chronica Minora.* Edited by Sir F. Madden. (RS 44) (3 vols.), London, 1866.

Paris, Journal d'un Bourgeois de, see Tuetey.

Paston Letters. 1422–1509. A new edition, &c., edited by James Gairdner. (3 vols.), London, 1872–75.

Paul, Sir J. B. "Processions," in the *Scottish Review* (xxx, p. 217), 1897. [This essay deals with the processional customs of man, and includes a passing reference to several mediæval pageants.]

[Peace Jubilee of 1814]. *An Historical Memento*, representing the different scenes of public rejoicing, which took place the first of August, in St. James's and Hyde Parks, London, in celebration of the Glorious Peace of 1814, and of the Centenary of the Accession of the Illustrious House of Brunswick. . . . (Illustrated.) London, 1814. [SA]

Peele, George. *Works.* Edited by the Rev. Alexander Dyce. Second edition. (3 vols.), London, 1829–39.

Ibid., edited by A. H. Bullen. (2 vols.), London, 1888.

Peele, George.

(*Show for 1585*). *The Device of the Pageant* borne before Woolstone Dixi Lord Maior of the Citie of London. An. 1585. October 29. Imprinted at London by Edward Allde, 1585.

Under the Latin "Verses written vnder the Armes of England" at the end of the pamphlet, stands: "Donne by George Peele Maister of artes in Oxford." [B (*Gough Lond. 122.1*): on the fly-leaf, in Farmer's MS.: "This is probably the only copy remaining. It was given up to me, as a Favour, at Mr. West's Auction for £0, 8*s.* 0*d.* I have seen a fine wooden print of Sir Wolstan at Christ's Hospital. See Stow by Strype." (This note is printed in *Harl. Misc.*, x, p. 351.)]

The pamphlet is reprinted in Dyce (1829), ii, p. 147; Bullen, i, p. 351; Price, p. 199; *Prog. Q. Eliz.*, ii, p. 446; *Hist. Leicestershire*, iv, p. 496; Strype's Stow's *Survey* (1720), ii, p. 136; *Harl. Misc.* (1813) x, p. 351. Cf. Greg, p. 22; Fairholt, pt. i, p. 24; J. G. Nichols, p. 100; *Gent. Mag.*, for August, 1824, p. 113.

(*Show for 1588*). "*Ye device of the Pageant* borne before the Righte honorable Martyn Calthrop, lord Maiour . . . George Peele the author," was entered on the Stationers' Register 28 October, 1588. *See* Arber, *The Stationers' Register*, ii, p. 504. Fleay, *Biographical Chronicle of the English Drama, 1559–1642.* (2 vols.), London, 1891, ii, p. 154, assigns the "device" to Peele; cf. *ibid.*, p. 402. Greg, p. 20; Fairholt, pt. i, p. 26, and *Gent. Mag.*, for August, 1824, p. 113, record the show.

(*Show for 1591*). *Descensus Astrææ.* The Device of a Pageant borne before M. William Web, Lord Maior of the Citie of London, on the day he tooke his oath, beeing the 29. of October. 1591. Wherevnto is annexed A Speech deliuered by one clad like a Sea Nymph, who presented a Pinesse on the water brauely rigd and mand, to the Lord Maior, at the time he tooke Barge to go to Westminster. Done by G. Peele Maister of Arts in Oxford. Printed for William Wright. [London, 1591.] [Gh.] Reprinted in Bullen, i, p. 361; Dyce (1829), ii, p. 155; *Harl. Misc.*, x, p. 68, and Gillespy, p. 66. Cf. Fairholt, pt. i, p. 27; J. G. Nichols, p. 100; Greg, p. 22; *Gent. Mag.*, for August, 1824, p. 113.

Pepys, Samuel. *Diary.* Edited by H. B. Wheatley, with Lord Braybrooke's notes. (10 vols.), London, 1893–99.

Perkins, Rev. F. L. *Up the Heights.* A Play with a Purpose. York, n. d.

Perkins, Rev. F. L. *Disinherited — ?* A Play-Pageant in aid of the Church in Wales. York [1914].

[Perry, Micajah]. *A Transcript of the Diary of the Proceedings, Habits* [costumes] *and Ceremonials observed in the Office of Lord Mayor of the City of London, in the Mayoralty of Micajah Perry, 1738–39.* Made in 1833, and presented to the London Corporation Library by the Town Clerk. [Gh, *MS. 15.*]

Another copy of the same MS. made "from one on vellum formerly in the possession of Mr. Woodthorpe, and which was destroyed by Fire at the Royal Exchange on the night of the 10th of January, 1838," is also in the Gh. [*MS. 16.*] A third, copied in 1787, is in the Gh [*MS. 267* (*no. 3.*)].

Peterborough, New Hampshire, Pageant. George P. Baker, Master. *Book of Words.* [Peterborough] 1910.

Petowe, Henry. *England's Cæsar. His Maiesties most Royall Coronation.* Together with the manner of the Solemne shewes prepared for the honour of his entry into the Cittie of London. Eliza. her Coronation in Heauen. And Londons Sorrow for her visitation. By Henry Petowe. London, 1603. [BM. Reprinted in *Harl. Misc.*, x, p. 342.]

Pewterers. *See* Welch.

[Philip II]. *See* Elder.

[Pickering Pageant. (Yorkshire.)] Gilbert Hudson, Master. *The Book of the Pickering Pageant* (*or Historical Play*). Arranged by Gilbert Hudson. August 10, 11, 12, 13, 1910. Pickering [1910.]

Political Merriment, see Brinsden.

Pollard, A. F., *see Tudor Tracts.*

Pollard, A. W. *English Miracle Plays, Moralities and Interludes.* Oxford, 1890.

Poole, Benjamin. *The History of Coventry. . . .* ("Embellished with numerous engravings.") Coventry, 1852.

Poole, Benjamin. *Coventry: its History and Antiquities.* Compiled . . . from authentic publications, ancient manuscripts and charters, corporation records, &c. (Illustrated by W. F. Taunton.) London and Coventry, 1870.

[Pope-burning.]

Londons Defiance to Rome, a Perfect Narrative of the Magnificent Procession, and solemn Burning of the Pope at Temple Barr, Nov. 17th 1679 (Being the Coronation Day [*sic*] of that Never-to-be-forgotten Princess, Queen Elizabeth.) With a Description of the Order, Rich Habits, Extraordinary Fire-works, Songs, and General Tryumphs attending that Illustrious Ceremony. [n. p., n. d.] [SA, B.]

(Cf. *Tracts relating to the Popish Plot*, 1679–82, in BM [*8133. h. 5* (*1–10*)] of which the fourth pamphlet is entitled:

The Scots Demonstration of their Abhorrence of Popery, with all its Adherents. In a letter from Edenbrough to a Friend in London, containing the Manner of Burning the Pope there in Effigie on Christ-Mass Day, &c. [? 1680].)

The Solemn Mock Procession: or the Tryal and Execution of the Pope and his Ministers, on the 17. of Nov. at Temple-Bar; where, being brought before the Figure of Q. Elizabeth, he receiveth his first Sentence; and afterwards led before the Statue or Tribunal of K. Charles the Second: on the other side he receives his Final Doom and Downfal, viz., to be burnt with all his Fry into Ashes, and the same to be scattered about, that thence might never spring hereafter in England one Popish Phenix. London, 1680. (Illustrated.) [BM. Cf. Fairholt, pt. i, p. 92, n. 2; Saintsbury's ed. of Scott's Dryden (18 vols., Edinburgh, 1882–93), vi, p. 237; North, *Examen* (cited *ibid.*, x, p. 370); Scott's Swift (19 vols., Edinburgh, 1814), ii, p. 408–10; Brayley, *Lond.*, iv, p. 80; Hone, p. 242.]

A Modest Apology for the Students of Edenburgh Burning a Pope, December 25, 1680, Humbly Rescuing the Actors from the Imputation of Disloyalty and Rebellion, with which they were charged in a Letter, &c. . . . London, 1681. [19 pp. Cf. BM, *T. 2* (28)* — a collection of tracts — p. 114.]

The Procession: or, the Burning of the Pope in Effigie at Temple Bar, or in Smithfield, on the 17th of November, 1681, being Queen Elizabeth's Birthday. Describing the several Pageants, and rare Devices of the Pope, Cardinals, Jesuits, Friers, and many others. As likewise a Pageant of several Effigies in a Pillory drawn by Horses upon a Sledge. Several painted Pieces, and Fire-works, &c. Far exceeding whatever has been exposed in this nature. With the signification of the several Hieroglyphicks. Humbly dedicated to his Holiness. [4 pp. 1681.] [BM, B.]

[This pamphlet is numbered 8 in the BM collection of *Tracts Relating to the Popish Plot*, and is also in the Bodl. (*Gough Midds. 32.*)]

A Dialogue upon the Burning of the Pope and Presbyter in Effigie at Westminster, Novem. 5, 1681. London, 1682. [B]

(Cf. Brayley, *Londiniana*, iii, p. 205; iv, p. 73; Brinsden; *Massachusetts Laws,* and chapter vii of the text, for a discussion of this pageantry.)

Porta Pietatis, see Heywood (sub anno 1638).

Porter, Elizabeth C. " A Pageant of Progress," in the *Outlook* for 23 November, 1912, p. 653. (Illustrated.) [The writer describes the Mount Holyoke Pageant, which celebrated the seventy-fifth anniversary of the founding of the College.]

Potter Heigham, *see* Parker.

Pouncy, H., *see* West Dorset.

Presentation in the Temple, The. A Pageant as originally presented by the Corporation of Weavers in Coventry . . . Edinburgh, printed for the Abbotsford Club, 1836.

[Preston]. *The History of Preston in Lancashire; together with the Guild Merchant,* &c. (Illustrated by 18 plates.) [E. Jeffrey.] London, 1822.

See also J. Taylor.

Price, J. E. *A Descriptive Account of the Guildhall of the City of London: its History and Associations.* London, 1886.

Prideaux, Sir Walter S. *Memorials of the Goldsmiths' Company.* (2 vols.), London, n. d.

Proceedings, or Minutes, of Committees for Conducting the Entertainment at Guildhall on Lord Mayor's Days (with accounts of expenses in some cases). Gh, *MSS.*

For 1790, MS. 25; 1794, MS. 26; 1795 and 1801, MS. 25; 1809 (with " Expences at Guildhall " on Lord Mayor's Day, 1815), MS. 148; 1821, MS. 27; two contemporary copies of the Minutes for 1822, MSS. 28 and 149; for 1823, MS. 29; for 1825, MS. 30; 1833, MS. 32; 1839, MS. 33; the accounts for 1847 (bound with the 1822 Minutes), MS. 149; the Minutes for 1848, MS. 34; 1849, MSS. 35 and 899; 1879, MS. 517. For 1824–25, *see above, under* Ceremonies.

Procession of the Lord Mayor's Show. London, n. d. (A colored panorama, folded in a cover. [HL.])

Puttenham, George. *The Arte of English Poesie.* London, 1589.

[Quebec]. *Les Fêtes du Troisième Centenaire de Québec, 1608–1908.* (Illustrated.) Quebec, 1911.

Quebec Pageant. Frank Lascelles, Master. *Historical Souvenir and Book of the Pageants of the 300th Anniversary of the Founding of Quebec, the Ancient Capital of Canada.* 20–31 July, 1908. (Illustrated.) Montreal [1908].

The Quebec Tercentenary Commemorative History. (Illustrated.) By Frank Carrel (and others.) Quebec, 1908. (This volume is cited as Carrel.)

Quenson, le Conseiller. *Gayant, le Géant de Douai; sa Famille et sa Procession.* (Illustrated.) Douai, 1839. [SA]

Raine, J., Jr. *A Volume of English Miscellanies.* Published by the Surtees Society (lxxxv), 1890.

Remembrancia, see Overall.

Rendle, William, and Philip Norman. *Inns of Old Southwark.* London, 1888.

Repertory. The MS. records of the Court of Aldermen of the Corporation of London. In the Guildhall Archives.

Reyher, Paul. *Les Masques anglais.* Paris, 1909.

Reynolds, George F. "Some Principles of Elizabethan Staging," in *Modern Philology* for April and June, 1905. Chicago.

Rhode Island Normal School. *A Victory Pageant,* 29 May, 1919. [Program in HL]

Riley, H. T. *Memorials of London and London Life.* London, 1868.
See also: Liber Albus, and Walsingham.

Ritson, Joseph, *see* Chestre.

[Robarts, Henry]. *The Most royall and Honourable entertainment, of the famous and renowmed* [sic] *King, Christiern the fourth, King of Denmarke, &c. . . .* With the royall passage on Thursday the 31. of July, thorough the Citty of London, and honorable shewes there presented them, and maner of their passing. By H. R. At London, printed for H. R. . . . 1606. [Gh]

Robert of Brunne, *see* Manning.

Robert of Gloucester, *see* Gloucester.

Rockwell, Ethel T. *Historical Pageantry: a Treatise and a Bibliography.* [The State Historical Society of Wisconsin, Bulletin of Information no. 84, July, 1916]. (Illustrated.)
[A six-page essay with an incomplete bibliography on pageantry.]

Rosny, Lucien de. *L'Épervier d' Or, ou description historique des Joûtes et des Tournois, célébrés à Lille au Moyen-Age.* (Illustrated.) Paris and Lille, 1839. [SA]

Rowell, G. A. "Notes on some old-fashioned English Customs: The Mummers, the Morris Dancers," &c., in *Folk-Lore Journal* for April and June, 1886.

Royal Oak, see Tatham (sub anno 1660).

Saddlers, *see* Sherwell.

[St. Albans]. *St. Albans and its Pageant.* The official souvenir of the Pageant held in July, 1907. (Produced under the direction of Herbert Jarman.) Various contributions arranged by E. W. Townson. London and St. Albans, 1907.

St. Johnsbury, Vermont, Pageant. W. C. Langdon, Master. Held on 15–17 August, 1912. *Book of Words.* St. Johnsbury, 1912.

[St. Louis]. *The Book of Words of the Pageant and Masque of St. Louis.* The words of the Pageant by Thomas Wood Stevens; the words of the Masque by Percy MacKaye. St. Louis, 1914. [HL, *Thr. 1211.74.*]

[St. Louis]. *Report of the Celebration of the Anniversary of the Founding of St. Louis.* 15 February, 1847. [St. Louis], 1847. [HL, *US. 25390.7.5.*]

[St. Louis]. "The Veiled Prophet." Frank Gaiennie, in the *Encyclopædia of the History of St. Louis,* by William Hyde and Howard L. Conrad, (vol. iv, p. 2370.) New York, Louisville, and St. Louis, 1899.

Salters, *see* Gillespy.

Saltmarshe, Colonel, *see* Solloway.

Sawyer, F. E. "The Sussex 'Tipteerers' Play," in *Folk-Lore Journal* for January, 1884.

Scarborough Historical Pageant and Play. Scarborough Castle Yard. July 9th to 13th, 1912. Gilbert Hudson, Master. *Book of Words.* Scarborough, 1912.

Schelling, Felix E. *The Elizabethan Drama.* (2 vols.), Boston and New York, 1908. [Chapter xv treats the history of the masque.]

Schenck, Frederic. *Foreign Chivalry at the Court of Edward III.* [Unpublished dissertation.]

Scherm, C. W. "Das Wesen der neuen Maske unter Heinrich VIII von England," in *Germ.-Rom. Monatschrift* for August–September, 1912. Heidelberg, 1912.

Scherm, C. W. "Englishe Hofmaskeraden bis 1550," in Koch, *Studien zur vergleichenden Literaturgeschichte* (ix, p. 406). Berlin, 1909. [This paper deals with the origins of the masque, and its development in the reign of Henry VIII.]

[Scotland]. *The Scottish National Pageant of Allegory, Myth and History.* To be held in the Grounds of the Scottish National Exhibition, Saturday, 13th June, 1908. . . . Edinburgh [1908]. [Program in HL.]

Scott, Sir Walter. *See* Somers; and his editions of Swift and Dryden, listed under Pope-burning.

Segar, Sir William. *Honor Military and Ciuill.* London, 1602. [BM, *9917. i. 5.*]

Settle, Elkanah, *see* F. C. Brown.

(*Show for 1691*). *The Triumphs of London*, Performed on Thursday, Octob. 29. 1691 for the Entertainment of . . . Sir Thomas Stamp, Kt. . . . Containing a true description of the several Pageants, with the Speeches spoken on each Pageant. All set forth at the proper Costs and Charges of the . . . Drapers. By E. S. (Epistle dedicatory signed "E. Settle.") London, 1691. [Gh, B (2 copies), HL, BM. Cf. Fairholt, pt. i, p. 109; J. G. Nichols, p. 117.]

(*Show for 1692*). *The Triumphs of London.* Performed on Saturday, Octob. 29, 1692 for the Entertainment of . . . Sir John Fleet, Kt. . . . Containing a True Description of the Several Pageants; with the Speeches spoken on each Pageant. All set forth at the proper Costs and Charges of the . . . Grocers. Together with an exact Relation of the Most Splendid Entertainments, prepared for the Reception of Their Sacred Majesties. By E. S. London, 1692. [Gh, B, BM. Reprinted in Health (3d ed.) appendix, p. 551. Cf. Fairholt, pt. i, p. 111; J. G. Nichols, p. 117; Gough, *Brit. Top.*, p. 342.]

(*Show for 1693*). *The Triumphs of London.* Performed on Monday, Octob. 30th, 1693, for the Entertainment of . . . Sir William Ashurst, Knight . . . Containing a True Description of the several Pageants; with the Speeches spoken on each Pageant. All set forth at the proper Costs and Charges of the . . . Merchant-Taylors. Together with the Festival Songs for his Lordship and the Companies Diversion. By E. S. London, 1693. [BM. Cf. Fairholt, pt. i, p. 112; J. G. Nichols, p. 117.][1]

(*Show for 1694*). *The Triumphs of London*, Prepared for the Entertainment of . . . Sir Thomas Lane, Knight . . . Containing a full Description of the Pageants, Speeches, Songs, and the whole Solemnity of the Day. Performed one [*sic*] Monday the 29 of October, 1694. Set forth at the Proper Cost and Charges of the . . . Clothworkers. London, 1694. [Gh, BM. Cf. Fairholt, pt. i, p. 113; J. G. Nichols, p. 118.]

(*Show for 1695*). *The Triumphs of London.* Performed on Tuesday, Octob. 29. 1695 for the Entertainment of . . . Sir John Houblon, Kt. . . . Containing a True Description of the Several Pageants; with the Speeches spoken on each Pageant. All prepared, at the proper Costs and Charges of the . . . Grocers. To which is added a New Song

---

[1] In a letter of 13 July, 1918, Mr. Bernard Kettle, Librarian of Guildhall, London, writes: ". . . In the recent Huth sale were three of Settle's pageants. Two we already had, but the third, Ashurst's pageant of 1693, we were anxious to secure. The Committee's limit of twenty-five guineas was, however, outbid by one of £28, 10s. — a good price for poor Settle's tosh! How he would have jumped at such a price for the original MS., when it is remembered he only received £6 for one of his efforts."

upon His Majesty's Return. By E. S. Published by Authority. London, 1695. [Gh, B, BM. Cf. Fairholt, pt. i, p. 113; J. G. Nichols, p. 118.]

(*Show for 1698*). *Glory's Resurrection; being the Triumphs of London Revived*, for the Inauguration of . . . Sir Francis Child, Kt. . . . Containing the Description (and also the Sculptures) of the Pageants, and the whole Solemnity of the Day. All set forth at the proper Cost and Charges of the . . . Goldsmiths. Publish'd by Authority. London, 1698. (Illustrated.) [Gh, BM. Cf. Fairholt, pt. i, p. 114; J. G. Nichols, p. 118. The illustrations are: The Amphitheatre of Union; the Goldsmiths' Laboratory; a Triumphant Chariot of Gold, and the Temple of Honour; they are reproduced in Brown, opp. pp. 122, 124, and 126.]

(*Show for 1699*). *The Triumphs of London*, For the Inauguration of . . . Sir Richard Levett, Kt. . . . Containing a Description of the Pageants, together with the Publick Speeches, and the whole Solemnity of the Day. Performed on Monday, the 30th Day of October, Anno 1699. All set forth at the proper Cost and Charges of the . . . Haberdashers. London, MDCXCIX. [Gh, BM. (The prefaces are signed "E. Settle.") Cf. Fairholt, pt. i, p. 115; J. G. Nichols, p. 119.]

(*Show for 1700*). *The Triumphs of London*, for the Inauguration of . . . Sir Thomas Abney, Kt. . . . Containing a Description of the Pageants together with the Publicke Speeche[s] and the whole Solemnity of the Day. Performed on Tuesday the 29th of October, 1700. All set forth at the proper Cost and Charges of the . . . Fishmongers. Published by Authority. London, 1700. [Gh. Cf. Fairholt, pt. i, p. 116; J. G. Nichols, p. 119.]

(*Show for 1701*). *The Triumphs of London*, For the Inauguration of . . . Sir William Gore, Kt. . . . Containing a Description of the Pageants, together with the Publick Speeches, and the whole Solemnity of the Day. Performed on Wednesday the 29th of October, 1701. All set forth at the proper Cost and Charge of the . . . Mercers. Published by Authority. London, 1701. [Gh, B. Cf. Fairholt, pt. i, p. 117; J. G. Nichols, p. 119.]

(*Show for 1702*). *The Triumphs of London*, At the Inauguration of . . . Sir Samuel Dashwood, Kt. . . . Containing a Description of the Pageants, the Speeches, and the whole Solemnity of the Day. Perform'd on Thursday the 29th of October. All set forth at the Cost and Charges of the . . . Vintners. Together with the Relation of Her Majesty's Reception and Entertainment at Dinner in Guild-hall. Publish'd by Authority. London, 1702. [Gh. Cf. Fairholt, pt. i, p. 118; J. G. Nichols, pp. 84 and 119.]

(*Show for 1708*). *The Triumphs of London* for the Inauguration of . . . Sir Charles Duncombe, Knight. Containing the Description (and also the Sculptures) of the Pageants, and the whole Solemnity of the Day. Performed on Friday the 29th of October, Anno 1708. All set forth at the proper Cost and Charge of the . . . Goldsmiths. Published by Authority. London, 1708. [Gh, B, BM. The Chariot of Justice — which is the same as the 1698 Chariot of Gold — forms the frontispiece of Fairholt's *Civic Garland*. The illustrations are: the Temple of Apollo; St. Dunstan; The Chariot of Justice. Cf. on this show, Fairholt, pt. i, p. 122; J. G. Nichols, pp. 119 f. F. C. Brown, p. 126, n. 5, points out that "the Guildhall copy has lost the 'sculptures,'" but that the BM and B copies have the cuts.]

Sharp, Thomas. *Dissertation on Pageants or Mysteries at Coventry*. (Illustrated.) Coventry, 1825.

Sharpe, Reginald R., editor. *Calendar of Letter-Books, preserved among the archives of the Corporation of the City of London*. (11 vols.), London, 1899 *et seq.*

Sharpe, Reginald R. *London and the Kingdom.* (3 vols.), London, 1894–95.

Shaw, Henry, *see* Munday (sub anno 1616).

Sherborne, Dorsetshire, Pageant. Louis N. Parker, Master. *In celebration of the twelve hundredth Anniversary of the Founding of the Town of Sherborne,* &c. By Louis N. Parker. (12–15 June, 1905), Sherborne, 1905.

Sherwell, John W. *A Descriptive and Historical Account of the Guild of Saddlers.* [London,] 1889.

Shirley, John. *The Triumph of Peace. A Masque presented by the Foure Honourable Houses, or Innes of Court . . . at White Hall, February the third, 1633. . . .* London, 1633.

Skinners, *see* Wadmore.

Smith, J. L., *see* Lancaster.

Smith, Lucy Toulmin. *The York Plays.* Oxford, 1885.

Smith, Toulmin. *English Gilds.* [EETS. xl.] With an introductory essay on guilds and trades-unions by Dr. L. Brentano. London, 1870; reprinted, 1902.

Smith, William, *see* King.

[Smith, William]. *Of a celebration of the King's Coronation-Day in the famous City of Bathe. A true Narrative in a Letter sent from thence to Dr. Charleton, Physician to his Majestie.* London, 1661. [B (*Wood, 537.17.*)]

Solemn Mock Procession, see Pope-burning.

Solloway, Rev. J., and Colonel Saltmarshe, editors. *The Historic and Heraldic Guide to the York Pageant.* York, 1909.

Somers, Lord. *A Collection of Scarce and Valuable Tracts,* &c. Second edition, revised, augmented and arranged by Sir Walter Scott. (13 vols.) London, 1809–15.

Songs, Duets, &c., in the New Pantomine called Lord Mayor's Day, or a Flight from Lapland. As performed at the Theatre-Royal in Covent-Garden. With the Grand Procession, &c. London, printed for T. Cadell, in the Strand, 1783. [Gh]

Sörgel, A. *Die Englischen Maskenspiele.* Halle, 1882.

Spenser Society's collection of Taylor's works " not included in the folio volume of 1630." Five collections (vols. 7, 14, 19, 21, and 25 of the Society's Publications, 1870–78).

Sprott, Thomas. *Chronica.* Edited by Thomas Hearne. Oxford, 1719.

Squire, John. (*Show for 1620.*) *Tes Irenes Trophæa, or the Tryumphs of Peace.* That Celebrated the Solemnity of . . . Sir Francis Iones, Knight, at his Inauguration into the Maioraltie of London, on Monday being the 30. of October 1620. At the particular cost and charge of the . . . Haberdashers. With explication of the seuerall shewes and deuices by I. S. London, 1620. [Gh. Reprinted in *Prog. James,* iii, p. 619. (The " Epistle Dedicatory " to the Mayor is signed Io. Squire.) Cf. Greg, p. 24; Fairholt, pt. i, p. 46; J. G. Nichols, p. 103; *Gent. Mag.,* for August, 1824, p. 116.]

Stevens, Frank. " The Giant and Hob Nob and their Story," in the *Salisbury Festival Book.* Salisbury, 1914.

Stevens, T. W., *see* St. Louis.

Stewart, Horace. *History of the Worshipful Company of Gold and Silver Wyre-Drawers.* (Illustrated.) London, 1891.

Stewart, Lila A., *see* Cincinnati.

Stone, Sir Benjamin. *Festivals, Ceremonies and Customs. Records of National Life and History reproduced from the collection of photographs made by Sir Benjamin Stone, M. P.* London, 1906.

Stow, John. *Annales, or a Generall Chronicle of England.* (Black-letter.) London, 1600.
Ibid., continued and augmented by Edmund Howes. London, 1615.
Ibid., London, 1631.

Stow, John. *Survey of London*. Corrected and enlarged by A[nthony] M[unday]. (Black-letter), London, 1618.

Ibid., corrected and enlarged by John Strype. (2 vols.), London, 1720.

Stow's Survey (from the text of 1603) with introduction and notes by C. L. Kingsford. (2 vols.), Oxford, 1908.

[Stow, John]. *Three Fifteenth-Century Chronicles*, with historical memoranda by John Stow. Edited by James Gairdner for the Camden Society. [London], 1880.

Strutt, Joseph. *Horda Angel-cynnan, or, a compleat view of the Manners, Customs &c., of the English people.* (3 vols.) Illustrated by 158 plates. London, 1774–76.

Strutt, Joseph. *Sports amd Pastimes of the People of England*, &c. London, 1801.

Ibid., enlarged and corrected by J. Charles Cox. London, 1903.

Strype, John, *see* Stow, *Survey.*

Stubbs, Rt. Rev. William, editor. *Chronicles of Edward I and II.* [Vol. i, includes the *Annales Londonienses* and the *Annales Paulini.*] (RS 76) London, 1882–83.

Sullivan, *see* O'Curry.

Symonds, John A. *Shakespeare's Predecessors.* London, 1884.

Tatham, John. *Dramatic Works.* Edited by J. Maidment and W. H. Logan. Edinburgh, 1879.

(*Show for 1657*). *London's Triumphs*, Celebrated the Nine and twentieth day of this present Month of October, 1657: in Honour to . . . Richard Chiverton, Lord Major . . . At the Costs and Charges of the . . . Skinners. By John Tatham, Gent. . . . London [1657, obliterated in the BM copy.] [BM. Cf. Fairholt, pt. i, p. 65; J. G. Nichols, p. 107; *Gent. Mag.*, for December, 1824, p. 514.]

(*Show for 1658.*) *Londons Tryumph, Presented by Industry and Honour:* with Other Delightfull Scænes, appertaining to them: Celebrated in Honour of . . . Sir John Ireton, Knight, . . . on the 29th day of October, 1658, and done at the Cost and Charges of the . . . Clothworkers. J. Tatham. London, 1658. [Gh, B (2 copies), BM. Cf. Fairholt, pt. i, p. 66; J. G. Nichols, p. 107; *Gent. Mag.*, for December, 1824, p. 514.]

(*Show for 1659*). *London's Tryumph*, celebrated the Nine and Twentieth day of October, in the year 1659. In Honour of the much Honoured Thomas Allen, Lord Mayor. . . . Presented and personated by an Europian, an Egyptian , and a Persian. And done at the Costs and Charges of the . . . Grocers. By J. Tatham. London, 1659. [B. Reprinted in Heath (3rd edition) appendix, p. 466. Cf. Fairholt, pt. i, p. 67; J. G. Nichols, p. 107; *Gent. Mag.*, for December, 1824, p. 515.]

(*Show for 1660*). *The Royal Oake*, with Other various and delightfull Scenes presented on the Water and the Land, Celebrated in Honour of . . . Sir Richard Brown . . . The 29th day of October in the 12 Year of his Majesties most happy, happy, Reign, An. Dom. 1660. And performed at the Costs and Charges of the . . . Merchant-Taylors, Being twice as many Pageants and Speeches as have been formerly showen, by John Tatham. London, 1660. [BM, B. Reprinted, Fairholt, pt. ii, p. 87; cf. *ibid.*, pt. i, p. 68; *Gent. Mag.*, for December, 1824, p. 515, and J. G. Nichols, p. 108.]

The Several Speeches made to the Honorable Sir Richard Brown, Lord Mayor . . . on Monday the Twenty Ninth Day of October, in the Twelfth Year of His Majesties most happy Reign, Anno Dom. 1660. With the manner of the Celebration of this Triumphant Day; and the various Scenes, Figures and Pageants; Representing the Royal Oak and its Pendant Leaves, that preserv'd and enshadow'd our Gracious Lord and Sovereign King Charles, from the hands of his Blood-thirsty Enemies. London, 1660. [Gh, C.]

Londons Glory, Represented by Time, Truth, and Fame: at the Magnificent Triumphs and Entertainment of His most Sacred Majesty Charles the II . . . at Guildhall on

Thursday being the 5th day of July 1660 and in the 12th Year of His Majestie[s] most happy Reign. Together with the Order and Management of the Whole Day's Business. London, 1660. [Gh, B, BM (3 copies), SA, C. Reprinted in his *Works*, p. 293.]

(*Show for 1661*). *London's Tryumphs*, Presented in several delightfull Scœnes, both on the Water and Land, and Celebrated in Honour to . . . Sir John Frederick, Knight and Baronet, Lord Mayor . . . At the Costs and Charges of the . . . Grocers. John Tatham. London, 1661. [BM, Gh. Reprinted in Heath (3d edition) appendix, p. 475; cf. Fairholt, pt. i, p. 68; J. G. Nichols, p. 108; *Gent. Mag.*, for December, 1824, p. 516.]

Aqua Triumphalis; being a True Relation of the Honourable the City of London's Entertaining Their Sacred Majesties upon the River of Thames, and Wellcoming them from Hampton Court to White-hall. Expressed and set forth in several Shewes and Pageants the 23. day of August 1662. Written by John Tatham, Gent. London, 1662. [Gh, BM, B (3 copies).]

(*Show for 1662*). *London's Triumph:* Presented In severall Delightfull Scænes, both upon the Water and Land: and celebrated in Honour of . . . Sir John Robinson . . . Lord Mayor . . . at the Costs and Charges of the . . . Clothworkers. London, 1662. [BM, B. Cf. Fairholt, pt. i, p. 71; J. G. Nichols, p. 109; *Gent. Mag.*, for December, 1824, p. 517.]

(*Show for 1663*). *Londinum Triumphans.* London's Triumphs, Celebrated in Honour of the truly Deserving Sir Anthony Bateman, Knight, Lord Maior . . . and done at the Costs and Charges of the . . . Skinners, the 29th of October, 1663. By John Tatham. London, 1663. [Gh. Cf. Fairholt, pt. i, p. 71; *Gent. Mag.*, for December, 1824, p. 517; J. G. Nichols, p. 109; Wadmore, p. 145.]

(*Show for 1664*). *London's Triumphs*, Celebrated the 29th of October, 1664. In Honour to the truely Deserver of Honour Sir Iohn Lawrence, Knight, Lord Maior . . . and Performed at the Costs and Charges of the . . . Haberdashers. . . . Written by John Tatham, Gent. London, 1664. [BM, B, Gh. Cf. Fairholt, pt. i, p. 71; J. G. Nichols, p. 109; *Gent. Mag.*, for December, 1824, p. 517.]

Taubman, Matthew.

(*Show for 1685*). *London's Annual Triumph:* Performed on Thursday Octob. 29. 1685. For the Entertainment of . . . Sir Robert Jeffreys, Kt. Lord Mayor . . . With a description of the several Pageants, Speeches and Songs, made proper for the occasion. All set forth at the proper Costs of the . . . Ironmongers. Composed by Matt. Taubman. London, 1685. [BM, B. Cf. Malcolm, ii, p. 45; Fairholt, pt. i, pp. 100 f., and p. 174; J. G. Nichols, p. 115. The pamphlet is reprinted from the Bodleian copy by Nicholl, pp. 306 f.]

(*Show for 1686*). *London's Yearly Jubilee:* Perform'd on Friday, October xxix. 1686. For the Entertainment of . . . Sir John Peake, Knight, Lord Mayor . . . With a Description of the several Pageants, Speeches and Songs, made proper for the Occasion. All set forth at the proper Costs and Charges of the . . . Mercers. Composed by M. Taubman. London, 1686. [Gh, B (2 copies), BM. Cf. Fairholt, pt. i, p. 102; J. G. Nichols, p. 115 f.]

(*Show for 1687*). *London's Triumph, or the Goldsmiths Jubilee:* Performed on Saturday, October xxix, 1687, For the Confirmation and Entertainment of . . . Sir John Shorter, Kt., Lord Mayor . . . Containing a Description of the several Pageants and Speeches made, proper for the occasion. Together with a Song, for the Entertainment of His Majesty, who, with His Royal Consort . . . honour his Lordship, this year, with their Presence. All set forth at the proper Costs and Charges of the . . . Goldsmiths. By M. Taubman. London, 1687. [Gh (2 copies), B (2 copies), BM. On the title-page of the

BM copy is a pencilled "excessively rare"; also the following MS. note à propos of Shorter: "He had a new Quarter to his Arms giuen him by K. Iames 2d. for receiving the Pope's nunc[io]. He was Grandfa[ther] to Catherine first wife of Sir R. Walpole Earl of Orford." *On this show see also*, Hone, pp. 257 f.; Fairholt, pt. i, p. 103; J. G. Nichols, p. 116.]

(*Show for 1688*). *London's Anniversary Festival*, Performed on Monday, October the 29th, 1688. For . . . Sir John Chapman, Kt. Lord Mayor . . . Being Their Great Year of Jubilee. With a Panegyrick upon the Restoring of the Charter. And a Sonnet provided for the Entertainment of the King. By M. Taubman. . . . London, 1688. [B (2 copies). Cf. Hone, p. 260; Fairholt, pt. i, p. 105; J. G. Nichols, p. 116.]

(*Show for 1689*). *London's Great Jubilee;* Restor'd and Perform'd on Tuesday, October the 29th, 1689. For the Entertainment of . . . Sir Thomas Pilkington, Kt. Lord Mayor . . . Containing a Description of the several Pageants and Speeches, Together with a Song, For the Entertainment of Their Majesties, who . . . Honour his Lordship with their Presence. All set forth at the proper Cost and Charges of the . . . Skinners. By M. T. London, 1689. [BM (2 copies, one imperfect), B (2 copies — one incomplete), Gh. The BM has three subsequent editions of the pamphlet, which was reprinted in Somers' *Tracts* (1751) Third Coll., iii, p. 33; *ibid.* (2d edition, 1814), xi, p. 584. Cf. also Fairholt, pt. i, p. 107; J. G. Nichols, pp. 116 f.] A reprint of this show was made in 1761:

A Description of the Several Pageants Exhibited on the 29th Day of October, 1689, Being the Day on which the late Sir Thomas Pilkington, Knt. Entered a Second Time on his Mayoralty . . . also two Songs, One to their then Majesties and the other to the Lord Mayor. The Whole being design'd for the Entertainment of King William and Queen Mary . . . was done at the sole Expense of the . . . Skinners: And is now published for the perusal of the several Companies of London, agreeable to the Recommendation of . . . Sir Matthew Blackiston, Knt. Lord-Mayor, and the Court of Common Council, held on Saturday the 3d of October, 1761, to the Livery Companies of the said City, for the Entertainment of their present Majesties, on Monday the 9th Day of November next, being the Day on which Sir Samuel Fludyer, Knt. and Bart. Lord Mayor elect will enter on his Mayoralty. [London, 1761.] [BM, SA]

Taylor, Arthur. *The Glory of Regality*. London, 1820.

[Taylor, John]. *A Brief Description of the Burrough and Town of Preston, and its Government and Guild, originally composed between the years 1682 and 1686.* With occasional notes by John Taylor. Preston, 1818.

Taylor, John, *see* Spenser Society.

(*Show for 1634*). *Triumphs of Fame and Honour* [for Robert Parkhurst of the Clothworkers Company. This is mentioned in Greg, p. 25; J. G. Nichols, p. 105; *Gent. Mag.*, for November, 1824, p. 413, and Fairholt, pt. i, p. 57. It is not included in the Spenser Society collections of Taylor's works "not included in the folio volume of 1630." I have not seen a copy of this pamphlet, nor had Fairholt.]

England's Comfort and London's Joy, &c. London, 1641. [8 pp., including "Verses presented to the King's own Hand by John Taylor." Illustrated with three woodcuts, showing the entry of Charles I from Scotland on 25 November, 1641.] [B (2 copies); reprinted in the Spenser Society's collection, iv, no. 7.]

Taylor Collection of Broadsides. In the Guildhall Library.

Ten Brink, Bernard. *Geschichte der Englischen Literatur*. (2 vols.), i, Berlin, 1877; ii, Strassburg, 1893. [*See* ii, p. 306, for mention of pageants.]

Thetford, Vermont, Pageant. W. C. Langdon, Master. 12, 14, and 15 August, 1911. *Book of Words*. White River Junction, 1911.

Thomas of Chester, *see* Chestre.

Thompson, E. M., editor. *See Chronica Roberti de Avesbury* [*s. v.* Avesbury]; *and* Murimuth.

Thomson, Richard. *Chronicles of London Bridge.* London, 1827.

Tingey, J. C., *see* W. Hudson.

Toland, John. *Miscellaneous Works.* (2 vols.), London, 1747.

[Torkington, Sir Richard]. *Ye oldest Diarie of Englysshe Travell: Being the hitherto unpublished narrative of the pilgrimage of Sir Richard Torkington to Jerusalem in 1517* . . . Edited, from Addl. MSS. 28561 and 28562, by W. J. Loftie. London [1884].

Tracy, G. L., *see* Marblehead.

Trevelyan, Marie. *Folk-Lore and Folk-Stories of Wales.* With an introduction by E. Sidney Hartland. London, 1909.

Triumphs of London, the. Performed on Monday October xxix, 1683. for the entertainment of . . . Sir Henry Tulse, Knight . . . London, 1683. [Gh, B. In pencil on the title-page of the Gh copy is written " by Thomas Jordan, city poet." The pamphlet is not attributed to Jordan in the catalogue of the Bodleian. *See* Jordan (sub anno 1683.)]

Troia Nova Triumphans, see Dekker (sub anno 1612.)

Tudor Tracts, 1532–88. With an introduction by A. F. Pollard. Westminster, 1903.

Tuetey, Alexandre, editor. *Journal d'un Bourgeois de Paris* (1405–49). Edited for the Société de l'Histoire de Paris. Paris, 1881.

Tyrrell, Edward, editor. *A Chronicle of London from 1089 to 1483.* London, 1827.

Udal, J. S. " Christmas Mummers in Dorsetshire," in *Folk-Lore Record* (for 1880, pp. 87 f.).

Udall, Nicholas, and John Leland. Verses for the entry of Anne Boleyn in 1533, reprinted in Arber, *Eng. Garner,* ii, pp. 52 f.; *Ballads from MSS.* (edited by Furnivall), i, pp. 364 f.; *Tudor Tracts, 1532–1588,* pp. 20 f.

Underhill, Edward. His account of the progress through London of Queen Mary before her Coronation is printed in Arber, *English Garner,* iv, pp. 84 f.

Unwin, George. *The Gilds and Companies of London.* London, 1908.

Veiled Prophet, The, see St. Louis.

[Victoria]. *The Visit of Queen Victoria to the City of London on . . . 9 November, 1837.* Collected by F. Hobler, 1836. [Gh, *MS. 36.*]

Vulson, Marc de. *Le Vray Théâtre d'Honneur et de Chevalerie.* (2 vols.), Paris, 1648. [SA]

Wadmore, James F. *Some Account of the Worshipful Company of Skinners of London.* . . . London, 1902.

Walker, Joseph C. " An Historical Essay on the Irish Stage," in *Trans. Royal Irish Academy* [ii, 3, pp. 75 f.] Dublin, 1788.

Wallace, C. W. " The Evolution of the English Drama up to Shakespeare," in *Schriften der Deutschen Shakespeare-Gesellschaft.* [Vol. iv.] Berlin, 1912.

Walpole, Horace. *Miscellaneous Antiquities,* &c. (No. 1.), Strawberry Hill, 1772. [BM, *188. a. 15.*]

Walsingham, T. *Historia Anglicana.* Edited by H. T. Riley. (RS 28) London, 1863.

Ward, Sir A. W. *The History of English Dramatic Literature.* (2 vols.), London, 1875.
Ibid. (3 vols.), London, 1899.

Ward, Edward. *The London Spy.* Fourth edition. London, 1709.

Warton, T. *The History of English Poetry.* Edited by W. Carew Hazlitt. (4 vols.), London, 1871.

Warwick Pageant. 2–7 July, 1906. Louis N. Parker, Master. *In Celebration of the Thousandth Anniversary of the Conquest of Mercia by Queen Ethelfleda.* Invented and arranged by Louis N. Parker. Warwick [1906].

Watermen, *see* Humpherus.

Webb, William, *see* King.

Webster, John. *Works*. Edited by Rev. Alexander Dyce. (4 vols.), London, 1830.

Dramatic Works. Edited by William Hazlitt. (4 vols.), London, 1857.

(*Show for 1624*). *Monuments of Honor*. [For John Gore, of the Merchant-Taylors' Company. I have not seen a copy of this pamphlet, which is reprinted in his *Works* (1857, iii, p. 225.) Cf. Greg, p. 25.]

Weir, Hugh C. "The Hudson-Fulton Pageant," in *The World To-Day*, for November, 1909.

Welch, Charles. *The History of the Worshipful Company of Pewterers of the City of London, based upon their own Records*. (2 vols.), London, 1902.

West Dorset Historical Pageant. Rev. C. F. Langford, Master. Bradpole, near Bridport, Dorset, 20–22 July, 1911. *Book of Words*. (A. M. Broadley and H. Pouncy.) Bridport, 1911.

Westminster, Matthew of. *Flores Historiarum*. Edited by H. R. Luard. (RS 95) London, 1890.

Wheatley, H. B., *see* Pepys.

Whitelocke, Bulstrode. *Memorials of the English Affairs during the Reign of King Charles the First*, &c. London, 1732.

[William III]. *An Account of His Most Excellent Majesty's Splendid Reception into the famous City of London; together with His Royal Entertainment in and through the said City on Tuesday the 16th of this Instant November, 1697*. [Gh, *Broadsides 7.17*.]

Williams, Benjamin, editor, *see Gesta Henrici Quinti*.

Williams, William M. *Annals of the Worshipful Company of Founders of the City of London*. [London, 1867.]

Winchester National Pageant. F. R. Benson, Master. Wolvesey Castle, 25–30 June, 1908. *The Book of the Words and Music*. Winchester, 1908.

Withington, Georgiana B. *A Children's Parade*. n. p., n. d. [1915] [HL]

Withington, Robert. "The Lord Mayor's Show for 1623," in *Publ. Mod. Lang. Assoc.* for March, 1915.

Withington, Robert. "Queen Margaret's Entry into London, 1445," in *Modern Philol.* for May, 1915.

Withington, Robert. *A Manual of Pageantry*. Indiana University Bulletin [xiii, no. 7.] Bloomington (Indiana), June, 1915.

Withington, Robert. "After the Manner of Italy," in *Journ. Eng. Germ. Philol.* for July, 1916.

Withington, Robert. "The Early Royal-Entry," in *Publ. Mod. Lang. Assoc.* for December, 1917.

Withington, Robert. "The Lord Mayor's Show for 1590," in *Mod. Lang. Notes* for January, 1918.

Withington, Robert. "A Civic 'Triumph' circa 1700," in *Journ. Eng. Germ. Philol.* for January, 1918.

Withington, Robert. "A Note on 'A Fragment of a Lord Mayor's Pageant,'" in *Modern Language Notes* for December, 1919. See the paper by Elizabeth D. Adams in *Modern Language Notes* for May, 1917, pp. 285 ff.

Wolgemuth, Fritz. *Riesen und Zwerge in der altfr. Erzählenden Dichtung*. Stuttgart, 1906.

Wright, Thomas, editor, *see* Maidstone.

Wriothesley, Charles. *A Chronicle of England during the Reigns of the Tudors*. (1485–1559.) Edited for the Camden Society by William D. Hamilton. (2 vols.), London, 1875–77.

Wyre-Drawers, *see* Stewart.

[Yale Pageant]. *The Book of the Yale Pageant.* 21 October, 1916. In Commemoration of the Two Hundredth Anniversary of the Removal of Yale College to New Haven. Edited by George Henry Nettleton. New Haven, 1916.

[Yale Pageant]. *The Yale Alumni Weekly* for 27 October, 1916. (New Haven.) [Francis H. Markoe was the Pageant Master.]

[Yale Pageant]. *See* Brian Hooker.

York. *See* Davies, F. Drake, L. T. Smith, *and* Solloway.

York Historical Pageant. Louis N. Parker, Master. 26–31 July, 1909. *Book of the Words.* [York, 1909.]

[York]. *The Book of the York Pageant.* Containing: C. E. Pascoe's description of the Pageant; "The Music of the Pageant," by R. S. Rose; "The Genesis and Evolution of Christianity," by the Rev. Dr. Solloway; "Ecclesiastical Costumes," by the Right Rev. Prior Cummins; "Sources of Costume Design," by Major and Mrs. Lindberg; "The Armorial Bearings of the Old Craft Guilds," by T. P. Cooper; "Norman and Plantagenet Armour and Arms, and Heraldry of the Pageant," by Colonel Saltmarshe. York, 1909.

Young, Sidney. *The Annals of the Barber-Surgeons of London, compiled from their Records and other sources. . . .* London, 1890.

NOTE: Recent English Pageants are pictured in the *Illustrated London News* (English edition) as follows:

Army (1910): 25 June, pp. 1016–19; 1021.
Bath (1909): 24 July, p. iv (supplement).
Bury St. Edmunds (1907): 6 July, pp. 18–19.
Cardiff (Wales) (1909): 31 July, pp. i and iv (supplement).
Chelsea (1908): 27 June, pp. 952–953.
Chester (1910): 16 July, p. 99; ("Behind the Scenes," 23 July, p. 144).
Colchester (1909): 19 June, pp. ii–iv (supplement).
Dover (1908): 25 July, p. 117.
English Church (1909): 5 June, p. 809; 12 June, p. 843; 19 June, p. i (supplement); p. 880 (G. K. Chesterton as Dr. Johnson.)
Gloucestershire (1908): 11 July, p. 43.
Liverpool (1907): 10 August, p. 191.
London (1911): 13 May, pp. 682–683; 20 May, p. 740.
Oxford (1907): 6 July, p. 3.
Pevensey (1908): 18 July, p. 79.
Porchester (1907): 6 July, p. 17.
St. Albans (1907): 13 July, p. 70; 20 July, pp. 98–99.
Sherborne (1905): 10 June, pp. 814–815.
Wales, *see* Cardiff.
Warwick (1906): 30 June, pp. 974–975.
Winchester (1908): 27 June, pp. 956–957. ("A Rehearsal" is pictured 23 May, p. 741.)
York (1909): 31 July, pp. ii, iii (supplement).

INDEX

INDEX

THE NAMES OF CHARACTERS IN PAGEANTS ARE IN ITALICS

CORRIGENDA ET ADDENDA

VOLUME I

PAGE 19, n. 8 [on p. 20]. *For* Ispwich *read* Ipswich.
34, n. 2. *For* 1882 *read* 1822.
35, l. 1. *For* Preston *read* Coventry.
44, n. 2. *Delete the apostrophe after* Doctors'.
51, n. 2. *For* Judas-burning *read* Judas-flogging.
54, n. 2. *For* Lebeaus *read* Libeaus.
58, n. 2. *For* Mathew *read* Matthew.
59, n. 2. *For* Gigantic *read* Gigantick.
63, n. 1. *For* Faitholt *read* Fairholt.
63, n. 2. *Add*: Cf. the giants at Antwerp in 1803 (below, p. 254) and in 1843 (below, p. 256).
77, n. 1. *For* februrier *read* feburier.
80, l. 3. *For* 1553 *read* 1554.
81, l. 6. *For* twenty *read* thirty.
81, l. 7. *For* this *read* mythology.
81, n. 4. *For* 111 *read* 169.
82, l. 21. *For* Anne *read* Catherine of Valois.
83, l. 11. *For* 1469 *read* 1468.
91, l. 11. *For* 1432 *read* 1342.
91, n. 4. *For* 1541 *read* 1341.
109, n. 1. *For* Gynewulf *read* Cynewulf.
123, l. 1. *For* latter *read* later.
124, l. 14. *For* 3 *read* 4.
125, n. 1. Mr. C. L. Kingsford (*Eng. Hist. Rev.*, April, 1919, p. 270) notes that William Packington "was the author of one of the French originals of the *Brut*."
126, n. 1. The mayor in February, 1313 (whose second term began in 1312) was Sir John Gisors, Pepperer. (See Stow, *Survey* [1618], p. 925; Gregory's *Chronicle* [ed. Camden Society] pp. 74 and 252.)
126, n. 1. *For* Augier *read* Aungier.
159, l. 9. *For* Minister *read* Minster.
162, l. 15. *For* an *read* au.
174, l. 4. *For* London *read* England.
190, n. 12. *Add*: Mr. Kingsford records "an account of the pageant for Philip of Spain in 1554 . . . in the Chronicle printed in *Camden Miscellany*, xii, 38." (*Eng. Hist. Review*, April, 1919, p. 270.)
209, n. 6. *For* Campian *read* Campion.
214, n. 3. *Delete the comma after* annis.
219, l. 17. *Delete the comma after* Bacon.
229, n. 2. }
230, n. 1. } *For* fols. *read* fol.
231, n. 3. }
230, n. 4. *For* London Love *read* London's Love.

CORRIGENDA ET ADDENDA

PAGE 231, l. 31. *Insert quotation-marks, ending the citation, after* behalf.

252, n. 1. *Add*: Cf. p. 51, n. 2, for mention of the burning of the giants, 24 April, 1685.

255, n. 3. *For* Faitholt *read* Fairholt; *for* contans *read* contains.

255 ff. On this royal-entry, see my paper: "Scott's Contribution to Pageantic Development—a Note on the Visit of George IV to Edinburgh in 1822," in *Studies in Philology* for April, 1920.

256, n. 4. *For* Lond. Illus. News *read* Illus. Lond. News.

256, n. 7. *For* Lord. *read* Lond.

VOLUME II

NOTE: In the 1783 pantomime, and in the 1907 Show, Sir Thomas Gresham, who founded the Royal Exchange, was represented. He was not a mayor of London, but was the son of Sir Richard Gresham, mayor in 1537. He laid the foundation of the Royal Exchange in 1566. [See *Three Fifteenth Century Chronicles* (edited by James Gairdner for the Camden Society, London, 1880), p. 135, and the biography of Sir Thomas in the *DNB*.] Sir Richard appeared in the 1906 Show (see his biography in the *DNB*) — and Sir John, his younger brother, who was sheriff the same year that his brother was mayor (1537) and who was mayor himself, ten years later, appeared in the Shows for 1889 and 1895.

PAGE 109. *Add*: I am indebted to Professor Kittredge for calling my attention, while this volume was in press, to a song entitled "Gog and Magog in Danger," published in *The Melodist* (London, 1828), ii, 201 f.; and to "The Lord Mayor's Show," a humorous monologue, with verses [to the air of "The Dog's-meat Man"] written by J. S. Wyburn, and sung by Mr. T. Jones, at the Rotunda, (*ibid.*, iii [London, 1829] 102 f.)

190. *Add*:

THE ROYAL TOURNAMENT [1920]

When a name grows too long it is often blue-pencilled. The Royal Naval, Military, and Air Force Tournament had become cumbrous by additions. In future it is to be known as the Royal Tournament, which is quite comprehensive. This year's exhibition will open at Olympia on May 20th, and will run until June 5th, during which time it will be seen by the King, the Queen, and other members of the Royal Family. Whereas last year's show was largely concerned with giving an idea of the war, this year's will return to colour and pageantry. The military history of Britain is to be illustrated. Grenadiers will appear in the uniforms of three centuries, and that they may appear correctly every armoury and military centre in the country has been searched. Of course, the war cannot be forgotten. The Royal Engineers will reconstruct a thrilling incident of bridge-building under fire; while Jerusalem and the Dardanelles will enter largely into the decoration of the great hall. — From the London *Times* [weekly edition, 7 May, 1920], no. 2262, p. 369.

222, n. 2. *Add*: Mr. G. K. Chesterton, as *Dr. Johnson* in the English Church Pageant at Fulham Palace, is pictured in the *Illus. Lond. News* for 19 June, 1909, p. 880. As an actor in a pageant, he has something to say about pageantry (*ibid.*).